D1523320

Maternal Metaphors of Power in
African American Women's Literature

Maternal Metaphors of Power in African American Women's Literature

From Phillis Wheatley to Toni Morrison

Geneva Cobb Moore

Foreword by Andrew Billingsley

The University of South Carolina Press

© 2017 University of South Carolina

Published by the University of South Carolina Press
Columbia, South Carolina 29208

www.sc.edu/uscpress

Manufactured in the United States of America

26 25 24 23 22 21 20 19 18 17
10 9 8 7 6 5 4 3 2 1

Library of Congress Cataloging-in-Publication Data
can be found at http://catalog.loc.gov/.

ISBN 978-1-61117-748-0 (cloth)
ISBN 978-1-61117-749-7 (ebook)

This book was printed on recycled paper with
30 percent postconsumer waste content.

In Memoriam

W. C. Cobb Sr.
1912–1992

and

Canary Beatrice Cobb
1913–2000

The concept of race is nothing but a whited sepulchre, a conception which in the light of modern experimental genetics is utterly erroneous and meaningless, and . . . should therefore be dropped from the vocabulary of the anthropologist, for it has done an infinite amount of harm and no good at all.

Ashley Montagu, ed., *The Concept of Race*

The ubiquity of the term *race* in modern discourse indicates that early-twenty-first-century Americans adhere to this creation myth with remarkable tenacity—in other words, that they believe that race is real and that race matters. In fact, however, like its worldwide counterparts, the American creation myth is the product of collective imagination, not historical fact. . . . The myth of race is, at its heart, about power relations. . . . Who benefited from these narratives of racial difference?

Jacqueline Jones, *A Dreadful Deceit: The Myth of Race from the Colonial Era to Obama's America*

The idea of America as a "Herrenvolk republic" did not spring Medusa-like out of the minds of white folk. It emerged only after the progress and demands of free blacks [who] compelled whites to clarify and make explicit their understanding of American republicanism as the white race's exclusive gift.

Paul Goodman, *Of One Blood*

Contents

Foreword

Great writers at their best often reveal significant dimensions of the histories and societies, cultures, and especially personalities of the people about whom they write. Consider, for example, the writings of Alexandre Dumas of France, Aleksandr Pushkin of Russian, Huan Soyin of China, Nadine Gordimer of South Africa, Chinua Achebe of Nigeria, Charlotte Brontë of Great Britain, and William Faulkner and Richard Wright of the southern United States of America. Left to the empirical investigation of historians and social scientists alone, the development of our knowledge of history, culture, and society would be far less imaginative and complete.

It is not that literary writers can replace historians and social scientists in depicting the interactions between people and their cultures and societies. But writers, often unlimited and unshackled by objective realities, can plunge beneath the social conditions of history to reveal what is true and shocking but also what might have been or what might still be in regard to human possibility. The relation between art and society can be illustrated by the artist or writer standing before his or her society, holding a mirror and making perceptibly visible to future generations what might otherwise be considered the foreign and complicated occurrences of history that influence human conduct or stifle human aspiration.

This work places the literary writings of influential and intellectual black women in their historical times, uniquely combining history and literature or presenting literature as history. As such, the study richly adds to our understanding of the black experience from the era of colonialism and slavery in Boston with the experience of the poet Phillis Wheatley to the horrors of plantation slavery in Harriet Jacobs's North Carolina and then the promise of abolitionism and the Civil War as witnessed in the diaries of Charlotte Forten Grimké—and this in just the first three chapters in this study. This book continues with the Jim Crow era of the Harlem Renaissance writers Jessie Fauset, Nella Larsen, and Zora Neale Hurston; progresses to the Caribbean experience as described in the novels of Paule Marshall; and then moves on to the civil rights movement and two novelists coming out of that experience, Alice Walker and Toni Morrison. The ambition of this examination opens up a Pandora's box of American history and the tragedy and transformation of African Americans. Enslaved and freed and perpetually existing in a state of rediscovering the meaning of freedom, its restrictions, and its possibilities, African Americans offer a different narrative on history from the one constructed by the mainstream media and the general society, as this book illuminates.

I was privileged to read the manuscript of this work when I was living and working in West Africa as a Senior Fulbright Scholar and Lecturer at the University of Ghana. It was there that I first met the author Geneva Cobb Moore, also a

Fulbright Scholar, teaching American literature at the university. I must confess that I initially read Professor Moore's manuscript as a social scientist and was immediately struck in each chapter by the crisis of the black family in slavery and freedom, especially as depicted in the literature that she has chosen to examine. Images of African American families have not fared well, generally speaking, in American scholarship. Scholars have been perhaps overly influenced by the downside of the black experience and have little understood, until quite recently, the creative pattern of adaptation that black families have had to adopt because of their unique historical situation. Black and white American scholars have been unduly influenced by their immersion in Eurocentric cultural perspectives, which largely dominate much of American education and the public discourse on the nuclear and middle-class family.

We are all, therefore, appreciative of Professor Moore's great effort and of her perceptive analyses of the works of leading African American women writers who, among other achievements, reveal the dynamic complexity of African American family structures over a wide span of time. It is possible in this study to trace the early identity of the black family from being ruptured and dispossessed to endeavoring to be made whole, intact, and self-sustaining. Among the writers treated here, Phillis Wheatley was kidnapped from her family in Africa, and Harriet Jacobs labored to maintain a basic but essential maternal relationship with the two children born to her out of wedlock after she had already lost her mother, father, grandmother, aunt, and uncles through their deaths or her fugitive-slave status in New York and Boston.

There is, however, one writer in this book, Charlotte Forten, with whom I am quite familiar because of my own research on the life of Robert Smalls, the black South Carolinian and Civil War maritime hero whom she met in Beaufort, South Carolina, on the eve of the Civil War. A writer-diarist, Forten provides an extraordinary glimpse into the world of the rare, black patrician family in antebellum America. Through Professor Moore's analysis of the *Journals of Charlotte Forten Grimké,* we see images of the black family as an expression of the rich cultural heritage and aspiration of free African Americans, establishing themselves as models for enslaved blacks. While much of what scholars have revealed to us about the African American people of this period is from the study of poor, enslaved people on southern plantations, Charlotte Forten's family life gives a striking contrast. She was born into a free black and wealthy family in Philadelphia led by her illustrious grandfather James Forten Sr., a wealthy sailmaker and philanthropist of various social causes, including abolitionism and women's rights.

After Charlotte Forten's mother died, young Charlotte was raised by several members of her extended African American family, including her father's three sisters and a free Negro family of abolitionists in Salem, Massachusetts, where she attended school. Within this social context of the extended African American family, whether in Philadelphia with her aunts or in Massachusetts with family friends, young Charlotte was provided with the support she needed to grow up in a safe and prosperous environment. Although, as Professor Moore clarifies, Forten still experienced the discrimination that virtually every black person endured during her generation, her experiences were far less traumatic than those of Harriet Jacobs, for example, who lacked both the freedom and the extended familial resources available to free Negroes such as Forten.

Among contemporary African American writers, both male and female, none has focused so resolutely on or been as successful in elucidating the triumphant but sometimes painful element of African American culture than the Nobel Prize–winning author Toni Morrison. Without the historical framework that Professor Moore uses to introduce and analyze Morrison's novels, readers could possibly be tempted to view the author's characters as saboteurs rather than the dispossessed victims of history. Social scientists who write and teach courses on the black family throughout history have often discovered Morrison's novels to be indispensable in illuminating the various issues facing the black family, whether in slavery or in freedom.

The sociologist Robert B. Hill and his studies *The Strengths of African American Families: Twenty-Five Years Later* (1999) and *The Strengths of Black Families* (2003), the sociologist Joyce Ladner and her book *The Ties That Bind: Timeless Values for African American Families* (2000), and the anthropologist Michelle Foster and her work *Black Teachers on Teaching* (1998) have all moved into the forefront of the fledgling movement among scholars to delineate the basic cultural beliefs that have sustained many African Americans. Among these essential values are those that writers such as Jessie Fauset, Zora Neale Hurston, Paule Marshall, Alice Walker, and Toni Morrison stress: namely, strong kinship and/or communal bonds, what Professor Moore refers to as the necessary work of these authors' female characters, their adoption of "maternal metaphors of power." Nuclear family systems, while desirable, were frequently not available to blacks in the slave community. But alternative familial relationships provided blacks with a sense of family and the support that it offered. As Professor Moore discusses, Pecola Breedlove of Toni Morrison's *The Bluest Eye* experiences a social death and then mental collapse because, as Morrison suggests, she is cut off from the two essential bonds of family life and community.

In my book *Climbing Jacob's Ladder: The Enduring Legacy of African American Families* (1994), I argue that the merits of kinship and community are the veritable pillars of the African American cultural heritage. These intrinsic values have an African origin, although European culture and the experience of slavery in America have influenced them in ways not always beneficial to the black community. Yet in each chapter here, Professor Moore reveals how the writers' own values and family backgrounds have had a profound impact on their writing and their visions in changing their world. She shows how each writer was influenced, in one way or another, by her family heritage.

The renowned African American writer James Baldwin once described himself as a "revolutionary," confessing that every time he sat down to write he was attempting to reveal why and how our society should be reformed. The women authors examined in this study have not claimed to have, to my knowledge, a raging revolutionary status. Yet each writer had catalyzed and continues to catalyze a reform movement, with a unique gender or maternal role in capturing the spirit of her historical moment and literally or symbolically "nurturing a wounded race," as Professor Moore states.

For a number of years I have argued that the way to understand the African American experience is to place the people within their historical context, something I believe this work does out of academic necessity. Students of literature, history, women's studies, race and ethnic studies, and culture and society will be enormously rewarded by the insight of these seven essays and the collective story they narrate of the historical black experience.

Andrew Billingsley

Preface and Acknowledgments

I remember telling my two sons, Kenny and Christopher, years ago that it would take about four years for me to complete this study. That was approximately twenty years ago. Since that time they have gone on to finish middle school, high school, college, and for Kenny, graduate school in Washington, D.C., and for Chris, to begin graduate school in California. Life happens while we are planning what we wish we could do, or what we wish we could accomplish in a set period of time, over which we sometimes have little control.

Nevertheless, this study has been completed with the encouragement and assistance of mentors and colleagues in Wisconsin and around the country, and in Africa, where I was a Fulbright Scholar from 1997 to 1998. The following are the names of individuals to whom I owe a debt of gratitude for reading and commenting on sections of the manuscript or the entire manuscript: George Adams, Richard Allen, Brian Altano, Robert Burrows, Kari Dako and A. Denkabe (University of Ghana), Joanne Glasgow, Jessie Grearson, Suzanne Griffin, Saidiya Hartman, Holly Hassel, Fred Hobson, Joe and Rebecca Hogan, Cynthia Huff, Linda Hutcheon, Julian Mason, John Knapp, Elena Levy-Navarro, Beth Lueck, Margaret Musgrove, Andrea Musher, Andrea Nye, Margo Peters, former dean Howard Ross, Geoffrey Saddock, Joan Schwarz, and Julie Smith. Special thanks to Mark Clinger, for his inspiration as I was writing chapter 7, and to the late Peter Gillette, Barbara Beaver, and Carolyn Wedin Sylvander. To Andrew Billingsley, who read the manuscript in Africa and who wrote the foreword, I am much indebted, as I am to the generous and gracious historian Eric Foner, who read and commented on an earlier draft of the manuscript. The late historian Arthur Schlesinger, in his seminar "Literature and Society," gave birth to the idea of this work. The two editors who provided me with considerable support are John Easterly, formerly executive editor at Louisiana State University Press, and Jim Denton, acquisitions editor at the University of South Carolina Press. To my benevolent, meticulous, but anonymous reviewers, I hope you can identify many of your fine recommendations in *Maternal Metaphors*.

"Archetypal Symbolism in Alice Walker's *Possessing the Secret of Joy*" was first published in the *Southern Literary Journal* 33. © 2000 by the Department of English and Comparative Literature of the University of North Carolina at Chapel Hill. Used by permission of the publisher, the University of North Carolina Press, www.uncpress.unc.edu.

"A Demonic Parody: Toni Morrison's *A Mercy*" was first published in the *Southern Literary Journal* 44. © 2011 by the Department of English and Comparative

Literature of the University of North Carolina at Chapel Hill. Used by permission of the publisher, the University of North Carolina Press, www.uncpress.unc.edu.

"A Freudian Reading of Harriet Jacobs's *Incidents in the Life of a Slave Girl*" was first published in the *Southern Literary Journal* 38. © 2005 by the Department of English and Comparative Literature of the University of North Carolina at Chapel Hill. Used by permission of the publisher, the University of North Carolina Press, www.uncpress.unc.edu.

"When Meanings Meet: *The Journals of Charlotte Forten Grimké*" has been re-printed partially from *Inscribing the Daily: Critical Essays on Women's Diaries.* © 1996 by the University of Massachusetts Press.

"Zora Neale Hurston as Local Colorist" was first published in the *Southern Literary Journal* 26. © 1994 by the Department of English and Comparative Literature of the University of North Carolina at Chapel Hill. Used by permission of the publisher, the University of North Carolina Press, www.uncpress.unc.edu.

Introduction

Signs of Regeneration in African American
Women's Literature

Ralph Ellison has stated, "Thus on the moral level I propose that we view the whole
of American life as a drama acted out upon the body of a Negro giant, who, lying
trussed up like Gulliver, forms the stage and the scene upon which and within
which the action unfolds. If we examine the beginning of the Colonies, the application of this view is not, in its economic connotations at least, too far-fetched or
too difficult to see. For then *the Negro's body* [emphasis added] was exploited as
amorally as the soil and climate." Identity politics is thus the real subject of this
study: the history shaping and making of events, identities, and national outcomes
and the intellectual-as-artist wrestling that power away from history and reshaping
events, identities, and national outcomes. In identity-theory scholarship, scholars
aver that individuals can exert control over the perception of their own identities
and who they wish to be, based presumably on natural gifts, opportunities, and
will power.[1]

Over a long, historical period of time from the colonial epoch and slavery to the
Civil War and Reconstruction, the emergence and reemergence of racial strictures led
to the caste barrier of a rigid Jim Crow system in 1892, firmly establishing the foundation of America's "Herrenvolk democracy," against which modern, black women
authors write just as their literary predecessors had written against slavery and the
early subjugation of African Americans. The sociologist Pierre L. van den Berghe
defines Herrenvolk forms of democracy as those that exist in a "parliamentary
regime in which the exercise of power and suffrage is restricted *de facto*, and often
de jure, to the dominant group." In a Herrenvolk democracy, which emerges as an
"ideological contradiction" between a country's professed love of democracy and
its practice of discrimination, the privilege of democracy is restricted to a valued
and superior caste over its known inferior and cultural Other.[2] Although Pierre van
den Berghe developed the theory of a Herrenvolk democracy, the Swedish sociologist Gunnar Myrdal, in his study of black/white relations in the 1940s, enunciated
the skewed but philosophical rationalization of the coexistence of democracy and
racism. The "partial exclusion of the Negro from American democracy," Myrdal
posits, can be attributed to his alleged inferiority, which justifies the "need for race
prejudice" as a "defense on the part of the Americans against their own national
Creed, against their own most cherished ideals" of liberty.[3] Having a subordinate

status, African Americans under slavery and in a Herrenvolk democracy of ratio-
nalized inequities after slavery faced an impermeable racial caste system, illustrated
in the literature of nine women writers from Phillis Wheatley to Toni Morrison.

Divided into two parts, *Maternal Metaphors of Power in African American Wom-
en's Literature* provides a literary history of the black experience from the colonial
and (pre)revolutionary era to postmodernity. Part 1, "Slavery and Abolitionism,
Freedom and Jim Crow America," traces the origin and development of the black
female writer's appropriation of feminine and maternal metaphors of power within
the rigidly proscribed public sphere of slavery and segregation, the liberal romanticism of the abolitionist era, and the spirited movement of the Harlem Renaissance.
Part 2, "A Conflation of History, Past and Present," analyzes their continuing quest
for liberation, though inner directed, and the contemporary novelist's adoption too
of feminine/maternal tropes, providing an overview of the West Indian and African
American bond in a lengthy, historical critique of dominating systems of power.

Rewriting history and rejecting the master narrative on race and identity, these
nine women writers reveal a desire to challenge the convention of their times,
singly and collectively. Many studies on African American women writers have focused primarily on theory and on a select group of writers whose literary achievements do not necessarily represent a long and sustaining narrative chronology of
American history. With the exception of the late Barbara Christian's pathbreaking
book *Black Women Novelists: The Development of a Tradition, 1892–1976* and Hazel
Carby's important study *Reconstructing Womanhood* (1987), which covers several
centuries, and several other works cited throughout my text, few studies have been
written on African American women writers as creating an uninterrupted narrative on history, race, identity, and literature. *Maternal Metaphors* attempts to join
a select list of scholarship on black women's literature as history, representing the
black experience while covering perhaps a greater period of time from Wheatley's
autobiographical poem in 1768 to Morrison's novel *Home* (2012) and closing with
a look at Morrison's 2015 novel, *God Help the Child*.

The thesis of my study can be summarized thusly: black women writers from
Wheatley to Morrison have created feminine and maternal metaphors of powers
to unhinge oppressive forces against blacks and women and others, and to assert
women's innovative powers of authority. These writers often adopt the feminine
and maternal body as a trope of justice and freedom and an emblem of women's
creativity in opposition to patriarchy and hegemony. Generally, women's feminine
and maternal nature of regeneration helps to explain these writers' persistent reliance on strong maternal images and characters that have a liberating political
function because of the uniqueness of African American history. Mother Africa,
Mother Country, Mother Earth, Mother Nature, and the Great Mother archetypal
tale of Demeter and Persephone are all maternal metaphors and narratives that attest to the veneration and privilege of the maternal body and the ideal of symbolic

and literal motherhood. In Africa, for example, the Earth and the River Niger are considered goddesses because they are sources of life, perhaps one explanation among many of Phillis Wheatley's overwhelming emphases on goddesses in select poems. Moreover, in their valorization of femininity, ancient artists from the Neolithic period illustrate through their cave drawings the ideas of women as mothers/goddesses. These paintings express too the emotional and psychological bonding of mothers and their children, of mothers and their communities.[4]

From the amniotic sacs in their wombs that shelter and nurture the fetuses to the mammary glands of their breasts that dispense milk and nourish the babies, mothers have a literal life-and-death power over their children. In the modern era, however, feminists often argue that Western culture with its entrenched patriarchy is matricidal. Pre-Oedipal societies venerated mothers, but post-Oedipal cultures from the age of Sophocles to Freud have challenged their real or symbolic maternal powers. Whereas in ancient and matrilineal societies mothers were the fonts of life, in patrilineal cultures mothers give birth to their children and relinquish them to a society, which then renders them powerless in determining their children's life courses.[5] In Freudian mythos separation from mothers, especially for boys, became a crucial marker of male autonomy and identity in patriarchal society. Elizabeth Fox-Genovese argues that in compensation for the loss of the mothers' power, the "ideology of motherhood that would rapidly develop into a full-blown ideology of bourgeois domesticity appeared to offer an ideal solution to the problem of women's place in the brave new world of individualism."[6] The relation between mother and child changed, diminishing the mother's influence. If Western culture was matricidal for white women, offered a compensatory mommy-track of bourgeois domesticity, what was it then for physically enslaved, sexually abused, spatially segregated black women, who, as Toni Morrison's narrator remarks in *Beloved*, often were denied the natural emotion of "desire"?[7] As if responding to this question, Alice Walker writes that the answer, like the question, is "cruel enough to stop the blood."[8] Because of their experience of slavery and segregation and their double oppressions as blacks and women (and triple oppressions as "foreigners" in Paule Marshall's fiction), "transgressive" female characters in black women's literature frequently discover the social impetus for radical activism to reform society.

Through their characters, black women writers rewrite the role of black women and challenge the political/national body of rules (from slavery to segregation) used to govern women and minorities' subordinate behavior. In *Philosophy and the Maternal Body*, Michelle Boulous Walker logically asks "whether this transgressive maternal space [for all women] can be useful for any feminist analysis given that, according to [Elizabeth] Grosz, it ultimately rests upon, and stands in for, a phallic paternal phantasy. We need to ask whether this space has anything to do with women and their voices."[9] The transgressive maternal and feminine space in black women's literature has a special function in creating a change throughout the scheme of things, political and social. To speak more directly to Michelle Boulous Walker's question, in Alice Walker's novels, for example, the phallic maternal-imaginary exists not as a replacement for male authority but rather in a pointed and militant opposition to women's real or symbolic castration. Before Boulous Walker even asked the question, however, Helene Cixous had very early radicalized the maternal space and generative power of the feminine body in the recovery of women's voices and humanity.

Like Ralph Ellison in the opening quotation, Cixous articulates the delicate operation that women, or in this case African Americans, must perform on themselves in taking back their bodies and reshaping their lives, their images, and their identities. Cixous avers, "Woman must write her body," *écriture féminine,* through which she must also inscribe "the endless vertigo of a history loosed like an arrow from all of men's history, from bibliococapitalist society."[10] Ellison's and Cixous's theories, respectively, on the auctioned, enslaved, lynched, and segregated black body-in-crisis as constituting a long, dramatic narrative of American history and the feminine/maternal body as being a weapon of spiritual renewal and rebirth for women comprise the "new constellations between body, history, language and politics."[11] That is, as an instrument of feminine power, the maternal trope can be used in a revision of history through women writers' adoption of visionary language, asserting the relation of self and community and triumphing over their political disenfranchisement: their voicelessness.

In this study two identical features of black women's literature across time and place illustrate the dramatic history of Ellison's "black body-in-crisis" motif and Cixous's *écriture féminine* thematic, or the artist-as-mother, procreating and nurturing life through her real or artistic textual and poetic body. With the exception of Nella Larsen's fiction (*Quicksand* and *Passing*) and several of Toni Morrison's novels (most notably *The Bluest Eye, Tar Baby, Jazz, Love,* and *A Mercy*), few of the writers' texts examined in this book have autobiographical selves or major fictive characters who remain bodies-in-crises. Noticeably, these writers and/or their characters are invariably changed, reborn, regenerated—radically transformed into something other than what they were intended to be in Cixous's "bibliococapitalist" society, where subordinate selves are consumed by a market economy.

Black women writers are, then, authors of "subversive" feminine texts and "transgressive" maternal spaces. They recast the black female body from a state of trauma to a site of regeneration, from an experience of slavery to an encounter with freedom, from a Herrenvolk democracy of Jim Crow and second-class citizenship to an expansive and aesthetic realm of beauty. As writers of "subversive" texts, challenging the status quo and re-creating images of women and blacks, these women writers assume a maternal function, as do the major female characters in Wheatley's poems, Harriet Jacobs's slave narrative, Charlotte Forten Grimké's Civil War journals, and the (post)modern novels of Jessie Fauset, Zora Neale Hurston, Paule Marshall, Alice Walker, and Toni Morrison. "A feminine text cannot *not* [emphasis added] be more than subversive,"[12] Cixous writes, using double negatives to stress emphatically the willed purposefulness of the female writers' reinscription of identity in political spaces previously denied to them and their heroines.

Throughout this study I use the terms "feminine" and "maternal" in the broadest possible sense—expressing an all-encompassing image of these writers' adoption of various maternal metaphors: 1) of maternal ethics in fostering caregiving in the community; 2) of the feminine/maternal body as a self-generating site of (re)production; and 3) of the maternal ideal and maternal imprinting as suggestive of women's roles in mothering, teaching, and performing the grunt domestic work of radical social reform. In each chapter the feminine/maternal figure, real or imaginary, emerges as the obverse of women's marginal status in society and invariably signifies the author's reinvented autobiographical self or female characters giving, protecting, and restoring life to others in a national and global setting, claiming the world as their territory, as pronounced dramatically in Alice Walker's bold work.

The maternal impetus toward regeneration for these women writers, as noted in their autobiographical works, or for their characters, as seen in their novels, sets these writers apart from others with what Patricia Meyer Spacks speaks of in another context as a "symbolic as well as literal significance."[13] I am not, however, using these terms "feminine" and "maternal" to assign to these women writers or their heroines the strict biological determinism of their sex and gender. I hope that it will be clear that with their distinct voices and their wide use of feminine and maternal powers of creativity they limit neither themselves nor their characters to the biology of their bodies. Writers from Wheatley to Forten Grimké and even Marshall, Walker, and Morrison (who have been accused of reverse sexism) represent their male subjects as also being capable of having the transformational impulse of their female subjects. Clearly, the capacity of providing and fostering care in the community is not limited by gender: in these texts caring men can "mother" too. But the male lacks the profound fecundity of the female body, its life-giving properties, and therefore the dominant maternal metaphors and images of regeneration in these women's literature are distinctively feminine.

Maternal Metaphors of Power in African American Women's Literature includes seven chapters followed by an afterword. Drawing upon the various theories of feminists from Carol Gilligan and Patricia Hill Collins to Luce Irigaray and Julie Kristeva, psychoanalysts from Freud to Lacan and Jung, and social scientists from Stephen Jay Gould to Michel Foucault and W. E. B. Du Bois, along with others, I examine the maternal iconography and counterhegemonic narratives of black women writers. Across their periods, genres, and literary influences, ranging from colonialism to postmodernism, these writers were all on the cutting edge of history, reforming their societies and capturing the national character of America's identity politics as well as the related history of the Caribbean experience, in the case of the Diaspora writer Paule Marshall.

Maternal Metaphors offers a sweeping though not complete "historicization of slavery—and freedom"[14] and the "*Herrenvolk* democracy" of the United States past the advent of World War II,[15] the time that van den Berghe limits it to but which the texts examined here show lasted much longer. The Jim Crow system of racial segregation crystallizes the theory of van den Berghe and Myrdal and what they had to say about American democracy, its practice or lack thereof for Negroes, a racial designation used before the era of the civil rights movement and the 1960s and cited throughout this study when appropriate. The ambitiousness of this literary project on America's Herrenvolk democracy, written over a period of fifteen years, is related in part to my study of the subject "Literature and Society" in a postgraduate seminar taught in 1989 by the historian Arthur Schlesinger Jr. at the Graduate School of the City University of New York. We examined the influence of the events of history and society on the writing of literature, which offers insight into lessons on the inherent struggle between the individual and social forces, appearing beyond her or his control. Moreover, female students in my "American Minority Women Writers" course often express a desire to place women's literature in its historical context, examining the connection between the writers' literary subjects and the forces against which they wrote, especially if demoralizing to themselves or their artistic vision of a more humane society. We learn that the study of literature, set apart from the sociopolitical dynamics that fostered its appearance, can frequently result in a failure to appreciate the writers' accomplishments in capturing the ethos of the age and contributing to our knowledge of the ascending and progressive nature of history based on the evolution of social thought and values.

The writers included in *Maternal Metaphors* were selected primarily because of their historical significance but also due to their popularity with students. Phillis Wheatley was a northern slave and harbinger of African American literature; Harriet Jacobs was a southern slave and provider of insight into the sexualization of plantation slavery; and Charlotte Forten was a free, wealthy Negro, less examined in literary studies but equally as important as her feted contemporaries, Harriet Jacobs and Frances Ellen Watkins Harper. The cosmopolitan and local-color writers of the Harlem Renaissance, Jessie Fauset, Nella Larsen, and Zora Neale Hurston, were producers of a literature of aesthetics, providing a counternarrative to the antiblack aesthetics of Jim Crow America. Paule Marshall, Alice Walker, and Toni Morrison are an admired triad of contemporary writers who offer differing yet poignant perspectives on the civil rights movement and history in general, past and present. Singly and collectively these writers provide an unremitting gaze into American history, describing its racial past as a prologue to its racial present and providing too an understanding of America's long, complex racial narrative: its failure and its promise.

Part One

Slavery and Abolitionism, Freedom and Jim Crow America

The works of the six writers discussed here contain a microscopic history of slavery, abolitionism, and black emancipation and then the rise of Jim Crow strictures, which sought to limit the newly acquired freedom of African Americans. Their genres are easily recognizable: Wheatley's religious poetry; Jacobs's slave narrative; Forten Grimké's Civil War journals; and Fauset's, Larsen's, and Hurston's early twentieth-century novels. Across their selection of literary genres, these authors provided the visible conditions of their times, which they experienced and/or confronted and described in their work. Based on the variety of their art forms, a set of critical and theoretical assessments is used to elucidate the uniqueness of their style, content, and meaning.

1 Phillis Wheatley's Seminaked Body as Symbol and Metaphor

As Roman imperialism laid the foundations of modern civilization, and led the wild barbarians of these islands along the path of progress, so in Africa today we are repaying the debt, and bringing to the dark places of the earth, the abode of barbarism and cruelty, the torch of culture and progress, while ministering to the material needs of our own civilization. . . . We hold these countries because it is the genius of our race to colonize, to trade, and to govern.[1]

As the opening quotation on empire and racial arrogance reveals, the image of Africa as the dark and vast unknown has a long and tortured history from the advent of the African slave trade in the fifteenth century to these postmodern times. In examining the iconography of Phillis Wheatley's seminaked body, marketed on Boston's slave auction block in 1761, we see her enslaved physical body as a pejorative symbol of the Dark Continent of Africa, pronounced in the rationalization of slavery and the construction of racial grids. Yet, Wheatley's body can also be interpreted as a metaphor of women's transformational power, for in coming to write, she gave new birth to herself and founded African American literature. As an artist, Wheatley represents the feminine-maternal capacity to regenerate life, although women as mothers have identities that go beyond that which are gendered and biologically determined. In her study *Philosophy and the Maternal Body*, Michelle Boulous Walker, like Helene Cixous before her, relates women's bodily power to their creative potential in opposition to the (in)stability of the father's universe.[2] Samples of Wheatley's poetry reveal from this perspective her appropriation of feminine and maternal metaphors of power in that she often demonstrates a gender-specific, nurturing, and transformational impulse in selected works, whether her autobiographical poem, political and religious poems, or elegies. Rebirth and regeneration are major motifs in her poetry, of which, as slave-turned-poet, she is the archetypal model.

Critics such as Robert Reid-Pharr who argue for the disestablishment of Wheatley as the harbinger of African American literature misread her significance as the first African American writer who established the precedence of black authors rewriting the body and human suffering via tropes of healing and recovery. Reid-Pharr posits, incorrectly, that because Wheatley was purchased and reared by the white Boston merchant John Wheatley and his wife, Susannah, she manifested "traits of an 'unfinished' literary training" and "an 'unfinished' racial identity." In an attempt to buttress his argument for a new assessment of Wheatley, he states that she lacked a "black subjectivity" and "black singularity." Wheatley, according to his reading, was "no Frederick Douglass," who distinguished masters from slaves in the Hegelian sense of the individual striving with the wisdom of historical consciousness and progress. "This is why I have pointed to Wheatley's interracial domestication in my efforts to disestablish her status as the original author of a noble Black American literary tradition," Reid-Pharr writes. Wheatley's seminal autobiographical poem "On Being Brought from Africa to America, 1768" demonstrates, he continues, that her "work does little to establish black specificity" because "she celebrates her enslavement."[3]

Yet this autobiographical poem serves as an example of how several Wheatley scholars, including Reid-Pharr, have misinterpreted her double-voiced poem on Christian hypocrisy, which she parodies. In coming to write, Wheatley not only was the first significantly published and celebrated black intellectual artist to re-create herself from a degraded slave to a famous author, but she also was the most cherished who reinvigorated the abolitionist movement. By the time of Frederick Douglass's emergence from slavery in 1838 to the publication of his first slave narrative in 1845, the abolitionist movement in America and London was well under way, having been advanced by Wheatley as early as 1773. From her autobiographical poem to her later poems and letters, Wheatley emerges as a moral and social reformer of her rigid colonial world. In her poetry she constructs the sociopolitics of civic mothering, caring and nurturing others and fostering a sense of community, beyond the circumscribed boundaries of race, gender, religion, science, and politics.

While drawing upon maternal metaphors of regeneration, Wheatley anticipated the principal tenets of maternal and feminist ethics that contemporary feminists from Carol Gilligan to Patricia Hill Collins attribute to women in their overarching maternal roles.[4] White and black feminists such as Gilligan and Hill have defined concepts of a feminist morality in terms of the self in relation to others in the community that the precocious Wheatley, as poet, clearly embraces. In her pathbreaking book *In a Different Voice: Psychological Theory and Women's Development*, Gilligan interprets white, middle-class women's definitions of themselves in terms of their relationship and connection with others, unlike their male peers who view autonomy and individualism as important self-defining values. Feminists such as Collins agree that women's maternal ethics of fostering care and building relationships symbolize a distinctly feminine characteristic and code of behavior. However, Collins posits that given the unique history of black men and women as enslaved individuals, black maternal and feminist ethics encompass a broader political and social agenda in reforming society in reference to the lives of black Americans. Their survival of slavery was a blow to the established order where their bodies had been given the marginal status of only an economic interest in the marketplace, as Ralph Ellison suggests in the introduction to this work.

On the threshold of a defining moment in history, Wheatley is one of the major precursors of the questing artist in society, advocating freedom and social and political justice on a much larger scale than Gilligan suggests about white women in particular. Wheatley is the first, African American female writer to combine the domestic politics of maternal and feminist ethics on a prominent level, for she wrote poetry that addresses the needs of individuals as well as the redressing of the entire national and global order vis-à-vis religion, science, peace, war, and later, slavery. For example, in her University of Cambridge (now Harvard University) poem, written before 1773, she refers to herself as an "Ethiop," synonymous with the whole of Africa. She uses her ethnic identity to admonish white college students to make the most of their privileges and opportunities, the luxuries of which are missing in Africa. Wheatley cites her hybrid status (as an African pariah and American Evangelical Christian) to contrast the indigenous but limited world of Africa to the unlimited realm of science in the West, thereby crossing and yet building a bridge across continents and disciplines. While the African scholar Adeleke Adeeko classifies this and other poems (in which Wheatley refers to her ethnic identity) as the poet's "African poems" of a "New World, Christian, subaltern voice," imitating her "masters and mentors" and denigrating Africa,[5] Vincent Carretta posits that her "exposure to Christianity, and to literacy, soon made her known to fellow believers,"[6] nationally and internationally.

Wheatley appropriates her religion "as a primary subject," giving her the "authority and power"[7]to speak to others, democratizing the hierarchy of race and class for the African outsider. In the Cambridge poem science and religion are morally juxtaposed as two determining forces of history. But the logic of science should not supplant, she implies, the importance of faith and religion. She explains, "Students, to you 'tis giv'n to scan the heights / Above, to traverse the ethereal space, / And mark the systems of revolving worlds / Still more, ye sons of science you receive / The blissful news by messengers from heav'n, / How Jesus' blood for your redemption flows."[8] Although the Cambridge poem does not specifically address the issue of race, Wheatley, the Ethiop, uses race and religion as yardsticks to check the inevitable proliferation of science against the students' cultivation of an inner spirituality. With her antithetical positioning of race, religion, and science, Wheatley, the self-deprecating and "untutored" African, appears to analyze subtly the inequality of race and opportunity while lauding the triumph of faith, a socially leveling force for her in an enslaving society.

Another illustration of her offering an olive branch of peace in this time after conflict and war is seen in one of her last poems, where she examines political power but applies feminine metaphors of positive social change to human advancement.

Wheatley's poem "Liberty and Peace," published in 1784, the year of her death, celebrates the achievement of the American Revolution. In this poem she uses gender-specific language to describe the human virtues of peace and freedom, which she characteristically feminizes. She writes,

> Lo! Freedom comes . . .
> "She moves divinely fair,
> "Olive and Laurel bind her golden Hair."
> She, the bright Progeny of Heaven, descends,
> And every Grace her sovereign Step attends;
> For now kind Heaven, indulgent to our Prayer,
> In smiling Peace resolves the Din of War.[9]

Justice and freedom, peace and nonaggression are intricately connected to a feminine psyche, but war and aggression ("Navies," "fraternal Arms," and "savage Troops") are firmly linked to a masculine imaginary. She feminizes the word "Columbia" and is believed to be the first to describe America as "Columbia, 'the goddess of freedom'": "The Sword resign'd, resume the friendly Part! / For Gailia's power espous'd Columbia's Cause." The goddess of freedom functions as a metaphor of tranquillity after the chaos of war. Considering her violent abduction from Africa, her transition from a state of innate freedom to one of colonial enslavement, done at the will of an avaricious African and European patriarchy, Wheatley's poetic inscription of feminine powers appears to register her distrust of dominating, imperial authorities. Historically the black female body, as with the example of Wheatley's youthful appearance at auction, has been a site of the configuration of black women's identity as indistinguishable from commodified objects, made visible in black women's socially ascribed roles as slaves, servants, and sexed bodies. Appreciably, Wheatley is the first to rewrite the history of race and gender subordination to international acclaim and social change, transcending her inauspicious beginnings.

The Origin of Phillis Wheatley: The Quintessential Slave Heroine

According to Julian Mason's introduction to Phillis Wheatley's poetry, on July 11, 1761, an enslaved and frail African female arrived at Boston's Feather Wharf[10] perhaps wearing only a ragged piece of cloth tied around her tiny waist. Kidnapped from her family in West Africa, probably by Africans, shipped on the slave ship *Phillis* to America, and sold to the prosperous and religious Boston merchant John Wheatley, the puny slave would later become known as a famous poet whose writings were cited by abolitionists to attack the institution of slavery. However, her inauspicious naming and identity (after the slave ship *Phillis*) were symbolically inscribed on her seminude body. Her body was displayed as a capitalist tool and product of the African slave trade and European expansionism, and she was forced to stand at auction, perhaps under the typical advertisement of the day: "A Parcel of Likely Negroes Just Imported from West Africa." The public, partial nakedness of Wheatley's developing body becomes a symbol of inscription, for on her body was written her foreignness, a politically and socially constructed identity, based on her color, gender, and culture.

The historian Winthrop Jordan has noted, "The Negro's color attained [its] greatest significance not as a scientific problem, but as a social fact. Englishmen found blackness in human beings a peculiar and important point of difference."[11] Within the cultural context of difference and foreignness, black peoples' color became an issue of debate over its origin, its cause, and its significance, particularly at a propitious time in history with the growth of imperialism and the slave trade. Slavery was seen by many as a necessary evil in the development of European capitalism, but the stigma of color mitigated this evil in the era of colonialism. Africans or Negroes became "subjects for a special kind of obedience and subordination" to Englishmen who were "energetically on the make," Jordan remarks, and "sought to possess for themselves and their children one of the most bountiful dominions of the earth"[12]: land as property. The early pejorative association of blackness with heathenism and difference was one that ascribed to blacks a certain identity, emblazoned on enslaved bodies of which Wheatley's becomes the prototype. She is perhaps the first clear model we have of an object-turned-subject with a conscious awareness that by writing she was giving birth to a new self, as seen in one of her epistles.

Wheatley's Seminaked Body: A Symbol of the Dark Continent

Wheatley's body was indeed a symbol of Africa and social death. As an illustration of this idea, we must consider the following occurrences: 1) the establishment of scientific racism in the eighteenth-century; 2) the John Hancock committee's affidavit on Wheatley's poetry; 3) John Wheatley's separate statement about his slave's uniqueness; and 4) Wheatley's writing of a short, autobiographical poem, "On Being Brought from Africa to America"—described as one of the most "reviled" poems in the African American literary canon.[13] The first of these, scientific racism, contributed to the overarching perception of blackness as a state of negation, a notion delineated in Carolus Linnaeus's book *Systema naturae* (1758), in which the Swedish botanist, who invented the term *Homo sapiens*, divided the human race into four categories. These classifications were based on skin color, temperament, physical stance, and geographical region, hence Native Americans, Europeans, Asians, and Africans. Native Americans were defined as "red, choleric, upright"; Europeans as "white, sanguine, muscular"; Asians as "pale-yellow, melancholy, stiff"; and Africans as "niger, phlegmatic, laxus," with capricious behavior.[14] Although Linnaeus did not design his scientific grid of taxonomy "in the ranked order favored by most Europeans in the racist tradition,"[15] Stephen Jay Gould explains, he nonetheless established a perception of race that clearly favored the "sanguine" European over others, especially the "capricious" African.

Perceptions of race as outlined in a grid form and as projected on Wheatley's diminutive body-in-crisis on a slave auction block helped to fix her body in the racist gaze of the dominating culture, leading to the undoing of her body as a human body. Hers was not a valued human body, except for reasons of economic exploitation. Empirical scientists such as Gould, social scientists from Michel Foucault to Jacques Lacan, and the feminist Luce Irigaray have theorized the disjunctive discourse on race and taxonomy and gender. To various degrees they describe the resulting fragmentation of identities, springing from an enduring low ranking of the cultural Other, ideas useful in a rereading of Wheatley. In *The Mismeasure of Man*, Gould argues that Linnaeus is not truly responsible for the scientific establishment of racist thought in the eighteenth century, although he influenced it. Gould reserves this infamous distinction, ironically, for J. F. Blumenbach, the German naturalist who did rank humans by their putative worth in a hierarchical ranking of the five categories of humans, including the Malay, with Europeans at the top and Africans at the bottom. "Blumenbach certainly thought that his switch from the Linnaean four-race system to his own five-race scheme—the basis for his fateful geometric shift . . . from cartography to hierarchy—arose only from his improved understanding of nature's factuality,"[16] says Gould. The irony of Blumenbach's fateful hierarchy is that he did not believe in the concept of black inferiority, having affirmed "the perfectibility of the mental faculties and the talents of the Negro," citing the example of "Phillis Wheatley of Boston, who is justly famous."[17] Blumenbach kept a copy of Wheatley's 1773 book of poems in his library. Still, Gould cites Blumenbach, not Linnaeus, as fixing the attitudes on racial worth, although Blumenbach was "the least racist, most egalitarian . . . of all Enlightenment writers on the subject of human diversity."[18]

Blumenbach and the racial grids that he and Linnaeus established confounded for Foucault the problem of life in the eighteenth century, a fact that Wheatley's harshest critics, Reid-Pharr and Adeeko included, seem to ignore. In his analysis of the age and its development of the systematic ranking of human bodies, Foucault interprets the period as a "grid of denominations." He singles out Linnaeus, who initially distinguished "the parts of natural bodies with his eyes, describes them appropriately according to their number, form, position, and proportion and he names them." Natural history and naturalists such as Linnaeus, Foucault posits, are concerned only with the "structure of the visible world and its denomination according to characters. Not with life."[19] Wheatley's poem to students at the University of Cambridge, written when she was only a teenager, says as much about the unfair dominance of science in the inflexible ordering of the universe, as Foucault would later theorize in his critique of dominating systems of power in that century. On a subliminal level, Wheatley could have been taking aim at the scientific structure of valuation that relegated her life to the social bottom. There-fore, her emphasis on religion gave her a voice beyond the subaltern and a higher social ranking in the community she was building.

While the human body can be defined as a mass of tissues, organs, and flesh, Linnaeus's and Blumenbach's critical moves to identify and rank specific kinds of bodies, giving them a certain significance or insignificance within a grid, commu-nicate an infinite number of meanings, not solely scientific but rather perceptual. Naming and identifying bodies to be accepted as the very things that are described can become, according to Lacan, "a pact, by which two subjects simultaneously come to an agreement" over the objects being named, and the "power of naming objects structures the perception itself."[20] That is, the perception becomes as great as the subjects-as-objects being named and defined. Hence the innocence of color per se is compromised by the various perceptions of color as rooted in something other than the purity of hue. In the novel *Moby-Dick,* for example, Herman Mel-ville establishes the perceptual differentiation of color in his manipulation of the reversal of color discrimination. Melville creates a white, albino whale whose per-sonified and malevolent whiteness psychologically reverses the trope of blackness as terror. But on Boston's Feather Wharf, the enslaved and unnamed black child was a symbol of a geographical location, an emblem of the sacrificial black body-in-crisis, marketed for the common good of a capitalist Western culture. With Lin-naeus's grid (rather than Blumenbach's, which came later) of Africa and Africans etched in the minds of society, the prodigy did not represent a youthful self with potential but a pagan people, fixed in a perceived identity.

As racial symbol, Wheatley could not go beyond this essentialist copy of race and identity. Theoretically, in the pairing of her quasi-nude body with the rheto-ric of her distorted image, Wheatley in the civilized New World represented the nakedness of Africa. Nowhere is the association of Africa with barbarism more explicitly demonstrated than in the statement of a prominent, all-white male com-mittee in Boston. Their affidavit on Wheatley's poetry was requested—no evidence exists of her meeting with them in public as Henry Louis Gates and Paul Gilroy logically assume[21]—when she decided to write poetry and become a published poet in London, not Boston, where publishers refused her book of poems for publi-cation. Her London publisher and her benevolent mistress, Susannah Wheatley, solicited a group of distinguished men in Boston to authenticate her poetry for a racist society that needed proof of her talent. Even as they authenticated her writings, however, these men denigrated her African body in a Cartesian mind/body separation that ironically objectified and celebrated Wheatley's mind while perceptually connecting her body to the perceived pagan body of Africa:

> To the Publick. As it has been repeatedly suggested to the Publisher, by Persons, who have seen the Manuscript, that Numbers would be ready to suspect they

were not really the Writings of PHILLIS, he has procured the following Attesta-tion, from the most respectable Characters in Boston, that none might have the least Ground for disputing their Original. We whose Names are under-written, do assure the World, that the POEMS specified in the following Page, were (as we verily believe) written by PHILLIS, a young Negro Girl, who was but a few Years since, brought an *uncultivated Barbarian from Africa,* [emphasis added] and has ever since been, and now is, under the Disadvantage of serving as a Slave in a Family in this Town. She has been examined by some of the best Judges, and is thought qualified to write them.[22]

Among the eighteen distinguished men signing the statement were John Wheatley, the master; John Hancock, the famous signer of the Declaration of Independence; and Thomas Hutchinson, governor of the Massachusetts colony. As documented evidence, the affidavit represents the power of a white, dominant and masculine authority to bring to public consciousness the work of an African writer, with their stamp of approval of Wheatley's reconfiguration of identity, beyond her doubly colonized body as African and New England patriot.

Although the affidavit anticipates the racist suspicions that Wheatley's literacy as a slave would undoubtedly raise, no less a prominent figure than Thomas Jeffer-son questioned her authenticity as a poet. In *Notes from Virginia,* Jefferson asserts that Wheatley's poems were "beneath the dignity of criticism" because "among the black is misery enough, God knows, but no poetry. Religion indeed has produced a Phyllis Whately [sic]; but it could not produce a poet."[23] According to Jean Fagan Yellin, Jefferson's *Notes* "embodies both an assertion of human liberty, and a classic statement of the racism which has prevented its realization in America."[24] Indeed, Paul Finkelman's *Slavery and the Founders* goes beyond hinting that Jefferson, iron-ically, was the most racist of the founding fathers. Unlike the others, especially Benjamin Franklin and George Washington, the Declaration of Independence au-thor was "blind" to the "talents, skills, or intellectual abilities" of blacks,[25] including those who labored freely for his comfort on his Monticello estate. In Jefferson's mis-spelling of Phillis Wheatley's name and his questioning of her authorship of poems ("published under her name"), he negates her identity twice while engaging in con-flicting criticism: he mocks her poems while suggesting that she is not really their author. Jefferson's criticism is consistent with the image of Wheatley and Africa as pronounced in the Hancock committee's statement, but with one critical difference.

When Jefferson remarks that "Religion" has produced Phillis Wheatley, he as-cribes to her a bodily transformation of identity but implies that only the West and its culture could have effected these changes, a proslavery argument for the civi-lizing of Africans. Unlike Jefferson, the Hancock committee describes Wheatley as intellectually gifted, but like Jefferson, they make a distinction between her mind and her body inscribed as "an uncultivated Barbarian from Africa." In the mind/

body split of Cartesian dualism, Jefferson acknowledges only the metaphysics of Wheatley's bodily metamorphosis from pagan body to religious body, while the Hancock committee recognizes her mind but describes her physical body as they perceived her native African continent: barbaric. When the Hancock committee described Wheatley as a barbarian, she had been living in the colonies for over a decade and considered herself an acculturated American, as we see in the famous George Whitefield elegy when she addresses the countess and tells her that "*we Americans* [emphasis added] revere / Thy name." Although she could not have become a citizen because of her race, she had become, biculturally, an American hybrid, as many Europeans did in immigrating to the colonies, where they secured their freedom and became citizens. That Wheatley was denied the status of even a cultural hybrid (except in her espousal of religion) reveals Jefferson's and the Hancock committee's refusals to see her as anything other than a *foreign* body in the national body politic. Several centuries later and in a postmodern America with its first African American president, Barack Obama, one sees this same kind of public denial of a black person's national-body citizenship by President Obama's right-wing "birther" critics, revealing the long arm of American history and identity politics, poignantly examined in Jacqueline Jones's study, *A Dreadful Deceit: The Myth of Race from the Colonial Era to Obama's America* (2013).

In both eighteenth-century cases, with Jefferson and the Hancock committee, Wheatley's mind and body are not reconciled in a whole, reciprocal relationship: the mind communicating to the body that acts as a vehicle or channel through which thoughts are processed and acted out in bodily language, gestures, and signs. Since Wheatley's mind and body are treated separately in both instances, it is clear that for Jefferson and the Hancock committee, Wheatley remained a fragmented body, a perception of a symbol, an embodiment of Africa, the dark unknown and unknowable continent. In her century Wheatley was placed in the unenviable position "of experiencing herself only fragmentarily, in the little-structured margins of a dominant ideology," as Irigaray remarks in another context on female subjugation. Irigaray goes on to comment that within her marginal positionality, the splintered woman (such as Wheatley here) can recover "only in secret, in hiding, with anxiety and guilt."[26]

If we view Wheatley's adoption of the double-voiced discourse in earlier and later selected poems and letters, then her psychic recovery from slavery and racial essentialism is related to her ability to manipulate language and voice subversively in a hostile, alienating society that saw her as unwhole. The Wheatley scholar Paula Bennett says as much when she writes, "Wheatley's manipulation of Western rhetorical and cultural conventions in the interests of her own poetic agency is nowhere more evident than in her handling of the elegy, or formal mourning poem."[27] However, even before the writing of elegies such as the Whitefield poem, Wheatley showed an uncanny manipulation of language in one of her first poems.

Just as she adroitly creates feminine images of the goddess of freedom and disrupts the traditionally putative low ranking of women, thought to be weak and emotional rather than strong and rational, Wheatley also controls language and voice in "On Being Brought from Africa to America." In this poem she subtly, or in Irigaray's word, secretly, attacks the hypocritical religious and slaveholding society in which she lives. But in her private correspondence, for example, her 1774 letter to Samson Occom, the Native American missionary, Wheatley was free to be less secretive. Speaking in a single voice, she describes Africa as a land of chaos but argues that Christians who enslave Africans to save them from paganism manifested a "strange Absurdity of their Conduct" because "God has implanted a Principle, which we call Love of Freedom" in "every human Breast."[28] Her diction of "every human Breast" is an all-encompassing yet incarnate maternal and life-supporting metaphor. It resounds with ideas of human essence and a healthful liberal egalitarianism, dominating Enlightenment discourse.

One other document pertains to Wheatley as an emblem of the Dark Continent. Her slave master, John Wheatley, submitted an official statement in support of Wheatley's 1773 publication of poems, which, perhaps unwittingly, reveals the falseness of the cultural assumptions of the West about Wheatley's place of origin but which she both refutes and mimics, perhaps showing her own confusion. John Wheatley writes, "Without any Assistance from School-Education, and by only what she was taught in the family, she, in sixteen Months' Time from her Arrival, attained the English Language, to which she was an utter Stranger before, to such a Degree, as to read any, [even] the most difficult Parts of the Sacred Writings."[29] By identifying Wheatley as a "Stranger" to the West, its language, and its culture, John Wheatley submits to, yet simultaneously challenges, the West's racist conceptualization of Wheatley and Africa as the barbaric cultural Other, but he also reinscribes her identity as prodigy.

Wheatley's ability to learn several different languages from English to Latin to Greek and to read the Bible and English and Greek literature with considerable facility contradicts Jefferson's claim that religion alone had produced Phillis Wheatley. Her education, Vincent Carretta explains, resembled that of highly educated white men and was superior to that of most white women, of whom "only about half" of the population was "sufficiently literate."[30] The Wheatley scholar Lucy Hayden identifies and traces Wheatley's classical allusions to Greek and Roman mythology in twenty-six of her first published thirty-nine poems,[31] with one of her earliest poems, "On Messrs Hussey and Coffin" (1767), containing several classical allusions and stressing the origin of her maternal metaphors of power. Yet even here, in a poem about men in Cape Cod who narrowly escaped a disaster while at sea, we can see Wheatley's signature invention of a feminine trope of positive maternal intervention in the men's rescue from danger. This particular trope of "powerful women [as goddesses] in powerful roles," as Gerda Lerner reminds us in *The Creation of Patriarchy*, is at odds with the "lifelong dependency of women on fathers and husbands [that] became so firmly established in law and custom as to be considered 'natural' and god-given."[32] In working against the fortification of that which was considered "natural" in the social dynamics of identity politics, Wheatley exuded a clearly defined, albeit subtle and subversive personal politics. That is, she epitomized and transcended the accepted discourse of the age, perhaps best summarized by the literary giant of the conservative neoclassical period, Alexander Pope, who paternalistically writes in his famous *Essay on Man*, "WHATEVER IS, IS RIGHT."[33]

In Wheatley's "On Messrs Hussey and Coffin" poem, she strikes a conciliatory tone and asks the weary men, "Did Fear and Danger so perplex your Mind / As made you fearful of the Whistling Wind? / Was it not Boreas knit his angry Brow / Did haughty Eolus with Contempt look down / With Aspect windy, and a study'd Frown? Had the soft gliding Streams of Grace been near / Some favourite Hope their fainting hearts to cheer." In this poem the Greek gods of the wind, Eolus and Boreas, have a violent, rupturing presence, endangering the men's lives while they are in rough waters. Having the power to delay Odysseus's return to Ithaca, Eolus, the keeper of the winds, reveals his terrible force in Homer's *The Odyssey*, the epic to which Wheatley most likely alludes in her treatment of the winds. The poem's image of the feminine and "soft" Grace, representing the three graces Aglaia, Euphrosyne, and Thaleia in Greek mythology, is one that projects maternal powers of compassion, leading to the protection of the men, had the goddess been near. We see, then, how the presence/absence of gods and goddesses can change the direction of this poem with Wheatley inflecting here a uniquely life-altering feminine imaginary in one of her early poems of comfort. These traits are associated with women, acting maternally. Given her rupturing experience in the New World, one can ask how Wheatley came to this kind of artistic temperament at such a young age.

Eighteenth-century critics who were suspicious of Wheatley's literacy and her ability to absorb knowledge and articulate her thoughts, through the art of poetry, exhibited a profound cultural ignorance of Africa and its indigenous ways of knowing. While African societies had formal and informal systems of education, most education involved what the European historian Basil Davidson describes as word-of-mouth learning in the "teaching of skills, customs, laws, traditions, and the like. It was done for the most part without the aid of writing and reading: the culture was non-literate."[34] Storytellers, musicians, and poets had remarkable roles in Africa's nonliterate culture, preserving African history as told by Griots in great literary events, which lasted for days. While scholars have traditionally differed on the identity of Wheatley's place of origin—Angola, Gambia, and Senegal being frequently mentioned—Carretta states that Wheatley, the sickly "refuge"[35] slave, came from the area connecting today's Gambia and Ghana. While no one can claim that she was a direct descendant of West African Griots, she nonetheless retained in genetic cultural memory the artistic skills associated with Africa's preliterate oral and cultural tradition and adapted these skills to a literate Western culture.

On occasion she recalled specific African cultural rites. This illustration of cultural memory was evidenced on the morning that the Wheatleys discovered her outside at the crack of dawn pouring water from a basin to the rising sun.[36] Of her early formative years in Africa, she could recall only the image of her biological mother pouring water on the ground before a rising sun. This ritual, John C. Shields argues, strongly implies that the poet's "parents were sun worshippers," an image consistent with the eighteenth-century symbol of Africa and Africans as pagans. Wheatley as poet, Shields submits, "syncretized the memory of her mother's sun worship with Christianity" in circular imagery of freedom and wholeness."[37] While Wheatley could not recall the symbolism of her mother's act, the eighteenth-century African writer and former slave Gustavus Vassa (or Olaudah Equiano) did remember the meaning. It was expressive of the natives' practice of honoring the Creator who *lived* in the sun (emphasis added), an embodiment of the Creator's splendid creation.[38] Wheatley's mother was not a sun worshipper but a believer who participated in traditional cultural rites honoring the Creator. In another essay Shields provides an analysis of Kant's dictum that the "feeling of the sublime never occurs 'in objects' but always results from a mental response to their contemplation,"[39] which applies more accurately to Wheatley's mother's morning rites of repose and contemplation, honoring the Creator, not the object of the sun.

The complexity of essentializing Wheatley's identity in the eighteenth century via scientific grids, cultural assumptions, and cultural ignorance about Africa is made no less complex by Wheatley, as we see in one of her first published poems. In the well-known and most "reviled" autobiographical poem, "On Being Brought from Africa to America," the teenaged Wheatley engages in a double-voiced discourse, which underscores the fragile nature of her existence in colonial Boston, particularly with its people to whom she spoke, but sometimes in a tied tongue. While ostensibly presenting herself in the image that the dominant society perceived her as (a "pagan" from Africa with the "diabolic dye" of blackness), Wheatley cleverly appropriates the symbol of the biblical Cain and turns the discourse around to criticize the hypocrisy of Christians:

> 'Twas mercy brought me from my Pagan land,
> Taught my benighted soul to understand
> That there's a God, that there's a Saviour too:
> Once I redemption neither sought nor knew.
> Some view our sable race with scornful eye,
> "Their colour is a diabolic die."
> Remember, Christians, Negros, black as Cain,
> May be refin'd, and join th' angelic train.[40]

The Wheatley scholar William Scheick argues that her metaphor of Cain is suggestive of the larger spiritual linkage of whites and blacks as "sin-darkened descendants of Canaan," for the idea of original sin "applies equally to both races."[41] With Wheatley's use of the biblical allusion to Cain, Scheick asserts that she draws on a popular motif of her age. Inhabitants of the period were fond of interpreting the outcast Cain as black, and Wheatley puns on Cain as an "oral corruption of Canaan," as a person and a place.[42] Canaan was Ham's son and Noah's grandson whom Noah cursed along with other descendants of Ham because of his filial disrespect of his father, whom he had seen naked. Canaan is also the native name of Palestine, the land given to Abraham and his descendants, and the site of the historical violence between Arabs and Jews. As Scheick asserts, the thematics of blackness, sin, and curses dominate the poem, but Wheatley maneuvers the image of color to portray whites and blacks as having a "shared Adamic heritage."[43]

In contrast to Scheick's interpretation of the poem as Wheatley's manipulation of image to contest exclusionary ideas of race, her autobiographical poem can also be read as a parody of race and racial violence. In stylized language Wheatley parodies the dominant group's legacy of imperialist violence and its denial of brotherhood and goodwill with black people, disproving Reid-Pharr's claim that Wheatley celebrates her enslavement and that Douglass was one of the first great slaves to contest slavery. While Scheick establishes the mark on Cain's forehead as colorless, his criticism focuses too much on skin color. He falls into the historical color trap of race and identity, accepting the image of blackness as a symbolic pejorative—that is, attributing to Wheatley the belief that "both races share a common heritage of Cain-like barbaric and criminal blackness" and that "white and black people are jointly a 'sable race.'"[44]

Even Betsy Erkkila, whose criticism of the tirade against Wheatley by Amiri Baraka in *Home: Social Essays,* which he published under the name LeRoi Jones in 1966, is well received, falls into the color trap. Although he could not have known of recently discovered poems and letters that place Wheatley in a different light, Baraka, as Jones, ridicules Wheatley. He chastises the poet for writing polite poems, which were "departures from the huge black voices that splintered southern nights."[45] Writing over thirty years later and with more information on Wheatley, Erkkila counters Baraka and also Alice Walker,[46] who criticizes Wheatley's description of the "golden hair[ed]" goddess of justice and peace. Erkkila identifies the blond goddess as the "insurrectionary 'Goddess of Liberty' . . . [who] stalks" injustices in many of Wheatley's poems, notably "Liberty and Peace," discovered and published after 1979. Up to the period of the Protestant Reformation, Gerda Lerner remarks, the "vast majority of women"[47] could not allude to other women in positions of power. Excluding her epic lamentation "Niobe in Distress for Her Children Slain by Apollo," which Wheatley adapted from Ovid's legendary *Metamorphoses,* her powerful goddesses address what still must have been something of a void of feminine power even a few hundred years after the Reformation. However, like Scheick, Erkkila finds in Wheatley's reference to Cain an emphasis on "the equality of [the] spiritual condition shared by whites and blacks alike"[48]—that of sin in color-coded language.

What critics appear to overlook in the autobiographical poem is Wheatley's lethal parody of the adult Christians' spiritual immaturity and hypocrisy. The line "Their colour is a diabolic die" critiques the Christians' racism and transcends the color trap and its perceived and ascribed pejorative symbolism. In a single line Wheatley undermines the authority of hegemony and its racialized discourse in a double-coded referentiality—theirs and hers, which imitates and mocks theirs. According to Bakhtin, this kind of parodic stylization of language is an "act of authorial unmasking . . . openly accomplished within the boundaries of a single simple sentence, merged with the unmasking of another's speech."[49] Rather than pairing blacks and whites as "sin-blackened" Cains, Wheatley holds the dominant group responsible for incurring the violent legacy of Cain, who murders his brother. But she uses a clandestine method of assault: what Irigaray associates with women quietly recovering their voice. The line "Remember, Christians" implies that colonists are not who they think they are: true Christians. Hence, Wheatley believes that she, the untutored African, has to remind them, to persuade them to harmonize their worldview with that of Christ and recognize the brotherhood of men. In London in 1787 the potter and abolitionist Josiah Wedgwood created the jasper medallion of a kneeling male slave pleading, "Am I not a man and a brother, too," a medallion housed in the British Museum but copies of which became fashionable antislavery icons in Europe and America. Wheatley—in the most "reviled" of her poems—had voiced the suppliant slave's plea almost two decades earlier.

Wheatley's Seminaked Body: A Metaphor of Feminine-Maternal Power

An equally powerful and countering visual image to that of the unnamed female child standing on Boston's Feather Wharf is that of the prepubescent female whose nascent womb and developing body are literally and metaphorically the lifeline of human society. Unlike a symbol, to be a "metaphor [is to] insist on the miracle by which things change their nature, become other than themselves, their substance dissolving into other things . . . a total aesthetic control everywhere within its domain."[50] Wheatley's goddess archetypes of regeneration describe the female's miraculous capacity of body, creative mind, and spirit, and her vision of the goddess metaphor emerges perhaps as her own reflection of the "deep Source of creativity and the Self-affirming be'ing of women . . . fulfilling the wholeness of what we are capable of being."[51] What Phillis Wheatley was capable of becoming was far beyond the symbols of what she represented for others, as seen especially in her writing of the George Whitefield elegy, the 1770 publication that catapulted her to international fame. Her self-genesis as an internationally acclaimed poet with the

Whitefield elegy recalls Cixous's theory of *écriture féminine* and highlights Wheatley's rejection of herself as described in affidavits and scientific studies on race and identity.

George Whitefield, the English evangelist to whom she ascribes the miraculous feminine power of transformation, across the boundaries of gender lines, was a controversial figure. He visited the American colonies many times but became ill and died during one of his visits. Above denominational lines that must have attracted the boundary-crossing Wheatley, he initiated the art of preaching outside to crowds underneath a tent during revival meetings in the South and the North. He opened his revivals not only to white Christians but also to outcasts: slaves and orphans, for whom he opened an orphanage in Georgia.[52] Loved and loathed, popular and unpopular in England and her colonies, Whitefield "had a wonderful power over the hearts and purses of his hearers," wrote the beloved, but notoriously penurious Benjamin Franklin. Upon attending one of Whitefield's crusades, Franklin confessed, "I silently resolved he should get nothing from me."[53] As Whitefield delivered his sermon, Franklin had second thoughts and "softened." After making a small contribution to the offering, Franklin became so impressed with Whitefield's oratorical skills that he "emptied [his] pocket wholly into the collector's dish, gold and all."[54]

A very different view of Whitefield was expressed by Alexander Pope, who satirized the overly dramatic evangelist in *The Dunciad* as an "ass" with "lab'ring lungs."[55] Wheatley, however, shared Franklin's admiration for Whitefield, rejecting and even rewriting Pope's profane criticism of him, for which Jefferson attacked her. In her elegy "On the Death of the Rev. Mr. George Whitefield, 1770," Wheatley alters Pope's image of Whitefield's "lab'ring lungs" to "lab'ring breath," a euphemism of Pope's harsh portrayal. She writes, "But though arrested by the hand of death, / Whitefield no more exerts his lab'ring breath."[56] In his continuing depreciation of Wheatley, Jefferson made reference to Pope's *Dunciad* and Wheatley's poetic license in countering Pope's description of Whitefield as an "ass" with "lab'ring lungs." Mocking Wheatley, Jefferson determines that the "heroes of the Dunciad are to her, as Hercules to the author of that poem."[57] In short, Jefferson denies Wheatley's talent and cultural hybridity as well as her entry into eighteenth-century letters.

However, her heroic treatment of Whitefield was based on her appreciation of his cosmopolitan views and the opening of his revival meetings to marginalized figures in the colonies. It is also likely that Wheatley was well acquainted with Whitefield, who perhaps stayed at John and Susannah Wheatley's estate overnight during his travels to Boston. Susannah Wheatley admired and supported him and other visiting ministers.[58] In capturing Whitefield's bold, dramatic style, Wheatley adopts the double-voiced discourse again, recalling Paula Bennett's critique of her "manipulation of Western rhetorical and cultural conventions" for her own artistic purpose. That is, "the dead for whom Wheatley stands in *loco mortui* say precisely what she as an African and a slave could not."[59] But this time she does so with the intention of also paying tribute to Whitefield's spectacular style and delivery:

> "Take him, ye wretched, for your only good,
> "Take him ye starving sinners, for your food;
> "Ye thirsty, come to this life-giving stream,
> "Ye preachers, take him for your joyful themes;
> "Take him my dear Americans, he said,
> "Be your complaints on his kind bosom laid:
> "Take him, ye Africans, he longs for you,
> "Impartial Saviour is his title due:
> "Wash'd in the fountain of redeeming blood,
> "You shall be sons, and kings, and priests to God."
>
> Great Countess, we Americans revere
> Thy name, and mingle in thy grief sincere;
> New England deeply feels, the Orphans mourn,
> Their more than father will no more return.[60]

In emphasizing Whitefield's ideas about the impartiality of Christ ("Impartial Saviour is his title due"), Wheatley refers to the evangelist's invitation to society's pariahs—the "wretched," "sinners," "Africans"—into the body of Christ, and she, following Whitefield's safe lead, shrewdly places these outsiders in solid rank with the mainstream of society: "preachers" and "Americans." Wheatley engages a traditional Anglo-American form, the elegy, but then appropriates its stylistic device to discuss the bane of American racism, furtively, while quoting Whitefield and thus reinforcing his dramatic but wholesome message of cultural and racial inclusion.

In the Whitefield poem, which according to Carretta brought Wheatley "almost instant intercolonial and transatlantic fame" in October 1770, "expanding her community of women supporters,"[61] Wheatley attributes the maternal practices of guidance and care to Whitefield in a reversal of gender roles. His social role of minister is akin to that of her archetypal goddesses in that both real and visionary characters exude an otherworldly authority—divine for Whitefield, classic for the goddesses—both of which trump that of the unpredictable secular world. Having him to transcend ascribed gender types, Wheatley elevates Whitefield to the nurturing world of the maternal, suggesting that men such as Whitefield can "mother" too and occupy the special place that feminists often reserve for women who foster a wider sense of community above that of self-interest. In her attempt to capture the power of Whitefield's persuasion and his belief in the equality of Christians (he argued, contrary to proslavery thought, that slaves possessed an immortal soul), Wheatley depicts a liberating spiritual realm of experience for social outcasts.

This new place of inclusion is denied to them in the exclusionary material world and in the autobiographical poem, where she pleads to hypocritical Christians for their acceptance into the spiritual community of believers. Several years later, in the Whitefield elegy, we can see her shifting her focus from the secular to the sacred, a more reliable space of nourishment with the paternal Whitefield as maternal-acting guide. Silenced by society, the ostracized could more likely find a voice in Christ's "impartial" realm.

When Wheatley wrote the Whitefield elegy, she made reference to Countess Selina Hastings (Whitefield's aristocratic English and Methodist patron) and sent a letter to the countess in which she, displaying social decorum, apologizes "for this my boldness" as an "untutor'd African." Subsequently she received an invitation to visit London.[62] Traveling in 1773 to England, she had her book of poems published and met with several important abolitionists, including Granville Sharp, with whom she toured the Tower of London.[63] Sharp was a leading British abolitionist who played a major role in the famous case of *Somerset v. Stewart* in London. James Somerset, a runaway slave, had brought a writ of habeas corpus against his master Charles Stewart of Boston, who had taken his slave to London and made plans to send him to a plantation in Jamaica. On June 22, 1772, Lord Chief Justice Mansfield ruled in favor of Somerset, citing the illegality of slavery in England, a free land, based on common law and laws established by Parliament. Wheatley's visit to London coincided with the excitement of the aftermath of the famous Somerset case, which had ramifications for runaway slaves stepping foot on free land, far beyond English territory. The critic David Waldstreicher writes that Wheatley "allowed her sympathizers to make her a celebrity in England. Lord Dartmouth [for whom she penned a poem] and Brook Watson, the lord mayor of London, invited her to visit and gave her books." "To the Right Honourable William, Earl of Dartmouth, His Majesty's Principal Secretary of State for North America, & C" is the poem celebrating his appointment and is noteworthy for at least two reasons.

First, the poem presents her alliterative and feminine-maternal signature of the goddess of freedom: "Fair Freedom rose New England to adorn / . . . . She shines supreme, while hated faction dies: Soon as appear'd the Goddess long desir'd," an image that, again, valorizes women's powerful roles as natural healers, driven by a sense of justice and morality. This positive illustration of female influence represents Wheatley's patriotic zeal shortly before the beginning of the American Revolution, showing the shortsightedness of the celebratory poem and the fact that there were some things in an imperfect human society that even a goddess could not fix. Although she sickens and languishes "at the view" of British tyranny in the colonies, Wheatley's goddess is endowed with the preeminence found invested exponentially in the age's "monolithic pretension": as writers would "try one last time for the affirmation of an orderly, over-arching structure"[64]—expressed in Wheatley's goddess poems and Pope's *Essay on Man*. However, human behavior cannot be mandated even though Wheatley was hopeful, not naive, which brings us to the second notable idea in this poem.

Wheatley was aware of the irony of a slave, even a celebrated one, speaking on the subject of freedom, so she addresses this contradiction. Her use of symbol and diction of "Tyranny with lawless hand / Had made, and with it meant t' enslave the land" connects the wrongs of British imperialism to the trauma of the African slave trade. She recalls her African family's lingering personal injury, "That from a father seiz'd his babe belov'd: / Such, such my case. And can I then but pray / Others may never feel tyrannic sway?" She links the symbiotic parent-child relationship on two levels: her own and the mother country with its North American colonies. Their suppression is the real and *safe* subject of the poem, not her piteous "case," which is a truncated analogy, embarrassingly signaling Africa's political castration with its inability to protect its defenseless children. While Wheatley was in London, the ubiquitous statesman Benjamin Franklin called on her, apparently, as Waldstreicher states, upon the request Susannah Wheatley made to a Franklin relative.[65] She knew what the famous visit would mean for the poet. Always with an eye toward history, Franklin notes in his autobiography that he "went to see the black poetess, and offered her any service I could do for her."[66]

Although she never met the countess, who was away when she and Nathaniel Wheatley (one of the Wheatley twins) visited London, the influential countess (with the assistance of Susannah Wheatley working behind the scene) had made the necessary arrangement for Wheatley to have her book of poems published. The abolitionists took note:

> A French official living in America during the war took surprised and rather bemused note of the sudden appearance of this remarkable prodigy, "one of the strangest creatures in the country and perhaps in the whole world." "Phyllis [sic] is a negress," wrote the Marquis de Barbe-Marbois, "born in Africa, brought to Boston at the age of ten [sic], and sold to a citizen of that city. She learned English with unusual ease, eagerly read and reread the Bible . . . and at the age of seventeen [she was about twenty] published a number of poems in which there is imagination, poetry, and zeal though no correctness nor order nor interest. I read them with some surprise. They are printed, and in the front of the book there are certificates of authenticity which leave no doubt that she is its author." Phillis Wheatley, "the negro poetess," became antislavery's most prized exhibit, her name virtually a household term for the Negro's mental equality.[67]

Other abolitionists in Europe were beginning to pay greater legal attention to the poet and her legacy too. After collecting evidence against slavery and its atrocities, in 1785 Thomas Clarkson wrote his dissertation, "The Slavery and Commerce of the Human Species, Particularly the African," submitted to Cambridge University. Appearing before Parliament, Clarkson read excerpts from Wheatley's book of poems and declared, "If the authoress was designed for slavery (as the argument [of innate Negro inferiority] must confess) then the greater part of the inhabitants of Great Britain must lose their claim to freedom."[68] Three years after Wheatley's death, Clarkson and Granville Sharp formed the Society for the Abolition of the Slave Trade in 1787. One of its twelve members was William Wilberforce, an aristocratic member of Parliament who became the most famous of English abolitionists: his long effort to end England's participation in the African slave trade is chronicled in the English/Hollywood production of the movie *Amazing Grace* (2006). The title of the movie is taken from the hymnal written by the redeemed slave-ship captain John Newton, who became a minister.

Having a short life, dying at the age of thirty-one, but leaving an engaging heritage, Phillis Wheatley was no mere biological entity, her body no symbolic Dark Continent: she was a major human event in the impending battle to end slavery. In America, Jupiter Hammon, a Long Island, New York, slave, published a religious poem in 1760 and is widely recognized as the first African American after Lucy Terry to compose and write and publish poetry. But Hammon's paean "An Address to Miss Phillis Wheatly [sic]" (1778) suggests his contentment to orbit the galaxy established by the stellar Wheatley. Prolific, she published the first book of poems by a black American and created a legacy of black women writers as public intellectuals. With this distinction, she shifted the racial politics of her identity, lauded in Europe, a fact noteworthy to Diaspora scholars such as Paul Gilroy. In *The Black Atlantic,* Gilroy opines that blacks from Wheatley to Douglass and Jacobs and Richard Wright represent a minihistory of the role that the crossing of the Atlantic has played in black Americans' developing awareness of the "instability and mutability of identities."[69] He remarks, "Notable black American travelers, from the poet Phillis [sic] Wheatley onwards, went to Europe and had their perceptions of America and racial denomination shifted as a result of their experiences there. This had important consequences for their understanding of racial identities."[70]

Gilroy suggests that Wheatley's identity as a poet of historical significance was made in London, which appears to be true. In her 1773 letter to Obour Tanner, a Rhode Island slave and Wheatley's alter ego, the poet writes of her London visit: "The Friends I found there among the Nobility and Gentry. Their Benevolent conduct towards me, the unexpected, and unmerited civility and Complaisance with which I was treated by all, fills me with astonishment."[71] Gilroy's claim that black American writers were renewed and emboldened by their Atlantic crossing is evidenced by Wheatley's letters and later poems, particularly her elegy on the death of the revolutionary patriot General Wooster, who died in 1777. With his dying breath, Wooster chastises the newly freed colonists who "hold in bondage Afric's blameless race,"[72] which in Wheatley's adoption of the double voice, again, is still a radical change from the supplicating Cain-like plea for blacks in the autobiographical poem. In another letter to an acquaintance, written after her return from England, Wheatley shows her clear self-genesis: "Since my return to America my Master has at the desire of my friends in England given me my freedom. The Instrument is drawn, so as to secure me and my property from the hands of the Executors, administrators. . . . I am now upon my own footing."[73] Wheatley's London publisher, her meeting with English abolitionists, and John Wheatley's decision to manumit her are all interrelated in that each recognized the new politics of identity that she brought to a hierarchal colonial society. In addition to discovering and publishing the Wooster letter in 1979, Mukhtar Ali Isani in 2000 provided a long list of the "expanded range" of media interest in Wheatley at home and abroad. This includes writings about Wheatley in newspapers and magazines in Boston, Rhode Island, New York, New Hampshire, and Pennsylvania as well as England and Ireland, all acknowledging the authorship/whereabouts of one of the most phenomenal poets of the century.[74]

However, despite Gilroy's assertion of black Americans' discovery of themselves in London, as the Wooster letter and the Isani listings prove, Wheatley's rebirth readiness was obvious the moment she picked up her quill to write and publish, first, occasional poems in newspapers and pamphlets beginning in 1767 in the Boston area, predating her London visit by at least six years. Local publishers had no problem publishing separate pieces of her work, but publishing houses found a larger book publication more problematic. Literally and metaphorically Wheatley wrote her way to freedom, establishing the precedence for Douglass and Jacobs of literate slaves becoming writers and authors and entering the public discourse on issues affecting their lives and identities. The most famous example is, of course, Douglass, who became lionized after the publication of his narrative. But in Wheatley's time, the act of writing and earning her own emancipation is remarkable; for as Foucault summarizes, "Up to the end of the eighteenth century, in fact, life does not exist; only living beings. . . . in the taxonomic sense of that word—in the universal distribution of beings."[75] While Gilroy insists that the newness of Wheatley's identity originated in her Atlantic crossing and the breadth of her European experience, I would argue that the seeds of Wheatley's regeneration had been planted as far back as Africa, with its preliterate culture. But Gilroy rightly observes the critical importance of Wheatley's international experience and, in fact, her globalization, which affirmed the transcendental and liberal spaces she invariably sought to occupy, inviting others to join her as she expanded the boundaries of eighteenth-century identity politics, both in her poetry and in her life.

After the trauma of her abduction in West Africa and her naked humiliation on the slave auction block in Boston, if she could still recall, imitate, and perform the act of her mother pouring water before a rising sun, then surely she retained something else of a wider, African ancestral worldview. This view holds, explains the African writer Malidoma Patrice Somé, that "to forget the way life used to be lived is to become endangered."[76] In traditional African society, the intersectionality of the health of the community and the well-being of the individual is perceived as an important and necessary linkage. Somé avers that individual "healing can be seen as a protection of life's energetic wheel, for only when all of the individuals in a community are healthy can there be health in the community itself."[77] African communal values and cultural rites are wholly consistent with feminist views on maternal nurturance, with an emphasis on the relational aspects of the individual and the community. In looking at the nature of the body of Wheatley's poetry, it is obvious that she was constantly in the process of re-creating communities beyond barriers of race and gender, social and physical illnesses, and even life and death. For example, of the thirty-nine poems published in the famous 1773 London volume *Poems on Various Subjects Religious and Moral,* thirteen poems are elegies while several are written to people who sustained a tragedy or needed to recover their health, which often involved travel, sometimes across the Atlantic. The titles alone of these poems reveal Wheatley's desire to ameliorate the misfortune of even anonymous others: "To a Lady on the Death of Her Husband"; "To a Lady on the Death of Three Relations"; and "To a Gentleman on His Voyage to Great-Britain for the Recovery of His Health." Wheatley's thematic of travel and health is one that Katherine Clay Bassard connects to her poetics of recovery on a more personal level, as she "writes/rewrites the Middle Passage in her poems,"[78] a metaphorical act of restitution.

Wheatley's African heritage, Atlantic crossings, cultural hybridity, and influential backing by the Wheatley family certainly made her, as Isani remarks, "precocious and extraordinarily mature for her years."[79] Moreover, her relationship with Susannah Wheatley, her maternal caregiver, can hardly be overestimated. As Wheatley reveals in another letter to Obour Tanner, Susannah Wheatley was no ordinary slave mistress. Upon Susannah's death in 1774, Wheatley wrote to Obour Tanner the following: "I have lately met with a great trial in the death of my mistress, let us imagine the loss of a Parent, Sister or Brother [for] the tenderness of all these were united in her—I was a poor little outcast & a stranger when she took me in. I was treated by her more like her child than her Servant."[80] In a letter to John Thornton, an English merchant and benefactor of missionaries, Wheatley describes Susannah as providing her with an "uncommon tenderness for thirteen years from my earliest youth—such unwearied diligence to instruct me in the principles of the *true* [emphasis added] Religion."[81]

Reid-Pharr expresses concern about the fostering of Wheatley's identity in an all-white household and, understandably, raises concern about her developing a "black subjectivity." But he rashly concludes that Wheatley had none. A white surrogate mother to Wheatley, Susannah Wheatley was a member of the dominant racial group. In instructing the poet on the merits of true religion, distinguishing it from the false religion parodied in the autobiographical poem, Susannah Wheatley obviously had a keener sense of the strategies required for her protégée to navigate the racial conflicts of experience. In her study of black children with white mothers, France Winddance Twine observes that "since white mothers who have African-descent children perceive them as not belonging to the same racial category . . . they may have more motivation to develop and/or articulate some forms of proactive antiracist strategies."[82] The degree to which Susannah Wheatley engaged in proactive race-based tactics will have to remain hypothetical since she left no record behind of her relationship with the poet, who, in contrast, rescued the Wheatley family from an otherwise historical obscurity.

We do have, however, Wheatley's letters as well as her poem to Susannah Wheatley, and both identify her as being the beneficiary of maternal nurturing, and as many feminists note, daughters learn the skill of mothering from their mothers. The Susannah Wheatley effect and Phillis Wheatley's indigenous African worldview together reveal that the poet's tendency to promote human relationships and communities over isolation and conflict came through an early associative network of influence. Obviously, Wheatley would not have had the artistic freedom to become a published poet without Susannah Wheatley's intervention and contact in Boston and London. We can glean from Wheatley's letters and poem the sincerity of their relationship. Around the time of her voyage to London, Wheatley wrote the poem "A Farewel [*sic*] to America. To Mrs. S.W." In this single-voiced poem, she openly addresses the anxiety of separation of surrogate mother and child: "Susannah mourns, nor can I bear / To see the crystal show'r, / Or mark the tender falling tear / At sad departure's hour; / But let no signs, no groans for me / Steal from her pensive breast."[83] "Breast" becomes a repeated maternal signifier of human nurturing in Wheatley's work, but this time with a deep emotional attachment.

For her part, Susannah Wheatley encouraged the poet to write, furnishing her bedroom with "light and in the cold season with a fire, in her apartment during the night. The light was placed upon a table at her bed-side, with writing materials, that if anything occurred to her after she had retired, she might, without rising or taking cold secure the swift-winged Fancy."[84] However, there is no record to indicate that Susannah and John Wheatley dissented against slavery or the Hancock committee's description of the poet as an "uncultivated Barbarian" from Africa. But the absence of dissent does not imply the presence of approval, and the biased statement may well have been recognized as the cost that Wheatley had to pay for making history. Yet the mistress, like her husband, defended slavery because they purchased Phillis and owned several other slaves, and her maternal benevolence was not extended to them. On one occasion when the weather became inclement, Susannah sent an elder servant to "take the chaise and fetch Phillis" after one of her reading performances in Boston. When the two arrived home, Susannah protested, "Do but look at the saucy varlet—if he hast't the impudence to sit upon the same seat with 'My Phillis.'"[85] The words of endearment "My Phillis" no longer suggest the ownership of property but rather the pampering of a poet who, nonetheless, writes Carretta, was not included in John Wheatley's will,[86] revealing the limits of romantic racial liberalism. Still, one wonders if the will would have been written differently if Susannah Wheatley had lived.

Nevertheless, Wheatley's present and future greatness had been established by her writing of occasional poems as well as her poems eulogizing and celebrating the luminary figures of the period such as Whitefield, Dartmouth, and, finally, George Washington. Several years after writing the Dartmouth poem, she wrote the poem celebrating Washington's performing "the work of war" against British colonialism, showing a private and public shift in opinion on colonial politics but also a return to her goddess metaphors. In this poem she provides Washington with the protection of Erkkila's insurrectionary stalking goddess of justice: "Proceed, great chief, with virtue on thy side, / Thy ev'ry action let the goddess guide. / A crown, a mansion, and a throne that shine / With gold unfading, WASHINGTON be thine."[87] The gendered association of her smiling goddess of freedom with peace in the Dartmouth poem and her stern goddess of war with aggression in the Washington poem provide insight into Wheatley's purposeful, shifting maternal metaphors, beginning with the image of "soft" Grace whose role is to comfort and protect in the Cape Cod poem. The function of these differing metaphors of authority is determined by the specificity of their mission in times of danger, peace, and war. Furthermore these powers are Wheatley's artistic embodiments of a necessary and obligatory feminine psyche at work in society, invoked to effect positive change and to amend a fallen social order, which had resulted in her enslavement.

After reading her poem celebrating him, Washington from his Cambridge headquarters responded to Wheatley. In a letter dated February 10, 1776, he wrote as an afterthought to his military secretary, Col. Joseph Reed, "I recollect nothing else worth giving you the trouble of unless you can be amused by reading a letter and poem addressed to me by Mrs. or Miss Phillis Wheatley." Washington referred to Wheatley's "great poetical genius" but feared having her poem published, due to his uncertainty of "whether it might not be considered rather as a mark of my own vanity than as a compliment to her."[88] In referring to the new instances of Wheatley's genius in his letter, Washington revealed his awareness of the poet, her work, and her celebrity, taking a different view of Wheatley from Jefferson's. The historian Joseph Ellis states that Washington did not "embrace the racial arguments for black inferiority that Jefferson advances in *Notes on the State of Virginia*" and that he "tended to regard the condition of the black population as a product of nurture rather than nature," with slavery being the "culprit."[89] It is tempting to think that the well-nurtured Wheatley helped to influence Washington's view, for he invited her to his headquarters: "If you should ever come to Cambridge, or near headquarters, I shall be happy to see a person so favored by the Muses, and to whom nature has been so liberal and beneficent in her dispensations."[90] Black soldiers and Wheatley probably challenged Washington's general prejudices against blacks who were reluctantly allowed to join the revolutionary army.

The historical meeting between George Washington, commander in chief, future president of the United States, and Virginia slaveholder, and Phillis Wheatley, former slave, the abolitionists' darling, and the harbinger of African American literature, is recorded in Benson J. Lossing's *The Pictorial Field-Book of the Revolution.* "I might give a long list of eminent persons whose former presence in those spacious rooms adds interest to retrospection, but they are elsewhere identified. I cannot refrain, however, from noticing the visit of one, who, though a dark child of Africa and a bondwoman, received the most polite attention from the commander-in-chief," he writes. Lossing comments that the poet "passed half an hour with the commander-in-chief, from whom and his officers she received marked attention."[91] Wheatley met with Washington in 1776. In her 1773 letter to David Wooster, she writes of John Wheatley's manumitting her, so it is unlikely that she was a slave in 1776, although Washington and later the historian Lossing connected her to bondage, probably because of the stigma of color. Notwithstanding her celebrated genius, the nature of race and racism in the eighteenth century was such that Wheatley was likely received as both genius and anomaly, attracting the polite attention of Washington. Because she was not easily reducible to the stereotype of race and identity, she represented the enlightened ideas of social progress, as Washington's giving his "marked attention" to her suggests.

From her meetings with Washington, Franklin, Sharp, Dartmouth, Watson, and the luminaries of her age to her poetry being read in Parliament by Clarkson and kept in the library of Blumenbach, Phillis Wheatley emerges as the first black American literary intellectual to enter the public discourse on race and influence social change, worldwide. In an age of racial grids, slave ships, and auction blocks, she wrote poetry in an unpoetic world, her creative impulse being consistent with Diaspora blacks who "devised means of willful persistence,"[92] as even Adeeko admits in general. In African American letters, Wheatley raised the bar for blacks writing politics into literature, challenging the status quo. Among early black female intellectual writers, she is unparalleled in historical firsts: the first writer of a published book of poetry; the first black poet to have positive access to preeminent revolutionary American and European figures; and the first black female writer to create a sustaining maternal image of women as goddesses, representing creative powers of regeneration. As her reputation has evolved, an original Wheatley letter written in 1774 was auctioned and sold in 2005 in New York for $253,000 at cash value. A desk that she used for writing sits in the Smithsonian Institution, and a writing table believed to have belonged to her is at the Massachusetts Historical Society in Boston.[93] Like many historians before him, Paul Goodman recognizes the historical merit of early black intellectuals. He observes that Africa and Phillis Wheatley were "no Dark Continent."[94] Over half a century later, in 1861, Harriet Jacobs, a North Carolina slave, would move into Wheatley's sphere, destined to challenge her nineteenth-century society's symbolic construction of the black body-in-crisis, this time as sexual object.

2 Harriet Jacobs's *Incidents in the Life of a Slave Girl*

A Freudian Reading of Neurotic and Sexed Bodies

Although George Fitzhugh stated, "The negro [*sic*] slaves of the South are the happiest, and, in some sense, the freest people in the world. The children and the aged and infirm work not at all, and yet have all the comforts and necessaries of life provided for them,"[1] *Incidents in the Life of a Slave Girl* (1861), written by the North Carolina slave Harriet Jacobs, provides clear evidence about slavery's all-consuming "curse" on blacks and whites alike, countering Fitzhugh's fantasy about the benefits of the peculiar institution. With her oft-quoted lines informing her readers that she and other former slaves could have told a different tale about slavery, Jacobs referred explicitly to the master discourse on slavery in the nineteenth century. Appropriating different kinds of maternal metaphors of power from Wheatley's stalking goddesses, Jacobs literally used her own material body in much the same way that the resurrected Wheatley cultivated her intellect and adapted Christianity as a religious exercise of self-empowerment. On a southern plantation where her sexuality played a far different role than Wheatley's feted intellect in the North and abroad, Jacobs was forced by history's peculiar institution of slavery to resort to sexual and bodily machinations, whether mutually seducing her chosen white lover or cross-dressing as a sailor in an effort to liberate herself and her children. Because of these machinations, Jacobs, as a female slave, was in a better, though unenviable, position than others to attack the deceptive master narrative, propagated by those such as Fitzhugh.

In their power to represent slavery as they wished it to be seen, slave owners demonstrated what Foucault pronounced, in another context in *Madness and Civilization*, as a systematic operation of social and political repression, in which madness "is responsible only for that part of itself which is visible. All the rest is reduced to silence. Madness no longer exists except as seen."[2] Appearing to live up to the ego ideal of themselves as benevolent owners of slaves who lived with their masters in a paternalistic community of white and black "families," slavocrats willfully deluded themselves in their neurotic reversal of reality. Freud's concept of the ego ideal that appears as a paradigm of human perfection—"expected of the higher nature of man"—is a component of the super ego.[3] With its positive and authoritative parental qualities and its values of decency and integrity, the superego (similar to the ego ideal) captures the projected image of the master-slave relationship imbibed romantically in the southern ethos of paternalism. However, the ego ideal lacks the superego's parental powers of constraint and becomes a defense mechanism for slavocrats, denying the conscience proponent of the superego that would be more punitive toward bad behavior.

Countering the master narrative on race and slavery and subverting the myth of the ego ideal, Jacobs's *Incidents in the Life of a Slave Girl* rips the veil off slavery's madness, making it visible. She exposes the pathological nature of slavery as a peculiar rather than benign patriarchal institution. "I am not disposed to paint their condition so rose-colored as the Hon. Miss Murray paints the condition of the slaves in the United States,"[4] she remarks in a comparison of slaves and the oppressed poor in England. The "subversive" genre of the slave narrative, as quasi-autobiography and historical document, and Jacobs's slave status in Edenton, North Carolina, where she was born in 1813, enabled her to record for her generation and posterity the sexualization of plantation slavery as a severe form of its neuroses. Authenticated by abolitionists and prominent citizens, the slave narrative allowed Jacobs to describe slavery as she lived it on the plantation, depicted as a harem. Far different from northern slavery, southern plantation slavery, writes Orlando Patterson, required the enslaved to perform "every known task" to man and woman, although "there was usually a primary use for which they were acquired," whether for labor and economic reasons or for sexual favors. Regarding sexual favors, Deborah Gray White remarks, "While some women remained the concubines of their white lovers and eventually obtained freedom for themselves and their children, just as many, if not more, were sold off to plantations where they shared the misery of all slaves."[5] The sexual subordination of black female slaves was institutionalized in the South, as Jacobs reveals, and one of her stated objectives was to avoid being victimized by this part of the system.

Thus the locus of *Incidents in the Life of a Slave Girl* is on Harriet Jacobs's enslaved, sexed body as property: as her master, Dr. Flint, reminds her, "Do you know that I have a right to do as I like with you, that I can kill you, if I please?" (41). Propertied bodies of slaves, especially slave women, often became sexed bodies after puberty, as Jacobs relates in describing her fifteenth year as "a sad epoch in the life of a slave girl" (26). She endured the anxieties of the plantation regime and frequently complained of bodily and mental pain. In her coupling of mind and body—"I was too ill in mind and body . . . to say nothing of my soul" (166)—she stresses the psychical and physical interdependency of the human body, Husserl's concept of body as an intermediary of the will.[6] Jacobs's ability to perceive herself as whole, despite her enslavement, is in contradistinction to the Cartesian dualism invoked by the Hancock committee in assessing Wheatley, separating her civilized Christian mind from her savage African body. Because Jacobs perceived body and mind as interdependent, she devised bodily strategies (from seduction to concealment and camouflage) to escape the twisted contortion of slavery and racial identity. I would posit, then, that her shrewd tactics to avoid suffering the "usual fate" of slave girls and women should be a challenge for scholars who represent her as a silent victim of rape. Along with her other forced role, that of the mad mother holed up in a garret, these staged performances eventually led to Jacobs's emergence from susceptible sexed body to responsible maternal body.

Jacobs's Sexed Body: A Symbol of Plantation Slavery's Neuroses

Like other black enslaved Americans struggling for self-definition, Jacobs experienced the constricted space of race and identity, not on an auction block as did Wheatley, but on a southern plantation where her sexed body played a fundamental role in her life as a would-be vulnerable female slave. As such, Jacobs was destined for early motherhood, but without its rights and privileges. Owned and claimed by Dr. Flint, Jacobs's sexed body emerges as a trope for the socially ascribed identity of female slaves and the institutionalization of slavery's erotic as well as neurotic sexual character. Nevertheless, Jacobs shows that masters and slaves often engaged in a contest of wills. This is observed in *Incidents in the Life of a Slave Girl* with the behavior of Dr. Flint, who pursues Jacobs obsessively and neurotically until his death (at which time his daughter and her husband track her down in New York) as she escapes his powerful reach, confessing that the "war of my life had begun" (17). Slavery was a war for the black body-in-crisis: self-ownership for the slave and object-property for the master. Jacobs's determination to protect her body from Dr. Flint is seen throughout the narrative.

As a young and perceptive slave girl, she was territorially aware of the falsity of the southern body-politic and its representation of slavery. "My master was, to my knowledge, the father of eleven slaves," she writes, but the slave mothers did not "allude to it, except in whispers among themselves? No indeed! They knew too well the terrible consequences" (35). Jacobs took note of the consequences of transgressing the unspoken law of the ego ideal and of female slaves' sexual subordination, and she devised strategies of resistance, using her sexuality to her advantage while fighting off her master, who represented a system that oppressed all women: not only the slave girl but also the slave mistress. For example, suspicious of her husband and jealous of Jacobs, Mrs. Flint slipped into Jacobs's bedroom, imitated her husband's voice, and "whispered in my ear, as though it was her husband who was speaking to me" (34). Jacobs's confession that she was "fearful for my life" conveys her sense of the materiality of her body, not only as object-property for the master but also as a target of envy for her mistress. Yet, Elizabeth Fox-Genovese, who believes that Dr. Flint succeeded in raping Jacobs, states that white slave mistresses "endured husbands who whored in the slave quarters" but "managed to come through with a striking lack of neurotic inhibition."[7] But Jacobs's description of Dr. Flint's wife's neurotic performance as the suspicious wife undercuts the idea that slave mistresses exhibited a "striking lack of neurotic inhibition." Saidiya Hartman too depicts Jacobs as a victim of rape, although "rape is only represented in terms of its effects—mute, pregnant women and near-white offspring." Thus "resistance is hopeless," as even Jacobs confesses, leading Hartman and others to argue that Jacobs, unable to discuss her rape by Dr. Flint, crafted her narrative rhetorically to convey "the impossibility of adequately representing the violence of slavery" and rape.[8] As will become clear, Jacobs dethrones Dr. Flint's lordship as master, contesting allegations of her as powerless rape-victim.

Incidents in the Life of a Slave Girl establishes a narrative pattern of Jacobs's detailing Dr. Flint's alternately nonaggressive and aggressive, neurotic-compulsive behavior and Jacobs's anxieties as inscribed on the body of her template and alter ego, Linda Brent, a subject of interest for most scholars. The preeminent Jacobs scholar Jean Fagan Yellin posits, "Harriet Jacobs had become 'Linda Brent,' but not to hide behind a pseudonym or to disappear under a fictitious name. As 'Linda' she had empowered herself to write about a life that as 'Harriet,' she could neither speak nor write."[9] I would counter, however, that Jacobs and *not* Linda Brent appears as the lone rational voice of *Incidents in the Life of a Slave Girl*, removed, as the fugitive and freed Harriet Jacobs was, from slavery's asylum of victims and perpetrators. Linda Brent's voice is muted, essentially, for she is nothing more than an instrument for Jacobs's remembered agony as a slave girl. On this template Jacobs necessarily transfers her recollected bodily pain and anguish, still apparently fresh and poignant as she frequently interrupts her discourse on the slave girl's experiences and speaks of her (the older Jacobs's) current emotions. In her narrative description of real and symbolic neuroses, Jacobs places the convenient protagonist, Linda Brent.

It is Brent who emerges as a quasi-autobiographical creation that allows the unyoked Jacobs a critical distance, as Yellin implies, but also allows her the adoption of a wise maternal voice as she outlines on Brent's sketched body her (Jacobs's) past agonizing experiences. Jacobs, not Brent, narrates the tale of slavery, approximately eighteen years after she had escaped slavery and Edenton in 1842, giving her the advantage of hindsight, eluding the slave girl Linda Brent as the presumed, but fictitious narrator. "I am still pained," Jacobs wrote around 1858, "by the retrospect" of slavery's wrongs, a confession indicating the passage of time and her growth and maturity in her own voice. Jacobs's retrospection is disclosed further in other such statements, as with her description of the slave mother who lost all seven of her children to a slave trader and whose "wild, haggard face lives *to-day* [emphasis added] in my mind" (13). Retrospectively too Jacobs recalls her daughter Louisa Matilda (Ellen in *Incidents*) being advised wisely not to reveal Jacobs's concealment in the garret. Jacobs writes, "And she never did" (158), in a distinctly historicizing voice, one separating the painful past from a calmer present, the maternal Harriet Jacobs from the anxiety-prone slave girl Linda Brent.

In separating the narrative past from the narrative presence and isolating a myriad of slave experiences, hers and others', from her present thoughts and emotions, Jacobs, as narrator, distances herself from Linda Brent. In distancing herself from the slave girl and the youthful slave mother and, by association, from the psychoses of plantation slavery, Jacobs, as the real narrator, emerges as saner than the experiences of slavery that she narrates notwithstanding the various roles she must adopt to emancipate herself and her children from slavery's mad clutches. Inside the slave community, for example, the slave girl's mad mothering performance of hiding in a garret, incredibly, for seven years, waiting for the time when she and her children could escape to freedom in the North, reflects an induced infirmity. Yet in Jacobs's narrating voice, this example of slavery's induced pathology in the slave girl is explained as a healthy reaction to an unhealthy society of propertied human bodies and their commoditization. In juxtaposition to this kind of environment and in a Victorian era that defined true womanhood by its purity, submissiveness, and gentleness, Jacobs, the real narrator, assumes, retrospectively again, a more cultivated and composed maternal voice.

This voice is transcendent of the squeamish Linda Brent, who as Jacobs's young double frequently trembles, screams, faints, and worries hysterically in her Jacobs-like contact with Dr. Flint, her owner, and Mr. Sands, her white lover. Although scholars might relate her individual hysterics to the genre of the sentimental novel with its celebrated heroine, popular in the nineteenth century, her symptoms and the narrative emphases on obsessive human sexuality suggest the total dysfunction of the wider environment, theoretically inseparable from the heroine. Jacobs's alter ego reacts to this sick social milieu, but only in Jacobs's recollective memory and controlling voice. Jacobs's *Incidents in the Life of a Slave Girl* subsumes and transcends women's sentimental narratives, implying that white women's middle-class Victorian fiction of manners could not possibly capture the harsh reality of slavery and slave women's lives. Within the context of the master/slave girl relationship, Jacobs delineates the larger society's personal and collective madness, which her obsessive-neurotic master, Dr. Flint, represents on a microscopic level. She had determined that slavery was a "curse" for both blacks and whites, as the philanthropist-abolitionist Gerrit Smith had concluded, specifically for whites, stating in a "public letter," "So debauched are the white people by slavery that there is not virtue enough left in them to put it down."[10] But the curse of slavery's degradation was written more painfully on the black body-in-crisis as seen in their acute physical and psychological torture. Trauma, as Freud theorizes, induces many pathological symptoms and problems, illustrated in *Incidents in the Life of a Slave Girl*, framing the narrative necessity of a Freudian reading of Jacobs's text as largely a psychoanalytical slave narrative on sex demanding our attention.

In turning to an exegesis of Freud's ideas of anxieties and neuroses relevant to Jacobs's descriptions of her master and her experiences, it is clear that Jacobs, while not having access to Freud's language, anticipated his theories on neurotic disorders and libidinal sexual drives. I want to clarify from the beginning that I am aware of many feminist scholars' rejection of the Freudian paradigm, which they have analyzed for its sexism and misogyny. Some feminists argue, for example, that while Freud may not reduce women to the function of their physical attractiveness and sexuality, men's sexuality is presented as more study-worthy, empirically.[11] Even male critics such as E. Fuller Torrey denounce Freud as "inherently misogynistic and patronizing. Freud said that women are more narcissistic than men and have 'little sense of justice.' He called girls 'the little creature without a penis.'"[12]

The basis of these strands of anti-Freudian criticism is found in Freud's "Three Essays on the Theory of Sexuality," where he discusses the perceived sexual differences between the sexes, distinguishing men and their sexuality from women. Freud argues that the "significance of the factor of sexual overvaluation can be best studied in men, for their erotic life alone has become accessible to research. That of women—partly owing to the stunting effect of civilized conditions and partly owing to their conventional secretiveness and insincerity," makes them objects less worthy of empirical investigation than men.[13] Freud's statements are sexist in tone and meaning, if not intent, for he disclaimed feminist charges against him for his biases against women. Despite his feminist detractors and his disclaimer, feminists such as Nancy Chodorow and Elizabeth Grosz posit that Freud's writings often provide psychoanalytical theories and models for feminists coming to an understanding of the ideological conceptions of sex roles in power relations between men and women.[14] Freud "depicts for us clinically and theoretically how men experience women,"[15] and this is particularly relevant to a reading of *Incidents in the Life of a Slave Girl,* where we see Jacobs and other slave women defined and treated in terms of their relationship with powerful men who devalue them. Just as Freud reveals a masculinist attitude toward women, Jacobs shows that this attitude was more pronounced in the slave community, due to the nature of slavery and the hysteria it created in many households.

Freud was indebted to his teacher Jean-Martin Charcot, who in the 1870s had taken an interest in hysteria as a mental illness with physical manifestations. Mark S. Micale hypothesizes the "late nineteenth century as the 'heroic period' of hysteria" and hysteria as "a classically Victorian neurosis . . . with its sexual confinement, emotional oppression, and social suffocation." Micale continues, "In the popular historical imagination today, the late nineteenth century is the age of hysteria, with Jean-Martin Charcot and Sigmund Freud serving as its representative personalities and Paris and Vienna its quintessential capitals."[16] Charcot thought hysteria to be a neurological problem, but Freud related hysteria to a repressed sexuality, a theory that resonated with interest for a sexually prohibitive Victorian society concerned with proper standards of behavior and conduct. Freud's notion also resounds with an epistemic violence for female slaves whose sexed bodies became likely ciphers for their masters' improper and unlicensed sexual drives. According to Freud, while neuroses have their origin in traumatic events, they assume a sexual pattern of behavior connected to the id, the powerful sexual instinct of passions. In the 1890s Freud had begun to study "sexuality as the fundamental cause of neurosis and its prominence in mental life."[17]

He developed theories for several of the symptoms of neuroses in an individual's behavior as characterized by obsessive thoughts, compulsive-aggressive actions, and high-level anxieties of hysteria and hypochondria, as related in the Jacobs-Flint war and the larger Edenton community. Additional Freudian theories on sexuality find primary support in *Incidents in the Life of a Slave Girl*, omitting their technical jargon. Although Freud created such terms as ego-libido, object-libido, object-cathexis, and libidinal cathexis of the ego, many of their descriptions appear to overlap. They are as well essentially indistinguishable, barring perhaps the emphasis on the subject in the ego-libido and the desired object of the subject in the object-cathexis libido, or simply, the desired sexual object. Dr. Flint's ownership of Jacobs's propertied and sexed body and his claiming "a right to rule [her], body and soul" (40) appear to represent Freud's libidinal object-cathexis hypothesis and perhaps other nineteenth-century hypotheses of neurotic disorders. Dr. Flint's lascivious attachment to his slave girl's body and her narcissistic resistance to him (based on her physical attractiveness and self-esteem) identify one of the more prominent psychological features of Jacobs's narrative: the old master's lust and the young slave girl's vanity.

Manifestations of plantation neuroses are presented graphically in Jacobs's relationship with Dr. Flint, especially in his nonaggressive, obsessive-neurotic thoughts of a sexual nature and his aggressive, neurotic-compulsive actions to satisfy his sexual desires and make her his sex slave. We have already witnessed at least one example of his neurotic thoughts about his ownership of his slave girl's body and his right to murder her with impunity, but his compulsive actions begin when he literally strikes her. In conjunction with the real threat that he faces in losing her as his presumed sex slave (that is, when she begins to form relationships with other men), Dr. Flint's actions increase in neurotic severity, for example, when he furiously cuts her hair. Yellin identifies Dr. Flint's cutting of Jacobs's hair as the nineteenth-century symbol of the status of the woman as a "whore."[18] But Jacobs is not *his* whore, which is the underlying reason for his frustrations. Individual narcissism also plays a significant part in the Flint-Jacobs battle, with his libidinal attachment and her persistent defiance of a "man forty years my senior." Dr. Flint's arrogance and notions of planter aristocracy are based on the prestige that he enjoys as a powerful property holder and master, although Du Bois states that behaviorally many slave owners were unrefined, parvenu slavocrats of the "cursing, whoring, brawling" type.[19] Even though she is a slave, Jacobs displays the development of a healthy ego-identity formation, based primarily on her proud family heritage and her good looks. Her grandmother is a well-respected property owner and community baker, and her parents, although slaves, are legally married. Her father is a skilled carpenter, hired to work on projects outside the slave community, where he travels freely.

As a result of her biracial background (her grandmother was the daughter of a South Carolina planter, and her father was the son of a white North Carolina farmer[20]), Jacobs was also alerted to the fiction of racial purity, which, similar to the ego ideal, falsely buttressed Edenton's hierarchy. A descendant of mulattoes, Jacobs was empowered by an "articulation of subaltern agency to emerge as relocation and reinscription" of identity, as Homi K. Bhabha relates of the power of the subaltern consciousness.[21] That is, Jacobs appropriated her hybrid status to question the authority of hegemony and racial authenticity, inquiring, "And then who are Africans? Who can measure the amount of Anglo-Saxon blood coursing in the veins of American slaves?" (47). Jacobs's query and race scholars' statistical analyses of blacks' racial amalgamation (70 to 80 percent of black Americans are mixed[22]) are intended not to reflect disparagingly on blackness but rather to question the essentialized category of race as Wheatley did, but with a different configuration. Moreover, Jacobs's query not only assaults ideas of history's racial essentialism but also foregrounds her discourse on the plantation as a legally institutionalized whorehouse.

A clearer source of pride for Jacobs is her sheer physical appearance and youthfulness as inscribed on the slave girl's developing and attractive body, which becomes a marked emblem of the vanity that Freud attributes to pretty women. As chairman of the Vigilante Committee in Philadelphia, the mulatto abolitionist Robert Purvis was moved to comment on Jacobs's beauty when she arrived in that city after fleeing North Carolina. Purvis described Jacobs as a "beautiful creature,"[23] even though he likened her to Byron's "Prisoner of Chillon" in her sad state of existence, her freedom in chains, a condition that followed her wherever she traveled, an indication of slavery's enduring trauma. In her previously published edition of *Incidents in the Life of a Slave Girl,* Yellin provides another example of Jacobs's acclaimed good looks and bodily voluptuousness with an illustration of the well-publicized advertisement that Dr. James Norcom (Dr. Flint in *Incidents*) submitted for his runaway slave girl, Harriet. Jacobs is described as a "light mulatto, 21 years of age, about 5 feet 4 inches high, of a thick and corpulent habit [bodily voluptuousness], having on her head a thick covering of black hair that curls naturally, but which can be easily combed straight. She speaks easily and fluently, and has an agreeable carriage . . . a variety of very fine clothes."[24] Dr. Flint's detailed description of Jacobs's body (her height, weight, skin color, hair, carriage, and attire) may have been legally required, but it suggests too his erogenous attention to her body as a sexed and propertied body, belonging to him.

In *Incidents in the Life of a Slave Girl,* the slave girl's beauty is a source of both pride and conflict for Jacobs in her self-confessed war with Dr. Flint, but it certainly provides her with an advantage, as Freud opines in general about beautiful women. Freud discusses the compensatory development of narcissism in women, which finds particular expression in the slave girl's relations with Dr. Flint and indeed in Jacobs's having survived slavery. Freud explains the compensatory relationship between women's beauty and their developing self-preservative narcissism: "Women, especially if they grow up with good looks, develop a certain self-contentment which compensates them for the social restrictions that are imposed upon them in their choice of object."[25] In the real world as well as in the narrative, Jacobs's beauty, like Wheatley's religion, countered and helped to lessen, socially and psychologically, her subaltern status, illustrating Freud's idea that beautiful women can use their beauty as a weapon in their struggle for self-empowerment and self-identity.

As the megalomaniac title of "master" signifies, slavocrats such as Dr. Flint wielded power over their slaves legally and psychologically, having advantages that Jacobs denies to him, including the rights to her body and the subsequent "rape" alleged by several critics but with no hard evidence. In a slave society dominated by the master's autocratic will and "lordship," as Hegel sweepingly describes the master's power, Jacobs's self-preservative narcissism (that is, keeping her hair styled nicely, dressing fashionably, and acquiring an education despite antiliteracy laws) serves her as a form of self-protection. That is, she is able to perceive herself as greater than her socially ascribed identity. "It seemed not only hard, but unjust, to pay for myself. I could not possibly regard myself as a piece of property" (210), she proudly rationalizes.

Here, Jacobs provides another example of slavery's pathology, slaves purchasing themselves, and she interrupts her discourse on slavery to distinguish herself from Brent, whose freedom has just been bought, reducing her to an object of exchange in Cixous's "bibliococapitalist society." In *Incidents in the Life of a Slave Girl*, Dr. Flint is consciously aware of his slave girl's narcissism and feels compelled to remind her, Jacobs writes, "that my feelings were entirely above my situation" (94). However, rather than dismissing Jacobs as a vain slave girl out of touch with reality, Dr. Flint is drawn further to her, suggesting that one of the charms of the narcissistic and sexual object lies in its inaccessibility. The charm also lies in the reality that "another person's narcissism has a great attraction for those who have renounced part of their own narcissism and are in search of object-love," Freud states.[26] Dr. Flint reveals his ego-withdrawal instinct when he occasionally stops pursuing his slave girl, who frequently outwits him. When he informs Jacobs, "I don't know what it is that keeps me from killing you" (65), he implies a form of respect for her narcissistic self-esteem, unusual for someone with her slave status.

Jacobs remarks that he frequently refers to her as a "lady" and promises "to give [her] a home of [her] own and to make a lady of [her]" (57). Dr. Flint's pronouncements represent his clever appeal to the vaunted Victorianization of female desire in the nineteenth-century's cult of true womanhood. The master flatters his slave girl and her cultivated self-image of the alluring but inaccessible ingenue: he appeals to her yearning for the sentimental values of the domestic life of home and family, but only as his concubine-slave or sexual object. He pleads with her, "You can do what I require; and if you are faithful to me, you will be as virtuous as my wife" (83). Although Jacobs rejects Dr. Flint's offer, he grounds his proposal in the era's feminine domestic ideal to which many southern white ladies aspired and from which all enslaved black women were excluded. Claudia Tate remarks that domestic Victorian ideas and desires form the basis of Jacobs's appeal in writing *Incidents in the Life of a Slave Girl*. Tate argues that Jacobs "depicted freedom not simply as escape from the political condition of slavery, but as the gaining of access to the social institutions of motherhood, family, and home."[27] In her study *The Feminization of American Culture*, Ann Douglas avers that the "cult of motherhood" in nineteenth-century America led to the establishment of "Mother's Day" and was a "precondition" of women's flattery.[28]

As an obsessive-neurotic master in pursuit of his slave girl, Dr. Flint begins to exhibit his most severe form of neuroses in his defusing of two important instincts, the sexual and death instincts,[29] both of which characterize his erratic behavior. His disorder includes symptoms of neurotic-compulsive actions such as speaking impulsively to Jacobs, blurting out and writing notes of obscenities, harming and inflicting bodily pain on her and her son, Benjamin [Jacobs's son, Joseph], and wishing danger or even death upon her and her young children, Benjamin and Ellen. Jacobs writes that in the beginning Dr. Flint began "to whisper foul words in my ear" and then swore that "he would kill me, if I was not as silent as the grave" (26, 28). Another element of the obsessive-neurotic type, as demonstrated in this last quotation, is his propensity for secrecy and slyness and a desire not to be found out, as Jacobs states, "[Dr. Flint] did not wish to have his villainy made public" (29). This last observance is indicative of the neurotic character's wish to keep up appearances and the public image of the ego ideal, or to preserve what Freud refers to as the "scatological practices, ceremonies, and so on, which they carefully keep secret."[30] Rape would have most assuredly blown his sly cover, as Jacobs shields herself from Dr. Flint's obscene rituals of making lewd signs and gestures and writing erotic letters to her that she, though literate, claims she cannot read.

While Dr. Flint's behavior has remained essentially nonaggressive, though prurient and neurotic, his aggressive neurotic actions increase as his sexual anxieties mount and his sexual ambitions are rivaled. We see this last form of behavior when Jacobs cultivates romantic relationships, first with the free colored carpenter and then with the white attorney Mr. Sands. About the colored carpenter Dr. Flint asks her, "Do you love this nigger? [and then] sprang upon me like a tiger, and gave me a stunning blow. It was the first time he had ever struck me" (40). Later he apologizes to her. Jacobs explains that Dr. Flint "thrust a note into my hand. . . . It expressed regret for the blow he had given me" (42). He also starts to build a house for her, and Jacobs is forced to acknowledge her narcissism: "When I found that my master had actually begun to build the lonely cottage, other feelings mixed with those I have described. Revenge and calculations of interest were added to [my] *flattered vanity*" [emphasis added] (59). When Jacobs enters a sexual alliance with the white Mr. Sands, Dr. Flint experiences rising fears and a greater ego-related competition, which the real and private correspondence between Samuel Tredwell Sawyer (Mr. Sands in *Incidents*) and Dr. James Norcom reveals.

In *Harriet Jacobs: A Life*, Yellin produces a letter that Sawyer had written to Dr. Norcom on July 2, 1828, when Jacobs was only fifteen years old but already in the year of her first pregnancy. In his letter Sawyer, a political candidate, pleads that "all that has passed between us of an unpleasant nature may be forgotten and buried in oblivion. On my part, I regret it exceedingly, and being far your junior in years, am free to admit that you have not been treated by me with that decorum which your age, your character and your standing in society merited."[31] Yellin inquires if Sawyer is cryptically and apologetically referring to his relationship with Jacobs (undercutting claims of Dr. Flint's rape of Jacobs and his paternity of her children), as he seeks Dr. Norcom's support. Moreover, the letter is a declaration of Sawyer's acceptance of the ego ideal in principle: he publicly acknowledges his personal failure of social decorum and apologizes to a man who shares his moral failings, making them comrades and combatants in the plantation's twisted human relations.

The Flint-Jacobs-Sands sexual triad in *Incidents in the Life of a Slave Girl* is representative of a competitive alliance of two white professional men, one a physician and the other an attorney, fighting over a female slave who is demeaned by both men. However, Dr. Flint, unlike Mr. Sands, who steadfastly represents the ego-libido when he withdraws his attention from Jacobs, is unable to extricate himself. Freud speaks of the ego-libido as similar to the object-cathexis in its sexual fixation, but the ego-libido "is finally drawn back into the ego, so that it becomes ego-libido once again."[32] Sands represents the ego-libido because he (while pursuing Jacobs, who admits her mutual seduction of Sands to foil her master) can and does lose his sexual interest in Jacobs. He becomes himself again and maintains in practice the passions of the ego ideal: he runs for Congress, leaves Edenton, and returns with a young white wife whom Yellin identifies as Lavinia Peyton of Virginia.[33] Interestingly, Jacobs describes the aging Mrs. Flint as unattractive, a second wife, who is "not a very refined woman," conveying a strong sense of her youthful vanity. However, Jacobs's narrative silence on the physical appearance of her real rival, the young Lavinia Peyton, is deafening, suggesting her sensitivity to their vexed relations.

When Jacobs writes of Sands's new wife being informed of his "parental relation" to her children (they had had two when he married Lavinia) and his commenting further that "their mother was a slave" whom, Jacobs adds, "he had represented to be dead," she implies his psychological attitude toward her as being dead sexually to him, now (153). So strange was southern plantation slavery that it produced its own vocabulary, for no rational language existed to clarify the knotted relationship between white fathers and their slave children, hence the ambivalent term "parental relation." Such diction loosely admits the white father's paternity while simultaneously denying his obligation of fatherhood. After Jacobs conspires to have Sands buy her children from Dr. Flint, they become their father's slaves in addition to being his children. Jacobs's daughter gives voice to the ambiguity of this relationship when she grieves her father's "parental relation" with her in Washington, D.C., where he takes her for a while but only as his legitimate white family's servant. She confesses, "I used to wish he would take me in his arms and kiss me as he did Fanny [his white daughter]; or that he would sometimes smile at me as he did at her. I thought if he was my own father, he ought to love me. I was a little girl then, and didn't know any better" (212). The daughter's yearnings and expectations are, of course, rational, but what she comes to realize is the irrationality of slavery, which prevented normal black and whites ties even between a father and his biological offspring.

Thus, Sands's affair with Jacobs is hardly ever threatened by his having acquired a zealous overattachment to her sexed body, unlike Dr. Flint, who does place a sexual valuation on her body as his property. While the married Mr. Sands ends his relationship with Jacobs as Samuel Tredwell Sawyer did upon his marriage, the equally married Dr. Flint is unable to liberate himself and become egolibido again. He cannot extinguish his passion for Jacobs's sexed body, implying his being yoked to his slave girl and becoming a slave himself, to lust. Skillfully, Jacobs reduces Dr. Flint to the "thinghood" of Hegel's master-slave dialectics, for he who once held the position of lordship has now become "the reverse" of what he is supposed to be.[34] Jacobs, the slave, having been assumed to be a "consciousness repressed within itself . . . will enter into itself, and change round into real and true independence,"[35] lording her skills over her old master and new slave, another reason for disbelieving the rape charges.

Predictably, Dr. Flint's most extreme display of crazed outbursts occurs with Jacobs's pregnancies. After the first, he "looked at [her] in dumb amazement," abruptly left the house, returned, and offered her an abortion. He then began to implore her to "obey [his] wishes," threatening her with "the fires of hell" and "grabb[ing] [her] arm as if he would have broken it" (61, 63, 64). Had he been able to force himself upon Jacobs and succeed in raping her, it is unlikely that he would have become so violent with her here, demonstrating his frustrations, unable to vanquish her, seductively or forcibly. With her second pregnancy, Jacobs experiences the shearing incident, which occurs as a result of Dr. Flint's ego-related humiliation. "When Dr. Flint learned that I was again to be a mother," Jacobs recalls, "he was exasperated beyond measure. He rushed from the house, and returned with a pair of shears. I had a fine head of hair; and he often railed about my pride of arranging it nicely. He cut every hair close to my head, storming and swearing all the time" (85). Dr. Flint's cutting of his slave girl's hair represents one of the dangerous passages he has reached as a compulsive-neurotic type in the narrative spectacle of his aggressive, sexually frustrated behavior. Symptomatically, the shearing incident represents the climax of the master's loss of self-control and self-mastery.

His compulsions are stepped up to the point that his obsessions lower him to the status of a pouting child, for example, when he sends Jacobs away to his son's plantation as her punishment. His infantilism is another characteristic of obsessive neurotics. Freud states that the "sexuality of psycho-neurotics has remained at, or been carried back to an infantile stage," related perhaps to the "sexual impulses of childhood."[36] The master's reduction and loss of status embroil not only his son on a faraway plantation but also the law. When Jacobs runs away, the Flint-Jacobs war is transformed into a wildly narcissistic battle of egos, which was always present though now more consciously deadly. Freud relates the death instinct to severe cases of neuroses: "the instinct of destruction is habitually brought into the service of Eros." There is an "instinctual defusion and the marked emergence of the death instinct" that exists "among the effects of some severe neuroses—for instance, the obsession neuroses."[37] Sublimating his sexual desires for Jacobs, Dr. Flint brings in the law in an effort to capture her. He posts the reward notices (physically describing Jacobs's body) and makes three trips to New York as she remains cramped in a garret in North Carolina, outwitting him.

From Sexed Body to Maternal Conduit: Jacobs's Self-Genesis

Jacobs's transformation from a sexual object to a responsible mother who comes into legal rights and possession of her own body and her own children is related to her forced adoption of theatrics. *Incidents in the Life of a Slave Girl* represents southern slavery as a form of theater, demonstrated in one example by Mrs. Flint's dramatic performance of assuming the identity of her husband and whispering into Jacobs's ear. For slaves, however, devising and performing acts of subterfuge were seen as strategies of resistance in their effort to liberate themselves. Frederick Douglass, Henry "Box" Brown, Ellen and William Craft, and Harriet Jacobs all achieved their freedom from slavery by appropriating the art of theatrics and disguising their bodies. They depicted the madness of southern plantation slavery as a psychodrama: one of autocratic masters and resisting slaves lured into patterns of deception. Living in such an environment, perceptive slaves who were aware of the gross fraud of slavery, as Douglass opined, played to the histrionics of their forced subjugation and repeatedly juxtaposed two radically different worlds of slavery: as a sociopolitical reality and a mad social experiment. Both invited slave resistance. Indeed, Kenneth Stampp and Deborah Gray White agree that slave resistance was a cornerstone of southern plantation life, with Stampp stating that resistance "forms a chapter in the story of the endless struggle to give dignity to human life." White concurs, offering that the reality of slave resistance assisted in "defining [an] aspect of female slavery, one that shaped relationships and identity."[38]

In her three performances as 1) seducer, 2) sailor, and 3) mad mother in the garret, Jacobs used her body creatively to thwart the paternal law against women and black motherhood. "I resolved to match my cunning against his [Dr. Flint's] cunning," she remarks and alters her body (142). Her body assumes a positive mediating function between her life as a slave and her life as a free woman and mother. In her three performances, Jacobs makes a distinction between slave women's sexed and reproductive bodies and their self-possessing maternal and nurturing bodies. In the former, slave women's reproductive bodies were like Wheatley's Dark Continent body: commoditized objects of exchange, symbolizing their degraded rank in society. However, in the South, slave women's bodies were further exploited, sexually and reproductively. For instance, although Wheatley lived an impoverished life after she married the free but indebted Negro John Peters in Boston, she nonetheless had a legal marriage and children who belonged to her. For Jacobs, a southern slave denied the privilege of marrying, the maternal function on the Flint plantation "was not enshrined with minimal or restricted rights," Saidiya Hartman remarks. In fact, the maternal function was "indistinguishable from the condition of enslavement and its reproduction. Motherhood was critical to the reproduction of property and black subjection, but parental rights were unknown to the law.[39] Yet, Jacobs defied southern law by using the tool that was used against her: her body. Therefore she transgressed the law, designed to strip her of her maternal rights, not to mention her natural rights to her own physical body.

First, Jacobs's forced seductress role is one that is fraught with the tensions of the Jacobs-Sands-Flint battle and the vulgar image of the black woman as sexually immoral. Rejecting the rape allegations, Yellin asserts that Jacobs, realizing the inevitability of single motherhood, had cunningly selected the white attorney to father her children, based on the Edenton model of Rose Cabarrus,[40] a slave girl whose wealthy white lover freed her and their children. Nevertheless, in becoming a single mother, Jacobs, the symbolic prisoner of Chillon, was haunted by the image of the easy black woman. From Philadelphia to New York, Boston, Washington, D.C., and London, places where Jacobs as social reformer traveled as a single mother in a Victorian era, she remained sensitive to her status. She was met with a polite but prudish British reception, for example, when she initially attempted to publish *Incidents in the Life of a Slave Girl* in London.[41] This is yet another illustration of the hardships Jacobs suffered, unlike Wheatley, who was well received in London even though she lived and died over a half century before Jacobs was born. In 1862, when her narrative was finally published in London under the title *The Deeper Wrong; or, Incidents in the Life of a Slave Girl,* the publication occurred a year after the American publication and the London serialization of John Jacobs's antislavery treatise "A True Tale of Slavery." Perhaps the British found Jacobs's *Incidents in the Life of a Slave Girl* too racy and thus unacceptable, a result of Jacobs's sexual agency in addition to her description of fornication, adultery, miscegenation, homosexuality, and hints of sexual perversion. The slave Luke, for instance, was made to perform sex acts for his "palsied" and "despotic" master that were, Jacobs relates, "of a nature too filthy to be repeated" (216).

In *Incidents in the Life of a Slave Girl*, even when she escapes slavery and should feel the elation of her freedom, Jacobs, the fugitive, is met with cautionary rebuke for being a single mother. The Reverend Jeremiah Durham assists her in Philadelphia on the Underground Railroad and inquires about the daughter whom Jacobs has mentioned. Jacobs confesses, "He was approaching a subject on [which] I was extremely sensitive. He would ask about my husband next, I thought, and if I answered him truly what would he think of me? He asked some further questions, and I frankly told him some of the most important events of my life. It was painful for me to do it" (182). Politely, Reverend Durham cautions her not to divulge her unwed status to others who may not be as understanding of her predicament, presumably as he and his wife, whom Jacobs represents as not very prying. Is this, then, one of the reasons why Jacobs pleads for the slave girl not to be judged by the same standard as others?

Jacobs's early life and the particular representation of the black woman as promiscuous were cultivated by the circumstances of female enslavement, but the image, according to Winthrop Jordan, also constituted a convenient and "logical explanation for the white man's infidelity." Jacobs's lover Mr. Sands, for example, was not subjected to the criticism that her defloration evoked, suggesting a different set of rules for masters and slaves, men and women. Jordan remarks, "If she [the black woman] was *that* lascivious—well, a man could scarcely be blamed for succumbing against overwhelming odds."[42] Even though Jacobs's text gives voice to this pejorative picture of female slaves, she crafts the image to demonstrate her individual will and agency, which are important to her. At a younger age Jacobs shows more political shrewdness than polite, free Negroes as well as her proud but grieving relatives. In a wise maternal voice she asks, "But why, thought I, did my relatives ever cherish hopes for me? What was there to save me from the usual fate of slave girls?" (66)

Second, like her calculated seductive performances, Jacobs's seafaring role is plotted to subvert history's and slavery's power over her. She again transforms her body when she darkens her face and cross-dresses as a sailor, playing the role of the dark phallic mother, a trope on male agency and power that progressively preceded Alice Walker's by approximately 110 years. Her new appearance as a "man" gives voice to ideas of female castration and helplessness in a patriarchal social order, recalling Freud's infamous description of females as suffering from penis envy. Jacobs's cross-dressing suggests, however, that a woman in search of independence must assume the assertive behavior of males just to gain access to public discourse, perceived stereotypically as the province of men. In her performing role as sailor, Jacobs explains, "Betty brought me a suit of sailor's clothes—jacket, trousers, and tarpaulin hat." She advises Jacobs to "put your hands in your pockets and walk rickety, like de sailors." Jacobs responds, "I performed to her satisfaction" and "passed several people whom I knew, but they did not recognize me in my disguise" (125). Betty is the slave-cook of the white slave mistress who harbors Jacobs after she leaves her first refuge at a friend's home. Jacobs's fears and hysteria threaten to ruin the benevolent mistress, whose dual role in slavery as slave liberator and slaveholder stresses the schizophrenic nature of slavery, as revealed earlier in Mr. Sands's buying and then giving away his own children.

As a "sailor" walking through the streets of Edenton unnoticed and undisturbed, Jacobs converges the powerful gender image of white males with the acceptable seafaring image of black males, as seafaring was one of the few occupations available to enslaved and free black men. Douglass dressed as a sailor when he made his escape from a Maryland plantation, and Jacobs describes her Aunt Nancy's enslaved husband as a "seafaring" man who eventually leaves slavery and Edenton freely in his own attire after his wife dies. Yellin states, however, that Jacobs's Aunt Betty's (Nancy in *Incidents*) husband was forced to leave Edenton permanently after Jacobs's children and relatives were jailed, a punishment for her disappearance.[43] Betty's husband believed that he had nothing to return to Edenton for, having been dispossessed of his wife, an act revealing his powerlessness as a free Negro in a system of racial caste.

Jacobs walks the streets freely in a man's attire, still manifesting symptoms of hysteria. She reveals the precariousness of her situation even though this second altering of her body gives her greater spatial freedom than the area she will be restricted to in her grandmother's crawl space, where she is headed. With the cook Betty warning Jacobs, "you's got de high-sterics" (121), the narrative emphasizes the evolving tenseness of Jacobs's situational identities from sexual object to seductress, single mother, runaway slave, and now cross-dresser. Jacobs's hysteria is related to her fears about her children and possibly to a repressed sexuality. These anxieties are physically manifested on her body as she complains when she moves into the narrow space created for her in her grandmother's house, a confinement that leads to her developing symptoms of hypochondria. While Freud likens the neuroses of hypochondria to an "organic disease," one that emanates from real, painful bodily sensations, he distinguishes the latter from the former. Organic diseases are based on demonstrable bodily changes, while hypochondriac illnesses are not but are almost solely affectations of a troubled mind and spirit, as we shall see with Jacobs in the garret. Nonetheless both diseases are related to the libido and real or perceived bodily changes, affecting the body to the temporary exclusion of the individual's interest in the external society, hence Jacobs's obsessive focus in the garret on the "dreary past" and the "uncertain future."

Reflecting on her seven-year imprisonment in the garret, Jacobs relates the organic changes of her body to the mental anguish she experiences, refusing to separate the symbiotic relations of mind and body or the organic from the inorganic. She muses, "I hardly expect that the reader will credit me, when I affirm that I lived in that little dismal hole, almost deprived of light and air, and with no space to move my limbs, for nearly seven years. . . . for my body still suffers from the effects of the long imprisonment" (166). Her conflation of the past and present has the effect of reminding her readers, once more, that it is she, the mature Jacobs, who is controlling the narrative and enunciating its meaning and its truth, beyond the fictionalization of her alter ego, Linda Brent. While the physical complaint for Jacobs was real, the tortured psychological basis of her illness is related to the trauma of her enslavement.

Third, as the forced mad mother in the garret, Jacobs voices symptoms of hypochondria that are evidenced in her "dismal hole" or garret, which is "nine feet long and seven [inches] wide" and with a ceiling only "three feet high" (128). Her multiple complaints of bodily "pains and ache" extend to "my limbs" being "benumbed by inaction"; "my face and tongue" being "stiffened" with the "lost" of "the power of speech"; and "my life" being constantly threatened (136, 137). She is "stupefied" with drugs, "herbs, roots, and ointment" and remains in bed "six weeks, weary in body and sick at heart" (137). Real bodily torments combine with mental anguish, especially in reference to her children: "Dark thoughts passed through my mind as I lay there day after day. I tried to be thankful for my little cell, dismal as it was, and even to love it, as part of the price I had paid *for the redemption* [emphasis added] of my children" (137).

In associating her life so closely with the lives of her children ("my life was bound up in my children," 113), Jacobs manifests the maternal desire to create for her children the mirror reversal of her life. She determines, "Whatever slavery might do to me, it could not shackle my children" (123), recalling Toni Morrison's maternal heroine Sethe in *Beloved,* who repeats, "It's my job to know what is and to keep them [her children] away from what I know is terrible" (*Beloved* 165, 1988 edition). In their emphases on the means by which the maternal nurturer is to ensure the freedom and livelihood of her generation of children, Jacobs and Morrison, though a century apart, employ the same timeless trope of grunt maternal work ("my job") to stress the discipline and responsibility of motherhood. Jacobs's emphatic desire to liberate her children is heavily invested in her strong sense of selfhood (neither she nor her children were property) and her natural acceptance of the virtues of motherhood, notwithstanding slavery's attempted usurpation of her maternal rights.

At this narrative juncture, Jacobs's self-confessed vanity and her maternal altruism in sacrificing seven years of her life to redeem her children's lives appear to be at odds. Freud is helpful here. He comments that narcissistic women who become mothers often transfer their narcissism onto their children with whom they experience an inseparable part of their maternal body, with the bodies of both becoming bound up as one. Even "for narcissistic women, whose attitude towards men remains cool, there is a road which leads to complete object-love. In the child which they bear, a part of their own body confronts them like an extraneous object, to which, starting out from their narcissism, they can then give complete object-love."[44] Freud's theory can be applied to Jacobs's attachment to her children, despite or perhaps because of her fragile identity and Dr. Flint's retaliatory promise, "Your boy shall be put to work, and he shall soon be sold; and your girl shall be raised for the purpose of selling well" and become a female slave breeder (99). These threats to the welfare of her children are what really force Jacobs to make plans for their escape to the North: "more for my helpless children than myself" (99).

In direct contrast to her pride about her appearance, Jacobs's maternal altruism is suggestive too of the self-sacrificing greatness of the maternal ideal, which she radically revises. Nineteenth-century advocates of the maternal ideal, as thematically expressed in Coventry Patmore's paean to white, middle-class, and upper-class Victorian ladies, paid tribute to women's genteel characteristics of sexual purity, docility, and sacrifice, but only in service to men. I explore the topic of the maternal ideal in greater detail in chapter 3 on Charlotte Forten Grimké and abolitionism. Suffice it to say here that Jacobs redefines the maternal ideal not only in terms of her devotion to her children, born out of wedlock, but also with her painful public disclosure in writing *Incidents in the Life of a Slave Girl* on behalf of the slave mother. Yellin cites this narrative as the "only slave narrative that takes as its subject the sexual exploitation of female slaves—thus centering on sexual oppression as well as on oppression of race and condition."[45] Yellin argues for the consideration of Jacobs as the "representative"[46] woman of the nineteenth century "because she shap[ed] her past from a private tale of shame of a 'slave girl' into a public testimony against a tyrannical system."[47]

Aside from her worries about her children's future, Jacobs's sexual abstinence in the garret could have intensified her bodily complaints, leading to problems of hypochondria. There are coded sexual references to Sands/Sawyer that are perhaps related to her bodily irritations in the "dismal hole." From approximately 1828 to 1833,[48] Jacobs and Sawyer had an active sexual relationship, but now, in the garret, the young slave mother has to repress or deny any emotional links to him, not to mention her own sexual drive. Jacobs expresses her angst toward her lover and the father of their children: "There was one person there [in Washington, D.C., where he had taken their daughter] who ought to have had some sympathy with the anxiety of the child's friends at home; but the links of such relations as he had formed with me are easily broken." In a cryptic reference to the past and their sexual relations, she grieves, "Yet how protectingly and persuasively he once talked to the poor, helpless slave girl! And how entirely I trusted him!" (159).

Jacobs's abrupt shift in language from the objective third-person "slave girl" or Linda Brent to the first-person pronoun "I" or Harriet Jacobs marks her more personal narrative input, beyond telling a story of slavery. Her shift also pits narrative past time against narrative present time, making it Jacobs's and not Linda Brent's remembered and current pathos. Jacobs's self-reference as a "poor and naïve slave girl" is rather self-serving, however, and belies other images of her as the performer, manipulator, and seductress cleverly adapting her body to meet her natural human needs, denied by the institution of slavery. While the first image of Jacobs as the "poor slave girl" is intended to appeal to her northern audience of abolitionists and feminists ("Reader, I draw no imaginary pictures of southern homes. I am telling you the plain truth" [36]), the other images of her suggest that Jacobs's performances were not limited to her coseduction of Sands: her seduction extended adroitly to her northern white audience as well.

The narrating of *Incidents in the Life of a Slave Girl* is structured to appeal to sympathetic audiences, to northern white women and mothers, with whom Jacobs wishes to identify even as she plays the roles forced upon her by history and the institution of slavery. In alluding to her sexual relationship with Sands, though, Jacobs exploits her image as a poor slave girl, which she invariably counters and contradicts. She attempts to use her rank as "poor slave girl" because of her cultivation of the picture of the suffering slave mother, holed up in the garret, versus the gallivanting white congressman who betrays her and their children. Jacobs having had what can be regarded as a satisfying sexual relationship with Sands/Sawyer for five years, resulting in two children, her abstinence for seven years could have played a functional role in her anxieties and hypochondria. It is not clear that Jacobs repressed her sexual desires: only that she did not engage in any sexual activity with her former lover. Any suppression of the awareness of sexual desire can be perceived as a logical response to her confinement in the garret, but still with her developing symptoms of bodily irritations.

For Freud, painful bodily symptoms often served a purpose, for instance, in this case, of keeping Jacobs from having to engage in sexual activity that would be traumatizing. Freud states that the "character of hysterics shows a degree of sexual repression in excess of normal quantity, an intensification of resistance against the sexual instinct (which we have already met with in the form of shame, disgust and morality)." Yet there appears "an instinctive aversion on their part to any intellectual consideration of sexual problems."[49] Freud characterizes hysteria as sexual in nature, and it is brought on by the repression of mental and emotional processes when the individual is unable to seek relief in the sexual drive—as we must imagine was the case with Jacobs, especially with Sands, a married man now.

Aside from her sexual restraint or repression in the garret, Jacobs was affected for years by her cramped position in her cell, leading to her and others fearing that she would become "a cripple for life" (142). When she flees to New York, she is haunted by the anxiety of the garret: "My greatest anxiety *now* [emphasis added as Jacobs indicates that she was perpetually experiencing anxieties] was to obtain employment. My health was greatly improved, though my limbs continued to trouble me with swelling whenever I walked too much" (189). In "A True Tale of Slavery," John Jacobs, visiting his sister in New York after her escape, recorded his reaction: "At first she did not look natural, after having been shut out from the light of heaven for six years and eleven months." There was always a reminder of her confinement and its permanent effect on her body. Yellin describes Jacobs's difficulty in just climbing stairs at Nathaniel Willis's New York Idlewild home, where she worked. According to Yellin, Jacobs also complained in a letter to Amy Post about the pain afflicting her womb. "The trouble dear Amy is with my womb[;] I cannot tell you how much I have suffered during my illness."[50]

As a symptom of a deeper psychic conflict, a few of Jacobs's fears for her life and her children's lives enabled her to express in bodily form the terror of her anxieties as a slave mother and even as a free woman working in New York, as a nurse to the Willis's baby and writing *Incidents in the Life of a Slave Girl* at night. As a disorder, short-term hypochondria can be perceived as a "deflector" and therefore "as a relatively safe way of letting a basic conflict partially express itself" on the body as a receptacle for mental anguish and emotional conflicts.[51] In this sense, hypochondria, like the pseudocharacter Linda Brent, the alter ego and template, can function to deflect the angst that Jacobs, the narrator, experienced. While Jacobs's muscles were atrophied, she never became, as she had feared, a "cripple" for life. I am not suggesting that Jacobs's bodily ailments were not serious: her letter to Amy Post about her visit to the doctor assures us that she had a serious problem with her womb because of a cyst or tumor. But as a part of her exposé of slavery's tyranny, Jacobs discloses that the greatest of her and other slave mothers' fears were induced by the perils of motherhood under the governance of the southern plantation system—unlike anything that George Fitzhugh described.

The role of motherhood consumed her in and outside of slavery's confinement. At the time that Jacobs mentioned her womb-related illness to Amy Post, she was convalescing in Cambridge, Massachusetts, during the period of the Anthony Burns fugitive-slave trial in 1854 (discussed in chapter 3), and after her battle with Harriet Beecher Stowe, with whom she fought over her daughter, Louisa. Stowe had written to Mrs. Cornelia Grinnell Willis, the wife of Nathaniel Willis, forwarding for verification the intimate details of Jacobs's life that Mrs. Willis did not know and that Post, at Jacobs's request, had sent to Stowe, seeking her assistance with the writing of *Incidents in the Life of a Slave Girl*. However, as William Andrews remarks, Stowe was not interested "in a creative partnership with Jacobs,"[52] and Jacobs would not permit the famous author to fictionalize her painful life in her forthcoming book, *The Key to Uncle Tom's Cabin*. Jacobs became angry with Stowe, who had refused Jacobs's request to take Louisa to England with her as a representative slave girl. Stowe thought that the British would "pet" a former slave, a remark that Jacobs found racially insensitive. These were Jacobs's additional anxieties, but the old ones (from slavery) were always with her.

In *Incidents in the Life of a Slave Girl,* Jacobs literally and figuratively places herself and her mad mothering performance within the wider subtext of the social malady in the Edenton slave community. Without the subtext of plantation slavery as a curse for the various social groups described (from slave mothers to slave fathers and white slave mistresses), Jacobs's actions emerge as separate and isolated from the environmental conditions inimical to her slave society. For example, in her apotheosis of Jacobs's performance and the "psychological warfare" she wages against Dr. Flint, Yellin represents Jacobs's maternal performance as a sleuthing act, smart and efficient: "From her cramped hiding place, she manipulates the sale of her children to their father, arranges for her daughter to be taken North, tricks her master into believing that she has left the South, and quite literally directs a performance in which Dr. Flint plays the fool while she watches, unseen."[53] In isolating Jacobs's ingenious performance from the institutional madness of plantation slavery, Yellin and other scholars only hint at the abnormal intrigues of the whole plantation regime.

This slave regime provoked in Jacobs the uneasiness that led to her three performances of countermadness. *Incidents in the Life of a Slave Girl* should not be read without the realization that Jacobs does not divorce her mad acts from the wholly institutionalization of madness under slavery's practices. In her maternal role, Jacobs is invariably reacting to her slave community, not acting on her own accord, but always in response to the neuroses of the wider slave community. In her own voice, Jacobs reiterates this idea: "I like a straightforward course, and am always reluctant to resort to subterfuges. So far as my ways have been crooked, I charge them all upon slavery. It was that system of violence and wrong which now left me no alternative but to enact a falsehood" (187–88). Thus, in performing the activities that Yellin incisively condenses, Jacobs engages in actions that outside slavery would be perceived as the neurotic reversal of responsible maternal work: fostering the preservation and care of children and the community. Almost everyone connected to Jacobs's secret hiding place—from her children to her grandmother to her white benefactor—is endangered. Indeed during her hiding in the garret, Jacobs admits that in "the midst of my illness, grandmother broke down under the weight and anxiety and toil" (136–37), a description revealing some of her reasons for not writing about her life in slavery while her grandmother was still alive. Yellin reports that only after her grandmother had died did Jacobs feel free to revisit her Edenton trauma and write *Incidents in the Life of a Slave Girl.*[54]

In manipulating the sale of her children to their father, Jacobs, from her garret, adopts a rational approach to an eerie scene of interpersonal human relations under the influence of slavery. As an enslaved mother, she had no power to protect her children. As a free white man of property, Sands, the children's father and new slave owner, had considerable discretion about the welfare of his children/his slaves. Jacobs understandably has the feelings of a "wretched mother" with "painful memories," and when she learns of Sands's impending departure for Washington, D.C., she literally crawls from her hole to "speak for my children" (140), risking everything. Although Sands describes Jacobs's concealment in Edenton as the "height of madness" (141), his representation of madness (restricted only to Jacobs's relatives hiding her) screens the wider social reality of the pathology of slavery, afflicting the entire Edenton community. Sands plays a major role in Jacobs's daring performances from propertied sexed body to seductive maternal body. Though now out of coinage, Adolf Meyer's theory of "psychobiology,"[55] or the concept of the individual as psychically the sum total of his or her environment, illuminates Sands's position in Edenton. In his own schizophrenic roles, Sands was Jacobs's lover, her children's "parental" relation, her brother's slave master, and Dr. Flint's competitor/ comrade, the latter of whom he defrauds by buying his own children who are legally the doctor's property. Yellin works out Sands's aberrant status differently, focusing on his relationship with Jacobs's brother, who was his slave, but also his functional brother-in-law and his children's uncle.[56] Sands's madness was not divorced from Jacobs's; both were fostered by slavery's neuroses.

With Ellen and Sands in Washington, D.C., and Benjamin in Edenton with his great-grandmother, two of Jacobs's three objectives for running away from the younger Flint plantation have been achieved. What remains is the freeing of her own body from the garret and slavery. When this final act is accomplished, she leaves the garret "faint in body, but strong of purpose" (176). In her emphasis on the body-will union again, Jacobs typically valorizes the will over the body yet signifies the maternal body as a creative site of regeneration. If Jacobs had died in the garret, her cell would have emerged, figuratively, as an example of the stillbirth of the maternal womb, which is instead the miraculous font of life. Her problem with her womb can be related to the constriction of her physical body, and this imprisonment is a reminder of slavery's debilitating impact on motherhood physically and emotionally.

However, Jacobs does not die in her crawl space, which can be viewed metaphorically as the functional process of her incubation and her long maternal labor. Jacobs, like Wheatley, gives birth to herself, a self-genesis: for the garret, no longer a prison, becomes instead a maternal incubator, paving the way for her emergence from slavery. Jacobs rises victoriously from her inverted cell, affirming the metaphor of the maternal body as a source of feminine replenishment in filial transgression of paternal law, which had sanctioned the maternal plundering of her reproductive slave body. Whether as seductress, sailor, or mad mother, Jacobs patiently executes her plan to deliver herself and her children from the stillbirth, death knell of slavery. She leaves the garret "faint" but "strong," heading north to freedom, signifying the miraculous impulse of the maternal body: the/life-spring of women's creative potential—literally and metaphorically.

In nineteenth-century society Jacobs had attained a position that many women in Victorian America coveted: motherhood. But as a slave mother on a southern plantation, she could neither enjoy the status of motherhood nor claim ownership of her children, neither marry the man of her choice nor possess a home protected by the law until much later in her life. In writing *Incidents in the Life of a Slave Girl*, Jacobs, the maternal conduit, placed the antislavery cause and maternal and feminist ethics before her personal trauma and embarrassment. In her letter to Amy Post, she pleads the cause of the slave mother: "I ask nothing—I have placed myself before you to be judged as a woman whether I deserve your pity or contempt—I have another object in view, the "Slave Mother.""[57] In representing the "poor Slave Mother," Jacobs had to divulge her experience because the slave mother was the fulcrum on which the reproduction of slavery rested. "Judgment," remarks Hazel Carby, "was to be passed on the institution of slavery, not on deviations from conventions of true womanhood."[58]

During and after the Civil War, Jacobs's activism on behalf of slave women and slave mothers places her in the pantheon of women as social reformers, but the irony of her new position was not lost on her. Yellin chronicles Jacobs's abolitionist and Reconstruction activities from London to Virginia, South Carolina, and Washington, D.C., where she raised money, taught children and adults, and had a school named after her and in her honor, the Jacobs's School. She also cared for orphans in addition to nursing Union soldiers. Other critics too cite Jacobs's work in refugee camps during and after the Civil War to "raise consciousness about the plight of the 'contrabands.'"[59] However, a lingering question remains about Jacobs's level of sensitivity about her unwed status and whether, in spite of her social reform work, it played a role in her presumed social ostracism from elite Negro society in a Victorian age. Jacobs had confessed to Post, "I have not the Courage to meet the criticism and ridicule of Educated people."[60] Nonetheless her aspirations and reform work placed her in the company of educated social reformers such as the youthful Charlotte Forten.

Yellin reports that the educated Grimkés, Forten and her husband, Rev. Francis Grimké of Washington, D.C. (Angelina Grimké's mulatto nephew), befriended Jacobs and her daughter, Louisa. Nevertheless mother and daughter remained outside the Grimkés' social circle. Forten Grimké never invited them to the "Friday night gatherings at the couple's book and flower filled Corcoran Street home, where works of painting and sculpture were studied and aesthetic criticism was read."[61] But in journal 3, August 11, 1862, the young diarist refers politely to Jacobs, twenty-five years her senior, as "Mrs. J," the "kindly, motherly friend" whom the motherless daughter sought for most of her life. As a single woman living in Boston, Forten nurtured friendly relations with the older Jacobs, relations not repeated when she became a married woman living in fashionable Washington, D.C. But Forten's husband had experienced the plague of slavery that Jacobs captures in *Incidents in the Life of a Slave Girl*. He fought off his white half brother's attempt to whip him and make him a personal house servant; he was not as successful when his half brother sold him to a Confederate officer. Francis Grimké escaped the South and slavery by running for his life, as did Jacobs, whom he eulogized in 1897.[62]

Harriet Jacobs's importance to her period and African American literary history is noteworthy in other ways beyond her writing of *Incidents in the Life of a Slave Girl* and her antislavery crusade. When Charlotte Forten entered African American literary discourse by relocating to the South to do the great work of regeneration, she did so in part because of her acquaintance with the elderly Jacobs. On August 17, 1862, the diarist noted Jacobs's influence on her decision to help the freed people: "Since Mrs. J. [politely assuming a marital status that Jacobs did not have] has given me such sad accounts of the sufferings of the poor freed people, my desire of helping them has increased."[63] In *The Harriet Jacobs Family Papers*, Yellin cites John Greenleaf Whittier's sister, Elizabeth, testifying to Forten's passion: "The young lady is heart and soul in her work—deeming it a sacred duty to devote life and talents to the improvement of her unfortunate race,"[64] putting her in the class of Wheatley and Jacobs. *Incidents in the Life of a Slave Girl* retains the poignancy of Jacobs's and other black women's desire for "home," "freedom," and "motherhood." But slavery, which had denied Jacobs that natural right, became the impetus for her involvement in radical abolitionism and her easy recruitment of the aristocratic Forten.

3 The Maternal Ideal

The Journals of Charlotte Forten Grimké

> My mother! my loved lost mother!
> Thou are hovering near me now!
> Oh! bless and lead aright thy erring
> child, and let it not be very long ere
> thou claimest her again for thine own!
> For I am very weary; I long for thee.[1]

A former member of Philadelphia's free and elite Negro society, Mary Virginia Wood Forten, Charlotte Forten's mother, died in 1840 at the age of twenty-six, when Charlotte was only a three-year-old toddler. The diarist keeps the faint but tender memory of her mother alive in her journals, however, asking her to bestow the gift of immortality and referring to her angelically as "hovering near me now" and possessively as "my own mother" who had a "pure and noble character" (210, 238).[2] By valorizing her mother in her diaries, Forten appropriates the Victorian trope of maternity and celestiality, an indication that she was emotionally invested in the nineteenth century's vaunted cultural paradigm of motherhood and femininity as the sine qua non of the female role and character. Forten's appropriation of the Victorian metaphor of the angel in the house and the paradigm of the maternal ideal along with her privileged family background in an enslaving antebellum America suggest her interstitial position: she was neither white, nor a sexualized female slave, nor a poor black free Negro; she was a black aristocrat, triply marginalized.

Forten's family heritage and her journals mark a crucial turning point in African American women's literature and black literary history. After Phillis Wheatley and Harriet Jacobs, who were literal slaves, Forten represents the origin of a new, emerging class of the activist-elite, black intellectual, female reformer, a prototype for Du Bois's "Talented Tenth." She was joined by other black women intellectuals such as Maria W. Stewart (1803–79); Harriet Wilson (1825–1900); and Anna J. Cooper (1858–1964), all becoming important chroniclers of the age and representing the emergence of black feminist thought on education and social justice not only for the enslaved but also for the so-called "free Negro." As social reformer, Forten, isolated by race, gender, and class, used her interstitiality or her elite marginality to mark and expand the space that could lie open to other talented black Americans. She was an aristocratic abolitionist who traveled to South Carolina to educate contraband slaves, and she captured in her journals one of the most meaningful events in America's history: the reading of the Emancipation Proclamation to a group of slaves. Harbinger and pariah, Forten was an important part of a series of interrelated historical events—from slavery and abolitionism to liberation and Reconstruction. The latter shaped black enfranchisement, educational reform, and the beginning of a more integrated, democratic society. In short, Charlotte Forten was on the cutting edge of a changing American society, and her journals chart the fledging democratization of America when blacks, no longer slaves, were in the process of becoming free citizens.

Important to a study of Forten are the background of her privileged family life, the theory of the maternal ideal and its radical feminist revision, and her symbolic, interstitial position as a free and wealthy black woman in antebellum America. An analysis of her journals with reference to the ideas of the maternal ideal, her representation of the age, and the theory of journal scholarship illuminates her evolving personas throughout her diaries.

While upper-class Victorian respectability was not truly within the grasp of enslaved or free black women, the class status of the Fortens of Philadelphia presented the diarist with the kinds of opportunities and experiences that made her a more likely candidate for such stature to a degree. The extraordinary patriarch of the family, James Forten Sr., born in 1766, was a free Negro; was educated by Quakers and influenced by the most prominent among them, Anthony Benezet; and was later commissioned as a powder boy during the American Revolution. In *A Gentleman of Color,* his biographer Julie Winch explains that he was a prisoner of the British and placed with other patriots aboard the ship *Jersey,* which sailed to England. He was released many months later in an exchange of prisoners but later returned to London, which, despite earlier accounts of its abolitionist activism, had become inhospitable to blacks. "When James Forten arrived in London, the abolitionist crusade was only just beginning," writes Winch. Indeed the "London Friends had responded to news that Parliament was about to authorize the resumption of the slave trade after suspending it during the War for Independence."[3]

Black Loyalists who fought for England's King George and then fled the colonies for freedom in London discovered that for the British, giving "all the rights of Englishmen to black people in Britain was another matter entirely."[4] In such an environment, James Forten looked to the British abolitionists for more encouragement about social reform, although it is not clear that he had ever planned to stay in London beyond the time of a youthful and adventurous visit. Forten was a Revolutionary War patriot but was influenced in his own life by the awakening of abolitionist sentiments in London. By the time of his visit, the attorney and abolitionist Granville Sharp (Wheatley's escort to the Tower of London) had successfully defended the acquired freedom of a Virginia slave, James Somerset. The slave's southern master had brought him to England, a free land, which, as Lord Mansfield ruled in the famed Somerset case in 1772, had therefore made the slave legally free.

James Forten left England in 1785 after only one year of residence but with more than a little knowledge about subjects as diverse as sailing and abolitionism, both of which were fated to play important parts in his life.

Returning to Philadelphia in 1786, the towering Forten, standing six feet tall, became an apprentice and later a foreman in a business owned by the friendly white sailmaker Robert Bridges, who taught him "the full range of the sail-maker's craft."[5] Forten became a "master craftsman," learning "how to measure not only lengths and widths and diagonals, but also how to calculate angles and make careful scale drawings for use in the loft." By 1798 James Forten, already an anomaly in antebellum America, had become even more so as a free Negro who had bought out the retiring Robert Bridges with the patronage of two white wealthy businessmen, Willing and Francis. "Probably because they had already employed Bridges and knew the quality of the work his loft produced," remarks Winch, "the partners gave Forten some of his first orders," playing a "crucial role" in the establishment of his career and the upper-middle-class status of the wealthy Forten family into which Charlotte Forten was born.[6]

As master sailmaker, James Forten amassed a fortune that Ray Allen Billington (who wrote Charlotte Forten's first, primary minibiography) estimates as being over one hundred thousand dollars by 1832. This was at a time when wages were pecuniary, and he hired or retained thirty to forty white and black employees.[7] Winch adds that in researching Forten's business background, she located letters attesting to his great wealth and the "surprise" with which he was met in others' greetings. "One recipient noted on the back of a letter that he had kept it as a curiosity because 'it was from a Negro-man';—a Negro-gentleman, I may say. He was in possession of a fortune made by his own industry," a fortune that later included vast real estate holdings.[8] A pious family man, James Forten had his wealth extended to include a large number of children. Remarrying after the early death of his first wife, he and his free-born second wife, Charlotte Vandine, his "beloved wife,"[9] had nine children. Seven of these included Robert Bridges, Charlotte Forten's father, named after the white sailmaker; James Jr.; Thomas Willing Francis, named after the rich patrons; William Deas, named after another white merchant; and daughters Margaretta, Sarah, and Harriet. All seven surviving Fortens became active members and even founders of educational reform and antislavery societies.

Abolitionism became a family cause. Since women were barred from the national antislavery societies, the Forten women, led by the matriarch, Charlotte Sr., founded the Philadelphia Female Anti-Slavery Society in the early 1830s. Harriet Forten married the wealthy mulatto abolitionist Robert Purvis, one of the original signers of the American Anti-Slavery Society Charter in 1833, the other signers being James Forten Sr. and the poet John Greenleaf Whittier. The patriarch's spacious Lombard Street home was a luxurious retreat for such abolitionists as Whittier, Wendell Phillips, Lydia Maria Child, William Lloyd Garrison, and England's George

Thompson and Harriet Martineau (who sent Forten a copy of her book *Hour and the Man*). In Boston, Lydia Maria Child remarked to the diarist that she had visited her grandfather's Philadelphia home when Charlotte "must have been a 'wee toddling.'"[10]

John Greenleaf Whittier wrote the poem "To the Daughters of James Forten" —"Sisters! The proud and vain may pass ye by"—encouraging them and denouncing the color prejudice they would likely encounter but from which their father's wealth shielded them since they were privately tutored and educated. The white abolitionist Samuel J. May, for example, described Forten's daughters as "lovely [and] accomplished." May also noted, however, that Forten had confided in him that "their education, evidently of a superior kind, had cost him very much more than it would have done, if they had not been denied admission into the best schools of the city."[11] Margaretta later founded her own school, at which Charlotte Forten would intermittently teach.

The Fortens were considered "old Philadelphians," a title defining their aristocratic standing in a traditional northeastern city of black pioneers and religious and social reformers, as described in W. E. B. Du Bois's study *The Philadelphia Negro* (1899). Philadelphia's colored aristocracy consisted of three groups of people: native Philadelphians such as the Fortens; a Caribbean group that established businesses in the city; and free-born mulattos from the South such as the South Carolina–bred Robert Purvis, whose wealthy English father had left him and his brothers a sizable inheritance. Like Whittier, Garrison was an admirer of the industrious Fortens. After visiting the Byberry country estate of Robert and Harriet Purvis, he wrote to a friend, "I wish you had been with me in Philadelphia to see what I saw, to hear what I heard, and to experience what I felt in associating with many colored families." Garrison found among the Fortens and Purvises "colored men and women, young men and ladies, in that city, who have few superiors in refinement, in moral worth, and in all that makes the human character worthy of admiration and praise."[12] The privileged Forten women were a picture of Victorian femininity.

Known for his Negro leadership in religious and civic activities, the progressive patriarch supported women's rights and initially funded and gathered Negro donors for Garrison's antislavery paper the *Liberator* (1831). Four years earlier Forten had lauded the founding of the first black, but short-lived, newspaper *Freedom's Journal,* to which he contributed letters of protest assailing colonization and defending black people's rights under his pen name "a Gentleman of Color." For over twenty years he led the opposition to the American Colonization Society, which sought to send free Negroes "back" to Africa while ignoring the plight of slaves in the South. Because of his patriotism during the American Revolution and his willingness to keep the British out of Philadelphia during the War of 1812, he helped to write the Resolution against the American Colonization Society. In doing so, he drew adroitly upon his native credentials: "WHEREAS our ancestors (not of choice) were the first successful cultivators of America, we . . . feel ourselves entitled to participate in the blessings of her luxuriant soil, which their blood and sweat manured."[13] Upon his death in 1842, he was given a hero's funeral: from three to five thousand Negroes and whites marched in the procession in a "real amalgamation funeral,"[14] the abolitionist Lucretia Mott noted.

Thus the elderly Harriet Jacobs would have encountered no problems in her recruitment of the youthful Charlotte Forten for the abolitionist cause. As James Forten's granddaughter, as her mother's daughter, she was the inheritor of a unique family tradition not only of wealth (which declined after the patriarch's death) but also of a sense of noblesse oblige. No less an abolitionist giant than Wendell Phillips reminded her of the role that she was destined to play in the crusade against slavery. "You owe this [her involvement] to the noble name you bear," he informed her.[15] Indeed, writes Winch, "James Forten cast a long shadow. His legacy was a complex one that both burdened and blessed his heirs" with the "constant pressure to live up to his example."[16] Perhaps with these words and the knowledge of the diarist's background in mind, readers can appreciate the import of one of her early entries in the journals, which describes her having a "craving for anti-slavery food" and a "longing for something higher and nobler than I have known" (261).

In September 1854 she entered in her diaries, "This evening Miss S[arah] B[rown] and I joined the Female Anti-Slavery Society. I am glad to have persuaded her to do so. I can only hope and pray that she will be true and courageous enough to meet the opposition which every friend of freedom must encounter" (141). The words "to meet the opposition" suggest that like her mother and her relatives before her, Charlotte saw slavery as a long struggle between the friends "of freedom" and their southern opponents. Since she was residing in Salem, Massachusetts, at this time, she would have joined the integrated Salem Female Anti-Slavery Society, established in 1834, and affiliated with the Garrisonian wing of radical abolitionism.

As radical reformers, the group called for the immediate end of slavery through moral suasion but was not entirely supportive of nonresistance while advocating women's rights as well. Through their fairs and lecture series, the Salem women "enjoyed hosting major figures of the antislavery movement and highlighting their society's role in connecting Salem to the larger world of abolitionism."[17] As a result of her association with this group and other similar female groups in Boston and Philadelphia, Forten came to know and to be associated with many of the great abolitionists of her time, who influenced her. Like her grandfather and her mother, Forten, doubly invested in the heritage of social reform, thought of slavery and racism as a war that she was more than willing to fight, and she was ready to enlist others who "will be true" to the cause. Her reasons for assuming a warriorlike attitude in combating the twin evils of her age were as much personal as they were moral and political.

In the opening quotation to this chapter, we see Forten's depiction of the inseparable mother-daughter dyad, grounded in Victorian sentimental literature but truly conveying her marginal position in antebellum America. Even as free and never-enslaved Negroes, Forten and her mother would not have had total access to the raced space of Victorian maternity and womanhood, and in this sense the diarist joins the rank of Wheatley and Jacobs, whose bodies were symbols of difference, though more intrusively than Forten's rich, free-born body. The Forten women embraced the values of Victorian upper-class women, but they were still outside the Victorian sphere of true womanhood. Coventry Patmore's popular Victorian versepoem "The Angel in the House" was a paean to conservative and upper-class *white* women who accepted their subordinate status as domestic angels in the house, residing within the circumscribed border of patriarchy. Forten's angel-mother was self-sacrificing too, like Patmore's domestic maternal ideal, who in his oft-cited line "loves with love that cannot tire." However, Mary Virginia Wood Forten's self-sacrifice as a former member of Philadelphia's Female Anti-Slavery Society was noble but problematic. That is, she was personally connected to the publicly degraded social body of slaves, whom she did not know but with whom she and her daughter emblematically shared the socially constructed and bodily configuration of race and identity. Thus, Forten's interstitial body can be likened superficially to Wheatley's Dark Continent body and Jacobs's sexed body: all *raced bodies* of the cultural Other. But Forten's proximity to the sacred tradition of the maternal ideal separated her from Jacobs, whom she knew, and Wheatley, whose poetry she read and whose "character and genius afford a striking proof of the falseness of the assertion made by some that hers is an inferior race" (92). In this direct line of literary descent, Forten and her diaries are akin to Wheatley and her religious poetry and to Jacobs and her slave narrative: they all recorded the politics of their age, against which they waged war, subversively. Forten's selection of genres, the diary, however, underscores her class status and her interest in Victorian ideas of the maternal ideal and domestic feminism.

The Maternal Ideal

A primary characteristic of the maternal ideal of the "Angel in the House" is the females' unswerving commitment to a sense of duty as wives, daughters, and especially as mothers. According to Ann Douglas, the cult of motherhood, like Barbara Welter's cult of true womanhood, celebrated the feminine virtues of purity and domesticity. Women's ideal domestic position as caring mothers was valorized in the influential works of some of the most popular nineteenth-century orators and writers and the "chief exponent of the doctrine of the feminine sphere," as Douglas refers to Sarah Hale and her influence on Victorian ladies.[18] Literary magazines, orations, tracts, books, and teachings from Sarah Hale's edited *Godey's Lady's Book* to Henry Ward Beecher's Sunday sermons, Catherine Beecher's *Domestic Economy*, and Harriet Beecher Stowe's *Uncle Tom's Cabin* (1852) had as the center of their discourse a ministerial praise of and the ethical instructions on women's proper behavior and feelings.

The reform-minded patriarch of the Beecher family, the Unitarian minister Lyman Beecher, established the tradition of reform that his progeny inherited, articulating the same or similar themes. As a minister, his son, Henry Ward Beecher, linked God to the superiority of women as mothers in that a "mother's love is 'a revelation of the love of God.'"[19] An avid participant at lecture series, Forten attended one of Beecher's lectures, and since he was against slavery (as certainly almost everyone whose lectures she attended was), she writes favorably of him. "This evening attended a lecture by Rev. Henry Ward Beecher of Brooklyn," she writes, and continues, "His manner is not at all polished or elegant, but he says so many excellent things with such forcible earnestness or irresistible humor, that we quite forget it" (121–22). Like other members of the Beecher family, Ward Beecher preached the merits of feminine power, and for Forten, his valorization of women and the maternal ideal excused his unpolished manners. His sister Harriet wrote the most popular novel of the age, valorizing maternal feelings. Her frail and dying, selfless and angelic Little Eva best expressed the cult of sentimentality, moral suasion, and moral redemption. Despite her youth, Little Eva dons the garb of the idealized mother and maternally admonishes her slaveholding society to feel and do "right." She then dies, ascends to heaven, becomes an angel, and anticipates the coming of Jubilee.

In many ways the Victorian idea of women and mothers possessing a sacred feminine principle of eternal love and moral discipline resonated with the diarist because she accepted the idea that it was women's maternal responsibility to uplift society and the individual. The vaunted idea of the feminine sphere found expression in Forten's poem "The Angel's Visit," and she therefore joins the rank of white male and female Victorian angelographers, but with a discourse on class, race, gender, and the body politic that articulated the triple paradox of her Victorian sensibility. In "The Angel's Visit," she imagines her "angel mother" visiting, nurturing, and sustaining her, reminding the daughter that she has the permanence of a "mother's love" even though the mother is dead and physically absent. But the mother's death, like Little Eva's, facilitates her apotheosis as a spiritual messenger from heaven who serves as a link between the two realms of immortality and mortality, giving her the maternal/celestial power over life and death, good angel over bad angel. As the good angel, Forten's mother chooses life for her weary daughter and urges her to "falter not; keep bravely on, / And nobly bear thy part" to become a maternal warrior, regenerating a slaveholding society, fulfilling her dead mother's aborted mission while she, though dead, hovers angelically in the background speaking to her daughter.

"The maternal ideal," avers Deborah Gray White, "achieved its quintessential expression in the writings of the mid-nineteenth century," and Charlotte Forten was one of its chief exponents. The maternal ideal was task oriented, and the celestial/maternal figure reminds her daughter that in an era of social reform she too has a role to play even though the all-knowing mother is aware of "the cruel wrongs that crush / The young and ardent heart."[20] In writing this poem, the diarist reveals her sensitivity to the Victorian ethos of a feminizing-ministering spirit who is the domestic angel in the house in physical body and earthly mind. However, Forten's dead mother has become a literal spirit-guide who takes the form of the celestial maternal. In this role the omnipotent mother knows the troubles of the world and has transcended them, functioning, unlike Patmore's domestic maternal ideal, as the immortal maternal ideal of perfection to which her daughter aspires. Like her mother, the warrior-daughter embraces the role of the duty-bound, Victorian maternal ideal but more radically so, outside the patriarchal borders of the home and into the ever-expanding field of grunt social reform.

The two concepts of the maternal ideal of *being* excellent and perfect in character and of *doing and performing* the dutiful work of mothers in the home coalesce more politically outside the home for Forten, as we see in her volunteering to participate in the Port Royal Social Experiment. Even though Forten was privileged by family background, her colored body connected her irretrievably to the bodies of the dispossessed and all those experiencing both "slavery and prejudice," as she laments in her first journal (67). This dispossession, this racial conflict became her "subversive" motivation to revamp the status quo and to undo social injustices, calling for the work of the maternal ideal.

The maternal ideal of being a worthy individual and the maternal ideal of doing greater social reform work outside the home and in society are evident in the philosophy of radical domestic feminism. As a new and emerging militant thought in the nineteenth century, radical domestic feminism redefined Patmore's provincial concept of the maternal ideal of submissive women, devoted to the well-being of men. This new maternal ideal was one that asserted women's power in the public world as well as the private realm. One sees the radicalization of the traditional women's space in the women's antislavery activities and fairs sponsored in Massachusetts, for example, by the Salem Female Anti-Slavery Society and the Boston Female Anti-Slavery Society. Forten belonged to both women's groups and participated in their fairs, as found throughout the diary in the descriptions of her activities. These included her baking pies and sewing garments, perhaps for fairs, fulfilling the Victorian "social expectations of virtuous upper-class femininity,"[21] while subversively challenging traditional gender roles. At these meetings and fairs, antislavery women presented and sold to the public such seemingly innocuous objects as pincushions and pot holders. Inscribed on these items, however, were antislavery sentiments and mottoes such as "Remember them that are in bonds" and "Am I Not a Woman and a Sister?," which were similar to the men's abolitionist slogan for male slaves, "Am I Not a Man and a Brother?" While these objects, made in the home, were both "radical and conservative," the rhetoric of the image "brought a public and political issue into the home, and enlisted home and mother in political action," acknowledging the home as "a political space."[22]

Although women could not be ministers in society as could Lyman Beecher or Henry Ward Beecher, they could influence and perhaps transform society as revolutionary angels, combining abolitionism and feminism, as Jacobs did in her self-appointed role as a maternal conduit and spokesperson for the slave mother. Embracing the slave mother's cause was not difficult for feminist and nonfeminist abolitionists because radical white women had come to regard the female slave's propertied body as similar to their own socially proscribed bodies. The feminist Karen Sanchez-Eppler distinguishes, however, the difference between these two bodies, observing that the unlikely comparison "obliterates the particularity of black and female experience, making their distinct exploitations appear identical" while the "two sorts of bodies were prisons in different ways."[23] Indeed in *Incidents in the Life of a Slave Girl,* the three women Jacobs, Mrs. Flint, and Mrs. Sands were all victimized to various degrees by oppressive male sexual power over women, but Jacobs's fears about her children and her welfare were unlike anything the other women experienced.

In a Victorian era that viewed motherhood and the maternal body of women as a site of sanctity, white women who appropriated the slave mother's pathos (rather than her body) as something that white mothers could empathize with were on more solid ground. Stowe knew this stern fact and proved it in the afterword to *Uncle Tom's Cabin.* She spoke directly to white mothers, making her appeal: "And you, mothers of America . . . by the sacred love you bear your child; by the motherly pity and tenderness with which you guide his growing years. I beseech you, pity the mother who has all your affections, and not one legal right to protect, guide, or educate, the child of her bosom!"[24] Having never been a slave mother, Forten would have appreciated Stowe's entreaty. Feminism and abolitionism were related, especially for women such as Forten who joined antislavery societies and even for Stowe, who never formally joined an antislavery society. These "isms" were connected to women's roles as mothers, a cultural role in a Victorian society across the fault lines of race and class. While Stowe was not speaking on behalf of women's antislavery societies, her maternal iconography and direct address to northern women as mothers can be seen as a trope of women's power to effect change.

Forten's Interstitiality in Society and African American Literary Discourse

Forten would have agreed with Stowe. Undoubtedly persuaded by the idea of women's literal and metaphorical maternal power to regenerate society, she drew upon this force in ways different from that of her white contemporaries who adopted self-assured public voices. White women emphasized a maternal function to placate men such as Patmore's maternal ideal or to resolve (like Stowe's northern mothers) an immediate challenge of domestic relations, either between husband and wife or North and South, vis-à-vis slavery. For nineteenth-century black women intellectuals such as Forten, Harriet Jacobs, and Frances Ellen Watkins Harper, the discourse on the maternal, the home, and the social body of slavery and its resulting legacy of discrimination refused the closure of immediate resolution and remained a daunting challenge, as we read in their literary works and letters. Attempting to remove the chains of black enslavement and the persistence of racism in the North as well as in the South, black women writers and intellectuals found an uneasy public voice in their writings and their antislavery affairs. "We meet the monster prejudice *everywhere*. . . . You must aid us," cried one black female officer to her white sisters in the Salem Female Anti-Slavery Society.[25]

Black female reformers were in an untenable position, whether as slaves like Jacobs or as free-born Negroes like Harper and Forten. Jacobs's fictive heroine, Linda Brent, and Harper's white-skinned protagonist in her serial fiction and Reconstruction novel *Iola Leroy* all struggle for Victorian respectability within a system that denied their legitimacy. Other real-life examples of the delegitimating of the black body come to mind. As seen through the racist gaze of many European males, the Hottentot Venus, the African Sarah Baartmann, became the "central image for the black female throughout the nineteenth century," and she was presented as a pathological object of ridicule in Europe. Yet it appears that the repressed sexuality and fears about sexuality among racist Europeans caused the Baartmann objectification. Due to the appearance of her large buttocks, Baartmann was put on display in London museums and at Paris balls. "When the Victorians saw the female black," Sander Gilman adds, "they saw her in terms of her buttocks," an erotic caricature of Baartmann, also another example of pseudoscientific racism and the desire of white male fantasy.[26] Between the image of the slave woman in antebellum America and Baartmann in Europe, the black female was attached to a stereotype that denied her distinctive characteristics and attributes, which all three women writers rejected in their own unique ways.

For example, Jacobs and Harper labored to describe their heroines' mixed-race lineage, which, while challenging ideas of racial authenticity, also further complicated their racial identity and subjectivity. A dispirited Victorian aspirant, Jacobs was pursued by her slave master, Dr. Flint/Norcom even as she unsuccessfully pursued Victorian standards of conduct. An antislavery lecturer, serial writer, and novelist, the indefatigable Harper, in her novel *Iola Leroy,* too manipulated the borders of race and caste, which the racially conflicted Iola as a white woman defends until she discovers her Negro ancestry and becomes enslaved. As a freed woman, Iola works as a nurse to Union soldiers and later for racial uplift, transforming her and her race's identity. A self-proclaimed "chaste and pure" Victorian lady, Charlotte Forten was haunted, like Jacobs and Harper, by the specter of the downtrodden racialized Other in a society that had particular views on race, gender, and class.

But Forten was also different from the widowed, laboring Harper and the enslaved Jacobs, whose scandalous, sexual experience forced her into the early role of teen mother, making her, in Jean Fagan Yellin's words, a "fallen woman"[27] in Victorian parlance. As a result of her "fallen" status, Jacobs repeatedly apologizes in the narrative and asks not to be judged harshly.

However, Forten's elite background isolated her even from her intellectual sisters: Jacobs, a former slave twenty-five years her senior; and Harper, a free, widowed Negro twelve years her senior. Neither a slave nor a widowed, free Negro, neither society's image of the maternal ideal nor a white, feminist-abolitionist, Forten, the black aristocratic abolitionist, surely felt her interstitial place in nineteenth-century society. Moreover, whereas the Salem Female Anti-Slavery Society, to which Forten belonged, was forced to develop creative projects to help free but impoverished black children in addition to slaves and fugitives, the Philadelphia Female Anti-Slavery Society, to which she also belonged, had a more genteel tradition because its members, including Forten's mother, had come "from Philadelphia's most substantial black families."[28] As a member of both societies, the marginalized Forten must have constantly renegotiated the contrary ramifications of her difference from one city and society to another, not to mention the racial "assumptions about membership" operating in Salem and Boston. "Although race was not mentioned directly in clauses dealing with membership qualifications," asserts Julie Roy Jeffrey, "the term 'lady' had race- as well as class-based overtones."[29] Could Charlotte Forten have been a "lady" in the Philadelphia society but a "member" in the Salem and Boston societies, with her moving in between the racial overtones of the former and the class-based understanding of the latter?

The very idea of a colored aristocracy in antebellum America was "so alien to most whites" that "it regularly encountered ridicule and scorn"[30] in public discourse as well as in journals and magazines, remarks Willard B. Gatewood. Forten's problems in antebellum society are mirrored by the uncertainty of her legacy in black literary discourse. In current scholarship, several critics perceive Forten as an anachronism, though for different reasons from those of nineteenth-century whites who had a monolithic view of blacks as slaves and servants. In our own time Forten has been dismissed by critics because just as she did not fit the peg of race in antebellum America, she also does not belong—as some scholars argue—in the paradigm that scholars have created for struggling heroes such as Douglass and Jacobs. In *Black Autobiography in America*, Stephen Butterfield asserts that African American authors each present a self in life writing that is dramatically different from the white Western self who forges an identity freely out of the raw material of life. Because of the historical forces that have shaped the black experience, the self that evolves in the African American narrative is a "soldier in a long, historic march toward Canaan,"[31] the biblical promised land of freedom. Butterfield refuses to include Forten in this struggle and describes her as the sheltered daughter of the black bourgeoisie. He misreads her journals as nothing more than the "sensitive response of an upper-class Negro girl, becoming a woman, attending an exclusive female seminary, deeply flattered by visits from prominent white abolitionists." He accuses Forten of sycophancy, of writing to such well-known poets and antislavery crusaders as "[Henry Wadsworth] Longfellow and [Charles] Sumner for autographs, unable to sever her mind from the bitter and horrifying reality of the four million poor blacks held in bondage far beyond her elegant living room."[32]

Even Joanne Braxton and Brenda Stevenson, while more sensitive to the complexity of Forten's identity crises, describe her nonetheless as culturally "distant" and more accepting of the "moral nobility" of whites than of poor blacks. Braxton notes, apologetically though, that Forten blamed the poor blacks' failure on the "unhappy circumstances in which these [poor blacks] are placed, [which] are often more to blame than they themselves."[33] Unlike Butterfield, Braxton acknowledges the difficulty of Forten's dilemma and places her in the tradition of black women writers struggling to develop a "political and artistic consciousness" while forging a public voice amid "shattering encounters with racism," an acknowledgment that a member of a new generation of Forten scholars posits more affirmatively. According to Erica Armstrong Dunbar's *A Fragile Freedom*, Forten's experience as a member of the African American elite allowed her entrance into the world of education and activism. Her social status granted her the opportunity to help herself, to help others, and to speak her mind."[34] Still, the overwhelming nature of Forten's identity challenges must be clarified to appreciate her labors.

Forten's perceived cultural distance and her "sheltered, upper-class" lifestyle in the nineteenth century and in African American literary scholarship point to two critical ideas. These are the construction of a rigid, racial grid where a colored aristocracy emerges as a cultural aberration outside the fixed hierarchy of race and class, and inside the grid of race, as an emblem of wealthy, free Negroes' sophisticated uselessness in the black struggle. However, in the late nineteenth century, enlightened whites had discovered the existence of a small but prominent mulatto and black middle-class group and had begun to "question the validity of the common notion that all blacks were upon an equal plane."[35] Forten was in the position to make such a distinction for those inquirers. Because of the racial class that she represented, Forten was on the cusp of a new, though small and growing Negro elite—as white society discovered and as William Lloyd Garrison describes in his private correspondence, and as Forten reveals in her journals. Although Butterfield finds Forten's diaries lacking the "literary value" of the slave narrative, he misses the true import of her life writings.

It is precisely because Forten did not share the experience of the majority of blacks as slaves or as free but impoverished Negroes that her journals *do* have the equivalent literary and historic value of the slave narrative. What critics ignore is Forten's chartering of a new territory in her journals, one leading to a greater extension of the meaning of identity and identity formation for aspiring Negroes becoming American citizens. They would be the beneficiaries of the creation of a free, public school and educational system created during the era of Reconstruction, which Forten helped to usher in. The Freedmen's Bureau, employing New England schoolmarms such as Forten, devised a free system of education that came to define, according to Du Bois, one of the hallmarks of the nineteenth century and the great age of reform. "The greatest success of the Freedmen's Bureau," Du Bois explains, "lay in the planting of the free school among Negroes, and the idea of free elementary education among all classes in the South."[36]

In the triple marginal space that Forten's raced body inhabited, she maternally labored toward the liberation of slaves, moved forward the idea of a wider black middle class, and ushered in the dawning of a new period of race relations. In the last of her journals, journal 5, she heralds the coming of Booker T. Washington and the Tuskegee Normal School, which was "entirely under *colored* management" (527), she boasts. Forten was not fitted comfortably to her interstitial position and discovered relief in the enlarging space of race and identity just as she found self-affirmation through the subversive act of journal writing, coming to a voice of empowerment, as Wheatley and Jacobs did, through the act of writing, *écriture féminine*. William Andrews asserts that for liminal blacks such as Douglass and Jacobs, and we might add for Wheatley and Forten, the "autobiographical act" of writing provided them with the opportunity to "affirm their liminality as a "potentialising phase in which indeterminacy signifies a host of possibilities, not simply a loss of center."[37] Such an act of self-affirmation was important to the motherless Forten, dutifully taking up the role of her dead mother, given her isolation in society and thus her attempt to bridge the chasm between self and others, blacks and whites, justice and injustice, as seen in her personal, though historic journals.

Forten's Journals and the Auto/Biography of Race

After being privately educated at home and in protest of Philadelphia's staunchly segregated schools, Forten moved to Salem, Massachusetts, in 1853/1854 to be educated at the liberal Higginson Grammar School and later the Salem Normal School. Robert Bridges, her widowed father, sent her to Salem to stay in the home of the affluent, free-born abolitionist Charles Lenox Remond, one of the most popular antislavery orators of the nineteenth century until he was overshadowed by the lionized Douglass. In Salem at the age of sixteen Forten began keeping a diary. In keeping a journal, she selected the form of discourse suited to her class, for journal or diary writing was associated with culture and gentility. The terms "journal" and "diary" are used interchangeably here, although journal writing is viewed as more elaborate than diary writing because of its details. Dual characteristics of diary discourse and autobiography proper are seen in Forten's life writings, for both elements of style describe her journals. Diary scholarship has identified the uniqueness of this genre of autobiography as having nonlinear, feminine features of the moment-to-moment writing one finds in the journal. Perhaps for sexist reasons, some male critics have dismissed diary writings as a result of their following a "non-masculine"[38] pattern of sporadic writing. Presumably, the diarist can see no coherent linear pattern emerging in the world being described. She therefore is seen as being stuck in the immediacy of the moment. In contrast, autobiography proper has a coherent, "masculine"[39] shaping of events without the spurts found in the diary, written with the random discursiveness of the form, as seen in the fragmented notations of such events as births, marriages, and deaths. But in her diary writing, the intellectual Forten avoided this kind of fragmentation.

In autobiography proper, one expects to find a solid core or a "totality rather than a quintessence"[40] of events. Forten's journals have such a symbolic core. Her journals are a hybrid of diary writing, autobiography proper, and racial biography. Through her journals readers can trace Forten's and America's developing maturity. When she began journal 1, for example, she was a teenager, making a round of antislavery fairs and meetings, but when she entered her last entry in journal 5, Forten was in her fifties, an aging romantic, enjoying a country free of slavery. As an adult, she ruminated on the past, on abolitionist warriors and heroes such as Whittier and Douglass. With her husband, the Reverend Francis Grimké, twelve years her junior, and other religious reformers, the progressive and perennially youthful Forten founded the Laura Street Presbyterian Church in Jacksonville, Florida. She refers to Jacksonville as a "good field for missionary work" (537), a reference to the scope of the radical maternal ideal and maternal and feminist ethics.

In Florida, Forten benefited from her friendship with the prominent educator-activist Bishop Daniel Alexander Payne of Philadelphia, of the vaunted African Methodist Episcopal Church. According to Julie Winch, Payne arrived in Philadelphia in 1835 and through Robert Bridges met the "venerable" James Forten Sr., as Payne recalled in his memoirs *Recollections of Seventy Years* (1888). He also would have been able to provide insight into the last days of the diarist's mother's life since he attended to her spiritual needs before her death. Payne was another link to the past, and Forten considered him and his influence essential to her grand maternal work in Florida. She explains, "Bishop [Daniel A.] Payne dined with us. It is a great pleasure to have him; he is so thoroughly interested in literature & all that is improving. What a grand example to the rising generation,—if they would only follow it" (523). With Payne, she expresses a desire to continue to aid the "rising generation" and establish a literary society for young people to provide them with "something higher than dancing & other frivolous amusements" (523).

Capturing the moment in Salem, however, the teen-diarist could not have foreseen the future and the many important roles she would play in Salem, Boston, South Carolina, and Florida and indeed in the country and her era, with the coming of the Civil War and Reconstruction. Forten therefore could not have shaped her diary discourse to reflect, as an autobiographer would have done, the climax of her life experiences. Yet when this privileged, free Negro traveled to the South to teach former slaves, to nurse Union soldiers, and to found a church, a fusion of two worlds—hers and the slaves'—occurred, significantly connecting her to the shared oppression and freedom of other black Americans. In these times Forten's private and personal diaries become auto/biography proper and historically rich documents chronicling the continuing saga of race, its social death in slavery and its rebirth in freedom.

In the diaries that make up *The Journals of Charlotte Forten Grimké,* the diarist emerges most consistently as a romantic visionary, influenced by the two notions of the perfection and performance of the maternal ideal. Written over a period of thirty-eight years, the journals reveal Forten's embodied, if paradoxical subjectivities of pariah and harbinger, motherless and dutiful daughter of the maternal ideal, doing her part, as had Wheatley and Jacobs before her, in regenerating her society. Forten does more than record the "passing events of my life," as she modestly announces at the beginning of her diaries: she captures and helps to transform the national ethos of her age, in both the North and the South. There are five journals: journal 1, Salem (Massachusetts), May 24, 1854–December 31, 1856; journal 2, Salem, January 1, 1857–January 27, 1858; journal 3, Salem, January 28, 1858–St. Helena Island (South Carolina), February 14, 1863; journal 4, St. Helena Island, February 15, 1863–May 15, 1864; and journal 5, Jacksonville (Florida), November 1885–Ler [Lee?] (Massachusetts), July 1892. In viewing the five diaries as hybrid forms of autobiography and biography of race and country, I find the following distinctions: journals 1 and 2 and in part 3 and 4 show the daily and yearly tensions between Forten's two worlds of an idealized inner harmony and a troubling social order; and journal 5 is her briefest diary.

The social disorder captured in the journals is reflected in the upheaval of slavery and the aftermath of the congressional passing of the Fugitive Slave Law in 1850, affecting the fugitive-slave case of Anthony Burns (1854), which became a rallying call for abolitionists. Several back-to-back events in the 1850s contributed to the decade's apocalyptic political atmosphere: the Kansas-Nebraska Act of 1854, which repealed the Missouri Compromise of 1820, prohibiting slavery in the Kansas-Nebraska territory; South Carolina representative Preston S. Brooks's caning of the abolitionist senator Charles Sumner in 1856; and the Dred Scott Supreme Court decision of 1857, declaring all blacks noncitizens. John Brown's violent revolt at Harper's (now Harpers) Ferry occurred two years later. According to Robert S. Levine's *Dislocating Race and Nation,* these last two events led even the lionized Douglass to advocate the possible immigration of blacks to countries such as Haiti and to remove himself to England, for his falsely presumed role in the Harper's Ferry disaster. In short, the 1850s brought about challenges for blacks, the abolitionists, and the country on the brink of a Civil War. "How strange it is that in a world so beautiful, there can be so much wickedness," Forten writes in journal 1 (70), anticipating the political explosiveness of the decade when many whites "found themselves for the first time sympathetic to abolitionists,"[41] who were perceived initially as zealots disturbing the status quo.

There are more than seven hundred entries in the first two journals alone, but journal 3 is the most symbolic of the diaries, covering a span of five years with more than three hundred entries. Of all five diaries, journal 3 is also the most elaborately written, as Forten records her experience in South Carolina. Forten's and her race's historic stride toward Canaan, the setting in the Bible of the emancipation of the Jews, is viewed through the prism of this third journal. If the journals were read as a novel, journal 3 would be the climax. Journals 4 and 5 are then anticlimactic. Journal 4 covers only a year and has more than one hundred entries, while journal 5, though written over a period of almost seven years, is the shortest and most sporadically written, with fewer than one hundred entries. In journal 3 Forten valorizes the reading of President Abraham Lincoln's proclamation as she describes standing by with Union officers and soldiers and weeping as she witnessed the outcome of a cause from which her grandfather had never wavered. Indeed in the 1820s "James Forten's pursuit of wealth clashed with his antislavery principles." The captain of a "ship that had been engaged in the slave trade, and was likely to be thus employed again, was in need of sails, and applied to him to furnish them; but he indignantly refused."[42] The patriarch's opposition to slavery was manifested not only in his business practices but also in his antislavery activism, which opened up an acceleration of protests from 1831 to 1861, leading to his granddaughter's defining moment in South Carolina.

At the beginning of her diaries, Forten narrates her intent: "A wish to record the passing events of my life, which, even if quite unimportant to others, naturally possess great interest to myself. I feel that keeping a diary will be a pleasant and profitable employment of my leisure hours" (58). The diary scholar Margo Culley misinterprets the phrase "even if quite unimportant to others," and the error raises the issue of Forten's interstitiality. Culley argues that Forten implies that "others might find her record of interest"[43] and misses Forten's sarcasm. Rather than implying that others "might" find her journals interesting, she assaults the arrogance of race, relegating her to the status of the cultural Other, unworthy of public interest. She assails dominant powers in her letter to Sumner after his caning, expressing the "deep gratitude and admiration with which you are regarded by a youthful member of that oppressed class which the white American finds guilty of a skin not colored like his own."[44] In her letter-writing campaign to abolitionists, Forten emulated her grandfather, who wrote to Garrison in 1831 that the *Liberator* "has roused up a Spirit in our Young People" and that "we shall produce writers able to vindicate our cause,"[45] a letter anticipating the diarist's emergence.[46] In stating her intent in keeping a diary, Forten uses the word "leisure," reminding the reader of her aristocratic class status.

The tensions in Forten's journals are marked by the self-navigating she was forced to do between her two dialectically opposed legacies—which, combined with her interstitiality, resonate with meaning throughout her journals and must dictate our reading of them. The first is the legacy of the sacred maternal ideal of *being* as represented by her dead but angelic mother, whose absence/presence in her daughter's life and journals reflects her profound loss and yet her visionary zeal to fill the maternal breach, which stirs "evangelical piety and moral commitment."[47] Forten fills this emotional space with romantic images of beauty in which she "luxuriates," as revealed by her nurturing maternal metaphors of Mother Nature as a construction of an ideal, whether she was in Boston or on the Sea Islands in South Carolina. She marks the gap by aligning herself with individuals whom she admired and who shared her cause. She did not merely write to them to ask for their autographs, as Butterfield claims. Conversely, the diaries reveal deeper and more personal yearnings for her involving her missing mother.

First, in the journals, Forten submits herself to the awful task of reconciling her life without her mother—a "primal anxiety"[48] of children, according to Freud, caused by their separation from their mothers or some highly valued objects, a thematic that Carolyn Dever traces in her study *Death and the Mother from Dickens to Freud.* The death of the mother as found in *Oliver Twist* and *Bleak House,* for example, precipitates a crisis of identity, one resolved by Oliver's and Esther Summerson's discoveries of their birthrights and maternal inheritances with all roads leading to the missing mothers.[49] In her diaries Forten acknowledges Dickens's sentimental power after reading "Little Dorrit" (204), and she identifies with the crisis of maternal loss and the quest for recovery. She confesses, "How often it comes over me!—this longing for a mother's love—a mother's care. I know there is none other like it. Dear, dear mother whom I have scarcely known, yet so warmly love,—who art now an angel in heaven,—my heart yearns for thee!" (210, 211, 238): a confession pronouncing her problems of identity. The crisis of the lost mother precipitated Forten's trauma of lost parental love. Her father remarried and "moved to Canada"[50] and then to England before returning home to fight in the Civil War, enlisting "with the 43rd Regiment, United States Colored Troops"[51] and becoming a unit leader. Forten was not close to him, as revealed when the ailing diarist received a letter from him and wrote in her diary, "A cold letter, it seems to me. He is sorry that my health is impaired, hopes that it will be better—just as any stranger might" (251–52). Her maternal loss without her father to fill the breach set in motion her journey toward self-recovery through tropes of an abiding maternal presence and maternal iconography.

Notably in the dead mother's absence Forten, as a teen and a mature woman, sought to cultivate relationships with maternal surrogates and with individuals she most admired. Mainly these were members of her own class: upper-class, educated, and liberal black and white abolitionists and feminists, maternal breach fillers, which explains, sadly, her fragile relationship with the "motherly" Harriet Jacobs. Forten dined with both Garrison and Whittier, describing the former as "beloved Garrison" and the latter as having a "noble" and "spiritual" face and being "the greatest Poet of Humanity" (141, 247). She boasts of the "honor" of walking "at a Boston's antislavery fair arm-in-arm" with Maria Weston Chapman, the beautiful and popular Boston Brahmin and principal officer of the female Boston Anti-Slavery Society, who was also the editor of Garrison's *Liberator* (175). Forten makes several references to "my lost mother" and repeats her desire to be near "Dear A[nnie], the only sister of my lost mother" (360). She claims Amy Matilda Remond, Charles Remond's wife, as a surrogate mother but grieves over her death, "the one almost a mother" (366), within a few years of Forten's arrival in Salem.

Haunted throughout the diaries by the permanence of her maternal loss, Forten presents herself in the image of the frustrated motherless daughter, notwithstanding the maternal ideal she aspires to cultivate. After reading Elizabeth Barrett Browning's epic poem "Aurora Leigh," about the "Unmothered Aurora" who "felt a mother-want about the world" because fathers love but "with heavier brains," Forten responds, "I, too, have known but little of a father's love" (251–52). In intimating her disappointment with her father and his withholding of parental affection, Forten signifies on Patmore's maternal ideal of love that "cannot tire," but only to suggest the mother's (idealized) "boundedness and existence as a separate person." Her indirect comparison of her mother and her father and their capacity to give or their decision to withhold love highlights her mother's extraordinary qualities. It is as if the motherless daughter had discovered, painfully, through the mother's absence, "that the whole world does not provide care" like the idealized mother does, increasing her mother's importance and the daughter's anxiety.[52]

In her analysis of Forten's post-Reconstruction writings and reviews on art for *Scribner's Monthly* in 1872 and the *Christian Register* in 1876, Carla Peterson furthers the discussion of the dialectics of Forten's ideal realm of beauty and the motherless, sober reality of the real world that she confronted. Peterson argues that the diarist "in one of her Centennial Exposition articles explicitly affirmed the realm of the aesthetic as one which the 'too painful' must be forbidden entrance." Forten selected a line from another Browning poem to illustrate her idea: "They say that ideal beauty should not enter the house of anguish." Peterson remarks that Browning's sonnet is rather a "meditation on Hiram Powers' Greek Slave statue," which must be used to crash and dismantle the "serfdom of this world." Forten therefore, according to Peterson's reading, "had come to recognize the violent co-existence" of "ideal beauty" and "anguish."[53] I would argue otherwise.

As Forten's appearances at antislavery meetings, fairs, and lectures in such cities as Philadelphia, Salem, Boston, Danvers, and Framingham attest, although she tried to draw a fine line separating her ideal realm from the real one, as Peterson remarks, she was never totally successful with this effort. When she announces in the journals "a longing for something higher and nobler than I have known" (261), she expresses a Victorian upper-class lady's sentiment, which shaped her cultural domestic sphere and which she expanded to include the work of the radical maternal ideal: that is, in her work outside the home as her lost mother would have encouraged her. Rather than admitting to the permanence of the "violent co-existence" of the realms of beauty and sadness, Forten, following her mother's advice, spent most of her young and adult life attempting to eradicate the physical and psychological violence of the outer world, which intruded on the ideal one where "liberty, glorious, boundless liberty reigned there supreme" (88).

Such an effort implies that Forten almost never lost faith in her vision, shaped by her love for her lost mother, and of Mother Nature and its healing properties, as she often describes in the diaries. "The ground was thickly carpeted with ferns of a most delicious green," she writes of her visit to the Sea Islands, "and to crown all we found Azaleas of a deep pink color and perfect fragrance. I think I never enjoyed anything so perfectly. I *luxuriated* in it" (474). Earlier in Boston she attended one of Emerson's lectures on Mother Nature, and she describes him less effusively as "peculiar-looking" but still "one of the truest of Nature's interpreters on the true beauty of Nature, and the pleasure and benefit to be derived from walking amid this beauty" (279). Mother Nature embodied for Forten the perfection of the maternal ideal of being and transformed her sober material reality, however briefly, from an abject to an elevated feeling, providing her with a social blueprint for how life can be. A legitimate question to ask of her diary keeping, then, is this: What is the relationship between the scope of her diary, the privileging of the detail of what and whom she read, the lectures she attended, and her own romantic self-fashioning in nature? The answer, with the diary as an outline for how she wished life to be, plays a significant role in her stride toward Canaan after the Anthony Burns case, which represented the harsh real world of the black body-in-crisis.

The Maternal Ideal of Performance: The Regenerative Impulse

The other legacy Forten inherited was that of the maternal ideal of *performance,* of actually *doing* the grunt work of a revolutionary social reformer, of metaphorically giving birth to a new-world order, as her angel-mother had encouraged her. The chaos of the outer world conflicted with Forten's aesthetics and romantic self-image as a genteel Victorian female, as seen in the diaries, and thus the dutiful image and work ethic of the militant maternal ideal was needed for effecting social change. Lori D. Ginzberg cites the feminist role models of Lucy Stone, Lucretia Mott, and Abby Kelley Foster for young women reformers entering the revolutionary movement, such as "Ellen Wright, Olympia Brown, and Charlotte Forten," all of whom "grew up with idols who were remarkable for any age."[54] But for the motherless Forten, her interstitial identity, her vision of the maternal ideal, and her activist family legacy were perhaps the greatest social impetus for her benevolent work, which found its first significant testing in the Anthony Burns case. In this hurtful outer world, Forten languished in despair over the fugitive slave Anthony Burns, who was captured in Massachusetts, a free state, but was returned to Virginia, a slave state. Grieving, "it is impossible to be happy now," an insecure Forten wavers, and her voice is drastically different from that of the secure, first person "I" that luxuriated in Mother Nature on the Sea Islands. Rather than focusing on her individual development in the journals, she now shifts her mood and possessively aligns herself with a downtrodden race: "A cloud seems hanging over me, over all *our* [emphasis added] persecuted race" (65).

In his study *The Trials of Anthony Burns*, Albert J. Von Frank provides a description of Forten, who attended Burns's trial in Boston. She was a "delicate, slender" young lady with a "finely chiseled countenance," differing dramatically from the tattered and bound Burns, with whom she identified. Von Frank inquires if the woman who cried out, "why is he [Burns] not man enough to kill himself,"[55] was Charlotte Forten, angered by the court ruling. She remarks in her diary, "Alas! That anyone should have the power to decide the right of a fellow being to himself!" (65). With her interest in Burns, Forten recognized the need to perform the work of the maternal ideal and to effect the regeneration in society that would have saved an Anthony Burns, and in the process she stabilized her own voice and identity. Black bodies, free and enslaved, were objects of scorn, and for slaves such as Burns, objects of property: they were bodies-in-crises. Foucault describes the docile body as trained and controlled by military-disciplinary regulations, and the trained military body begins to resemble the reliability of state-assault weapons. It is not a stretch to suggest that Burns's body had at least one characteristic of Foucault's body of the state.

Burns's body was a trope of state power to such a grotesque degree that he symbolized a bit actor in a circus where a white judge, a white jury, white attorneys, and a predominately white public fought over his mangled body. Abolitionists such as Remond, Stephen S. Foster, and Foster's wife, Abby Kelley Foster, spoke at rallies on behalf of Burns and against Massachusetts's authorities becoming "minions" of the South. What is notable about the Burns trial is his body. As a testimony to his slave experience, his "hand is broke, and a bone stands out from the back of it, a hump an inch high, and it hangs almost useless from the wrist, with a huge scar or gash covering half its surface."[56] During the trial, it was stated that his master had "mortgaged" him to another master, from whom Burns had escaped but who therefore had "no right to say to Burns that he may or may not come or go."[57] Burns was propertied real estate. On June 2, 1854, Judge Loring, who cited the legality of the Fugitive Slave Bill and was influenced by the proslavery politics of Franklin Pierce, the president of the United States, ruled in favor of Burns's return to Virginia.

At the time of the final hearing, Burns was dressed in a "rather fine new suit of clothes, and he appeared as "an impressive-looking fellow" in his young twenties.[58] Burns's new clothes were a gift from his jailers, "who probably knew that slaves got such outfits only when they were being dressed up as merchandise."[59] While legal and illegal attempts were made to secure Burns's freedom, in the end armed soldiers led him in chains through the streets of Boston. He went back to Virginia and slavery in the midst of a public outcry, summarized by Wendell Phillips: "Burns, there isn't humanity, there isn't Christianity, there isn't justice enough here to save you."[60] Burns's body represents the awakening narrative of the people in Boston, especially of abolitionists in the North. They used the Burns case as a rallying call for a renewed commitment to keep Massachusetts free from southerners in search of fugitive slaves. Phillips expressed the outrage that the people against the state felt. He also articulated his angst, leading to his renewed commitment, "I vowed anew before the ever-living God [that] I would consecrate all the powers He had given me to hasten the time when an innocent man should be safe on the sacred soils of the Puritans."[61] Burns's body remained even for Phillips, one of Forten's maternal breach fillers, a means to an end toward the freedom of Massachusetts from the tainted politics of slavery.

Reactions to the Burns trial and its decision are telling of the tumultuous times of the 1850s. Visiting in Boston during the trial, Harriet Beecher Stowe remained cautiously silent, "not now eager for controversy," Von Frank states, although she presented a copy of *Uncle Tom's Cabin* to an ex-captain of the policemen in Boston. The captain had resigned his position after Judge Loring's fateful decision.[62] After the public storm against him, Judge Loring was eventually removed from office. Forten, however, wrote of the experience, appropriating the collective personal pronoun "our" and in emotion and tone conveying an unsteady voice associated with the trauma of the black body-in-crisis. "Our worst fears are realized," she laments; "I can write no more" (65–66). She had personalized the tragedy to such a degree that she experienced emotional paralysis.

While not a slave, Forten was a victim of discrimination. Even at the liberal Higginson Grammar School in Salem, whose principal Mary Shepard befriended her, Forten faced racial prejudice from her classmates, who barely acknowledged her, although the school noted Forten's intellectual superiority.[63] In an early diary entry she pleads, "Would that those with whom I shall recite to-morrow could sympathize with me in this; would that they could look upon all God's creatures without respect to color, feeling that it is character alone [that] makes the true man or woman?" (67). As a precocious teenager, Forten had verbalized an idea, a yearning that future black intellectuals and civic and religious reformers such as Martin Luther King Jr. would repeat almost one hundred years later. In "I Have a Dream," King echoes Forten when he expresses the hope that "my four little children will one day live in a nation where they will not be judged by the color of their skin, but by the content of their character."[64] It is worth noting that in terms of her ideological, cultural, and sociopolitical stance, Forten represented the vanguard of black intellectual thought and its exegesis of liberal social and moral doctrine. Given her reaction to the Burns debacle and her own personal trials, it would have been hard for her to suppress the maternal regenerative impulse that took her to South Carolina to reconcile the painful outer world with her perfect inner vision.

Bridging the Gap: The Port Royal Experiment of Democracy and Literacy

With her historic participation in the Port Royal Experiment, Forten did more than bake pies, attend rallies, and write to famous abolitionists for autographs while indulging her fantasies in the journals, under lock and key. She manipulated the conservative politics of the Victorian maternal ideal when she relocated to South Carolina. In journal 3, where she names and feminizes the diaries as "Dear A," she describes the turning point, the "significant meeting place between the individual and the outer world" that illumines both in autobiography.[65] In naming the journals here, Forten superimposes on them an identity that symbolizes their authority in being the instrument by which evidentiary proof is provided of her resolving one of the major conflicts of her life. With an understanding of the tensions of Forten's identity, Edmund Wilson comments in *Patriotic Gore* on her opportunity to resolve them: "Charlotte Forten *was saved* [emphasis added] by the war when she was still only twenty-five," a hyperbole, of course, but one that underscores the intensity of Forten's identity crisis. Because of her involvement in the shaping of American history, Wilson finds that Forten "fills in a curious corner of the complicated Civil War picture."[66] The dutiful daughter also fulfills one of her dead mother's most earnest dictates to do her part in transforming America.

After Abraham Lincoln's election, eleven states seceded from the Union, and this act brought on the war in 1861. The Civil War transformed southern life as Union soldiers occupied southern territory and created enclaves in such places as South Carolina and its coastal areas. These enclaves were havens for fugitive slaves and territorial bases for expeditions into Confederate land, causing a disruption of plantation slavery.[67] As a slave state, South Carolina contained the largest black majority of all southern states, and many slaves retained certain aspects of African culture, including religious practices, social customs, and languages. Finding communication with the contrabands difficult, a Union general requested the War Department on January 15, 1862, to send northern educators to the Sea Islands to instruct the contrabands. After Sherman captured portions of South Carolina, the Bostonian Edward L. Pierce, a lawyer-abolitionist, was selected to oversee a program to relieve the suffering of the poor and to educate contraband slaves, hence the birth of the Port Royal Experiment. Whittier advised Charlotte to apply for permission to become a part of this project, and she leaped at the opportunity for the "high and noble" calling of the maternal ideal of performance, with women working for the social regeneration of society. Indeed at the age of eighteen, she wrote of being "born as we are to the stern performance of duty rather than the pursuit of happiness" (137), a revision of Thomas Jefferson's statement on individual aspiration in contradistinction to the mantra of sacrifice, characterizing the great age of reform. Eric Foner refers to the Civil War as America's "unfinished revolution,"[68] alluding to the incompleteness of Jefferson's declaration of the individual's rights, especially when each slave was still counted as only three-fifths of a person.

Since Forten had already declared war on slavery, she was determined to relocate to the South and be a part of this "unfinished revolution." So fervent was she about the revolutionary cause that when the Boston Commission denied her application there, she traveled to "abominable" Philadelphia and received permission to go on behalf of that agency. On October 22, 1862, she left Philadelphia for the Sea Islands. Excluding a two-month northern vacation, due to her frequent headaches, which were perhaps caused by personal and social tensions (she died in 1914 of a cerebral embolism), she stayed on the island for approximately seventeen months. She would return several years later, 1865–71, to teach at the Robert Gould Shaw Memorial School in Charleston. In South Carolina, Forten's first soldierly march to Canaan as a "friend of freedom" took her to the harsh world of the slaves, and a better script could not have been written for her.

Forten's Role in Mothering the Race to Freedom

In the literature of Reconstruction and racial uplift, the black female reformer became a prominent figure in the kind of civic mothering with which Forten and Jacobs were engaged, but Forten more officially so as a New England schoolmarm. In her study *Mothering the Race,* Allison Berg calls attention to the different kinds of dialectics that female reformers such as Forten would have faced in elevating duty and sacrifice over personal ambition and autonomy. The "imbrication of motherhood and race at the turn of the century," Berg remarks, "spurred reconstructions of womanhood on both sides of the color line." Berg cites Laura Doyle's suggestion that the "very concept of a race mother depends upon a system of racial patriarchy in which mothers reproduce bodies not in a social vacuum, but for either a dominant or a subordinate [racial or ethnic] group."[69] Berg's and Doyle's concerns suggest the theory of the biological determinism of motherhood and race and its social implication in regard to mothers and their defenselessness in a patriarchal and racist culture.

But critical feminist theory on sacrificial motherhood, leading to the arrest of individual female ambition, is one that Forten would have necessarily rejected because she would not have accepted its feminist premise. For Forten, female ambition was not stymied by a cultural motherhood, civic or biological, but rather was intimately connected to it, at least during this critical period of black nation building. History was moving forward, and ideas were changing. The process of social improvement was itself an act of creation, literally and metaphorically linked to the promise of social and personal regeneration for all, notwithstanding the Jim Crow laws to follow. Forten's brand of feminism, based on freeing *all* members of the race, was not entirely connected to the familiar rhetoric of white women and feminism, which included ideas of parity with white men that had led to the 1848 Seneca Falls convention in New York. As Edmund Wilson suggests, with some exaggeration, the ambiguity of Forten's identity, based primarily on the politics of race and class formation, was such a problem that only a war of the magnitude of the Civil War could resolve it and personally "save" her.

Nevertheless even Forten's position as a New England schoolmarm reflected her interstitiality in society: as a wealthy black, educated woman. Overwhelmingly the New England schoolmarm was an elite white woman by education and birth, usually affiliated with the clergy or missionary organizations. Initially, Forten felt marginalized in South Carolina and had prepared herself to dislike Pierce of the Port Royal Experiment, due perhaps to the Boston agency's denial of her first application. After meeting Pierce, though, she confessed, "His manners are exceedingly pleasant—I can't help acknowledging that, [but] I had a preconceived dislike for him because I had heard that he said he 'wanted no colored missionaries nor teachers down here'" (464). As a New England schoolmarm at the Penn School a few years before the official creation of the Freedmen's Bureau in 1866, Forten anticipated the drive for the development of public schools. At the Penn School, the work of the New England schoolmarm, the sentiments of antislavery, a revolutionary version of radical domestic feminism, and the maternal ideal and benevolence all came together at a significant moment in history. Led by its founder, Laura Matilda Towne of Pennsylvania, and her assistant Ellen Murray of New England, the Penn School was a precursor to the founding of public schools everywhere, set in motion by visionary feminist-abolitionists. What "most distinguished these teachers from other wartime relief workers," Lori Ginzberg remarks, "was their explicit commitment to antislavery and their sense of their war-work as a continuation of abolitionists' efforts."[70] Many teachers were "living among the former slaves, teaching schools of as many as four hundred students, and struggling to provide food, clothing, and health-care in areas isolated and threatened by warring armies, compris[ing] the obvious next step in the moral battle to end slavery after the military one was well under way."[71]

While the men fought the war, the women were engaged in a different kind of battle. As maternal surrogate, taking up the cause of her warrior mother, Forten found in her young South Carolina charges a chance to mother the race. She records in her journals, "Dear children! Born in slavery, but free at last? May God preserve to you all the blessings of freedom, and may you be in every possible way fitted to enjoy them. My heart goes out to you. I shall be glad to do all that I can to help you" (391). Forten emulates her maternal celestial guide, following her dead mother's advice to bear her part while valorizing the birth of a new generation of free African American children to be educated and whom she instructs like a maternal conduit, determining what and whom they should read: "Talked to the children a little while to-day about the noble Toussaint [Haitian slave revolt leader]. They listened very attentively." She then adds instructively, "It is well that they sh'ld know what one of their own color c'ld do for his race. I long to inspire them with courage and ambition" (397–98). Forten's desire to teach the children the values of "courage and ambition" stresses the work of the maternal ideal and feminist ethics—transforming not only the social order but its citizens as well.

Despite the benevolence of her intentions, Forten experienced difficulties in relating to the island's poor blacks, according to Dorothy Sterling, who adds that she was condescending and "patronizing" to them.[72] Sterling's criticism reveals one of the difficulties Forten must have faced in her transitioning from the domain of the maternal ideal of the good and the beautiful to the real domestic fieldwork of maternal labor. She encountered enslaved blacks whom she had idealized from a romantic distant, but what she actually witnessed was a collection of "crude little specimens," ravaged by slavery (499). Sterling states that Forten was not entirely comfortable with the culture of slavery. "Despite her appreciation [for] the islanders' songs," writes Sterling, Forten "concentrated on teaching her pupils new music: the John Brown song and two hymns by Whittier, the 'Song of the Negro Boatmen,' written in a synthetic dialect." Sterling notes the "irony of [Forten's] teaching a New England version of the boatmen's song to Sea Island children who heard the genuine music of Negro spirituals every day."[73]

Forten's reaction to slave society was far more complex than Sterling initially cites, however, and the contrabands' reaction to her was equally revealing. Those born into bondage and imbibed with the politics of white supremacy must have experienced a culture shock upon meeting an educated colored aristocrat who was also a woman. Initially the contrabands questioned the authority of "dat brown gal"[74] and had to be persuaded to wait on her in much the same way that they served and waited on whites such as Pierce, Towne, and Murray. But Forten became "the pet and belle of the island"[75] among Union officers and abolitionists, who were familiar with the James Forten legacy; and the contrabands, upon hearing her play the piano, abandoned their aloofness and commenced to tell her their stories, their lives.

When the slave mother "Old Suzy" was asked if she would like her former master to return to the abandoned plantation, her answer qualifies as a classic one for feminists critical of slavery's distinctive character of maternal abuse. Old Suzy informed Forten, "No, indeed, missus, no indeed dey treat we too bad. Dey tuk ebery one of my children away from me. Dey's orful hard, Missis" (399). In hearing Old Suzy's fractured narrative of maternal love, loss, and sacrifice, Forten had the benefit of being there in person, playing the part of an understanding mother, assuaging the grief of those whose cause she, her late mother, and her family had pleaded. Despite the persuasiveness of Sterling's remarks, Forten bonded with many of the people she met and came to love them and their traditional Negro spirituals. She was moved by the singing of Negro spirituals, as even Sterling admits, especially those of the "Negro boatmen" who sang "Roll, Jordan, Roll," which she describes as "grand" because of the men's "sonorous tones." The Negro boatmen made slender boats from cypress logs, and these boats were used for transportation until the roads and bridges were repaired and built.[76] As she entered and left the coastal areas and traveled to Beaufort to meet Harriet Tubman, these boats were Forten's main mode of transportation, and the boatmen were her guides and entertainers.

Since Forten did write to Whittier to ask him to compose a song in dialect for the boatmen and children, she was indeed, as Sterling comments, unaware of the irony of asking a white New Englander to write a song in Negro dialect. It is therefore difficult not to conclude that Forten on occasion not only demonstrated her own cultural and class elitism but also, like Wheatley and Jacobs, gave expression to feelings of Anglophilia, perhaps the insidious result of centuries of slavery and racism. Yet, Forten was aware of the superiority of Negro spirituals, as indicated in her observation of the former slaves' funeral rites: "There was a Negro funeral at the burying ground. We c'ld see the crowd of people and hear them singing hymns;—not their own beautiful hymns, I am sorry to say. I do so fear these will be superseded by *ours* [emphasis added], which are poor in comparison, and which they do not sing well at all" (477). When we compare her expression of "our fears" for Burns earlier and her adoption of the same pronoun to indicate her cultural association with northern white Americans, we get another glimpse of Forten's renegotiation of identity and of Du Bois' theory of black Americans' double consciousness as blacks and as Americans.

Like Wheatley and Jacobs, Forten was forced into a dominating grid of race, but one that the privilege of her birth and class had upset, leaving her at various times in between identities: a racial and cultural insider here, but an outsider and cultural hybrid there. Like Sterling, Carla Peterson argues that Forten emerges as an objective ethnographer of primitives, whom she found "strange,"[77] as revealed in her unguarded comments on contrabands and their folk culture. Peterson's description recalls Butterfield's, Braxton's, and Stevenson's suggestions that Forten was remote from the folk, although Peterson notes Forten's gradual feelings of familiarity with them. Her unique identity is invariably a problem for most critics. But in the *Atlantic Monthly* article "Life on the Sea Islands" (1864), she expresses her appreciation for the considerable survival skills and cultural authenticity of the enslaved. Although she mocks their individual shortcomings, she also assaults ideas of white supremacy. She pleads the cause of the folk against the "haughty Anglo-Saxon race . . . who, North as well as South, taunt the colored race with inferiority while they themselves use every means in their power to crush and degrade them."[78] Forten's outrage refutes criticism that she was racially alienated from suffering Negroes, notwithstanding her class snobbery.

Forten's marginalized positions are not necessarily contradictory. Rather than interpreting her association with the dominant cultural group as a rejection of slave culture, readers could perhaps accept instead the sheer complexity of her cross-cultural persona in a racialized society. Even Peterson acknowledges that Forten's journals "betray a sensitive awareness of the complex process of trans-culturation that was unfolding on the Sea Islands" and that she witnessed and captured in her writings. Forten became an eyewitness to the "back-and-forth traffic between dominate and subordinate cultures as, for example, the freed people learned Whittier's songs and the white abolitionists the Negro spirituals."[79] Forten was again on the threshold of history and experienced the emergence in the South of a legitimate, bicultural American society, one in which folk and traditional exchanges were very early being made between two different racial and social groups and classes: one privileged and the other underprivileged. These exchanges manifest the emergence of a heterogeneous American society, North and South, which therefore necessitated a new kind of interracial understanding.

In her meeting on the Sea Islands with the archetypal maternal warrior Harriet Tubman, the proclaimed "General" and "Moses" of black people, Forten met the "Folk" par excellence. Heroically, Tubman single-handedly led approximately three hundred enslaved men, women, and children to freedom in Canada and the North. When "Moses" greeted the "soldier," the old world of black subjugation came face-to-face with the patrician society of the black aristocracy. Both Tubman and Forten in their historic meeting acknowledged implicitly that regardless of class, education, wealth, and status, African Americans have a shared cultural heritage of oppression. To be sure, Forten revealed as much in her journals when she wrote upon meeting Tubman, "My own eyes were full as I listened to her—the heroic woman!" (442). Unlike her treatment of Old Suzy and her ungrammatical fractured narrative, which Forten presents unedited, the diarist's handling of Tubman and her equally fractured language suggests one soldier's valorization of another: she does not "mother" Tubman, who instead "mothers" a weeping Forten.

Forten's treatments of Old Suzy and of Tubman's mininarratives on slavery are noteworthy: she gives actual voice to the authenticity of Old Suzy's poignant but ungrammatical narrative of maternal grief but respectfully controls Tubman's story of heroism. "How exciting, it was to hear her tell the story. And to hear her sing the very scraps of jubilant hymns that he [the male slave whom Tubman led to freedom in Canada] sang," she writes (442). By suppressing Tubman's voice, Forten protects the unschooled Tubman. Known for her boast and figure of speech, Tubman proclaimed her own victory as "General" in the Underground Railroad: "I nebber run my train off de track, and I nebber lost a passenger." Sterling reports that when Tubman arrived in Beaufort in May 1862 and addressed the Gullah-speaking people, she remarked, "Dey laughed when dey heard me talk, [but] I could not understand dem, no how."[80] What Forten would have described as "ungrammatical" in the speech of Old Suzy and Tubman is explained in Geneva Smitherman's study *Talkin' and Testifyin'* as blacks creating their own style of language, as found in Ebonics or black English. In denying the heroic but illiterate Tubman a voice, Forten wanted to shield her maternal breach filler from the snobbery of her Victorian elite group. At the same time, Forten vicariously experienced the virtue of the performing maternal ideal that Tubman so clearly represented. In forwarding Forten's essay "Life on the Sea Islands" to the *Atlantic Monthly,* Whittier referred to her experience in South Carolina as a "labor of love."[81] This particular description of her maternal achievement affirms the power of the domestic maternal ideal, as seen in her handling of Lincoln's Emancipation Proclamation.

On Thursday, New Year's Day, 1863, when Lincoln's proclamation was read to a standing group of soldiers and children, Forten captured in her diaries this historic moment for posterity: "It all seemed, and seems still, like a brilliant dream. As I sat on the stand and looked around on the various groups, I thought I had never seen a sight so beautiful. There were the black soldiers, in their blue coats and scarlet pants, the officers of this and other regiments . . . and crowds of lookers-on, men, women, and children. Immediately at the conclusion, some of the colored people— of their own accord sang 'My Country Tis of Thee.' It was a touching and beautiful incident" (429–30). Her raison d'être for participating in the antislavery crusade, finishing her dead mother's mission, is related to this momentous occasion and the realization of black liberation. On this day the motherless daughter and Forten family heir crossed the ultimate threshold of freedom and citizenship initially conceived by those who bore her. She grieves, however, in journal 4 over the death of Robert Gould Shaw (with whom she had socialized the night before) and the members of the all-black Fifty-fourth Massachusetts Regiment in their failed but "noble" attempt to take Fort Wagner. The movie *Glory* is based on Shaw's letters, which are archived in Harvard's Houghton Library. Forten reflects on the meaning of Shaw's death to his wife and mother, and she revisits the emotional space left by her own mother's death, a vacuum now experienced by Shaw's wife and mother. "I know it was a glorious death. . . . But oh, it is hard, very hard for the young wife, so late a bride, for the invalid mother, whose only and most dearly loved son he was; —that heroic mother who rejoiced in the position which he occupied as colonel of a colored regiment. Oh what must it be to the wife and the mother" (497). Her empathy appears to be a reproduction of her own grief twenty-three years after her mother's death. For Forten, Shaw's wife and mother represent the principle of the maternal ideal in their commitment to duty, responsibility, and sacrifice, causing her empathetic understanding.

Still, one cannot ignore Forten's revelations in the diaries detailing her un-happy times. In Beaufort there were reminders of the complexity of her identity. A few Union soldiers in South Carolina freely used the word "nigger" in her pres-ence. "The little Commissary, himself, Capt. T.," she records, "is a perfect little popinjay, and he and a Colonel somebody who didn't look any too sensible, talked in a very smart manner, evidently for our especial benefit. The word 'nigger' was plentifully used, whereupon I set them down at once as not gentle [men]" (389). She experienced difficulties with other Union soldiers and, according to Peterson, also faced racism at the Penn Center. In her diary Laura Towne refers to the contrabands as "darkies" and "niggers" and to the northern teachers as "nigger teachers," as Pe-terson reminds us. Despite her obvious prejudice, it should be noted that Towne spent the rest of her life at Penn Center, living, working, and finally in 1901 dying there; she is buried in the churchyard across from the center, which has become a historic site and community center. As another example of the murkiness of racism, Towne offered a rejoinder to a racist in South Carolina who thought "the whole race of niggers ought to be swept away." She writes in her diary, "I told him my business was with that race and that they would never be swept away."[82] The great age of reform broadened these reformers' vision on a racial level for Towne and a class level for Forten: it was responsible for making their grand vision greater than their personal prejudices.

A Wistful Fondness and the End of an Era

Journals written over a period of time permit the emergence of contradictory and maturing selves in their open-ended discursiveness. In journal 5 a matronly Forten reflects wistfully on the abolitionist warriors of the past, including Douglass, whom she knew and visited but omits mentioning in journal 1 and dismisses in journal 2. Her mature reflection is significant because of what it reveals about the nature of diary writing and her evolving persona as maternal warrior. Her earlier treatment of Douglass in her diaries prompts theoretical insight into diary literature as a form of discourse adverse to a rigidly fixed persona per se. Forten's adult fondness for the dying but heroic Douglass in journal 5 is different from her youthful dismissal of him in earlier journals. Her omission of any mention of Douglass in journal 1 is noteworthy because she discusses so many radical antislavery orators, but Douglass was the most radical of them all, advocating eventually that slaves use violence to free themselves.[83] Elizabeth Cady Stanton recalled Douglass's impact on audiences: "Around him sat the great antislavery orators of the day . . . earnestly watching the effect of his eloquence on that immense audience[;] all the other speakers seemed tame after Frederick Douglass who stood there like an African prince, majestic in his wrath."[84] Douglass overshadowed Remond and broke with Garrison. Loyal to Remond, with whom she stayed, and friendly with Garrison, whom she adored, young Forten in journal 2 finds Douglass lacking a "heart worthy of so great, so gifted a mind" (240). At forty-six, after traveling to the South, she had gotten a glimpse of slave society and recognized Douglass as a hero-reformer who had performed the work of the maternal ideal. The essay "At the Home of Frederick Douglass" (Francis Grimké Papers, Moorland-Spingaen Research Center, Howard University) elevates him to the status of those whom she revered.

Housed in Howard University's Moorland-Spingarn Collection, *The Journals of Charlotte Forten Grimké* is a time capsule of the great age of reform. The people mentioned in the journals form a Who's Who in nineteenth-century America. Regarding the maternal function, the journals provide an important description of Forten's coming-of-age, deferential to the voice of her long-gone, yet angelically present mother "hovering" over her daughter and encouraging her mission in American history. The idea is that Forten in the maternal womb had been given a life already mapped out for her in the struggle of the black body-in-crisis. Thus her success is not only because of her appropriation of the European tradition of the rhetoric of "sympathy and sensibility" in the journals, leading to action as progressive whites adopted the black cause, leading to democracy, as one scholar contends.[85] Rather, Forten's success is witnessed in the role she played as Mary Virginia Wood Forten's daughter, committed to completing the task of mothering a race to freedom. Moreover she adopted language that bore witness to the fragmented worlds of a privileged heir who unified those two worlds.

The Civil War "unleashed a dynamic debate," writes Eric Foner, "over the meaning of American freedom and the definition and entitlements of American citizenship, a debate that continues to this day."[86] Forten participated in that historic debate. Written to the moment and yet transcending the momentariness of diary discourse, her journals allow generations to experience her private and public worlds, their friction and their resolution at one moment in time, unparalleled in importance for the emancipation and citizenship of black Americans.

4 Antiblack Aesthetics

Jessie Fauset, Nella Larsen, Zora Neale Hurston, and Jim Crow America

"Beauty evokes a pleasurable response. It makes us feel a part of something larger than ourselves."[1] "Who shall describe Beauty? The problem of the twentieth century is the problem of the color line."[2] As these two quotations suggest, the pleasurable idea of beauty and its comely aesthetics were at odds with the strict color line of Jim Crow America and its treatment of the "contaminated" black body-in-crisis. Thus the works of Jessie Fauset, Nella Larsen, and Zora Neale Hurston represent another turning point in the literature of African American women writers, especially in their early twentieth-century development of modern aesthetic metaphors of beauty and the feminine body. From Fauset's golden-colored Maggie Ellersley, who has a lean body resembling calla lilies, to Larsen's global traveler Helga Crane, who pursues "freedom and cities," and Hurston's widowed Janie Crawford, who becomes a feminist folk model, a new image of the black female body is born. This image becomes a powerful figure, which experiences the expansiveness of beauty; transcends, for the most part, race, gender, and class oppression; and reveals the lofty, yet common aspirations of the Negro people to be treated decently as members of the human family.

After Charlotte Forten's victory of emancipation in South Carolina, the reemergence of racial strictures in American society proved Pierre L. van den Berghe's theory of the dichotomizing system of Herrenvolk democracies "that are democratic for the master race but tyrannical for the subordinate groups." The development of Jim Crow laws also revealed "how flexible and adaptable the structures of white supremacy were"[3] and how the "color line" of Jim Crow America continued to map out the conditions of life for Negroes, but their innovative protest. Hence, Fauset's, Larsen's, and Hurston's reconfigurations of the black body from repressed and destitute to rising and self-endowed reflected the radical idea that beauty and aesthetics mattered to the new Negroes, a historically disinherited people.

In developing the aesthetics of racial and gender identities, Fauset, Larsen, and Hurston expressed a contrasting bourgeois and village-folk culture that worked to sustain and reify Negro lives during a tumultuous Jim Crow period. In this chapter, their major novels are discussed through the prism of the aesthetic principles of Booker T. Washington, W. E. B. Du Bois, Kant, and Adorno. An emphasis is placed on the novelists' appropriation of the feminine and maternal body as a trope of regeneration in overcoming the humiliating, antiblack aesthetics of Jim Crow racism and gender oppression. First, though, it is necessary to foreground their superb achievements, for they faced major challenges in their aesthetic production of beauty images against the antiblack aesthetics of their Jim Crow times as well as the legacy of slavery with its pre-aesthetic representation of color as a badge of shame. Many scholars of the Harlem Renaissance have defined the period and its "conflicting ideological forces" of "racial nationalism and bohemian celebrations of black exoticism" leading to "the aspirations of the new generation for democratic freedom."[4] But no scholar to my knowledge has examined the pre-aesthetic and anti-aesthetic barnacles that these writers confronted in their miraculous recovery and contribution to the spirit of a black American regeneration.

Aesthetics and the Anti-Aesthetics of Racial Identity

Aesthetics played a fundamental role in the metaphorical representation of the free colored body, aesthetics related, of course, to that of the Harlem Renaissance with its celebration of color and the cultural productions of the Negro artist in art, dance, fiction, poetry, music, performance, and sculpture. The Harlem Renaissance, 1919–40, was a great cultural awakening of Negroes under the leadership of a boundary-crossing and educated mulatto and black elite whom Du Bois referred to as the "Talented Tenth" and Alain Locke described as the "New Negro" in his titular work of 1925. During this period a concentration of talent in Harlem created a collective racial ethos, one unprecedented in American history. Although Fauset, Larsen, and Hurston were named the rear guard of the Harlem Renaissance and were seen as behind the advance guard of a male bastion led by the poet Langston Hughes, they in fact presented revolutionary and cultural inscriptions of the female body that depart dramatically from history. Their aesthetics of a colored bourgeois and cosmopolitan feminine body and a free-spirited folk body challenged the antiblack aesthetics of the juridical and national social body of Jim Crow America. After the Civil War and emancipation, Jim Crow laws recircumscribed the bodily spaces of Negroes, announced in the semiotics of public signs reading "For Whites" and "For Coloreds." In a literary and historical dialogue on race and representation, the Harlem Renaissance and Jim Crow society offered two diverging images of the body, respectively positive and negative, revealing that bodily images of Negroes never have been, historically, a nonneutralized area of public discourse.

Bodily expressive art as found in the dancing of Florence Mills and Josephine Baker, or the instrumental playing of Duke Ellington and Louis Armstrong, or the writing of Jean Toomer's *Cane* and Nella Larsen's *Quicksand* (novels with moving mosaics of bodies) announced a certain arrival of the mobile black body. This emergence was unqualified in its multidimensional and artistic creation, its politics, and its reach, which was far into, for example, the black arts movement of the more militant 1960s, with its absence of white patronage and its resounding Afrocentric

ethos, advanced by Zora Neale Hurston. With a new attitude fostered by the returning and angry Negro soldier to a segregated America after fighting for democracy abroad in 1919, the Negro artist was further motivated in the development of
progressive racial images. By the end of World War I, the "radical" Negro, Nathan
Huggins states, was "already serving notice that the Negro of postwar America was
going to be much more militant than his prewar brother."[5] The new "militancy"
was articulated clearly in Langston Hughes's manifesto "The Negro and the Racial
Mountain" (1926), a literary document proclaiming the Negro artist's autonomy
and radicalism, not only from white America but also from the conservative and
prescriptive art and politics of black America. This autonomy included a stepping
away from the conservative politics of Du Bois, for example, who advocated a
program of black aesthetics that favored the middle-class fiction of Fauset and
Larsen over Claude McKay's works of "debauchery" and those of the liberal white
member of the Harlem Renaissance and "Niggerati," Carl Van Vechten. McKay's
Home to Harlem and Van Vechten's *Nigger Heaven*, novels of Harlem's nightlife and
licentiousness, made Du Bois want "to take a bath."[6]

At the heart of the Harlem Renaissance writers' literary productions is the racy
or respectable cultural representation of the black body. Du Bois favored images
of the Negro that were cultured and striving and that imparted and transmitted
knowledge about Negro aspiration, talent, and yearning for social justice, a creation that would grant the Negro's rightful place in American civilization. Based on
his response to the short-lived magazine *Fire!* (1926), it is doubtful that Du Bois
would have thoroughly embraced Hurston's complete appropriation of folk dialect
and art, replete with the racial epithet "nigger" and lacking the narrative gentility
he admired in Fauset's and Larsen's novels. According to David Levering Lewis,
the "Young Turks," consisting of Hughes, Hurston, Wallace Thurman, and others,
produced the radically independent magazine *Fire!* with an expressive zeal: "fy-ah'
gonna burn ma soul." In response, Du Bois "confined himself to a terse, one-line
notice [of the magazine's publication in *Crisis*]," but *Fire!* folded after one issue for
lack of resources and interest.[7]

Even though the Hurston scholar John Lowe posits that she had an "antipathy
for Du Bois," who is represented by characters satirized in *Jonah's Gourd Vine* as
"elitist blacks,"[8] Hurston was capable of assuming various political voices, compli-
cating her views on politics and people. For example, in a letter to Du Bois dated
June 11, 1945, she refers respectfully to him as the "Dean of American Negro Artists."[9] After the Harlem Renaissance was history, she continued to acknowledge Du
Bois's overwhelming influence on the movement. Hurston, like Fauset and Larsen,
created aesthetics that acknowledged in many ways the Negro promise in a demoralizing period, which attempted, in turn and in antiblack aesthetics, to dislodge
the black body and voice of Negroes, countering the Harlem Renaissance writers'
overwhelming, aspiring metaphors of self-agency.

In his study *The Anti-Aesthetic: Essays on Postmodern Culture,* Hal Foster defines the term "anti-aesthetic" as the gaudy artlessness of mass culture, in its production and consumption of objects and materialism in postmodern society.[10] The anti-aesthetic, according to Foster, is a crass display of tastelessness to the nth degree. Although I borrow the term "anti-aesthetic[s]" from Foster, I use it differently to denote the continuing denigration of the black body-in-crisis in mainstream society: that is, the denial of its colorful beauty and its possibilities as well as its native citizenship. Jim Crow America painted its own unattractive and contaminated or anti-aesthetic portrait of Negroes, legally in the case of *Plessy v. Ferguson* (1896). However, social codes of segregation to the "nth degree" had followed the Civil War with, in Du Bois's words, "infamous pieces of legislature,"[11] detailing in the Black Codes the freed people's spatial bodily limitation.

Distinguishing slavery's treatment of the black body from Jim Crow's, Walter Benn Michaels argues that in the *Plessy* case, the Louisiana Supreme Court's ruling of "physical differences" between whites and blacks marked a "new development in racial thinking" after slavery, one ominously opening up another affirmation of white supremacy.[12] Homer Plessy was declared Negro because he was only "seven-eighths Caucasian and one-eighth African,"[13] a diabolical mathematical configuration stressing the one-drop rule of color. Since Plessy had a so-called determinate amount of African blood coursing through his veins, he was declared a Negro and relegated to the space allotted to his race—in the rear of railroad cars. According to Michaels, the *Plessy* ruling did more than just remove blacks from the paternal relations many white southerners believed the two groups enjoyed under slavery. The *Plessy* case also repudiated the "paternalist prewar race relations" between white masters and black slaves in the South, casting "blacks out of the [national] family so that Northern and Southern whites . . . can finally become brothers."[14]

Citing the shibboleths of Nordic supremacy in the 1890s, even in white liberal magazines such as the *Nation,* the *Atlantic, Harper's Weekly,* and the *North American Review,* C. Vann Woodward gave early voice to Michaels's metaphor of North/South white brotherhood and the resulting legal/social ostracism of the Negro. "Just as the Negro gained his emancipation and new rights through a falling out between white men," Woodward posits, "he now stood to lose his rights through the reconciliation of white men."[15] Dedicated to the belief of white supremacy, Jim Crow society, North and South, put forces into play that guaranteed a "cumulative weakening of [black] resistance to racism."[16] From the "poll taxes" levied against impecunious Negroes trying to vote in the South to the extension of segregated public facilities in the South and the North, Jim Crow laws effectively controlled policy and social thought, aimed against black citizenship. Negroes were denied or given restricted access to basic accommodations in society, including public transportation, public schools, public parks, jobs, neighborhoods, hospitals, and restaurants. The Jim Crow policy of separate but equal facilities reinstituted the subjugation of Negroes, reinscribing the black body as untouchable and different from that of the white and national "American" body. Blacks and whites were to "live the effects of their national identity directly on the body, registering," Lauren Berlant remarks, "the subject's legitimacy, according to the degree to which she [or he] can suppress the [bodily] 'evidence.'"[17] While "passing" white-skinned Negroes could "suppress the evidence" of bodily identification, the white-skinned Homer Plessy preferred not to pass. With his decision, he exposed the supremacist discourse of Jim Crow laws but also the fluidity and antiessentialism of racial identity denied by juridical laws.

Moreover, the lynching of black bodies, as many as 78 in 1896 and 123 in 1897,[18] an increase a year after the *Plessy* ruling, disclosed the violence and racial anxiety of the period facing all Negroes, including the Harlem Renaissance writers. Movie and theatrical pictures of Negroes further exploited the heated racial feelings. The media extravaganza of D. W. Griffith's *Birth of a Nation* (1915), for example, presenting screen images of the free black male lusting after white women, received support from no less a figure than President Woodrow Wilson, who viewed the movie with a select audience in the White House. Jim Crow America, with its pejorative legal, public, and media control over the images of the black body, provided a backdrop of the times, defining the overwhelming problems facing positive black aesthetics. In several respects, then, the Harlem Renaissance writers clearly had their work cut out for them.

At least four challenges awaited writers such as Fauset, Larsen, and Hurston. First, the development of a black aesthetic is burdened by the holocaust of American slavery and its harsh pre-aesthetic discourse on the colonized and enslaved black body as propertied and unattractive. According to Winthrop Jordan, the colors "black" and "white" were "emotionally partisan" to slave-trading Englishmen as "no other colors" were, and they "so clearly implied opposition."[19] The pre-aesthetics of slavery attempted to strip blacks of the experience of art and beauty even before they had a chance to demonstrate their love of beauty and their talent on a significant scale to the world and be accepted as cultural producers of knowledge and beauty. American slavery and its pre-aesthetics of propertied bodies had built a far-reaching formation of multiple abject concepts, which encased the Negro, according to Alain Locke, in a "damaged group psychology."[20] In his study of a psychohistory of slavery and racism, Joel Kovel examines the technical schema of the propertied black body and posits one theoretical conundrum confronting a developing black aesthetic, underscoring the interplay between hegemonic power and ethnic-identity struggle. For Kovel, the "American slaver did not simply own the body of his black slave . . . [but] went one step further in cultural development" by reducing the "human self of his black slave to a body" and then "a *thing*" in a world marketplace.[21] This economic production occurred as "the Westerner was changing his entire view of reality—and changing reality in accordance with his new conception of it."[22]

Second, Kovel's argument suggests another problem facing the development of a black aesthetic. Lacking the power of agency, the Negro, as a member of an ethnic group, was at the mercy of a powerful white hegemony, malevolent or benign: its laws, politics, and media productions. From the advent of slavery as a "civilizing" mission of cultivating pagans (that is, Phillis Wheatley, the "uncultivated Barbarian" from Africa) to the era of abolitionism as a recognition of the brotherhood of men, each new historical reality reproduced accompanying racial symbols. One of these symbols appeared most famously during the abolition period in the plaque of an enchained black man, no longer a heathen, but a fellow brother, kneeling and pleading, "Am I Not a Man and a Brother."[23] As a minority, the Negro generally lacked the power of agency on a national scale, which was not related to a kinder, gentler, and counterhegemonic movement on his or her behalf since white hegemony was not necessarily monolithic. A case in point is the famous relationship between the celebrated Frederick Douglass and the white abolitionist William Lloyd Garrison, from whom Douglass broke *after* he founded and published the *North Star.* Douglass claimed his autonomy from Garrison, Wendell Phillips, and other paternal white abolitionists, but not before he and the abolitionists, abroad and at home, had secured his freedom. On his own and as a fugitive slave, Douglass evinced no such agency.

That the Harlem Renaissance occurred at the time it did in the 1920s underscores Kovel's point about the power of hegemony and the construction of reality with an emerging set of ideas, confluent with yet another reality. Although atypical of Kovel's Western slaving prototype and yet like the abolitionists before them in having the power to refashion ideas on race and identity, liberal white intellectuals and artists from Eugene O'Neill to Horace Kallen in the 1920s assaulted early twentieth-century notions of racial purity and one hundred percent Americanism. O'Neill's *The Emperor Jones* (1920), a vehicle for Paul Robeson's introduction on Broadway, had a "great impact on the Harlem Renaissance."[24] O'Neill dared to present a black male as a protagonist, introspective and not foolish, though brooding and superstitious to the sound of beating drums in the primitive background. Although removed from slavery, the Negro was still a priori defined from the outside, although from a less hostile but still controlling force, which is the point Kovel makes about the suprapower of political and cultural hegemony.

For Renaissance scholars such as George Hutchinson, the interracial networking evident at the turn of the century in the new publishing interest in black writers by magazines such as the *Nation* and book publishers such as Boni & Liveright and Knopf made a necessary commitment to the ethos and growth of the Harlem Renaissance. White/black networking did challenge the reductive notions of white supremacy even if the "white allies" of the movement were, as Hutchinson concedes, not entirely "above American racial ideology."[25] But Hutchinson's acknowledgment proves the validity of Kovel's argument of the rather unbroken and demonstrative retention of hegemonic public discourse crippling the Negro. Negro reliance on white patronage, not entirely removed from the conditioning of white supremacy, was problematic, as evidenced by Hurston's and Hughes's relationships with the white philanthropist Charlotte Osgood Mason, who was attracted to the Negro's "primitive" identity as most authentic. Horace Kallen too proves an interesting case in his self-confessed liberalism.

In his influential essay "Culture and Democracy in the United States" (1924), Kallen created the term "cultural pluralism"[26] and articulated a philosophy of an aggregate cultural experience that influenced the social impetus toward multiculturalism and hinted at black inclusion. A Jewish immigrant, Kallen responded to a tide of publications such as *A Study of American Intelligence* (1923), by Princeton University's Carl Campbell Brigham, which claimed Nordic superiority and Negro, mulatto, and hybrid-immigrant degeneracy. Kallen's article influenced the attack on Nordic supremacy, anti-immigration policy, and a rising Ku Klux Klan, whose membership increased after the public screening of *Birth of a Nation*. Nevertheless even Kallen could not envision Negroes as having an equal place in this new modern, multicultural America, with the exception of elitist blacks such as Alain Locke, his former student at Harvard. John Dewey criticized his Columbia University colleague for his segregationist views and indirect support of Jim Crow policy, but to Kallen, "most blacks" were just "too different."[27]

Third, in light of the fluctuating, Western binary image of Negroes, enslaved and propertied or alien and exotic, Renaissance writers were challenged to define a black cultural authenticity and desire, irrespective of a propagandistic pre-aesthetic and anti-aesthetic sense of its negation. Where, for example, inside the always already embodied Negro was the culturally authentic Negro, given the pervasive and synthetic historical images besmirching the black body-in-crisis? Booker T. Washington and W. E. B. Du Bois identified two differing aesthetic philosophies for the manacled Negro of history. Washington's famous quip—"You can beat me being a white man, but I can beat you being a Negro"[28]—expresses the responsibility of a black aesthetic ideal to forward ideas of blacks being and doing what they know best on a practical level. A former Virginia slave and educated at Hampton Institute, Washington observed that "in order to lift them [Negroes] up, something must be done more than merely to imitate [a] New England education,"[29] leading to the development of his bootstrap philosophy and the launching of his industrial program at Tuskegee. Although practical, Washington's domestic program for Negro education and the teaching of essential but basic skills such as carpentry and mechanics led Du Bois to criticize his "singleness of vision."[30]

Since the historical black experience in America does not exactly constitute a normalizing cultural discourse on self-development for African Americans, Washington and Du Bois entered into a lively exchange, which led to at least two of several ideological positions on the black aesthetics taken up by Fauset, Larsen, and Hurston. Washington's self-serving depiction of educated blacks with "high hat, imitation gold eye-glasses, [and] a showy walking-stick"[31] was intended to lure frightened whites to his side. As carpenters and blacksmiths, Washington's Negroes would know their place but would also become economically viable and self-sufficient in their honest labor. Since the classically educated New Englander Du Bois, from Fisk, Harvard, and the University of Berlin, carried a walking stick, the icy disdain with which Washington appeared to have held liberally educated blacks served to exacerbate the pain of his menial goals for Negroes. On another level, Washington's black aesthetic agenda of domestic simplicity had the potential to "disregard the superficial for the real, the appearance for the substance, [the] great and yet small, learned and yet simple."[32]

Du Bois debated and embellished Washington's policy and widened the pathway taken by writers such as Larsen and Fauset, whose professionally educated characters as doctors, artists, and educators would otherwise be viewed in the satirical light of upward-bound Negroes, ridiculed by Washington for the purpose of allaying the fears of whites. While Washington's Negroes were not moving too fast for their own good, Du Bois advocated a cultural *and* political black aesthetic program, beyond Washington's agenda of domesticity or even away from Immanuel Kant's classic definition of art and beauty as pure judgments of taste and experience, unrelated to politics. Kant distinguishes "free beauty" from "dependent beauty" in that the former provides an unconditional, purposeless, and pure aesthetic presentation of beauty, while the latter maintains a conditional and adherent concept of beauty in relation to its purpose.[33] Whether in terms of free or dependent beauty, Kant's aesthetic theory, unlike Du Bois's, forwarded the idea of art for art's sake without art being used as a weapon for political purpose.

A black aesthetic program for Du Bois, however, was a part of a wholly purposeful and political design of creative protest, geared toward racial regeneration. Art *was* political. Between the crushing discourses of the crude, pre-aesthetics of American slavery, with its flesh branding of propertied bodies on the auction block, and the new, anti-aesthetics of the black body, segregated and policed in Jim Crow America, Du Bois determines in "Criteria of Negro Art" (1926) a specific direction for the Renaissance writers. He defines the writers' "bounden duty" to create, preserve, and realize an ethic of beauty, truth, and goodness as a "great [political] vehicle" for providing a "universal understanding" of the Negro cause.[34] While Du Bois's essay sparked Langston Hughes's protest of artistic autonomy in the "Racial Mountain," it nevertheless succeeded in establishing a course for Negro artists, as Hurston's letter to Du Bois acknowledges. Black cultural authenticity was to be linked to a new phenomenon, one recognizing and yet overcoming the lowly influences of history through liberal advancement of education, supplanting a Washingtonian emphasis on an important but limited cultural norm.

Although Darwin T. Turner chides Du Bois for not defining beauty per se in his pronouncement of a black aesthetic ideal and for equating beauty with truth in an enigmatic John Keats fashion,[35] Du Bois implies the presence of morality in beauty and aesthetics. The kind of art that combines protest with moral goodness and human grandeur, speaking to the highest ideals of humanity, could perhaps influence positive human change and racial outcome. Already critical of Washington's program of accommodation at Tuskegee and his Atlanta Exposition Speech of 1895 embracing Jim Crow strictures, Du Bois further exploded their difference on the development of a black aesthetic agenda when he remarked that the "new young artists have got to fight their way to freedom," becoming "free of mind, proud of body and just of soul to all men."[36]

A fourth challenge they faced in coming to a black aesthetic program was that Fauset, Larsen, and Hurston inherited the artist's mission of creating beauty while simultaneously moving outside the sphere of a personal debilitating reality, revealed in each writer's own experience with Jim Crow racism. In *Aesthetic Theory*, Theodor W. Adorno analyzes the conflicting relations between the artist in society and his or her social reality and experience. Adorno indirectly communicates the difficulty of Du Bois's manifesto for black artists to fight their way to freedom while creating art. "Aesthetic identity," writes Adorno, "seeks to aid the nonidentical, which in reality is repressed by reality's compulsion to identity,"[37] which is doubly the case for the isolated writer of color. Works of art can become, Adorno asserts, bold "afterimages of empirical life insofar as they help the latter [the artists] to what is denied them outside their own sphere and thereby free it from that to which they are condemned by reified external experience."[38] To illustrate Adorno's idea of reality's resistance to the artist's building of an aesthetic identity and the necessity of the artist's afterimages of self or people, consider the musical compositions by slaves in the South, where antiliteracy laws intensified their suffering of unpaid labor. In the language of "ungrammatical profundity,"[39] these slaves created Negro spirituals as an empowering counterracial narrative, defying the master discourse on the pre-aesthetics of racial identity. With the creation of Negro spirituals of freedom, the slaves forged afterimages of themselves as musicians, singers, and composers. Afterimages helped to stabilize the identity of subjugated people from their otherwise destabilizing identity as chattel.

Significantly, for Fauset, Larsen, and Hurston to achieve the high level of culture and consciousness that Du Bois demanded, these three modern writers had to move outside the historical and contemporary markers of black identity. They had to see themselves and their people as something other than they were declared to be in Jim Crow America. Therefore this discussion of the four challenges of a black aesthetic program is intended to articulate the inherent difficulties that Fauset, Larsen, Hurston, and other Harlem Renaissance artists faced in the 1920s and 1930s. As black female writers, Fauset, Larsen, and Hurston inherited a tradition of major racial fault lines: 1) the humiliating pre-aesthetics of slavery; 2) the anti-black aesthetics of Jim Crow law; 3) the Western media's control of racial images;

and 4) each artist's own daunting experience with racism. *Quicksand's* narrative riposte that "even unloved little Negro girls must be somehow provided for"[40] is more factual than fictional in its description of Nella Larsen's alter ego Helga Crane, deserted by her white mother and unwanted by her white stepfather, as was Larsen. She reveals the struggle of the Renaissance writer in her quest to create afterimages of black existence unencumbered by subjective realities. As Renaissance writers, Fauset, Larsen, and Hurston communicate an ambitious aesthetic program combining the tenets of Washington's, Du Bois's, Kant's, and Adorno's theories: domestic and practical; aspiring and political; transcendent and sublime aesthetic principles, as well as the afterimages of Negroes. Such an aesthetic adornment of Negro life as crafted by these three writers suggests, in the words of Houston Baker, their miraculous "spirit-work."[41]

Jessie Fauset: Midwife of the Harlem Renaissance

Fauset personifies the hardworking, all-around, feminine genius of the Harlem Renaissance. Her four narratives of racial and maternal regenerative power are rooted in her proud, middle-class background, resulting in her emphasis on Negro respectability and aesthetics, foregrounding maternal ethics. The seventh child of Annie Seamon Fauset and the African Methodist Episcopal minister Redmon Fauset, Jessie was born in New Jersey in 1882. She was reared, however, in Philadelphia and educated at Cornell University, where she was a Phi Beta Kappa member, the University of Pennsylvania, and the Sorbonne, where she became fluent in French. Fauset could trace her ancestors to the 1700s, biographical data that illuminate her authorial emphases on family heritage and "old Philadelphians," a Victorian signifier on a politically active black aristocracy similar to Charlotte Forten's family. The Forten surname is cited in Fauset's novel *The Chinaberry Tree*, linking the liberal, college-aspiring character Mallory Forten to that family's history.

As a student at Cornell, Fauset wrote to Du Bois in 1903, after reading *The Souls of Black Folk*, expressing her admiration and seeking employment assistance for the summer of 1904, thus attaching herself to the Renaissance man. Du Bois was able to help Fauset find a teaching position in the South, which she had preferred. "I know only one class of my people well," she confesses, "and I want to become acquainted with the rest,"[42] a statement implying her difference from but sense of connection to the common folk of Booker T. Washington's territory. Many of the characters in Fauset's novels are educated at ivy-league universities such as Harvard and Dartmouth, and they become doctors and lawyers, members of a rising black elite in Harlem, a suggestion of her espousal of the principles leading to Du Bois's development of the "Talented Tenth" theory. But Fauset also applied Washington's aesthetic principles to her literature, though clearly showing a preference for Du Bois's ideological position on affirming the Negro's elevated, cultural aspiration.

Fauset's own maternal role in discovering and nurturing young Harlem Renaissance writers such as Langston Hughes, Jean Toomer, Claude McKay, and Countee Cullen has been noted. She is described as the "mid-wife" of the Harlem Renaissance, and the publication of her first novel in 1924 was the galvanizing event for the movement, one formally introducing the Negro renaissance and its literary impetus at the Civic Club in New York. Representing the Negro intelligentsia, Charles Johnson of the National Urban League, Alain Locke, James Weldon Johnson, and Du Bois heralded Fauset and the new writers. The renaissance artists were also surrounded by a supporting cast of white editors, from Frederick Lewis Allen of Harper to Carl Van Doren of *Century* magazine. The Harlem Renaissance's white supporters prompted Robert E. Washington's chilly observation, supported by Kovel's criticism on the power of cultural hegemony, that "favorable recognition by white American elites was the yardstick most middle-class blacks used to determine whether blacks were making racial progress."[43]

Du Bois also brought Fauset into the National Association for the Advancement of Colored People (the NAACP) as editor of the *Crisis* from 1919 to 1926. Afterward the disciplined Fauset began to associate with Du Bois "not as subordinate, but as an accepted equal,"[44] attesting to her value as an intellectual and social force. According to Fauset's biographer Carolyn Wedin Sylvander, Fauset had "extensive power and influence in the day-to-day running of *The Crisis*" and "near full responsibility for the *Brownies' Book*" for children, although she was denied patriarchal "credit by historians and critics of the 1920s, including Du Bois."[45] He had anticipated the Harlem Renaissance as early as 1915, in his call in the *Crisis* for "art and literature" that would "loose the tremendous emotional wealth of the Negro and the dramatic strength of his problems."[46] Fauset had answered that summons. Assuming multiple roles, she was midwife to the Harlem Renaissance, editor of one of the most powerful magazines of racial uplift, the *Crisis,* and the author of four novels richly imbibed with the aesthetic principles of the aforementioned philosophers but especially those of Du Bois.

While Fauset was the midwife of the movement, perhaps her greatest known public success was as a novelist. Her four novels, *There Is Confusion* (1924), *Plum Bun* (1928), *The Chinaberry Tree* (1931), and *Comedy, American Style* (1933), have received a mixed reception in traditional and feminist scholarship. Described alternately as the prim and proper "Jane Austen of Negro literature,"[47] an author of "uniformly sophomoric, trivial, and dull" fiction,[48] and a conservative woman writer who denies her female characters' autonomy,[49] Fauset has been misrepresented and underappreciated, as has her artistry. In her fiction Fauset's ability to capture a tense, historical moment of Negro Herrenvolk status underscores her power to transcend the angst of her Jim Crow society, as Adorno stipulates successful artists must do. In doing so, Fauset creates art that captures a racially inscribed hierarchy, but which she allows most of her aspiring characters to transcend as aesthetic models for the new Negro.

Fauset's characters are seated in the balcony of Jim Crow theaters, and they ride on Jim Crow buses, demonstrating the antiblack aesthetics of the Negro as different and undesirable. But Fauset supplants these pejorative images of the body with her own aesthetic metaphors of art, color, fashion, nature and the maternal sublime, and supple feminine bodies. While Barbara Christian remarks that Fauset ignores the depressing conditions of blacks in the 1920s and 1930s, we can see, in fact, how instead she refuses to allow her characters' history to overpower the beauty that they discover inherently in life, a position Fauset took in her own life. Although from a middle-class background, she faced the pain of exclusion in middle school, where she was ignored; in college dorms at Cornell, where she faced segregation; and in her professional career, where she had been denied a teaching job in Philadelphia "because of my color."[50] Her eventual success was marked by her belief, as expressed in a letter to Du Bois, in "race pride, self-pride, self-sufficiency . . . and the necessity of living our lives, as nearly as possible, absolutely."[51]

There Is Confusion: The New Feminine-Maternal Body, Maggie and Joanna

Although they are a study in contrast, Maggie Ellersley and Joanna Marshall are dominant female characters in *There Is Confusion,* Fauset's first ambitious novel filled with pre-aesthetic reversals of the denigration of color and the black body. What the two female characters Maggie and Joanna have in common, however, is the culture of beauty in which Fauset places them, one in beauty shops and the other in dance performances. Each character's sheer physical attractiveness is highlighted by the aesthetics of color, flowers, bodily agility, and female creativity and ingenuity, evidenced by Maggie founding her own beauty parlors and Joanna dancing in the Dance of the Nations and playing multicultural roles to show America's unacknowledged diversity. Fauset's image of female characters is groundbreaking in that she combines various colors of beauty—from Maggie's yellowness and Joanna's brownness to Vera Manning's whiteness—to suggest a kaleidoscope of Negro color, removed, though not entirely, from the typically light-skinned heroine of nineteenth-century fiction. With the characters Maggie and Joanna and the men they marry, Fauset gives voice to the aesthetic principles of Washington and Du Bois, teaching the effectiveness of both ideologies to a degree.

Maggie is described as a "yellow calla lily in the deep cream of her skin, the slim straightness of her body" (57; subsequent references to Fauset's novels are cited in endnotes). While the calla lily is not to be found in Gauguin's postimpressionist paintings, his colorful art of Tahitian women could be the model Fauset used for her description of Maggie Ellersley. Long, elegant, and spiral-shaped, calla lilies are found in Europe and North America, and yet Fauset's visual images of color and flowers evoke a feminine aesthetic resemblance to several of Gauguin's Tahitian paintings, including *The Woman with the Flower* (1891), *The Month of May* (1899), and *Maternity* (1899). These are postimpressionist portraits of gold and yellow, tall and fleshy women, which project the purposeful deportment of Fauset's ultrafeminine character Maggie. With the postimpressionist adoption of color in the 1890s, painters such as Gauguin could have anticipated the vibrant explosion of color during the Harlem Renaissance and the noble though primitivist image of Negroes. Gauguin's audacious use of color and island women as models of beauty led to the cultural shock of the European bourgeoisie with a *"succés de scandale."*[52] Based on the bourgeoisie's reaction, it is reasonable to assume that the pre-aesthetic representation of the crudity of color had its designed effect on European and American racism, which only a revolution of the magnitude of the Harlem Renaissance could colorfully undo in America.

Fauset contests slavery's pre-aesthetic denigration of skin color and the black body. While white was usually perceived as more aesthetically appealing than black, Fauset reverses slavery's pre-aesthetics and creates afterimages of race and color. Her characters live in a world of warm and lively colors, accenting their lives, and the black body is redefined in terms of the characters' appearance, skin tone, and a wide spectrum of hues. Pointedly, Fauset distinguishes color from whiteness, which her narrator describes as lacking vibrancy: "They're [gray and beige colors] all right for those palefaces. But colored people need color, life, vividness" (132). In the novel *Passing*, Nella Larsen adopts Fauset's reverse pre- and anti-aesthetics of color in Clare's description of her life as a passing Negro: "this pale life of mine[;] I am all the time seeing the bright pictures of that other that I once thought I was glad to be free of" (145).

By attacking slavery's legacy of color discrimination, Fauset recalls Kant's concept of dependent beauty and its reliance on personal taste and preference. Colors have this beauty too, Fauset submits, since prejudice for or against color is based on subjective judgment rather than universal approval or disapproval. The pre-aesthetics of slavery and the antiblack aesthetics of Jim Crow society (re)fashioned the positive, evaluative standards of whiteness, but Fauset deconstructs the myth of color and beauty as apolitical and fixed. She also assails the hypocrisy of European racial discrimination. While miscegenation was a social taboo and even illegal, "white men of every social rank," Winthrop Jordan writes, "slept with black women" in "an irreconcilable conflict between desire and aversion for interracial sexual union."[53] In the creation of the white-skinned character Vera Manning, Fauset sketches a mininarrative of slavery and miscegenation and the falseness of racial categories. When Manning's mother rejects her daughter's dark-skinned lover, the dental student Harry Proctor, Fauset exposes also the intraracism of blacks and their cramped aesthetic vision in regard to race and color, troping on Alain Locke's theory of the "damaged group psychology" of Negroes.

The literary critic Deborah McDowell acknowledges Fauset's exploration of the color code in her novels but criticizes the prominence it is given in Fauset scholarship, especially in critics' emphasis on Fauset's creation of light-skinned characters. While Fauset's other three novels have light-skinned heroines, the major protagonist of *There Is Confusion,* Joanna Marshall, is brown skinned and represents Fauset's spectrum of color as a realistic political statement of history and miscegenation. McDowell correctly asserts that Fauset appropriates a hierarchy of class and color "as a *function* of a complicated set of relationships: cultural, social, economic, and political."[54] I would add that the complications are recorded not only in the relationships of Fauset's white-skinned and dark-skinned characters, but also in her ambitious endeavor to contest the pre-aesthetics of race and slavery. Fauset manipulates the rhetoric and image of color and advances ideas of a new aesthetic, one based on the criteria of individual desire.

Color and class discrimination are both reconfigured in *There Is Confusion.* Members of the working-class poor, who Fauset does not ignore and who are represented by characters such as Maggie Ellersley, aspire to improve their condition. Maggie has "no background" (115) but desires to marry into a proper family such as the Marshalls or Byes. Her plans to marry the elitist Joanna Marshall's brother, Phil, who is studying to be a surgeon, are thwarted by the maternal-acting Joanna, who thinks Maggie's "lowly aims would only be a hindrance to him" (86–87). After a failed marriage to a gambler, Neal, who tries to kill her when she learns of his real identity and leaves him, and after failing also to persuade Joanna's rejected lover Peter Bye to marry her, Maggie becomes self-reliant, casting her bucket in Washingtonian fashion where she lives. With her husband's background as a gambler and his identification with the anti-aesthetics of crime of the Harlem underworld, Maggie is reduced to a position of vulnerability, resulting in her assuming a moral agency for her own life. When she makes the practical decision to attend beauty school and become a hairdresser, Fauset rewards her, emphasizing the polarization between Harlem crime and Harlem culture and affirming Maggie's transformational impulse.

Following her reconciliation and marriage to Phil, the new Maggie adopts a higher ambition to "inaugurate a chain of Beauty Shops" (261). She learns too of "the beauty inherent in life itself, the miracle of health and sane nerves, of the ability to make a living, of being helpful to others" (256), lines expressing Fauset's personal philosophy as pronounced in her letter to Du Bois. The aesthetic appeal of beauty shops and hairdressing is valuable and ornamental, and it dramatizes the growth and development of Fauset's working-class poor, whose ambition she champions, as evidenced in Maggie's case. While Addison Gayle accuses Fauset of being a spokeswoman for a disappearing Negro bourgeoisie who adopts "Nordic manners" and "Nordic culture,"[55] Fauset's emphasis on Maggie's working-class background proves that her literature was not wholly restricted to the bourgeoisie.

Furthermore, Fauset's letter to Du Bois shows that the values of Western society were not *raced* values per se, as Gayle implies, but rather were nonraced ideas that could originate in experience for anyone. One of Fauset's European critics, for example, traces her deracinated ideas on freedom to, among other factors, her "extended traveling on the European continent," where the "freedom" she experienced throughout France—in Paris, Avignon, Marseilles, Arles, Nimes, and Carcassonne—"is a freedom [that] she expresses in spatial terms."[56] This is, of course, in opposition to the spatial limitations of Negroes in Jim Crow America. Apparently the globe-trotting Fauset did not believe that white Americans owned cultural values, despite the skewed, pre-aesthetic training of race and slavery hammering the notion into the minds of Negroes.

Defying these kinds of limitations in her first novel, Fauset gives the surname of Marshall to her heroine, Joanna, who, as her last name indicates, is the book's marshalling force, exuding maternal wisdom despite her initial ostracism of the "lowly" Maggie Ellersley. Through Joanna's characterization, Fauset combines the aesthetics of art and the discipline of the maternal body as antidotes to the politics of Jim Crow exclusion and despair. The maternal-acting Joanna nurtures herself and Peter, whose Jim Crow experiences in medicine threaten his career as a surgeon when he temporarily quits medical school out of frustration only to become an entertainer. Joanna's Jim Crow trials, however, serve only to strengthen her resolve to become great. "It is true," the narrator explains in free indirect discourse reflecting Fauset's broad views, "that she had seen her own people hindered, checked on account of color, but hardly any of the things she had greatly wanted had been affected for that cause" (163).

Although the French dance instructor initially refuses to take black students into his studio because "the white Americans like not to study with the brown Americans," Joanna eventually convinces him to instruct the black students there in the evenings (95–96). She pursues dance because she believes, as her French instructor intimates, that "if there's anything that will break down prejudice it will be equality or perhaps even superiority on the part of colored people in the arts" (97). Fauset articulates Du Bois's and Locke's views on the importance of the Harlem Renaissance artist's fight for freedom, a belief that Du Bois and Locke would later find naive in light of continuing discrimination, which drove Du Bois into exile in Ghana, where he died in 1963 on the day of Martin Luther King Jr.'s "I Have a Dream" speech. Nevertheless, in the novel Joanna Marshall is described as belonging to the "better class of colored people" (49). She is "brown" and slender and has a "passion for beauty" (20), particularly music and dancing, as noted by her French instructor. "Not ordinary dancing," but "beautiful things that are different from what we see around here," she explains (45). When she performs onstage, she is a "rosy brown vision" in a "misty colorful robe" (131). Fauset uses Joanna's supple body to rewrite the social order in a Du Boisian manifestation of the aesthetic blending of art and politics. Joanna's dance performance in the "Dance of the Nations" becomes a metaphor for the cultural pluralism of American society in that as a dancer she assumes the identity of a multicultural America.

In "The Face of America: Performing Race and Nation in Jessie Fauset's *There Is Confusion*," Jane Kuenz argues that in the "realm of performance," many of the contradictions of race, class, and gender are played out. When Fauset stages a theatrical production of the "Dance of the Nations" and the principal white female dancer refuses to assume the "black" role of "America," Joanna agrees to play the three parts: white, black, and Native American. As "white" America, Joanna's blackness is "conveniently masked," making her "typically American," aesthetically and nationally. When the white audience applauds and asks to see the face behind the mask, Joanna complies, but she answers the audience's shock of recognition with this gem of maternal wisdom: "I hardly need to tell you," she pleads, "that there is no one in the audience more American than I am. My great-grandfather fought in the Revolution, my uncle fought in the Civil War and my brother is 'over there' now." While Kuenz posits Joanna's speech as representing Fauset's trope on history and race relations and the "native credentials"[57] of black Americans, Fauset could also be alluding to the melting-pot theory of multiculturalism, which had found expression in New York several years before the 1920s.

An avid reader, as was Charlotte Forten, Fauset was probably aware of Horace Kallen's popular essay "Democracy versus the Melting-Pot," published in the *Nation* in 1915. Kallen's essay responded to the rising intolerance directed against hyphenated Americans who were not Americans of Anglo-Saxon ancestry.[58] Undesirable eastern European immigrants from Italy, Poland, and Hungary experienced an ethnic exclusion in defense of "real" Americans retaining a democracy traceable to that founded by "their" founding fathers, largely their Nordic ancestors. A Herrenvolk democracy, then, was defined as the inalienable rights of one hundred percent pure Americans, leading to anti-immigration restrictions against the socially perverted, that is, eastern Europeans and Asians, especially Jews and Chinese. Citing the mobility of groups and their evolving assimilation in the adoption of language, clothes, and manners and in their acceptance of intermarriage, Kallen found the emergence of a "new" American race, a healthy melting pot of diversity, comparable to a symphony orchestra of many parts.[59] Locke's description of the "New Negro" in his titular essay reflects the era's emphasis on all that was thought "new" and thus fostered a particular excitement about its possibility. Although Locke adopted the popular term "new" to stress the "newness" of the "new" Negro, all said, the new Negro was not a part of Kallen's ideal cultural pluralism.

Interestingly, the immigrant-Jew Kallen traces the emergence of the assimilated American to the blending of European stocks, including Jews, Danes, Slavs, Poles, and so forth. In another related essay, Kallen questions "whether Negroes should constitute an element in this blend."[60] The new freedom sweeping through early twentieth-century America and the perception of foreigners as a "menace"[61] were related to economics in the public concern for resources and the real or perceived threat of a growing population competing for jobs. While finding the country's bias against immigrants geared more toward "the economic situation" than "cultural or spiritual" relations, Kallen cites the quote "by their fruits shall ye know the soils and the roots"[62] to argue in favor of the acceptance of immigrants. His quotation can be interpreted as grounds for the fair evaluation of "new" Americans or as mockingly reactionary to the ethnocentrism of the one hundred percent Americans, whom his essay addresses.

In *There Is Confusion*, Fauset perhaps hints at Kallen's racism and parodies his statement "by their fruits shall ye know the soils and the roots" in the slave Isaiah Bye's parodic revision: "By *his* fruits shall ye know—me" (29). Born into slavery and the property of the white Quaker Byes in Philadelphia, Isaiah cultivates and nurtures the white Byes' peach orchards, enriching the Byes not only by performing free bodily labor but also by producing prosperous and beautiful orchards. "By rights part of them [peach orchards] ought to belong to us," Isaiah's enslaved father confesses (30), another reminder of black economic dispossession. As a black inheritor of his family's economic deficiency, the character Peter Bye is bitter toward whites because of the exploitation of his great-grandfather and grandfather and the denial of blood relations with the white Byes and American first-class citizenship. Thus, Fauset's narrative trope on American history suggests that in Kallen's excluding blacks from the multicultural society that he was advocating, he imitated the master narrative of race that he simultaneously invoked and disavowed on behalf of European immigrants.

As the novel's young and developing maternal figure, Joanna offers comfort to Peter Bye and influences him to return to his original career goal to be a surgeon. Joanna's future surgeon husband, Peter is an Old Philadelphian who finds it "easy to learn things about the body" (44), suggesting its wonder and his surgical potential and skill. His own body is a "dark arresting beauty" (21). When Joanna initially meets Peter and demands to know (more like a mother than a lover) what he plans to do with his life, on cue he answers, "'A surgeon' . . . expressing a resolve which her question had engendered in him" (44). He begins a relationship with Maggie because she is less demanding of him than Joanna, but he comes to realize that he "had been nothing without Joanna" (188). As an early feminist model, Joanna asserts her independence in the arts and refuses to marry Peter until he becomes a man of great ambition. After the two reunite and marry, Peter reminds Joanna that she must give up her career, an order to which she calmly responds, "Of course, of course." For Fauset's feminist critics, these lines of submission are evidence of her ambivalence about the modern woman's place in a patriarchal society.

Sandra M. Gilbert and Susan Gubar criticize Fauset's starched ideology of woman's place and her perception of the "New Woman as a white woman, whose feminism the black woman must repudiate in order to reinvent the masculinity of black men."[63] Likewise, Hazel Carby opines that "Fauset adapted but did not transcend the form of the romance,"[64] where female characters marry at the end. Kuenz offers that Fauset rather than contradicting herself about women's place in society, as independent artists or devoted wives, gives voice to an ideological tension between traditional and modern women's roles.[65] Moreover, I would argue further with Kuenz that like Charlotte Forten, Fauset viewed racism as more of a problem for blacks than the sexism that black women faced in the early twentieth century. The historian Rayford Logan has described this period as the "nadir" of race relations, and Pierre L. van den Berghe calls it the "golden age" of Western racism from 1880 to 1920.[66] Gender would become just as important as race in the works of Paule Marshall, Alice Walker, and Toni Morrison, but at the time that Fauset was writing, after 1920, she still perceived racism as a greater threat than gender discrimination.

To the extent that black women could "mother" children and therefore "mother" the race to achieve social and political parity, Fauset only winked at early feminism in order to more fully combat the challenge of racism through the metaphor of the wise maternal and marshalling force of Joanna. Sara Ruddick defines women thinking maternally as "one kind of disciplined reflection among many, each with identifying questions, methods, and aims."[67] While not "free from its flaws,"[68] maternal thinking as a discipline requires from Joanna the same kind of self-mastery that she demonstrated as a dancer, artist, and would-be feminist. Feminists tend to ignore Fauset's treatment of Joanna as a maternal force to be reckoned with, and they also overlook Peter's and Joanna's lines following her submission of "Of course, of course" to him. These unacknowledged lines suggest Fauset's conjoining the traits of feminism and maternity. Peter explains, "For, if there should be children, I want, Oh, Joanna, I hope. . . . if they are like me they'll have so much to fight, and they'll need you to help them" (284–85). With these lines, Fauset identifies Joanna's autonomous feminist virtues, not exclusive of her maternal drive, and the pattern of success that she establishes as a single woman of remarkable "mental clarity" (175). The emphasis on Peter's faith in Joanna, that she would know how to mother colored children in a rigid Jim Crow culture, pronounces a practice of maternal discipline and thinking that goes beyond the self, implying Joanna's wideness of spirit and versatility of talent.

As the critical discourse above illustrates, Fauset displays dual and complex personas in her novels as a writer with a modernist-Victorian temperament, promoting a budding feminism while also lauding the traditional values of motherhood and home. Joanna is initially presented as a picture of the rising feminist woman, but she is also patterned after both her father and her mother. Fauset describes Joanna's parents as Victorian and only necessarily modern, reflecting the author's jockeying between the comfort of tradition and the uncertain march toward modernity. Joel Marshall, the patriarch of the Marshall family, is a self-made caterer whose wife stays in the background of the domestic sphere as the Victorian maternal ideal. He, rather than she, becomes the model of success and diversity for Joanna. He employs blacks and whites and is "one of the first colored men in Harlem to possess an automobile" (109). Fauset flirts with the idea that in order to become successful women must become like men, but her authorial flirtation appears only as a compromise to her well-established agenda of the domestic Victorian family of manners and values, as a bulwark against the dissembling nature of Jim Crow racism.

Perhaps due to the ambitiousness of Fauset's aesthetic purpose and her complex feminist, Victorian-modernist leaning, Robert Bone has famously described *There Is Confusion* as a novel that is "nothing if not well titled."[69] But the book's title refers to the "confusion slavery threw American life" into (245) and the heroic effort of Fauset's characters in their struggle to achieve a normal life at home and abroad, despite the prejudices they face in medicine, in the army, at dance schools, in theaters, on buses, and in other places of ubiquitous Jim Crow politics.

Plum Bun: Passing versus the Memorialization of Aesthetics

Fauset's second novel, *Plum Bun,* focuses on the era's phenomenon of white-skinned Negroes passing for white to avoid the negative, social effect of Jim Crow laws. Deborah McDowell asserts that the "passing plot constitutes a major state in Angela Murray's coming-of-age" and "that plot cannot be separated from the marriage plot, which constitutes the structural core of the novel."[70] Indeed approximately two thirds of the narrative addresses the passing motif, beginning with the protagonist Angela Murray's parents' death, after which she leaves home for New York and passes for white, and continuing with her attendance at the Cooper Union Art School as an art student. The action progresses to her romance with the white playboy Roger Fielding. The marriage plot is connected to the passing plot but is subsumed by it. However, the dead mother's echo of the value of home and its authenticity resounds, finally, with mental clarity for the born-again Angela, who confesses her desire "to see Philadelphia again" (360).

With the description of Angela's body as an "atrophied body" (207), Fauset suggests the anxiety of racial passing and breaks with the nineteenth-century literary discourse on passing as a desirable alternative to facing racism. After James Weldon Johnson's *The Autobiography of an Ex-Colored Man* (1912), a novel of a passing black man's racial and mental turmoil, Harlem Renaissance writers such as Fauset were more apt to treat the trope of passing as one suggesting "cultural confusion" and "existential angst,"[71] rather than discreet racial accommodation to racism. Fauset's treatment of passing, like Johnson's, stands in contrast to her forerunners in the nineteenth century, most notably William Wells Brown, whose novel *Clotel* (1856) features the white-skinned quadroon Clotel as a "Real Albino" who is "admitted by all to be the most beautiful girl, coloured or white."[72] Brown's Clotel fits pre-aesthetically in the "dominant racist definitions of womanhood and beauty."[73] While critics accuse Fauset of a similar artistic proclivity, it is clear that she is capable of breaking with the pre-aesthetic definitions of women, race, color, and beauty.

Indeed, Angela can be linked superficially to the experience of fugitive slaves who, unlike Angela, necessarily ran away from their families and slave communities in quest of freedom. Fugitives were forced to live lives shrouded in secrecy and mystery. Unlike the fugitives, Angela is not forced into her exile: she is not a slave but rather is a second-class citizen who desires first-class rights and privileges that she believes she can acquire only as the white woman Angele Mory. But like the fugitives who also changed their names, she is led to deny her birthright, her family and community, and her own darker-skinned sister Virginia before the white Roger Fielding, her beau. Angela is really a fugitive from the naturalness of her own body. She identifies her passing as a "secret" to her visiting sister Virginia (242), who contrasts Angela's life to her own as an "open life [with] no secrets, no subterfuges, no goals to be reached by devious ways" (243), implying the immorality of passing. Indeed more recent criticism on passing as an early twentieth-century phenomenon defines passing "by its nature" as a "secretive affair"[74] that caused "various attitudes" among blacks, ranging from frustration to ambivalence. However, Fauset rejects these ideas and is clear in her condemnation of passing.

With Angela's desire "to see Philadelphia again," Fauset begins to restore her to her nonpassing and natural body and the black Philadelphia community, to which she returns toward the end of a long narrative. Through musical aesthetics, Fauset induces in Angela a longing for home, emphasized throughout the narrative with the deceased mother (dead but still powerful even in death) calling her passing daughter "home." The "memorialization of aesthetics"[75] is a concept expressing the remembered pleasurable moments from the past as recalled by the individual, especially in moments of despair and pathos. The beautiful past as nostalgically memorialized and the hurtful present as painfully lived now are intertwined simultaneously, highlighting a past cultural pleasure in the midst of a present cultural void, as the mother's echoing voice reminds her.

Passing and the memorialization of aesthetics are at loggerheads in Plum Bun, with the former representing the false values and the material accoutrements of modernity in the form of sports cars, playboys, New York City apartments, and admittance into mainstream society. The Philadelphian community, in contrast, reflects a Negro culture driven by values of home and heart, in spite of its citizens' Jim Crow, second-class status in mainstream society. To appreciate the strategy of musical aesthetics that Fauset employs to bring Angela "home" and the role played by her dead mother, we need to look at the background that Fauset creates for Angela, one relevant to her family identity, and then discuss the phenomenon of passing in the early twentieth century and relate the racial proscription of the time to her desire to pass. A brief but extremely important scene of musical aesthetics in *Plum Bun* leads to Angela's regeneration, recalling Kant's aesthetic theory of art and morality.

Fauset's background of Angela's home life in Philadelphia is intended to illustrate the type of secure family from which she becomes detached in New York and to which she ultimately returns. A family of four, the Murrays live on Opal Street, and their lives revolve around the ritual of family, community, church, and the "awesome beauty" of music and the piano, which Angela's sister Virginia plays (25). Domestically the Murrays maintain and supersede Booker T. Washington's fundamental cultural values of practical aesthetic coherence, embedded in the immanence of family and stable economics. The father had been a "coachman," and the mother had worked as a "ladies' maid" and "dressmaker," but she retired upon marriage because her husband had worked his way up, financially. He buys a modern "Henry Ford, four-seater" (51), a house, and fashionable furniture, of which the Murray Chair becomes an heirloom—all examples of the family's rising economic status in modern society. Mattie, the wife, thought her husband "was God" (33), and she, Junius believed, was "a perfect woman, sweet, industrious, affectionate and illogical"—Fauset's facetious image of a condescending Victorian depiction of woman as helpless and yet as moral guide and companion, the domestic maternal ideal.

Typically Victorian but necessarily modern, the family shops—the white-skinned mother and Angela in fine, Jim Crow–segregated department stores. These stores are, of course, off-limits to blacks, so mother and daughter must "pass" for Caucasian. In passing for reasons of convenience, the mother did not mind: that is, until she is forced to ignore her husband, Junius, and her daughter Virginia on the streets. She then maternally warns Angela, "Life is more important than colour" (73, 333), meaning that they should be themselves even though they will no longer enjoy their freedom as "white women." Mrs. Murray's maternal advice, what Sara Ruddick identifies in another context as the "discipline of maternal thought,"[76] establishes one of the criteria for the mother being able to determine the success or failure for her children. Mrs. Murray's admonishment is also a social corrective to Angela, the errant daughter, who has taken the adventure of passing seriously because of the false freedom given to her and for which many light-skinned Negroes passed for white, a cultural phenomenon of the early twentieth century.

Indeed to avoid rabid Jim Crow strictures from 1900 to 1910, as many as twenty-five thousand Negroes passed for white.[77] It is estimated that during the period of the Harlem Renaissance between ten thousand and twenty thousand white-skinned Negroes crossed the color line annually.[78] Visual images of their bodies as "white" but their "true" identities as "black" demonstrated a guise of racial indulgence that had reached a peak form of fabrication in Fauset's and Larsen's era. Before the publication of *Plum Bun*, the NAACP's magazine *Crisis* editorialized in its

April 1915 issue that the concept of a biologically pure race, heralded at the time, was an accepted American racial myth,[79] as Harriet Jacobs queried and as Fauset dramatized in her novel over half a century later. That Jacobs and Fauset, having lived worlds apart, were protesting the same myth of biological and racial purity suggests that the concept of an American national bodily identity as conspicuously white was not to be hampered by facts. The historian Philip A. Klinkner remarks that despite the known fiction of race, "white Americans felt under relatively little pressure to end Jim Crow segregation in the 1920s"; this included President Warren G. Harding, who endorsed Jim Crow strictures but whose own racial heritage had always been questioned.[80] In the 1920 presidential campaign, the *New York Times* published a genealogy of candidate Warren G. Harding's family tree because of the racial "shadow" of his background. Harding had insisted that he was the descendant of a "blue-eyed stock from New England and Pennsylvania." Privately a somber, though flippant Harding whispered to a friend, "One of my ancestors may have jumped the fence."[81]

The biological racing of the body, which Larsen treats as a deadly social farce in *Passing,* is, in Fauset's hands, another opportunity to impart the wisdom of the maternal figure, represented by Angela's mother, whose "maternal instincts were sound" (16). After Angela's mother dies, her maternal advice becomes a narrative echo of the dead mother calling the lost daughter home from the "market." The novel's title alludes to the nursery rhyme "To Market, to Market / To buy a Plum Bun / Home again, Home again / Market is done." One can read "market" as Deborah McDowell and Ann duCille do, respectively, as a trope on black women's sexuality, in general, and Angela's free love experience in a "coupling convention"[82] with Roger Fielding, in particular. In duCille's and McDowell's feminist readings, the novel becomes one "brimming"[83] with sexual innuendoes and black female sexual desire, unhinging Angela from her maternal moorings. McDowell and duCille emphasize the sexual play on "bun" and Angela's sexed body as a locus of sexual desire. However, "market" also represents the larger, modern commercial world of Angela's passing interests.

Angela's light-skinned body is a metaphor of social coding and significance, "ready to receive, bear, and transmit meanings, messages, or signs, much like a system of writing."[84] When Angela recognizes the significance of the coded body and that what others believe one to be, one therefore is, she makes her decision to pass. She shares her new insight with her grieving but "lovely-bronze" colored sister Virginia: "It isn't being coloured that makes the difference; it's letting it be known" (78). Her body therefore becomes a surface on which race and identity are inscribed. "Why should I shut myself off from all the things I want most," she rationalizes; "clever people, people who do things, Art—travel and a lot of things which are in the world for everybody really, but which only white people, as far as I can see, get their hands on" (78, 46).

The language in which Fauset couches Angela's rationalization for passing is affective here, impressing upon her audience the real and practical disadvantages of the Jim Crow system that could cut Negroes off even from the visual, aesthetic beauty and pleasure of art and travel. As the white art student Angele Mory at New York's Cooper Union, Angela freely moves between both black and white worlds. But the dark-skinned art student Paulette Powell, who cannot pass, is limited in her contact and, in fact, has her fellowship to study abroad rescinded when an outside American committee discovers her racial identity. According to Cheryl Wall, Fauset bases this particular illustration of the anti-aesthetics of the Jim Crow system on a factual incident involving the dark-skinned sculptor Augusta Savage.[85] Savage studied sculpting at the Cooper Union and was awarded a fellowship to study in Fauset's beloved France in 1923. The fellowship, however, was rescinded when her racial identity was made known. In fusing fact and fiction in the Paulette Powell case, Fauset, on one hand, represents Angela's passing for white as an immoral thing to do and, on the other hand, makes readers sympathetic to her decision to pass, based on the real missed opportunities blacks faced.

For Angela, New York City, as a modern metropolis, has "jostling shops" of mass commercialism and "towering buildings [which] dwarf the importance of the people hurrying through its narrow confines" (87). Fauset's description of early twentieth-century architecture gives rise to Hal Foster's theory of the anti-aesthetic in art as that which emotionally distances the individual from history and subjective experience. Foster argues that the "anti-aesthetic" in modernism and postmodernism "signals that the very notion of the aesthetic, its network of ideas, is in question here." The query includes, for example, "the idea that aesthetic experience exists apart, without 'purpose,' [and] all but beyond history, or that art can now effect a world at once (inter)subjective, concrete and universal—a symbolic totality."[86] Art replaces lived, subjective experience.

While Angela has escaped the antiblack aesthetics of Jim Crow strictures in Philadelphia, in New York City she faces a different kind of danger, as Foster suggests in another context of the fantasy of modern creation: its design, as if in a vacuum, without the particularity of history, experience, value, and meaning. Similarly, Angela's passing, which she finds liberating, nevertheless deprives her of a particular point of reference, culturally and historically. As the white Angele Mory, she has no relatives, no family background, no history, personal or collective. As two opposing forces of authority, modernity's disrupting influence of materialism without specific cultural referentiality and Angela's mother's wise maternal advice are in a battle competing for Angela's soul. Though ignored, the wise mother offers to her daughter a resisting narrative of identity to the empty cultural production of modernism. Although Angela is tilted toward the New York world of dazzling "things," her imprecise diction stresses her imprecision of identity, hinting at the moral ambiguity or wrongs of her social compromise.

Fauset's dwarfing architectural motif of the individual in modern society reflects Angela's personal dilemma of having the freedom of expression but within an imprisoned body of pretensions. She hides her identity from Roger Fielding, who compromises her, refuses to marry her, but places her in an apartment as he moves through the city in a "blue car," a dazzling image of the modern single man. The playacting between the two ends when Fielding tires of her and brings a truth to a relationship based on fraud: "You knew perfectly well what you were letting yourself in for. Any woman would know it" (231). Perhaps McDowell has her strongest feminist reading of *Plum Bun* as a novel of sexual innuendo in her analysis of the tryst between Angela and Roger, the nature of their relationship, based on free love without marriage for him—a position compromising Angela's already embattled integrity. Fauset, posits McDowell, "capitalizes on the multivalent sexual implications of the title 'Plum Bun' [and] the suggestions in 'bun' or 'tail,' vulgar terms for sexual intercourse, [which] are clear, as are those in Roger's name, a noun for penis as well as a verb for copulation."[87]

Whether Fauset (whom Claude McKay and Arthur Huff Fauset, her half brother, described, respectively, as "prim" and a member of the "closed decorous circle of Negro society"[88] and who loathed coarseness of any kind) was consciously aware of her authorial Freudian inclination is a matter of conjecture. The tension in *Plum Bun,* though, is as much aesthetic as it is sexual. That is, Angela is caught in the middle of two culture wars: one modern and commercial, and antithetical to the interest of Negroes; and the other historically striving and determined to create a viable tradition and community through assertions of self-autonomy. Fauset describes Angela as becoming "Homesick," but "she hardly knew for what" (91), implying her dissatisfaction with her current life and her gradual remembrance of the cultural moorings of her home life. Her past, her family, and especially her mother loom in the background of her New York City experience.

She hears the voice of the wise maternal figure: "And once more her mother's dictum flashed into her mind. 'Life is more important than colour.' This, she told herself, was an omen, her mother was watching over her, guiding her" (266). The dead mother embodies the value of familial and cultural connection and the memorialization of the aesthetics of home: its rhythm, its music, its sound—all functioning as a narrative refrain, resounding in a brief but significant scene, ignored by Fauset critics. Walking on Fourteenth Avenue, Angela stops and gazes at the culturally diverse crowd. She then finds herself drifting to "those listening countenances usually at the playing of old Irish and Scottish tunes. She noticed then an acuter attitude of attention; the eyes took on a look of inwardness, of utter remoteness." Although the listeners were "varied" in number and ethnicity, they were all "*caught in a common, almost cosmic nostalgia*" (91, emphasis added). In this poignant setting, with instrumental music playing to a groundswell of the characters' emotions, Fauset illustrates the universal appeal of music in its ability to jar the memory and foster nostalgia for something of lost value such as home and the familiarity of what it represents. The fact that the music is instrumental, wordless and abstract, in its aesthetic appeal suggests Kant's idea of "free beauty." This is beauty freed from a fixed and determinate purpose and having the pure, unadulterated judgment of taste for each of its listeners, foreign and native.

Fauset uses this scene of musical aesthetics to imply the universal phenomenon of cultural homesickness and to relate Angela's alienation from her roots to that of the immigrants, living in a foreign land, which gets personal when one considers Fauset's decision to return to America after living in France. *Plum Bun's* characters' "cosmic nostalgia" for homes around the world in Scotland, in Ireland, in Philadelphia rests on the assumption of their cognitive sense of knowing and relating the heartstring sound of music to the distant, yet familiar echo of home. In listening to the music, they become transformed, emitting physical and psychological changes, evidenced by inward-looking eyes and transfixed bodies. That Fauset places Angela in a crowd of European immigrants whose perceived cultural foreignness in America is linked to that of a native-born Negro American passing for white suggests the author's strongest rebuke of passing Negroes. Fauset treats them as motherless aliens and orphans, as traitors, living in false bodies both inside the skin and in the Jim Crow public body of retrograded race relations, which by passing and denying her race, Angela unwittingly endorses.

Fauset's deft manipulation of musical aesthetics to reveal her characters' mixed emotions, their delight in hearing music, but their pain in reflecting on their alienation has the effect of showing how the memorialization of aesthetics can touch and influence lives, knowingly and morally. Based on her cognitive ability to listen, hear, and reflect, Angela is forced to apply the heartstrings of symphonic music to her felt loss and dislocation in New York City. Her problem now is no longer one of aesthetics and the juxtaposition of pain and pleasure, but rather one of morality. By passing for something that she is not, Angela becomes immoral, not only personally but also collectively, abetting a system whose privileging of whiteness is based on its fabricated pre-aesthetic and anti-aesthetic construction of color as offensive and undesirable.

Kant comments on the morality of art, which one can find implicit in Fauset's appropriation of instrumental music and its cognitive effect on Angela's emotions. In *The Critique of Judgement,* Kant remarks that the fine arts of culture, while being inferior to the free, natural, and purposeless beauty of nature, still has nature's superior capacity to appeal to "the play of our cognitive faculties," as opposed to our mere sensations of feelings.[89] The fine arts are "a mode of representation" that have "the effect of advancing the culture of the mental powers in the interests of social communication," writes Kant.[90] There can exist, then, a moral kinship between the fine arts and the individual's cognitive responsiveness to that which the arts awaken from its slumber. The indication here is that Angela is morally dead, but the music that she hears, her dead mother's echo, and her resulting cognitive reflection on the significance of its stirrings bring her closer to reversing her immoral decision to pass.

The memorialization of aesthetics in the music Angela hears has the effect of the wise maternal in that both serve as ethical guides in bringing Angela home. *Plum Bun* can be read, then, as a beckoning maternal narrative with the unethically dead daughter becoming spiritually reborn and returning to Philadelphia because she remembered its authentic cultural context of family and community. Angela's moral awakening, attributed to the power of the dead mother and musical aesthetics, is also linked to Paulette Powell's losing her scholarship, the final racial insult for Angela. "Because Miss Powell isn't going to France on the American Committee Fund . . . I'm not going either. And for the same reason. . . . I'm colored too" (347), she confesses to reporters and thus publicly retrieves her just balance. The novel concludes with the marriage plot: Virginia marries Matthew Henson, whom Fauset proudly names after the first black man to reach the North Pole; and Angela weds the dark and suffering art student Anthony Cross. But it is rather harsh to satirize Fauset, as Hazel Carby does, for "saving" her heroines from their hard-won autonomy. The marriage plot, like the home plot, is a part of Fauset's signature of empowering her characters with unique family backgrounds, education, and achievement as Adorno's afterimages of Negroes, representing their sense of overcoming Jim Crow hardships.

The Chinaberry Tree and the Maternal Sublime

The Chinaberry Tree represents Fauset's recurrent themes of historical black/white blood relations, inter/intraracism and class snobbery, the devastation and irony of black ostracism, and the Du Boisian aspiration and fight for black transcendence of racial barriers. The novel's major character, the half-white Laurentine Strange, is a fashionable dress designer who, like Maggie Ellersley and Joanna Marshall, emerges as another new image of the modern black woman. While Ann duCille stresses Fauset's aesthetics of fashion, placing it in the context of modern African American women's history and ancient African women's society,[91] the Chinaberry tree is the most important, maternal-like symbol in the novel, representing several ideas. Indeed the tree is as much a major "character" as is Laurentine Strange, the heroine. In multiple ways the tree unifies the themes, characters, and images in the book, so that the text can be perceived as coherent rather than chaotic although overwritten with many characters and themes, as critics complain about Fauset's overwrought plots. Yet the Chinaberry tree symbolizes Kant's aesthetics of "free beauty" and represents the transcendent sublime. Devoid of a preconditioned concept of beauty, free beauty exists, a priori, unrelated to an "interested" as opposed to a "disinterested" subjective purpose, though having a universal appeal as, for example, great varieties of beautiful flowers do but without any expressed political purpose.

Fauset describes the tree as having a calming, nurturing effect on the novel's troubled characters and relationships and having, like the memorialization of musical aesthetics in *Plum Bun*, a maternal function of guidance and protection. To summarize, the novel is centered on two incidents, the first of which is an old romance between the married, white Colonel Halloway and his mother's beautiful black maid, Sarah Strange. Their affair results in the birth of Laurentine, the "cursed" daughter of her parents' doubly illicit union, based on race and class barriers. Like her wayward mother, Laurentine is shunned in Red Brook, New Jersey, society. Before he dies, the colonel purchases a house for his ostracized lover and daughter and plants a Chinaberry tree in the yard. His equally banned daughter is educated as a dressmaker to wealthy white women and, later, affluent, colored doctors' wives, one of whom receives a pair of red lounging pajamas. As a designer, Laurentine refashions the image of black women from poor and hapless to stylish and sophisticated. Through her association with enlightened doctors' wives, Laurentine meets and marries the colored physician Dr. Denleigh and becomes one of the women "lifted," as Hazel Carby sharply asserts, "from the abyss of scandal and gossip" by "professional black men."[92]

The second major incident involves the possibly incestuous relationship between Judy Strange's (Sarah's sister) daughter, Melissa, and Malory Forten, her unknown half brother. Malory is the son of Judy's married lover with whom she briefly runs away, but she returns alone with the child, Melissa. Because the character Melissa believes she can identify her biological father as the man her mother married, she treats Laurentine with contempt, mimicking the class snobbery of the black social body, which, in turn, is set apart from the dominant white and national body. When the provincial townspeople, having withheld knowledge about the biological relationship between Melissa and Malory for most of the narrative, finally disclose their connection, the incestuous flirtation ends. Melissa marries Asshur, a "bronze hero" who attends "a good agricultural college" and plans to be a farmer, even though Melissa wishes "he was going to be a doctor" (75). She initially rejects Asshur for the greater-aspiring Malory Forten, the college student with the famous last name. Once more through characterization, Fauset conveys the Washington/Du Bois strategies for Negro social advancement on both an agricultural and a liberal level that she, conflictually, through Melissa's initial rejection of Asshur, contests but then concedes as a practical course of direction for Asshur.

Many critics describe *The Chinaberry Tree* as the weakest of Fauset's novels because of its overwrought plot involving miscegenation, adultery, and incest within a Victorian context of class snobbery and domestic relations. Robert Bone early reduced *The Chinaberry Tree* to a "novel about the first colored woman in New Jersey to wear lounging pajamas."[93] With his caricature Bone relegates the meaning of Fauset's aesthetics of fashion and beauty to something he finds artificial and meaningless. But he fails to see the significance of a colored dress designer placed in the illustrious tradition, as duCille remarks, of African women's "weaving and wrapping of cloth"[94] and developing a chic sense of exquisiteness and, not co-incidentally, the respect of self-autonomy. Like her aesthetics of color in her other two novels, Fauset's aesthetics of fashion and the sublime in *The Chinaberry Tree* affirm black existence and show a successful and cosmopolitan group of Negroes, collapsing the essentialist proscription of race and identity. In the foreword to the novel, Fauset announces one of her major narrative intents in presenting "something of the homelife of the colored American who is not pressed too hard by the Furies of Prejudice, Ignorance, and Economic Injustice" in Jim Crow America (ix).

In other words, except for their historical and racial banishment to the margins of society, Negroes, Fauset insists, are just like other people and must be seen and treated with the same sense of social justice. Through her characters' cultural advancement, Fauset asserts their civic equality. This was, however, a risky undertaking because in asserting the racial and cultural identicalness of Negroes to a white cultural hegemony, Fauset was also denying the permanent harmful effect of centuries of racism and discrimination that many blacks could never overcome, as Richard Wright's *Native Son* explosively clarifies. It is on this basis of Fauset's representation of successful Negroes that critics such as Barbara Christian criticize her for ignoring lower-class blacks' plight, although, as discussed in *There Is Confusion*, she does not ignore them but rather transforms them. Fauset's aesthetic program was, then, multilayered, even beyond her appropriation of various aesthetic philosophies from Kant's to Du Bois's. She creates vivid images of the racial wars menacing Negro characters but for whom she finds a way out.

One of Adorno's afterimages in *The Chinaberry Tree* is the tree, which represents numerous forms of transcendent beauty and is a stabilizing, maternal force for Fauset's characters such as Joanna Marshall in *There Is Confusion* and Mrs. Murray in *Plum Bun*. After the troubled and brooding character Melissa "sat under the Chinaberry Tree with Asshur," for example, "her weary mind suddenly [became] calm, her hurt heart, finding [a] balm" (81). What Fauset describes as a "balm" here expresses the moral purposiveness of the sublime. Kant distinguishes the sublime from the aesthetic pleasure of beauty in that the former does not require the kinds of labored discussions, relating to distinctions of beauty, free or dependent, that the latter does. Rather, the sublime presupposes an individual's "'susceptibility' to moral feelings,"[95] without any effort to induce these feelings, as we see with Fauset's Melissa merely sitting under the tree with Asshur and becoming reassured. There is a distinctive spiritual feature of Fauset's tree because it has the capacity to evoke feelings beyond human expression.

Aesthetically the Chinaberry tree is a true representation of Kant's free beauty, and in its referential symbolism it embodies an abiding and comforting maternal presence, protective of others with its "thick foliage" and "circular shadow" (16), like a caring mother leaning over her children. While no definite reason is given for the white Colonel Halloway's planting of the tree (thus the absence of the concept of dependent beauty), the tree's planting symbolizes the transcendent love he bore for his family's colored maid, Sarah, over the impediment of race and class. Before he dies he makes provisions to care for Sarah and their daughter, Laurentine, provisions obstructed by his legal white wife, although her daughters finance Laurentine's education as a dress designer, a tacit acknowledgment of their relationship.

Aside from its other identities, the Chinaberry tree mainly reflects Mother Nature and is the natural symbol of openness in a novel of secrets and deceptions. Sitting under the tree, individuals and couples are drawn to its maternally nourishing capacity because it personifies an image of beauty that resists the anti-aesthetics of oppression and repression, which are part of Red Brook's social reality. Although shunned by Red Brook black and white society, the symbolically named Strange mother and daughter "could not . . . leave this beauty, this calm, the promise of the Chinaberry Tree" (17). The ostracized and unmarried Laurentine "went out in the chilly night and sat for hours under the Chinaberry tree and sought answers to questions of the future" and "something very clean and sweet and bracing to rescue her soul from this welter" (13). As an indicator of her protection from something artificial and unreliable—for example, her relationship with Philip Hackett, who abandons her—Laurentine was "conscious . . . that she had never stood under the Chinaberry Tree with Philip Hackett" (61). After she marries Dr. Denleigh, Laurentine and her mother, Melissa, and Asshur sit under the tree, which is a "Temple" emanating "the immanence of God" (341).

With its capacity to extend its maternal and regenerative powers to those seeking its shelter, the tree further represents the morally redemptive function of art as opposed to the powers of negation in the larger mainstream society. We are reminded in this novel of the Jim Crow policy, again, as colored characters are forced to "sit in a special section [of movie theaters] reserved for their kind" (33). This particular description of Jim Crow segregation in public entertainment in *The Chinaberry Tree* reveals a near-totalizing asphyxiation of Negroes in the 1920s when we recall Fauset's depiction of other forms of discrimination in *There Is Confusion* and *Plum Bun*. In light of such anti-aesthetic images of blacks as personae non grata, Fauset's afterimage of the Chinaberry tree stands for what Adorno describes as the sublime "untouchability" of beauty in resistance to a daunting social reality. The tension between beauty and reality is resolved because "beauty establishes a sphere of untouchability," and works of beauty "become beautiful by the force of their opposition to what simply exists."[96]

Besides the tree and its green, leafy foliage, the novel is replete with the lushness of color, moving beyond the bodily panorama of white, bronze, tan, and the brown skin tones of Negroes. While Laurentine is light-skinned, she polishes and reddens her face with colorful "rouge" of "a beautiful flush." She wears a "smart, green felt hat" and a "green cloth coat with its high mink collar," and both "fitted so beautifully, so snugly" (35). Fauset's saturating the blushing and colorful Laurentine in the shade of green is suggestive of the heroine's partnership with Mother Nature, which shelters her. Gloria T. Hull famously complains, however, that Harlem Renaissance writers such as Fauset celebrated a wide-ranging aesthetics of color, but the "entire spectrum was still not as widely accepted in real life where the same old light-minded hierarchy operated."[97] Yet the variety of natural and aesthetic hues invoked by Fauset, Larsen, Hurston, and others in the Harlem Renaissance relayed their superior consciousness of color's rich variegation, even if the writers were still struggling with the deeply rooted and pre-aesthetic legacy of slavery and color, as Hull suggests. Indeed the color dynamic of Fauset's vast program was cataloged in Larsen's *Quicksand* in the variegated "dozen shades" of Negroes from "sooty black, shiny black, taupe, mahogany, bronze" to "copper, gold, orange, yellow, peach, ivory, pinky white, pastry white" (90). These writers were simply but also radically on the cutting edge of redefining color, the black body, and beauty in ways that had not been done so purposefully before.

Comedy, American Style: The Tragedy of Color Mania

In her introduction to *Comedy, American Style,* Thadious Davis cites the novel's contrasting critical assessments by William Stanley Braithwaite and Alain Locke to illustrate the early and intense debate about the value of Fauset's oeuvre. While Braithwaite thought that *Comedy* placed Fauset "in the front rank of American women novelists" along with Sara Orne Jewett, Edith Wharton, and Willa Cather, Locke cavalierly dismissed the novel. Locke thought that Fauset's "characterization" was "too close to type for the deepest conviction," her "style" too "mid-Victorian," and her "point of view fall[ing] into the sentimental hazard, missing the deep potential tragedy of the situation on the one hand, and its biting satire on the other."[98] When *Comedy* is read as a satire on the inversion of maternal nurturance, though, Locke's denunciation of Fauset as "missing the deep potential tragedy of the situation" can be seen as mistaken and Claude McKay's criticism of Locke as too "high handed,"[99] as rather precise, at least in this instance. Through the tragedy of the archetypal bad mother, Olivia Blanchard, Fauset allows racism and racial passing to reach their satirical but logical climax in the mother's destruction of family and self, showing the power, social and psychological, of Jim Crow politics.

As a single woman, the white-skinned Olivia keeps a boardinghouse near Harvard Square and eventually marries one of its promising medical students and moves to Philadelphia. After she marries the darker-skinned Christopher Cary, fretting about the color their children might take, she succeeds in "marrying her [light-skinned] daughter off" to a French professor, reinforcing the historicized notion of the sexualized black female body as an object of exchange. After slavery and during minstrel performances, white "men were routinely encouraged to indulge in fantasies"[100] about black women, a concept Fauset plays on in pairing Teresa with a little-known, white Frenchman of aristocratic appearance. He is impoverished but white and assumes, like the new Terese, a false social role. Of Olivia and Christopher's three children, Teresa, Christopher Jr., and Oliver, only Oliver cannot pass and is treated like a Filipino or Mexican butler when Olivia entertains her white friends. In the end Oliver commits suicide and Teresa has a miserable life in France. Christopher Jr., who refuses to pass, lives in harmony and marries the half-white Phebe Grant. He practices medicine with Christopher Sr., who forces Olivia into permanent exile in France.

In specific reference to Olivia's home, *Comedy, American Style* is satirically devoid of the memorialization of aesthetics found in *Plum Bun's* Murray home, with its musical aesthetics and maternal voice rescuing Angela. Rather, *Comedy* is in opposition to the caring maternal model established in *Plum Bun* and constructs in minstrel-like tradition the counterfeit nature of the maternal and race and gender as written on the body. In Eric Lott's *Love and Theft: Blackface Minstrelsy and the American Working Class*, Lott, citing David Roediger's term of minstrel shows as white "blackface-on-Black violence," posits that minstrel shows in the early twentieth century sought to negotiate "'imaginary' resolutions to intractable social conflicts."[101] The white body as a performing black body constructed images of Negroes as ingratiating and grinning "coons" and "darkies." While Lott cites the minstrel performances as "Janus-faced figures"[102] in their racial dualism of the body, demonstrating superior Anglo-American culture and gross primitivism, the black body-in-crisis was still the site of a market economy as it was in slavery.

With her creation of the Anglophiliac Olivia Blanchard, whose surname is linked to racial bleaching, Fauset tropes on the minstrel image of white-faced Negroes such as Olivia passing and validating the superiority of Anglo-Saxon heritage to the detriment of responsible maternal practice. As a discourse on the absurd, *Comedy* is perhaps Fauset's parting shot at the relentlessness of Jim Crow discrimination. Unlike her other three novels, *Comedy* extends Fauset's (il)logical depiction of race and color mania run amok, a grotesque realism of the anti-aesthetical "triumph" of the legacy of slavery as fostered in a rabid Jim Crow system that forces a mother to deny her own son. Within the context of a racist cultural tradition, Fauset appropriates and satirizes the pre-aesthetics of race and color as originated and established by slavery and offers a tragic reversal of racial uplift and the Victorian maternal ideal.

As the archetypal bad mother, Olivia Cary creates a home life marred by a cold deflection to the anti-aesthetics of maternity as well as race, which the young Oliver, Olivia's Janus-faced, darker self-loathing, and masculine namesake, recognizes. At home the mother fed Oliver "the same food, watched over and satisfied his physical welfare . . . [but] she never sought his company . . . took him riding or walking as she did the others, never bestowed on him more than the perfunctory kiss of salutation" (42). As another illustration of Olivia's maternal neglect, Fauset describes her home furnishings as indistinguishable from, let us imagine, the comfortable heirloom of the morris chair in *Plum Bun*. In contrast to Mrs. Murray's lovely home, Olivia's house is frequently "done over": furniture "intensely new and different and uncomfortable" would replace that considered old (43), one set of furniture distinguished from the other only by its newness. The memorialization of aesthetics regarding the home and nostalgia for what it represents applies only to the home life of the darker-skinned Marise, Teresa's former friend, whom Olivia denies because of her darkness, performing the work of Jim Crow authorities. While Teresa has no fondness for the home that Olivia refashions for the Cary family, she does recall Marise's home as "large" and "old-fashioned" and with plenty of "noise, laughing, singing, and romping as you pleased" (43). Teresa's recognition of the aesthetic joys of Marise's home life serves to illuminate the absence of aesthetic pleasures in her own.

Fauset's contrasting emphases on color and aesthetics of the dark-skinned Marise's and the light-skinned Teresa's homes are suggestive of Marise's family being more in tune with the cultural authenticity of Negroes than the falsely passing Negro family under Olivia's dereliction of maternal duty. Through Olivia's cold-hearted maternal detachment and rejection of traits traditionally linked to mothering and caring (such as warmth and nurturing), Fauset subverts the dominant Victorian paradigm of femininity, domesticity, and motherhood, permitting the self-destructive consequences of racism. *Comedy, American Style* subversively trumps the mother's power with that of the system's supraforce of command. Olivia's obsession with race, color, and materialism leads her to destroy the lives of most of her children, most notably Oliver. A sympathetic character if only because of her powerlessness before greater Jim Crow social forces, Olivia merely submits herself to a machinery of power regarding racial attitudes but suffers the predictable outcome. Due in part to the fraudulence of passing, white-skinned characters such as Olivia are engaged in a social drama of their own minstrel-making. While Fauset rescues Angela Murray from disaster, with her dead mother calling her "home," she allows Olivia Cary to become entangled in identity crises to depict the deep morass of race and passing.

Citing Fauset's earlier poem "La Vie C'est La Vie" as a heralding thematic of "matrilineal heritage, racial history, and women's lives and passions," Thadious Davis finds *Comedy* a blistering satire on race and maternity within the modernist environment in which Fauset was writing. Davis stresses Fauset's bourgeois emphasis on American modernity to suggest Olivia's overzealousness to be identified with mainstream culture and Negroes achieving a social status often denied to them. By "means of clothes, homes, cars, [college] degrees, jobs, furnishings, and travels of her characters," states Davis, Fauset reveals "that not all black people are rural,"[103] or illiterate, as whites performing in black-faced minstrel shows depicted.

However, *Comedy* is a tragedy of maternal failure, and rather than focusing only on Negro success, Fauset stresses the hazard of maternal failure in this particular instance. For example, through the characterization of Olivia's deadly maternal skills, Fauset broadens her critically representative portrayal of the maternal as all-wise and all-nurturing. As evidenced by her novels, Fauset's mothers are a study in contrast, from the nurturing Victorian maternal ideal in *There Is Confusion* and *Plum Bun* to the stereotypical image of the sexually "impure" and isolated mother and daughter in *The Chinaberry Tree* and the selfish, loveless mother in *Comedy, American Style*. Young Oliver's beautiful potential and aesthetic sensibility are indicated in his desire to be "a musician" of "music that told something" (193). Yet in the final analysis, Fauset suggests that his desire is not enough to combat an oppressive maternal force. In spite of feminists rebuking her for marrying off her heroines, Fauset appears to attribute the power of liberating lives to the feminine work of the progressive maternal figure, as represented, for example, by Mrs. Murray and the young and developing maternal figure Joanna Marshall.

Whereas the chaos of the rabid Jim Crow external social order is never allowed to penetrate the inner sanctum of the Marshall and Murray homes in the first two novels, the final two narratives reveal modernity's disturbing encroachment on the home and the physical maternal body. Although revived in *The Chinaberry Tree* by the omnipotent power of the tree, the troubled maternal in *Comedy* is left to its own faltering devices. Young, male, and therefore vulnerable, Oliver suffers from his mother's acting out the performance of whiteness; thus the child becomes Fauset's lasting symbol of the tragic consequences of maternal breakdown and the necessity of maternal wisdom. Yet Fauset's appropriation of the maternal body and maternal metaphors of empowerment is not nearly as extensive as Larsen's and Hurston's, perhaps due to the autobiographical nature of their novels.

Nella Larsen: Tragic Motherless Daughter

All the women writers previously discussed in *Maternal Metaphors* have been, ironically, motherless daughters: Phillis Wheatley, Harriet Jacobs, Charlotte Forten, and Jessie Fauset. While Wheatley was kidnapped into slavery and torn from her mother, Jacobs's, Forten's, and Fauset's mothers died when they were still quite young. All were reared lovingly and responsibly, however, by relatives and/or surrogate maternal figures, symbolizing a transcendent principle expressed in their literature. As can be seen in their writings and achievements, these women writers adopted authorial personas that perhaps assume the idealized power of the missing mother and that give voice to supportive maternal ethics of caregiving, both politically and personally. The deaths of their mothers may have forced motherlessness upon them, but a sustaining apotheosis of the dead and therefore ideal mother soon followed, as evidenced especially in Forten's diaries and Jacobs's slave narrative.

Unlike these writers, Nella Larsen experienced a different kind of motherless-ness because her white mother did not die but left her, due to the unrelenting pressure of Jim Crow racial caste. Born April 13, 1891, in Chicago to a Danish mother and a Danish West Indian father, Larsen experienced a traumatic isolation in childhood. In her quasi-autobiography *Quicksand,* Larsen's protagonist, Helga Crane, visiting Denmark, expresses an anger that the author perhaps felt. When the character of the Danish artist Herr Axel Olsen proposes to her, Helga declines, providing a mininarrative on race and maternal neglect that Larsen repeats in various guises throughout the text: "I couldn't marry a white man. . . . It's racial. Someday maybe you'll be glad. We can't tell, you know, if we were married, you might come to be ashamed of me, to hate me, to hate all dark people. My mother did that" (118). In Harlem, Helga expresses again the agony of her and presumably Larsen's birth and childhood: "Of that white world, so distant, so near, she asked only indifference. . . . Sinister folk, she considered them, who had stolen her birthright" (77).

Larsen scholars exploring Helga's mental and emotional confusion and attempt-ing to define the author's query "But just what did she want" (45) offer various explanations. Allison Berg remarks that by attempting and failing to live beyond the racing of her bodily identity, Helga "sinks instead into a maternal quicksand" of having multiple babies with an illiterate minister to stress her feelings of psychic entrapment. Through Helga's fatal "quicksand" maternity, Larsen presents mother-hood as a form of depletion for the artist in patriarchal society, says Berg.[104] Larsen caricatures Negro uplift through eugenics too, states Berg, as suggested by Helga's snobbish Naxos colleague James Vayle, who complains that "very few Negroes of the better class have children" (132). The European scholar Lena Ahlin argues that what Helga wants is what Larsen herself was after: "freedom from racial dis-crimination as well as for family and a sense of belonging,"[105] a search that neces-sitates Helga's journey to Europe away from Jim Crow America. Nevertheless, Ann Hostetler posits that in America, in Helga's inability to "find a cultural mirror that corresponds to her image of herself," Larsen "dared to explore the failure"[106] of Negro heroines, unlike Fauset, whose "light-skinned heroines"[107] often triumph over the system. But Hostetler plays down Fauset's Olivia Cary, whose overwhelm-ing failure at motherhood conflicts with the ideal aesthetic image of beauty, ma-ternity, and race and reflects Fauset's willingness to critique sad maternal figures. Helga's motherlessness and homelessness, not just her cultural aspirations, are at the center of her complications.

Thadious Davis explores the mystery surrounding the author's childhood with her family in America, specifically in Chicago, in regard to her light-skinned father's death, passing, or disappearance and her white mother's remarriage to a white man and the significance of the new marriage for the dark child, Nella. Davis remarks, "It is possible that Marie Larsen denied the child particularly if Peter Larsen no longer wanted the responsibility or the stigma of a stepdaughter of color."[108] In 1907 Larsen's mother traveled with her to Fisk University, where Nella was enrolled in the three-year high school preparatory program with only one year to complete. However, Davis finds that in spring 1908 the mother visited Larsen but shortly thereafter Marie Larsen left both Fisk and her family for good, disappearing from her daughter's life altogether.

When the lone but aspiring Larsen married the physicist Elmer Imes in 1919, writes Charles R. Larson, she "must have been the envy of many of her friends" because he "had a Ph.D. in physics . . . at a time when most black Americans had not graduated from high school."[109] Trained as a nurse, Larsen found another career with the coming of the Harlem Renaissance, from which she "derived a great amount of satisfaction."[110] Yet, Larsen's two novels reveal an irreconcilable striving to be reunited with her mother; before she died alone in New York in 1964, she attempted to contact her white half sister, Anna, who still denied her, although she later inherited Larsen's estate.[111] None of the other black women authors in this study shared the complex social context of mother-daughter relations that Nella Larsen experienced and that resulted in the maternal haunting in her novels of a mother and daughter separated because of the dictum of race.

Between the era of the 1960s and 1970s, miscegenation and the mulatto body still carried the stigma of lawlessness that Larsen and her mother must have faced in the 1890s and 1900s. Indeed in her second novel, *Passing*, Larsen's narrator, Irene Redfield, makes reference to the 1924 legal case of Leonard Kip Rhinelander, a white scion of Huguenot descent, and Alice Beatrice Jones, a mulatto who married him and was later sued for race deception. Jones was victorious because her attorney, having her strip to the waist before an all-white male jury, proved that her husband must have known her race as well as he knew her body, disproving Kip's father's claim of Jones's fraud. The Jim Crow culture of segregation had changed slowly over time. Indeed until the late 1960s miscegenation, as an anti-aesthetic assault against blacks, was still a crime in as many as seventeen American cities, primarily located in the South.[112] The Commonwealth of Virginia, for instance, did not abolish the anti-miscegenation laws until 1967, a result of the victorious *Richard and Mildred Loving v. Virginia* decision. In 1958 the white Richard Loving and his black American wife, Mildred, were arrested in Virginia for being married. To avoid incarceration, they moved to Washington, D.C., where the American Civil Liberties Union defended them in court.[113] Two generations later, in her Larsenesque novel *Caucasia*, Danzy Senna created a self-styled mulatto, Birdie Lee, whose white mother knows history and briskly informs her that her half-white body is "against the law" and "a federal offense."[114]

Probably absorbing the encumbrance of the "federal offense" of miscegenation in her own era, Larsen's abandoning mother married again, but this time within her "race." According to Thadious Davis, the mother listed only herself, her husband, and their all-white daughter, Anna, on the Cook County, Illinois, census records,[115] omitting Nella Larsen's name and identity. Without the colored child as bodily evidence of her breaking a Jim Crow and federal law and a racial and social taboo, Marie Larsen reentered mainstream society without the yoke of the child's raced body being linked maternally to hers. However, for Nella Larsen, a country obsessed with assessing the value of the body based on race had stolen her "birthright." In *Quicksand*, Larsen establishes the idea that the white mother was as much a victim of Jim Crow racism as she was but less tragically. "Her [Helga's] thoughts lingered with her mother long *dead* [emphasis added]," writes Larsen, a "fair Scandinavian girl in love with life, with love, with passion, dreaming, and risking all in one blind surrender" (56) and not fully appreciating the moral judgments she would incur and be unable to withstand emotionally.

Larsen subtly presents her mother, a foreign woman in America, as prey to its patriarchal legal system. In *Subjectivity, Identity, and the Body: Women's Autobiographical Practices in the Twentieth Century,* Sidonie Smith theorizes that subordinate women are "subject to man's authority and theorizing because, if unmanned and misaligned, she will subvert the body politic."[116] However, manned and aligned, the subordinate woman will resist "embracing encumbering identities in service to family, community, and country,"[117] an apt characterization for Larsen's portrayal of her mother. Thus, Larsen emerges as the permanent victim of racist, patriarchal laws of encumbrance living in the twilight zone of the mulatto, neither black nor white, perhaps leading to her miming and burlesquing both black and white societies as no other writer was capable of doing in her time. As a novelist, Larsen describes bourgeois Negro society as shallow and imitative and the white public as guilty of childhood larceny. While Du Bois praised Larsen's *Quicksand* because it met his criteria for a developing black aesthetics in articulating the Negro problem while communicating aspirations for unfettered existence, Larsen shows no real affinity with race. Indeed she caricatures too Booker T. Washington's practical aesthetic program of domesticity with her description of Helga's experience at the backward, Tuskegee-like southern college Naxos. Larsen stresses the "drab" existence of Negroes whom Helga personally "hated" just as she "loathed" too "the viciousness of white people" (38, 80).

Quicksand's Dialectical Aesthetics of Beauty and Tragedy

In her aesthetic strategy that rejects the public, antiblack context of race, Larsen, like Fauset, draws upon art, color, clothes, music, feminine maternal bodies, and home furnishings to modernize the image of the Negro woman. Her initial portrayal of Helga is elegantly poetic. Helga's body is slim and golden, and her "fragile stockings and underthings and the startling green and gold negligee dripp[ed] about on chairs and stool" (44), a scene resembling the unruffled "green freedom" of Wallace Stevens's poetic "Sunday Morning." Stevens's aesthetics of ambiance, consisting of the "Complacencies of the *peignoir,* and late / Coffee and oranges in a sunny chair,"[118] memorializes, in Adorno fashion, the calm afterglow of Sunday mornings. Unlike Fauset, Larsen establishes another articulation for her aesthetic reproduction. Her crafted sophistication is not totally related to Negro "uplift," as we see with Helga's decline and her critical assessment of uplifting Negroes such as the characters Anne Grey and Dr. Anderson. Although Du Bois praised *Quicksand* and Helga Crane as "typical of the new, honest, young fighting Negro woman,"[119] Larsen was more interested in divulging the cultural pretensions of racial solidarity and Negro disingenuousness.

Home furnishings in *Quicksand* are revealing of character and desire; for instance, Helga's strewn-about clothes on fashionable chairs are an indication of her beautifully languorous mood and aesthetic taste. Larsen's narrative description of Anne Grey's fashionably decorated home in Harlem, though, contrasts with the atmosphere of the lived life emitted from Helga's room. Looking around the interior of Anne's home, Helga catalogs the home furnishings belonging to Anne and to which she, Helga, is drawn because of her "aesthetic sense" (76). Yet Anne's beautiful home furnishings such as the "Duncan Phyfe, rare spindle-legged chairs" and the "lacquered jade-green settee with gleaming black satin cushions" are there as collectibles, still-life repositories for Anne. As a proud member of the black bourgeoisie in Harlem, the "brownly beautiful" Anne is dedicated to racial uplift activities and "hates" white people, but her possession of the Scottish-style Duncan Phyfe chairs, Eastern rugs, Chinese tea chests, and Japanese prints denies the racial reductionism that she otherwise embraces. Her hypocrisy of race is seen too in her preference for Pavlov over Florence Mills and John McCormack over Paul Robeson. While Anne professes love for blacks and subscribes to the "complaining" Negro magazines, she imitates the behavior of cultured whites and their gracious lifestyle.

The Scottish-finished Duncan Phyfe chairs in *Quicksand* recall the English-made morris chair in *Plum Bun* in their Europeanized aesthetic adornment of the occupants' homes. But Larsen and Fauset use these objects differently to convey a distinct sense of their characters: for Larsen, Anne's ostentatious character; and for Fauset, the Murrays' culturally enriching aspirations, coexisting with their deep cultural roots. Helga notices that Anne's aesthetic objects are there to be seen, as if on display in an art gallery, not in a life with a purpose. But in *Plum Bun* the morris chair is actually used and has a functional utility as well as an aesthetic sense of beauty and is a part of the daily lifestyle of the Murray family. Indeed, Angela Murray recalls her mother sitting gracefully in the chair.

Larsen appears to embrace Kant's distinction between the fine arts of beauty and the sublime, as opposed to the soulless arts that lack a "certain something that would make it [art] more than just an artificial version of a beautiful natural object."[120] For Fauset and Larsen scholars, herein lies a major difference between the two writers' aesthetic styles of soulful and soulless art reflecting cultural pretension, enrichment, or loss, though Addison Gayle indicts both writers for affecting Nordic cultural values. Fauset's rejection of "raced" cultural values has been pointed out, but Gayle's criticism that "no adoption of Nordic manners or expropriation of Nordic culture could change the way whites perceived them," as Negroes,[121] misses the mark for Larsen too, for Larsen appears to have contempt for the black bourgeoisie, and her narrative description of Anne Grey's home and character allows her to provide a subtle social commentary on the black elite's class affectation, which Gayle also ridiculed.

In like manner does Larsen appropriate musical aesthetics in *Quicksand*, critically aligning and yet distinguishing herself from Fauset again. Dvorak's New World Symphony is to Helga Crane what the instrumental composition is to *Plum Bun*'s immigrants and Angela Murray: a memorialization of aesthetics in regard to a nostalgic recognition of the loss of something of value and pleasure. In visiting America, Dvorak was drawn to the native music of Negro spirituals and thus composed his New World Symphony, influenced by the Negro soloist Harry Burleigh, one of his students at the National Conservatory in Boston. Dvorak defined Negro spirituals as "beautiful and varied" because they were genuine expressions of the "product of the soil" of America.[122] Written in four movements, the symphony has a luring, universal theme of homesickness, a musical motif, which the black American jazz pianist Art Tatum captured in his rendition and proceeded to rename "Goin' Home" in the folk dialect of Zora Neale Hurston's Negroes of the southern soil.

In the structuring of events that leads Helga to the moment when she attends a concert in Denmark and hears the "wailing symphonic undertones" of the New World sound, Larsen musically devises what Hayden White refers to as a "solution to a problem."[123] White remarks that "narrative might well be considered a solution to a problem of general human concern, namely, the problem of how to translate *knowing* into *telling*" in ways that are "generally human rather than culture-specific."[124] At the time that Helga hears the New World tune, Larsen writes, "Her definite decision to go was arrived at with almost bewildering suddenness. It was after a concert at which Dvorak's 'New World Symphony' had been wonderfully rendered. Those wailing undertones of 'Swing Low, Sweet Chariot' were too poignantly familiar. They struck into her longing heart and cut away her weakening defenses" (122). Given the repetition of Helga's experiencing "always a feeling of strangeness, of outsideness" (57), Larsen could very well have appropriated Dvořák's New World Symphony to reflect the tragic irony of the tune for Helga, a motherless daughter in Denmark away from America.

In structuring the narrative juxtaposition of Helga's hearing music that makes her long for "home" while revealing her actual spiritual/maternal "homelessness," Larsen articulates the social problems engineering Helga's lonely situation. Writing into the narrative the musical aesthetics of Dvorak's haunting symphony, Larsen *names* Helga's tragedy of homelessness in both America and Europe, at odds with the overview of scholars such as Paul Gilroy and Lena Ahlin, who write of African Americans searching and perhaps finding a sense of belonging in a freer Europe. Unlike Fauset's Angela Murray, who has a *home* to which she can return in the black community in Philadelphia, Helga has no such *home*, no such sense of belonging, in Europe or Jim Crow America and, most importantly, no mother, dead or alive, calling her *home* to the beautifully haunting sound of instrumental music, an expression of Kant's transcendent sublime. "I don't seem to fit here," Helga says of the Booker T. Washington–styled college, with the refrain of not belonging, which follows her to Chicago, Harlem, Copenhagen, Harlem again, and back to the South—there always being for her "a feeling of strangeness" (52, 57).

Her dead mother's brother rejects her after giving her money to travel to Denmark, but Helga turns away from those who try to assist her, with or without good reason. While she is visiting her uncle and maternal aunt in Copenhagen, Herr and Fru Dahl attempt to marry their beautiful niece off to the famous artist Axel Olsen, perhaps to increase their status. But Helga rejects their patronage and remembers a love for Negroes, whom she had previously despised. In Jim Crow America, Helga had earlier rebuffed Mrs. Hayes-Rore, a possible maternal surrogate whom she had encountered, but resisted the "lemony-yellow" and wealthy "race-woman" who can be likened to Anne Grey. Mrs. Hayes-Rore is a classic representative of the Negro bourgeoisie who loathes whites and thinks of race mingling and thus Helga's half-white body as "beyond definite discussion" (72), as if her body is not real. Helga could never find her niche, a problem that Thadious Davis traces to Larsen's missing white mother: "The paternal legacy that she carried out of Chicago was the emotional baggage of familial rejection and color consciousness, and her maternal legacy was emotional ambivalence toward women and African Americans."[125]

George Hutchinson, in *In Search of Nella Larsen: A Biography of the Color Line*, presents a hauntingly vivid and psychological portrait of Larsen in ways similar to Davis's. Nonetheless he argues with Davis's "facts" and interpretations, regarding especially Larsen's travels to Denmark, her remembrance of Danish children's games, and her relationship with her white mother and African Americans. He does not attribute, for example, Larsen's personal difficulties to the racial reductionism of whites and blacks, particularly in her dealings with her white mother. The biography repeats, in one chapter, Hutchinson's rebuke of Larsen's critics, primarily prominent women of color, who fail to appreciate her profound insight into the racial labyrinth, a motif "sublimated, even unwittingly repressed" in Larsen scholarship, which seeks to emphasize her maternal repudiation and the culture of segregation "against which she wrote."[126] He opines that the transcultural Larsen was better equipped than most writers of the Harlem Renaissance to critique race on both sides, black and white, and to offer a more incisive picture of its complexity. Psychologically and socially Hutchinson finds that Larsen renders race as a "modern, transnational racial labyrinth," signified in the naming of the Naxos

college after the island Naxos in Greek mythology where Ariadne is either left pregnant by Theseus or rescued by Dionysus. The abandonment motif is more fitting
for *Quicksand*. After sailing to Delos, Theseus instituted a "commemorative dance
known as Gernaos, 'the Crane,' after the bird whose movements resembled the
twistings and turnings of the Labyrinth,"[127] similar to the racial maze from which
Helga Crane cannot escape, urging another critic to declare her bodily entrapment.

According to Hutchinson, Larsen's scholars are too eager to denounce and kill
off the white mother and assail white racism in what he describes as their "critiques of the pigmentocracy and the ethics of black solidarity against racist oppression."[128] Larsen's work, if we follow his line of criticism, has been misread by
these critics who would limit themselves to a strict racial reading of *Quicksand* in
support of Larsen and against the racism and maternal abandonment she suffered.
But Hutchinson's criticism is reductive too, from a racialized perspective, and as a
result, he ignores some of the more acute observations that black feminists make
about Larsen's work and with which he agrees.

Thadious Davis, Claudia Tate, and Hazel Carby are among the black feminists
whom Hutchinson cites in the text and endnotes of "*Quicksand* and the Racial
Labyrinth" but who actually appear to read Larsen's texts *Quicksand* and *Passing*
as more racially complex than Hutchinson acknowledges. In her biography, *Nella
Larsen, Novelist of the Harlem Renaissance*, Davis not only cites the problem of maternal neglect for Larsen but also, like Hutchinson, criticizes the "class-conscious
circle of African Americans."[129] *Quicksand*'s black bourgeoisie at Naxos, in Chicago,
and in New York represents for Davis the intolerant circle of bourgeois Negroes
stressing family connections, as Fauset does in her novels, but who, in fact, made
Larsen feel and regret her homelessness.[130] Larsen's repetition of the word "home,"
ironically, in fact stresses her alter ego's rootlessness: "And, oddly enough, she
felt, too, that she had come home. She, Helga Crane, who had no home" (62–63).
Davis seems to understand, however, that as limited as Larsen's black bourgeois
characters are, the importance of family, money, education, and status (what Helga
superficially seeks) was appropriated in one instance as a form of overcompen-
sation for their racial discrimination, a point highlighted in Gunnar Myrdal's *An
American Dilemma*.[131] To overcompensate for their social ostracism, Myrdal notes,
Negroes of Fauset and Larsen's time relied on developing strategies of coherence as
a resistance to racial caste, stressing their accomplishments to gain self-respect and
control over their humiliatingly segregated lives.

In her reading of *Quicksand*, Claudia Tate notes Larsen's fictive and symbolic
killing off of the betraying white mother as suggested in Helga Crane's "fatal" child-
bearing. Tate's essay "Desire and Death in *Quicksand*," to which Hutchinson refers,
and her study *Psychoanalysis and Black Novels*, published a year after Hutchinson's critical essay, pronounce Helga's decision as "overdetermined" in rejecting
the white Olsen, "who stands as a surrogate for all those white people who have

rejected her."[132] Helga's brash decision, as both Hutchinson and Tate observe, collapses important distinctions between the novel's intolerant white Americans and the more urbane Europeans. En route to Denmark, the Scandinavian cursor invites Helga to eat with him on the steamer. Once in Denmark, the artist Olsen proposes to Helga, and her maternal aunt, who dresses her in exotic clothes, shoes, and earrings, acknowledges the beauty of her rich skin color. No white American was capable of treating Helga with that kind of civility, given the Jim Crow pressures they lived under and to which they succumbed, as Hutchinson argues and as Tate in her text agrees.

Carby, along with other feminist critics, advances theories of the sexed, black female body as a Western stereotypical image from which Helga recoils, repressing her sexuality before finally imploding. After her failed attempt to seduce Dr. Anderson, who marries Anne Grey, a dejected Helga marries Reverend Green, a "fattish yellow man" and southern minister. His dirty fingernails and unwashed "fat body" symbolize her fall and the anti-aesthetics of dirt that a rabid Jim Crow system associated with the perceived bodily contamination of Negroes, and that resulted perhaps in Booker T. Washington's overemphasis on cleanness in *Up from Slavery*. At the beginning the aesthetically driven Helga is presented in the cosmopolitan feminine image of Wallace Stevens's attractive heroine in "Sunday Morning," but she becomes an exotic body, perceptually in Europe and literally in America. Hutchinson cites Carby's displacing of Helga's female body from America to Europe as (in a paraphrase of Carby's description) an "issue of white fascination with the exotic and primitive during the Harlem Renaissance." Carby's theory suggests, Hutchinson argues, that the "phenomenon pertains more to white Europe's view of African Americans than to white America's—which is by no means a flattering observation to either side."[133]

But the discourse on the sexed and voyeuristic black female body before and during the Harlem Renaissance is not a question of flattery for white Americans and Europeans. It is rather a fact of historical record in a Western market economy: going back to Phillis Wheatley standing, youthfully, seminude on the Boston auction block; the Hottentot Venus, Sarah Baartman, displayed in museums in Paris and London; and Harriet Jacobs, chased around Dr. Flint/Norcom's southern plantation. Despite Hutchinson's protest, Carby's criticism has a valid historical context, even if limited to the Renaissance in Harlem. Carby's and Tate's discussions of Helga's sexuality place her in the pathological and sexual identity of black women's history for Carby but with issues of Freudian psychology for Tate, the latter being more problematic.

Helga's conflicted racial, sexual, and psychological desires are incisive reminders of the complexity of Larsen's devastating critique of racial socialization. But Tate is mistaken, I believe, in defining Helga's desire as finally "incestuous," as a longing for the missing black father rather than the abandoning white mother.[134] Tate opines that Helga remains incoherent until she resolves her feelings of desire for her father.[135] In her "sensual self-projection"[136] and seduction of Reverend Green, who displaces the lost father, Helga experiences "the 'rites of a remote obscure origin'" that Tate relates to the "obscure origin" of the Freudian "primal scene."[137] In this scene Helga relives "the horror," which "held" her and which Tate relates to a child's observation of the "spectacle of sexual intercourse between the parents."[138] In Tate's reading, Helga remembers the "primal scene" and "fantasizes" about sex with the father, replacing the mother and fulfilling a repressed yearning and "reinforc[ing] her meager self-esteem."[139] Tate's argument stresses the importance of the "daughter-father plot" and Helga's "identificatory love and desire for the father," a reading elevating the text's "unnamed father" and emphasizing the "ambivalence toward the lost mother."[140]

While Helga is seen as and even acts out the role of the oversexed primitive, her true desire is not sexual but rather is maternal. Helga wishes to return to the comfort and bodily warmth of the maternal womb, a place of natural primal safety before racist Western patriarchal law took hold of the mother and daughter bodies and separated them. Helga's bodily narcissism/dejection complex is rooted in what Julie Kristeva calls the symbolism of the "personal archeology"[141] of abjection, resulting from an unsuccessful attempt to release the hold of the maternal, a victim too of patriarchy. In Helga's yearning, the mother's body becomes what Kristeva refers to as "a lost territory" and a "fantasy"[142] in the "idealization of the relationship that binds"[143] mother and daughter. Helga briefly and sporadically idealizes her problematic relationship with the white mother whom she longs to retrieve. Although she ruminates on her father's life, as Tate asserts, and forgives him for abandoning her, her identification with him is based on her new understanding of the forced and "irresistible ties of race" (122), not on incestuous desire.

Furthermore, while Tate admits but dismisses the fact that Larsen never names Helga's father throughout the entire narrative, the significance of this detail cannot be denied. In Hayden White's language, the "impulse to rank events with respect to their significance for the culture or group that is writing its own history . . . makes a narrative representation of real events possible."[144] Critics have already agreed that Quicksand is Larsen's quasi-autobiography. The chronological ranking and thus significance of Helga's/Larsen's maternal and paternal experiences and the repetition of the words "mother" and "mother's death" confer an importance on the lost mother who is named while the missing father remains unnamed. The father is never named or identified and is, in fact, hardly mentioned. In contrast, the mother is named and singled out as "Karen Nilssen" (61)—no maternally ambiguous figure here. Through the memorialization of aesthetics, Helga idealizes the mother: "There was her mother whom she had loved from a distance and finally so scornfully blamed . . . appeared as she had always remembered her, unbelievably beautiful, young and remote" (155). The white mother is presented as someone who loved her colored daughter and tried to keep her, but whose maternal insistence resulted in "ugly scarifying quarrels" with the white stepfather (56), an example of Sidonie Smith's encumbering patriarchy saving a "misguided" woman. In Denmark, Helga's maternal aunt reminds her of her mother's love. "She wanted to keep you, she insisted on it, even over his protest, I think. She loved you so much, she said" (108).

To Helga, the absent mother is emotionally, if not physically, dead as she copes with her traumatic lost. Symbolically the mother is presented as dead several times: "Her mother's death" (57); "Miss Crane, a friend of mine whose mother's dead" (74); and "Helga had been relieved that Anne had never returned to the uncomfortable subject of her mother's death" (75). In Carolyn Dever's study *Death and the Mother from Dickens to Freud*, maternal absence or death is the primal loss for a child and is compensated, in Freudian analysis, by the *"fort-da* game."[145] This game functions as a compensation for maternal loss and attempts maternal replacement for the child. In playing the game of *"fort-da"* or "gone there," the motherless child identifies the mother's disappearance and protects her/himself with the "weapon of language, a concept suggestive for the rhetorical analysis of maternal loss in narrative fictions."[146]

In Larsen's narrative emphasis on the mother's rather than the father's death as the most important event in Helga's life, Larsen ranks, as White theorizes in another context, one of Helga's most important experiences and creates a therapeutic game of fixing the mother's position as dead and gone. Through Larsen's authorial repetition of the *"fort-da"* game, Helga, and perhaps the author herself, takes psychic refuge in the commonplaceness of the mother's death, as often as it is repeated and therefore becomes common and emotionally acceptable. Since Karen Nilssen's death is repeated throughout the text, Helga's attachment to her mother and her subsequent loss explain the poignancy of her unfulfilled desire. Thus, in marrying the minister, Helga attempts not to replace her lost father, as Tate argues, but to experience Allison Berg's "fatal maternity" with a twist. Becoming a mother, Helga relives the pain of her mother's leaving but supplants, in Adorno's aesthetic sense of afterimages, the painful image of maternal abandonment with one of maternal devotion and sacrifice. Although her body is emaciated from childbirth, Helga muses, "But to leave them would be a tearing agony, a rending of deepest fibers. She felt that through all the rest of her lifetime she would be hearing their cry of 'Mummy, Mummy, Mummy'" (161).

Here, George Hutchinson has his most poignant analysis of the novel and what he believes, correctly, that many feminists overlook: the twin motif of Helga's homelessness and her motherlessness. "Critics wishing for a different kind of feminist conclusion to the novel," he asserts, "have missed the tragedy and power of this scene." These feminists are "apparently unable to recognize that the voice Helga hears is her own, crying for the Danish mother that 'race' in America has stolen from her."[147] Larsen's loyal though weakened maternal imago recuperates the painful memory of maternal loss even if Helga's "long, slender body" (92), of a glamorous Sunday afterglow, is changed forever.

Passing: Motherhood, Maternal Obsession, and Racial Farce

Passing presents Larsen's acerbic critique of imperial Jim Crow social taboos even or especially in regard to marriage, a matter of the heart rather than the law. Larsen treats Jim Crow convention and light-skinned Negroes' subsequent passing as an absurd metaphysical farce of race. She shares Fauset's authorial disdain of racial passing, but rather than appropriate the memorialization of aesthetics to bring her character Clare Kendry "home," Larsen instead kills her off, highlighting the tragic folly of passing while also underscoring Clare's white husband's final recognition of their common humanity. Cheryl Wall incisively identifies the characters' frequent masking, laughing, and joking[148] and the absurdity of their choices and situations. But Wall does not relate these farcical characteristics to the genre of farce, as perhaps Larsen, as farceur, intends in farce's wild burlesquing and illumination of the illogicality of her characters' choices in their rabid Jim Crow society.

In her critique of *Passing,* Wall focuses on the psychic cost of the characters' masquerade, resulting in Clare's fears of being socially unmasked as a Negro and Irene's deviousness leading to Clare's fatal fall. Irene therefore, according to Wall, becomes a "psychological suicide, if not a murderer." Larsen's *Passing* reveals, Wall further asserts, the "psychological displacement experienced by middle-class black women"[149] in the rigid racial boundaries of the period. But *Passing* also emerges as another maternal narrative with an extreme inversion of Larsen's maternal neglect as seen in the character Irene's maternal obsession. *Passing* can be read most significantly as a racial farce. As Larsen's last novel, *Passing,* like Fauset's *Comedy,* reveals a more acerbic attitude toward race and her Jim Crow environment, one lamenting the unbroken domination of the social powers against the helplessness of the individual, by and large.

As farce, *Passing* has a strategic pattern of social masking and joking in one very important scene where Clare's racist husband berates interracial marriage before her and two passing Negroes. These two elements of farce, masking and joking, are apparent in *Quicksand* too, for example in Helga's conversation about her biracial identity with Mrs. Hayes-Rore, the proud race woman; both women "slipped on masks" (72) to avoid the discomfort of truth in the reality of miscegenation. In her refutation of Dr. Anderson's description of her as a "lady" of "dignity and breeding," Helga laughingly retorts that the "joke is on you . . . my father was a gambler who deserted my mother, a white immigrant" (72, 54–55), a farcical reversal of black bourgeois vanity, which Larsen loathed. These scattered incidents of a masking and burlesquing of truth in *Quicksand* reveal Larsen's initial impulse toward farce. Nevertheless they lack the sustaining social masquerade of jokes, laughter, and secrets found in one main scene in *Passing.*

In a brief overview of the plot, set in Chicago and New York, *Passing* brings together two childhood friends, Clare and Irene, who meet accidentally on the rooftop restaurant of the Jim Crow, Drayton hotel in Chicago and immediately begin to stare at each other, but not from recognition. In Chicago to visit her ailing father, the New Yorker, Irene Redfield, temporarily and conveniently passes for white to receive service at the hotel, as Larsen explores other kinds of passing, ranging from permanent passing to part-time and temporary passing. The novel's two heroines, Clare Kendry and Irene Redfield, are a study in contrast and represent different and extreme ideologies on race, desire, and motherhood—from reckless maternal carelessness to maternal overprotection and obsession.

Irene, the doting mother, experiences a sense of adventure and "aesthetic pleasure" from watching the "exquisite, golden, fragrant" Clare, the carefree mother who permanently passes for white and marries a white international banker. While Irene stays home with her two sons, Clare's daughter, Margery, is "left in Switzerland in schools" (233, 239), away from Clare, who believes "that being a mother is the cruelest thing in the world" (227), as much for the passing socialite mother as for her neglected daughter. Married to the "extremely good-looking" and "deep-copper" skinned physician Brian, the olive-skinned Irene passes, part-time or inadvertently, only for the temporary convenience of entering Jim Crow hotels and department stores or when she is mistaken for being white and can quickly get a taxi (213, 214).

Larsen's emphasis on the women's beauty and Irene's staring at Clare and being attracted to her has prompted two prominent scholars, Deborah McDowell and Judith Butler, to read *Passing* as a lesbian text. Moreover, Thadious Davis provides details of Larsen's New York City social life that lends support to McDowell's and Butler's readings, and another Harlem Renaissance critic describes in detail "Harlem's world of drag balls and gay night clubs," frequented by whites and blacks such as Carl Van Vechten and Bruce Nugent.[150] But Brian refers to "sex as a joke," not because he and Irene have a passionless marriage, as McDowell contends, but due to Larsen's caricature through Brian of Negroes trying to manage livable, normal lives of marriage, family, and professionalism in a suffocating Jim Crow milieu. The narrative clarifies that Irene knew that Brian "loved her, in his slightly undemonstrative way" (221), and Brian maintains a flippant attitude about virtually everything, sex included. Although he is a professional, Brian alludes sardonically to the theory of racial uplift and Du Bois's mantra for the "Talented Tenth": "Uplifting the brother's no easy job. Lord, how I hate sick people . . . their stupid, meddling families . . . smelly, dirty rooms, and climbing filthy steps in dark hallways" (217). His blasé attitude encompasses a range of life, and he desires to relocate to South America perhaps more for its racial tolerance than for its perceived sexual freedom for gay as well as straight people.

According to McDowell, Irene's "awakening sexual desire for Clare" begins at the Drayton hotel, and McDowell refers to Clare's subsequent letter/envelope to Irene as a "metaphoric vagina"[151] that Irene "hesitates to open," fearing that its "'contents would reveal' an 'attitude toward danger.'"[152] Butler too stresses Larsen's description of beauty and sex as hints at "what can and cannot be spoken" during the 1920s and "what can and cannot be publicly exposed," and critics following in the footsteps of McDowell and Butler comment on the "*reality* [emphasis added] of a homosexual longing between Clare and Irene."[153] In her biography of Larsen, Davis refers to the "lesbian undertone"[154] of *Passing* as viable, considering Larsen's relationship with a "literary and theater"[155] group in New York, who were open in their homosexual and bisexual behavior. Yet Davis posits further that other "attractions are at work" in Irene's "aesthetic attraction to whiteness: white values, white standards of beauty." As an illustration of these standards, Davis cites Clare's description as a "blond, pale, ivory" beauty.[156]

Irene, I would argue, is physically drawn to Clare at the Jim Crow hotel, but not to Clare's sexuality or whiteness. Rather, through the two women's scrutiny of each other, Larsen appears to be cryptically alluding to Jim Crow spotters in public places, which denied the admittance of Negroes. Jim Crow establishments often hired as spotters Negroes who were light-skinned enough to pass for white and could identify other passing Negroes to the unsuspecting white management. The passing Negroes were then asked to leave.[157] Irene could be staring at Clare because she believes she might be a spotter: "Very slowly she [Irene] looked around, and into the dark eyes of the woman in the green frock at the next table. But she evidently failed to realize that such intense interest as she was showing might be embarrassing. . . . it was Irene who was put out. Feeling her colour heighten under the continued inspection, she slid her eyes down" (178). Other lines in the novel are more revealing about Clare's possible identity as a Jim Crow spotter, rather than a lesbian prowler. Irene wonders, "Could that woman, somehow know that here before her very eyes on the roof of the Drayton sat a Negro" (178)? Larsen hints at white management's reasons for hiring Jim Crow spotters. "White people were so stupid about such things," her narrator voices, "for all that they usually asserted that they were able to tell; and by the most ridiculous means, finger-nails, palms of hands, shapes of ears, teeth, and other equally silly rot" (178). Details such as these are revealing of what spotters were looking for in identifying passing Negroes. Like Mark Twain in *Pudd'nhead Wilson,* Larsen critiques white supremacy's obsession with racial purity: down to the craft of palmistry as a racial determinate, causing Twain's passing Tom Driscoll to retort that "a man's own hand keeps a record of the deepest and fatalest secrets of his life."[158]

Aesthetically, Irene and Clare are two competitive women in self-fashioned worlds of beauty. It is not a "white" standard of beauty per se that attracts the stylish

Irene, who gathers Clare's letter in her aesthetically pleasing "black crepe de chine lap" (208), Larsen's emphasis on the exquisiteness of Irene's dress and taste. Discovering that Clare is not a spotter, Irene is attracted to the whole aesthetic package that Clare represents as an artistic production, as Lauren Berlant suggests.[159] The slender Clare is also described in postimpressionist imagery as a woman "sweetly scented" and "fluttering" in a "dress of green chiffon whose mingled pattern of narcissuses, jonquils, and hyacinths" recalled "chill spring days" (176). Clare resembles the visual transcendental experiences of beauty and taste in the "strict immanence of the spirit of artworks"[160] and afterimages. So Irene's attraction to Clare is largely aesthetic.

Although representative of two differing maternal types, Clare and Irene have similar aesthetic tastes and functions. Clare wears a red dress and red lipstick, and Irene Redfield's surname associates her, like Clare, with a self-made aesthetic world of passion and beauty that both women cultivate. A risk taker, Clare gives birth, confessing, "I nearly died of terror the whole nine months before Margery was born, for fear that she might be dark" (197). Through Clare's confession, Larsen illuminates the "black-baby myth,"[161] which is the fear of exposure that passing women of color felt during childbirth because "nobody wants a dark child" (197). While Clare believes motherhood to be "the cruelest thing in the world," Irene responds differently. Without apparent distaste, she remarks, "One of my boys is dark. . . . We mothers are all responsible for the security and happiness of our children. . . . I take being a mother rather seriously. I *am* wrapped up in my boys and the running of my house" (227, 228, 240).

Irene's boys' gender ("the mother of sons, too!"), though exclaimed, makes her job that much more cumbersome. Larsen expresses this in *Quicksand* as well, when Helga initially refuses marriage and motherhood because they provide only "more dark bodies for mobs to lynch" (104). The historian Leon F. Litwack relates the story of Negro soldiers in 1917 going off to military camp while "hoisting banners that read 'Do Not Lynch Our Relatives While We Are Gone,'"[162] attesting to real concerns in Larsen's historical fiction in the 1920s. In *Passing*, Larsen's Irene therefore becomes overprotective of her sons regarding their premature awareness of sex and their overhearing conversations about lynching and "learning the word 'nigger'" (263). Maternally intent on protecting her children, Irene informs Brian that he is "not to talk to them about the race problem." Her emphasis on maternal ethics in fostering the growth of her two boys shields them from what she perceives as racial knowledge threatening their security. Jim Crow society forced on Irene an exaggerated response to motherhood, but the nonmaternal Clare compliments the obsessively maternal Irene, "I haven't any proper morals or sense of duty, as you have" (240). Despite Irene's maternal zealousness, Larsen theorizes motherhood as moral obligation, not mere biological imperative, which is another dim reminder of her childhood.

As farceur, Larsen appropriates the style and value of farce in her characters' performances of race to (un)mask social identity constructions and the blurring of race and identity. Because Larsen was personally aware of the dissembling pressure of society for Negroes, based on the notion of their race as fixed and immutable, she employs in this narrative on passing the style of farce that goes "in its depth," Eric Bentley avers, "right at things" in its "unmediated vision."[163] That is, farce allows Larsen to get closer to the truth of the illogicality of her Jim Crow times through a miming and mocking of truth and logic. One of the most vivid scenes in *Passing* where the farce-plot of the absurd, masquerade and social masking, and laughing and joking all come together coherently and merge into a farcical tour de force is when Clare, her white husband, Jack, and the passing Irene and Gertrude discuss race. They are in an elegant Jim Crow hotel off-limit to Negroes.

The drama of this racial farce scene is somewhat masked and subdued by Clare and Jack Bellew's aesthetically pleasing and posh, blue-draped Morgan hotel room in Chicago, the ambience of which invokes an air of romanticism, cloaking the tragedy that lies beneath the surface. Clare's husband, the white Jack Bellew, calls his wife "Nig" because as she ages her skin darkens, and he adds, "I tell her if she don't look out she'll wake up one of these days and find she's turned into a nigger" (201). After the "joke," Bellew "roared with laughter"; Gertrude "added her shrill one"; and Irene "gave way to gales of laughter." The laughter at the "joke" of Clare being a Negro springs from its essential closeness to the truth as well as the three women's knowledge of Irene's and Gertrude's true identities. Clare, assuming self-agency by masking her otherwise hated Negro identity, confidently "handed her husband his tea and laid her hand on his arm with an affectionate little gesture" (201), mocking his hatred of Negroes, his unsuspecting explanation of her color.

Characterized as going "right at things," Larsen's racial farce imitates but inverts the socially constructed hierarchy of race, as her characters mask and conceal a secret. The author then forces laughter from three of the four characters who know the "secret" and thus see the real "joke." A braggadocio, Bellew, a play on the word "bellow," meaning loud and hollow, emerges as the butt of his own racist joke, though he boasts, "I know you're no nigger, so it's all right. You can get as black as you please . . . since I know you're no nigger. I draw the line at that. No niggers in my family" (201). With their forced and continued laughter, Larsen infuses her black characters' uneasiness not only with the throb of felt racial subterfuge, but also with the knowledge of the desperate and precarious nature of the truth. Irene is keenly aware of the danger in Clare's home and resents it. The situation was "absurd, her reason told her as she accepted Bellew's proffered light for her cigarette" (201).

While farce elicits laughter from the masked Clare, who is breaking a Jim Crow law as well as a social taboo, farce can also turn into tragedy, as it apparently does with her. Traditionally farce maintained an "unwritten contract between *farceurs* and their audiences . . . that the characters will" ultimately "come out of their ordeals unscathed, because the audience must be permitted to laugh." However, Albert Bermel remarks that "the contract has undergone revision," and death "has become a legitimate subject for farce," with characters dying and coming back to life or their deaths farcically enacted.[164] Larsen adopts this last enactment of a real but theatrical performance of tragedy, resulting in Clare's tragic fall and death. In appropriating the dialectic aesthetics of truth and falsehood in beauty images, Larsen turns the farce of sophisticated banter into a farce of tragedy. Returning to Harlem to attend Irene's Negro Welfare League party, Clare falls to her death. When Bellew, suspicious of her identity after he "spots" the nonpassing Irene with a visibly colored woman, follows and confronts her, Clare "got up from her chair, backing a little from his approach" (271). Whether Clare falls or is pushed from the window, plunging to her death, Larsen does not make clear, but the image of Clare's body falling and shattering signifies the antiblack aesthetic horror of Jim Crow laws and social attitudes and their fatal outcome. Larsen does clarify Bellew's heartfelt "agony" (like Helga's white mother's pain) and Irene's "shaking body," with both conveying a network of meaning regarding patriarchal laws and human desire.

Larsen creates a visual and rhetorical finale that mocks Clare's and Irene's self-ish or altruistic, incorrect or correct maternal efforts, relating character dissembling not to the women's psychic state but to the larger and unreasonable world of the Jim Crow legal system. In the grief of Clare's exposure and death, the social critic/author Larsen places real-life judgment against the lies of society and its larger fabrication of the essentialism of race and identity. In a sense, Clare's passing for white is a parody of society's racing the body, but to her benefit, more or less. Jim Crow strictures force Clare to mimic the deadly social game of racing the body and falsifying biological identity. Although consumed by irrational thoughts of losing Brian to Clare, as Cheryl Wall suggests, the maternal Irene does not cause Clare's death: Jim Crow America does—just as it takes Helga Crane's mother away from her.

In *Passing*, Larsen redefines the trope of racial passing, unmasking society as a learned social game of behavior, stripped of its pretentious order and harmony. The character Irene comes to regret her complicity in Clare's racial deception and her denial of affiliation with a race that she proudly embraces. Irene, Gertrude, and Gertrude's white husband, who knows her race and hides her secret, all wear social masks, playing the game of race in America. Their social masking and Gertrude's husband's complicity indicate, as Jacquelyn McLendon theorizes, that "passing" does not only relate to the body; it also connotes a "state of mind,"[165] influenced by society. Masked bodies within the larger social masking of mainstream society are then complicit and "coterminous with the cognitive mask [of the individual and society] that structures how we perceive both the world in general and our social interaction within that world."[166]

The crime of interracial marriage fictively treated in *Passing* was factually pronounced in the sensational case involving Kip Rhinelander and Alice Beatrice Jones. The Rhinelander case, which Larsen obviously followed, held a special poignancy for her, perhaps more than for any other Harlem Renaissance writer. In reflecting on Jack Bellew's possibly divorcing Clare before her death, Irene refers to the legal precedence of racial deceit by noting, "There was the Rhinelander case" (261). In *Love on Trial: An American Scandal in Black and White,* Earl Lewis and Heidi Ardizzone describe Alice Beatrice Jones's forced disrobing before a jury that was hearing her white husband's case against her of race fraud. Jones's white male attorney insisted that she "show the jury her legs and torso to prove that her race was obvious [to her white husband] in her physical appearance,"[167] her body being more clearly colored than perhaps her face because of cosmetics. In a repeat of the youthful Phillis Wheatley's dissembling at a slave auction in 1761, Jones's mature body also became an exhibit in 1924, though for different reasons. The Wheatley-Jones bodily exploration from the colonial period to the modern era marks the long arm of patriarchal law in its manipulation of the black female body: a site of exploitation and voyeurism.

Jones wept at her disrobing even though the white male jury ruled in favor of her voyeuristic bodily evidence. Attorney Davis concluded that "had it not been for the public inspection that put their love on trial, the two might well still be married and out of the public's view."[168] Jones's white English mother lived with her, her dark English-Caribbean husband, and two additional mulatto daughters. The mother, who loyally attended the trial, was attacked for breaking the racial taboo of miscegenation, even though it is doubtful if her husband had ever considered himself a Negro or subscribed to America's racial definitions. Ever vigilant, Du Bois followed the case and commented that "if Rhinelander had used this girl as concubine or prostitute, white America would have raised no word of protest. . . . It is when he legally and decently marries the girl that all Hell breaks loose and literally tears the pair apart."[169]

It is difficult to know precisely how the Rhinelander case influenced Larsen's writing of *Passing.* Both are tales of the public spectacle made of interracial marriage in the 1920s, although it can be argued that the fictive Bellew had no knowledge of Clare's colored identity. Despite Jim Crow laws, his emotional unraveling —"Nig! My God! Nig!" (271)—implies his love for his wife and the tragedy of a legal system that dictates human feelings with a predictable tragic outcome. Both the Rhinelander case and *Passing* add to the exhibition made of interracial marriage, the iconic value of motherhood, marred also by racism for Alice Beatrice Jones's mother and fictively for Clare and Irene even though both women took separate, yet drastic approaches to maternity. *Quicksand*'s Helga suffers from marriage and motherhood too but differently. Her perplexing marriage to the uneducated Reverend Green, with whom she has five babies, can be read as a farcical tour de force, but of the elitist pretensions of the black bourgeoisie and the argument for eugenics, made by James Vayle. In free, indirect discourse, Larsen's omnipotent narrator foretells Helga's fall, due largely to the "accumulated unreason in which all values were distorted or else ceased to exist," as Larsen has her narrator caution (39). The farcical elements of the Rhinelander case were perhaps related to a distortion of values: seen through the prism of societal logic, held up to ridicule in Larsen's novels.

Although Larsen's untidy endings in *Passing* and *Quicksand* are bothersome to her critics, they are necessarily farcical. This is, I submit, her authorial signature too, because farce allows her to assault through laughter and tears that which is viewed as logical, legal, and rational in a period that was irrational, barring blacks not only from the aesthetic pleasure of art, as Fauset reveals, but also from the necessary places of hospitals, theaters, parks, hotels, and so forth. As Jessica Milner Davis avers, "Farce enshrines the element of unreason" and provides a "release from rationality,"[170] although violently in Larsen's texts. Her unfortunate family background and the sharply aggressive nature of farce, especially in *Passing,* simply did not permit the kind of romantic and balanced endings of, say, Jessie Fauset's primarily wholesome narratives.

Zora Neale Hurston: The Local Colorist of Folk-Village Aesthetics

Born in Notasulga, Alabama, in 1891, Hurston moved with her family to Eatonville, Florida, an all-black community that had been incorporated as an independent town in 1887. Hurston biographers Valerie Boyd and Robert Hemenway note the impact that the fruitful history of Eatonville had on her developing consciousness and the healthy racial ethnocentrism that she took with her when she left. Boyd relates the founding of Eatonville to Booker T. Washington's self-help philosophy as "Negroes are made to feel the responsibilities of citizenship in ways they cannot be made to feel them elsewhere . . . [;] they have an opportunity to discover themselves" because "racism was no excuse for failure."[171] Washington's practical aesthetic program, in its simplest demand on the domestic, was unquestionably more suited to the fiction of Hurston than to either Fauset or Larsen.

As a Harlem Renaissance writer, Hurston felt a duty to distinguish the Eatonville folk from the cosmopolitan characters found in Fauset's and Larsen's fiction as well as the typically disparaging portrayal of Negroes in Jim Crow society. "Zora Hurston searched hard for a way to transfer the life of the people, the folk ethos," writes Robert Hemenway, "into the accepted modes of formalized fiction. She knew the folkloric context better than any of her contemporaries."[172] Through the genre of local color, Hurston found a way to emphasize the village aesthetic of folk characters, imbibed with Booker T. Washington's bootstrap teachings of the respectability of domestic life and labor. Unlike Fauset's and Larsen's characters, Hurston's characters are not physicians or attorneys but rather carpenters and day laborers, projecting an aesthetic realism of folklife for which Hurston was early criticized.

Richard Wright and Ralph Ellison thought that her "black-minstrel"[173] characters humored a patronizing white audience. But Alice Walker celebrated Hurston, the foremother of black feminist writers, and had a monument erected at the site of her burial in a Jim Crow potter's field in Fort Pierce, Florida. Hence, Hurston stirs emotions on both sides. While Hurston has been described alternately as minstrel, anthropologist and ethnographer, voodoo priestess, feminist, and folklorist, her real significance as a writer of folk aesthetics is best summarized by Robert Hemenway: "Zora was concerned less with the tactics of racial uplift than with the unexamined prejudice of American social science. She became a folklorist at a time when white sociologists were obsessed with what they thought was pathology in black behavior, and when the discipline of anthropology used a research model that identified black people as suffering from cultural deprivation. Hurston's folklore collection refuted these stereotypes by celebrating the distinctiveness of traditional black culture, and her scholarship is now recognized by revisionist scientists questioning the racial assumptions of modern cultural theory."[174]

In Hurston's emphasis on Negro dialect and humor, geography and setting, culture and social customs, folk aesthetics are linked to the tradition of local color. Because the Eatonville villagers were the models for Hurston's factual and fictive folksy, cultural richness, I find that she emerges most clearly as something that few critics, with the exception of Robert Bone, have written about significantly: a local colorist of folk-village aesthetics. Bone avers that Hurston "reverted to her folk tradition as a moral touchstone. That is what accounts for her impassioned defense of black folk culture: its pungent language; its flair for storytelling; its hoodoo magic." In her oeuvre, Bone opines, Hurston "insists on the vernacular, refusing to forgo the common speech, just because she is a graduate of Barnard."[175]

Local color as a genre and technique emerged after the Civil War in 1868 with Bret Harte's "fresh pictures of California mining camps." But nineteenth-century manifestations of local color often painted a rather shallow, genteel picture of life.[176] Local color as a concept has undergone, however, considerable changes because of writers such as Mark Twain, William Faulkner, Eudora Welty, and Zora Neale Hurston, eminent local colorists capturing the distinctive quality of southern life. Critics now acknowledge the national or even universal dimensions and implications of regional literature and see it as echoing certain moral and historical truths about our humanity. In his classic compilation *The Local Colorists,* Claude Simpson cites Hamlin Garland's famous announcement that "only a native is equipped to write successful local fiction" because of the "depth of understanding necessary for more than a superficial view of picturesque oddities." In creating "the illusion of an indigenous little world,"[177] the local colorist captures not only the sounds and sights of the region, but also the people's mannerisms, mind-set, dialect, and most significantly, mode of living. The local-color writer describes the day-to-day existence that distinguishes one cultural group of people from another in their approach to living lives subtly influenced by social milieu and physical landscape.

Early in life Hurston recognized the importance of her luxurious Florida land-scape. In her autobiography, *Dust Tracks on the Road* (1942), she describes her home and the natural aesthetics of beauty surrounding it. These included two big Chinaberry trees; Cape Jasmine bushes with hundreds of "fleshy, white fragrant blooms"; fruit trees of guavas, grapefruits, oranges, and tangerines; and fish in the surrounding Florida lakes. Hurston describes Eatonville as a "city of five lakes, three croquet courts, three hundred brown skins, three hundred good swimmers ... two schools and no jail house,"[178] a black utopia. It is a place where the villagers gather at Joe Clarke's store porch to tell tall tales (what Hurston jovially refers to as "lies") on a daily basis. Because of these wildly told stories, Hurston writes that the store porch was the most interesting place "I could think of. I was not allowed to sit around, naturally. But, I would and did drag my feet going in and out, when-ever I was sent there for something, to allow whatever was being said to hang in my ear."[179]

Florida's rich topography, the Eatonville community, and Joe Clarke's store porch are permanent, village-aesthetic features in Hurston's local-colorist works. From living in an all-black town to attending an all-black school to inheriting an all-black oral tradition, Hurston revives her cultural upbringing. When she writes in "How It Feels to Be Colored Me" that she is not "tragically colored" and does not belong to the "sobbing school of Negrohood who hold[s] that Nature somehow has given them a ... dirty deal,"[180] we look to the proud heritage of the Eatonville village to appreciate her pride. This folk inheritance of racial pride was no easy feat in the Jim Crow decades when people of color were made to feel their apartness from the rest of humanity in a Herrenvolk democracy of master and subordinate groups.

This illustrious heritage did not make Hurston immune to Jim Crow antag-onism. In her essay "My Most Humiliating Jim Crow Experience," she details a painful personal narrative of Jim Crow medical practices. Hurston's white patron, Charlotte Osgood Mason, had made an appointment for the ailing writer with a white Brooklyn specialist, obviously failing to mention Hurston's color. When Hurston arrived at the doctor's office, he was "very unhappy" to see her and di-rected his nurse to take her to a private room, which she identified as the linen closet with "a pile of soiled linen." After the hurried examination, Hurston "got up, set my hat at a reckless angle and walked out, telling him that I would send him a check, which I never did." Despite her humiliation, Hurston writes, "I went away feeling the pathos of Anglo-Saxon civilization. . . . I know that anything with such a false foundation cannot last. Whom the gods would destroy, they first make mad."[181] Hurston articulates a desire to revolt against a system that had attempted to demoralize her, demonstrating what Samira Kawash describes as the stormy "cosmic upset" in *Their Eyes Were Watching God*, when Hurston uses natural forces to destroy the social order, which she then re-creates and from which a regenerated Janie Crawford emerges.

Undefeated by racism, Hurston emerges as a local colorist of folk aesthetics, influenced by the Columbia University scholar and anthropologist Franz Boas, a German émigré. Like Horace Kallen, another immigrant, Boas believed in a theory of the developing, American melting pot of diversity, but unlike Kallen, Boas viewed Negroes as making a distinctive contribution to the melting pot because of the authenticity of Negro folklife. He encouraged Hurston as a Barnard college student to develop the anthropological tools required to return to Eatonville to collect and study the rich folk material produced spontaneously on Joe Clarke's store porch. Boas also questioned the theory of Anglo-Saxon superiority in the early twentieth century, positing that it is "hardly possible to predict what would be the achievement of the Negro if he [or she] were able to live with Whites on absolutely equal terms."[182] Boas's observation was radical for his time because not only did he question blacks' Jim Crow second-class citizenship, but he also went further to suggest the unfairness of an American society that attempted to arrest the cultural development of its members.

Boas and Hurston knew that unlike black northerners, black southerners had retained, as Charlotte Forten recorded in her journals, distinct Africanisms, due to the rigidity of a southern antebellum and postbellum racial system, which kept whites and blacks separated. Hurston's return to the South and Florida was essential to her development as ethnographer/novelist of local culture, to her legacy as a precursor of Afrocentric scholars, causing a Hurston scholar to suggest that readers often feel an "intimacy" with her that is not felt with Fauset and Larsen. This is due to a "combination of [Hurston's] narrative, ethnographic, epistolary, critical, and biographical discourse."[183] Influenced by Boas as well as her rich racial heritage in Eatonville, Hurston was impatient to return home. In *Mules and Men* (1935), written before but published after *Jonah's Gourd Vine* (1934), Hurston writes, "I hurried back to Eatonville because I knew that the town was full of material and that I could get it without hurt, harm or danger. . . . As I crossed the Maitland-Eatonville township line, I could see a group on the store porch. I was delighted."[184]

"Gold's Folktale": Female Emergence in the Realm of Patriarchy

One of the folktales Hurston retells is a curious blend of the villagers' healthy racial ethnocentrism, rooted and nurtured in a region that appears lovely but primeval, with their hilarious racial stereotyping. Gold, the narrator of this tale from *Mules and Men*, is a bold, big-boned woman who enters the male-dominated sanctuary of Joe Clarke's porch to tell the story of how God "gave out color":

one day He said, "Tomorrow morning, at seven o'clock sharp, I aim to give out color. Everybody be here on time. I got plenty of creating to do tomorrow, and I want to give out this color and get it over wid. Everybody be 'round de throne at seven o'clock tomorrow morning." So next morn-ing at seven o'clock, God was sitting on His throne with His big crown on His head. . . . Great multitudes was standing around the throne waiting to get their color. God sat up. . . . looked west, and He looked north and He looked Australia, and blazing worlds were falling off His teeth. So He looked over to His left and moved His hands over a crowd and said, "You's yellow people." . . . He looked at another crowd . . . and said, "You's red folks!" . . . He looked towards the center and moved His hand over another crowd and said, "You's white folks!" . . . Then God looked way over to the right and said, "Look here, Gabriel, I miss a lot of multitudes from around the throne this morning." . . . Gabriel run off and started to hunt-ing around. Way after while, he found the missing multitudes lying around on the grass by the Sea of Life, fast asleep. So Gabriel woke them up and told them . . . "Old Maker is might wore out from waiting. Fool with Him and He won't give out no more color!" . . . they all jumped up and went running towards the throne, hollering, "Give us our color! We want our color! We got just as much right to color as anybody else." . . . [they were] pushing and shoving. . . . God said, "Here! Here! Git back!" . . . they misunderstood Him, and thought He said, "Git black!" So they just got black, and kept the thing-a-going![185]

In this tale Hurston blends the aesthetics of laughter, joy, and humor of the common folk, their grouplike ethos and self-determining posture, far away from the shadow of the dominant, Jim Crow gaze. Through humor Hurston has the towering-feminist Gold, representing maternal omnipotence, deflect the tragedy of racism by visualizing blacks as complicit in the "crime" of their color. In *The Ideology of the Aesthetic,* Terry Eagleton remarks that Freud thought of humor as "a kind of triumph of narcissism, whereby the ego refuses to be distressed by the provocations of reality in a victorious assertion of its invulnerability." Freud be-lieved that humor had the capacity to transform an otherwise "threatening world into an occasion for pleasure; and to this extent it resembles nothing as much as the classical sublime."[186] Hurston's practical aesthetics of humor are elevated to the status of Kant's sublime because of the transcendent quality they offer to the villag-ers. Aside from the humor that Hurston describes to reveal the aesthetic adornment of the villagers' common everyday lives, Gold's tale is interesting for its insights into power relations. With Gold's tale, Hurston achieves several significant feats.

First, Hurston reverses male dominance and power in a patriarchal setting where men traditionally dominate women. Her physical description of Gold as black and big-boned is a radical departure from Fauset's and Larsen's long and lean, sexy, yellow and tan feminine bodies. Although Deborah Plant contends that the mulatto female such as Janie Crawford is "highly suspect in Hurston's work" and that the light-skinned Hurston "admired" her father's yellow skin color and gray-green eyes,[187] Hurston resists rigid racial coloring. Plant later admits in *Zora Neale Hurston: A Biography of the Spirit* that the "essential Zora defies knowing in any factual sense."[188] Indeed, Hurston is quite versatile in her work. For example, beginning with her early short fiction, "John Redding Goes to Sea" (1924), "Drenched in Light" (1924), "Spunk" (1925), "Sweat" (1926), and "The Gilded Six-Bits" (1933), brown-skinned male and female protagonists govern her work, leading to Joel Williamson's description of the Harlem Renaissance as an artistic "browning" of America, a fusion of blacks and mulattoes.[189] Decidedly not yellow and not feminine, Gold and her big black body represent the physiological function of the masculine imaginary, strong and powerful, as she, an outsider to Eatonville society, muscles her way onto the porch and wields knowledge to the crowd, daring them to question her maternal authority to speak.

Second, Hurston shows the depth and security of local black southerners who can narrate racial jokes at their own expense and yet in doing so appear to give credence to the widely held stereotype of their lazy, whining, and complaining nature. Moreover, Hurston gives voice to this particular racist thought in her satire *Moses, Man of the Mountain* (1939) with a Negro Moses leading slaves out of bondage to freedom. But when their liberation is threatened, the former slaves seek Pharoah and turn on Moses as a "stray man that nobody don't know nothing about," an incongruity that saddens Moses, who realizes that freedom is "a funny thing," not "permanent" but to be earned "fresh every day."[190] Between her authorial display of folk pride and flippancy, there emerges a self-described cosmic Hurston who attacks racism and defends her racial braggadocio and caricature. Hurston remarks in *Dust Tracks on the Road* that "our lives are so diversified, internal attitudes so varied, appearances and capabilities so different, that there is no possible classification so catholic that it will cover us all,"[191] defending, perhaps, her various positions.

Third, through Gold's tale Hurston portrays everyday villagers as transformed into poets and mythographers, daring to penetrate the mystery of God and creation and to understand the complexity of race and skin color. Personally, Hurston understood that Jim Crow laws and policies were designed to have a "'psychological' purpose—to promote in the minds of blacks, by daily 'physical evidence' of exclusion, a sense of doomed fatalism in a world where whites, seemingly, are 'First by Birth, eternal and irrevocable.'"[192] The closed Eatonville environment, however, shielding the villagers from this daily fatalism, enabled them to create Adorno's afterimages of themselves, redefining their identity, as marked by the charm of black dialect and verbal art. That is, Hurston distinguishes herself and her characters from Fauset and Larsen and their elite characters who speak acceptable English. In contrast to Hurston's use of dialect to entertain the village characters, Fauset and Larsen occasionally appropriate Negro dialect to show a character's illiteracy and to pronounce the standard and educated English of their favored bourgeois class. For example, Larsen's humble speech pattern for the maid, Zulena, in *Passing* ("She says, ma'am that she'll be able to go" [262]) differs from that of the maid's professional employers, the polished Dr. Brian and Irene Redfield. Additionally, Carolyn Wedin Sylvander writes that the "heavy use of dialect always bothered Fauset." Perhaps Negro dialect disturbed Fauset because "that characteristic alone was enough to relegate a Black to the bottom of any heap in her growing-up years for mocking, scornful humor."[193] Whereas Fauset associated heavy Negro dialect with black cultural degradation, Hurston presents it as natural and unpretentious and as reflective of the authentic folk lifestyle. According to Robert Bone, Hurston "rescued"[194] the common Negro vernacular from the distortion of a socially degraded language.

Fourth and finally, there is more, significantly so, to Gold's tale. Whether or not Gold and other unschooled, illiterate, and poor southern blacks realized it, they were reviving and celebrating an ancient African tradition of oral expression. As evidenced by Gold's storytelling ability, Hurston appropriates the precolonial aesthetics of memorialization in marked contrast to Fauset's and Larsen's uses of classical and Scottish-Irish airs. In Hurston's folk aesthetics, there are no European home furnishings, no morris chairs, no Duncan Phyfes, no piano solos, and no symphonic sounds of classical music calling passing or confused Negroes "home." Hurston's villagers are already *home* in the most authentic sense of the word— culturally, spiritually, and physically. Her appropriation of the memorialization of aesthetics (especially in storytelling) tropes on Africa in a variety of cultural forms, and her novels are picturesquely in the style of the Harlem Renaissance's major black artist, Aaron Douglas. His African-inspired *Heritage*, depicting tall and angular blacks in their natural milieu, offers a vivid picture of Hurston's strong, animated villagers. The Aaron Douglas–Zora Neale Hurston connection appears to be no accident. According to Amy Helene Kirschke's *Art in Crisis: W. E. B. Du Bois and the Struggle for African American Identity and Memory,* Du Bois pictured African art on the cover of *Crisis* magazine throughout the 1920s. Douglas's 1927 portrait of a black woman shouldering and lifting the globe, appropriately titled "The Burden of Black Womanhood,"[195] could well have been the inspiration behind one of Hurston's most famous lines about the black woman being the "mule" of the world, repeated in *Their Eyes Were Watching God.*

In her black ethnographic depiction of the Eatonville folk culture, Hurston has been criticized for displaying a "colonial imagination," but she clearly reveals a decidedly precolonialist ethos. Hurston reconciles the folk with their indigenous cultural heritage before European colonial contact. Yet in her reflection on European colonialism as it relates to Hurston's works, Hazel Carby writes that Hurston "shares this romantic and, it must be said, colonial imagination. Her representation of Eatonville in *Mules and Men* and in *Their Eyes Were Watching God* is both an attempt to make the unknown known and a nostalgic attempt to preserve a disappearing form of folk culture." For Carby, Hurston stands as an ethnographer *outside* the folk, but it is clear that she shared folk culture and wore two hats as she collected folk material and reveled in it. Carby argues that Hurston's "anthropological work . . . concentrated upon the cultural 'other' that existed within the racist order of North America."[196] But in pre-European contact there is no "cultural other," and no authorial and theoretical doubleness for Hurston as black writer and quasi-European gazer. As a local colorist, Hurston revives black oral tradition and rewrites black folk as subjects, not objects, because of how she was personally situated in the Eatonville aesthetics of Joe Clarke's porch culture.

As a writer with an Afrocentric perspective, Hurston creates folk characters who are informally schooled, unlike the formally educated characters in all four of Fauset's novels and in Larsen's two narratives. In *A History of West Africa*, Basil Davidson writes that while some learning in West Africa involved formal education, most learning was received by word of mouth, especially in the "teaching of skills, customs, laws, traditions and the like. It was done for the most part without the aid of writing and reading: the culture was non-literate."[197] In *Africa: Before They Came*, Galbraith Welch states that the oral history of Africa as told by Griots or oral historians was the essence of Africa's mind. Welch explains that in the "bookless regions and in the old *pre-colonial days* [emphasis added] the recital by a specialist was a big element in popular life," akin to the production of a stage play or a great literary event. European travelers were mesmerized by many speakers' deliveries, reporting that a Griot "would deliver an historical discourse for days on end, his narrative interspersed with *apropos* songs and pantomimes."[198] On Joe Clarke's porch, Hurston has the villagers perform the orality of African's precolonial and nonliterate tradition.

Anthropologists, psychologists, and social scientists unfamiliar with West African history and culture would not be equipped to understand the symbolism of Gold's tale and Hurston's interest in reporting it. As Hemenway states, many of these professionals simply dismissed villagers such as Gold as culturally deprived. Similarly, in *Black Culture and Black Consciousness*, Lawrence W. Levine writes that while Joel Chandler Harris, a real cultural outsider, became famous for popularizing the tales of Uncle Remus, he was "as blind as he could be to some of the deeper implications of the tales he heard and told."[199] Undoubtedly familiar with the Uncle Remus tales and Joel Chandler Harris's reputation for creating happy, docile "darkies," Hurston in her fiction refutes such a stereotype and uses a woman as a strong, culture-bearing maternal figure to do the refuting, thus representing the maternal as a counterforce to patriarchy. Hurston subtly revises the texture of the folk environment as formally unschooled but informally well educated in their African cultural tradition and roots.

Joe Clarke's store porch was not only a place for entertainment and cultural exchange; it was also an aesthetic haven, with the village theater embellishing the daily. Poetically transformed, the villagers created the illusion or perhaps the reality that no other world existed or mattered. Two favorite Hurston remarks to be found in her fiction are "the porch laughed" and "the porch was boiling now." Her use of metonymy stresses the communal gathering on the porch and the towns people's enjoyment. The tall tales also had the distinction of breaking the monopoly of daily tedium, encouraging the aesthetic adaptation of the Negro "furthest down" into a Griot, a poet, a philosopher, and a powerful matriarchy. Their revolutionary self-reconstruction was one that resisted hegemony and their cultural othering through a celebration of themselves. According to Levine, "in the midst of the brutalities and injustices of the Antebellum and post-bellum racial systems, black men and women were able to find the means to sustain a far greater degree of self-pride and group cohesion than the system they lived under ever intended for them to be able to do."[200] These were Adorno's afterimages of individuals, defying their cultural othering in society, presenting themselves as being more than they were given credit for being.

This is precisely Hurston's position as a local-color writer, showing and emphasizing the great self-sustaining power of black people, especially women. That is, the heroines Gold, Lucy Pearson in *Jonah's Gourd Vine*, and Janie Crawford in *Their Eyes Were Watching God* constitute another "new" image of black women. While Deborah Plant asserts that "more often than not, Hurston endowed women with a weak will and cast them in the stereotypical mode of emotional or financial dependents,"[201] Hurston's Gold, Lucy, and Janie do not fit this pattern.

Jonah's Gourd Vine: Valorizing the Maternal Body

Hurston lost her mother when she was approximately nine years old, joining the ranks of motherless black women writers. In *Dust Tracks on the Road,* she expresses her loss in a typically inimitable way: "Mama died at sundown and changed a world. That is, the world which had been built out of her body and her heart."[202] John Lowe remarks that Hurston "began *Jonah* in an attempt to understand her father by fictionalizing him,"[203] but her maternal deification of Lucy Pearson (Hurston) in *Jonah* returns the narrative to the locus of the maternal body. Like the black women writers before and after her, Hurston associates the maternal body with life, creativity, and sacrifice, but she details John Pearson's maternal plundering of it, which the daughter/writer regathers and deifies. The mother-daughter attachment in *Jonah's Gourd Vine* becomes the paradigmatic relationship, framing the shift in the parents' troubled marriage, the mother's death, and the daughter's responsibility to the dead but revered mother. In framing her father's abuse of the maternal body, Hurston focuses on the mother as the foundation of the marriage and family and attempts to recuperate the maternal body as a privileged site of existence.

As the following quotation implies, Hurston comes to terms with her father, a minister, and his infidelity, which perhaps led to her mother's shortened life. "My father had been killed in an automobile accident," Hurston reflects, "[but] in reality my father was the baby of the family. With my mother gone and nobody to guide him, life had not hurt him, but it had turned him loose to hurt himself."[204] From his beginning "across de Creek" to his collision with a train, John Pearson lives and dies as a tragic phallic symbol. Hurston reverses Jacques Lacan's image of the "imaginary dominance of the phallic" and the "castration of the mother."[205] As phallic symbol, John Pearson asserts his male sexual dominance in his illicit affairs with multiple women, including "Big 'Oman, Lacey, Semmie, Bootsie and Mehaley." But his adulterous relationships with these women "merely called for action" (31),[206] a suggestion of his phallic drive. Although his wife, Lucy Pearson, weak from multiple childbirths, suffers and dies as a result of heartbreak and spousal abuse, Hurston represents her as a stronger figure, both intellectually and spiritually, than her husband. In the process of narrating her mother's story, Hurston, from a folk-aesthetic, local-color perspective, frames the narrative around folk morality and ethics in Eatonville, in regard to family life, with Lucy as the maternal model of fidelity.

Village aesthetics and ethics are observed when church members call a conference to subtly chastise their minister, John Pearson, about his affair with another woman. Because of Pearson's "bold and unusual" demeanor with regard to his anatomical statue as well as his oratorical skills, the members become cowed. Cleverly an official approaches Pearson and rhetorically chastises him: "Look heah, Elder Pearson. Ah reckon you don heard dat some dese niggers is throwin' lies 'bout you and some woman over 'bout Oviedo. Ah ain't tole yuh nothin', and you be keerful uh dese folks dat totes yuh news"(103). This implicit criticism of Pearson's adulterous behavior is followed by more explicit criticism from Lucy. She later asks her husband to identify his Sunday text, to which John answers, "Iss Communion so Ah reckon Ah'll preach de Passover Supper in de upper room." Lucy warns him, "Don't you preach it" (104). The sacredness of holy community, John's sin, and the quiet but festering anger of the church membership are too incongruent for the pure-hearted Lucy.

Although John has had numerous affairs, his relationship with Hattie Tyson threatens his marriage and ministry. To save her family, Lucy pleads with him, "John . . . you kin keep from fallin' in love wid anybody, if you start in time" (102). Unknown to John, Hattie Tyson has a secret weapon for enticing him, which he finally learns from his best friend, Hambo, who informs him "bout all dat conjure and all dem roots she been workin' on you. Feedin' you outa her body" (14). John Lowe remarks that in the *Journal of American Folklore*, Hurston cites in her essay "Hoodoo in America" that women seeking to make men love them resorted to a hoodoo practice of putting "urine or menstrual discharge" in their food.[207]

Hurston therefore relates Hattie Tyson's sexed but infertile maternal body to that which is soiled and unclean, unlike Lucy's.

Hurston contrasts Lucy's intellectualism and cleanliness with John's action-driven and fleshly encounters with women and his overall general debauchery. When Lucy initially meets John in a school setting where her uncle is the teacher, he is "amazed at the number of things to be learned. He liked to watch Lucy's class recite" (26). Although he begins to attend school, Lucy is more advanced, superb in spelling, and "kin speak de longest pieces and never miss uh word" (350). While the narrator describes Lucy as "perfect," John is associated with Hurston's rendition of the folk fabliau, a characteristic device distinguishing his lowly over-the-creek origins from Lucy's (35). Attempting to court her, he asks, "Don't you do nothin' but warm uh chair bottom?" and the "clean" Lucy, associating "bottom" with sexual connotation, promptly responds, "Oooh, John Buddy! You talkin' nasty" (32).

While *Jonah's Gourd Vine* begins and ends with descriptions of John's early life and his death, respectively, between these events Hurston portrays the gradual decline of a marriage and writes what Hayden White refers to as a "discourse of the real,"[208] effecting a narrative style detailing the family's dissolution. Tracing Lucy Potts's early life at home with her strict but caring parents, to school where she excels, and then to her courtship and marriage to John Pearson, Hurston draws a vivid picture of the death of the mother, aesthetically and literally. The love letters that John and Lucy exchange before the marriage and the aesthetic game of "Hide the Switch" that they play—similar to the game Missy May and her husband Joe play in "The Gilded Six-Bits"—stress their love and unity before he finally destroys it—just as Missy May's adultery almost ends her marriage. One of the ways that Hurston identifies strong unions is by the couples' easy physical access to each other, suggesting their natural and vital bodily contact, the loss of which is signified by the absence of aesthetic play.

The small-framed Lucy Pearson, who increases in weight to ninety-five pounds and has seven children, suffers not from childbirth, as some critics posit, but rather from her husband's incorrigible philandering. Hurston's representation of maternal wisdom places Lucy in a sacred feminine sphere, violated by her husband's phallic transgressions. It is Lucy who suggests to John that he become a carpenter: "You knows how tuh carpenter. Go ast who want uh house built, and den you take and do it" (94). This is how he gets his start in Eatonville and the job to which he returns after he leaves the church. On Joe Clarke's store porch, Sam Mosely acknowledges Lucy's maternal power: "Anybody could put his self on de ladder wid her in de house. Dat's de very 'oman Ah been lookin' fuh all mah days" (94). Similarly in "Sweat," Walter Thomas, speaking to the men on the porch, lauds Sykes's smart but equally abused wife Delia Jones as a woman, saying, "Ah'd uh mah'ied [married] huh mahseff if he hadnter beat me to it."[209] Delia, like Lucy, has a small body, but the narrative emphasizes her "spiritual earthworks" and "triumphant indifference"[210] to her husband.

Aesthetically too Hurston balances small women's physical frames and the men's seemingly towering and all-powerful stances over them with descriptions of the women's unique psychological/spiritual powers of coherence, disrupting male authority and mediating the women's wifely role as the feminine repressed. Deborah Plant's contention that Hurston frequently "endowed women with a weak will"[211] is true only to the extent that they *appear* to be weak, largely from a feminist perspective. Hurston's narrative description of maternal weakness or paternal strength through the guise of physical appearance belies her greater emphasis on the recognition of character identity through final outcome. Often, Hurston depicts a character's integrity by what happens to her or him, as we see with Sykes being bitten by the snake he had brought into his home to bite and poison Delia, who had predicted that he would "reap his sowing," as Lucy's John does.

Although John Pearson has never stopped having affairs, his relationship with Hattie Tyson is the turning point in the novel. Lucy identifies Hattie and sees her letters to John lying carelessly around the house "where mah chillun kin git holt of 'em," dismissing her own pain to protect her children's innocence. A pregnant Lucy links her ailing maternity to the other woman (108). Helpless, she prays and voices maternal anxiety, not for herself but for the unborn Isis/Zora: "Lawd lemme quit feedin' on heart meat lak Ah do. Dis baby goin' tuh be too fractious tuh live. . . . if Ah meet dat woman in heben, you got tuh gimme time tuh fight uh while. Jus' ruin dis baby's temper 'fo it git tuh did world. 'Tain't mah fault, Lawd, Ahm jus' ez *clean* [emphasis added] ez yo' robes" (98).

Symbolically the mother's bonding with the daughter begins in the maternal womb, not only with the umbilical cord but also with their linguistic connection, and continues after birth. While Lucy's other babies are announced anonymously, "Isis" (Zora) is named and fussed over. "One night as she sang the sleep song to the younger children she noticed a sallow listlessness in Isis, her younger girl" (100). The mother's anxiety, the daughter's illness, the father's sexual immorality, and Hattie Tyson's conjuring are presented in rapid succession in fewer than ten pages, two of which detail Tyson's visiting a conjuror. In detailing these narrative events, Hurston suggests a tragic relationship between the philandering father's fatal attraction and the saintly and clean mother's illness.

Hurston demonstrates a narrative exaltation of the maternal metaphor before and after Lucy marries the lowly John Pearson. Her authorial emphasis on the aesthetics of cleanliness may be related to the influence of Booker T. Washington, as John Lowe suggests. Washington's *Up from Slavery* valorizes the cleaning of the body and clothes and even homes, yards, and buildings as a virtue of character. Washington says, "I learned there [at Hampton Institute] for the first time some of its value, not only in keeping the body healthy, but in inspiring self-respect and promoting virtue," and he continues, "I never see a filthy yard that I do not want to clean it."[212] Born a few miles from Tuskegee Institute, Hurston, unlike Larsen, who stressed the drabness of schools such as Tuskegee, found Washington and his enterprise worthwhile. The dignity of labor and work for uneducated Negroes living in the South, a few generations removed from slavery, is celebrated in Hurston's oeuvre.

Hurston, adds Deborah Plant, praised Washington, and in her review of the book *The Jeanes Teacher in the United States*, she even sounded like him, adopting his conservative and controversial racial politics. "There is no patronizing attitude toward a minority group, nor glossing over the unfortunate facts of the Negro being in part responsible for lack of progress by his own indifference to consequences,"[213] Hurston writes. Hurston was shaped not by the assimilationist models of black bourgeois success theories but rather by black models of self-reliance, and the implication of her Washington-like rhetoric turns her toward a hegemonic cultural view in politics, which she otherwise shuns in her fiction. Politically, Hurston was controversial, but she was faithful in her fiction to the portrayal of the indigenous world of characters such as Lucy who live above the systems of racial caste and patriarchy.

John Lowe incisively relates the thematic of water and cleanliness in *Jonah's Gourd Vine* to the idea of John's rather than Lucy's salvation on a concrete and neo-Puritan level, although the image of Lucy's cleanliness also has significant meaning in terms of her character development. Lowe writes, "The idea of judgment also looms large, as represented by the fiery thunderbolt; it becomes coupled with washing/cleansing aspects of both water and fire, which in fact are dominant images throughout the novel, echoing the powerful neo-Puritan motif,"[214] as seen in Washington's slave narrative. Lowe adds, "To maintain pastoral control and piety, however, one must constantly publicly 'wash' one's soul clean, as John attempts to do in this story," while "Lucy later claims that John can't wash himself clean from sin"[215] with water.

Lucy is suggesting to John a different kind of cleanliness, one not linked to water and the body but linked rather to the soul and spirit. Because Hurston presents her as the embodiment of spiritual regeneration, Lucy's spotlessness, unlike John's cleanliness, which is based on water, forgiveness, and church doctrine, is related to her total ascending nature—maternally, spiritually, and intellectually. Hurston therefore presents Lucy as John's superior, as Lowe acknowledges, but not on the basis of Lucy's pedigree.[216] Unlike his affairs with his mistresses, which demand only physical action, his relationship with Lucy requires "words and words that he did not have" (31). As mother and wife, Lucy requires more from the phallic-gratifying minister than he is capable of giving, and she dies because of his sins, becoming the proverbial sacrificial lamb.

In Lucy's death scene, Hurston recalls her own mother's death and her need to recuperate her mother's voice that would haunt her long after her mother had died. The image of the mother calling to Isis, "Stop cryin', Isie, you can't hear whu Ahm sayin'" is one that constructs the mother and the maternal body as a sacred hieroglyphic text that only the daughter Isis/Zora can translate. Having understood what her mother wanted her to do with her life (to get an education) and with the mother's dying body (to stop the folk ritual of removing the pillow from under her head), the daughter honors only the former. She fails, however, to achieve the latter because of the folk surrounding her mother's deathbed. This failure would disturb the adult Hurston for the rest of her life, as she explains in *Dust Tracks on the Road*: "She [the mother] had felt that I could and would carry out her wishes, and I had not."[217]

Perhaps this failure evoked Hurston's psychological and literal endeavor to retrieve the lost maternal while she lived in Jacksonville, Florida. In *Dust Tracks on the Road* she explains, "I had an experience that set my heart to fluttering. I saw a woman sitting on a porch who looked at a distance like Mama. . . . Maybe she was not dead at all. They had made some mistake."[218] Learning that a mistake had not been made when she comes upon the strange woman turning away from her, Hurston had attempted nevertheless to recover her mother and the lost, nurturing maternal body. Like Larsen, she participated in the Freudian "*fort-da*" game, naming and locating the mother's unacceptable site of disappearance and, in a sense, protesting the mother's death, which had led to the daughter's profound loss.

While Lowe compares Larsen's Helga Crane to Hurston's Lucy Pearson as a demonstration "that the maternal role frequently subtracts substantially from a woman's potential for creative expression,"[219] I would argue that neither artist makes such a claim. Larsen's Irene Redfield expresses herself through the aesthetics of fashion and Negro social events *while* nurturing and obsessing over her two boys. Since *Quicksand* and *Jonah's Gourd Vine* are quasi-autobiographical novels, Larsen and Hurston write about personal mother/daughter experiences of anxieties, resulting in the daughters' psychological and literal losses. That Larsen and Hurston were themselves childless neither endorses nor refutes their novelistic representations of the maternal body and motherhood. Through *Quicksand's* and *Jonah's Gourd Vine's* literary maternal metaphors, the authors present analyses of the crises of mothering, dissecting maternal trauma in its twin oppressive patriarchal and racial spheres.

Their Eyes Were Watching God: Janie's Quest for Maternal *Jouissance*

Valerie Boyd and Robert Hemenway have identified *Their Eyes Were Watching God* as also autobiographically based. According to Hemenway, the "impetus" for this love story "came from Zora's affair with a man of West Indian parentage whom she had first met in New York in 1931" and then again in 1935.[220] Boyd identifies the "tall, dark brown, magnificently built" Percival McGuire Punter, a twenty-three-year-old Antiguan, as the young man whom Hurston, forty-four years old in 1935, fell in love with, or as Hurston confessed, "I did not just fall in love. I made a parachute jump."[221] The relationship was doomed from the start, however, not because of the difference in ages but as a result of Hurston's free-spiritedness: she could not give up her career, as the jealous Punter had demanded. Outwardly, asserts Hemenway, Hurston was "calm," but Punter was "hurt" when she left him to travel to the Caribbean. While Punter was "confused, wondering if she was 'crying on the inside,'" Hurston, writes Hemenway, "gave him her answer in *Their Eyes Were Watching God.*"[222] The novel describes the passionate love affair between Janie Crawford, forty, and Tea Cake, twenty-five years old.

Several critical interpretations are important to an analysis of *Their Eyes Were Watching God* as a text of Janie's quest for and final achievement of maternal *jouissance*. Henry Louis Gates Jr., John Lowe, Molly Hite, and Samira Kawash were helpful here in that they rendered influential readings of the novel that practically capture the breadth and depth of Hurston's schematic/thematic achievement in rewriting Jim Crow and gender boundaries. In his much-cited analysis of *Their Eyes Were Watching God* as an aesthetically, "speakerly text"[223] with the strategy of a narrative frame, Gates heralds Janie as an emerging pedagogue. As a local-color text, the novel presents Janie's oral tale as her entrance into black patriarchal space after her first two husbands, Logan Killicks and Jody Starks, attempt to control her voice. Pheoby is Janie's "true pupil."[224] Lowe discusses *Their Eyes Were Watching God* as continuing *Jonah's Gourd Vine's* discourse of maternity with the liberated and childless Janie replacing the traditional, suppressed maternal Lucy Potts.[225]

For Hite, Hurston's reconfiguration of the trope of mothering is linked not to the birth of a child but to the "production of a powerful narrative," Helene Cixous's theory of *écriture féminine*. Janie's framed narrative "enjoins a world view and a series of prescriptions about how to live." After effectively revising Nanny's slave narrative of "de nigger woman" as "de mule uh de world," Janie assumes "the maternal function" and rewrites the discourse on race and women, thus liberating herself and perhaps others like her.[226] Kamish offers Hurston's "cosmic upset" theory as a "meaningful transformation" of a racially violent social order, trumped by the equally violent and angry hurricane. Nature's moral force, captured in the storm, disrupts life on the muck where dead white and black bodies are segregated for Jim Crow burials, as required by law. With Tea Cake dead, Janie emerges as the new modern woman, unattached and free, sauntering into Eatonville wearing not the crepe de chine dress of Fauset's or Larsen's bourgeois female characters, but gender-crossing blue jeans, which show "yo' womanhood" (Hurston, *Their Eyes Were Watching God*, 4; subsequent references given parenthetically in text).

"Ah been a delegate to de big 'ssociation of life" (6), confesses Hurston's heroine Janie Crawford. Compare Janie to Larsen's Helga Crane, whose inner sense of freedom is thwarted because she initially seeks acceptance aesthetically from an urbane world of "clothes and books" and the "sweet-mingled smell of Houbigant and cigarettes . . . and sophisticated tuneless music," or to Fauset's Angela Murray, who is equally frustrated. Angela is denied entrance into a mainstream society of "clever people, people who do things. Art . . . travel and a lot of things." Such comparisons suggest what Hurston's folk aesthetics do for African American women's literature: they invest and empower it with a woman who celebrates the nakedness of her existence and the driving force of her individuality without looking to the trappings of society for approval.

The readings by Gates, Lowe, Hite, and Kamish all affirm Janie's bildungsroman through a speakerly and feminist, social impetus, aided by natural cosmic forces, thunderously proclaiming a black woman's hard-won arrival. Since *Their Eyes Were Watching God* is passionately sexual in desire and ultimate fulfillment, the multiple themes of Janie's coming-of-age can all be collapsed into Hurston's metaphor of maternal *jouissance*, sexual and spiritual enlightenment, both initially denied to Janie. Julie Kristeva theorizes that in a symbolic patriarchal social order, "the vagina and the *jouissance* of the mother are disregarded," even though the mother "experiences *jouissance* and bears children." Procreation exists, but only "in the name of the father," and female sexuality is usurped by a patriarchal "mis-recognition" of the maternal body.[227] Although not a biological mother, Janie embraces maternal ethics and comes to mother and nurture folk women and the younger Tea Cake, who confesses, "Ah feels lak uh motherless chile round heah." Responding to Tea Cake's childhood needs, Janie maternally "soothed and soothed" him (164–65).

The term "maternal *jouissance*" is used here to posit Janie's total illumination, sexual and social, educational and spiritual, as a woman returning to the village after experiencing the expansiveness of beauty in the "horizon," transcending Jim Crow shadows, due to Hurston's explosive "cosmic upset." Fueled by the rationalism of the Greek *Kosmos* of human institutions being "governed by *logos* and *nomos*,"[228] Kamish's fascinating theory of cosmic disruption in *Their Eyes Were Watching God* nonetheless overlooks the divine energy behind Hurston's storm. A minister's daughter well versed in sacred literature, Hurston rewrites several biblical events to reflect Janie's bodily transubstantiation from the asexual to the sexual, and the maternal and sacred. The storm in *Their Eyes Were Watching God* is a sacred trope on Noah's flood and perhaps represents Hurston's personal/political deconstruction of a Jim Crow system that had humiliated her, reminiscent of Wheatley's rewriting of the infamous Middle Passage via tropes of healing and recovery. The hurricane in *Their Eyes Were Watching God* has the effect of an authorial remaking of society, not only in "the force of resistance to [a violent social] order,"[229] as Kamish posits, but also in Hurston's universalizing principle of the one-life motif as found in Samuel Taylor Coleridge's *The Rime of the Ancient Mariner.*

Up against the storm, the embattled white authorities even discriminate between dead black and dead white bodies, urging grave diggers to make "coffins fuh all de white folks" but to sprinkle "quick-lime" over the black bodies (163). With

Tea Cake's retort "dey think God don't know nothin' bout de Jim Crow law" (163), Hurston parodies the overdetermined racism of Jim Crow social convention and the white men's imperious behavior in deciding burial rites for the dead. In Genesis, God laments earthly corruption and directs Noah to build an ark to save himself and selected others before "I do bring a flood of waters upon the earth, to destroy all flesh, wherein is the breath of life, from under heaven."[230] Like Noah's flood, Hurston's storm is "on a cosmic scale" of "two hundred miles an hour wind," and it brings together humans, white and black, and animals and fish. The image of "Water everywhere. Stray fish swimming in the yard. . . . frightened cattle. . . . bodies fully dressed" represents a significant alignment of creatures, great and small (152, 153, 162). Hurston appears to allude to the moral didacticism of Coleridge's ancient mariner, who acquires an understanding of the divinity of the one-life theme, barring secular distinctions and the Logos of human institutions in the social order, the message of Hurston's cosmic storm.

Janie identifies the "big burst" of thunder and lightning as God's work, saying, "Ole Massa is doin' His work now. Us oughta keep quiet" (150), attributing the force of the cataclysmic turn of events not to the accident of *Kosmos* but rather to the purposeful work of God. Whereas Kamish relates the storm to the "*Kosmos* in classical Greek usage" and the philology of the "original reference to order,"[231] Hurston implies a sacred figurative construction. Like the biblical flood, the hurricane in *Their Eyes Were Watching God* reaches a climax and then a calming. A rabid dog bites Tea Cake, whom Janie must kill in self-defense. Afterward she emerges as an autonomous woman after being associated with three men, two of whom attempted to dominate her, and the last, Tea Cake, of whom she regrettably is forced to kill.

Throughout the narrative Janie becomes freed from a tradition of women's racial and gender confinement, as represented by Nanny and slavery, her mother and sexual promiscuity, and three husbands who represent male authority in various guises. Moreover, Hurston names the novel in this stormy cosmic section: "They seemed to be staring at the dark, but their eyes were watching God" (151). The storm, Janie's ultimate transformation, and the naming of the novel suggest, like the aftermath of Noah's flood, a departure from the old and a preparation for the new. The storm signifies omnipotent power and creativity, like a woman giving birth and transcending human authority.

Structurally, Hurston devises *Their Eyes Were Watching God* to reflect Janie's struggle for *jouissance*, not merely voice, as some feminists maintain in comparing Janie's disembodied voice to Alice Walker's Celie in *The Color Purple*.[232] In her early beginning with Killicks and Starks, Janie does not achieve *jouissance*: the fat Killicks is physically undesirable, the aging Starks impotent. Aesthetically, Hurston devises and Janie frames the narrative of the flood significantly at the end of the text, after she achieves her goal, graphically described in Janie and Tea Cake's lovemaking. After an argument, Tea Cake "hurled her to the floor and held her there melting her resistance with the heat of his body, doing things with their bodies to express the inexpressible." Janie "arched her body to meet" Tea Cake's, and "they fell asleep in sweet exhaustion" (132). This is perhaps the first explicit, passionate literary portrayal of lovemaking in black women's fiction. At the beginning of the novel, Janie's aesthetic vision of the leafy, blossoming pear tree, representing her sexual awakening, reflects too her dream of a Garden of Eden paradise, Hurston's second biblical trope, with its fruit trees of permissive and forbidden knowledge.

Hurston continues to employ the image of fruit, knowledge, and maternal *jouissance,* as her description of Janie's reentering of Eatonville shows: her "firm buttocks" resemble "grape fruits in her hip pockets" (2). John Lowe remarks that the "figuration of Janie's buttocks and breasts as grapefruits and weapons" appears to signify on women as traditional sexual objects. Janie's body as a female "weapon" suggests, Lowe continues, that she "embodies, in short, a mystery" to male ego and lust and the possibility of female rebirth.[233] But in the biblical context, the fruit image further reveals Janie's deeper aesthetic yearning for life, beauty, self-knowledge, and *jouissance,* forbidden to women just as "the fruit of the tree which is in the midst of the garden" of Eden is forbidden to Adam and Eve. As the rebellious woman, Eve, in biblical lore, rejects God's patriarchal law and acquires forbidden knowledge along with Adam, whom she seduces.[234]

Janie's character reconfigures Eve's: Janie's desire for the blossoming pear tree indicates her initial aesthetic and sexual longing, finally achieved. In describing Janie's triumphant return to Eatonville and stressing her body parts (that is, "firm buttocks," "great rope of black hair," and "pugnacious breasts"), Hurston details her transfiguration, linked to *jouissance.* After Tea Cake confirms to her, "You got me in de go-long," Janie "lit up like a transfiguration" (100). Janie's image alludes to Moses's shining transformation on Mount Sinai after seeing God and receiving the Ten Commandments, whereupon "the skin of Moses' face shone,"[235] as does Janie's in Hurston's third biblical allusion.

Janie assumes a maternal role, as Molly Hite posits, instructing the domesticated subordinate, Pheoby, described as a "pupil" by Henry Louis Gates Jr. but who can also be interpreted as Janie's "daughter." Pheoby divulges to the maternal Janie intimate details of her dissatisfying marriage, revealing what Kristeva names as the loss and/or denial of maternal *jouissance.*[236] As Pheoby makes her way to Janie's house at dusk, a female character warns her, "De booger man might ketch you," but Pheoby tellingly replies, "mah husband tell me say no first class booger would have me" (4). While Janie and Pheoby are presented as childless, Hurston nevertheless appears to relate the power and creativity of the maternal body not necessarily to childbirth but to self-knowledge and sexual satisfaction. Other women share Pheoby's dissatisfied conjugal status, as Hurston's omniscient narrator details in a barrage of questions, highlighted by dashes, stressing the women's breathless envy of Janie: "What she doin' coming back here in dem overhalls? . . . —Where all dat money her husband took and died and left her . . . —Where she left dat young lad of a boy she went off here wid?" (2).

From a local-color perspective, Hurston illuminates the emotional hunger of married women's stunted lives in provincial communities, no longer aesthetic havens for independently driven women unable to use their bodies as the towering Gold does to remove themselves from under the thumb of patriarchy. Hurston's handling of women's gossipy behavior tropes on the anti-aesthetics, which are related in a twisted way to the Jim Crow politics of social degradation. According to Rachel Blau DuPlessis, Hurston, who had worked as a manicurist in a black-owned Jim Crow barbershop that catered to white customers, had decided that race per se was a "determinate that itself could be overruled by class and economic self-interest."[237] In her characters' jealous opposition to Janie's new identity, Hurston reveals their psychological internalization of the antiblack aesthetics of Jim Crow racism. That is, these characters' unhealthy digestion of negative self-images contrast with the healthy racial sense of characters such as Gold, suggesting Hurston's various aesthetic positions that critique women's development. The character Pheoby symbolizes the denial or death of maternal *jouissance,* but Hurston permits Janie to express her discovery of *jouissance,* thus offering Pheoby a paradigm to rebuild her life. Hurston allows Pheoby to voice the point of Janie's maternal lesson: "Ah done growed ten feet higher from jus' listenin' tuh you, Janie. Ah ain't satisfied wid mahself no mo'. Ah means tuh make Sam take me fishin' wid him after this," demonstrating her longing for *jouissance* (182–83).

Zora Neale Hurston had successfully returned home to the folk, giving them renewed life in her literature. In *Mules and Men,* Hurston confesses that she did not return to Florida "so that the home folks could make admiration over me because I had been up North to college and come back with a diploma and a Chevrolet." She had returned to Eatonville as "Lucy Hurston's daughter, Zora."[238] The daughter's return home suggests the permanent value of the mother's nurturing skills and the daughter's honoring of the maternal body in death as well as in life. But Hurston, like Fauset and Larsen, is not limited to this maternal trope alone. Indeed in their America these three women authors made "A Plea for Color?" (*Quicksand* 51), as Larsen articulates, bringing a recalcitrant America into a new world of multiculturalism.

For Werner Sollors, "ethnic literature of the first half of the twentieth century shows a remarkable concern for the American world of modernity,"[239] including the world of aesthetics in art, fashion, beauty, and the reconfiguration of the proverbial black body-in-crisis. Even with Helga Crane's "geographical moves and her constant sense of not being at home,"[240] Larsen, like Fauset and Hurston, had shown that modern America is home for African Americans, though a more troubled home in Larsen's narratives. They were in myriad ways "bound to the land . . .

soiled by the land, a claim that drew on their roles within agricultural economies as well as the ideological and social privations caused by racism[;] African Americans had not only earned a place at the table"; they had also been the "very foundation on which the table could stand."[241] In their mosaic of color and aesthetics, folk and cosmopolitan, these authors presented a diversifying "collage-like reality" of the gradations of color of black Americans, imbued with qualities of "dynamism and fluidity."[242] They met the four challenges laid out at the beginning of this chapter and absolved the colored body from the pre-aesthetic bane of slavery, changing the literary image of black women forever. Carby names Larsen's Helga Crane as the "first truly sexual female protagonist in Afro-American fiction."[243] Hurston's Janie Crawford emerges from her experience of *jouissance* competing for that distinction. However, it is Fauset's description of Maggie Ellersley's long and lean "calla-lily body" that represents the beginning of all three novelists' rich assortment of feminine images, revealing Adorno's theory of the untouchability of beauty, beyond the reach of these Harlem Renaissance writers' mortifying Jim Crow time.

Part Two

A Conflation of History, Past and Present

Paule Marshall, Alice Walker, and Toni Morrison are contemporary writers who nonetheless conflate history—that is, they do not limit their work to one time frame but move from the slave era to the Jim Crow period, to the civil rights movement, to our current postmodern age. In their conflation of time, they appear to collapse the boundaries separating one era from another, as if to suggest that the social progress made (in abolishing slavery or Jim Crow segregation, for example) did not really effect the changes required. For this reason, each of these writers develops the theme of the importance of a character's inner well-being. I use a different set of critical and theoretical tools to analyze their creative achievements, based on the uniqueness of their particular style.

5 Maternal Imprinting
Paule Marshall and the Mother-Daughter Dyad

It was here that they brought 'em. . . . And the minute those Ibos was brought on shore they just stopped, my gran' said, and taken a look around. . . . Well, they seen everything that was to happen round here that day. The slavery time and the war my gran' always talked about, the 'mancipation and everything after that right on up to the hard times today. Do you know what the Ibos did?. . . . I do.[1]

In several ways the above quotation is representative of Paule Marshall's appropriation of mother-daughter metaphors in her literary oeuvre. Marshall politicizes the relationship between surrogate or blood mother-daughter figures, stressing the regenerative nature of these roles in the African American and West Indian quest for coherence. Without exception, Marshall's major characters seek an interior liberation from the chaos and confusion of oppression, and this innate sense of well-being is soul reclamation, as each of these characters retrieves his/her lost or distorted essential self. By insisting on her characters' reclamation, despite oppressive conditions, Marshall succeeds Zora Neale Hurston and anticipates the spiritual interior discourses of Alice Walker and Toni Morrison. Marshall then radically breaks with her literary predecessors, whose early abolitionist, social-reform activism, and literary accomplishments empowered her to envision new strategies of resistance, but still ones that ensure black group survival without looking to hegemony for change. This shift from social to personal regeneration is not related to a feminist backlash or a second feminist wave after the first wave of black and white women's institutional reform, but rather it is connected to Marshall's repudiation of dominant frames of power as being truly committed to black interests.

Born in 1929 in New York City to Barbadian immigrant parents, Paule Marshall is described as a writer who reconnects Africa, black America, and the West Indies, leading one critic to describe a Pan-African moment in *Praisesong* as "an important model of diasporic nationality."[2] Marshall's cultural uniqueness helps to explain her and Lorraine Hansberry's authorial distance in their first major publications, *Brown Girl, Brownstones* (1959) and *A Raisin in the Sun* (1958), respectively, the former attracting the attention of the Harlem Renaissance's Langston Hughes, who invited Marshall on a European book tour, as she recalls in her abbreviated memoirs *Triangular Road* (2009). Although Hansberry and Marshall had belonged in the 1950s to the black artistic group Association of Artists for Freedom and sought to address new civil rights issues as writers, the endings in their first important productions are telling of their visions. While Hansberry's Walter Younger family celebrates the dismantling of Jim Crow laws in 1954 by moving to an all-white Chicago suburb (where they are not wanted), Marshall's Selina takes a significant detour and leaves America altogether, traveling to her ancestral home, Barbados. Hence even in her seminal novel and in an era that appeared to be promising for the traditionally isolated black American, Marshall launches a journey homeward for the bicultural Selina.

Through her characters Marshall drives home the similarities of the oppressive nature of black peoples' experiences with colonial powers, and she tries to bridge the cultural gap between two suffering groups of people: black Americans and West Indians. The slave legacy left each group with injured psyches and fragmented souls (Alain Locke's "damaged group psychology"), a condition that no civil rights movement focused on legal issues could remedy, as Marshall's novels suggest. Uprooting the deeply entrenched Caliban/Prospero, black oppressed and white oppressor mentalities requires, Marshall implies, radical surgery, which only spiritual regeneration can evince, akin to Houston Baker's mantra of the "spirit-work" of the Harlem Renaissance but with a diasporic difference. "What really needs doing," cries Merle Kinbona of *The Chosen Place, the Timeless People*—the character that Marshall told the literary critic Daryl Cumber Dance she loves—is "the all-out change you and I know is necessary" (226). Some scholars, however, refuse Marshall's vision and reject her bicultural emphasis on black Americans and West Indians, but for more personal reasons.

In *Crisis of the Negro Intellectual*, Harold Cruse accuses Marshall of having "divided loyalties"[3] because of her West Indian parentage. Yet, Cruse acknowledges her distrust of white American liberals who were "opposed to change that [was] not gradual."[4] While the latter observation might help to explain Marshall's disaffection and distrust of the incessant clamor of integration movements of the 1950s and 1960s, the first (about her divided loyalties) clearly rankles her. In her interview with Daryl Cumber Dance, Marshall years later addressed Cruse's criticism and his disparaging comments regarding her American heritage by West Indian parents. "It used to hurt and exasperate me years ago—the disclaiming part of it—and still does to some degree," she confessed. "But I simply go on being who I perceive my life and my work to be. And I like to think of myself and my work . . . as a kind of bridge that joins the two great wings of the black Diaspora. And my principle [sic] imperative is to give expression to the two cultures that created me, and which I really see as one culture. All o' we is one."[5]

Due to their history of racial violence and slavery, black Americans and West Indians, Marshall asserts, share a common plight. Evidence of their shared history is presented in Mary Prince's slave narrative, one of the first of its kind. Like Frederick Douglass and Harriet Jacobs, Mary Prince, a late-eighteenth-century West Indian slave, experienced the inhumanity of slavery and authored a compelling slave narrative. *The History of Mary Prince, a West Indian Slave, Related by Herself* (1831) is an important slave account and appeared in the *Anti-Slavery Reporter.* Prince was an eyewitness who captured the horror of slavery in the West Indies, and she is believed to be the only author of a British-Caribbean slave narrative.[6] She gives details of her birth, the physical treatment of slaves, the auctioning off of herself and her siblings, her marriage to a free colored man, her escape and return to slavery, her final escape, her death wish, and, as did Jacobs, the sexual abuse of female slaves. West Indian slavery was worse than American slavery. With a lucrative sugar cane industry in the West Indies, slavery there was an entrenched way of life. Hilary McD. Beckles writes that Barbados, for example, represented even in 1650 the wealthiest "agricultural colony in the hemisphere" because of the imported African expert skill in successfully cultivating sugar cane, a staple crop in Marshall's brilliant novel *Chosen Place.* However, the success of slavery in the West Indies led to early deaths for overworked slaves. Reportedly, George Washington once threatened to send one of his slaves to the West Indies as a form of punishment "because 'this fellow is both a rogue and a runaway.'"[7] Mary Prince's narrative is proof of the historical reality that black Americans and black West Indians suffered a similar fate and that "slavery, wherever it prevails, produces similar effects."[8] Marshall adopts this attitude, which Harold Cruse at the time had failed to realize.

Because the civil rights movement in the United States did not effect an "all-out change," due in part to the intransigence of the country's Herrenvolk democracy, Marshall gives only an obligatory nod to the movement and its much-heralded success of integration in three of her novels: *Praisesong for the Widow; Daughters;* and *The Fisher King.* Yet with only a footnote to contemporary history, Marshall places the locus of her historical novels on a romanticized and mythical past because of the need for "all-out change" and the relentless, homeostatic conditions of racism. Marshall explained her authorial preference for a mythical past to Dance as an "antidote to the lies" of history: "I'm interested in discovering and in unearthing what was positive and inspiring about our experience" and how "I as a woman—a black woman—and a writer [can] continue to function and to grow in a society that almost daily assaults my sense of self."[9] Consequently, Marshall rejects Ann Petry's literature of social protest as found in *The Street* (1946) and Lorraine Hansberry's literature of social integration as seen in *A Raisin in the Sun.* She espouses instead Frantz Fanon's ideology that in the "struggle for liberation" black intellectuals must "go farther [sic] than [the] cry of protest" and crystallize "the national consciousness" by using black history as a guide.[10] Marshall's maternal warriors lead the way, and their daughters' regenerative capacity ensures a sense of continuity, hence the significance of the mother-daughter dyad.

This chapter includes an examination of Marshall's signature gesture of pairing mothers and daughters to effect personal transformation while appropriating history, myth, and ritual to offer her protagonists liberating ideas on individual aspiration and fulfillment. In her study *Mother Imagery in the Novels of Afro-Caribbean Women*, Simone A. James Alexander attributes the significance of Marshall's emphasis on mothers to the "potent symbolic force" of mothers as "female precursors" for their daughters who inherit the "authority of authorship."[11] But I argue that Marshall ambitiously rewrites the African Diaspora using the influence of maternal imprinting through African tales, myths, and rituals to impress upon the mothers' daughters the importance of black resistance to personal and racial denigration. Maternal imprinting, defined as mothers' ability to successfully nurture their daughters' or sons' consciousness and thus their personality, involves the schematization of a talismanic object and a style of behavior.[12] Marshall creates formidable African warriors whose magical powers to fight oppression and win back their innate freedom assure their canonized stature. Her literary oeuvre of mythical heroes and heroines, having the aura of Roland Barthes's "rhetoric of the image,"[13] signifies the black ontological experience of war (recall Ralph Ellison's statement), struggle, and survival. One becomes by mere association with this oppressive history a woman warrior and not just an author of authority. Indeed, Marshall describes the heroine Avatara as a would-be "Dahomey woman warrior of old" (*Praisesong* 130).

In Marshall's novels, mothers emerge most often as liberating women warriors who teach their daughters ways to survive oppressive forces of class, gender, and race. Frequently the warrior-mothers and their tales of talismanic African warriors are at the heart of their maternal imprinting, literally or symbolically. Marshall's first novel, *Brown Girl, Brownstones,* which details the Caribbean immigrant experience in New York City before, during, and after World War II, has no literal African tale of warriors to imprint on the minds of Silla's blood daughters, Ina and Selina. But Silla is a figurative warrior who casts herself in the shadow of redoubtable African warriors to set an example for her daughters. She makes a ritual of hard, spirit-sapping work "so you can keep your head up and not have these white people push you 'bout like you's cattle" (*Brown Girl, Brownstones* 172).

It is no accident that Marshall's daughters and son are young and that their mothers indoctrinate them during their most early, impressionable years. Myths and rituals are recognized as means of social imprinting. Myths are mentally associated with rites, which are physical illustrations of myths. By learning the myths of the cultural group and by performing its rites, children become socialized into their society and function as a natural part of it.[14] At the core of the myths and rituals in Marshall's first four novels is, of course, black history: it is a history that Marshall rewrites to give pride of heritage to her characters and to enhance their sense of self. Marshall's revisionist history is intended also to energize and encourage her characters to overcome their marginal societal status. Marshall's mothers appropriate history, myth, and ritual to spiritually inspire and teach; their daughters and son accept their imprinting and even return to the memory of it as wandering adults to reclaim an interior freedom. In *Brown Girl, Brownstones*, however, Selina spurns her mother's patterning of bourgeois materialism as strategies for coping with racism because she seeks a more meaningful healing.

Brown Girl, Brownstones: Silla and Selina in War and Love

Over thirty years before the publication of *Daughters* with its mother-daughter dyad, Marshall established in *Brown Girl, Brownstones* (1959) her signature approach of focusing on maternal warriors and daughters, distinguishing herself as an early "feminist" even before the publication of Betty Friedan's groundbreaking book, *The Feminist Mystique* (1963). In her book Friedan gives voice to women's mystical powers of creation and renewal. Marshall, like Walker and Morrison, resists labels, however, and her early emphasis on women's creative force is not related to feminism per se but is related to the female models in her family, as she describes them in her autobiographical essay "From the Poets in the Kitchen." In Marshall's novels, maternal metaphors of regeneration, as captured in the mother-daughter dyad, are more explicit and blood related in *Brown Girl, Brownstone* and *Daughters* than in any other Marshall novel. In the quasi-autobiographical novel *Brown Girl*, Silla and Selina represent Marshall's wide-ranging discourse on the discord and harmony of what Adrienne Rich calls the emotional "cathexis between mother and daughter" in its "most painful estrangement" and "deepest mutuality."[15] Both emotions are brilliantly illustrated in *Brown Girl, Brownstones*.

The maternal imprinting here is different for Selina, though still political. Silla Boyce, whom Selina calls "the mother," as if she is *the* major figure in a race war, has internalized the Protestant ethic of hard work, bourgeois materialism, and American capitalism. She uses Faustian tactics to acquire "security" and, like Faust, damns her soul and destroys her marriage. Silla justifies her multiple jobs as domestic, factory worker, landlord, and cook "so you can keep your head up" (172). When Selina tells her mother that "some people don't care about those things" that Silla's money can buy, the daughter's rejection of what she believes is harmful maternal imprinting is imminent.

Brown Girl, Brownstones features the most archetypal mother-daughter confrontation within the scope of the author's rich and vivid description of the West Indian immigrant experience. Marshall's Silla, a Barbadian immigrant, like European and Asian immigrants, comes to New York in search of a better existence. Because her first novel details the black immigrant experience, Marshall has been compared to Anzia Yezierska, a Jewish immigrant and novelist from the 1920s, who described the immigrants coming to America circa 1880–90. But Marshall's immigrants in *Brown Girl* have little in common with Yezierska's immigrants in *BreadGivers* (1925). Jewish immigrants fled pogroms in Eastern Europe, but in America, away from religious persecution and murderous anti-Semitism, many Jews prospered, especially in New York's garment district, as Yezierska demonstrates with the character Berel Bernstein, a clothing manufacturer. Examples of Jewish social mobility are evidenced in *BreadGivers*, from characters gaining an entrance into the markets of real estate and jewelry to the fashion and manufacturing industry and the media. Jewish immigrants are white, and Barbadian immigrants are black. In *Caribbean New York*, Philip Kasinitz summarizes what is obvious to Marshall: "if West Indians look like immigrants when compared with other blacks, they still resemble other blacks when compared to white immigrants."[16] Any attempt to compare Marshall to Yezierska and to suggest her authorial indebtedness to a Jewish immigrant novelist must end there, after acknowledging that both bear witness to the American immigrant experience. But the differences in these experiences span the distance of the Jews' Hester Street milieu and the Barbadians' or Bajans' Brooklyn brownstones, from which the whites flee.

Bajans such as Silla leased and bought brownstone apartment homes after a massive immigrant and nonimmigrant white flight in Brooklyn. Even the Chinese immigrants in Amy Tan's *The Joy Luck Club* find their comfortable niche in American society as the mothers flee war and communism in China to come to America to give their daughters "Chinese character, but American circumstances."[17] In their search for harmony and balance, or yin and yang, Tan's Asian Americans become what the political scientist Andrew Hacker has referred to as "upwardly mobile" Asians, or probationary whites.[18] Not only do Tan's immigrants, like Yezierska's, absorb the full-blown spirit of American capitalism, but Tan's mothers too are infected with a particularly Americanized brand of racism. When the mother Lindo takes her daughter Waverly to a Californian hairstylist for a "Shirley Temple" style and Waverly emerges with an "uneven mass of crinkly black fuzz," the mother grieves the daughter's "Negro Chinese" looks.[19] West Indian immigrants of the 1920s and 1930s were New York immigrants in a city of other immigrants, but race structured their lifestyles and limited their opportunities. While they entered a prosperous American society, they also joined the ranks of black Americans, one of the country's most oppressed minorities. West Indians, though, sought ethnic distance as they believed black Americans were "overly preoccupied with racial slights and barriers."[20] Marshall's Bajans come to realize, however, their own restrictions despite their aspirations.

Selina's mother, the "strong-made body" Silla, laments, "Just because your skin black some of these white people does think you can't function like them" (16, 102). Her father, Deighton, complains, "They's all the same, lady-folks. Here and in Bimshire [Barbados] they's the same. They does scorn yuh 'cause yuh skin black" (83). This sad awareness causes the Bajans to form their own business association and credit union from which black Americans are excluded because the Bajans wish to keep their cultural distinctiveness. They isolate themselves from the ranks of America's oppressed minority and begin a rivalry that Marshall continues in *The*

Fisher King. The motto of the Bajan Association is boastfully uttered by one of its members: "We ain white yet. We's small-timers. . . . But we got our eyes on the big time" (221). The organization is seen as "a sign that we has a *business* mind!" With her illustration of such negative ethnic imprinting, Marshall describes children imitating their parents, snobbishly forming their own youthful association only to give scholarships to college-bound Bajans.

While Marshall's narrator suggests Silla's imitation of "whiteness," Deighton is without the same description. These different responses to racial ostracism lie at the heart of the novel: pitting conforming Bajans against nonconforming Bajans, black Caribbeans against black Americans, and Silla against Deighton and, finally, Silla and Selina fighting each other. Selina's life is fraught with the tensions of this conflict, which becomes a war, played out dramatically against her mother. The Bajans' yin and yang aspiration is so thwarted by American racism that they find themselves making false enemies of husbands and wives and mothers and daughters.

Marshall disavows "a Manichaean brand of dualism that sees matter, flesh, the body, as inherently evil" for her Bajans. Presumably, Bajans "had never heard of the mind/body split" in their ubiquitous references to each other as "soully-gal" or to something or someone as "beautiful-ugly," terms used to describe the wedding of Deighton Boyce and Gatha Steed's daughter (see Marshall, "From the Poets in the Kitchen"). Nevertheless, as Abdul R. Jan Mohamed posits in *Manichean Aesthetics,* a negative dualism in literature reflects a Manichaean dialectics of colonized people and their colonizers psychologically in Marshall's work. Whether or not the Bajans ascribe to beliefs of the principles of a fundamental dualism of existence, the nature of the characters' lives in *Brown Girl, Brownstones* reveals this split.

The oppositional dialectics invested in *Brown Girl* and in the mother-daughter dyad merit attention and scrutiny, for key players are not seen for being the victims they truly are as they wrestle for an identity. Characters such as Silla embrace the ethos of American materialism and buy brownstone houses as a defense against racial vulnerability. Characters such as Deighton shun the ethics of compensatory bourgeois appendages and subsequently drown, literally. There is then a fundamental dualism in the novel: in choosing assimilation and acculturation, Silla becomes severed from her racial past; in electing to remain indigenous to his heritage, Deighton appears stagnant. Assimilation and nonassimilation, salvation and damnation, white and black, love and hate are dualistic forces in the novel with which the characters contend, making them combatants. Yet in the afterword of *Brown Girl, Brownstones,* Mary Helen Washington writes that the novel "is thus one of the most optimistic texts in Afro-American literature, for it assigns even to an oppressed people the power of conscious political choice: they are not victims" (322). Regarding the mother-daughter bond, Gloria Wade-Gayles adds that Silla and Selina's conflict is that of an "adolescent rebellion against a cold and domineering mother."[21] But witnessed through the prism of fundamental dualism, *Brown*

Girl is a tragedy, and the characters are victims. Selina, whom Marshall describes as an "old" adolescent, does not rebel against Silla, as Wade-Gayles posits, but against something much larger than Silla. Selina is at war against the dualistic forces that symbolically destroy Silla and literally kill Deighton. In the end the psychological violence of racism motivates Selina to find freedom away from America.

While there are no ancient African warriors in *Brown Girl, Brownstones*, paradigmatically Marshall uses the beginning and ending of World War II (book 3, "The War") to indicate the nature and context of the Boyces' warring existence in the 1940s. Silla and Deighton are at war with each other; the mother, as warrior, is forced to fight against her own husband. At the beginning of the section, the "news of the bombing" unleashes "hysteria" and "shattered Sunday's tedium" (65). Silla has decided to betray Deighton by selling the Barbadian land he has inherited from his deceased sister. Damning her soul, she writes home in Deighton's name and urges and achieves the sale. With the money she plans to buy the brownstone that the family has been leasing and take a "lesson" from "the Jew landlord" and lease rooms. From the beginning Deighton, an illegal immigrant, has wanted to use his inheritance to return home and build a house in Barbados. He confesses to Selina, "Barbados is poor-poor, but sweet enough. That's why I going back," to reclaim his essential self (11).

To Silla, the forceful maternal figure, the war that her life has become must be matched with equal force, but Deighton, whose emasculation in Barbados is continued in America, is resigned to his mediocre fate while still revering his ancestral home. He sleeps in the sun parlor and keeps a concubine. When Selina visits "the mother" at the war-defense factory where she works, the daughter notices that only "the mother's own formidable force could match that of the machines" (100). While Deighton takes life easily and remembers Barbados as poor but sweet, Silla cries to Selina, "Nice? Bimshire nice? . . . Lemme tell you how nice it is. You know what I was doing when I was your age? . . . picking grass in a cane field from the time God sun rise in his heaven till it set. . . . working harder than a man at the age of ten" (45). Pained by the remembrance of her poverty, Silla has "no time for gaiety." At Gatha Steed's daughter's Fifth Avenue "beautiful-ugly wedding," Marshall describes the guests as "two warring camps" (136). Almost all of the guests are against the "wuthless Deighton," who has eschewed their acculturated American lifestyle.

While the mother is a big, "dark force" but a necessary figure of support, the father is needed too. The mother-daughter dyad is therefore compounded by Deighton's triangular influence, which is transformative for Selina. Both Deighton and Silla claim Selina, so she is caught in the crossfire of a parental war. Silla refers to her as Deighton's child, while Deighton has called her "yuh mother child, in truth" (91). However, Deighton has granted her a reprise from an otherwise tumultuous mother and daughter relationship.[22] Though defeated, Deighton impresses upon

Selina the shallowness of Bajan materialism and provincialism and the importance of ancestral strivings. At the wedding Silla and Deighton still apparently maintain an unspeakable passion for each other, but she rejects him. He stumbles away saying, "Oh God, why," and his downfall begins.

Afterward, Deighton injures his arm in a machine at work, an injury symbolic of his displacement in an industrialized America. He joins a religious fraud's "family" and abandons his own family, including Selina, who visits him at the Harlem temple where he lives. During the visit, the fifteen-year-old Selina is "embarrassed" for her father and others who are equally deceived: "She felt suddenly old and terribly wise, while they seemed to her like children" (166). An irate Silla turns Deighton over to the police as an illegal immigrant. While homeward bound Deighton jumps or falls into the water and drowns. At the end of book 3, Silla receives a cable announcing her husband's death while soldiers scream "the goddamn war's over" (186). Although she dislikes the mother for the "pain of her childhood," Selina also loathes Silla for betraying and contributing to the death of her father.

The greatest conflict in the novel is Selina's emotionally confusing hatred and love, rejection and acceptance of her mother. Mary Helen Washington's incisive summation of the dyad bears repeating: "The relationship between Silla and Selina Boyce is so full of mystery, passion, and conflict that it may well be the most complex treatment of the mother-daughter bond in contemporary American literature."[23] Silla's betrayal unleashes Selina's rage, resulting in their private war. Calling her mother "Hitler," Selina "sprang" at Silla with "envenomed eyes and [a] frenzied shout" while a guilty Silla "stumbled across the room" (184). Selina fights her mother but later "sag[s] helplessly against" her breast, falling asleep and sinking "into the curve of Silla's neck" (185). Lovingly the mother caresses her daughter, with her maternal body functioning as a pillar of major support.

Selina has always recognized, Marshall writes, that without Silla, the mother-warrior, "the world would collapse" (46). But it is not until she faces racism herself and its dismantling effect that Selina appreciates her mother's formidable strength. The tall and big-breasted African American matriarch, Miss Thompson, bridging the two cultures, had forewarned Selina that "maybe someday you'll understand your momma and then you'll see why she does some of these things" (215). Although Selina feels at one with the women and especially Silla, she decides to visit Barbados. Like the Great Mother Demeter upon losing her daughter, Persephone, Silla cries, "Going 'way. . . . Oh God, is this what you does get for the nine months and the pain and the long years putting bread in their mouth?" (306). The strong tie of the umbilical nexus between mothers and daughters and sons (appearing in virtually all of Marshall's novels) first appears in *Brown Girl, Brownstones*. Marshall has Selina's boyfriend Clive articulate the permanence of this maternal connection: "Mothers? Hell, they seldom say die! Fathers perhaps. Like my poor father. But not mothers. They form you in that dark place inside them and you're theirs.

For giving life they exact life. The cord remains uncut" (262). By having Clive rather than the emotionally invested Selina comment on the force of maternal love, Marshall provides a seemingly "unbiased" and thus acceptable pronouncement on maternal attachment.

Clive's speech is perhaps more properly directed to the mother-daughter bond, classically illustrated in the Demeter-Persephone tale. Indeed, writes Adrienne Rich, "There is nothing in human nature more resonant with charges than the flow of energy between two biologically alike bodies," so that "the loss of the daughter to the mother, the mother to the daughter, is the essential female tragedy."[24] Although black feminists such as Mary Helen Washington decry the ubiquitous facilitation of the Demeter-Persephone myth as the paradigm for the mother-daughter dyad,[25] it is difficult to imagine a more powerful example of a mother's anger and pathos upon losing a daughter. As goddess of the earth's vegetation, Demeter threatens to end the earth's fertility until Persephone is returned to her from Hades, even in a compromise. The mother-goddess insistence remains one of the greatest illustrations of the dyadic connection. Silla's Demeter-like lamentation about her separation from Selina is related to her maternal labor, first, as a mother with emotions traced to the mother-daughter nexus formed in her womb, and second, as the major provider for her family. Although she rejects Silla's imprinting, Selina understands the greater oppressions that have shaped her mother's response to it, and she marvels at the strength of the maternal warrior who had chosen not to drown.

Drowning has been interpreted as an image of black male "castration symbolism"[26] by male scholars who see Marshall, Alice Walker, and Toni Morrison as contributing to black male stereotypes. *Brown Girl, Brownstones,* for example, contains an array of black male characters, from Selina's Clive to Silla's Deighton, who experience inertia or death in stark contrast to assertive and fertile maternal figures. Silla, Florrie, and Virgil form a supportive network of women who comfort each other and discuss community affairs, gender specifically. In graphic language they celebrate the female characters' aggression but criticize male characters' weakness: "Look at Eulise Bourne. She buying another [house] despite the worthless husband"; and "Vi Dash on Fulton Street crying poor, but she buying the second house. . . . and the husband is nothing but a he-whore" (73). In discussing Deighton's concubine with Silla, Virgil, with her "perennially burgeoning stomach," tells the "suffering-soul" Silla, "But Deighton oughta stop. . . . Nobody din say he can't have the hot-ass woman, but [come] dear his own got to come first" (31). Unsympathetic to the male and sympathetic to the female, the women stress the wives' material success, despite obstacles in and outside their communities.

Born out of necessity, not choice, Marshall's maternal warriors such as Silla are like Brecht's Mother Courage, who informs an army sergeant how she got her name: "They call me Courage, sergeant, because when I saw ruin staring me in the face I drove out of Riga through cannon fire with fifty loaves of bread in my wagon.

They were getting moldy, it was high time, I had no choice."[27] Similarly, Marshall's Silla is forced by circumstances into her maternal-warrior role out of necessity, not choice. The experiences of black people, Marshall intimates, threaten their lives: a threat they must fight, a war motif, which Ralph Ellison had expressed several years before Marshall's publication of *Brown Girl, Brownstones*, showing Ellison's influence on her work. In *Invisible Man* (1952), the grandfather informs the grandson, "Son, after I'm gone I want you to keep up the good fight. I never told you, but our life is a war."[28] Silla's struggles typify this war, making the personal, as feminists argue, the political in the social realm.

The question is, do black women writers' female characters fight this war more effectively than their male characters? Since Marshall's *Brown Girl, Brownstones* is autobiographical, the answer to this question is a resounding yes, as Marshall explains: the experiences of black male characters in the novel often reflect the author's own past. Deighton abandons his family for a religious fraud in Harlem just as Marshall's father had abandoned his family. Like Zora Neale Hurston, Marshall appears to have written her first novel to reconcile her feelings for her father and to valorize the maternal body. Marshall's father, Samuel Burke, she writes, "abandon[ed] us to a cycle of poverty and my mother's rapid decline into bitterness, cancer, and an early death. . . . It's taken me a long time and much interior work to get over my anger at him."[29] *Brown Girl, Brownstones* depicts these family complications and understandings.

The Chosen Place, the Timeless People: Bournehills, a Maternal Landscape

In her second novel, Marshall adopts a more formally ritualistic mother-daughter-warrior patterning. The African warrior tale of the Cuffee Ned slave rebellion in Barbados in 1675 is impressed upon the young villagers in *The Chosen Place, the Timeless People* (1969), which contains a symbolic and liberating mother-daughter dyad, though one even more sweeping in nature than in *Brown Girl, Brownstones*. Marshall's Barbados is the mythical Bournehills, which the author describes alternately as a primordial tragedy and a "vast warm womb" (25). Bournehills also represents Carl Jung's mother imago, the lush "island landscape" here,[30] and Merle Kinbona, the island's heroine, is the feminization of the maternal womb. Sent to Bournehills to study the conditions of the island, the American researcher Allen Fuso tells his supervising researcher, Saul Amron, that Merle has "become too much a part of the place. In a way I can't explain, she somehow is Bournehills" (118).

Bournehills and Merle have a dual function: to (pro)create and educate a new world order of an island and a people raped and ravaged by Caribbean slavery. Images of female fecundity abound in this novel, expressing the author's thematic emphasis on rebirth and renewal. Merle's aging matriarchal housekeeper Carrington is a "tall, full-bosomed, maternal figure" who has "great breasts that had been used, it seemed, to suckle the world" (110, 403). In addition, at the end of the novel two women, Gwen and Milly, await the birth of their children: the latter's "stomach was as large now . . . as Gwen's had been all along" (471). Even Bournehills is presented as an island of "endless cane fields covering the breast of the land" (95). The primary maternal bond is between Bournehills and Merle Kinbona.

Like the island, Merle has been dispossessed, and her personal tragedy mirrors the island's political and economic rape, as evinced by its perpetual mudslides and land shifts. When Marshall initially describes Merle, her personal chaos is immediately apparent. The daughter of a white slavocrat, who bred her black mother, Merle was ignored by Ashton Vaughan, her father. Later he sends her to England to study. In London, she meets and marries an East African and has a daughter. But after her English lesbian lover divulges their earlier affair, the African leaves Merle and takes their daughter back to Africa. Merle spends fifteen years in London and then returns to Bournehills, where islanders describe her as the woman who "has been through enough to set out the strongest head" (33). In Bournehills for eight years, Merle drives a "beat-up Bentley," dresses in African print dresses, and wears English earrings but Barbadian bracelets. Her internal chaos is apparent as she struggles for cultural unity. Having witnessed, as a child, her mother's murder by her father's white wife, having been deprived of maternal imprinting, and having been the product of a small island raped by slavery, Merle's ontological tragedy is a facsimile of the island's.

In her penetrating essay "*Chosen Place, Timeless People:* Some Figurations on the New World," Hortense J. Spillers remarks, "Any attempt to summarize *Chosen Place* is ultimately frustrating since single threads of it disappear into the whole, integrated fabric." Nevertheless, Spillers offers "a simple pattern of four concentric circles as a useful paradigm for grasping the novel's dynamically related parts." These include "four circles of involvement-myth, history, ritual, and ontology."[31] I believe that a fifth circle can be added: black surreal time, a radical restructuring of Western linear time with its cosmic periodicity. Black time is centered on a "mythic concept of time," and with it a sense of surrealism replaces a linear and technical construct of time.[32] Time stands still in Bournehills, for in the village there is no Western sense of time. This allows Marshall's beloved villagers to beat back the profane Western time of their ancestors' enslavement and subsequent cultural incoherence.

Although Spillers suggests that *The Chosen Place, the Timeless People* cannot be thematically summarized, Marshall foreshadows the theme in the epigraph to the novel: "Once a great wrong has been done, it never dies. People speak the words of peace, but their hearts do not forgive. Generations perform ceremonies of reconciliation, but there is no end." Her most politically and historically ambitious novel, dense and well over 450 pages, *The Chosen Place, the Timeless People* is an epic lamentation of Caribbean slavery and the fracturing of the Caribbean mind. "*Fractured* means broken, splintered, or ruptured," writes Joyce Pettis, and "in the traditional literary sense, *psyche* refers to the invisible soul that complements the physical body, a presence rooted in myth, but validated through psychology." Pettis continues, "Thus, a fractured psyche affects identity and threatens psychic survival, unless it is repaired."[33] In all of her novels Marshall relates black cultural healing not to integration movements but to knowledge of an ancestral foundation and a (re)staging of history. In this novel Marshall brings together the major characters or countries involved in the slave trade to effect cultural healing: Merle Kinbona of the West Indies; Saul and Harriet Amron from the United States; Sir John Stokes of England; and Merle's husband, who appears in name only, from Africa. Through these representations and narrative actions, Marshall revisits history, using maternal imprinting, ritual, and myth to restabilize black life.

With their rich and abundant arable soil and their lucrative production of sugar cane crops, West Indian colonies such as Barbados were lands of exploitation and not colonies of settlement, as Mary Prince implied in distinguishing proper British behavior in England from colonial British action in the Caribbean. From 1626 to 1807 Barbados imported approximately half a million slaves from West Africa. Yet in 1834 only eighty-two thousand were on the island to receive emancipation, due to the high mortality rate.[34] Barbados was called "Little England," and the island kept its English seventeenth-century assembly well until 1966, the year of its independence.[35] With absentee European or British landlords, Caribbean slave society was managed by "a debased backwater from the mainstream of European culture,"[36] but blacks were excluded even from this group.

Despite the people's social exclusion, many historians have commented that no other European colony was so convinced of its British or European "heritage" as these islands.[37] Because blacks outnumbered whites, color distinctions were therefore shrewdly created by the whites to enable them to control and manipulate the slaves.[38] Whites distinguished free colored people from slaves by freedom and by color.[39] Marshall captures the Caribbean color fetish in all four novels but especially in *The Chosen Place, the Timeless People*. The "near-white" Hinkson apologizes to the American researcher Saul Amron for a local, "noisy argument," assuring the American that "we are not a people given to such outbursts. We're much too British for that" (61). The dark-skinned Lyle Hutson studies law in London but returns to the island speaking in a "clipped Oxonian accent," wears a dark Oxford robe in the hot tropical sun, marries a near-white woman, and keeps a white mistress. Of all the exploited colonies, Barbados emerges, perhaps, as the most color conscious of them all.

Merle Kinbona, the heroine Marshall loves, asks, "Who put us so" and then answers her own question: "Those English were the biggest obeah [black magic] men out when you consider what they did to our mind" (105, 67). *In the Castle of My Skin,* by the Barbadian writer George Lamming, captures this magical dimension of the Caliban-Prospero metaphor rather well: "Today, I shudder to think how a country, so foreign to our own instincts, could have achieved the miracle of being called Mother."[40] Marshall faithfully mirrors the islanders' colonial mental bondage symbolically by the refining process of islanders transforming "crude" dark sugar from the canes into "refined" white sugar in the factory.

Even her most militant islander and villager, Ferguson (who proclaims the return of the seventeenth-century African warrior Cuffee Ned), is incapable of escaping the Prospero magic. He boasts of what he plans to tell Sir John Stokes of London about the inoperative cane rollers upon Stokes's annual visit to the Cane Vale factory. Through narrative semiotics, Marshall establishes British imperial attitude, behavior, and dress code as Sir John arrives in a "black stately Rolls," dressed "for a safari," and sporting an "imperious air." Studying the cane rollers in the factory of the British-owned Kingsley and Sons firm, he sees the need for new rollers but imperiously approaches Ferguson, the would-be warrior. Yet when Sir John stares and challenges Ferguson to speak, "no sound came." Saul Amron, the American who has witnessed Ferguson's impassioned speeches about the African warrior Cuffee Ned, has to "look quickly away" (222), having recognized the humiliating effect of race and class subordination.

For colonized subjects such as Ferguson, there is, in Frantz Fanon's words, a myth to be faced. The "Negro is unaware of it as long as his existence is limited to his own environment, but the first encounter with a white man oppresses him with the whole weight of his blackness."[41] Marshall highlights the profound pathos of the lingering effects of slavery, its psychological impact on mental health and social behavior. Compare Ferguson's humiliating experience with Sir John to that of the Ibos' miraculous walk on water back to Africa in *Praisesong*. Whether the "rhetoric of the image" is one of defeat for Ferguson or victory for the Ibos, Marshall provides an artistic rendering of the power of self-disclosure, via inaction and insecurity for Ferguson or action and reclamation for the Ibos.

We have an example of one of Spillers's four concentric circles, of the ontology of the Bournehills characters, ranging from the professionals such as Hinkson and Hutson to the nonprofessionals such as Ferguson, class and education notwithstanding. Even Merle Kinbona, in her chaotic form of dress, symbolizes the native insecurity of the islanders' identity. Marshall's description of their confused life in Bournehills reflects the historical reality of West Indian slavery. But Anthony Trollope's much-cited observation of West Indian society after slavery, in 1860, was more stigma than genuine lamentation: "How strange is the race of creole Negroes—of Negroes, that is, born out of Africa. They have no country of their own, yet they have not hitherto any country of their adoption. . . . They have no idea of country, and no pride of race."[42] Trollope's comment is ironic in its evasion of European enslavement of Negroes and invidious in the British author's articulation of racism. Yet the West Indian scholar Kenneth Ramchand asserts that islanders are indeed in search of an identity,[43] and in *The Chosen Place, the Timeless*

People, Marshall launches her villagers into a journey of self-discovery from their ontological insecurity to their ontological security.

Once again she appropriates social and maternal imprinting from ritual, myth, and history to facilitate these changes. Marshall reappropriates the Cuffee Ned slave revolt in Barbados in 1675 to teach history as a guide to the islanders. Conventional history has it that Gold Coast African warrior Ned and thirty-five slaves were routed and executed by the British when a female slave revealed their conspiracy to overthrow colonial rule.[44] Marshall's villagers tell a different tale. During the West Indian Carnival—when social and political realities are conveniently dispensed—the villagers, led by Ferguson and Stinger, his ally, perform the Pyre Hill revolt, an annual ritual. Ceremonially dressed, Ferguson becomes Percy Bryam, the white master, and Stinger becomes Cuffee Ned, the African warrior. As the heroic Ned, Stinger captures the white enslaver and then leads him victoriously to his just execution. Ferguson and Stinger's impassioned performance has the mark of authenticity, so real is their need to fill the breach between social reality and psychic desire.

An elder villager approaches Ferguson as Bryam and remarks, "It serve you right, Percy Bryam. . . . You ain't had no business doing the people's bad" (289). While the professionals Hinkson and Hutson are embarrassed by the carnival display, preferring a less threatening tourist attraction, Marshall suggests that for the villagers, the carnival is a political necessity. The theme of the carnival, "All o' we is one," is socially inclusive for them. Additionally the Cuffee Ned revolt allows the villagers to reclaim their worth as human beings. Ferguson boasts that Cuffee Ned held "off the whole damn British regiment," and then he proclaims, "He's goin' come again" (134). The idea is that only a revolt of this magnitude, with the oneness of mind of the warriors, can change an island that the author describes alternately and symbolically as both a "tragedy" and a "womb." These diverse descriptions refer to Bournehills's history of slavery, but also to its metaphorical and maternal readiness for rebirth.

Bournehills and Merle have a dyadic relationship. Merle teaches the Cuffee Ned revolt to young students, her "daughters," imprinting it on their young minds. Describing Merle as a tall, maternal figure, sketched like other maternal warriors to resemble Paule Marshall's formidable grandmother Da-duh, Leesy remarks, "She was telling the children about Cuffee Ned and things that happened on the island in older times." Leesy explains that Merle endangered herself because "the headmaster wanted her to teach the history that was down in the books that told all about the English" (32). Merle changes the English canon and loses her job, signaling Marshall's reference to the constant furor and debate over the traditional Great Books canon and its multicultural challenge for diversity (to add more women and minorities) and thus a revision. Merle protests the politics of the established canon, fighting the English version that "made it look like black people never fought back" (32). In maternally imprinting the Cuffee Ned lore on children, Merle assumes the warrior-guise of Marshall's forceful mothers.

Marshall's heroine also reveals the essentialness of the African oral tradition. Orality replaces Western literary tradition and catapults its speakers and listeners into the nonliterate culture of African society. The oral tradition, accompanied by ceremonial rituals, ruptures the tradition of Western dominance through written language. We see the importance of oral narration in the local school, where Merle impresses upon the children of Bournehills the importance of the African Anancy trickster tales. Merle tells "another episode in the life of Spider, the wily hero of the Anancy tales; narrated throughout the islands, Anancy, though small and weak, manipulates and defeats the stronger enemy" (224). While the children sit obediently listening, one imagines the future metamorphosis of their physical landscape, Bournehills. Marshall describes them as storing all that they hear for future use. The children's vision of their human community will go far beyond the traditional British authority and the imperial Sir John Stokes.

In *The Chosen Place,* the imprinting of children or daughters begins a process meant to move forward Marshall's authorial new-world order. The daughters in Marshall's novels are not just the fruit of the first womb; in addition they represent the second womb and a second chance to refashion a world. Merle's return to Bournehills, after being lured away to London and chaos by colonial forces beyond her control, sets in motion her own rebirth in addition to the island's. As a maternal figure, representative of the island's "vast warm womb," she is given the opportunity to reinvent herself.

Merle and Saul, a Jew who knows something about oppression, are bonded historically and emotionally. When the two have an affair, Saul's wife, Harriet, an American descendant of wealthy slavocrats, confronts Merle, the colonial subordinate. Harriet imperiously attempts to bribe Merle to send her back to London, back to mental slavery. This classic confrontation between the colonizer and the colonized, the dominant and the subordinate has different results from those of the Ferguson/Sir John debacle. Merle affirms her new identity as matriarchal nurturer and maternal imprinter, informing Harriet, "I can't be bought. Or bribed. . . . I've grown wise in my old age" (441). This defiant statement leads her to reclaim her heritage. She must return to Africa and claim her lost daughter, who will be the recipient of her mother's imprinting. Merle's planned route to Africa is noteworthy as she forgoes the usual route north to London via New York. Instead she flies "South to Trinidad, then on to Recife in Brazil" and then on to Africa, a new route of a symbolic, diasporic reconnection.

History, myth, ontology, and ritual do indeed make up the basic structure of *The Chosen Place,* as Spillers avers. The fifth unique dimension of black time, however, enables Marshall to emphasize the cultural distinctiveness of the island, its rejection of profane Western time, and its need for rebirth readiness. The critic Keith

Sandiford cites the appearance of black time in *Praisesong* with the Ibo landing and reclamation of their lives from the grip of Western time.[45] But this is an act, whereas in Bournehills, black time is an all-encompassing ethos. Again, Marshall employs female fecundity to stress change. Stinger's Gwen has a dual function in the novel: as a pregnant woman, she is waiting to give birth to Marshall's new society. The maternal waiting reflects black time symbolism; for example, to Saul's wife, Harriet, it seems as if Gwen has been pregnant for an extended time, beyond the Western linear time of nine months. Harriet has come to view Gwen's protruding stomach as a "tumor," a medical dysfunction, while Gwen assures her that she and the baby are healthy. Gwen will give birth in her own time.

Diametrically opposed views about the nature of Gwen's pregnancy allow Marshall to transform Western linear time into African mythic time, for a mythic concept of time is indigenous to traditional African societies. Only recently has Africa emerged from the period of myth into the age of mainstream history. The linear concept of Western time, however, is practically foreign to African societies. African time is harmonic or synchronic, nonlinear, and typical of agrarian societies. Western time is technical or diachronic, linear, and expressive of industrialized cultures. African conceptualization of time is shaped by lifestyles, and rituals convey a sense of timelessness, effacing mechanical and cosmic linearity.[46]

Having their humanity negated by their enslavement, having their freedom marginalized by their minority or third-world status, blacks, Marshall intimates, must in turn negate and nullify Western, first-world time. This negation and marginalization of profane time are everywhere in the novel. Ferguson's face is described as an ancient Benin mask, and Merle's face resembles an ancestral Bantu's. Harriet notices that even the Bournehills children are primordial-like. She observes "the manner of children in Bournehills, their almost frightening reserve, the old way they had about them" (178). Such is the description of Gwen and the female villagers in the cane factory. Gwen places the gathered sugar cane sheaves on her head and moves "confidently down" a precarious slope "as did the other women, her head weaving almost imperceptibly from side to side under its load"—"reminiscent of those child dances from Bali" (161). Even the natural order of the universe participates in the African surreality of time. Marshall writes that "instead of rising to its zenith as it should have as they approached noon, [the sun] appeared to drop closer, so close finally [that] it looked as though the men could reach up and touch it" (161). Gwen's pregnancy manifests the surreality of this African time.

Marshall makes considerable use of the characters Gwen and Harriet to achieve one of her signature focuses on female fecundity and rebirth. Gwen stores eggs that she sells to the Bournehills postmaster, who is to disseminate these tropes of a rebirth readiness throughout the island. While caring for Gwen's children in the mother's absence, Harriet imperiously decides to break and cook the eggs, to the suppressed befuddlement of the youths. Egg symbology contains past/present/

future historicizing conflicts from the natives who store the eggs, to the postmaster who buys them, to Harriet, who arrogantly breaks them—examples symbolizing the colonial yoke of imperialism. Marshall implies here the vulnerable manipulation of lives of the Diaspora, in need of a new beginning as Marshall's fecund mothers and maternal imprinter, Merle, await the long awaited: regeneration.

Praisesong for the Widow: The Maternal, Powerful Enough to Return from the Dead

In the opening quotation to this chapter, great-aunt Cuney, Marshall's wise ancestral figure, is the maternal figure, and her great-niece Avatara is the obedient respondent whose statement "I do" affirms her rite de passage into mythic maternal discourse. In *Praisesong for the Widow* (1983), Marshall's third novel, the legacy of the Ibos' walk on water back to Africa is an inspirational tale, and great-aunt Cuney narrates the details to Avatara. The story that Marshall's characters refer to, of the Ibos walking on water back to Africa after looking into the future and seeing black suffering into perpetuity, is one of Marshall's finest literary images. Marshall chooses one of the most autonomous of tribal groups in Africa, the Ibos, to perform an independent and rebellious act against black enslavement. Historically the Ibos were noted for their creation of multiple village governments because of their enterprising spirit and their distrust of authority. Marshall alludes to this particular feature of the Ibos, as detailed briefly in Basil Davidson's study *West African History*.[47] The Ibos' regeneration is illustrated by their return to Africa, and great-aunt Cuney keeps their act alive.

Roland Barthes's "rhetoric of the image" symbolism casts considerable light on great-aunt Cuney. Her appearance, manner, demeanor, and name all suggest her authority and mission, and she could be viewed also as Jung's embodiment of the maternal imago. Her vesting rituals are performed religiously when she visits the site of the Ibos' "unrecorded miracle," the landing in Tatem, South Carolina. She wears the same clothes and puts them on in ritualistic fashion, one after the other, following the same process each time, like a soldier preparing for war.[48] Marshall describes Cuney as so "straight" and "large-boned" that she resembles a "tree" (32). Trekking through the woods to the coastal area of the Ibo landing with Cuney is Avatara, whom Cuney names, assuming maternal authority. The nomenclature (Avatara as a divinized being with a messianic mission) symbolizes the child's function. Duty bound, Avatara follows Cuney into the woods, imitating the matriarch by donning her imaginary second belt, but real "field hat," and playing "a silent game of Take a Giant Step" to keep up with the aunt, her maternal imprinter.

At the landing Cuney narrates the Ibo miracle to the child: "It was here that they brought 'em. They taken 'em out of the boats right here where we's standing." After describing the Ibos' look into the future, their prescient awareness of black displacement, and their Christ-like walk on water back to Africa, Cuney regards her great-niece "in silence" when she asks, "But how come they didn't drown, Aunt Cuney?" (39). To the old woman, who has accepted myth as an act of faith, the question is absurd. She rebukes the child, "Did it say Jesus drowned." Twice a week the surrogate mother and child make the holy pilgrimage to the Ibo landing, and Avatara is reminded, on this occasion, of the importance of the mind-spirit and body-flesh split, a different kind of Cartesian dualism from that experienced by Phillis Wheatley, the "pagan" Christian. The child repeats her grandmother's adage, "Her body she always usta say might be in Tatem, but her mind, her mind was long gone with the Ibos" (39). In an oppressive environment, care of the mind-spirit is Avatara's essential lesson. From the age of seven until "the age of ten," Avatara believed the "far-fetched story of people walking on water," so thoroughly had the maternal surrogate indoctrinated her (42).

With the Ibo legend and the additional social imprinting provided by her New York family in their annual summer outings to Bear Mountain, Avatara is launched securely into life. At Bear Mountain she "would feel what seemed to be hundreds of slender threads streaming out from her navel and from the place where her heart was to enter those around her. And the threads went out not only to people she recognized from the neighborhood, but out to those she didn't know as well" (190). Marshall's "threads" and Avatara's "navel" are diasporic connections, gathering black New Yorkers (Americans and West Indians alike) "to loll on the grass and eat fried chicken and potato salad" and, most importantly, "to lay claim" to "God's heaven" in a Jim Crow society before its legal dismantling (192). Rituals such as these family gatherings are functional because they give substantive form to human life.[49] Marshall illustrates the ritualistic functioning of myth too in having Avey, a married woman, take her husband, Jay Johnson, to the South Carolina home left to her by her now-deceased great-aunt Cuney. She narrates to him the "apocryphal tale," and he suspends disbelief and responds, "I'm with your Aunt Cuney and the old woman you were named for [the gran']. I believe it, Avey. Every word" (115).

The importance of ritual is evinced further in Avatara's married life. On visits to South Carolina, she and Jay "chang[ed] to the Jim Crow seats in the rear once they reached Washington." The Negro spirituals of "The Southerners, the Fisk Jubilee Choir, Wings Over Jordan," the dancing and singing after work, and their "small rituals . . . had made Sundays a special day." There is as well the sweet ritual of their romantic love, which soon results in two baby girls. When the rituals fade, something essential to their spirits is lost, and physical fatigue overwhelms them. The forces that lure the adult Avey away from the maternal and social imprinting of her youth, even of her young married life, coincide with and are symbolized by Jay's climb to material prosperity. After the "fatal Tuesday" when Avey accuses Jay of infidelity (while she is carrying their third child), rather than abandon her, he works relentlessly, and "the man Jay used to become at home . . . went into eclipse during the years following that near-fatal day" (116). With a "face which bore Jay's clear imprint," not great-aunt Cuney's, Avey fails to note the change, or she notices it "but did not dare to stop and reflect" (13, 116).

Jay and Avey become obsessed with the myth of the American dream and its materialism and lose their essential selves. He works several jobs, and their praise songs of Sunday afternoons are replaced by marital discord. Twenty years later, with three adult children, their small Halsey Street apartment, and their rituals all a distant memory, Avey and Jay, who has become the more formal Jerome Johnson, move to North White Plains, New York. Their false security is represented by the trappings of "insurance policies, annuities, trusts and bank accounts . . . small sheaf of government bonds and other securities" (88), all that Marshall's Selina rejects. With a change of names, Marshall indicates the characters' willful amnesia of ancestral strivings and cultural rituals, intended to give spiritual security and meaning to a black existence mired in the misery as seen all around them.

This oppression is more evident to their daughter than it is to her forgetful parents. Marion, the youngest and most conscientious daughter, participates in the "Poor People's March in Washington" and calls home collect. But Avey "almost refused to accept the call she had been so annoyed" (140). When Jerome Johnson dies "with a stranger's cold face laughing in Mephistophelean glee," his wealthy widow begins to take annual cruises to the Caribbean with friends, over Marion's objections. The ritual of a cruise, predominantly of white passengers, mocks her earlier cultural grooming. The name symbolism of the cruise ship the *Bianca Pride* and her North White Plains home reveal Avey's loss of cultural roots. Aboard the cruise, however, her life of sophisticated uselessness is called into account by the reappearance of great-aunt Cuney, returning from the dead. The maternal imprinter comes back from the other side to reclaim her lost surrogate daughter in a dream that Avey describes as so real that she palpably feels the physical struggle between the "mother" and her "daughter."

Great-aunt Cuney's love is so strong for her adopted daughter, Marshall suggests, that her return from the dead is imminent and emphasizes the depth of her maternal care. The aunt's plea to Avey, "Come / O will you come," is a sermonic call with profound theological revelations. Although Marshall, like Richard Wright and Ann Petry before her and Alice Walker and Toni Morrison after her, eschews orthodox religion, *Praisesong for the Widow* is, ironically, a theological novel. Marshall's oft-repeated, authorial condemnation of orthodox religion is apparent in *The Chosen Place, the Timeless People* and *Brown Girl, Brownstones*. Merle screams to a character who asks for prayer, "Heathen. . . . If I thought for a moment prayer did any good I'd have prayed for myself" (261). In her inimitable use of language as a political weapon, Silla remarks to her friend Iris, "The rum shop and the church join together to keep we pacify and in ignorance" (70). Yet the idea of spiritual reclamation in *Praisesong* is linked symbolically to Judeo-Christian properties of water baptism, spiritual anointing, and altar calls, and the sermonic call of providence is repeated throughout the text. The adult Avey recalls the religious imprinting of her youth and the ministerial Easter resurrection sermons: "The stone to the sepulcher was gone" and "Call Him" (198, 202). Interestingly, after Avey leaves the *Bianca Pride*, cutting short her cruise at the next port of call, takes a taxi to an island hotel, and walks in a trance toward a remote place, she meets Lebert Joseph, who beckons, "Come. . . . You must come in" (180). In listening to Avey's struggles, Joseph hears the "Gethsemane she had undergone" (172). Thus it is not easy for contemporary black writers to reject *all* aspects of orthodox religion, the bedrock of the slaves' survival.

Beginning with the Ibos' Christ-like walk on water, continuing with Avey's recollection of her childhood Easter Sundays, and concluding with her ritualistic baptism and rebirth, Marshall links African mythology and ritual to Christian symbolism in their healing belief systems. Lebert Johnson is described as an "Old Testament prophet, chronicling the lineage of his tribe." He convinces Avey to accompany him to the Carriacou Excursion to honor the "Old Parents, the Long-time People" and to "Beg Pardon" for the "Away" or diasporic people, their excursion being based on reality. In her symbolically titled memoirs *Triangular Road*, Marshall describes her travels to Grenada and the small Carriacou inlet to which the islanders journeyed to participate in the "Beg Pardon" ritual. She writes, "It was long past midnight when the elderly dancers finally tired. They had acknowledged their [diasporic] nations," making such an impression on the visiting Marshall that "the idea for a novel I would write almost a decade later [1983] later grew out of this overnight trip." While these Carriacou/African Diaspora ceremonies for the dead have no real significance for new-world black Americans, the reality-based ceremonies for the dead on Carriacou have a definite meaning for Africans—the influence of which "is taken for granted in many Caribbean communities,"[50] setting Marshall apart from other writers in this study. Conversely, Marshall appropriates Nina Simone's lyrics—"he forced my mother my mother / late / One night / What do they call me"—to portray the profane/sacred fetish of color in the black/mulatto community, resonating with meaning for black Americans but not for Africans unfamiliar with Nina Simone's cultural tropes.

As a diasporic writer, Marshall faces certain cultural challenges. Readers come across her cryptic, bicultural references earlier with her luminous description of Barbados, as the mythical island of Bournehills. Marshall writes, "It was the Atlantic this side of the island, a wild-eyed, marauding sea the color of slate, deep, full of dangerous currents, lined with row upon row of barrier reefs, and with a sound like that of the combined voices of the drowned raised in a loud unceasing lament" (106). According to the historian Edward Brathwaite, "The people of Barbados know this coastline—wild, Atlantic, and rocky. But how many, looking down on that surf . . . realized . . . that Barbados, the most easterly of the West Indies, is in fact *the nearest to Africa.*" Brathwaite emphasizes that "no major Barbados writer known to me had ever made the point."[51] While the Middle Passage tragedy is recognizable in the "voices of the drowned" for black Americans, the coastal area of Barbados with its proximity to Africa is probably a remote thought. These are the beautiful difficulties that Marshall faces as a diasporic writer attempting to bridge two cultures, African American and African Caribbean, which fail to understand the other's cultural signs.

Marshall's religious symbolism, however, is more clearly recognizable, here and elsewhere. The schooner that Avey and Joseph and other islanders board is described as a "scarred and battered" relic, which has a "crudely carved figurehead of a saint" wearing sandals and a "long girdled robe" and holding a "crucifixion in its hands." Aboard the boat Avey begins to vomit and experience the "massive contractions" of a suffering woman giving birth to herself, as Marshall links the power of religion with the miracle of the feminine-sacred, or what Kristeva refers to as "an implacable maternal force, a 'divine' omnipotence, [which] very often dominates the female psyche."[52] Indeed in her novels Marshall's Greek allusion to Demeter and Persephone, Christian tales of suffering and redemption, and maternal images of birth all sweepingly project (via pagan and religious tropes) a transcendent feminine principle in opposition to laws or suppositions of women's powerlessness. In *Praisesong for the Widow* other miracle-working women join Avey and assist in her divine mission on the island: chanting, bathing, and laying their hands on Avey's body, anointing her new birth and reclaiming her. Indeed, cites one Marshall critic, her "characters' spiritual maturation includes the resolution/integration of grief resulting from the death of a loved one, resurrection/reclamation of self after the character's own metaphysical death, and/or reunification with others after estrangement from the black community,"[53] which is what we see here.

Other symbols of Judeo-Christian religion are discovered, and the number three emerges as the most significant one. From the beginning of the novel, Marshall's creative use of the number three signifies Avey's rebirth and revival, a theme rooted in the Judeo-Christian meaning of the death-burial-rebirth cycle of Christ. Rituals of myth, maternal experiences, and imprinting through the number three manifest Marshall's overwhelming emphasis on ontological regeneration via cultural and metaphysical symbols, and the number three is abundantly represented. It is the number of children Avey has, and her third daughter, Marion, is her savior figure. It is Marion who warns her mother about the *Bianca Pride* and its infamous Versailles Room, where Avey becomes ill eating a parfait, which in nomenclature represents the French palace where imperial powers "divvy[ied] up India, the West Indies, the world" (47).

Thomasina, Clarice, and Avey are the three friends who take the annual cruise, but it is Avey who becomes ill and recalls "the dream three nights ago" when great-aunt

Cuney visited her. Seeking an isolated spot on the ship to finalize her plans to leave, Avey enters the "Three Deck" passage to the library. All the discomfort she now feels comes after "three years that she had been coming to the islands" (70). With "mystifying clarity" Avey begins to recognize the significance of the "crucifixes" and other objects she had viewed "three days ago in Martinique" (83). The Carriacou Exchange is for two or three days, and there are three drummers. All islanders speak patois, the official language, for two or three days. Within these three days that Avey hears the language of patois, the critic G. Thomas Couser observes, she is taken back to the "aural memory" of her South Carolina roots. "The initial reactivator of Avey's ethnic consciousness is, significantly, an aural memory." The patois spoken by natives on Martinique, Couser continues, "faintly echoes the Gullah spoken by the older blacks in Tatem, South Carolina, where she had summered as a youth. The aural memory thus reawakens her condensed cultural memory, which was transmitted orally."[54] Through aural memory, ritual, song, and dance Avey is transformed and sees "a hole the size of a crater where her life of the past three decades had been" (196).

Avey emerges from the Carriacou journey having been prompted by a dream and the appearance of great-aunt Cuney, the eternally powerful maternal figure. Avey will become like Coleridge's wide-eyed, ancient mariner, "the obsessed old sailor" who "stoppeth one of three" to repeat the lesson she had learned. Avey learns the lesson that all of Marshall's heroines must learn: "that the darkness contained its own light" (232). Marshall suggests that black people were their own saviors, hence her avoidance of social movements—and, incidentally or not, the title of Alice Walker's book of meditations, *We Are the Ones We Have Been Waiting For* (2006). Great-aunt Cuney's maternal mirroring of the Ibo legend, the New York summer gatherings on Bear Mountain, and Avey's and Jay's early spiritual and romantic rituals evoke a schema of narrative events that find final expression in the Carriacou Exchange. But only Avey, and not Jay, lives to experience Marshall's rebirth motif.

Some black male scholars argue that black female writers have castigated black male characters, emotionally and psychologically, and others challenge Marshall's authorial decision to kill off Jay while saving and celebrating his widow, Avey, whose complicity in their bourgeois climb to success betrays her maternal imprinting. "If Marshall is to escape the charge of reverse sexism," argues Keith Sandiford, "the only defense possible is one coherent with her mythic theme: though she makes Jay a paragon of black manhood (conscientious, resourceful, and sensitive), he lives too entirely in the illusion of self-sufficiency."[55] That is, Jay has not benefited from maternal imprinting, and unlike his wife, Avey, he does not have the necessary foundation to fall back on when he goes astray.

Sandiford's criticism seems tenable until we acknowledge that even with maternal imprinting, Marshall's male characters go astray. Compare Jay's absence of maternal imprinting and his subsequent loss of self with Primus Mackenzie's maternal patterning in *Daughters* and his eventual identity collapse despite his childhood imprinting. In *Daughters*, Primus's mother asks him, "Tell me, why am I sending a little boy still in short pants to live all the way in big Fort Lord Nelson? Why am I putting the only boy child I have in this world—my heart string, *oui!*— in some big school where he won't know a soul?" (161). Because the child does not understand, the mother informs him, "It's so he'll understand from the early how things go in this world. . . . how to carry himself in this life" (161). Primus's maternal nurturing influences the formation of a proud male ego, but he is lured away from the imprinting by the trappings of capitalism, before finally being reclaimed by his wife and daughter. Thus, Sandiford's theory is untenable, for even with maternal mirroring Marshall's male characters such as Primus Mackenzie falter on their own accord.

It is apparent that Marshall, Walker, and Morrison do display an affinity for their endearing maternal characters. Accordingly their writings challenge the accuracy of the feminist assertion that race is such a primary marker in American society that issues of gender are secondary in their importance to black women writers.[56] This may have been the case for eighteenth- and nineteenth-century black women writers such as Phillis Wheatley, Harriet Jacobs, and Charlotte Forten, who placed their emphases on institutional reform in regard to race, with Jacobs making a special plea for the slave mother even though it meant revealing some of the embarrassing events in her life. But Marshall shows gender and race as important markers of her female characters' identity, perhaps rooted deeply in a collective history where women were major players who hardly received the recognition they deserved until now. In her travels throughout the South after slavery, for example, Frances Ellen Watkins Harper observed that black women endured the work of "unremitted labor"[57] in the home and in the field. Slavery as an institution attempted to destroy the black family. "Reproducing the slave labor force required," writes the historian Herbert Gutman, "only the simple biological dyad 'mother and child.' The social dyads 'husband and wife' and 'father and child' were not essential."[58] The family, the children, were largely the responsibility of women who understood how the economic and political control of black men had necessitated the women's ascendancy to power (such as Brecht's Mother Courage), which Marshall acknowledges in her illustrative dyads.

Daughters: The Long Shadow of an African Monument

The blood mother-daughter dyad in *Daughters* (1991), Marshall's fourth novel, includes the characters Estelle and Ursa Mackenzie. Estelle Mackenzie continues Marshall's maternal mirroring of African warriors who resisted humiliation and bondage. When her daughter is only two, Estelle takes Ursa to the Great Monument of Will Cudjoe and Congo Jane, two warrior-lovers, on the mythical

Caribbean island of Triunion. "Stretch all the way up and touch Congo Jane's toes," the mother commands her daughter. Marshall writes that Ursa as a child "did as she was told, leaning dangerously over to her left to get at the other colossal pair of feet" (*Daughters* 14). The image of the two warriors is a liberating reminder to Ursa as a troubled adult that unity between men and women is possible.

Although Marshall's novel *Daughters* is dedicated to her father and brother, the book is thematically about a victorious mother and daughter, Estelle and Ursa, and the rupture of contemporary male-female relationships on various levels: romantic and political, external to the maternal imprinting of the colonial alliance of Will Cudjoe and Congo Jane, two African warriors. But with its multiple characters, mininarratives, competing voices, and epistolary narrative breaks, *Daughters* is a demanding novel. Marshall's own description of the book's theme reveals why: "*Daughters* is about people, politics, culture, history, race, racism, morality, marriage, children, friendship, love, sex, the triumph and sometimes defeat of the human spirit, as well as a few other things I threw in for good measure."[59] The "few other things" include an array of women, the daughters of the title, who have an impact on Ursa's life in one way or another. Ursa, in turn, is the little girl of all these older daughters, now maternal characters (2). She is the unifying character in a text that presents the reader with a commuting between a colonial past and a postcolonial present.

Critical of the novel, Heather Hathaway identifies the narrative structure and fragmentation of *Daughters* through its "postmodern and post-colonial contexts." She argues that the novel's "fragmentation of narrative voice as well as of geographic and temporal location . . . gives the text an ambiguous sense of both self and place."[60] The novel's two settings, New York and the Caribbean, its various characters, and their heteroglossia speech acts all represent Marshall's ambitious effort to uncover, across time and space, the problem of the crises of identity affecting colonial and postcolonial blacks. As she does with all of her novels after *Brown Girl, Brownstones,* Marshall fashions a romantic image of a diasporic past and colonized blacks who worked effectively for change and then uses this model for postmodern blacks trapped within a historical system that continues to enslave them, psychologically and politically.

Unlike the celebrated and united colonial blacks, represented by the monument of Will Cudjoe and Congo Jane, postmodern blacks as couples are presented as disunited, unable to effect the transformation of character that would link them nobly to Marshall's model coconspirators of change. Despite the text's narrative problems as Hathaway articulates, Ursa, led by her mother, Estelle, *is* the unifying character in the text who arrests the commuting between an elevated colonial past and a troubled postcolonial present. Ursa's voice is the major voice of the text. Marshall describes and connects a chaotic group of relations across geographic locations in New York and in the Caribbean. Estelle and Ursa, the mother-daughter dyad, function to ameliorate the discursiveness of the text and the dysfunctional male-female relationships.

Marshall describes broken relationships between male and female characters; ordinary social and political life magnifies the tension between them, young and old. For example, two teenage girls, one wearing a maternity top and the other holding a baby, assume maternal roles but seek financial assistance and travel a "mental distance" to answer basic questions. Even the mature Mae Ryland and the middle-aged Sandy Lawson, "coleaders" of a political campaign to help elect Lawson as mayor of Midland, a small black community in New Jersey that needs revitalization, are crippled. When Lawson becomes mayor, he abandons the vision of revitalization that he had shared with Mae, and he becomes a puppet of white businessmen. Over her objections, Lawson approves the construction of an expressway through Midland for the benefit of white suburbia.

In New York, Ursa's relationship with her boyfriend, Lowell, is also conflicted. Middle-class beneficiaries of the civil rights movement, Ursa and Lowell are two of the "Young and the Restless Upwardly Mobiles" in "black face." Having left graduate school to become an associate director of research for a Fortune 500 company, Ursa leaves there too and seeks a more meaningful career as a freelance researcher conducting studies on black life in Midland, New Jersey. Lowell Carruthers is an assistant manager of employee relations at Halcon Electronics. Like Ursa, he has a vision of a service career, which is as a college recruiter for minorities. Unlike Ursa, however, Lowell does not have the courage to change positions even though he is unhappy with his corporate job, where he is dominated by whites, as Sandy is in New Jersey. *Daughters* opens with Ursa aborting Lowell's baby; the abortion, like the teenage pregnancy and Sandy's betrayal of Mae, signifies the failure of relationships.

Despite their corporate titles and education or their absence of education and young pregnancy, these male and female characters are adrift in a sea of unworkable relationships. Viney, Ursa's friend, echoes Arthur Miller's desperate character Willy Loman in *Death of a Salesman*, dramatically expressing the novel's sense of urgency: "The woods are on fire out here . . . and we need everybody that can [to] tote a bucket of water to come running" (102). This theme is repeated when Ursa fails to write a graduate thesis on the fraternity of black male and female slaves, a topic her white professor rejects because he doubts the accuracy of the subject. He informs her that it is "highly doubtful" that relations between the sexes even during slavery were viable, although Ursa believes otherwise as a result of her maternal imprinting of the Will Cudjoe–Congo Jane legend. Away from her maternal patterning, Ursa, like the others, exists in a postmodern, splintering mass of humanity.

As a parallel plot to the American identity crisis, on the mythical Caribbean island of Triunion, Ursa's father, Primus Mackenzie, loses his shared vision with his wife, Estelle, an African American who bridges the two wings of the diasporic cultures. As the prime minister, Primus forgets his promise to aid the villagers and begins to build his own empire and supports a foreign-backed investment plan to build a resort hotel on government land for wealthy white tourists. Primus also has adulterous affairs, maintaining a relationship with Astral Forde, the near-white manager of his hotel and his "keep-miss," the Caribbean nomenclature for "mistress." Through name symbolism, from Estelle to Astral and Celestine, Primus's devoted childhood nurse-housekeeper, the critic Dorothy Denniston identifies Marshall's stellar constellation of female characters in orbit, circling Primus. Star imagery, Denniston states, "dominates *Daughters*" and evokes a "radiating influence [that] women can exert in the universe."[61] Star imagery is not, however, limited to Primus, who represents the color fetish and the concubine history of a slavish colonial past. The Will Cudjoe and Congo Jane monument is surrounded by a horizon of stars, one facilitating Estelle and Ursa's vision, built stone by stone, of male-female cooperation rather than strife and conflict.

Estelle and Ursa's dyadic relationship is one of the closest in Marshall's oeuvre of literary mothers and daughters, representing the sum of the author's long discourse on female networking, beginning with *Brown Girl, Brownstones*. When Estelle takes Ursa, the child, to the Will Cudjoe and Congo Jane monument, Marshall writes that Ursa "couldn't ever remember calling [her mother] anything but Estelle, [who] had gotten down on her knees at the base of the statue" and lifted Ursa to her shoulders (13). Will Cudjoe and Congo Jane stand tall "on a pedestal," and Jane's "head appeared to be grazing the sky" even as she carried a musket in her hand. Commanded to touch the toes of the warriors, Ursa "did as she was told" and looked "to find Orion, the hunter, and the North star" (54). For fugitive slaves, the North Star was a specific symbol directing them to freedom. Likewise, Estelle instructs Ursa, vis-à-vis the monument, to gaze on the sky and the stars and to see the importance of the free horizon.

All five of Marshall's novels employ African warriors or European tug-of-war imagery to illuminate the tension between the individual and society and the individual's battle readiness. In *Daughters*, Ursa undergoes the usual, compensatory rite of passage in preparation for her inevitable social battles. Estelle rushes Ursa's childhood training so she can move to America and take her mother's place in the civil rights movement. Ursa explains that her mother was "always in such hurry for me to grow up. As soon as I turned twelve she went rushing off to town and bought me a training bra" (98–99). In America, despite her own crippling times, Ursa recalls her childhood days, her mother's influence, and the "Great Monument" of Will Cudjoe and Congo Jane. These anchoring markers of Ursa's identity, particularly her visits to the monument, become a narrative refrain and serve as a unifying trope for what Heather Hathaway otherwise identifies as the disjointed narrative structure of *Daughters*.

From the cases of Sandy and Lowell in America and of her father, Primus, in the Caribbean, Ursa recognizes a pattern of male transgression across the Diaspora

and grieves, "Nothing changed," a reference to the injured psyche of the historically dispossessed. Ursa's long-awaited visit to Triunion has the main purpose of
returning her to the vision of her maternal imprinting. With Estelle's help, Ursa
sabotages the elections by giving to Justin Beaufils, her father's challenger, Primus's
prospectus for the resort-hotel building, which in effect is a plan that continues
the exploitation of black islanders. With the disclosure of Primus's intent, the natives vote him out of office, restoring him to his original status, and elect Beaufils,
making him and his wife inheritors of the Will Cudjoe–Congo Jane legacy. After
the elections, the pain from Ursa's abortion that once cut "across the well of her
stomach" but has now "vanished" (407) becomes associated with her repossession
of her body and her vision.

Jean-Francois Lyotard's description of the "postmodernist condition,"[62] of the
loosening or even the erosion of the social bond of individuals in a society, unstable and ungrounded, leading to the fragmentation of identity, is one that concerns Marshall. Her romance with an African past is in contrast to her assault on a
postcolonial system of power that continues to entangle the individual. Although
her novels end rather tidily with heroines expressing her ultimate faith in their
transcendence of social realities, Marshall's suspicion of "progress" and its vaunted
materialism, as seen in novels from *Brown Girl, Brownstones* to *Daughters,* remains
unabated. What the characters Silla, Jay, Sandy, and Primus share, irrespective of
gender, is the will to power through the acquirement of wealth. Silla betrays Deighton; Jay betrays himself; Sandy betrays the black New Jersey residents; and Primus
tries to betray the Triunion natives. Marshall confessed to Daryl Cumber Dance
"a number of concerns that have preoccupied me for years" and "my hope for
reconciliation, cooperation, love, and unity between black women and men,"[63]
hence the importance of the monument as a cultural trope of unity and the dyad as
working to restore the vision.

The Fisher King: A Child Shall Lead Them

The Fisher King (2000) breaks with Marshall's African warrior tale and mother-
daughter dyad. Nevertheless in this novel the characters of the maternal figure,
Hattie Carmichael, and her adopted eight-year-old son, Sonny, continue Marshall's
maternal patterning of warring historical figures. As a title, *The Fisher King* is taken
from an Indo-European ancient myth of an ailing knight, keeper of the Holy Grail
in a cultural wasteland. With his drawing bloc, Sonny, the cultural healer, pictures
himself as the armed knight, protecting the artist and artistic autonomy in society.
In his drawings he "protects," by standing guard, the legacy of his grandfather
and namesake, the gifted jazz pianist Sonny-Rett Payne. Young Sonny also bears
the responsibility of bridging the chasm between family rivals. Although Sonny
is male, Marshall endows him with nurturing characteristics normally associated
with females. Sensitive and caring, feeling a "balloon in his chest," and slipping

his hand into Hattie's to comfort her, he emerges as the unifying force in a novel of ethnic and adult conflicts.

Marshall's fifth novel departs from the largely positive maternal sketches of her other novels. Here she extends to male characters a perceptible pattern of responsible imprinting usually associated with mothers and the author's recognition of women's power. While *The Fisher King,* short and lean, lacks the development of her other works, it still provides a microcosm of the kinds of cultural and racial intolerances that one finds in her oeuvre. Marshall redresses her perceived "black male castration" problem by creating strong male characters, especially with her creation of Edgar Payne, the affluent black "Dutch burgher" who buys, renovates, and sells houses and nurtures his grandchildren and Sonny (90). Furthermore, with her emphasis on the young male, Sonny, as cultural healer, Marshall suggests again, as in *The Chosen Place,* her hope for a younger generation. The fundamental necessity of maternal and paternal imprinting and the chaos caused by their absence are illustrated throughout the book.

Marshall presents a flawed group of women as mothers from one generation to another. As a way of introducing the different kinds of irresponsible mothering in the text, whether in traditional households, foster-care environments, or postmodernist pop culture, with its destabilization of the familiar norm, Marshall portrays several "bad" mother types. Ulene Payne is the West Indian mother of Sonny-Rett Payne, the jazz great and "disobedient" son, and his older and "obedient" brother, Edgar Payne, the director of Brooklyn's Reclamation, Restoration, and Rebirth housing project. At the urging of his widowed and hardworking mother, the young Sonny-Rett studies and masters the piano, playing the classics of Bach and Beethoven to maternal approval. When he matures and begins to harmonize Eurocentric and Afrocentric melodies and cultures by blending Bach with Art Tatum and Count Basie, the mother, "tall and stern," dismisses his individualism and misidentifies his artistry as "Sodom and Gomorrah music" (95, 137).

Sonny-Rett leaves home, joins the military, and becomes an expatriate in Paris, taking with him the African American Cherisse, whom he marries, to both of their mothers' dismay. Her mother, Florence Varina McCullum-Jones, also a well-off widow, refers to West Indians as "monkey chaser[s]" who "ruined the block" and blames Sonny-Rett for spoiling the career the mother had envisioned for her daughter in Hollywood as another Dorothy Dandridge or Lena Horne (33, 38, 41). The feud between Ulene and Florence symbolizes Marshall's recurring discourse on West Indian and African American conflicted relations, a subtheme in *Brown Girl, Brownstones* and *Daughters.*

That Marshall persists in novelizing the intraracism of diasporic blacks demonstrates her desire to illuminate other kinds of prejudices that exist, outside the powerful parameter of white racism, as well as her determination to correct the problem by reinforcing the idea of ethnic and individual equality. Because of their ethnocentric and maternal intolerance, both mothers lose their son and daughter, due to the "one-way" view they have of seeing the world, their cultures, and their ambitions for their children. The family therapist Barbara Rogoff theorizes that through the "one-way" prism that some families adopt to view the world, they, in fact, attempt to reduce or avoid ethnic conflicts. Rogoff argues that reducing ethnocentrism "does not require us to give up our own ways to become like people in another community, nor [does it] imply a need to protect communities from change. If we can get beyond the idea that *one* way is necessarily best, we can consider the possibilities of other ways, seeking to understand how they work."[64] This too is Marshall's viewpoint. *The Fisher King* is full of examples of hostile rejections, based not only on ethnicity and race but also on class and nationality, as Marshall links one kind of intolerance to another. In America, Hattie, the former neglected foster-care child sexually harassed in one foster home and unable to get her hair combed in another, is rejected by her best friend's mother, barred from Cherisse's middle-class home. In Paris, Parisians and Algerians are embroiled in cultural clashes of another kind, traceable to French imperialism in the North African country and the "intrusion" of "foreigners" on France's native soil, the irony of their hostility lost blindly on the Parisians. Marshall binds up these global hatreds and makes a novelistic commentary on Rogoff's "one way" optical system that families, racial groups, and countries have of gazing on the cultural Other, frequently with devastating consequences.

From Paris, attempting to escape their intolerant mothers and American racism, Sonny-Rett and Cherisse beckon Hattie. Hattie has matured as a singer, a businesswoman, and a road manager for Sonny-Rett. She also becomes his lover and a member of the "Inseparable Three" in Paris (186). Marshall's penchant for the number three continues here in *The Fisher King* after *Praisesong for the Widow*, where she uses it to greater appeal, associating it with Judeo-Christian rites, which is not the case here. Sonny-Rett makes "three" classic albums in 1948; his Parisian apartment is "big enough for three"; and back in New York, Hattie is ordered to bring Sonny-Rett's grandson "three days hence" to see his West Indian great-grandmother (187, 189, 42). The number three and its symbolic nomenclature (for example, it is related in *Praisesong* to the three days of Avey's spiritual regeneration in the Judeo-Christian sacred rituals of death, rebirth, and regeneration) is fitted only to Sonny-Rett's grandson. He is the novel's cultural unifier who represents the salvation of the third generation of Paynes. With Sonny-Rett's mysterious death in a Paris subway station, where he is either pushed or falls to his violent death, Marshall extends Parisian racism against Algerians and Africans to black Americans. Even great jazz musicians such as Sonny-Rett, who represents past expatriates warmly embraced in postwar France, experience the brunt of European racism in the 1960s/1970s. The social change that Marshall illustrates in Paris has the effect of increasing the violence of intolerance in the novel and the further splintering of identities. The familial, ethnic, racial, individual, and global discord pins down her general motif of the widening net of the postmodernist condition, unrestricted in the force of its strength and its reach. Marshall uses Sonny-Rett's death and Cherisse's illness and death to develop Hattie's role as maternal imprinter.

Sonny-Rett and Cherisse's daughter, JoJo, has left home after seeing Hattie and Cherisse in an erotic-lesbian position, as Marshall continues here with a flirtation of homosexuality as begun in *The Chosen Place*, in which Merle has a lesbian affair with an Englishwoman. Marshall risks criticism of homophobia because in both texts the lesbian affairs, treated abruptly and critically, are used against the women: Merle's husband kidnaps their daughter and returns to Africa; and JoJo runs away. Yet one may argue that Marshall's novelistic experimentation with individual bodies -in-crises across sexual and racial, ethnic and class fault lines shows her intersecting link of discourses on intolerance. Although JoJo, described as an errant, "runaway girl-mother," returns to Paris, she abandons her baby, Sonny. Fathered by an East African who is forced to leave Paris, baby Sonny emerges as the descendant of Marshall's three diasporic wings: African, Caribbean, and black American, succeeding Selina's and Ursa's bicultural identities as West Indian and African American. Hattie becomes his caretaker and his "fathermothersististerbrother," his everything, so that at the age of eight, Sonny has a New York family he has never seen because Hattie is afraid of losing him. But the triply multiethnic Sonny has a status that transcends her cultural isolationism.

Marshall's character Hattie is no Merle Kinbona: that is, Hattie lacks Merle's breadth and depth of character, but she performs the work of the maternal imprinter for Sonny, first selfishly and then more carefully in her maternal patterning. She is both the bad and the good maternal surrogate, having had no maternal model to follow. Hattie's "maternal concern" is like her "ordinary, unremarkable body": excessive in personal neediness, expressed in trysts with both Sonny and his wife and in her desire to remedy her nurtureless, motherless past by smothering her young charge (73, 195). In discussions on the context of maternal emotional dissatisfaction, Vivien E. Nice explains that "because of her [the mother's] own neediness in teaching her daughter [or son] to look after others, the mother may offer herself as the first 'candidate' for the daughter's nurturing skills." While the mother's relating to "her daughter may revive the mother's own feelings of loss of early nurturance from her mother (the mother is a 'motherless daughter,' too); she may therefore look to her daughter to make up for this [loss]."[65] Hattie is modeled after this description. She and Sonny have a reciprocal nurturing relationship, despite her leaving him at night with an alcoholic neighbor so that she can support the two of them by working as a wardrobe mistress in a seedy Parisian club.

Yet, Hattie takes Sonny on daily strolls through well-kept Parisian streets, and they visit the "renowned Parisian *immeubles*," where he views the "mascaron of Joan of Arc" and his favorite statue of the "mustachioed Hessian soldier" (61, 63).

These gender-specific monuments, like the statue of Will Cudjoe and Congo Jane, serve as a frame of reference in spite of their European origin. The stone-faced heroine and hero express a particular code of virtue worth fighting for and that the young boy, if not Hattie, emulates. He draws pictures of "medieval castles and fortresses and armored knights" and of his grandfather, over whom he, as one of the armed soldiers in the drawing, stands guard, "protecting" him just as he looks after Hattie, slipping his hand into hers to soothe her.

With her creation of the character Edgar Payne, young Sonny's paternal great-uncle who, with the help of an attorney, locates him in Paris, Marshall announces a change of direction in her depiction of black male characters, foreshadowed by her brief use of paternal imprinting in *Brown Girl, Brownstones*. Marshall now provides a strong character with the economic and spiritual means to perform the rites of passage for his sons and daughters. By planning a memorial concert for his brother, Sonny-Rett, Edgar Payne persuades Hattie to return to America with young Sonny, who will live with him, his wife, and his grandchildren, who are recovering from their parents' divorce. Sonny's cousins too live fragmented lives: they stay with their grandfather Edgar but spend "part of the summer" with their mother, who attends law school in the South, and visit their father, who has remarried and lives in California (154). Marshall continues with her description of a postmodernist society of disintegrating bodies, but she also develops the black male figure as a cultural anodyne to this social fracturing, unlike the male splintering portrayal in *Daughters*. In New York, where he will stay, Sonny experiences his uncle's "outsize hands riding piggyback on his. Colossal arms encircling him. Larger-than-life face bent close to his. The man smell. A different, more powerful aura that wasn't about creams and lotions" (49). Sonny hears childhood stories about his grandfather (stories Hattie could not have narrated), and he begins to bond with his cousins. He attempts to heal the rift between his two ancestral relatives, his maternal and paternal great-grandmothers. By leaving a twig of Florence's ancestral tree in Ulene's home, Sonny, the cultural healer, reminds the aging women of their common heritage.

From *Brown Girl, Brownstones* to *Daughters*, Marshall's male characters such as Deighton, Jay, and Primus are either economically or spiritually unable to offer their daughters the kind of positive social patterning that Marshall usually ascribes to responsible mothers and surrogates. Joyce Pettis remarks that through fiction, Marshall "illustrates how race, class, and gender oppressions dovetail and overlap and how they are inseparable from the world of work and capitalist profit. Her characters' fates suggest that industrialization is antithetical to spiritual and physical survival for nonwhite workers."[66] With *The Fisher King* and the character Edgar Payne, Marshall breaks with her proclivity to demonstrate, as Pettis claims, that capitalism and industrialization have compromised black men's spirituality. Edgar

Payne, the shrewd but successful businessman, devoted father, grandfather, uncle, and paternal imprinter, suggests otherwise.

Through her novels Marshall attempts to answer the question, what is the Caribbean connection to black American women's literature? In her insistence on reconnecting the descendants of the African Diaspora, Marshall brings a Pan-African perspective to black American women's literary tradition. Although the "African heritage is fragmented, perhaps not 'authentic' in the narrow sense of the word, these fragments are what mark [diasporic blacks'] identity." Even if Africa "as a pure, ancestral place is unreachable," blacks in the Diaspora "have put down roots in the shifting, routed ground of the diasporic place,"[67] as another critic incisively summarizes Marshall's cultural and literary ideas. Moreover, with her reliance on maternal metaphors of power, Marshall reveals an artistic connection to her predecessors and successors, insisting that despite their specific cultural distinctions in language, religion, and socialization, black Americans and West Indians and Africans are bonded by history. She eschews the civil rights movement's issues for the most part, suggesting the interior psychic work that must be done in the black psyche, a position that Alice Walker adopted after her fieldwork during the civil rights movement and after the shattering 1960s political assassinations that arrested social progress. So important is Marshall's contribution to the black female literary canon that if she had not come along, as the proverbial axiom resonates with a spirit of arrogance, we would have had to invent her.

6 The Phallic Maternal

Alice Walker's Novels of Archetypal Symbolism

Mr.__ ast me the other day what it is I love so much bout Shug. He say he love her style. He say to tell the truth, Shug act more manly than most men. Speak her mind. Shug will fight, he say. Just like Sofia. Mr.__ think all this is stuff men do.

Since the *anima* is an archetype that is found in men, it is reasonable to suppose that an equi- valent archetype must be present in women; for just as the man is compensated by a feminine element, so woman is compensated by a masculine one.[1]

In *How Free Is Free? The Long Death of Jim Crow,* the historian Leon F. Litwack remarks on the hope and aspiration of the leader of the civil rights movement, Dr. Martin Luther King Jr. (1929–68). For Litwack, as for others, including Alice Walker, King was the "Face of the Movement," inspiring the masses while understanding the challenges of American history facing them. Litwack writes the following summation: "King had always scoffed at the notion that civil rights legislation alone had created a level playing field. He asked Americans to think of it as a track meet. If a man is entered at the starting line in a race three hundred years after another man . . . he would have to perform some impossible feat to catch up." The March on Washington, August 28, 1963, was one such feat, drawing the nation's attention to civil rights and attracting hundreds of thousands of Americans and applauding King's now-famous speech "I Have a Dream." A year later he received the Nobel Peace Prize in Norway. The Civil Rights Act of 1964, initially filibustered by southern senators, was another major feat, a bill, signed into law by President Lyndon Johnson, that banned discrimination against blacks in employment and in public accommodations. However, "by the end of the 1960s, the hope that had once sustained King and the movement" was gone.[2] After leading a campaign for the rights of striking garbage workers in Memphis, Tennessee, on April 4, 1968, the peaceful dreamer was murdered. In *Meridian,* Alice Walker, the civil rights activist/author, provides a literary obituary of the 1960s, a period of change and upheaval.

Unlike Paule Marshall, Walker does not give an obligatory nod to the movement: she describes the major aspects of it in her first two novels but afterward points her readers in another direction. Thus a major motif of individual regeneration marks the distance that Walker has traveled in her career. From a civil rights activist/author committed to changing society in *The Third Life of Grange Copeland* and *Meridian*, Walker becomes a transnational womanist/activist devoted to the psychological process of self-healing across fault lines in *The Color Purple, The Temple of My Familiar,* and *Possessing the Secret of Joy.* Because the social order is slow to change and progress, because beloved leaders are assassinated and masses left leaderless, Walker emphasizes the importance of the inward journey to effect positive, lasting change. She represents female characters as maternal nurturers but also as the phallic maternal, as the opening quotations attest. One of the first African American novelists to win the Pulitzer Prize for fiction, Walker in her award-winning novel *The Color Purple* assaults the politics of gender socialization that lead to women's subordination and docility, and she charts the inward journey to wholeness.

The two quotations that open this chapter are significant in this reading of Walker's works because each suggests the cultural exchangeability of "masculine" and "feminine" traits with which Walker invests her characters, particularly her female characters to protest women's *learned* social behavior in society. In *The Color Purple,* the character Mister seemingly validates the theory of essentialized gender behavior, believing that the female characters Shug and Sofia "act" like men because they fight and talk back to their antagonists. He implies that they "perform" a male function atypical for women vis-à-vis core gender qualities of passivity and submissiveness attributed to them. For example, docility is a characteristic that the protagonist Celie absorbs before she realizes that it is not an inborn trait but rather is a learned social behavior. In Mister's typical espousal of traditional theorizing of men's and women's gender constitution, he mimics societal expectations of gendered bodies. Unwittingly, however, he implies that gender can also be perceived as a matter of performance, as the critic Judith Butler has theorized.[3]

In the second quotation, Carl Jung's animus, one of his four archetypal patterns of human behavior, stresses a "masculine" element in the woman who projects a unique, powerful drive such as Walker gives to her "male-acting" female characters. But this drive is one that Jung does not associate with women in the traditional sense. In women, he remarks with psychoanalytical bias, "*Eros* is an expression of their true nature, while their *Logos* is often only a regrettable accident. It gives rise to misunderstandings and annoying interpretations in the family circle and among friends."[4] Walker's heroines reveal that women's Logos is not a regrettable accident but rather a fundamental and rational urge for those seeking expression in their otherwise constrictive environment. Walker rejects the sexism inherent in public and psychoanalytical discourses while illuminating archetypal concepts of human behavior to disclose ways that women and African Americans have been conditioned psychologically to accept their subordination in society.

That is, there is a pattern in Walker's oeuvre in which she initially describes female characters who are weak and passive as they are taught to be but who, as a result of an awakening, rise up in defense of themselves and others. For Jung, crises have a long, unconscious history, and the individual's inability to resolve the conflict between the ego-centered world and the personal and collective uncon-scious, manifested by archetypal symbols, evokes problems of identity that Walker relates to her characters' socially stunted lives in a racist Jim Crow or sexist mi-lieu. Therefore, in order to effect regeneration, Walker forces her characters to *perform* new gender roles, invoking an essence of character (Jung's animus arche-type), which the author posits is already there, submerged in the subconscious, but which she pushes to a conscious level by creating a crisis.

This chapter explains Walker's appropriation of psychoanalytical theory to subvert ideological positions on race and gender construction and to reveal the psychic determinism necessary for individual regeneration unrelated to social movements for change perhaps because of the tragedies that interrupted or even halted the civil rights movement. Walker's use of archetypes enables her to probe the deep-rootedness of her characters' subjective thought in terms of race, gender, and sexual-identity formation. Using the unlikely tools of feminism and psycho-analysis, she creates a particular female-centered framework and posits the appli-cability of psychoanalysis in discovering social patterns of thought, even as she resists several psychoanalytical/theoretical prejudices, as feminist theorists from Irigaray to Kristeva have urged women to do.[5]

Within the framework of these theoretical tools, this chapter analyzes her major novels: *The Third Life of Grange Copeland* (1970); *Meridian* (1976); *The Color Purple* (1982); *The Temple of My Familiar* (1989); and *Possessing the Secret of Joy* (1992), works that have a clear phallic maternal metaphor of Logos and desire. In his essay "The Signification of the Phallus," Jacques Lacan, seemingly avoiding Jung's bias, defines the phallus as the "organ, penis, or clitoris" and disavows the explicit sexualization of the symbol while positing it as "without regard to the anatomical difference of the sexes" because "in a more primordial sense" there is "the phallic mother." Lacan's male defenders comment on the "hermetic obscurity" of his writings but disavow too the sexualization of the phallus even though the term refers to male reproductive organs.[6] A privileged signifier of Lacan's Logos and desire, phallus does imply male dominance, despite the denials, and Lacan's diction, like Jung's, is shot through with masculinist bias. As the critic Barbara Johnson theorizes, even on "the most elementary level, the phallus is a sign of sexuality as difference, and not as the presence or absence of this or that organ."[7] Walker's radical revisionist metaphor of the phallus as representing female desire for self-empowerment tropes on and reverses a ruling, patriarchal shrine of penis/phallic worship whereby women of the "little penis," as Freud described them, are objects and not subjects.

Initially as objects, female and maternal bodies are strewn violently across the global landscape in Walker's fiction, victims of spousal despair, prostitution, suicide, murder, incest, gang rape, and female genital mutilation. From her home-town of Eatonton, Georgia, where she was born in 1944, to her adopted world-community that stretches from South America to Africa, Walker connects wom-en's bodily oppression across geopolitical fault lines. Refusing to valorize maternal bodies in a violent patriarchal and racist society, she presents a pattern of male violence against women's bodies that one finds rooted in her background. Accord-ing to Walker, at the age of thirteen she viewed a dead mother's shattered body in the funeral home where her older sister Ruth was employed as a hairdresser. The woman's drunken, impoverished husband had aimed a rifle at her and shot her in the face, just as Brownfield in *The Third Life of Grange Copeland* shoots and kills his wife, Mem, a name "rooted in 'French *la meme,* meaning the same,' implying women's universal" oppression.[8] Walker's own childhood maiming in the eye by her brothers, who were playing with a BB gun, is perhaps another psychobiograph-ical intrusion into her oeuvre as seen in the rebellious Sofia's "blind[ing] in one eye" (*The Color Purple* 91). With the publication of *Warrior Marks* (1993), a book on female genital mutilation that she coauthored with the Indian feminist Pratibha Parmar, Walker traveled to West Africa, where she connected her personal experi-ence in America to that of young girls in Africa waiting to be castrated in the ritual of infibulation. The title *Warrior Marks* refers to women surviving genital mutila-tion and becoming "warriors" rather than passive "victims."

The discussion that follows focuses on what I see as Walker's important refer-ence to an interrupted civil rights movement and thus her necessary development of phallic maternal metaphors of women's warlike usurpation of patriarchal and racist forces against minorities, blacks and women. Because the term "phallic ma-ternal" has opposing but powerful connotations of women's sex and gender, I use the term to suggest Walker's inversion of psychoanalytical biases favoring men and her suggestion that women must assume power over their own bodies. While the phallic maternal is capable of nurturing others, it is not limited to that function as women seek self-nurturance and self-empowerment, what Irigaray asserts women are not expected to do in a society relying on women's support of patriarchy.[9] Par-ticular attention is paid to Walker's application of Jung's four archetypes and the animus as a Lacanian phallic signifier of her characters' desire for power over their lives, their bodies. Her female characters' archetypal behavior as maternal phallic figures that learn to fight for their and others' rights, sometimes violently, distin-guishes her from many other writers in this study, who largely use maternal met-aphors in a nurturing capacity. Before an analysis of her novels and her depiction of the civil rights movement in the first two, it is useful to examine Jung's four archetypes.

Jung's well-documented break with Freud occurred because of his inability or unwillingness to accept Freud's restricted view of the libido as the sexual drive of fulfillment. Believing that the libido, or the urge toward life, extended beyond mere sexuality to a wider and hypothetical élan vital, or life energy, Jung stressed the individual's widened consciousness. This is a concept that Walker embraces, as can be seen in her emphases on her characters' inner well-being as exuded in the archetypal "Self" of harmony. The four archetypes are the following: 1) the persona/ mask, or false wrappings of society, acquired by the individual; 2) the shadow, or the dark side of the duality, such as a Mr. Hyde within Dr. Jekyll, 3) the anima/ animus, or maternal Eros, feminine spirit in the man and the paternal Logos, or masculine soul, in the woman; and 4) the Self, the essence of human wholeness, the individual par excellence. For Jung, archetypal patterns of behavior must be integrated into the world of the ego, forced to acknowledge that the ego-centered consciousness is not self-sufficient, does not exist independently, but is "subordinate to the self and is related to it like a part to the whole."[10] To reach the wellness of the individuation process, the experiential path to wholeness, the individual must overcome his/her personal/social distortions before being awarded with the enlightenment of the Self.

For Walker, women and minorities' acquired social behavior obstructs their discovery of the Self, that is, without a radical re-visioning of themselves and their world, usually evoked by authorial crises, resulting in their epiphany. Of the five novels discussed here, only *Possessing the Secret of Joy* is specifically Jungian; the others, beginning with *The Third Life of Grange Copeland*, are loosely but significantly based on these archetypes. Still, it is possible to analyze Walker's pattern of introducing male and female characters who are stifled by social customs, repressed by personal complexes that Jung theorizes must be made conscious to effect a healing. Upon reaching this level of consciousness, Walker's characters manifest the archetype of the animus/anima, what Jung describes as a powerful drive because it is "instinctual" and "full of animosity" at injustice but has "a positive aspect." Jung adds, "In the same way that the *anima* gives relationship and relatedness to a man's consciousness, the *animus* gives to woman's consciousness a capacity for reflection, deliberation, and self-knowledge."[11]

I use the term "phallic maternal" to capture what I see as Walker's willful and sometimes ribald description of female characters' assumption of a male/phallic sovereignty, or in other words, weak female types losing their passiveness and developing a warlike or mannish fortitude to effect personal and social regeneration. Walker's radical reconstructions of female characters (Lacan's phallic signifier of power and desire, and Jung's archetypal anima of positive intervention) coalesce in her maternal metaphors of power. Her first maternal-phallic protagonist, Grange Copeland, obviously male, is an emasculated sharecropper who regains his manhood, but Walker feminizes him in a disruption of gender ascription and in his transformation as his granddaughter's élan vital. In her feminization of a male character, Walker implies that black male characters' regeneration is linked to self-knowledge and to an appreciation of women, but not necessarily to nuclear family ties as constructed in bourgeois family systems.

The Third Life of Grange Copeland: Grange as the Phallic Maternal

In Georgia a pre–civil rights movement Grange Copeland is an ego-fractured sharecropper in a Jim Crow setting who assumes the mask of "boy" to the white neo-plantation owner Mr. Shipley. Brownfield witnesses his father's frozen persona when Mr. Shipley visits the fields and Grange's face becomes "an unnaturally bland *mask*" (emphasis added, 9–10). He also expresses the *shadow* archetype as a misogynist who abuses and abandons his wife and child, runs away to New York, and prostitutes women of color to white men. Grange experiences the archetypal Self not through psychoanalysis but through the living of several lives. When he returns to Georgia, a transformed Grange, in light of the coming civil rights movement, becomes the Great Mother archetype who nurtures and dies for Ruth, his granddaughter. Walker illustrates Jung's idea that the magnanimous Self exists in contradistinction to the petty and self-absorbed world of the ego, which "can do nothing against the self" but can participate "freely in the wider world of [the self's] objective interests."[12] Even Josie, Grange's former mistress and wife, recognizes Grange's achievement when she informs Brownfield, "He *bigger* than us, Brownfield. Grange thinks about the world and Ruth's place in it" (310).

Before Grange reaches this state of self-enlightenment, Walker connects his metamorphosis to his psychic recognition of his emasculation and misogyny and women's status in a sexist culture. She describes the lives of three generations of Copelands: Grange, Brownfield, and then Ruth, who becomes Grange's "duty" (279), an indication of his espousal of the tenets of maternal ethics in providing care to others. As the last unscathed female of his three granddaughters, Ruth represents a new generation of women after the deaths of Margaret, Grange's first wife, and Mem, Brownfield's wife, and her two sisters' sexual and social degradation. While Daphne goes insane, Ornette becomes "a lady of pleasure" (303), as Walker initiates another pattern, this one parodying the sexed and abused bodies of women. The majority of female characters are defined by their sexuality and/ or procreative function. This includes the educated Mem, whose body becomes a receptacle in which her husband plants "a seed to grow that would bring her down in weakness and dependence and to her ultimate destruction" (46). Walker treats women's pregnant bodies as sickly and nauseating, subverting the dominant Victorian paradigm of motherhood and purity and exploding the black bourgeois patriarchal model of families and generations in post-Reconstruction America.

The historian Kevin K. Gaines argues that the development of a black bourgeois ethic of success and morality was based on a conflicted and flawed intellectual idealism that presupposed the prominence of black patriarchal families in

America as "preconditions for fundamental human rights." Gaines concludes that the "tendency to locate the problem [of racism] in the bodies and behavior of African Americans rather than in their lack of citizenship, political rights, and ultimately, in social inequities, persisted."[13] However, in *The Third Life of Grange Copeland,* Walker rejects the conservative black ideology of racial uplift through patriarchal values of family formation, due to the complications of a developing black patriarchy in a racialized society. Her critique of the Victorian and post-Reconstruction "black family romance"[14] of an inspiring, conservative patriarchy is based on her perception of the impoverishment and emasculation of black men and the accompanying castration of black women living in "an oppressed colony" of black-on-black violence (Afterword, *The Third Life of Grange Copeland* 343).

The Third Life of Grange Copeland presents a cultural conundrum for black male characters as inheritors of masculinist structures of power but also as objects of white patriarchal facilitators of race, representation, and identity. In several ways Grange resembles the castrated maternal as a man inheriting patriarchal systems of power that, as a black man, he is unable to access in a Jim Crow, peonage society. His exclusion from this society is evidenced by the lynching of black men, especially in Walker's native Georgia. It was in Georgia that one of the most heinous crimes of lynching was committed in 1918, when a black man and a pregnant woman were lynched in a "lynching orgy."[15] The woman's fully developed fetus was severed from her dangling body. The NAACP's angry rhetoric of Georgia's "lynching orgy," conflating gendered and lynched black male and female bodies, signifies the sexualization of power and desire in a phallocentric discourse. In the novel even Grange's wife, Margaret, comes to realize the conflict of identity that he as a black man inherits. As Walker's omniscient narrator reflects, "in her plantation world the mother was second in command, the father having no command at all" (250).

That Grange has a penis but is excluded from the realm of phallic power only exacerbates his frustration. He seeks tragically to regain his masculinity by treating women's sexed bodies as "cunts." As a pejorative, cunt refers "almost exclusively to women and expresses the utmost rancor"[16] about men's attitudes toward women and their bodies, which is the objective of Walker's profane descriptions of women's sexual relations with men. Grange's wife concedes that his relationships with other women are more sexual than loving: "You'd think he'd be satisfied," Margaret grieves, "me feeding him and her fucking him" (22). Margaret too submits to affairs and even has a "bastard" child with her white boss, but she poisons herself and her child, acts that can be perceived as a causal effect of her and Grange's mutual and symbolic castration. After his wife's death and his spiritual metamorphosis, Grange sees that Margaret's problems were rooted in his own troubles. He confesses, "I mean . . . the crackers could make me run away from my wife, but where was the *man* in me that let me sneak off, never telling her nothing about where I was going . . . never telling her how wrong I was myself" (288). Grange's realization and confession are tied theoretically to Jung's archetypes, especially to the shadow.

Jung writes that the recognition of the "dark aspects of the personality as present and real" in individuals "requires much painstaking work extending over a longer period of time."[17] Through Grange's confession, Walker describes the persona and the shadow as consuming Grange with self-loathing, but his moral reparation makes his resistance possible. Nevertheless the rhetorical question implicit here is, what happens when the individual, unlike Grange, resists the recognition of the dark side of the personality? With Brownfield's portrayal, Walker links the tragedy of moral resistance to the consciousness of the shadow "bound up with projections," as Jung writes, "which are not recognized as such, and their recognition is a moral achievement beyond the ordinary."[18] Described as a character for which "Introspection came hard" (233), Brownfield rejects responsibility for his failed life, projecting his inadequacies onto others, again unlike Grange, who recovers from his self-inflicted and socially induced tragedies.

In describing Grange's new behavior, symbolizing Jung's archetype for the "feminine soul in the man," the anima, Walker implies that he assumes a maternal agency for Ruth, his mythological Demeter to his Great Mother archetype. As the first representation of Walker's description of the phallic maternal, Grange, the formerly emasculated black man, regains his phallic supremacy, but with a maternal twist. He learns to nurture and protect Ruth, building her a home and even brandishing a gun to keep Brownfield and the white sheriff off their property. Before Grange is shot and killed, dying for her, Ruth describes him as "softer than [she] had ever known him," while Brownfield was "a *shadow* from a very painful past" (emphasis added, 284). Grange had insisted that she "trade her jeans for dresses" and bought her "jars of Noxzema and Pond's hand cream" and, for her initiation into womanhood, "napkins, a belt, and lovely talc that smelled like a warm rose" (297, 271). Ruth, in turn, had taught Grange about the perils of hatred, even against whites, whom he grudgingly acknowledges as social reformers and civil rights workers (333). Here, Walker pays tribute to northern white civil rights activists and college students who flooded the South along with black civil rights workers in the 1960s, participating in sit-ins, voter registration drives, the integration of universities, and the Mississippi Freedom Summer of 1964, where a thousand or more activists registered voters, including a youthful Alice Walker. Influenced by the spirit of the age, Grange's transformation is noteworthy.

In her analysis of this novel, the literary critic Maria Lauret rightly posits that it "can be read as a *Bildungsroman* about Grange, and not Ruth as scholar Madhu Dubey sees it." Yet, Lauret questions the "miracle" of Walker's shift from domestic violence and southern history to Grange's development and the civil rights movement.[19] Since *The Third Life of Grange Copeland* spans several periods from World War I to the early 1960s, Walker presents readers with what Melissa Walker identifies as the "lives of isolated individuals whose personal dramas are initially played on the fringes of history." However, these lives and fringes "collide with historical events [with] *Grange* expos[ing] the devastating consequences of the racist practices of the twenties and thirties." The characters and events trace the "beginning of the struggle against such [racist and historical] practices."[20] Rather than making a narrative shift, as Lauret complains, Walker instead ties Grange's new identity to the nascent civil rights movement, which teaches the practice of nonviolence, which he rejects, and self-love, which he accepts and discovers in New York. He attempts to save a pregnant but deserted blond who prefers to drown rather than accept the saving hand of a "nigger" (217), her animosity and death influencing, ironically, his rebirth.

Walker therefore connects Grange's regeneration not only to the civil rights movement, and his recognition of Martin Luther King Jr. as a "man" who stood up to powerful forces, but also to women. These females are Ruth, the motherless daughter who needs him; the dying, abused blond whose defiant racism reanimates him; and, Margaret, his first wife, whose suicide he regrets. By providing Grange with a manly and self-sacrificing role model such as King and with female characters who have been brutalized by a racist and patriarchal culture, Walker again subverts typical masculinist thinking. The new Grange discerns how the fusion of racism and sexism threatens the loss of center for males and females, black and white. Grange informs Ruth, "The mean things I've done. . . . Think of me, when I'm gone, as a big, rough-looking coward. Who learned to love himself only after thirty-odd years. And then overdone it" (223)—a statement of his moral redemption.

Grange Copeland's achievement of masculinity and freedom is grounded in the ideal of manhood as represented by Martin Luther King Jr. in life and death. In two of her collections of essays, *We Are the Ones We Have Been Waiting For* (2006) and *In Search of Our Mothers' Gardens* (1983), Walker pays tribute to the martyred King. His resistance forced her to realize, "I would never be able to live in this country without resisting everything that sought to disinherit me" (144). She recognizes King as the "One Fearless Person for whom we had waited" (144), as she states in *The Three Lives of Grange Copeland*. But in *We Are the Ones We Have Been Waiting For,* written long after King's martyrdom, she realizes that "we discovered a tender, radiant certainty" because "we knew we had been completely loved. I firmly believe there is no wholeness for a people, no promised land in view, until this happens."[21] To a lesser degree, Grange's martyrdom, loosely reminiscent of King's, is also based on his willingness to love and die for an ideal much larger than himself, Ruth and her young generation, evidence of the widened consciousness of Jung's powerful Self par excellence.

Meridian: Subverting the Maternal Ideal

In contrast to Grange Copeland's feminization, Walker's masculinization of the female protagonist Meridian is the first opportunity we have of seeing her original development of a passive female protagonist who morphs into the phallic maternal. In *Meridian,* Walker realizes her classic signature of creating the metaphor of the phallic maternal for women largely through her appropriation of symbols. That is, in dress and behavior, Walker's heroine, Meridian, changes radically from an unhappily married and dutiful, pregnant wife and mother to a civil-rights' advocate whose androgyny is illuminated by her donning a man's cap and dungarees and resting in a sleeping bag, described as a "cell" (23). These symbolic investments are viewed as accoutrements of Meridian's conscious physiological battle and the unconscious, subliminal life force that sustains her in a chaotic society. As a cell, the sleeping bag tropes on the female reproductive cycle and the maternal womb as a safe space for rebirth readiness when Meridian's conscious and unconscious lives are reconciled. Small in stature, Meridian learns to face huge army tanks protesting hegemony, its Vietnam War and its southern racism, resisting forces with the sheer power of her vision of a more caring and nurturing society.

The narrative structure of the novel, the iconoclastic descriptions of traditional black motherhood and maternal bodies-in-crises, the protagonist's conformity and nonconformity, and the crises that provoke Meridian's archetypal behavior of Jung's animus/Lacan's imaginary phallus all lead to her metamorphoses, but also to her emotional paralysis. Divided into two time periods, *Meridian's* narrative past provides insight into the daily activities of the civil rights workers and eulogizes the movement's martyrs. The narrative present follows the flashback of the narrative past with Meridian leaving the North for the South to live "like Civil Rights workers used to do" and to finish the unfinished business of the era, attempting to save its children (31). In stylistically separating and yet grouping together the narrative past and present, Walker provides an overview of the 1960s and that decade's ethos, clarifying the struggle for King's beloved community of inclusion. With Meridian's growing conceptualization of a wider maternal responsibility, Walker attacks the ideology of motherhood, the Victorian maternal ideal that justified female domination.

Meridian ridicules the Victorian maternal ideal of the self-sacrificing mother who loves with love that cannot tire. Within the context of the novel and throughout Meridian Hill's matrilineal heritage, Walker presents and then ruptures a narrative minihistory of women's bodily oppression. The narrator describes a history of black women's lives and reveals their subjection to authority, locating the heroine within this matrilineal tradition. Meridian thinks of her mother, Mrs. Hill, the mother of six children, as "Black Motherhood personified." Her creativity is likened to typical slave women stifled by their reproductive bodies (96). On the Saxon slave plantation in Georgia, the West African slave Louvinie, a weaver of tales, has her tongue clipped for telling the master's children tales of horror. After her silencing, her tongue is buried under a tree on the plantation, and the magical *talking* tree becomes the Sojourner tree, named after the archetypal mannish woman Sojourner Truth, the towering slave who bared her breast to show her womanhood, claiming a voice at a convention of white women activists. But the tree, like women's voices of creativity, is later destroyed during a campus riot.

White and black female bodies are presented, again, as victims of patriarchy in different ways. Illustrating the deadly patriarchal restrictions placed on one white woman's sexed body, Walker writes an abbreviated and twisted parody of the maternal ideal. A blond "mummified white woman" becomes a carnivalesque spectacle of Jim Crow policy, as black children must wait until "their day" to witness her remains. The woman's mummified body becomes a source of revenge for the husband who murdered his wife because she had "gone outside the home to seek her 'pleasuring'" (22, 20), defying the husband's guardianship of her propertied body. A white, liberal New York civil rights worker, Lynne Rabinowicz, is abandoned by Truman, her black husband, and gang-raped by those for whom "her body [was] . . . conquered territory" (160). Her biracial daughter, Camara, is raped and murdered, as is the young, abandoned Wild Child, who is refused burial on the black women's college campus but whose casket is placed "beneath the Sojourner tree" as rebellious students sing the civil rights anthem "We Shall Overcome" (48).

With the character Meridian Hill, Walker launches an assault against the more "orthodox" passions of the female body, which lead, predictably but respectfully, to pregnancy and motherhood. Walker appropriates Meridian's fecund and developing body to neutralize, if not renounce, the pregnant maternal body as a projection of fecundity and health. During her pregnancy, an unhappily married Meridian critiques her bodily changes as fundamentally abnormal and unattractive. In the beginning months of her term, she "grew and grew and grew, as pregnant women will. Her skin, always smooth as velvet, became blotchy, her features blunted; her face looked bloated, tight" (63). When Meridian, the young, abandoned, and divorced mother (with a high IQ), receives a scholarship to attend college, her mother scolds her about putting her young son up for adoption: "I always thought you were a *good* girl. And all the time, you were *fast*" (87). Meridian puts her baby up for adoption, and as a college student she aborts Truman's baby, seizing control of her body, her life.

Her being perceived as "fast" can be reinterpreted as her developing a desire to reclaim her body, defying the scripted maternal identity imposed on her because she "could not live up to the standard of motherhood that had gone before" (91).

In another but related context, the feminist theorist Moira Gatens argues that social scientists from Lacan to Merleau-Ponty and Paul Schilder "offer an account
of the body image which posits that a body is not properly a human body, that is,
a human subject or individual, unless it has an image of itself as a discrete entity,
or as a *gestalt*."[22] Of Meridian's female ancestors, only Feather Mae, her paternal
great-grandmother, has this gestalt self-image, but she is described as "mad" because of her out-of-the-body experiences when "the spirit lived, set free in the
world" (58), unrestricted by patriarchal and racial boundaries and consistent with
the image of the phallic maternal. In positioning Meridian as an inheritor of her
great-grandmother's "mad" tradition, Walker marks madness as the "rational"
sphere of the phallic maternal resisting gendered and racial ascriptions of identity.

The major crisis that Walker creates to refashion Meridian's character from that
of the masked persona is traced to implosive/explosive occurrences. As a young,
deserted wife and mother about to inherit her mother's destiny, she observes her
baby, "whom, even then, she had urges to kill," demonstrating the willful motivation of the archetypal animus to save herself, that is, manifesting an instinctual impulse of self-preservation. Passively the young mother sits and watches television,
but she is startled by a news flash that changes her destiny: in 1960 the bombing
of a home and the subsequent death of three children make Meridian "aware of the
past and present of the larger world" (72, 73). Walker's narrative inclusion of early
1960s bombings is a reminder of the altruistic character of civil rights workers who
entered the South and endangered their lives knowingly. While King is also the
face of martyrdom for the movement, others, less known and often anonymous,
were sacrificed too.

Young men such as James Chaney, Andrew Goodman, and Michael Schwerner,
one black Mississippian and two white New Yorkers, respectively, have their names
enshrined in civil rights history, along with the names of countless activists who
died for their cause of racial justice. In 1964 Chaney, Goodman, and Schwerner
were killed in Mississippi after they attempted to investigate a church bombing.
Moreover a white civil rights activist and mother of five, Viola Liuzzo of Michigan, was shot and killed in Alabama in 1965 after the Selma-Montgomery freedom march. But the 1963 church bombing on a Sunday in Birmingham, Alabama,
which killed four little black girls, shocked the world, and angered Americans, led
to the passage of the Civil Rights Act in 1964. The names of Addie Mae Collins,
Cynthia Wesley, Carole Robertson, and Denise McNair were placed alongside those
of King, Malcolm, the Kennedys, and others, including Liuzzo, in the opening second chapter of *Meridian* (33). This literary obituary of the young and old, of white
and black, of male and female, of politicians and nonpoliticians evokes the pathos
of a Greek tragedy, recalling the unrelieved trauma of a long decade.

Symbolically the lynchings, killings, and bombings in the South performed the
work of a black communal castration, a sign of the people's helplessness, leading

in the novel to Meridian's radical quest for self-empowerment, or for the imaginary phallus as a trope of desire to reverse the social order that threatens her life, her community. Unlike other Walker females such as Mem in *The Third Life of Grange Copeland,* for example, who briefly threatens Brownfield with a gun as a symbol of her desire for phallic power, the nonviolent Meridian eschews guns and violence. Instead her body becomes a weapon, her phallic symbol of power in confronting injustice. Throughout the novel Walker's omnipotent narrator describes Meridian's body in a variety of ways that suggest her body as rejecting domestic and self-sacrificing motherhood, on one hand, but becoming a cipher for absorbing others' pain, on the other, assuming a wider maternal function in the politics of social reform. Meridian uses her lean but powerful body to stand before trucks and tanks and to register intimidated black voters. In the novel Walker represents this one aspect of the movement when young activists approach the home of a docile black woman, who tells them, "I wants to feed y'all real good, 'cause I don't believe in voting" (102). Still determined on another level, Meridian decides to lift and carry the dead Wild Child and to insist on a proper burial for her. She even leads a group of children to a Jim Crow facility in resistance of Jim Crow laws and fiercely stands up to bombs and tanks. Yet she refuses the deadly force of violence.

Her role as the daring phallic maternal is consistent with that of the nonviolence that King advocated in his civil rights book *Why We Can't Wait,* after which Walker patterns Meridian's nonviolence. As part of the civil rights movement's nonviolent campaign that stressed the resisting body as a peaceful weapon, King heralded the willfully subjected body. He describes the activists' pledge and the importance of nonviolence: "We proved to them [the infamous Bull Connor, Birmingham's chief of police who ordered the use of attack dogs, fires hoses, and policemen against activists] that we needed no weapons—not so much as a toothpick. We proved that we possessed the most formidable weapon of all—the conviction that we were right." Walker's descriptions of Meridian's body as a weapon of discipline and force and her frequent retreat to the cell/maternal womb could be connected to one of King's ten pledges: to "strive to be in good spiritual and bodily health."[23] Meridian's bodily paralysis, however, forecloses any achievement of Grange's élan vital, as Walker genders their difference.

In his provocative essay "Reading the Body: *Meridian* and the Archeology of Self," Alan Nadel traces Meridian's paralysis to the ill health of her violent southern society and traces her recovery to *écriture féminine.* He argues that the "first chapter of the novel makes clear the connection between Meridian's body and the body-politic when, after leading a successful protest (by staring down an armed tank), Meridian's body suffers a seizure of paralysis that necessitates her being carried home by four men."[24] When she sees the abandoned and neglected Wild Child, initially she also "withdrew to her room . . . for a long time" (36). Nadel cites the feminist Elizabeth Meese's description of the "body" as the "site where the political and the aesthetic interpret the material." Also he interprets Meridian's writing poetry as Walker's popularization of French feminists' theory of *écriture féminine*, of "writing located in and authorized by a fundamental female experience: 'writing the body,'" in order "to recreate [*sic*] the world," Nadel writes, with a "refusal of earthly boundaries," argues Katharyn Privett.[25] However, Nadel's multiple metaphors of the links between the political body, the aesthetic body, and Melissa's creativity can be broadened to stress the maternal body's recuperative powers as represented by her regenerative "cell."

With the book's finale—Truman's returning to Meridian's home and "shakily" entering her "sleeping bag" (220)—Walker reconfigures the image of Melissa's emotional paralysis in the first chapter and establishes the necessity of women's grunt maternal work, as Nadel implies in describing Melissa's art and protest activity. However, Walker goes further. In the book's two opening and lasting images of Melissa's paralyzed body and her worn cell/sleeping bag, which Truman enters, Walker reinforces her signature and pronounces a distinction between a racist, patriarchal culture's debilitating impact on blacks and women and women's bodies as having a regenerative capacity. In her collective attacks on the maternal ideal, on nuclear family systems' repression of female creativity, and on the language and law of Lacan's symbolic ruling order, Walker pulverizes systems of power that exploit and kill the spirit of American citizens, treated as pariahs. As Walker's first androgynous female protagonist of resistance, Meridian sets a new precedence for those that follow, namely *The Color Purple*'s Celie, whose regeneration is connected not to a movement that can die with its martyrs but to her growing awareness of the sanctity of the inner self in the most deplorable of social environments.

The Color Purple: Celie's Rewriting the Body and Lesbian *Jouissance*

Illiterate, "black and ugly," docile and silenced, bodily beaten and sexually abused by her stepfather and her husband, Celie represents the nadir of women's battered lives. Her sister, Nettie, recollects, "You said your life made you feel so ashamed you couldn't even talk about it to god, you had to write it" (136). In her re-creation of Celie from an abject persona to an androgynous, articulate, bisexual individual/ entrepreneur of her own company, Walker combines multiple phallic signifiers of power and desire, symbolized by Celie's grammatically fractured letters to God and the creation of Shug as Celie's maternal imago and lover. Celie's *écriture féminine* and lesbian *jouissance* mark another radical turning point in Walker's novels: she appropriates the genre of the epistolary novel, secret and private, to stress Celie's alienation and yet desire for authority of voice and authorship. With Celie's lesbianism, Walker boldly enters new territory, validating women's homosexuality as instinctual and legitimate. Significantly, although she has been raped by her stepfather, is the mother of two children, and is married to Mister, Celie has never experienced an organism. Her lesbian *jouissance* with Shug (similar to and yet dissimilar from Janie's with Tea Cake in *Their Eyes Were Watching God*) marked Walker's novel as her most controversial until the publication of her erotic novel *By the Light of My Father's Smile* (1998).[26]

While *The Color Purple* garnered two prestigious awards, the American Book Award and the Pulitzer Prize, the American Library Association has cited it as one of the ten most banned books in America.[27] Walker's raw explicitness of homosexuality and language established her reputation as the brilliant but controversial "womanist," that is, black feminist. After the success of *The Third Life of Grange Copeland* and *Meridian*, in which the phallic maternal is restricted to a retrieval of that which was lost, sexually and socially for the equally castrated Grange and Meridian, *The Color Purple* breaks rank with the past. Here Walker pursues not civil rights per se but rather female sexual pleasure, which she equates, like Hurston, with spiritual *jouissance*. Jung's individuation process does have a theoretical religious function whether or not one is a believer, for it is linked to the Self's feelings of harmony and peace, not with religious orthodoxy.[28] Walker's elevation of female *jouissance* to the status of a sacred, religious feeling of a widened consciousness reveals her authorial shift. She moves from solely advocating a redressing of the external conditions of society in the civil rights era, as we see in *The Third Life of Grange Copeland* and *Meridian,* to demanding the psychological development of women, as seen in *The Color Purple*.

The biblical "howl" or rage of *Meridian* is traceable to the aborted civil rights movement and the 1960s political murders, brilliantly pronounced in Walker's literary eulogy of martyrs. For the historian Litwack, the 1960s, like the Reconstruction period of the 1860s, when the dutiful Charlotte Forten traveled south to educate former slaves, reflected the "major efforts" of the U.S. government to make "legislative, executive and judicial commitments to black freedom and civil rights." Later, however, "despite court decisions and legislation, despite agitation, marches, and confrontations," racism persisted, King lay dead, and blacks were "forced to endure" what they had always endured: violence and humiliation.[29] Perhaps this tragic mood and realism set the stage for Walker's novelistic retreat from though not abandonment of social justice. Her new emphasis in *The Color Purple* on women's self-development without looking to power systems to effect change (predating *We Are the Ones We Have Been Waiting For*) has the purpose of placing the supremacy of change not in a movement for equal justice but in the hands and bodies of women. Thus, Celie's magical metamorphosis in *The Color Purple* reflects this new direction.

With Celie as persona or frozen mask, her condition could not have been more hopeless; but as an exemplar of the female Self, her transformation could not have been more miraculous. Walker's dominant metaphors of power, *écriture féminine* and the lesbian phallus, are empowering to Celie. Through her writing Celie transforms herself from an interiority denied validity and expression in the outer world to the consciousness of an élan vital celebrating life, the "stars," and "Everything" (292). She assumes the behavior of Jung's archetypal Self, but with a critical interrogation, due to her lasting and negative depiction of males. Of the first of these, *écriture féminine*, Celie's (re)writing her body, Walker achieves several feats in bringing Celie to maturity and *jouissance*. Celie's letters, never read by anyone and reflecting what Henry Louis Gates Jr. describes as her "unspeakable medium," has the effect of projecting a "body that holds this hidden self."[30] As a phallic signifier of the autobiographical act of self-recovery, the self-inscribing letters in present tense ("I feels") represent Celie's desire to bridge the abject world of her ego's domestic experience with her questing journey to locate her inner god, Jung's inviolate Self.

Walker, then, presents two Celies: 1) the lowly, passive *experiencing* Celie of the disembodied voice; and 2) the hopeful, aggressive *narrating* Celie with the self-referential voice, making her "letter writing" a subversive and rebellious act of self-recovery.[31] Walker's achievement in reconciling Celie's two voices and rendering her a conscious maturity to reflect her evolving growth is at the heart of the novel's rich depth. The narrative techniques that Walker uses to accomplish her objective, which is Celie's gradual self-mastery, are examined here, distinguishing the *experiencing* Celie from the *narrating* Celie.

Of the lowly, *experiencing* Celie writing to God in secret, Walker reveals the fathomless depth of her degradation: "Dear God, He [her stepfather] beat me today cause he say I winked at a boy in church. I may have got something in my eye but I didn't wink. I don't even look at mens. That's the truth. I look at women, tho, cause I'm not scared of them" (6). Because she has Celie write letters that are not spoken and not read, Walker manipulates the epistolary form of the novel, suggesting that what was done to Celie—the beatings, the rapes—not only are forbidden and offensive but also "test the limits of discourse." Thus, Celie's early conversations with herself establishing her innocence unwittingly describe too the poverty and crudeness of her social environment: with her "body" being "subject to the whim of locations"—horrifically, her own home.[32] Her initial persona of abused innocence communicates the crimes committed against her, foreshadowing her thinking of herself as a "baby" (39) when she meets Shug. This foreshadows too her maturity and *jouissance* as an older *experiencing* Celie, who becomes bold enough to confront Mister with the fighting or warring spirit of the phallic maternal.

With the *narrating* Celie, Walker deftly projects her coming to character and narrative authority. Initially, Walker presents Celie as a recorder of her experiences, her childhood innocence, for example. She is not an omnipotent narrator, as we see when she records her shock upon discovering her real father's identity, which removes her from the stigma of incest even as she assumes a personality and reprimands God, "My daddy lynch. My mama crazy. All my little half-brothers and sisters no kin to me. My children not my sister and brother. Pa not pa. You must be sleep" (183). But as a mature narrator, Celie not only rewrites and analyzes her experiences but controls other characters' representations as well: we come to know these characters only by what Celie chooses to reveal about them, sometimes subtly. Celie's writing is the first indicator of her having a powerful inner drive of subjectivity, which gradually comes to fruition. In the middle of the novel, Walker gives her the power even to transfer her narratorial authority to others, namely to Nettie when she writes to Celie from Africa, "Dear God, This the letter I been holding in my hand. 'Dear Celie'" (122).

However, Celie is an unlikely autobiographer and protagonist, unprivileged and yet writing letters and assuming the authority of an author, so the legitimacy of her authorship can be questioned. That is, we are permitted to ask, why does Walker give Celie the authority to (re)write her life? Her narratorial authority is supposed to be an earned privilege, "not an absolute, something inherent in a specific individual or in that individual's discourse: [it is] something to be earned."[33] Since Celie represents the silencing of women and the oral folk tradition of non-literate, impoverished southern women, Walker invests her with the authority of Everywoman. Because she experiences the nadir of maternal experiences, at one point having her children taken away from her as if she were a slave mother, she not only endures to tell her story but also lives to experience *jouissance*. Walker implies that Celie's victory over oppressive forces gives her the authority of authorship. Walker celebrates her victory when the mature experiencing/narrating Celie's voices are fused, and with this double force she informs Mister, who has berated her for being poor, black, and female, "I'm pore, I'm black, I may be ugly and can't cook, a voice say to everything listening. But I'm here" (214). This act of talking back to her antagonist is an indication that she has learned how "to fight" even after the young narrating/experiencing Celie had weakly confessed to Nettie, "I don't know how to fight" (18).

Celie's spousal relations with Mister present Walker with the opportunity not only to stress her growth but also to reveal her archetypal behavior of the anima, her Logos, her maternal phallic drive to be distinguished from the lesbian phallus of her sexual *jouissance*. This is when the mature experiencing/narrating Celie's voices are again fused and the evidence of her fiery maturity is apparent. After reporting that Shug has informed her that Mister has kept Nettie's letters from her, a pugilistic Celie understands what this violation means and writes of feeling "a lightening in the head" and standing with a razor in her hand "crazy for Mr. ___ " (125). Having noted Celie's cognitive awareness of being victimized, having described what she perceives as the rational urgency of her avenging violence against Mister, Walker then has Celie list a group of items as if in a psychoanalytical framework of one of the novel's motifs: her development over Mister's phallocentric control. These are Nettie's letters "locked up tight" but which she steams open and reads, "strut[s] a little bit," and again gives Nettie narratorial authority: "Dear

Celie, the first letter say" (131). The letters, like Celie's writing, frame her growth. That Mister hides the letters in a trunk with pieces of Shug's underwear and "nasty picture postcards" identifies him as the possessor of the phallus and women's bodies. With the trunk, Walker has the older, narrating Celie hint wittingly at Mister's subconscious, his Jekyll/Hyde shadowy Self, which is not reconciled with his conscious life, hence his stunted life.

Walker's symbolic discourse on Mister's phallogocentricity and Celie's lesbian phallic *jouissance* leads to an unrefined description of sexual acts, which perhaps caused the book's banning in some American libraries. In her narrative description of her sex acts with Mister, Celie shows herself still to be a "virgin," as Shug describes her because she has never experienced *jouissance* with Mister, who "plunge in" to do "his business" (81). Whereas the maternal phallic is represented by Celie's learning to fight like the "male-acting" Sofia and Shug, the lesbian phallic is manifested by her sexual maturity. Shug teaches her about her body, her clitoris of sexual excitement: "right down there . . . is a little button that gits real hot when you do you know what with somebody. It git hotter and hotter and then it melt" (81). The clitoris/button is Walker's trope on Freud's description of the clitoris as a "little penis" and as a signifier of Lacan's phallus of desire, as she inverts the image and the privileging of the male genitalia and valorizes the female clitoris. The two women "kiss" and "touch," and Celie feels "like a little lost baby" (118) and not an object in Mister's sexual embrace, prevented from experiencing *jouissance*.

In Celie's union with both the maternal body of nurturance and the lesbian body of *jouissance*, Walker emphasizes the togetherness, the touching of two female bodies. Bodily contact manifests itself also in Celie's quilting and communion with Sofia, but especially in her bodily pleasures with Shug because of the undeniability of her *jouissance*. Irigaray stresses bodily touching as a definitive difference in female/male sexuality within a "dominant phallic economy" where the "penis [is] the only sexual organ of recognized value."[34] For Irigaray, women's sexuality and autoeroticism differ from men's in that the fertile and erotic female body has multiple organs of arousal, from the "fondling of the breasts, touching the vulva, spreading the lips" to "stroking the posterior wall of the vagina."[35] Walker's graphic description of Celie and Shug's touching offers a glimpse of Irigaray's theorizing on the pleasures of the female body, removed from the shadow of the masculine imaginary and existing autonomously, as Judith Butler theorizes in her essay "The Lesbian Phallus and the Morphological Imaginary."[36]

Like Irigaray, Butler distinguishes the symbolism of the lesbian phallus from the Lacanian signifier of the phallus. While the latter assumes a symbolic imaginary of power systems, heterosexual and in the name of the father, the former seeks its own sexual symbolic signifier of desire vis-à-vis the lesbian body, as we find with Celie and Shug's encounter. Butler too valorizes the lesbian body as whole, lacking and displacing nothing in theories of sex and gender; that is, homosexuality is not a surrogate for heterosexuality. Similarly, in *The Color Purple*, Walker questions so-cially proscribed gender and sex roles with the creation of her first female bisexual protagonist.

Celie experiences *jouissance* with another woman, and Walker presents lesbian sexuality as a prototype of lesbian phallic *jouissance*, pertaining to Celie's attraction to Shug, whose body she worships. "First time I got the full sight of Shug Avery['s] long black body with it black plumb nipples," she writes, "I thought I had turned into a man. . . . I wash her body, it feel like I'm praying" (51). However, Walker complicates the lesbian phallus as existing outside the binary gender/sex param-eters of social thought and heterosexual coupling when she has Celie thinking of herself as having "turned into a man" because of her attraction to Shug. Walker mirrors Celie as a by-product of social norms, evidenced in her parroting of Mister, who beats the young, experiencing Celie. When Harpo asks Celie what he should do to tame the mannish Sofia, the innocent narrating Celie tellingly responds, "Beat her. I say" (38). In her confusion, the mature Celie comes to question the rules under which she lives: "He love looking at Shug. I love looking at Shug. But Shug don't love looking at but one of us. Him. But that the way it spose to be. I know that. But if that so, why my heart hurt me so?" (77), challenging the norm of heterosexuality and society's disdain for same-sex coupling. Through her letter writing, her archetypal behavior, and her lesbian experience, Celie (re)positions herself in a text that has stirred heated critical debates.

Primarily because of Walker's lesbian coupling, the critic bell hooks argues, Walker invites criticism and rebuke. Walker, hooks posits, fails to give voice to one of the most contentious debates of our time, same-sex relationships, and she con-tends that *The Color Purple* fails then as a test of social reality. "Homophobia does not exist in the novel," hooks complains, and "Celie's sexual desire for women and her sexual encounter with Shug is never a controversial issue even though it is the catalyst for her resistance to male domination, for her coming to power." While hooks continues that Walker "makes the powerful suggestion that sexual desire can disrupt and subvert oppressive social structures because it does not necessarily conform to social prescriptions," she finds that this "realization is undermined by [Walker's] refusal to acknowledge it [lesbianism] as threatening, dangerous."[37]

However, one can argue that in her critique, hooks conveniently ignores Walk-er's subtle critique of homosexuality, homophobia, and social rebuke. While hooks does not acknowledge Walker's attempt to reconcile polemically charged views on homosexuality, Walker does address sexual theories and the social formation of gender roles. Celie wrestles with her feelings for Shug in a scene that hooks ap-parently overlooks even though it is one that represents Walker's acknowledgment of the perceived abnormality of homosexuality. Moreover, dominant, mainstream notions of heterosexual coupling are presented in the older, narrating Celie's com-plaint that Sofia and Harpo "always try to set me up with some man" because they believe that "womens love just by accident, anybody handy likely to do" (267). If Walker does not engage in a sustaining narrative refutation of the women's relationship, as hooks demands, then perhaps it is due to her advocating the type of social indifference to same-sex relationships that Teresa de Lauretis seeks in her essay "Sexual Indifference and Lesbian Representation."

It is clear that in her authorial representation of lesbianism and the absence of narrative disorder and chaos, Walker posits lesbian phallic power as an intimate behavioral reflex, outside the boundaries of the binary gender construction of male/female heterosexuality. Shug and Celie do not make a conscious decision to have a lesbian relationship; they just do. The problem that Walker suggests is connected more profoundly to conceptions about the individual and sexual identity, not the lesbian body per se, a point that Barbara Smith avers in "The Truth That Never Hurts: Black Lesbians in Fiction in the 1980s."[38] Another problem, however, is that Walker's authorial perspective does represent, as hooks remarks, a minority point of view, which makes her accountable to address a mainstream perspective in anticipation of affective reader-response criticism in the contested terrain of author, text, reader, and social responsibility. To a degree Celie's comments about others trying to fix her up with a man attempt to do just that. Celie's lesbianism, though major, is only one of Walker's symbols of the manipulation of gender and sexual roles.

Another is seen in Celie's androgynous fashion for male and female characters, a dress code recalling Meridian's androgyny, which is linked to her archetypal behavior of the warring phallic maternal. In *The Color Purple,* Walker also manipulates the androgynous dress code of pants to query gender roles and patriarchal law regarding women's bodies on the basis of male/female physiology, as Celie's initial rejection of wearing pants indicates. Shug, as maternal imago, suggests to Celie, "let's make you some pants," to which the socially conditioned Celie answers, "What I need pants for? I ain't no man" (152). In wearing pants, characters and their bodies become gender neutralized, and Walker specifically unmarks the body through fashion, just as she does through sex, the archetypal symbols of the anima/animus, sexuality, and even physical height, as the image of Sofia's "amazon" sisters as pallbearers pronounces. Interestingly, it is Sofia who wears pants, and Celie, the ingenue, who begins to notice: "I see Sofia dragging a ladder and then lean it up gainst the house. She wearing a old pair of Harpo pants" (64). By the end of the novel, the older narrating/experiencing Celie wears and designs pants for everyone (218), positing the slippage of gender identity, this time through fashion. "Androgynous individuals," writes Richard A. Lippa, "can be flexibly masculine or feminine, depending on the situation," and can "define a new standard of mental health and adjustment."[39] Androgyny signifies the gender expansiveness in the novel, which affects everyone, as we see when the new, domesticated Mister assists Celie in sewing pants.

While Celie valorizes the subaltern of the female Other, her unchanging representation of male characters challenges her narrative objectivity throughout the text, which has led to assaults against Walker by prominent black male critics. For example, when she stops writing to God, Celie explains to Nettie that it is because "the God I been praying and writing to is a man. And act just like all the other mens I know. Trifling, forgitful and lowdown" (199). If the experiencing Celie is limited in her narrative scope to personal encounters with a certain kind of man, then why does the young and mature, narrating Celie categorize all men as "lowdown"? Celie's "distanced self-narration"[40] between the fourteen-year-old of the erased "I am" and the forty-four-year-old entrepreneur of Folkspants, Unlimited, is transformed in body, signified by her aging maternal body like "any woman's body going through the changes of age" (266). But her unrelenting harsh attitude toward men remains static even though she presents Mister as having been regenerated too, a striking inconsistency.

A maelstrom swirled around the publication of *The Color Purple* and the subsequent Steven Spielberg movie, which, as Walker's biographer Evelyn C. White hints, was symbolic of poetic justice, as it premiered in Walker's Jim Crow, hometown theater, which had once segregated black and white theatergoers.[41] The maelstrom, however, was largely due, for black male critics, to the movie's and the novel's depictions of black male characters and fatherhood. There is too the narrating Celie's consistent, benighted description of black male characters and the semiotics of male identity. In the absence of her cognitive awareness of others' growth, namely, male characters' growth, the narrating Celie is fixed irrevocably in the experiencing Celie's mental agony about men. Celie's representation of male characters reflects a narratorial bias that these critics attribute personally to Walker. Despite her friendly reconciliation with Mister, for instance, the mature Celie narrates an unchanging attitude toward all men: "Mr. ___ done ast me to marry him again, this time in the spirit as well as in the flesh. I say Naw, I still don't like frogs" (290). Although Walker generally attacks binary constructions of identity, one of the binary structures of the novel consists of Celie's Bildungsroman through the pleasure of her lesbian body, but male agency only through pejorative signifiers of phallic authority. These are the ubiquitously erect penis, the gun, the African ritual of female circumcision and clitoral castration, and Mister's locked trunk of sexualized female possessions, which includes a picture of a nude, white female.

Appearing to overshadow or compete with Celie's *jouissance,* a masculine "rephallization"[42] (Derrida's term for recovery of the castrated phallus) is achieved by the male characters' subjection of women's bodies, often impregnated. For the most part, black fathers are depicted as erect phallic symbols, having an erotic narcissism connected to Freudian discourse on the pleasure principle.[43] Walker's decision to fuse the narrating and experiencing Celie's discourses on men, from start to finish, has the propensity to collapse the space of time from narrative past to narrative present. In the condensing of time, there is an emerging contradiction involving the experiencing/narrating Celie's growth from mask to maternal phallic and lesbian phallic *jouissance* and Self of inner peace and yet her spiritual blockage in terms of her first and lasting image of men as "frogs." However, for her transforming male characters such as Grange and Mister, Walker appropriates a feminine principle of attachment and relatedness to dislodge the Freudian/Lacanian model of the masculine imaginary of dominance over the female body whereby male characters become "frogs."[44] *The Color Purple* is an antiphallocentric novel celebrating Celie's spiritual/sexual *jouissance* in a culture antithetical to characters' achievement of Self, calling for their revolt and regeneration, especially Celie's.

The Temple of My Familiar: Lissie, the Archetypal Wild Woman

A self-described, mythological narrative of the past five hundred thousand years, Walker's *Temple of My Familiar* is broader in scope than *The Color Purple* while still celebrating female sexuality and subjectivity, but Jungian archetypal symbolism is limited here to several examples of the female character Lissie's behavior. A sexual libertine, she assumes the activity of the ego-libido male while her husband is subordinated to the role of the long-suffering but understanding female, Walker's role reversal of male-female relations. However, their narratives are compounded and complicated by other competing mininarratives. *The Temple of My Familiar* is Walker's longest and most ambitious novel. Challenging on several levels and boasting over fifty characters, it remains for readers a book "often begun and seldom finished."[45] The literary critic Constance S. Richards discusses the book as "the second in Walker's trilogy of Pan-Africanist novels,"[46] after *The Color Purple* and before *Possessing the Secret of Joy*. Yet, *Temple* is also a precursor to ideas of psychotherapy, developed more clearly and elaborately in *Possessing*. For example, the effective rendering of Tashi's psychoanalysis in *Possessing the Secret of Joy* can be traced to Walker's early appropriation of hypnosis in Fanny's resolving repressed memories about her racial trauma with southern whites in *The Temple of My Familiar*. In a text "often begun" but "seldom finished," Walker adapts art and psychology to indicate the spiritual healing properties of the combination. Her major characters are artists and/or academicians seeking to harmonize their knotted existence. "Artists," the omnipotent narrator informs us, are "messengers" who have "the responsibility for uniting the world" (123). To harmonize their lives, characters must remember their past, reconcile their problems, and retrieve the temple of their familiar: their inner sacredness, sublimated by society.

Across geopolitical time and space, characters in *The Temple of My Familiar* inherit the postmodernist condition of fragmentation and splintering that Walker attributes to the original grounding of Western history, depicted by the advent of the African slave trade, the Spanish Inquisition, gender dominance and subordination, and so forth. From South America the feather artist Zede flees to North

America because of colonialism. In Baltimore, New York, and California, respectively, the artists Hal and Lissie, the academicians Suwelo and Fanny, and the rock star Arveyda, who marries Zede's daughter, Carlotta, an academic, all wrestle with racism, sexism, spiritual displacement, and death. In West Africa the playwright Ola, Fanny's father and *The Color Purple's* Olivia's lover, uses the theater to fight African neocolonialism because "drama deals at a highly concentrated, more intense level with the contradictions of social existence."[47] Ola marries the English Mary Jane Biden to enable her to acquire African citizenship, to remain in Africa to teach art to disturbed children, and according to Richards, to challenge the "preservation of the colonial government's ban of interracial marriage."[48]

The central character in the narrative, the artist Lissie, is Walker's wild woman, demonstrating Jung's archetype of the anima; she gives voice to one of the book's unifying themes: the importance of reclaiming the temple of familiar. Lissie places herself inside/outside of cosmic Western time in recalling her past lives as pagan, witch, slave, goddess, and pygmy who went to live among her cousins "the apes" and animals, which is "the only dream memory of peace that I have" (87). Through dream memory, Lissie remembers her ancient selves, recalling the loss of her temple of familiar in her attempt to imprison a winged creature that flies away and symbolizes the loss of her free spirit as an archetypal wild woman. Readers can examine Lissie as a study of the psychological nature encoded in her function as the anima archetype: she resists domestication, fights "like the devil," and in a reversal of the masculine phallic imaginary, has multiple affairs that lead to pregnancies, with Hal delivering her babies, "though none of them were mine" (108). Lissie's wildness is further captured by her photographer/lover Henry Laytrum in "thirteen pictures of thirteen entirely different women" (90–91). She lives out her untamed nature with Suwelo's Uncle Rafe in Baltimore, where she and Hal live. About her wild nature Lissie and Hal reach an understanding, but "before we reached it, we had, both of us, shed rivers of pain" (108).

Through Lissie's character, Walker evokes a mythical, romantic past and offers an alternative model of women and society before Freud, the evolution of patriarchy, and the dawning of civilization. Ancient art, important in the narrative, provides inscriptions of women as goddesses on cave walls and on tombstones and as statuettes, celebrating their life-nurturing and sustaining properties. While acknowledging J. J. Bachofen's regard of patriarchy's ascendancy, Gerda Lerner cites his influential work on the valuation of women in the "dim past": "At the lowest, darkest stage of human existence [mother-child love was] the only light in the moral darkness. . . . Raising her young, the woman learns earlier than the man to extend her loving care beyond the limits of the ego to another creature. . . . Woman at this stage is the repository of all culture."[49] *The Temple of My Familiar* reconstructs the modern loss of the ideal of women and the maternal as the "repository of all culture" and then laments its passing in the post-Oedipal epoch of "murders, rapes, torture, wars, abandoned children" (246, 275).

Walker conjures the dim past of matriarchy and shuns the Christian Madonna image of woman as self-sacrificing woman and mother. The free-spirited Lissie ruminates sardonically, "If I am not mistaken it is only in Poland that Our Black Lady, the Great Mother of All—Mother Africa, if you will—is still openly worshiped. Perhaps that is why it is said of the Poles that they are none too bright" (196). Walker's mythologizing and historicizing of time reflect a maternal/paternal bifurcation of society and tradition: undeveloped but peaceful even with animals in mythic maternal time; civilized but bereaved and displaced in patriarchal discourse. A postmodernist novel describing characters' "identity fragmentation," *Temple* "creates a mythic re-visioning of female empowerment and the encroachment of patriarchy, conjur[ing] an originary narrative to explain the inception of patriarchal societal relations and racial difference."[50] This novel may fail as a myth, lacking a meaningful and sustaining development of character, metaphor, and metonymy that readers can follow, as Richards argues.

Yet in *The Temple of My Familiar,* Walker continuously relates individual transformational processes to psychoanalytical patterns of health that have become her signature. Lissie pronounces Jungian ideas of the individual necessity of working out blockage, and she subjectivizes the individuation process: "It is against blockage between ourselves and others—those who are alive and those who are dead—that we must work" (355). As she implies, Jung's Self is not accessible to those who harbor animosities, for the virtue of the Self is predicated on the premise of reconciling opposites, that is, the reconciliation of the conscious, personal, and collective unconscious. A reconciliation of opposites is acquired through acts of forgiveness, a Walker trademark: Grange Copeland attempts reconciliation with Brownfield and Josie; Meridian, with Truman and Lynne; Celie, with Mister; and Lissie, with Hal and whites. As a novel of dreams, visions, and psychotherapy, *The Temple of My Familiar* is challenging, on one hand, but anticipates, on the other, one of Walker's most successful though painful novels on Jungian archetypes.

Possessing the Secret of Joy: Tashi's Phallic Castration and Protest

Possessing the Secret of Joy is a novel about civil and human rights on an international scale for African women who face bodily mutilation in rituals that they are made to embrace because of tradition. Significantly, Walker's patterning of Jungian archetypes is unmistakable throughout this text, and it is possible to follow her narrative delineation of archetypal patterns of persona/mask, shadow, anima/animus, and Self in the psychoanalytical structure in which Jung places them. Tashi, Walker's African heroine, experiences sexual trauma, and this bodily traumatic event alerts her to the limitations of the ego-centered consciousness and the profound but unconscious suprapersonal forces interfering in a creative and positive way with the ego. As witnessed in *The Third Life of Grange Copeland*, mental crises have an unconscious history, and one's inability to resolve the conflict between the ego-centered world of the self and the personal and collective unconscious (manifested by archetypal symbols) evokes crises. While Tashi experiences the individuation process to wholeness, Walker habitually gives greater voice to the inner power of the individual to change and mature spiritually, a psychoanalytical discourse that enables the author to acknowledge and yet downplay the power of society and tradition over individual will.

In *Possessing the Secret of Joy*, Walker strips Africa of the romantic image bestowed upon it by Paule Marshall, black writers in the 1960s, and the Harlem Renaissance artists of the 1920s. This novel is a contemporary and radical feminist rebuke of a patriarchal tribal god who "liked it tight" and ancient and modern African leaders who kept their penises while African females, bodily mutilated, lost their vulvas and the experience of *jouissance* (238, 244). In addition the novel is a political diatribe against the social disease of tribalism/sexism, responsible for Tashi's psychological maiming. With her dilemma consisting of renouncing the egoism and false pride of African tribalism and discovering a unique inner voice, Tashi creates an alter ego in the imaginary Lara, the rejected cowife in one of her stories. Tashi's complex about the sight of blood and her repression of archetypal images and their truths are the contributing causes of her mental instability.

Tashi's psychic wounding begins with the death of her older sister Dura, whom she sees bleed to death from a botched "bath," a euphemism for female genital circumcision. There are three types of female circumcision: *sunna* circumcision, referring to the removal of the prepuce or vaginal foreskin; clitoridectomy, referring to the detachment of the clitoris; and infibulation, referring to an excision of both sides of the vulva, which are scraped raw and sewn together, often in less-than-sanitary conditions. Infibulation leaves only a small opening for the vagina, which can give heightened sexual pleasure to a man during intercourse but which also makes urination, menstruation, intercourse, and especially the birth process not only painful for women but also life threatening. True to her willful sexual revolt and revolutionary politics, Walker dedicates *Possessing the Secret of Joy* with "Tenderness and Respect to the Blameless Vulva," choosing for her female characters the most radical form of female circumcision: infibulation.

Surreptitiously, Tashi has gone to the place of the baths in her village, has heard her sister Dura's screams, and has seen the bloody aftermath of the "operation," but she represses the memory of the experience and retains only a phobia of blood. As a result of this repression and her silence, she later submits herself to the African tradition of scarification (a different kind of bodily maiming) and even later, as a young woman, to infibulation. With an inflated ego, she informs an objecting Olivia, the African American missionary in Africa and sister to Adam, whom Tashi marries, "All I care about now is the struggle for our people. You are black, but you are not like us. We look at you and your people with pity [for] you barely [possess] your own black skin" (22–23). When she begins to awaken to the truth about her culture and the pain inflicted on women, however, Tashi confesses, "I was crazy."

Tashi goes to have her face scarred with identifying tribal marks and sees "pot-bellied" children with "dying eyes" and "old people" lying on "piles of rags" while the village women make "stew out of bones" (24). Unable to reconcile the impoverishment of her culture with the cultural arrogance she exudes, Tashi develops a "passion for story-telling" and slips into madness. To chronicle Tashi's descent into madness and her resulting fragmentation, Walker creates six personas: Tashi, the troubled African child who submits to the tribal rites of scarification and circumcision and upon whom silence is imposed; Evelyn, the scarred adult Tashi who becomes an American citizen; Tashi-Evelyn, the African American whose cultural duality is dominated by the nightmarish remembrance of her African past; Evelyn-Tashi, the Americanized African whose cultural selves coalesce into a picture of herself as a wounded American (167); Tashi-Evelyn-Mrs. Johnson, the aging matriarchal composite of selves who confesses to killing M'Lissa, the mutilator or tsunga (a Walker neologism), and who reconciles herself with Lisette, Adam's mistress, and Pierre, Lisette's son by Adam; and Tashi Evelyn Johnson Soul, who achieves the Jungian Self upon her reconciliation of opposites, resistance to social lies, and acceptance of death for her "crime" of alerting other women to her conviction that resistance to lies, imposed through silence upon suffering women, is the real secret of joy.

This last pronouncement is Walker's attempt to dispel the myth of racist anthropology propagated by Mirella Ricciardi in her book *African Saga* (1982), which holds that black people can survive anything, including all their sufferings, because they possess "the secret of joy." In her typical labyrinthine configuration of text and context, Walker constructs seventy-two narratives: forty-two narratives by the multiple Tashis; and a combined thirty discourses by Olivia, Adam, and Benny, Tashi and Adam's retarded son whose skull was crushed in the birth process. Within the thirty narratives are also stories of Lisette and Pierre; M'Lissa, the African tsunga; and Mzee or "Uncle Carl," the Jungian analyst. By focusing on Tashi's narratives, we can see the archetypal symbolism and the Jungian patterns of the individuation process. To avoid confusion, all six personas are referred to here as simply Tashi.

"And what about your dreams?" asks Mzee (25), the Swiss psychoanalyst to whose tower in Switzerland Tashi has been taken for analysis by Olivia and Adam, whose French mistress, Lisette, is a niece to Mzee. By implication Walker espouses Jungian dream symbology.[51] Jung has written of the importance of dreams, averring that there is nothing accidental about dreams, which come from a place that is not really human. Dreams have a "compensatory function"[52] in alerting the conscious mind to disaster or expressing the anticipatory as well as the good and the beautiful. Citing the autonomy of the unconscious realm of dreams, Jung writes that "even when asleep we dream." One therefore "cannot afford to be naïve in dealing with dreams" because they "originate in a spirit of the beautiful and generous as well as the cruel goddess."[53] By appropriating the dream motif and placing Tashi in Mzee's "tower" (Carl Jung built his own private tower in Zurich, which he called his place of maturation and which Walker visited[54]), she brings together the dynamics of Tashi's conscious, personal unconscious, and collected unconscious thoughts—which Jung believed to be essential in the individual's quest for psychological well-being.

Tashi's dream of imprisonment in an African tower that resembles a "termite hill" (239) is symbolic of the personal unconscious as the collective unconscious. Tashi is the queen termite with the broken wings (239, 232)—reproducing her own kind as scurrying termite workers (Africans) care for her needs because she is the sacrificial maternal breeder. Tashi is Everywoman, Walker's cultural trope for African females experiencing the bath and bodily mutilation. However, Tashi reveals this dream not to Mzee but to Pierre, whom she, as an ego-centered personality, initially rejects. Mzee's showing of a film of his visit to an African village with ritual ceremony of initiation jars Tashi's repressed memory of Dura's death and causes her to reveal her dream. The showing of the film is as deliberate as Mzee's desire to give Tashi "a very large bag of clay" (87), an early reference to clay fertility dolls symbolic of a magical, strong autoerotic matriarchal society, which is now denounced by the males for political purposes. Jung often used art in his analyses of patients, believing that art and its creative expressions could unlock the hidden world of dreams in the unconscious. Walker uses art in *Possessing the Secret of Joy* and in *The Temple of My Familiar,* a novel not explicitly Jungian, to reveal her Jungian tendency to connect art, psychology, and mental health.

After viewing the film, Tashi draws and paints a foot and fighting cocks, but there is a giant "strutting" cock that waits for the "insignificant and unclean" vulva that the "foot" will toss to it (75). Realizing that the giant cock is really a hen and that the foot belongs to M'Lissa, the tsunga who has operated on Dura and killed her, Tashi recalls her visit to the village bath and acknowledges Dura's "murder" (83, 116) and the women's participation in the murder. All is part of Walker's authorial pronouncement on the hierarchy of oppression, with women colluding with men against other women and therefore participating in their own oppression. Indeed later M'Lissa pleads to Tashi that Catherine (their mother) had helped to hold Dura down for the operation that killed her. Through M'Lissa's voice, Walker responds to Mzee's criticism that black women are difficult to analyze because they cannot bring themselves to criticize their "Mothers." This is a reference to black women's collusion with the social forces holding them down either through their imposed silence ("don't tell") or through more direct methods of collusion with their oppressors. Both cases are presented here.

On awakening, Tashi confesses, "I felt as if I were seeing the cause of my anxiety for the first time. There was a boulder lodged in my throat. I remembered my sister Dura's murder . . . exploding the boulder" (83). The boulder explodes further when a retiring Mzee introduces Tashi to Raye, a powerful African American analyst, who coaxes Tashi to discuss her own "bath" experiences. Raye bonds with Tashi and upsets again the silence imposed upon her. Raye does this by visiting a dentist who performs periodontal surgery on her guns, and the surgery, soreness, and healing of her gums represent, she comments to Tashi, her "puny" effort to comprehend the subject's emotions. Here, Walker refers to Jung's theory of the "participation mystique,"[55] whereby a person attempts to feel, empathize, and identify with another's experience. As a result of her revelations, Tashi is forced to see the falseness of her masked self as "Completely woman. Completely African. Completely Olinka"—reflecting the petty world of the selfish ego. She confesses to having had an "outlandish outsized image of myself" (64, 22).

Having given voice to the first of Jung's archetypes, the persona, Walker describes the second, the shadow, which is superimposed upon Tashi and manifested in her aberrant behavior. Tashi's shadowy personality is childish and awkward, though not necessarily malevolent unless it becomes integrated into the anima/animus archetype, which is more forceful than the shadow because it is convinced of its rightness. Walker writes of Tashi's shadows, illustrating the archetypal image on several occasions. For example, years after she marries Adam and relocates to America as a "wounded American," an adult Tashi returns to Africa to seek vengeance on M'Lissa, whom she confronts: "A proper woman must be cut and sewn to fit only her husband, whose pleasure depends on an opening it might take months, even years to enlarge. Men love and enjoy the struggle, you said. For the woman. . . . But you never said anything about the woman, did you M'Lissa?" (224). Tashi continues, "I am weeping now, myself. For myself. For Adam. For our son. For the daughter I was forced to abort. There is caesarean section, the aborting doctor had said. But I knew I could not bear being held down and cut open. The thought of it had sent me reeling off into the *shadows* of my mind" (emphasis added, 224).

The victims of Tashi's shadowy self are Benny, her son, and Pierre, Adam's son by Lisette. She "frequently and with little cause, no cause, boxed Benny's ears," making him "squeal and cringe"; and she hurls stones at Pierre when he comes to visit Adam, while the "cabby ran up to Pierre, grabbed him under the arms and dragged him out of sight" (144–45). Jung states that awareness of the dark shadows requires painstaking work, as Lissie remarks, giving distinct voice to Walker's psychoanalytical impetus. Walker's treatment of her heroine's rage and healing therapy over an extended period of time, after which Tashi recognizes and loses her shadow, is, it appears, quite realistic.

As Tashi-Evelyn-Mrs. Johnson, facing execution in Africa, the mature and shadowless Tashi writes to her husband's dead mistress seeking reconciliation, acknowledging, "Pierre has been such a gift to me" (277). Walker makes considerable use of the black French character Pierre, a bisexual. Through him she treats homosexuality as nonaberrant and explores the religious symbolism of stones, Jung's symbol of wholeness. When she finally allows Pierre, a student at Berkeley, to visit her in California, Tashi muses, "He has told me he likes men as well as he likes women, which seems only natural, he says, since he is the offspring of two sexes as well as of two races. No one is surprised he is biracial; why should they be surprised he is bisexual" (174). Pierre interprets Tashi's dream of imprisonment in a tower that is cool, tall, and dark with "millions of things moving about me in the dark" that are "forcing something in one end of me, and from the other they are busy pulling something out" (26–27). Near the end of her life, Pierre informs her of Africa's "strong identification with the termite" that "has kept a place for males in its society." As the desexed (broken wings) queen termite of her dream, Tashi, the prisoner, is "stuffed with food at one end . . . having your eggs, millions of them, constantly removed at the other"; afterward she is expected to die (233).

In *Possessing the Secret of Joy*, African women who are bodily mutilated, violently and deliberately, are depicted as sacrificial maternal breeders in a patriarchal and polygamous tribal society. Female circumcision therefore becomes a "sacred" or religious rite of passage intended to make a woman fit for marriage: "no man would marry" a "loose" or uncircumcised female whose "clitoris, like a penis, can rise" (235). The village elders believe that God "created the tsunga," and it is a religious taboo to break the silence surrounding what Walker presents as a psychic trauma, which women have endured for centuries in Africa and the Middle East. In the novel's afterword she cites statistics at the time that indicate that ninety to one hundred million women living today have experienced this torturous rite of passage (283). The African critic Olakunle George in his essay "Alice Walker's Africa: Globalization and the Province of Fiction" cites the Netscape data engine of 581,830 Web sites at the time for female circumcision and 23,090 Web sites for genital mutilation, evidentiary numbers of a worldwide interest in the trauma of the rites, which counter his criticism of Walker and other global feminists as cultural interlopers.[56]

To help Tashi recover from her trauma, Pierre, a student of anthropology, has immersed himself in her dementia, consulting a number of books in order to interpret her dream. Initially rejected, like the biblical Christ, he has become for Tashi the sacred "corner" stone that she once hurled at him. As such, Pierre symbolizes Walker's use of stones, which is not accidental here or in *The Temple of My Familiar*. The South American character Jesus in *Temple* believes that by guarding the village's "three small stones," he is preventing the villagers' foreign enslavement. In *Possessing the Secret of Joy*, M'Sukta is the sole survivor of an African matriarchal tribe. M'Sukta is put on racist display in Condon's "Museum of Natural History," and she is called "the African Rosetta stone" (72, 233). The cover of *Possessing* shows a photograph of "the hand of the author touching Jung's alchemical or philosopher's stone, carved by Jung in 1950" (frontispiece to *Possessing the Secret of Joy*). This stone is cube shaped and covered with inscriptions; in its center is a tiny replica of a man whose physical encirclement or encapsulation resembles the eye's pupil.

Jung had such a stone in his garden in Zurich. In the Middle Ages the "philosopher's stone" symbolized humankind's ultimate achievement of psychic wellness. Medieval alchemists had aspired to find "the secret of matter in a pre-scientific way, hoping to find God in it, or at least the working of divine activity," believing that the philosopher's stone embodied the secret of this energy."[57] In the individuation process, stones symbolically represent the Self, but Tashi, in Walker's hierarchical appropriation of Jungian symbolism, must experience the third stage of the individuation process, the anima/animus archetypes, or the fighting maternal phallic of Walker's man-acting female characters. Presenting what appears to be a natural male/female duality, Walker subverts and exposes traditional Africa's rejection of this duality and the autonomous rights of pleasure and gratification for women as the phallic maternal. Rhetorically she attacks "primitive" African society and its cultural female rites of castration of the "clitoris." Again, it is Pierre, Tashi's "gift," who assists her in her development, explaining the concept of the female soul of the male and the male soul of the female. This theory is nullified by Tashi's society because "Man's life was not capable of supporting both beings: each person would have to merge himself in the sex for which he appeared to be best fitted" (175), Walker's obvious sexual pun on socially ascribed sexual roles. Her gender-specific language mocks the patriarchal ethos of Tashi's Olinka society and its political/ moral biases that justify the suppression of females.

Indeed, Walker is most profane in that God, as presented in sacred African tribal lore as the ultimate signifier of the powerful phallus, had excised an "erect clitoris" that resembled an erect phallus and then "fucked the hole that was left" (234–35). In her rejection of the power drive of patriarchy and religion, Walker eschews religious orthodoxy, much like her contemporaries Paule Marshall and Toni Morrison. Marshall's characters' attack on orthodox religion has been discussed, and in *Beloved*, Morrison's Baby Suggs is most effective as an "unchurched" preacher in the Clearing. In *The Third Life of Grange Copeland*, Grange and Ruth "came to church" but "giggle[d] in serious places" (280). *Possessing the Secret of Joy*'s Raye avers, "Religion is an elaborate excuse for what man has done to women" (235). Walker does not shun the Jungian idea of the individuation process as containing a sacred, religious function, however. Thus her unorthodox treatment of organized religion does not obscure her apparent espousal of the theological divine in the individual, hence her attraction to Jung over Freud and Lacan. Nevertheless, Tashi, on the journey to the Self, reveals the animus stage of her development when she confronts and attacks M'Lissa, the tsunga.

Of the male or Logos and rational soul coexisting in the female gender, Jung writes that the "*animus* corresponds to the paternal *Logos* just as the *anima* corresponds to the maternal Eros," though the female "consciousness is characterized more by the connective quality of Eros than by the discrimination and cognition associated with *Logos*."[58] Jung also remarks that the anima/animus archetype is "uncommonly strong" (unlike the shadow self, which can be discerned and discarded) and is not easily dismissed because it has "an unshakable feeling of rightness and righteousness."[59] Under the influence of this archetypal image, one can plunge into the murderous depths of the shadow's childish behavior as Brownfield does in *The Third Life of Grange Copeland*. Tashi has, in fact, the killer instinct of a mythological murderer of women, Bluebeard: she willfully kills the tsunga who has called herself and others like her "torturers of children" (22).

Tashi, unlike Bluebeard, kills to avenge female suffering, the mutilation of the female and maternal body, and to affirm female sexuality and *jouissance,* a murderous act that illustrates the dual quality of the anima/animus as possessing both "good" and "bad" qualities. The critic Olakunle George describes Tashi and M'Lissa's relationship as "not simply that of a vengeful daughter getting rid of an evil ancestor" but as Tashi's representation of "every new generation" having a duty to "immolate its predecessor in order to fulfill a self-defined historical mission."[60] But Tashi and M'Lissa are represented in terms of good and evil, and it is the former's "goodness" or "rightness" in murdering M'Lissa, the killer of children, that illuminates the cumulative effect of Walker's bringing together all of Tashi's six different personas to underscore the naturalness of the battle and the victory of "good" over "evil." Tashi's different personas become her just and willing accomplices.

In *Possessing the Secret of Joy,* Walker vitalizes the Jungian notion of the anima/animus feelings of righteousness and rightness by having Tashi's six multiple selves all assume the responsibility for M'Lissa's murder. For Walker's readers, these multiple confessions can be confusing, but Tashi's act of murder is so logically "right" in its final appearance that her multiple selves want to claim credit for the feat, which explains the initial confusion of her multiple confessions. Dressed like an American but speaking like an Olinka, Evelyn leaves America to return to Africa to kill M'Lissa and is accused of murdering a "monument" (163). But it is Tashi who thinks of leaping up and strangling M'Lissa after listening to the stories of her painful life as a "tsunga" (224). Tashi confesses to Olivia her innocence of M'Lissa's murder, and yet Tashi-Evelyn-Mrs. Johnson states, "I did it." While on trial, the latter writes to the deceased Lisette, "Tomorrow morning I will face the firing squad for killing someone who many years ago killed me" (267, 274).

This is a dizzying discourse. It is also, however, a pointed illustration of Jung's conceptualization of the "unshakable feeling of rightness" of the anima/animus archetypes, and not coincidentally of Walker's subversion of Jung's sexist ideas that "Eros is an expression of their [women's] true nature, while their *Logos* is often only a regrettable accident."[61] Walker's idea of poetic justice is presented in Tashi's premeditated killing of M'Lissa, who anticipates and even foresees "the murder of the tsunga, the circumciser, by one of those whom she has circumcised" (208). But it is not for M'Lissa's murder that Tashi Evelyn Johnson Soul is executed. Although a tsunga and a "national monument," M'Lissa as a woman is expendable. Tashi dies for breaking the silence surrounding the misery of women's lives. Exposing the cruelty of a phallocentric society, Tashi challenges patriarchy, contributes to its waning authority, makes signs of protest (a radical American custom), and appropriates the colors of the African flag. Thus, Walker merges global traditions, creating a nexus of African and American cultural unity and dispelling the myth of feminists as the cultural Others.

Walker's diasporic, cultural, and feminist epistemology is not in conflict but rather is complementary in its broad antithesis to a Western and an African masculine phallic hegemony. Walker's having Tashi comment, "I was crazy" may reflect, as George opines, on her Western imperialist bias against the culturally untranslatable. Yet, Walker writes of hearing in Ghana the "testimonies" of villages of women who "were overpowered as children and irreparably wounded. I notice that for some of the women speaking, it is as if a dam has burst. They tell their stories over and over, with the same stunned amazement that there is a circle of faces mirroring them," hearing them.[62] The book *Anything We Love Can Be Saved: A Writer's Activism*, from which this quotation is taken, was published in 1997, and *Possessing the Secret of Joy* was published in 1992. The five-year interval of time makes the latter work prophetic in Walker's representation of the fragmentation of women's identity, the violation of their bodies. This fragmentation is caused by their oppression but also by their silencing.

In conclusion, Tashi achieves the Jungian Self, the union of opposites par excellence, at the end of the novel when she reconciles the personal and collective unconscious contents of the Self and mends her relationships with others, particularly Pierre and Lisette. Most notably, Tashi has accepted the truth of her personal experience, as opposed to the lies of the social order, benefiting the male. Resistance to the lies of female inferiority and subjugation brings her the secret of joy. In turn, she shares this joy of resistance and truth with other women who attend her execution, bringing ancient fertility dolls, "wild flowers, herbs, seeds, beads," and "ears of corn" in a feminist celebration of women's harvest and coming-of-age

(193). Even in the final lines of the novel, Walker's illustration of the Jungian archetypal Self is clear when Tashi Evelyn Johnson Soul faces a firing squad, hears a "roar as if the world cracked open," and is "satisfied" (281). With this lasting image of Tashi's death and rebirth, Walker links women's renewal on a global scale to the individual dynamics of psychic change, not political movements.

Olakunle George denounces Walker's book and treatment of female mutilation as the reductionism of an alien culture that she, an "American of African descent"[63] and a Western cultural outsider to boot, cannot understand. In his choice of authorities, George shifts Walker's discourse on female circumcision, positing the "cultural untranslatability"[64] of the experience that Walker represents as primitive and from which the African female must be saved. George argues a cultural inscription of the practice, citing Françoise Lionnet's legal case study of African and Muslim females in France who make the voluntary choice of castration, even in violation of French law. George borrows too from Gayatri Spivak's distinguishing of the suttee as subjective agent who wants to die in cultural rites of sacrifice and the suttee as passive victim who must be "saved" by global feminists. Spivak heralds the Indian woman's self-agency, denied by transnational feminists such as Walker, George remarks, who are seeking to connect and end women's bodily victimization around the globe from America to Africa. As agents, the Indian and African females are "active bearer[s]" of a "context-specific subjectivity."[65]

If Walker is sticking her Americanized cultural nose in another continent's business, as George implies, then she is also rewriting the text of her own childhood abuse as the "wounded I,"[66] as other critics and George argue. Indeed, Thadious Davis cites Walker's background and the South in particular as "central to the work she produced throughout the 1970s and 1980s" and even the 1990s with *Possessing the Secret of Joy.* Walker emerges as a "paradigm shifter" because she had the courage to undertake "the breaking down of oppositions, those that as Foucault suggests have 'remain[ed] inviolable, that our institutions and practices have not yet dared to break down.'"[67] Walker attempts to do so in the novels discussed here with her assault (before it became politically correct) on the interlocking systems of power on race, class, sex, gender construction, the bourgeois ideology of motherhood, religion, family systems, and even violence in the black community. In the South she experienced the brutality that led to her connecting women's oppression across geographical fault lines—all this while rescuing Zora Neale Hurston from the obscurity of a Jim Crow potter's field in Florida. While it appears that George accepts Walker's autobiographical insertions as a Georgian writing about racist America, he rejects her autobiographical intrusions as a transnational womanist/feminist criticizing Africa. Here is an example of a critic attempting to have it both ways.

Possessing the Secret of Joy resists, however, his and other critics' ideas of Walker's cultural interloping, criticism that was anticipated, pronounced, and rejected in *The Color Purple* with Nettie's dictum from Africa that "OUR COMMUNITY COVERS THE

WORLD" (241). Walker's biographer Evelyn C. White attributes Walker's enlarged authorial vision about civil rights to several influences in her life, including Muriel Rukeyser, one of Walker's Sarah Lawrence College literature professors. White cites Walker's confession that "Muriel had a very large imagination that wandered over vast terrain. More than any specifics about structure or technique, she taught me that it was possible to be passionate about writing and to live in the world on my own terms."[68]

Beginning with *The Color Purple* and moving on to *The Temple of My Familiar* and *Possessing the Secret of Joy,* Walker's novels increasingly position her as a global author attempting to illuminate cross-cultural signifiers of the maternal body in a crisis and using her own experience in Georgia as a reference. Invariably in interviews and essays she speaks of "plac[ing] myself in the body" of a scarred child, for example a boy enduring the ritual of facial scarification, as she recalls of her trip to Ghana. She discusses in the documentary *Warrior Marks* the "partial blinding I suffered as a child," which she links to African women's sexual "'blinding,' caused by the excision of the clitoris."[69] As an advocate for global civil and human rights and Amnesty International Ghana, Walker visited Accra after the publication of *Possessing the Secret of Joy,* making the personal radically political with her activism that began as far back as the civil rights movement, enshrined in the revolutionary decade of the 1960s.

7 Bodily Evidence
Toni Morrison's Demonic Parody of Racism and Slavery

As Ira Katznelson states, "Much of the Negro community is buried under a blanket of history and circumstance. It is not a lasting solution to lift just one corner of that blanket. We must stand on all sides, and we must raise the entire cover if we are to liberate our fellow citizens." Toni Morrison has claimed, "My job becomes how to rip that veil and teach a history that is unrecorded and untaught in mainstream education."[1]

The first African American to win the Nobel Prize for literature, Morrison is one of the most celebrated American and African American women writers in the world. In presenting the Nobel Prize to Morrison in 1993, the Swedish Academy acknowledged the "visionary force"[2] of her oeuvre and her remarkable fictional but fact-based representation of the African American historical experience. That is, after Wheatley, Jacobs, Forten, Fauset, Larsen, Hurston, Marshall, and Walker, Morrison's work subsumes *all* the history covered by these writers and at once lifts the "blanket" and rips "the veil" off the various corners of the black experience. In covering such a long span of history, she reveals that American history has dramatically challenged and even altered the lives of black Americans from the development of slavery to the structuring of the Black Codes, rigid notions of beauty and citizenship, Jim Crow laws, and other de facto forms of discrimination. Morrison captures and mirrors the tragedy and transformation of African Americans by adopting several essential narrative devices of parody and pastiche, semiotics and metaphors, and allegory to portray black life in America, teaching untaught history in order to liberate Americans.

To re-create and teach the oft-neglected reality of African American history, Morrison relies on the ancient genre of parody, a derivative of the Greek term *parodia,* which found its earliest expression in Aristotle's *Poetics.* In reconstructing and deconstructing American history as it pertains to the lives of African Americans, Morrison lifts parody from the "dust-bins" of literary history, and the genre reemerges, according to Robert Phiddian, as the "secret sharer of deconstruction."[3] In the aftermath of postmodernism, parody and deconstruction become weapons by which writers such as Morrison can question the established "truths" of the master discourse on race. Therefore, Morrison appropriates parody in her reconstruction and then deconstruction of history to query and restore truth "by reducing the lie [of the master discourse] to an absurdity," as Bakhtin remarks on the function of parody.[4]

For example, in a compromise reached between northern and southern delegates in Philadelphia in 1787, America's founding fathers (several of whom were slaveholders) determined that a black person as a slave should be legally and bodily inscribed as "three-fifths" a person in the U.S. Constitution. In Morrison's demonic parody of slavery, the novel *Beloved* contests the politics of a slave-market economy and capitalism and the politicization of black people's humanity when the Ohio fugitive slave mother Sethe, no longer a commodity, stands up to Schoolteacher, her master, in the woodshed. Although she must sacrifice her daughter, Beloved, Sethe reclaims the fullness of her humanity as a person and as a mother who establishes her maternal rights to her children. They are *not* to be returned to the slave plantation in Kentucky. In fighting back, she overthrows the shackles of her forced subordination, which is based on the diabolical, mathematical configuration of her proscribed racial identity as "unwhole," a fraction of humanity, as blacks were conveniently described in the Constitution.

In parody's active engagement "in intertextuality"[5]—that is, in its play with and on an accepted master discourse—it assumes a parasitic relationship with its host genre. The critic Gerard Genette refers to the two elements in this relationship as the "hypotext" or original model and the parodic "hypertext" that imitates the primary source.[6] Parody thus feeds on its own invited host,[7] deconstructing and illuminating the host's absurdities and hypocrisies about, in this case, the coexistence of liberty and freedom and enslavement and subjugation. For Morrison, these unfortunate inconsistencies as revealed in the Constitution and the Declaration of Independence provide the founding ideals, ironically, of American democracy, leading ultimately to the country's Herrenvolk republicanism.

Parody and pastiche can often be fused, but they have different impulses. In his essay on *Beloved*, Rafael Pérez-Torres discusses the novel as an example of narrative pastiche. He makes a distinction between parody and pastiche as elaborated in Fredric Jameson's *Postmodernism, or, the Cultural Logic of Late Capitalism*. While Jameson defines pastiche as blank parody without real motive and as parody's replacement ("parody finds itself without a vocation: it has lived, and that strange new thing *pastiche* slowly comes to take its place"[8]), Pérez-Torres claims that *Beloved*, in its multiple narrative discourses, emerges as pastiche. He remarks, "The novel deploys a narrative *pastiche* in order to contest history as a master narrative."[9] If pastiche is "blank parody" but lacks parody's "ulterior motive,"[10] then *Beloved* as a narrative pastiche is weakened because it lacks parody's decentering impulse against Western "history as a master narrative." That is, pastiche is devoid of parody's political intentionality.

Parody is often politically motivated, policing accepted and conservative boundaries of authority, ridiculing ideas of "intruders," debunking artificial boundaries, and unmasking their false construction. By refuting established truths, parody, unlike pastiche, becomes sharply polemical. Simon Dentith avers, "Parody is the favoured mode for performing these acts of debunking, carrying out just that polemical function which . . . defines it; parody therefore enters into the very texture of the novel . . . establishing its claims for a more realistic apprehension of human life."[11] Since Morrison has stated that her novels must be political as well as historical,[12] one can reasonably argue that parody is her genre of choice. However, I find that in her experimental novel, *Tar Baby*, Morrison blends pastiche with parody and other genres and forms, including references to the Hollywood film *Guess Who's Coming to Dinner*. Although *Beloved* is the most radically parodic of Morrison's novels (before *A Mercy*), due to its subject matter of human slavery, demonic parody informs the basic narrative structure of basically all of Morrison's novels: with their fiery images and motifs of the African American experience in America as a living segregated hell.

Demonic parody differs from simple parody in its apocalyptic representation of an unbearable world of evil. Simple parody has multiple applications in a variety of discourses: whether it is employed playfully, for example, in Miguel de Cervantes's parodic critique of romance and chivalry in *Don Quixote* (1605) or satirically in Jonathan Swift's mock epics of the intellectual authority of ancients and moderns in *A Tale of a Tub* and *The Battle of the Books* (1704). Swift appropriates parody to police the conservative boundaries of the ancients (with whom he agreed) against the moderns, whose abstract metaphysics he distrusted.[13] In contrast to Cervantes and Swift, Morrison is neither playful nor romantic in her quest to teach the hellish history of African Americans. Indeed in *Beloved*'s dedication to "Sixty Million and more" black African and black American slaves, she invokes in number alone the holocaust of slavery and the unimaginable sufferings of the untold and unknown number of lives sold, auctioned, lost, kidnapped, murdered, maimed, or "disremembered." While demonic parody shares parody's political impulse to debunk false arguments, it goes further, namely, in its reconstruction of demonic imagery to mirror a world turned upside down because of the unnaturalness of evil.

In his classic study *Anatomy of Criticism*, Northrop Frye emerges as one of the first critics to identify the wild, demonic strain of parody set loose from its twin in its representation of "real" experiences as opposed to those conjectured or imagined by literary parodists. Frye mentions "demonic parody" or "the radical demonic form" of parody many times in the section titled "Theory of Archetypal Meaning (2): Demonic Imagery." Here, Frye suggests the extension of parody from an imitation of art forms to a replica of real-life experiences of apocalyptic and hellish violence. As examples, Frye refers to Dante's *Inferno*, George Orwell's *1984*, Arthur Koestler's *Darkness at Noon*, and Jean Paul Sartre's *No Exit* as texts of "an existential hell" in these authors' portrayals of "real life." Frye argues the following: "just as apocalyptic imagery in poetry is closely associated with a religious heaven, so its dialectic opposite is closely linked with an existential hell, like Dante's *Inferno*, or with the hell that man creates on earth, as in *1984*, *No Exit*, and *Darkness at Noon*, where the titles of the last two speak for themselves. Hence one of the central themes of demonic imagery is parody, the mocking of the exuberant play of art by suggesting its imitation of 'real life.'"[14] With its emphasis on an apocalyptic society of devilish machinations against human beings, the genre of demonic parody illuminates Morrison's narrative imagery of the banishment of African Americans to the tormented space of a segregated hell within American mainstream society, first as slaves and then as Jim Crow or Herrenvolk second-class citizens.

If demonic parody allows Morrison to re-create and teach untaught American history, then her appropriation of spatially segregated places (as we find, for example, in the Jim Crow community, cemetery, parks, and railway cars in *Sula*) enables her to link the "contamination" of the segregated black body-in-crisis to the prejudices of a national body politic that is racist. With such a narrative description of Herrenvolk blacks and mainstream whites, she conveys the sense of a wholly unhealthy society, discriminatory beyond that which is practicable, as when Nel misses her grandmother's funeral because of Jim Crow laws for railway passengers. Whether confined and restricted to plantations in the South or to urban ghettoes in the North, African Americans, Morrison shows, have experienced historically a constricted spatiality, one marked by their perceived difference within an organizing superior/inferior grid of race. Constricted and demarcated spaces for blacks in Morrison's work represent a denatured parody of the wider spaces that whites have reserved only for themselves. The sociologists Douglass S. Massey and Nancy A. Denton posit in *American Apartheid: Segregation and the Making of the Underclass* that as a group African Americans remain the most segregated citizens in America, more spatially "hypersegregated" than either Asian or Hispanic Americans.

The "high level of segregation experienced by blacks today," up to one-third of the total group, the authors report, "is not only unprecedented compared with the experience of European ethnic groups; it is also unique compared with the experience of other large minority groups, such as Hispanics and Asians." African Americans' segregated spaces and social immobility play a significant role in Morrison's demonic parodies, as indicated by the semiotics of her characters' physical boundaries and bodily disfigurements—evidence of forced subordination. Such bodily disfigurements are seen, for example, in *The Bluest Eye* with Mrs. Breedlove's flopped foot or in *Beloved* with Sethe's scarred back, personal symbols of their trauma. But as one critic asserts, "disability in Morrison occupies a complex position. Unlike the category of race, which, in commentary on her work has often been interpreted as a sociological marker of the condition of black people in America [as Massey and Denton opine], it would be a mistake to take disability in her work in the same sociological vein."[15] That is, Morrison transforms her characters' disabilities into meaningful acts of sacrifice, rebellion, and even regeneration, joining the rank of the eight women writers previously discussed.

Semiotically the breakdown of bodily and cultural spaces is linked, especially in social theory, to ideas of individual marginality. In *Volatile Bodies*, Elizabeth Grosz remarks on the significance of the body/space corollary: "The body must be regarded as a site of social, political, cultural, and geographical inscriptions, production, or constitution," and bodily images are not isolated from the surrounding society. Rather, these bodily markings are representations of society as seen in *Sula*, especially. Accordingly, the body "is not opposed to culture, a resistant throwback to a natural past; it is itself a cultural, *the* cultural product."[16] Grosz continues, "The body image is the condition of the subject's access to spatiality (including the spatiality of the built environment)."[17] In Morrison's novels, the layering of space for African Americans always already prefigures a symbolic, disfigured bodily identity for them, regardless of their class and economic status. This can be witnessed in *Song of Solomon* with the white policemen's harsh treatment of Milkman, the son of a real estate tycoon, and Guitar, Milkman's impoverished, fatherless friend. Economically, Guitar and Milkman are far apart, but theoretically, in terms of race and identity, they are linked. The black legal scholar Derrick Bell cites the Constitution as being primarily responsible for legally originating the pejorative social discourse on race and the distorted bodily identity of African Americans. Bell argues that the Constitution's "three-fifth" clause is the "root reason for the inability of black people to gain legitimacy." The Constitution skewed the image of the enslaved and explains, Bell asserts, why African Americans "are unable to be taken seriously when they are serious and why they retain a subordinate status as a group that even impressive proofs of individual competence cannot overcome."[18] The radical abolitionist William Lloyd Garrison tore up a copy of the Constitution, which he described as a proslavery document.

Morrison's archetypal maternal heroine Sethe recognizes the illegitimacy and false construction of the body politic and the accompanying spatial strictures of black society and identity. Her lucid recognition spawns her revolt, as she laments the denaturalization of her enslaving cosmos in recurrent bodily imagery suggestive of the subversion of nature as inscribed on lynched black bodies hanging from trees. Sethe cries, "Fire and brimstone all right . . . hidden in lacy groves. Boys hanging from the most beautiful sycamores in the world" (*Beloved* 6). Bodily disfigurements and racialized spatial boundaries emerge as corollaries of the African Americans' segregated world and become fit subjects for Morrison's demonic parody of American history. "I propose," Ralph Ellison remarks, "that we view the whole of American life as a drama acted out upon *the body* [emphasis added] of a Negro giant, who, lying trussed up like Gulliver, forms the stage and the scene upon which and within which the action unfolds."[19] The basic, primary hypotexts of Morrison's parodic hypertexts are patriarchal law and racial boundaries as written on the black body-in-crisis from slavery to a restricted Herrenvolk freedom.

As a creative anodyne to the parodic, disfiguring social body of racism and patriarchy, Morrison, like her literary sisters, uses the maternal-womb metaphor to suggest the female's regenerative and recuperative abilities. She appropriates the maternal body as an emblem of the female's special gift and power. Here, in the imaginary space of the maternal womb, the individual can seek shelter, comfort, or rebirth. A safe space for the disempowered, the maternal womb (physical and metaphorical, as with *Sula's* Bottom) becomes a spatial and metaphorical innovation that emerges as an alternative to the existing, fragmentary cultural order. As noted in chapter 1 on Phillis Wheatley, Michelle Boulous Walker reiterates Helene Cixous's idea of the mother as metaphor, a claim that links women's bodily power above that which is biologically determined to their creative spirit, facilitating the radical undoing of paternal pain and repression.[20]

In many of Morrison's novels—*Tar Baby* (1982), *Jazz* (1993), *Love* (2003), and *A Mercy* (2008) being the exceptions—the maternal exists in stable opposition to the social instability of a racialized space as well as the limitations of a restricted black patriarchy. Morrison's wise and nurturing mothers represent maternal metaphors of power: *The Bluest Eye's* Mrs. MacTeer; *Sula's* Eva; *Song of Solomon's* Pilate; *Beloved's* Baby Suggs and Sethe; and *Paradise's* Consolata, along with a community of women in her novel *Home*. Men too can "mother," as Morrison shows in *Beloved* with Paul D and in *Love* with Sandler, but the image of women as primary nurturers is sustained in her narratives. Women's bodily power of giving birth places them in unique metaphorical and spiritual spaces of feminine power and sexuality, though often reduced to notions of strict biological subjugation in a racist-sexist patriarchal discourse.

The novels *The Bluest Eye* (1970), *Sula* (1972), *Song of Solomon* (1977), *Beloved* (1987), and *Paradise* (1998) are discussed in chronological and thematic order. Toward the end of the chapter, Morrison's additional novels that are atypical of her signature in representing the presence, acceptance, and dominance of a wise maternal force, excluding her two novels, *Home* (2012) and *God Help the Child* (2015), are analyzed. In fact, these novels appear to describe the chaos and confusion that occur when there is a rejection or an absence of maternal ethics. However, with the first-named novels, the discussion begins with an analysis of Morrison's appropriation of symbols and metaphors to mark characters and to create a distinction between those accepting of a constricted racial and Herrenvolk spatial identity and those resisting these proscribed places. Female characters who resist the social order typically use the extraordinary and magical powers of their bodies to heal their disabled communities.

The Bluest Eye: Jim Crow America and the Cultural Womb of Stillbirth

"My eyes. I want them blue," pleads a socially driven insane Pecola Breedlove to the false prophet, Soaphead Church, who is so genuinely moved by Pecola's innocence and pathos that even he, a religious fraud, writes a poignant letter to God on Pecola's behalf. Culturally and psychologically Morrison correlates the Breedloves' dysfunctional familial body to the stilted, spatial body of the 1940s and Jim Crow restrictions. In theory and practice, the politics of ascribing and fixing a physical space within society is designed not only to map the boundaries of existence for subordinates but also to authenticate racial identities of a beautiful superior and ugly inferior caste. The psychologist Jean Baker Miller states, "Once a group is defined as inferior, the superiors tend to label it as defective or substandard in various ways. These labels accrete rapidly. Tragic confusion arises because subordinates absorb a large part of the untruths created by the dominants." One Morrison scholar adds that *The Bluest Eye* specifically presents "psychological models of racism, stigmatism, [in the characters'] judging by appearance, and [dominant] hierarchies of emotions" and beauty.[21] Thus the untruths to which these two critics refer include ideas on the subjugated group's beauty, intelligence, and capacity. In a segregated society such as that created by Jim Crow laws, the accreted labels of the politics of race and identity and thus mainstream acceptability were intended to separate the dominants from the subordinates, who were made to feel their Otherness even in the appearance of family structure.

In *The Bluest Eye,* Morrison plays on the intertextuality of the hypotext of the Dick and Jane primer and her radical parodic restylization of the primer. There is in the restylized primer an implied suffocation of space that challenges the mythological sphere of the all-American family as being all white, all middle class, and all normal. The original hypotext of the primer reads, "Here is the house. It is green and white. It has a red door. It is very pretty. Here is the family. Mother, Father, Dick, and Jane live in the green-and-white house." Morrison's parodic hypertext "feeds" on the original hypotext but semiotically suggests the Breedloves' squashed space and identity problems with its lack of traditional spacing: "Hereisthehouseitisgreenandwhiteithasareddooritisverypretty . . . Hereisthefamilymotherfatherdickandjaneliveinthegreenandwhitehouse." The invented space of the hypotext of the Dick and Jane primer, representative of hegemony with its dominating racial politics, is grotesquely ridiculed in the *unspaced* letters of the parodic hypertext. It suggests the Breedloves' asphyxiation of identity.

The semiotics of the asphyxiated space set aside for Jim Crow citizens who are denied access to the healthier and wider spaces of hegemony is in contrast to the ideal text/space of Dick and Jane, creating grotesqueries of assigned social spaces. In her knotted compression of the Dick and Jane primer, Morrison engages the play of parody to attack the primer's mythological construct of space, hegemony, and race. In doing so she readily exposes the binary opposition of nonsegregated space for the "ideal" white family and segregated space for the "real" black family, dominants and subordinates residing in two different realms with two different realities, one beautiful and attractive, and the other ugly and unattractive. Morrison also assaults the bourgeois vacuity of the primer, the absurdity of a "pretty" house for the dysfunctional Breedloves with their two hopeless parents, errant son, and "ugly" daughter. Confined to the narrow space of an inner-city slum, the Breedloves live in a storefront house, which the drunken father burns down before he rapes his own daughter, Pecola, creating a familial hell, which demonically parodies the external hell of their suffocating, Jim Crow environment.

Morrison's character Pecola symbolically represents this claustrophobic, hellish space. Pecola's own cramped life begins in her mother's womb, spreads to her Jim Crow social milieu, and culminates with her father's raping of her pubescent body. As a result of the rape, she gives birth to a stillborn baby in a sterile society that denies African Americans access to its public places and aesthetic spaces of beauty. "Black people were not allowed in the park" (105), as Morrison's omniscient narrator reminds us of one of Jim Crow's laws regarding public spaces and racial boundaries. African Americans were systematically segregated from whites in restaurants and theaters, on trains and buses, and in residential communities and churches, hospitals and cemeteries, and even parks: wide-open spaces. Morrison joins Jessie Fauset in naming and stressing these places/spaces that were off-limits to black people, calling attention to the strange and out-of-the-ordinary creation of laws that would restrict their inhabiting the most natural of places/spaces in society. The historian C. Vann Woodward comments that as far back as slavery, the free Negro in the North and the slave in the South "lived in a society dedicated to the doctrine of white supremacy and Negro inferiority."[22] In this Herrenvolk democracy and through the force of the law and the power of the media, North and South alike sought to superimpose on society specific racial views by the manipulation of space in residential areas, on public transportation conveyances, and in the production of beauty images, an aesthetic space from which blacks were also excluded, making their isolation from society essentially complete.

A product of the South and virulent Jim Crow practices, Pauline Breedlove, Pecola's mother, has scripted on her own body the politics of subordination. Born in Alabama as the ninth of eleven children, Pauline was wounded at the age of two when she stepped on a rusty nail that injured her foot, causing her bodily deformity that mirrors her emotional limitations as a wife and mother. Pauline migrates to Ohio and marries Cholly Breedlove, an abandoned, emasculated alcoholic. Even before she gives birth to Pecola, a pregnant Mrs. Breedlove dismisses the fetus in her womb as ugly and unwanted, suggesting that she is maternally impaired. She envies and absorbs the ubiquitous, aesthetic images/spaces of beauty taken by American blond icons, namely Greta Garbo, Betty Grable, Ginger Rogers, and Jean Harlow, after whom she attempts to model herself once she becomes pregnant and wants to "look like Jean Harlow" (123, 125). But she is not white and not blond, and thus she becomes instead a ridiculously dark parody of the blond Hollywood icon, attempting to enter the forbidden space of beauty and aesthetics while becoming a symbol of the hapless maternal body.

As a domestic, Pauline seeks relief from her constricted world of ugly deformity in the spacious home of a wealthy white family, where her skin glows, inauthentically, "like taffeta in the reflection of white porcelain" (126, 107). The mother-daughter dyad is loveless and distant, indicated by Pecola's reference to her mother as "Mrs. Breedlove." However, at her white employers' home, Mrs. Breedlove becomes "Polly," a girlish name implying her impenetrable racial/spatial barriers as a black woman and a mother. As a demonic parody of Dick and Jane's mother, Mrs. Breedlove radically counters the tranquil, domestic image of the ethereal "Mother" in the mythological space of the primer. She is not a powerful maternal cure for an ailing culture and daughter, but rather a symptom/victim of cultural and social engineering. "Each culture or society organizes mothering, pregnancy, birth, and child care to fit the economics, religion, and scientific beliefs of that time and place,"[23] writes Jane Silverman Van Buren. The Dick and Jane primer and the Breedloves' parodic enactment represent these parameters of motherhood and society.

In the established social parameters of the primer and Morrison's deconstruction of its cultural construction, the primer's ideological role for the mother comes under scrutiny. Morrison unpacks the mythical notion of motherhood versus its grotesque reality in *The Bluest Eye*. Race, gender, and class domination encode the primer's politicization of a white, middle-class standard of the ideal mother and family while Morrison parodically decodes the mythological construct and provides a cultural "deviation" from its attractive idealized norm. In doing so she shatters the myth of the primer as politically neutral and reveals its racist media agenda in creating a hierarchy based on race and class but from which the Breedloves are excluded on a physical and an aesthetic level. Throughout her development in the Jim Crow South and North, Mrs. Breedlove and her family emerge as cultural distortions of the mythical norm.

At home, at school, and in the community, Pecola is assaulted because she represents a painful deviation from the white-beauty norm, which pervades the text. Her mother dismisses her as ugly, her teachers refuse to call on her, and the students refer to her as "black and ugly." In contrast, the mulatto Maureen Peal becomes a surrogate for the white image of beauty in the primer and on Hollywood posters. Eyes "genuflected" before her, representing a possible breakdown of the grid of aesthetic space for African Americans who look "white" and do not drastically threaten the dominating public sphere of race, beauty, and space. In contrast to Maureen's body language of beauty, the damaged Pecola walks home with her head bowed, reflecting her despairing psychic state as a result of the abuses heaped upon her. She stops at Yacobowski's Fresh Vegetable, Meat and Sundries Stores to buy three Mary Jane candies, which are wrapped in the image of a blond girl. A white immigrant, Mr. Yacobowski stares at her in a white dominating gaze of hatred, although he lacks Pecola's native citizenship and credentials. As she passes the home of the socially aspiring blacks Geraldine, Louis, and Junior, she is referred to as a "nigger," the most disparaging racial epithet.

Semiotics of black people's color fetishism permeates *The Bluest Eye*, from their idolization of blond movie stars and near-white African Americans to their affection for white baby dolls. The social psychologist Kenneth Clark found this attraction for white dolls damaging enough to conduct "doll tests" on black children in several southern and northern states in the 1940s and 1950s, which, writes the historian Risa L. Goluboff, the NAACP used as evidence before the Supreme Court of the "psychological damage" of racism.[24] Clark and his wife, Mamie, also a social psychologist, documented the harmful effect that white dolls had on black children in Jim Crow America. With an abundance of cultural images and icons from white dolls, Mary Jane candy wrappers, and Hollywood blond actresses, Morrison pulverizes Pecola's world and psyche with white/black semiotics of bodily differences and dead-end spaces. In this world there is no hope of escape, Jean Paul Sartre's no exit, as Morrison foreshadows in her parodic, cramped spaces of the primer. Pecola is psychologically pulverized on a daily basis, a theme tragically climaxing with her father's injection of semen into her developing womb.

Born in Georgia, abandoned as a child, and now unsuccessful as a man, Cholly Breedlove rapes his daughter Pecola twice. The rape represents a twisted parody of the nice father in the Dick and Jane primer, as Cholly subverts the role of the model parental figure. In *A Theory of Parody,* Linda Hutcheon posits, "Parody, then, in its ironic 'trans-contextualization' and inversion, is repetition with difference. A critical distance is implied between the backgrounder text being parodied and the new incorporating work, a distance usually signaled by irony."[25] The only similarity between Cholly and the ideal "Father" of the primer is that both are cultural productions: the model Father is projected as being gainfully employed, economically viable, politically significant, paternally responsible, and spatially unrestricted. A product of the Jim Crow South, unfathered and unloved, unemployed and unemployable in the Jim Crow North, Cholly is a demonic perversion of the perfect Father. He becomes paternally irresponsible because he is engulfed in a culture that denies his manhood.

Cholly's rapes and Pecola's pregnancy and stillbirth delivery radically parody the primer's representation of responsible paternal ethics in the ideal family. Ironically, his incestuous behavior underscores the only source of material value that he possesses in a patriarchal society: his penis. As a phallic marker of power in patriarchy, Cholly's penis is a symbol of masculine aggression, a characteristic that he, unlike the ideal Father, is allowed neither to develop nor to display in society but can subversively act out in his tortured, private hell. A drunken Cholly mistakes Pecola for her mother the first time, but he wantonly rapes her again in Morrison's demonic parody of one of the seven deadly sins: lust. The demonic imagery of a lecherous father suggests his final, infernal difference from the idealized cultural production of Dick and Jane's Father and reveals his total entrapment, even sexually. All spaces and exits are closed to Cholly; he has, in Sartre's words, no exit from his tortured hell.

Morrison's narrative imagery of rape, incest, and maternal carelessness becomes a familial parody of the Dick and Jane primer, capturing and defining the torture of Pecola's world. But in contrast to these fragmented and fissured representations of identity, Morrison also appropriates maternal metaphors of transformational power, setting up a binary opposition often found in her novels of spirited survivals. In *The Bluest Eye* and in many of her other novels, Morrison counters the hatred of society with the prevalence of love feasts, an Old Testament commandment of *agape* and *philio* acts of love for the community, particularly a disabled community of pariahs. In contrast to Mrs. Breedlove, the archetypal mother Mrs. MacTeer is a powerful maternal figure who not only conducts warfare on her daughter's illness before it takes "holt" on her like an enemy but also attempts to mother the essentially motherless Pecola.

As a surrogate mother, Mrs. MacTeer takes Pecola into her home and metaphorically into the comforting space of her maternal womb after Cholly burns down the Breedloves' storefront house. In the reassuring physical space of her home/womb, Mrs. MacTeer hums, and she bathes Pecola and gives her doses of maternal affection and nurturance when Pecola begins "ministratin." In coming to "womanhood" with her menstrual period, Pecola discovers the power of her own female body even before Cholly rapes her and distorts the power of the maternal force. The act of bathing, synonymous with a water baptism, represents a spiritual respite for Pecola. She enters into a bonding relationship with Mrs. MacTeer, sharing the adopted mother-daughter dyad. A nurturing mother, Mrs. MacTeer also keeps a garden, organically demonstrating with the vast womb of Mother Earth the like-minded principle of life and creativity of the feminine-maternal body.

The three jolly whores, Marie, Poland, and China, too represent the loving maternal figure. Unlike Pecola's and her mother's distorted bodies, asserts Vanessa Dickerson, the three whores' bodies freely belong to women who have learned to "subvert the external gaze" of social registry and who, like Mrs. MacTeer, offer Pecola maternal affection. This calls into question Tracey L. Walters's analysis of Pecola as having "no one" (not even temporarily) who can save her in the mode of the mythical Persephone-Demeter dyad.[26] In naming the whores, however, Morrison goes far beyond the confines of their concern with proper gender behavior and the social registry of their small, midwestern community. Freely engaged in the oldest profession for women, prostitution, the three whores are political symbols of power and evince the kind of maternal concern for Pecola that is shared by the wise matriarch, Mrs. MacTeer. She is the would-be maternal savior for Pecola if circumstances had not been so overwhelming for Pecola, as Morrison deliberately makes them, causing us to feel the sheer pathos of the young girl's ordeal.

Morrison's naming of the three whores signifies the force of their identity: they are Marie, Poland, and China because they are named after foreign countries that resisted invasion. The Maginot Line, loosely configured in Marie's naming, was an erected French fortification built in the 1930s to guard against a German invasion. Poland was a French ally. Like the Maginot Line, the Great Wall of China was constructed to keep invaders out in the early history of China. Since *The Bluest*

Eye is set in Ohio in 1941, the era of World War II, Morrison parodically names the whores after countries of resistance, inscribing on their feminine bodies a like-minded militarism against intrusive, foreign bodies of a disabling power, whether at home or abroad. Like Mrs. MacTeer, the whores display their own peculiar type of maternal ethics; although they are not biological mothers, they know the importance of fostering love. They refer affectionately to Pecola as "dumplin" and are concerned that she is appropriately attired in inclement weather. "Where your socks?" (51), they lovingly ask her.

The transformative power of maternal love, received intermittently in the novel, is not enough, however, for Pecola to wage constant warfare against the multiple forces of destruction that she encounters. In her first novel Morrison uses demonic parody, syntactically and sexually, to overwhelm and pummel the reader with the emotional reality facing Pecola, ultimately destroying her. In *The Dialogic Imagination,* Bakhtin describes the parodying of literary languages that fail to capture reality truthfully as a "parodic destruction of syntactic structures" in "accented words."[27] In her parodic destruction of the syntax of the Dick and Jane primer, Morrison inverts the idyllic image of family, individuals, and society to capture the Breedlove family's unrelieved suffering.

The literary critic Philip Page suggests that by creating "such an inverted world, Morrison begins" in *The Bluest Eye* "an artistic exploration of fusion and fragmentation" developed in subsequent works. Inversion, states Page, "embodies a doubleness, a division between right side up and up side down. In *The Bluest Eye,* Morrison initially posits the split, the violence and trauma of divided lives, in bleakest terms."[28] While "inversion" plays an important role in parody's intertextual play on its host genre, without the blunt force of demonic parody and its critical intent, readers can misconstrue what Morrison really achieves in writing *The Bluest Eye.* What Page refers to as Morrison's signature style of "inversion" is, in fact, presented here as her signature style of radical demonic parody, of which inversion, like irony, is a characteristic but not a genre, wholly simulating and criticizing history as an uncontested master text.

Rather than simply portraying an "inverted world" of a primer turned upside down, *The Bluest Eye* emerges as the first of Morrison's novelistic portrayals of the black American experience as a monstrous projection of Frye's existential hell. As a genre, demonic parody permits Morrison to revisit, graphically, the historical restrictions placed on the lives of African Americans. In response to her uncovering of these historical realities, she poignantly protests, "We are people, not aliens. We live, we love, and we die."[29] One of the difficulties for Morrison's readers, however, is that the original hypotext of the master discourse and the parodic hypertext must be recognized in their narrative interplay for a full understanding of the history being taught in her parodic unmasking. Without an understanding of the original host on which Morrison's parodic critique feeds, the leveling of established hierarchies would lose the power of attack that she clearly intends for them to have. It is akin to a building crumbling to the ground but without eyewitnesses there to mark the collapse. In works after *The Bluest Eye,* Morrison moves beyond Frye's demonic imagery of a fiery hell without the possibility of redemption, a direction that suggests her new emphasis (like her contemporaries Paule Marshall and Alice Walker) on the recovering capacity of the maternal figure after the failure of the nonmaternal Pauline.

Sula: The Bottom as Dispossessed Maternal Womb

It is equally as important to recognize Morrison's artistic use of demonic parody in her second novel, *Sula,* as it is in *The Bluest Eye.* Without such a critical analysis of parody in the text, Morrison's parodying of history and black economic dispossession during Reconstruction is lost in translation. Simon Dentith remarks that one "of the features of parody is that it depends for its effect upon recognition of the parodied original, or at least, upon some knowledge of the style or discourse to which allusion is being made."[30] For example, although their separate studies of *Sula* are incisive, Deborah McDowell and Gurleen Grewal analyze the novel in ways that suppress its parodic hellfire.

In a well-regarded feminist reading of *Sula,* McDowell writes, "*Sula* glories in paradox and ambiguity, beginning with the prologue, which describes the setting, the Bottom, situated spatially in the top. We enter a New World here, a world in which we never get to the 'bottom of things.'" McDowell finds that the titular character, Sula, inherits a "female heritage" (after Eva, her maternal grandmother, and Hannah, her mother) that is "an unbroken line of 'manloving' women who exist as sexually desiring subjects rather than as objects of male desire." Moreover, McDowell finds that "Sula's sexuality is neither located in the realm of 'moral' abstractions nor expressed within the institution of marriage that legitimates it for women."[31] For Grewal, *Sula* is a "book of wounds and schisms, losses and injustices at the individual and collective level[s]," and the novel represents the history of a segregated community[32] in Ohio, Morrison's home state, a favored setting.

A parodic reading of *Sula,* however, allows readers to find the underlying cause of things, to get to the bottom and to understand that the Bottom itself is a symbolic maternal womb of black economic dispossession similar to Paule Marshall's Bournehills. The Bottom represents Morrison's sarcastic comment on what happened economically to many African Americans after the Civil War and Reconstruction (1865–77). *Sula's* hypotext, then, is a postemancipation America where the newly freed slaves sought and were promised abandoned real estate land and economic opportunity while believing that their free slave labor was a result of what Du Bois described as "Theft on a mighty scale."[33] The Freedmen's Bureau had seized the slave barons' property of land and real estate, holding in its possession approximately eight hundred thousand acres of southern land, which belonged legally to slavocrats who had lost "between two and three billion dollars" in nineteenth-century currency after the slaves' liberation.[34] On May 25, 1865, President Andrew Johnson, a southerner, issued the Proclamation of Pardon to southern rebels, who subsequently regained control of their property, which had been assumed by some slaves who had already planted cherished gardens. When Union general Oliver O. Howard (the first director of the Freedmen's Bureau and a founder of Howard University) traveled to the South to inform the freedmen and freedwomen of the pardon, one woman burst into song with the Negro spiritual "Nobody Knows the Trouble I've Seen." The sympathetic General Howard "wept."[35] Thusly the segregated space of the Bottom represents Morrison's parodic hypertext of the original hypotext of the failed Reconstruction promises.

In *Sula,* the birth of the Bottom had come into being as a result of a "nigger joke" when a "good white farmer," representing patriarchy and the law, promised freedom and a piece of bottomland to his slave, the dispossessed, if he would "perform some very difficult chores." After the slave completed his tasks, however, the farmer realized that he did not "want to give up any land," particularly the fertile land of the valley. Appearing apologetic, the shrewd farmer deceived the trusting, freed slave into believing that "valley land was bottom land" up in the hills because when "God looks down it's the bottom" (5). Through hegemonic discourse and the farmer's manipulative use of language, Morrison parodies acerbically the era's promise of land reappropriation, aborted by President Johnson. Parodically the white farmer seriously mimics President Andrew Johnson's attitude.

As descendants of the freed but economically deprived slaves, *Sula's* characters reside in the Bottom, a semiotic marker of their status in hegemonic society and discourse. In the Bottom, Morrison re-creates the near total asphyxiation of the Jim Crow culture of spatial boundaries, where the characters are cut off from the oxygen of normal space and growth. Black passengers are seated in the Jim Crow sections of trains, black patients are placed in the "colored ward" of the hospital, and Sula's body is taken "to the colored part of the Beechnut Cemetery" (150). Parodying spatial boundaries of segregation, Morrison unmasks the reductio absurdum of Jim Crow regulations; such an absurdity is clear when Nel and Helene are forced to change trains several times on their way to Louisiana, stopping in Alabama, Kentucky, and Tennessee in obedience to the laws of spatial segregation on trains.

As a result of Jim Crow policy and its inconvenience, Nel and her mother arrive too late to see Nel's dying great-grandmother, who has passed away shortly before their arrival. In this particular scene, Morrison reveals the absurdity of Jim Crow law while disclosing its terrible, practical, and everyday effect on people's lives. As Grewal remarks, *Sula* "seethes with desire," but this desire is not limited, as Grewal suggests, to the loftier aspirations of men such as Ajax, who wants to fly an airplane, or Jude, who wants meaningful employment, or Sula, who seeks self-expression.[36] Indeed, like Nel and Helene, all of these characters have a more practical desire: a longing for simple fairness to arrive in time to bid a loved one farewell, to sit comfortably in a clean railroad car, and to be allowed to use the bathroom. These are all natural human longings that Morrison illustrates were denied unconscionably to black Americans.

The Bottom is a bottomless pit of hell for characters with aborted ambitions who are trapped within the impenetrable walls of a history of dispossession. Virtually every character in the novel is associated with the imagery of fire and water similar to the rain of fire found in the seventh circle of hell in Dante's *Inferno,* an intolerable heat reserved for violent offenders and suicides. Innocent of the behavior of Dante's hell-raisers, Morrison's characters are instead victims of the "crime" of color, similar to Richard Wright's Bigger Thomas in the 1940 novel *Native Son.* But *Sula* is a novel of raging and cooling imagery of fire, ice, and water, suggesting another Morrison work (even before the publication of *Beloved*) about a black holocaust due to the characters' lost inheritance, thwarted ambition, and spatial limitations in the Bottom.

From the most minor and diminutive of characters to the appearance of significant major characters, all live in the fiery furnace of the Bottom. Such characters include Teapot and Chicken Little, whose names signify on the proverbial tempest in a teapot and the apocalyptic town crier who warns, "The sky is falling." The World War I veteran Shadrack is named after the biblical Shadrach, who is placed in a burning furnace with Meshach and Abednego. Sula visits Nel and asks for "Lots of ice, I'm burnin' up" (96). After she dies, Sula's death is described as a "sleep of water" (149). Nel is linked to calm, tepid water until she develops "her very own howl" (108). Nel's husband, Jude, feels the heat of "rage, rage" (82), while Ajax takes "piping-hot water" baths (128). The matriarch, Eva, feels a "liquid trail of hate" for her estranged husband BoyBoy, who returns to the Bottom with his girlfriend (35). Toward the end of the narrative, the characters angrily rush to the tunnel that the men were "forbidden to build" because of Jim Crow employment practices, and at the river they smash bricks and experience a river baptism with the "blazing sunlit ice rapidly becoming water" (161).

Rage, fire, and water are biblical symbols of the apocalypse and Armageddon, of destruction and death, but also of rebirth, baptism, and spiritual regeneration— all images of Morrison's signature binary oppositions. Fire and water and the isolationist politics of Jim Crow laws underscore the characters' disjointed lives and unfulfilled yearnings in the Bottom, with the Bottom functioning as one of the most important symbols in the book. In her analysis Deborah McDowell remarks, "Not only does the narrative deny the reader a 'central' character, but it also denies the whole notion of character as static essence, replacing it with the idea of character as process."[37] But the setting of the Bottom *is* a unifying character/womb that represents the promise of a regenerative maternal womb, again like Marshall's vast warm womb of Bournehills, set against the flames of a dispossessing history and spatial Jim Crow limitations. Appropriating feminine and maternal imagery, Morrison's narrator describes the Bottom as "rich and fertile" and "sheltered" like a fetus in the placenta of a woman's womb (5–6), an indication of the citizens' rebirth potential even while the Bottom is depicted too as sterile land, a parodic countertext to history. Indeed the book begins with a description of the Bottom as a "nigger joke"; continues with the image of a maddened Shadrack, World War I, and shell fire; and ends with the Bottom being drenched in frozen rain.

Images of fire, ice, and water dominate those of blossoming pear trees, another symbol in the novel, which conveys an image that is not consistent with that of the Bottom, which is struggling for rebirth. Sula and the images of pear trees in the novel can be compared, as critics suggest, to Zora Neale Hurston's Janie Starks and her vision of blossoming pear trees in *Their Eyes Were Watching God.* Hurston uses blossoming pear trees to link them to Janie's vision of self-development, beauty, imagination, yearning, and growth, but Morrison shuns this kind of positive linkage. Unlike the beautiful pear-tree imagery in *Their Eyes Were Watching God,* the pear trees in *Sula* are cited only four times, and Sula's growth is not associated with them. Pear trees are mentioned in the razing of the Bottom, in the front of Eva's home during BoyBoy's visit, and in Sula's recall of her life's monotony (1, 30, 35, 147)—all negative imagery perhaps representing Morrison's parodic troping on Hurston's significantly life-affirming pictures for her heroine Janie.

Rather, holocaust imagery is more dominant: fire and water are mentioned approximately sixty-eight times, mirroring the people's blisteringly hot inferno but also their aspirations, which do not include maternal desire and nurturing for the sake of the community for the independent Sula. The matriarch Eva implores Sula to marry and "have some babies." Sula replies, "I don't want to make somebody else. I want to make myself" (92). McDowell rightly analyzes Morrison's critique of "common assumptions about the SELF" as "unified, coherent, stable, and known,"[38] a false ideology that Sula rejects. The semiotics of the walls of life in the dispossessed Bottom restrict self-development even for Sula. As the matriarch, Eva offers maternal advice to Sula that is not intended to inhibit her self-expression and the quest for self, as McDowell argues. Rather, Eva wants to inscribe on Sula's wayward body the maternal ethics of caring for someone other than herself, for caring for others in an isolated community struggling simply for air.

One can indeed posit, as McDowell does, that in her own inimitable way Sula unites the community, if only against her because of her affairs with married men, including her best friend's husband, Nel's Jude. As the narrator explains, the community and jealous wives coalesce, convinced that "Sula's evil changed them in accountable, yet mysterious ways. Once the source of their personal misfortune was identified, they had leave to protect and love one another" (117). However, Eva's notion of maternal ethics is based on an understanding of women's nurturing capacity, which is mutually healing and transformative for Sula and the community of women and men, as demonstrated by the maternal Nel, whom one critic describes as a "conventional counterpart" to the unattached Sula. Also, as Patricia Hill Collins remarks, "For women of color, the subjective experience of mothering/motherhood is inextricably linked to the socio-cultural concern of racial ethnic communities—one does not exist without the other."[39] The expansive maternal, as one of social concern for self and the wider community, is an idea that the wide-spirited Eva attempts to share with the self-absorbed Sula.

Eva exists in opposition to the emotional and psychological instability of a social order represented by Jim Crow laws and her husband's abandonment. Both a biological and a surrogate mother, the omnipotent Eva has the power of life and death over her charges in the Bottom, and she becomes a healthful anodyne to the historically and spatially dislocated. After BoyBoy abandons their family, he leaves an impoverished Eva with "$1.65, five eggs, three beets and no idea of what or how to feel," but "the children needed her" (32). With a bodily sacrifice in a grotesque parody of the kind of female agency she is forced to assume to become a nurturing mother, Eva loses a leg to collect money from an insurance policy. She then saves her family, and when Hannah asks if she ever loved them, the tired matriarch responds, "I stayed alive for you" (69)—self-preservation grounded in the ethics of maternal nurturing.

While her maternal body temporarily functions as a parodic critique of the desperate enactment of the kind of motherhood open to her in the Bottom, she appropriates her maternal body to become a lifeline for her children and the community. Eva also uses her own body when she rushes to save a burning and dying Hannah and "to cover her daughter's body with her own" (75), an illustration of the emotional depth of her mothering capacity. However, she makes the difficult decision to burn her drug-addicted son, Plum, dousing him with gasoline and fire because there was no room "in my womb. . . . I couldn't birth him twice" (71). Even so, there was room enough in her heart as she "rocks" him and holds him "close" (72) after her tough, mother-love decision to end his misery. As a biological and communal mother, Eva becomes a maternal trope for the schema of life and death in the Bottom, an image captured in Plum's dying but optical view of her resembling the "great wing of an eagle,"[40] an Old Testament image of God gathering the imprisoned Jews and taking them out of Egypt "on eagles' wings."[41]

As an inclusive maternal metaphor of godly power who contests Jim Crow exclusion, Eva becomes an emblem of the depth of parody, which can move beyond the polemics of assault. The literary critic Margaret Rose relates the "depth of parody" to its ability to transcend "superficial verbal forms" and "the very deepest principles governing another's discourse. Moreover, parodic discourse itself may be used in various ways by the author: the parody may be an end in itself. . . . to further other positive goals."[42] In Eva's maternal performances as birth mother and death mother, Morrison makes a vivid distinction between the disdainful, bodily politics of cultural boundaries and the maternal function of caregiving, illustrated too in *The Bluest Eye* in the maternal roles of Mrs. MacTeer and Marie, China, and Poland.

With her decision to adopt neglected young boys in the Bottom, whom she names and identifies as the Deweys, Eva extends her maternal womb-room, nurturing the boys to become a trinity, holy and inseparable. Likewise she opens her womb-home to the soulful Tar Baby, whose racial identity as a black or white man is ambiguous to all, although the omniscient Eva identifies him as white. She assists, moreover, the suffering and saintly Nel in reaching an understanding of her own moral limitations after Sula dies. In the metaphor of her expanded maternal womb, Eva personifies the whole womb of Medallion, Ohio, redressing the wrongs of a dispossessing history of slavery and Reconstruction that positioned blacks at the bottom.

Alternately described as a complex novel of fragmentation and of paradox, *Sula* may be more accurately read as another demonic parody of racial boundaries but also as a counterreligious parody of salvation and one woman's maternal function of self-sacrifice and deliverance. Eva is that wide-spirited woman. Diane Gillespie and Missy Dehn Kubitschek cite *Sula*'s maternal emphases on nurturance and its demonstration of the "inadequacy of the traditional male-centered psychology" of self and autonomy. In this reading, these feminists believe that the novel shows "that men raised to be autonomous, contained selves become alienated and unhappy." While the "women's lives do not run smoothly, they are raised to be selves-in-community."[43] This is the lesson that Eva attempted to teach Sula. Although white feminists such as Carol Gilligan, Sara Ruddick, and Virginia Held have expressed the unique psychological development of women and their relational inclination, the socialization of citizens in a community has always been a tool of survival for the black community. This is clear in *Sula* through Eva's actions and in her advice to Sula. In an interview Morrison heralded the community as both a refuge and a haven: "In the black community where I grew up, there were eccentricity and freedom, less conformity in individual habits—but close conformity in terms of the survival of the village, of the tribe."[44] Eva, the maternal character, represents the body and voice of survival/community.

Song of Solomon: Paternal Law versus the Maternal Spirit of Sacrifice

The Bible, maternal ethics, socially inscribed black bodies, cultural boundaries, and demonic parody play significant roles in Morrison's literature, beginning with *The Bluest Eye* and *Sula* but increasing in greater magnitude in *Song of Solomon*. Morrison reveals that virtually everything is subject to parody, in its negative and positive, profane and sacred discursive polarities. Divided into two books, *Song of Solomon* presents a "commuting" between both books and parodied subjects thematically, semiotically, and picturesquely. In the essay "Are Parody and Deconstruction Secretly the Same Thing," Robert Phiddian states that parody can indeed distance the reader "from identification with both the model discourse and the parodic text, setting us on a constant commuting between deconstructed and deconstructing poles/venues." In this instance readers fail to "arrive at a 'true' understanding" of either texts "because each constantly displaces the other."[45] Book 1 and book 2 follow Phiddian's parodic fluctuations, but the magical protagonist Pilate arrests the commuting between both books: one of violence and the other of *agape* love and Christ-like sacrifice.

In book 1 Morrison's hypertext parodies the historical hypotext of the naming and identifying of blacks after the Civil War, their exclusion from the professional space of medicine and real estate, and their violence as victims who unfortunately perpetrated the violence against them. The male protagonist Macon (Milkman) Dead III is the inheritor of a name that signifies the hypotext of the legacy of slavery and whites having the power to name blacks indifferently, yet significantly. Mercy Hospital is renamed, parodically, "No Mercy Hospital" because of its refusal to grant the town's one black doctor hospital privileges. The Seven Days gang, which targets whites, is a parody of the Ku Klux Klan and the killing of blacks; both engage in acts of racial hatred and violence.

The critic Ralph Story identifies Robert Smith's violent suicidal leap as both a heroic and a revolutionary act of the racial solidarity of the Seven Days,[46] based on Guitar Bains's boast, "And if it [revenge] ever gets to be too much like it was for Robert Smith, we do that [commit suicide] rather than crack and tell somebody" (159). In contrast to Story's critique of the "racial solidarity" of the Seven Days, Morrison appears to interrogate black male solidarity in her sarcastic description of the "Blood Bank," a demonic parody of black-on-black urban crime in cramped spaces of identity where oppressed blacks perform the violent work of hegemony in acts of self-sabotage. The image/semiotics of the men's blood flowing "freely" in their segregated spaces is an ironic inversion of their spatial immobility, which mocks their violent excesses.

Demonically parodying their violence, the narrator is caustically sarcastic: "They believed firmly that members of their own race killed one another for good reasons: violation of another's turf (a man is found with somebody else's wife); refusal to observe the laws of hospitality (a man reaches into his friend's pot of mustards [greens] and snatches out the meat); or verbal insults impugning their virility, honesty, humanity, and mental health" (100). The function of sarcasm in this verbal parody of black-on-black crime stresses the banality of self-perpetuating violence in an always already violent social order, with which blacks must contend. In the narrator's attack on the Seven Days and Guitar Bains, who ultimately attempts to kill even his best friend, Milkman, Morrison again extends her use of parody.

With her multiple uses of demonic parody, Morrison critiques the representation of beauty in *The Bluest Eye,* economic dispossession in *Sula,* and naming and identity in *Song of Solomon,* and in each of these works she addresses the violence of spatial politics and the social order. She reveals an absence of bias in her selection of parodic targets, notwithstanding controversy, especially regarding black-on-black violence. As with other scholars' criticism, Ralph Story's analysis of the Seven Days' racial solidarity appears incisive on its own merit, without recognition, as Dentith states, of "the style or discourse to which allusion is being made." However, failure to recognize the intertextual play between the Seven Days and the Ku Klux Klan, between No Mercy Hospital and discrimination in the field of medicine, and between the Dead family's name and the legacy of slavery makes Morrison's parodic practices practically invisible, once again.

Book 2, in contrast to book 1, which contains symbols of materialistic bodies and their physical and social death, tests Robert Phiddian's theory of the constant commuting between the parodied text and the parodying text. In book 2 Morrison offers her readers a picturesque haven of Arcadia, with its emphasis on beauty and peacefulness, annexed from the chaos of book 1. While book 1 symbolizes Macon Dead's paternal law of acquisition and possession, book 2 represents the maternal sacrifice of life, captured in Morrison's religious parodic reenactment of Golgotha and the Crucifixion, with a woman, Pilate, as the Christ-like figure of *agape* love.

Arresting the commuting between the parodic hypertext and the parodied hypotext, Pilate in her bodily sacrifice is a unifying metaphor for both books in *Song of Solomon*, even with the novel's sacred and profane parodies that can evoke reader anxiety. Pilate's name and rhetorical question "What is true in the world?" (149) are a religious parodic hypertext of the biblical hypotext of the New Testament and Pontius Pilate, who asks flippantly, "What is truth?"—as he hands Christ over to a mob to be crucified. Although her father names her vengefully after Pontius Pilate because God did not save his wife, the life-affirming Pilate is a powerful maternal metaphor of Morrison's (re)appropriation of the master discourse on gender and cultural politics.

Morrison shows, however, that with a metaphorical linkage, the commuting between hypotext and hypertext can be desisted. This is done with a flexible character such as Pilate, who collapses the breach of parodic discourse and shifts the locus of the dialogue away from violence and onto the interiority of identity, as when Milkman discovers his name and his real identity. In book 1 Pilate is responsible for Milkman's birth since she created the magic potion that induced in Macon Dead a desire for his spurned wife, and she practices the art of voodoo to persuade him not to abort the baby. In addition, Pilate cooks Milkman's first perfect egg. His awakening desire to be more than he is is echoed in his plea "I got a right to be what I want to be, and I want to be a egg" (166). Pilate acts as a maternal conduit between the narrow paternal and racist constrictions of Milkman's society in book 1 and his rebirth in book 2.

A classic Bildungsroman, *Song of Solomon* traces the rebirth and transformation of Milkman Dead as rituals of lovelessness and death form the pattern of book 1 in

Morrison's third novel, which spans the period of Jim Crow America to the early 1960s. Continuing to appropriate the Bible to suggest its importance to African Americans, Morrison takes her book's title from the Old Testament narrative "Song of Solomon." From 961 to 922 B.C. Solomon was king of Israel and the black son of David and Bathsheba, and his name is associated with wisdom, a characteristic that Morrison connects to the maternal and to Pilate as well as to Milkman's quest for identity. Death, life, and resurrection are the narrative schemata of his maturation in the text. As the symbolism of his surname, Dead also reveals that his relationship with his father is basically nonexistent as a result of his father's obsession with power.

As a real estate investor in Michigan, Macon Dead II experiences racial discrimination, and Morrison parodies this particular form of racism in the professional field of real estate with Macon's knowledge that as a "Negro he wasn't going to get a big slice of the pie" (63). However, even with Macon Dead's limited success, he links the value of life to the accumulation of property, treating his adult daughters and his wife as appendages of his wealth. He denies them his love. In his advice to Milkman, Macon valorizes ownership of property over self-knowledge and communal bonds, and he denigrates the maternal in a classic, though general paternal fantasy of self-making: "Pilate can't teach you a thing you can use in this world. Maybe the next, but not this one. Let me tell you right now the one important thing you'll ever need to know: Own things. . . . Then you'll own yourself and other people too" (55).

Theoretically, Morrison sets up relationships between Macon, Milkman, and Pilate that reveal Milkman's struggle for his soul. He wrestles with materialism versus spirituality and a patriarchal independence versus a connected, maternal, and black cultural sphere, represented by Pilate. Macon's bourgeois capitalist advice underscores the fissures of identity in his family and community, and his dialogue with Milkman becomes "the sign of a failure of relationship," as Carol Gilligan explains in her analysis of paternal aggression and violence. Gilligan continues, "As women imagine the activities through which relationships are woven and connection sustained, the world of intimacy—which appears so mysterious and dangerous to men—comes instead to appear increasingly coherent and safe." The literary critic Qin Sheng offers a cultural context in which we can place Gilligan's overarching remarks about women when she argues that Morrison makes known the role that "African American women" such as the fictional Pilate have played "in the reconstruction" of black cultural heritage to effect healing.[47] Although Morrison is sympathetic to the discrimination Macon faces in public and professional spaces, she rejects his cultivation of false values as a way to gain control of his emasculated body and embattled male ego and embraces the life-sustaining values of the maternal Pilate.

Furthermore, Morrison's narrator describes Macon as a victim of ironic self-parody, for he participates in rituals of his own social death. As an oppressed black male who overcompensates for his marginality by robbing others as a landlord, Macon reverts to the same patriarchal Western greed responsible for scripting the racial and cultural boundaries that have circumscribed spaces for African Americans and limited his life. As a testimony to the emptiness he feels in his small, ego-centered world, Macon walks by Pilate's house but "heard the music. They were singing. All of them. Pilate, her daughter Reba, and Reba's daughter, Hagar," and he "walked on, resisting as best he could the sound of the voices that followed him" (28). Singing in Morrison's narratives is often a sign of the characters' resistance to oppression and their soulful and spiritual regeneration. As Gay Wilentz remarks, "Even Macon, who deserted his sister, sees the house as a place of music, warmth, and caring, not realizing that he has destroyed the music in his own house," but "three generations' worth of women in Pilate's house can live and breathe and sing in harmony."[48] As an embodiment of black bourgeois society and paternal law, Macon recognizes in himself and his family a sense of loss; however, his male bourgeois "fantasy of self-genesis"[49] prevents him from seeking the transformation that Milkman desires and seeks, primarily from women in Morrison's sweeping display of maternal ethics.

My reading of *Song of Solomon*'s Pilate as a Christ-like maternal figure differs from that suggested by other scholars but suggests too the various roles that can be assigned to her. Like Eva, Pilate is wide-spirited. Joseph Skerrett's treatment of Pilate focuses on her as a looming embodiment of a female blues singer, a teller of tales, and a teacher who instructs Milkman and Guitar how "to talk properly."[50] Wilentz and Marilyn Sanders Mobley see her, respectively, as an exemplar of Afro-centricity and an alternative voice in the community. Wilentz and Mobley offer two different, yet similar images of Pilate. In appropriating Henry Louis Gates Jr.'s theory of the double-voicedness of signification in the black community and Bakhtin's concept of the heteroglossia of speech acts, Mobley connects Pilate's storytelling and song of flying Africans to the children's songs and communal voices in the narrative, significantly. As cultural bearer, Pilate carries the "narrative thread" of the song of flying Africans that links other heteroglossia voices in a dialectic structure of "call and response."[51] Her song offers an alternative image of black identity with a woman, as Sheng and Wilentz remind us, assuming the responsibility for transmitting and maintaining generational and cultural continuity.

As one of Morrison's most authentic and androgynous characters, Pilate emerges as such a mystical figure that virtually any careful scholarly analysis of her function in the narrative is not only plausible but also necessary in order for readers to appreciate the expansive scope of her magic. To Skerrett's, Wilentz's, Sheng's, and Mobley's multiple descriptions of Pilate as teacher, blues singer, Afro-centric cultural bearer, and voice of the community, add the sacred biblical image of the loving sacrificial lamb who teaches Milkman and Guitar not only how to "speak properly" but also how to forgive, live, and die. Pilate's absence of a navel suggests her sacred and miraculous conception. Like Christ, she is unattached to corporeality and thus freed from the Jim Crow racial strictures/markings of a disabling society. Pilate assumes, like Eva, a wider maternal function, unlike Ruth, who breast-feeds Milkman well beyond his infancy and manipulates the maternal body to overcompensate for her loveless marriage to Macon Dead. Skerrett's reference to Milkman and Guitar's greeting of "Hi" to Pilate (who would prefer the more correct greeting of "Hello") gives Morrison another occasion to teach and parody a minihistory of lynching in the South.

Understandably, Skerrett's criticism misses the parody of this history, just as Morrison's parody of black-on-black violence is overlooked in Story's interpretation of black men's "racial solidarity." Skerrett's and Story's otherwise legitimate criticisms reveal the risks that Morrison takes as a parodist whose play on that which is essentially absent from the text challenges readers to know her cryptic historical allusions. Without knowledge of Morrison's use of parody, critics will miss her authorial intent. For example, Robert Phiddian cites Brian McHale's analysis that the "flicker between parody's vacillation between presence and absence" represents an "anomalous spacing of discourse observable" in "the simultaneous moment of parody and *difference*." Phiddian then argues, "Parodies stand for the things they displace, but they do not merely repeat them, as translations aspire to do, or extend them like imitations. They displace, distort, differ, and defer."[52] Indeed, Pilate's retort and rejoinder to Milkman and Guitar's colloquial greeting of "Hi" presents Morrison with another opportunity to give lessons in history. In Pilate's correction of the men's greetings, she describes them as "the dumbest unhung Negroes on earth" (37). Such a description represents Morrison's hypertext, playing on the tragic hypotext of a reported lynching of 3,386 black people in the South from 1882 to 1930.[53]

When Guitar and Milkman break into Pilate's home to steal what they believe is a bag of gold, they foreshadow and eventually parody the two biblical thieves who hung on crosses with Christ at Calvary. The narrative configuration of their identity as two thieves is encoded further, but stereotypically, in a case of racial profiling as white police officers stop them in a search "for the Negro that killed that boy" (205). In this example of racism, Morrison targets and criticizes police harassment of any black body seen in the area of a crime. She uses demonic parody here not to distort or defer but rather to depict the volatility of black male bodies/identities-in-crises subjected at any time to searches and the destabilization of identity for the rich Milkman as well as the poor Guitar. Despite Milkman's status as a wealthy black man with his friend, the two are stopped and subjected to police brutality because of their race and gender. When the two are taken to jail and the real nature of their crime is revealed, a gracious Pilate tells the police an African "trickster tale" about the stolen bag of bones just to free Guitar and Milkman (208). In her trickster tale of bones, lynchings, and jokes played on an old woman,

Pilate (re)stabilizes Milkman's and Guitar's black-male bodies/identities. She therefore rescues them from a hostile public sphere while relating a tortured history of white male aggression against black males to which, by inference, she connects the "innocent" white police officers.

Morrison opens book 2 on a note of brotherly/sisterly love, as if this book takes its clue from 2 Corinthians and the Apostle Paul's most cited rejoinder to Christians to "live in peace" (13:11). Conversely, Milkman's sister First Corinthians is perhaps so named to signify on the hellish contentions in book 1, similar to the Apostle Paul's reference in the first letter to the Corinthians of the "divisions among you" and "contentions among you" (1:10–11). In the spirit of the apostle's second letter to the Corinthians, Morrison concludes *Song of Solomon* with Pilate's sacrificial act of *agape* love, as she sacrifices her own life for Milkman, whose rebirth in the womb/cave in Danville forecloses Macon Dead's symbolic paternal order of lovelessness, materialism, and violence.

Milkman arrives in a town with the rich, verdant beauty of the countryside. Still looking for the bag of gold, he walks to a cave and comes upon a body of water, in which he wades after removing his socks and Florsheim shoes. Signifying the maternal womb, the Danville cave's walls constrict, and Milkman drops "to his knees" and stretches "out on his stomach" (255). Emerging from the cave/womb, he travels to Shalimar, Virginia, still looking for the bag of gold, but is further initiated into manhood by men who teach him how to hunt and get close to Mother Nature and by women (with names such as Sweet, Grace, and Susan Byrd) who bathe him and identify his paternal grandmother, Sing. It is here that he learns the myth of the flying Africans and recognizes what Mobley refers to as the "narrative thread" of Pilate's culture-bearing song, a fragment that he connects to the children's song and uses to recognize and reclaim his lost genealogy, his real gold. When he returns to Michigan to inform others of his discovery, it is Pilate, the ethnic cultural bearer, who returns to Virginia with him to bury her father's bones, to bear witness to Milkman's genealogical discovery, and then to die for him.

In her religious parodic hypertext of the biblical hypotext of Golgotha, the site of Christ's Crucifixion, Morrison creates a sacred religious parody of Christ's death. She blots out the profane enactment of paternal hatred and violence in book 1, arresting Phiddian's commuting between intertextual discourses. The biblical Golgotha or Calvary is the place of a skull, a name signifying the site of Christ's Crucifixion on a hill in ancient Jerusalem. That Morrison chooses a woman to re-enact the Crucifixion of the male Jesus Christ further strengthens the image of the female and the maternal figure as embodying the creative spirit of the supernatural. Images of women as transformational spirits abound in book 2, from Circe, who beckons Milkman with the sermonic call "Come, come," to Susan Byrd, whose surname implies and affirms a transcendent feminine principle (242). Morrison's omniscient narrator carefully describes the scene of Milkman and Pilate's walk, which was "a long way to the top, but neither stopped for breath. At the very top, on the plateau, the trees that could stand the wind at that height were few" (339). At the top, Pilate "opened the sack while Milkman dug," and the two buried her father's bones taken from the sack, which Guitar, who has followed Milkman, believes contains real gold. At this moment Guitar shoots at Milkman but hits and murders Pilate, who dies, like Christ, professing her love for humanity: "I wish I'd knowed more people. I would of loved 'em all" (340). Carrying the cross/burden of the community like Eva, Pilate, like Christ, dies between two thieves: a redeemed and spiritually renewed Milkman and an unredeemable Guitar, the paternal assassin of the nurturing maternal body.

My reading of Pilate as a Christ-like figure adds to all other images of her as African cultural bearer, teacher and philosopher, and the healing and singing voice of a fragmented community. She is the overarching picture of the maternal sacrificial lamb. She gives her life to save the lives of others. According to her reading of Pilate as an African cultural bearer concerned with the health and well-being of the community, Wilentz remarks that Pilate is critical of Hagar and Milkman's incestuous first-cousin relationship, which can "breed" trouble. In her emphasis on the elders' attention to background in mate selection to avoid the peril of tribal interbreeding, Wilentz posits that Pilate, like an elder, makes no distinction between "cousin" and "brother," as Hagar maintains in justification of her incest. Pilate asks Hagar and Reba, "I mean what's the difference in the way you act towards 'em? Don't you have to act the same way to both? Then why they got two words for it 'stead of one, if they ain't no difference?" (44). Wilentz believes that Pilate's question suggests her rejection of incest between any blood relations. But as a personification of Christ, Pilate cites the word "brother" to suggest *philio* acts of love. Brotherly/sisterly love transcends the barriers of race, class, gender, and sex. The community has already rejected Hagar and Milkman's incestuous relationship, so Pilate's criticism must go beyond the obvious. In her rejoinder Pilate reminds Hagar and Reba of a greater act of love, found in book 2 but not in book 1. The first book is a replica of Northup Frye's hell on earth, fraught with the hateful tensions between Hagar and Milkman, Macon and Ruth, Macon's son and daughters, whites and blacks, blacks and blacks, and a Herrenvolk and Jim Crow order of American "liberty" and "democracy."

After *The Bluest Eye*, which presents her tragic vision of what happens to black children who enter a hostile public space unprotected by the nurturing maternal force, redemption for the most part becomes a dominant motif in Morrison's historical narratives. In an interview Morrison confessed to the impact of her own faith on her work: "The Bible wasn't part of my reading: it was part of my life. The New Testament is so pertinent to black literature—the lamb, the victim, the vulnerable one who does die but nevertheless lives."[54] Despite the dialectical complexity of one dying in order to live, Morrison implies here and in Pilate's death and

Milkman's rebirth a process of creation, which is stronger than the act of negation violently impinging against it.

Beloved: The African American Holocaust of American Slavery

Clearly the most demonically parodic of Morrison's novels, possibly until the appearance of *A Mercy, Beloved* is a chronicle of the black holocaust of the Middle Passage and southern plantation slavery, with their structural spaces of the strict confinement of the black body-in-crisis. Due to the outrageousness of the subject matter, slavery, *Beloved* abounds with characters reenacting Frye's parodic rituals of the hell on earth created by man. At the heart of the novel is, however, a poignant tale of maternal love, sacrifice, and loss, hence the missing number three from the address 124 Bluestone Road, symbolizing the absent child, Beloved (which one of my students originally identified in class in the early 1990s). Sethe lovingly but willfully sacrifices Beloved to prevent her from living a far more prolonged social death as a slave. Morrison's characters reenact the biblical concept of good and evil and the final conflict between these two forces at Armageddon, which is restaged in the woodshed when Sethe overthrows a power system that has dehumanized her. With Sethe's confrontation, Morrison, who believes in the spiritual power of redemption, goes beyond Frye's imagery of an existential hell without redemption and delves passionately into the possibility of regeneration. The missing number three signifies Sethe's maternal sacrifice, which haunts her until Beloved returns.

A human face is placed on the institution of slavery in Morrison's re-creation of the Margaret Garner tragedy, the original hypotext of the parodic hypertext *Beloved*. Garner was a young slave mother who killed her daughter in 1856 (Morrison cites the year 1855) after being followed and apprehended by her master in Ohio, the free state that offered, literally and metaphorically, the fugitive slave an alternative space for the reshaping of her identity. With *Beloved*, Morrison resurrects the lives of black American slaves, traditionally represented in textbooks as faceless, being shrouded in cold facts and statistics. While *Beloved* retells the Margaret Garner story, Morrison demonically parodies the larger slave experience as reconstructed and deconstructed in slave narratives, which she confesses to reading "for sustenance." Indeed the critic Robin Dizard asserts that nineteenth-century "slave narratives inform *Beloved*": possibly from *Slavery in the United States: A Narrative of the Life and Adventures of Charles Ball, a Black Man Who Lived in Maryland, South Carolina and Georgia as a Slave under Various Masters* to Solomon Northup's *Twelve Years a Slave* and John Parker's *His Promised Land*. This last narrative relates the now-famous tale of the Ohio mother (Harriet Beecher Stowe's Eliza in *Uncle Tom's Cabin*) who braved the icy Ohio River, similar to the pregnant Sethe, to free herself and her child.[55]

In *Beloved*, Morrison mimics the following slave experiences, all primary hypotexts of the parodic hypertexts: 1) the Middle Passage; 2) the branding and breeding of slaves; 3) the hiring out of time and naming of slaves; 4) benign and malevolent slavery, slave punishment, slave escape, and revolt; and 5) the legacy of slavery, Jim Crow, and de facto discrimination. Each of these five hypertexts is discussed specifically—but within the broader context of slavery: its weight of memory and its sites of trauma from slave ships to plantations and even, ironically, to the Clearing—after illuminating why *Beloved* is more of a demonic parody than a pastiche of oppressed voices.

The reenactment of these historical experiences of slavery and the African Diaspora as iterated in the characters' discordant narrative voices is suggestive of pastiche, according to Rafael Pérez-Torres. Pérez-Torres also remarks that the "play of the novel is not simply a *pastiche* of various narrative forms. Rather, it is a conjoining of different discourses, a tracing of their different social significance." Pérez-Torres continues in his qualification of the novel as more than pastiche when he asserts that *Beloved* "works to weave together into one narrative stories [that are] seemingly as dissimilar as those by Sethe and Paul D. Throughout, the text highlights the various processes by which stories, traditional and contemporary, oral and written, historical and fictional, are told."[56]

But what Pérez-Torres refers to as "different discourses" within the genre of pastiche emerges here within the genre of parody as one masterful and unified discourse on the different forms that oppression takes, whether for male or female slaves, or white indentured servants such as Amy Denver. If it can be argued, as Pérez-Torres suggests, that Morrison appropriates pastiche in *Beloved* as one of the narrative forms that the novel assumes, then pastiche is present in the novel only as an element of Morrison's larger demonic parody of slavery. Like parody, pastiche is related to the grotesque, but major differences between the two exist. Distinguishing the neutrality of pastiche from the politics of parody, Margaret Rose remarks that pastiche, while a "much more recent term than parody," is neither "critical of its sources, nor necessarily comic."[57] Like Jameson and Foster, Rose defines pastiche as freed from the deployment of critical discourse, serious or comic, which would otherwise undermine *Beloved*. In each parodic reenactment of oppression in *Beloved*, Morrison's use of parody functions to "serve the purposes of realism . . . because it [parody] holds up to ridicule those falsifying"[58] notions of power as not subject to contest, ideas Sethe rejects.

Vis-à-vis slavery, Morrison associates the trauma of slavery with the weight of memory, as experienced by the enslaved on specific sites. These sites range from tightly packed slave ships to confining southern plantations and even hauntingly so at the Clearing, which Sethe visits with Denver and Beloved after Baby Suggs's death. Even at the Clearing with its semiotics of the wooded, natural, and open space of bodily freedom for slaves reclaiming their humanity, Sethe feels oppressed; her "spirits fell down under the weight of the things she remembered" (98). More than just the haunting baby of Sethe's infanticide, Beloved becomes, as another Morrison critic argues, "the physical manifestation of suppressed memories" and "an embodiment of the repressed past" who "pries open suppressed memories and emotions" of those who need to seek recovery from their traumatized past.[59] Beloved's supernatural appearance at 124 Bluestone Road precipitates the characters' retrieval of memory and their lives.

Morrison creates a dizzying narrative circularity (similar to Walker's *Possessing the Secret of Joy*) that suggests how memory works as characters are forced to recall fragments of their lives, here and there, as jarred by an object, an image, a question, or a newspaper clipping. In *History and Memory after Auschwitz*, Dominick LaCapra cites Freud's analysis of the significance of "memory-work" to the past, present, and future and, importantly, to healing. "Memory-work," to use LaCapra's term, functions to open up the past, to critique it, and possibly to offer to traumatized clients a "situational transcendence of the past that is not total, but is nonetheless essential for opening up more desirable possibilities in the future."[60] "Memory-work" in *Beloved* is intended to unpack memories about the distortion of the slaves' lives in their efforts to come to terms with a past declared too painful to remember, which is one function of demonic parody: to give further life to that which it parodies in order to force us to remember it so we will not repeat history's traumatizing experience. Before the maternal/communal exorcism of Beloved (who takes on the demonic characteristics of slavery), she appears to emerge as the psychological "analyst" of the repressed Other, as Linda Krumholz suggests. Beloved also becomes an incarnate objective correlative. Her associative memory (of past and present) and jarring questions provide the emotional cathexis for the characters' archaeological digging, the unearthing of America's black holocaust.

She extracts from each major character something of value that each is forced to recall. Beloved asks Sethe, "Tell me your diamonds"; requests of Denver, "Tell me how Sethe made you in the boat"; and demands of Paul D, "Call me my name" (60, 76, 117). In demanding from each character their personal stories and voices of a wedding, a birth, and/or an emotional shutting down (what Pérez-Torres perceives as pastiche in separate narrative form), Beloved leads them to excavate and perform their own "memory-work."[61] Beloved's role of listener and the characters' roles as storytellers can become implosive, as evidenced by the shattering of the "tobacco tin lodged in" Paul D's heart (113), which Beloved pries open in her purposeful seduction of the battered male slave's body: "Red heart, Red heart, Red heart" (117). Sethe too, for example, "had to do something with her hands because she was remembering something she had forgotten she knew. Something privately shameful that had seeped into a slit in her mind right behind the slap on her face and the circled cross" on her mother's branded and mutilated body on a southern plantation (61). Sethe's mother's battered body takes on the physiological form of her experiences in Frye's demonic world "turned upside down," with the mother's marked body grotesquely mimicking the denatured society of slavery, the denatured trope of motherhood as distorted.

More than a sign of slavery's pathology, however, battered bodies from Sethe's mother's to those of Sethe and Baby Suggs represent Morrison's twisted parody of slavocrats' subversion of the private and sacred domain of motherhood. These maternal bodies are an oxymoron for black slave mothers who were property primarily. In *The Female Body and the Law*, the feminist Zillah R. Eisenstein posits that the law, appearing neutral while occupying the space between patriarchy and phallocratic discourse, really "constructs and mirrors patriarchal social relations through its phallocratic interpretations of truth. The law names reality."[62] Eisenstein's description of the law as that which can generate and privilege reality in a patriarchal and racialized social order helps to explain the contradiction between the nineteenth century's valorization of white, middle-class motherhood, on one hand, yet the subversion of black motherhood, on the other. Slave mothers, as blacks and considered to be only three-fifths of whites as declared in the Constitution, suffered an anatomical distortion that determined their "just" treatment at the hands of slavocrats. Beloved's hunger for her mother, however, represents Morrison's narrative eclipsing of the patriarchal law of subversion regulating mother-child relations but not obstructing the higher laws of nature, as in a daughter's natural yearning for her mother.

As an example of the first slave experience mimicked by Morrison in *Beloved,* the character Beloved becomes Morrison's parodic hypertext and collective symbol of the African Diaspora, the original hypotext. In her own storytelling, she describes to Denver the "crouching" on slave ships during the Middle Passage: "'I'm small in that place. I'm like this here.' She raised her head off the bed, lay down on her side and curled up" (75). While critics may view Beloved's curled-up bodily position as fetal, it is possible to identify her crouching behavior as Morrison's trenchant anatomical parody of the cargo of slaves experiencing the infamous Middle Passage. This cross-Atlantic voyage of trauma for Africans lasted for sixty days or more for those who survived. Beloved describes to Denver, "I'm small in that place . . . Hot. Nothing to breathe down there, and no room to move in" (75). Later in the stream-of-consciousness section of the novel, Beloved cries, "'I am always crouching The man on my face is dead The men without skin bring us this morning water to drink daylight comes through the cracks and I can see his [the dead slave's] eyes We are all trying to leave our bodies behind" (210). Her unpunctuated words suggest a body-spirit split that emphasizes the unacceptable spaces of identity allotted to blacks by whites. The words "place," "hot," "no air," "down there," "no room," and "cracks" describe not a woman's womb but rather the tight bottom of a slave ship, perhaps a kind of inverted womb that gives birth to that which slavery has contorted. In other words, the dehumanization of enslaved individuals began on the slave ships where slaves were made to lie on unplaned boards in their own excrement. Daniel Mannix's study *Black Cargoes,* for example, describes the tight packing of slaves as detailed in the diary of a former English slaving captain, John

Newton, who had a conversion and wrote the popular hymn "Amazing Grace"—
"that saved a wretch like me." For reasons of profit, slaves were so abnormally
stowed, writes Newton, that they resembled books upon a shelf, which "could not
contain one more."[63] The crouching trope, which Douglass, Wright, and Ellison
appropriate to describe slaves, Bigger Thomas, and evicted Harlem residents, respectively, presents the rhetoric of an image that is intended to go beyond a critique
of power to show its base effect on humans.

Second, Morrison suggests that the breaking in of slaves began during the Middle Passage and on slave ships but was demonically refined on the plantations in
the branding and breeding of slave bodies, male and female. Beloved forces Sethe to
"rememory" (to create a mental picture accompanying the person, place, or object
to remember) her mother, "Ma'am," a native African, whom Sethe associates with
a dancing antelope, indigenous to Africa. Beloved asks, "Your woman she never fix
up your hair?" (60). Here, Morrison parodies the slaves' hazy recollection of parentage and birth, for Sethe wonders if she was born in Louisiana or North or South
Carolina. In a parody of the slaves' hazy recollections of the places of their birth
or even their birth dates, Morrison alludes perhaps to Douglass, who writes that
slaves came no closer to identifying their birthdays than as during "planting-time,
harvest-time, cherry-time, spring-time, or fall-time."[64] All Sethe remembers is that
her mother was branded: "Right on her rib was a circle and a cross burnt right in
the skin" (61). Baby Suggs, the paternal grandmother of Beloved and Denver, was
victimized to such a degree that she walked like a "three-legged dog," and yet she
provided her master with his human property. Caricaturing the breeding of slaves,
another form of the sexed denigration of the black maternal body, Morrison's narrator mimics and mocks the "nastiness of life," for Baby Suggs's "eight children
had six fathers" (23). Slave breeding was a sanctioned method for slaveholders to
increase their wealth. The historian John Hope Franklin writes that one southern
planter boasted of his "uncommonly good breeders."[65]

Feminists theorizing about patriarchal dominance in a nuclear family within a sociopolitical economy have grounded their protest against proscriptive biological and
reproductive imperatives that inadvertently mock the trauma of black mothering,
historically. Under slavery the "law's concern with mothering exclusively involved
questions of property: diminution in the value of slave property, if the slave female
was unable to reproduce, or disputes regarding the conveyance and loss of property,"
explains Saidiya Hartman.[66] Slave mothers were treated like animals, as Morrison
indicates in the description of Baby Suggs's crooked walk like a "three-legged dog"
and in Schoolteacher's nephews' milking of Sethe as if she were a cow. They were
as mothers, however, the economic foundation of a profitable slave society.

Morrison deconstructs the hierarchical race/class paradox of the slave system,
revealing its false dichotomy. Without the slaves' bodily performances in free physical and sexual labor, the riches of the slave economy, which created an "aristocracy

without nobility,"[67] would have dried up. Thus mothering for black women under slavery challenged their essentially feminine and innate instincts toward nurturance because of the negation of their maternal rights/rites and the bonds of mother-child attachment. Recognizing and affirming the oxymoron of black-slave mother, Paul D reflects on the "risk" of mother love: "Risky, thought Paul D, very risky. For a used-to-be-slave woman to love anything that much was dangerous, especially if it was her children she had settled on to love" (45). With Paul D's interior dialogue, Morrison voices the complex dilemma of the nineteenth century regarding the Victorian paradigm of motherhood and the establishment of Mother's Day, a valorization of motherhood coexisting with slavery and the (dis)establishment of black maternity.

Morrison's male characters are committed to this "risky" business of maternal nurturing. The narrative image of nurturing males such as Paul D, who promises to care for Sethe, argues against the theory of a black-male castration complex in the works of Morrison: the portraiture of Cholly in *The Bluest Eye*, BoyBoy in *Sula*, and Macon Dead in *Song of Solomon*.[68] From Paul D to Halle, Sixo and Stamp Paid, and even to the collection of forty-six men in Brandywine, Georgia, who worked in tandem to free themselves from chains because "one lost, all lost" (110), Morrison's male characters are committed to the maternal practice of caregiving. Maternal ethics exist in contradistinction to the demonic parodic rituals of the dehumanization of slaves on slave ships and plantations. Indeed, Paul D can be likened to the ultrafeminine and long-haired Amy Denver, who informs an ailing Sethe, "I'm good at sick things" (82), speaking the language of the maternal. This same caring motif is reified in Sixo's relations with Patsy, for whom he dies, and in Stamp Paid's Underground Railroad activities with Ella, with whom he "ferries" runaway slaves to freedom. Moreover, Sethe chooses to marry Halle rather than one of the other men on Sweet Home Plantation because of his loving treatment of Baby Suggs, his mother.

Third, the naming of the other men on the plantation, Paul A, Paul D, and Paul F, represents Morrison's parodic reference to the enforced anonymity of slaves, the original hypotext on which the parodic hypertext feeds. In his first slave narrative, Douglass illustrates how arbitrarily slaves were named, relating one master's naming of two slaves who were father and son but distinguished from each other by an adjective: Old Barney, the father, and young Barney, the son.[69] While naming rituals confer on the enslaved an amorphous identity, consistent with legal and social theories proscriptive of their marginality, the hiring out of the slaves' time further revealed the economic parameters of their existence. Sethe's Halle gives up "five years of Sabbaths" to hire out his time and purchase Baby Suggs's freedom because he is "so in love with his mother" (11). According to Douglass, this particular exploitation of slave labor was considered a privilege for slaves who were trusted to travel to other plantations on their day of leisure, Sunday. However, they worked for wages often delivered to their masters, who gave the slaves a percentage of their own pay, an example of what Frye calls the evil machinations of the social order. In contrast to illustrating the many ways that male slaves as property were bodily and financially circumscribed in a patriarchal hierarchy, Morrison constructs significant mininarratives of males to provide a vision of men committed to the life-affirming values of grunt maternal work. As the exhausted, archetypal maternal nurturer, Sethe learns that the culture of maternal work is not rigidly encoded or defined by biology, race, sex, and gender, as evidenced in her rescue by the white Amy Denver and the black males Stamp Paid and Paul D. At the end of the novel, it is Paul D who rescues Sethe and adopts the rhetoric and image of mothering: "I'm a take care of you, you hear?" (272).

Fourth, as a slave of both Master Garner and Schoolteacher, the eviscerated Sethe has experienced two different kinds of slavery: benign and malevolent. Slavery is tolerable under Mr. Garner's rule but turns intolerable upon Schoolteacher's arrival after Garner's death. Baby Suggs makes the distinction between the two kinds of slavery, reflecting upon the Garners' running a "special kind of slavery, treating them like paid labor, listening to what they said, teaching what they wanted known. And he didn't stud his boys. Never brought them to her cabin with directions to 'lay down with her,' like they did in Carolina" (140). Still, Paul D wonders, "What would he have been anyway—before Sweet Home—without Garner?" (220). In a profane verbal parody, perhaps of Douglass's elegant metaphor of beautiful ships on the Chesapeake Bay, Morrison has Paul D deflate the difference between the two kinds of slavery, assaulting the question of slavery's distinction as negligible. Douglass contrasted his enslavement to "beautiful vessels . . . loosed from your moorings."[70] In a verbal parody of Douglass's elegant metaphor, Paul D appropriates the rhetoric of anger and the analogy of a free cock to stress slavery's vulgarity: "I watched that son of a bitch grow up and whup everything in the yard. Mister, he looked so . . . free. Mister was allowed to be and stay what he was. But I wasn't allowed to be and stay what I was" (72). Arguably, Baby Suggs's characterization of Garner's brand of slavery is intended to convey the nonconformist ethos of slavery's economic order on some plantations, while Paul D's profane verbal parody mimics the unethical vulgarity of any form of slavery. It is this last that *Beloved* gives final voice to, expressed by the religious Bodwins, the white brother and sister abolitionists: "We don't hold with slavery, even Garner's kind" (145), which was more tolerable than Schoolteacher's "kind."

Morrison accomplishes a major feat in her parodic characterization of the religious Schoolteacher, who represents the proponents of the diabolical three-fifths clause in the U.S. Constitution. Although Schoolteacher engages in a number of outrageous practices, including stopping Halle from hiring out his time and whipping and lynching slaves with impunity, one of his most narcissistic displays of power is the measuring of the slaves' craniums. This act is a demonic parody of nineteenth-century scientific racism. In *The Mismeasure of Man,* Stephen Jay Gould presents J. F. Blumenbach's illustration of the taxonomic "racial geometry" of skulls (1865 and 1895), a pyramid of race skulls from the "intermediary" Oriental and American Indian to the "Caucasian ideal" and the "degenerative" Malay and African.[71] Carrying notebooks, the religious hypocrite Schoolteacher mimics this historical hypotext of racial taxonomy; he lists the slaves' animal and human characteristics in separate columns, attempting to teach them, Sethe explains, "things we couldn't learn" (191). This is a reference to the three-fifths constitutional clause.

Although there are multiple climaxes in *Beloved,* Sethe's discovery of Schoolteacher's scientific project represents a major turning point in the novel, Albert Camus's moment of tragic lucidity. Significantly, the narrative juncture of Sethe's epiphany is related to her maternal function as she explains to Beloved, "No notebook for my babies and no measuring string neither. What I had to get through later I got through because of you" (198). With this confession, Sethe describes an internalized maternal law that resists the patriarchal law of society. Sethe, the maternal nurturing figure, stands in opposition to Schoolteacher, the flesh-and-blood representation of the law and Christian hypocrisy. In a proliferation of images that signify on Schoolteacher's difference from Mr. Garner, Morrison's most persistent sign is one that tropes on scientific racism, religion, and the law. While these cultural/political tropes may form an unholy alliance of the power of science, the church, and the state in the nineteenth century, especially in regard to the sanctioning of slavery, they are interlocked in sustaining a formidable, tripartite representation of power. These relational powers appear to be unimpeachable, etched bodily on the slaves even before the creation of the law: legitimating their crouching position during the Middle Passage; their auctioning on the slave auction block; their studding and breeding practices; their anonymous naming; and their physical and economic boundaries.

Despite the reality of relational powers that Schoolteacher represents, his measuring of the slaves' craniums, which launches Sethe's maternal revolt, appears outside slave culture as absurd and ungraspable. Jacques Barzun's analysis of the illogicality of "race-theorizing" as illustrated by mid- to late eighteenth-century scientists such as Linnaeus and Blumenbach and as vividly parodied in *Beloved* bears repeating here. Barzun avers that to follow the history of race-theorizing "is to be enmeshed at once in a tangle of quarrels, a confusion of claims, a knot of facts and fictions that revolt the intellect and daunt the courage of the most persistent. In its mazes, race-thinking is its own best refutation."[72] Hayden White's theory on the "logic of metaphor" inside slave culture, however, shows how even a rational argument against race-theorizing, such as Barzun's, can fail to envisage the aphrodisiac of what becomes "therapeutically efficacious"[73] in culture. White argues, "Cultural practice or belief can be adjudged absurd only from within the horizon of expectations marked out by those practices and beliefs that would make it either 'unthinkable' or, if thinkable, 'unconscionable.'" White remarks that from "the standpoint of a truly objective social science, no belief is inherently absurd if it provides the basis for an adequate functioning of the practices based on it within the total economy of the culture in which it is held."[74]

White's and Barzun's theories are relevant in understanding Morrison's creation of Schoolteacher. Morrison adopts the genre of demonic parody to illustrate White's "adequate functioning" of Schoolteacher's cultural practices while opposing them with what Barzun calls a "knot of fact and fictions that revolt the intellect." She thus plays on and fuses the rationalism buttressing both theories, imitating and exposing the complicated, double-sided, mock seriousness of racism as "empirically" grounded but also as reductio ad absurdum. Although the novel contains multiple parodies (demonically profane and verbal but also religiously sacred), the parody of scientific racism is more than a parodic spectacle of prejudice, as explored through the character of Schoolteacher. Race-theorizing about intelligence has become canonical since the founding of race taxonomy by the Swedish botanist Linnaeus (1758), its development by the German naturalist Blumenbach (1795), and its continuing development as evidenced by the success and controversy of books such as The Bell Curve (1994). Hence, Morrison can logically, if facetiously, describe Schoolteacher as a religious scientist, the "kind who know Jesus by His first name," because in his society his practices would not have been inconsistent with the dominant thought of the day (37). Douglass and Jacobs describe cruel slave ministers/masters who were deeply pious in their devotion. Even though Sethe, alone, escapes Schoolteacher's abuse, he has the legal right to remand her to slavery, back to spatial subordination on the southern plantation, because of the 1850 Fugitive Slave Law, whose passage revealed the long arm of the law.

The ideological conflict between Schoolteacher's sinister representation of Sethe's maternal body as "having at least ten breeding years left" and Baby Suggs's maternal advice to Sethe that "I should always listen to my body and love it" implies the dialectics between the identity politics of hegemony and those of counterhegemony (149, 209). At 124 Bluestone Road, Baby Suggs further counters the politics of conferred racial identity when she calls the traumatized slaves into the Clearing, a metonym for body-soul catharsis, rebirth, and regeneration. Urging men, women, and children to participate in what emerges as a sacred religious parody of an Old Testament ritual of feasting, song, and dance, she says, "all your inside parts that they'd just as soon slop for hogs, you got to love them" (88). Baby Suggs's maternal power is based primarily on love and nurturance in act, deed, and instruction. Love becomes the political weapon of the weak and enslaved: self-love and communal love but also bodily love, regarding the value of their lives. The "unchurched" but holy preacher Baby Suggs teaches the enslaved what the white abolitionist Bodwin learned from his father: "His father, probably, a deeply religious man who knew what God knew and told everybody what it was. Edwin

Bodwin thought him an odd man, in so many ways, yet he had one clear directive: human life is holy, all of it" (260). This religious sphere of holiness in Baby Suggs's Clearing reifies the humanity of the enslaved.

Sethe, the maternal, having learned to love her body and its fruits, allows motherhood to define her identity, and she embraces the maternal function as "my job to know what is and to keep them [her children] from what I know is terrible" (165). Feminists who read *Beloved* as developing "the idea that maternal bonds can stunt or even obviate a woman's individuation" and who see Sethe as the "Devouring Mother archetype" residing in a "matriarchal world turned in on itself and the pathology inherent in such female fortresses"[75] misrepresent the maternal Sethe. Rather, the "pathology" of Sethe's behavior in killing her daughter is instead a demonic reenactment of slavery's twisted vision of black motherhood in which Sethe is forced to sacrifice her loved one and herself to become a nurturing mother. What does it mean, then, when mothers can express human agency *only* through grotesque, parodic versions of what they would otherwise do? In contrast to the cited feminist reading, Mae Henderson sees the importance of true motherhood to Sethe, for her "womb functions as an image of corporeal interiority, the counterpart to Sethe's psychic interiority," which her "maternity privileges [with] interiority and [therefore] marks Sethe's entry into subjectivity."[76] Henderson's criticism emphasizes the sacredness of motherhood to Sethe's identity, above that inscribed on her scarred back and reproductive womb by slavery, as depicted in Morrison's parodic rituals of slave breeding and milking.

Perceiving her children as an extension of her idealized self, the self that is untainted by slavery, Sethe attempts to step outside the crude rituals of slavery's notions of black motherhood and its negation. She becomes inseparable from her children with full awareness of the sacredness of her womb, her body, her life, and her children—their lives. Like Eva, Sethe transforms her marked body and creates a greater maternal space for herself and her children. Psychically, as a consequence of motherhood, Sethe sees herself as "big . . . and deep and wide and when I stretched out my arms all my children could get in between. I was *that* wide" (162). Motherhood and maternal rights are at the center of the slave's rebellion in *Beloved*. It is the only rebellion in the novel that is fraught directly with the tension and force of the biblical Armageddon. With the staging of the final conflict between Sethe and Schoolteacher, the parodic hypertext of the historical and religious hypotexts of the Margaret Garner tragedy and the biblical Armageddon, Morrison creates one significant difference. Garner used a butcher knife to slit the throat of her baby daughter, while Sethe takes a handsaw, a more forceful and crude weapon. In distinguishing between Garner's and Sethe's weapons of choice, Morrison reveals the full force of her authorial fury directed at human slavery: the buying, selling, branding, breeding, deeding, whipping, lynching, and murdering (with impunity) of human beings. The fight between Sethe and Schoolteacher is between good and evil.

In the book of Revelation, at the sound of thunder a white horse of purity, a red horse of war, a black horse of judgment, and a pale horse of death "go forth" to seek vengeance against evil in the final conflict. In *Beloved*, Morrison's biblical parody of Armageddon begins with a description of the "dark and coming thing" of "THE four horsemen," the sheriff, Schoolteacher, his nephew, and a slave catcher (147, 148). With the inversion of the biblical four horsemen seeking godly revenge, Morrison might have in mind a play on the infernal parody found in John Milton's *Paradise Lost,* especially the demonic parodic trinity of Satan, Sin, and Death. But Schoolteacher's "righteous look" reinforces the legality of his mission, while Sethe, "squatting in the garden" nurturing a different kind of life, the greater womb of Mother Earth, immediately "flew" into the woodshed to kill her children. She succeeded in taking the life of only one, Beloved (157, 163). Sethe performs this act of infanticide wordlessly because of what she reclaims in resisting slavery: the other two-fifths of her humanity. Morrison perhaps alludes to this occurrence when she writes the lines "more important than what Sethe had done was what she [had] claimed" (164). Sethe's speechlessness demonstrates, according to Bakhtin's theory of parody, the force of the parodic unmasking of lies because "language is conventional and false, maliciously inadequate to reality." The truth "reverberates only in the parodic and unmasking accents in which the lie is present. Truth is restored by reducing the lie to an absurdity."[77] At this moment when Sethe overwhelms Schoolteacher, Barzun's race-theorizing trumps White's theory.

Fifth and last, Sethe's infanticide is not an act of despair but rather a sacrificial act of love. She takes Beloved's life in order to save her from the absurd, defined as an irrational world of "impoverished logic,"[78] as signified by the three-fifths clause. Sethe's killing of Beloved is not a personal performance alone, however; she becomes a tragic heroine who strikes a blow at the institution of slavery. For Camus, a revolt such as Sethe's "cannot expect any compensation for its lucid, lonely, and continued effort. It is a revolt without hope: it defends its truth, that perishable flame which leaped forth one day from the burning centre of consciousness. And the heroic zeal of this revolt seeks for nothing except to prove human grandeur."[79] Since *Beloved* is a novel of the redemption of the humanity of the enslaved, Morrison rejects Camus's and Frye's theories of existentialist and infernal hopelessness, as Paul D's final words of maternal promise to Sethe suggest. A realist, Morrison nevertheless defers to the theorists' point of view on the demonizing influences of power, as she realistically illustrates the intransigence of the culture of dominants and subordinates vis-à-vis the legacy of slavery. Semiotically the "filthy talking sheets" of the Ku Klux Klan (52) and the strictures of Jim Crow law demonstrate that legacy as evidenced by Paul D and Sethe's walk in town. Walking down a road,

Paul D and Sethe step aside and retreat, temporarily, into the space of subordination to allow four white women to pass before them. The women's arrogance is
indicated by their "shoes loud on the wooden walkway" (129). Despite the legacy
of slavery and racism, *Beloved* stylistically represents Morrison's demonic parody of
slavery and thematically one mother's resistance.

Paradise: Utopia and Dystopia in the All-Negro Community

Paradise is a demonic parody of a utopian community founded paradoxically
on elitist notions of difference and exclusivity. American blacks parody American whites, valorizing and privileging skin color. In this case the prized color is
black as represented by the characters' "eight-rock blackness": the deepest color
of black as found in coal mines. For her parodic hypertext, Morrison has taken a
little-noted event in history that occurred on April 22, 1889, when the American
government opened unoccupied land in Oklahoma to settlers; thousands of freed
blacks traveled to the state to found a number of all-Negro communities. According to Mozell C. Hill's essay "The All-Negro Communities of Oklahoma: The Natural History of a Social Movement," blacks primarily moved westward to found
their own communities and open spaces to escape white domination and to orga-
nize a social experiment based on freedom, prosperity, and autonomy. Southern
blacks migrating to Oklahoma, remarks Hill, were eager to "live without enduring
the social and psychological pressure of the super-ordinate white caste." Yet once
they settled into the utopian all-Negro communities, these southerners began to
experience "virtually the same inter-caste relations that had stimulated them to
emigrate from the South."[80] In *Paradise*, Morrison parodically traces the origins of
a black utopia community in Oklahoma, which dissolved in 1907. She historically
expands it to include a demonic parody of dystopia, due to the black patriarchal
community's requisite prejudices against the out-group of light-skinned Negroes,
whites, and free-spirited women, leading to the violence and radical changes in the
novel up to the 1960s/1970s.

Morrison appropriates demonic parody to reconstruct, deconstruct, and mirror the obvious contradictions of discriminating and intolerant utopian societies.
However, she also expresses an authorial understanding and even admiration for
those Negro pioneers who settled in frontier Oklahoma settlements in order to preserve their sense of dignity and to escape racial proscriptions unabated by the Civil
War and Reconstruction. The narrator's dictum of race places Booker T. Washington's ideas of domestic self-reliance over Du Bois's philosophy of a liberal education
for an aspiring black middle class: "In their view Booker T. Solutions trumped Du
Bois problems every time" (212). However, as Philip Page argues in relation to the
town's changing mottoes "Be the Furrow of His Brow" and "We Are the Furrow,"
there is no one "accurate" way of reading or ascertaining a singular meaning in these
or other lines. Morrison places value on a multiplicity of meanings in her novels.[81]

In an all-Negro community of self-reliant men and women, Booker T. Washington's focus on such practical domestic issues as the development of a homestead came to embody the fundamental principle of all-Negro communities in Oklahoma. This was seen in such cities as Langston, Taft, Rentiesville, Tatums, Summit, Vernon, Redbird, Clearview, Wybark, and Boley, the last city visited by Washington in 1905. He lauded the achievements of men imbued with his teachings of self-sufficiency.[82] Nevertheless, by parodically targeting a black patriarchy's failure to live up to its own ideals of utopian community, Morrison critically places an African American discourse on freedom and independence, posits Katrine Dalsgard, within the cultivated boundaries of the European-American tradition of race and "exclusivity." Morrison therefore illuminates the discrepancy between a "morally superior self-narrative" and "actual cultural practices."[83]

The original hypotext to Morrison's parodic hypertext includes the period of the 1630s, the deep, historical roots of the European and Puritan tradition of establishing a "city on a hill" in the New World while simultaneously enslaving Africans and murdering and banishing Native Americans to reservations. This is the subject of her novel *A Mercy;* however, *Paradise*'s strong black patriarchy mimics this particular Puritan tradition with disastrous results for everyone but especially for a group of free-spirited women looking for their own kind of salvation. The black-skinned and dignified founding fathers, led by Zechariah Morgan, nicknamed "Big Papa," bequeath to his son Rector Morgan, called "Big Daddy," a legacy of hard work and communal care. This legacy of self-sufficiency is entrusted to Rector's twin sons, Deacon and Steward, named symbolically as custodians (that is, "Big Brothers") of Ruby. Emulating the old founders' success in building Haven, the first utopia, the new founders, led by Deacon and Steward, found the new utopian community of Ruby but struggle with changes brought on by war and drought in 1932 and 1949. With its aesthetically pastel-colored houses, enormous green lawns, scented lavender air, and lush flower gardens "snowed with butterflies," the town of Ruby is named in memory of the twins' dead sister and has street names of St. Luke, St. Mark, St. John, and St. Matthews. Ruby is populated by 360 citizens who live ninety miles away from the nearest city and seventeen miles from an assortment of women in the Convent. Ruby is a secure, sacred oasis naturally and biblically. Unlike the insecure, edgy characters in Morrison's novel *Jazz,* these townspeople have a bank, a store, three churches, and a school. Young people memorize the poetry of Paul Laurence Dunbar, learn Negro history, and perform an annual Nativity play that elevates black utopia and self-segregated spaces to the beatific status of the birth and caregiving of Christ.

The ultrafeminine Soane, married to Deacon, makes lace, keeps a weed-free garden, and carries a crocheted purse. Her sister, Dovey, married to Steward, tends a flower garden at a second home, which is kept unlocked until Steward begins to lock the door, signaling a crisis of identity not found in *Tar Baby*'s Eloe, an open utopia. This event signals too the radical transformation of the citizens' paradise that had been virtually ensured by the seemingly but not actual incestuous inter-breeding of proud "eight-rock" families and a generational continuity of fellow eight-rocks. Steward's locking of the door is related to a series of tragic changes: Soane's and Deacon's losses of sons in the Vietnam War; Dovey's miscarriages; Sweetie and Jeff's incurably ill children; and the painted insignia of a black militant fist over the communal "Oven." Page cites the Oven as a unifying symbol of the community and as a protest "against the abuses that the community's women had suffered in white people's kitchens, spatial examples of confined domestic places. The Disallowing, as it came righteously to be called, justified the exclusionary dogma of Ruby and of the eight-rock families within Ruby."[84] In Orwellian lan-guage, the critic Patricia Storace remarks that the Disallowing becomes a sacred experience in which "the disallowed become the elite disallowers."[85] As the "elite disallowers," however, the disallowed themselves come to parody the chief pig in George Orwell's *Animal Farm*, Napoleon, who rewrites the pigs' declaration of equality in the language of Double Speak to justify the new dogma of exclusivity because some of the pigs are more equal than others.

The Oven is also a symbol of the old founders' and the new founders' successful utopia, which is threatened by an emergent dystopia. For now, the characters' mis-fortunes signify the encroachment of turbulence and change in a town of eight-rock immortals, citizens "racially untampered" with and "free of adultery too," with the exception of Deacon's brief affair with Consolata, who is conveniently demonized. The citizens' intolerance of change forms the friction of the narrative, especially for the Orwellian Big Brother custodians of the dream, Steward and Deacon. While retaining in his mind's eye the pictorial image of "nineteen summertime ladies" with "verbena scent" and "creamy, sunlit skin" (110, 109), Deacon invokes the historical moment of a founding era and looks upon the Convent women as a "flaunting par-ody of the nineteen Negro ladies" (279). The women become the proverbial scape-goats for the all-Negro community's ailments. The gender specificity of Deacon's vision of women at the Convent ideologically represents the dialectics of power be-tween the formidable patriarchy of Ruby and the enfeebled women at the Convent. This disparity of power relations between the strong and the weak foreshadows and influences the men's decision to contest and murder that which threatens their utopian space. Katrine Dalsgard correctly states that as Ruby's drama unfolds, "it has close parallels to the Puritan master narrative of the nation's bringing itself to the point of apocalypse through its failure to live up to its founding ideals."[86]

In an analog to the Salem witch trials in the early 1690s, during the waning days of Puritanism, Morrison demonically parodies the arrogance of eight-rock patriarchy and its scapegoating propensity when the men decide to storm the Convent with guns (in Alice Walker's language, weapons of their phallocentric power) and kill the women. In a mission supported by the elderly, puritanical Reverend Pulliam and led by the twin Big Brothers, Deacon and Steward, nine men rush to the Convent, a haven for battered women but which the men have reconfigured as a "dark and malevolently" infernal place "disconnected from God's earth" (18). Like *Beloved*'s religious slavocrat Schoolteacher, the eight-rock men use religion to legitimize their violence against women as the "Others." In the European-American exceptionalist tradition of "Othering" their targeted victims, the eight-rock men assume a similar position in their denunciation of the women as "lesbians" (double pariahs), dangerous interlopers in a restricted sphere where women's identity "rested on the men they married" (110).

Dalsgard, however, posits that Morrison's appropriation of the European origins of the exceptionalist discourse "has a different historical meaning to blacks than to whites,"[87] due to a history of oppression and rejection. Black nationalism, as Dalsgard's argument goes, becomes a necessary "counter-discourse that works in the service of a separate black nation."[88] Even in the service of Dalsgard's black nationhood, though, Morrison suggests the necessity of a universal and an ethical imperative for the common good of humanity, transcending all boundaries and historical fault lines of gender, race, color, and class. Without the establishment of such ethical standards, the radical parody of black men as the Orwellian "Thought Police" of spatial and aesthetic boundaries lacks a clear distinction from a demonic parody of white hegemonic power in Morrison's other novels, particularly *Beloved*.

The Convent is a major transformational symbol and space in *Paradise*, passing from the sexed-possessed space of men to the sacred habitation of women who transform it into a place of healing for battered bodies and souls. The proliferation of sexed, female body parts and images from the Convent's male ownership appears to reduce women to tropes of male sexual aggression and power in a misogynist representation of women as pornographic objects in a post-Freudian society. In *Imaginary Bodies,* Moira Gatens states, "Recent feminist research suggests that the history of Western thought shows a deep hatred and fear of the body. This somatophobia is understood by some feminists to be specifically masculine and intimately related to gynophobia and misogyny."[89] As a former "embezzler's folly," the mansion/dive reflected its previous owner's lust for power. There were "female-torso candleholders," "nipple-tipped doorknobs," "brass male genitals," and "alabaster vaginas" that cigar-smoking men used as ashtrays in which "the glowing tip of their cigars was slowly building a delicate head" (72)—a pun on the men's sexual perversity. After the embezzler's arrest and relinquishment of space, several Catholic nuns retrieved the mansion/dive and changed it into a maternal space of regeneration, a home and teaching institution, first for Arapaho girls and later for any troubled body.

Mary Magna, the Mother Superior figure, rescues the current proprietor and emerging Mother Superior figure, Consolata, from the "shit-shewn paths" of a Brazilian ghetto in South America. Before and even after Mary Magna's death,

Consolata reciprocally mothers and nurses her and then assists other girls and women in their spiritual/bodily metamorphoses. With the biblical names of her two heroines, Morrison suggests the divinity of the women's mission. Mary Magna is a coinage of the Virgin Mary as Mother of Christ, and Magna is a derivative of Mary Magdalene, one of Christ's first female disciples, whom he rescued from a life of promiscuity and a patriarch-led stoning. Additionally, the name Consolata in Spanish means to console and comfort. Through the naming and identifying of these two maternal figures, Morrison establishes in *Paradise* an association of caring and nurturing as principally though not wholly distinctive female and feminine characteristics, mutual and reciprocal as Ondine tries unsuccessfully to convince Jade in *Tar Baby* and as Baby Suggs passes on to Sethe in *Beloved*. In contrast, the sexual images of women as desiring but perverted sexual objects in the mansion/dive convey the social implication of women's bodily distortions, a gender socialization of men that is inconsistent with ideas about "the unity and wholeness of the body, its completion." In the collection of essays in *Toni Morrison and the Bible*, one scholar traces the coming "wholeness" of the women's lives and bodies to Consolata's "reinvention of life at the Convent." Morrison has her incorporate other kinds of sacred rites, including "African Brazilian modes of worship" to subvert "European-originating Christian theology" while "drawing on South American slave heritages."[90]

In having Consolata perform these other religious/cultural rites to effect healing, Morrison, like Paule Marshall, pays tribute to the black Atlantic diasporic connection, building a wider sense of community. In pursuit of the "unity and wholeness" of the female body across geographical spaces, the troubled females seek relief at the Convent with Consolata as the wise maternal conduit. Four women arrive at the Convent from different regions of the country. From Maryland, Mavis is the fleeing, scatterbrained housewife who suffers from spousal abuse and guilt, having accidentally caused the death of her twins by leaving them in a hot car with the windows rolled up. With post-traumatic stress symptoms, Grace comes from the Bay Area as a backpacking hippie who fled the sight of body bags, dog tags, and race riots. Seneca, a midwesterner abandoned by her teenaged mother, Jean, has escaped from the neglect of foster homes and sexual predators. Pallas is a West Coast victim of rape and maternal betrayal and paternal neglect: her mother sleeps with her daughter's boyfriend, and her wealthy father is self-absorbed. The four women are potential goddesses wounded by tragedy, as implied in the classical, mythological names of three of them: Grace, named after the Greek/Roman goddess of charity and beauty; Seneca, after the Roman philosopher-tragedian; and Pallas, after Pallas Athena, the Greek goddess of wisdom. Mavis is simply a feminine name, one perhaps foreshadowing her vulnerability in a patriarchal society.

Essentially covering the country's 1960s/1970s political/social landscape, Morrison presents a fictional panorama of women as cross-sectional bodies-in-crises in a cross-cultural parody of the times. Many of their crises are personally and politically related, and their bodies are virtual sites of the "social, political, cultural, and geographical inscriptions" of (post)modernity.[91] While these women's problems are connected to the violence of the social order, Morrison appropriates what Bakhtin identifies as the parodic stylization of language[92] to mimic the ethos and chaos of the age. Since parody suggests an authorial criticism and even a negation of the original hypotext, Morrison, as the Old Testament moralist, appears to be critical of the irreverence of life in a violent sociopolitical order, which characterized the 1960s and 1970s. For example, when the hippie Grace phones home to San Francisco, her grandfather asks sardonically, "World change enough to suit you? Everybody dead anyway, King, another one of them Kennedys, Medgar Evers, and a nigger name of X" (65). Through narrative references to the political assassinations of the 1960s and elsewhere the violence of the Vietnam War and the televised Watergate hearings, which led to the resignation of President Richard Nixon in 1974, Morrison links the women's personal traumas to the country's national, contemporary social hell. Parodically these women's tortured bodies reflect the age's politically chaotic landscape. In the Convent, symbolic of a large maternal womb, they seek rebirth and regeneration.

"My child body, hurt and soil, leaps into the arms of a woman who teach me my body is nothing, my spirit everything" (263). With her innovative creation of the template as a metaphor for the contouring of women's bodily pain, Morrison moves beyond the traditional Judeo-Christian imagery and biblical tropes of healing as found in *Song of Solomon* with Pilate and Milkman's trek to a symbolic Golgotha. In *Paradise*, Morrison links women's bodily transformation to the imprint of a healing template and incorporates, in this novel with a South American Mother Superior, cultural practices and rites indigenous to the Mother's mystical religious background in Brazil, unfettered by Catholicism, an orthodox and a religious sphere. The Convent is transformed into the space of a metaphorical maternal womb, and the women are naked like fetuses in a placenta of water, as they give spiritual birth to themselves.

We see this new birth as it begins with Consolata giving ritualistic expression to Morrison's blending of religion and South American spiritual mysticism, cultural beliefs, and practices. Mavis, Grace, Pallas, and Seneca lie on the floor naked. Consolata walks around them and paints silhouettes of their bodies, which are illuminated by the softness of candlelight, reflecting the comforting warmth of the reborn. Each female is asked to locate the source of her pain and to confront the "monsters that enslaved her." While they have visions of the sea, the supernatural woman Piedade emerges and sings to the women, who are "altered" in the rhythm of the birth experience (263–65). Piedade and Consolata function as midwives who assist with the women's mind/body/spirit regeneration. Page argues that the template and the women's "loud dreaming" or spoken dreams are "self-representations through which they are able to gain much-needed perspectives on themselves and each other." Page, though, incorrectly argues that the women are "self-destructive" and must get "outside their hitherto closed, self-destructive egos . . . to see themselves, to interpret themselves, and thereby to begin to cure themselves. The templates are analogous to fictional selves, doubling the self."[93] In stark contrast to Page's criticism, the image of water and the women's nakedness suggest something other than a picture of women in turmoil because of their "self-destructive egos." Since Morrison parodically mirrors and relates the women's pain to the social unrest of the 1960s and 1970s, their bodily reconfiguration can occur only when they have left the chaos of a self-destructive world, which they must leave behind to become rejuvenated and whole, the society being sickly satiated with murderous violence.

While *Paradise* begins dramatically and cryptically with the line, "They shoot the white girl first," race is not, in fact, an issue in this feminine/spiritual realm. With the narrative pronouncement of Pallas's Caucasian ethnicity, Morrison demarcates the racial boundaries of society with which the women had naturally dispensed as they focused on that which connected them (personal and social pain) rather than on that which separated them. It is in the maternal realm of peace at the Convent that the men erupt with their guns and "shoot the white girl first," ending a utopia that had already become a dystopia. As Deacon and the proud eight-rock blacks discover, human utopia is not a fait accompli, which suggests that Morrison shares Orwell's tragic vision of human utopia as an oxymoron. In a cycle of crises, redemptive sufferings, and rebirths, Morrison moves the action away from the domestic drama of the shooting (no female bodies are found, indicating the women's magical transformation) and places it, inclusively, within the larger and traditional Judeo-Christian context of suffering, remorse, and forgiveness. When one of the four deathly ill children dies, the citizens of Ruby are placed "in the awkward position of deciding to have a real and formal cemetery in a town full of immortals" (296), an acknowledgment of their imperfection and mortality.

In the final section of the novel, appropriately named "Save-Marie," the death and funeral of Save-Marie marks the official end of utopia and the beginning of a period of redemption for a town mourning the inevitable: the loss of its child, its innocence, and its vision. The narrative punning on Save-Marie is a beckoning plea to "save me," symbolizing the men's and the town's new redemptive mission. While a few of the men remain smug though physically wounded by Convent women who, no longer fragile, fight back, Wisdom Poole "fell on his knees and wept." Shedding his Big Brother cover, Deacon takes a "barefoot walk" in public for becoming "what the Old Fathers cursed: the kind of man who set himself up to judge, rout and even destroy" (302). Evincing their new military spirit, the four women also retrace significant steps, not in redemption but rather in celebration of their evolution from battered women to women warriors. The four women also experience the final cycle of healing, regenerating themselves as Morrison forces them to confront the lives they had left behind.

From *The Bluest Eye* to *Paradise,* Morrison reconstructs little-known events in America to illustrate and teach a history that is "unrecorded and untaught" in America's public schools. However, she goes beyond Frye's view of radical demonic parody in that she invariably turns the fiery violence of history into moments of redemption. In her narrative patterning of demonic parody and a paroxysmal turn of events that challenges the order of things, such as Sethe's meeting Schoolteacher in the woodshed, Morrison essentially moves her narratives to a higher ground, making her novels almost wholly moral texts thematically. Her particular emphasis on the maternal body and its recuperative powers not only feminizes her texts but also places the locus of cultural rejuvenation on women's creative and bodily powers as life-giving and life-sustaining agents. As noted by Caroline Rody, Morrison centers "her history in the bodies of daughter and mother" and "locates the historical where it has least been recognized": in "the female body," the "primary generator of history."[94] Whereas Rody focuses on "magic" to describe black women's bodily transformation and power in Morrison's novels, Morrison suggests that her characters' "magic" is that which comes naturally to them as Diaspora survivors. The trope of magic, related specifically to Beloved's return as the "magic black daughter"[95] traveling from the other side to "recover" the maternal, provides a potent racial countertext to hegemony. Morrison speaks of "magic" as a natural force of black people: "Black people believe in magic. Once a woman asked me, 'Do you believe in ghosts?' I said, 'Yes, Do you believe in germs?' It's part of our heritage."[96] That heritage, for Morrison, has a great maternal presence and healing effect: "One of the nice things that women do is nurture and love something other than themselves. Instinctively, perhaps, but they are certainly taught to do it, socialized to do it, or genetically predisposed to do it."[97]

Tar Baby, Jazz, Love, and *A Mercy:*
The Rejection/Absence of a Loving Maternal Force

The four novels discussed in this section are the exceptions to Morrison's oeuvre, that is, in her representing an accepted or looming maternal authority that exists in steady opposition to the social instability of a racialized space as well as the boundaries of black patriarchy. While the novel *Tar Baby* preceded *Jazz, Love,* and *A Mercy* by over a decade, it nonetheless introduces the maternal thematic that Morrison continues later, relating it to a protagonist's wretchedness when she or he fails to profit or reap the benefits of maternal metaphors of renewal. In each of these narratives, there is no Great Mother archetype whose judgment or steady appearance makes a significant difference in the lives of the rejecting and lost characters. Perhaps Jade's waywardness in *Tar Baby,* Joe Trace's eccentricity in *Jazz,* and the erotic exhibitionism of virtually all of the characters in *Love* are related to the denial or the dearth of an overarching maternal champion such as *Beloved*'s Baby Suggs, a maternal void which Joe Trace characterizes as "this nothing." *A*

Mercy follows a different trajectory from those in the other three novels because the mother sacrifices her daughter, lovingly, but with different results.

Tar Baby

Tar Baby is a metanarrative and a fictionalized critique of the distinct development of an individualized and postmodern African American ethos, one represented by the high-fashion model Jade, who rejects maternal nurturance. As a metanarrative, *Tar Baby* revisits the motif of maternal ethics, or the lack thereof in thematic emphasis, but in formal structure the narrative is terribly complex because of its blending of the tenets of postmodernism, including parody and pastiche. *Tar Baby* consists of multiple forms and genres, which then function as a unitary whole to suggest the problematic of race relations at home and abroad at a time when others flouted women and minorities' success (as seen in the portrayal of the model Jade) during the civil rights era. However, Morrison, like Marshall, gives only a polite nod to racial integration, not because the civil rights movement did not achieve the expurgation of racism from society, as Walker laments in *The Three Lives of Grange Copeland,* but for other reasons. Morrison's reluctance to embrace the ethos of integration is predicated on her belief that there is a "new capitalistic, modern American black, which is what everybody thought was the ultimate in integration. To produce Jadine, that's what it was for. I think there is some danger in the result of that production."[98]

In her criticism of the dangerous production of a slender, self-absorbed, high-fashion model Jadine or Jade, whose success is determined by her Europeanized bodily appeal to mass bourgeois consumerism, Morrison implies the synthetic reproduction of capitalism in postmodern society. According to the critic Jean Baudrillard, elements of postmodernism are inseparable from a "new era of communication" that "invades our minds in a pornographic way, ejecting all interiority, injecting the exterior world of television and information . . . without resistance."[99] Morrison uses semiotics to connect Jade to predatory imagery of lush material "progress," seemingly without her interior reflection or regard for the consciousness of identity that is stressed in the commercialization of her attractive body. Indeed, Jade reveals a libidinal phallic conquest of power as she lies "spread-eagled on the fur" of a coat made from the skins of ninety baby seals, a cutting image of her subversion of the maternal motif (112). In contrast, her nurturing Aunt Ondine represents the wise maternal authority who offers her another way of looking at the world. Without demanding anything from Jade, Ondine pleads, "All you need is to feel a certain way, a certain careful way about people older than you are" (281). Nevertheless, Jade's response, "You are asking me to parent you. Please don't. I can't do that now" (281), reveals her rebuff of the maternal instinct.

In *Maternal Thinking,* Ruddick explains that Ondine's advice to Jade is the very definition of maternal thinking. Because Ondine provides information about the welfare of others, daughters or even surrogate daughters such as Jade learn how to be daughters "when mothers speak" and learn how to listen without accepting "the conditions in which [traditional and domestic] mothers have been disdained and their work devalued."[100] However, Jade's response, like Sula's to Eva's request, mimics a male-gendered conception of autonomy, separation, and self-interest over a maternal emphasis on the importance of relationships. While Sula places the sacrificing Eva in a nursing home, Jade ignores Ondine and abandons her. In contrasting Jade's world of commercial success (she appears on the cover of *Elle* fashion magazine) with Ondine's realm of maternal caregiving, Morrison creates vivid distinctions between the two. A host of female characters from Ondine to Son's Aunt Rosa and Therese and the coterie of women appearing in Jade's dream attempt to transform her by reappearing as maternal metaphors of regenerative power. "What do you want with me," the model dreamily asks the women who offer her their magical breasts as symbols of women's capacity to give birth and nurture. In resisting the maternal body, Jade becomes the prodigal daughter.

Clearly, maternal discourse in the novel is not intended to deny Jade's individuality, but it does proffer through her maternal contacts the ideal formulation of unity and community, lying beneath a complex and fragmented society. "Kill your ancestors," Morrison adds, and "you kill all," a statement that tropes on the primary starting point or the foundation for order, clarity, and self-realization for African Americans living, as they do, in a country where "whiteness is posited as the unraced norm." But blackness is schizophrenically both "invisible and hyper-visible," a configuration of the psychodrama of "race" and also a "dramatizing of oppositions" in *Tar Baby*.[101] Whereas maternal ethics and Jade's denunciation of them make up one of the major themes of the novel, motley forms and time periods constitute the narrative hybrid of *Tar Baby*. The book makes historical/literary references to the following ideas and issues: France's seventeenth-century colonization of the Caribbean; Uncle Remus's late nineteenth-century tale of the Tar Baby as told to the journalist Joel Chandler Harris; the black utopian communities that sprouted up after the Civil War and during Reconstruction; and detailed here, Stanley Kramer's popular civil rights movement film *Guess Who's Coming to Dinner*. As a narrative collage or pastiche, each of these cultural references speaks specifically to a differing historicity, spanning a period of three hundred years or more and making the narrative appear disjointed. Pastiche, Hal Foster writes, "deprives styles not only of specific context, but also of historical sense: husked down to so many emblems, they are reproduced in the form of partial simulacra" because history "appears reified, fragmented, fabricated."[102]

Tar Baby, therefore, resembles a time warp because much of its sweeping history is collapsed or condensed, resulting in an assault on the establishment of neocolonial identities during the apocalyptic Christmas dinner scene, which is a racial parody of Kramer's politically correct Hollywood movie. At the Christmas dinner Valerian and Son, dominant and subordinate, respectively, exchange roles of prominence as Morrison tropes on Kramer's film. For its time period, *Guess Who's Coming to Dinner* (1967) represented what the film critic Laura Mulvey characterizes as "radical" cinema in a "political and an aesthetic sense." Radical cinema "challenges the basic assumptions of the mainstream film," which reflects the "psychical obsessions of [the] society which produced it."[103] An avant-garde film, *Guess Who's Coming to Dinner* withstood criticism. Indeed, as the liberal white mother of a daughter who plans to marry a black doctor, Katharine Hepburn won an Academy Award for best actress, and the picture was nominated for best picture. The film lost to the equally prominent civil rights–era movie *In the Heat of the Night,* which earned Rod Steiger an Oscar as the transforming, southern racist sheriff who develops a relationship with the intelligent, northern law officer, played by Sidney Poitier, who also appears in Kramer's movie. In a civil rights period, Hollywood had caught the spirit of the civil rights movement for equality and attempted to shift the racial divide from that of race to that of class and culture. Perhaps no other film represented the ethos of this period as clearly as Kramer's *Guess Who's Coming to Dinner,* for it reflected what Mulvey describes as a "skilled and satisfying manipulation of visual pleasure."[104]

The movie had a prominent, all-star cast, from Katharine Hepburn and Spencer Tracy as the white liberal parents, to the highly esteemed actor Sidney Poitier as the black research physician Dr. John Wade Prentice. Poitier's character's education, looks, and polysyllabic name all formally pronounce his importance. Although Mulvey asserts that "politically and aesthetically *avant-garde* cinema" remains a significant "counterpoint,"[105] perhaps to the white male bastion of the social order, Kramer's handsome characters as well as the movie provided the American public with a satisfying glimpse into the interweaving politics of race, class, culture, and gender. Nevertheless, Morrison's adept description of the Rastafarian-looking Son, sporting dreadlocks and named monosyllabically, as if to stress informally his fractured lifestyle and his lack of credentials, emerges as a parodic tour de force of *Guess Who's Coming to Dinner*'s well-intended racism. If Jade is a parody of the liberal parents' white daughter, then the formally uneducated, Rastafarian-appearing Son is an unkempt parody of clean-shaven, magna cum laude graduate, and physician Dr. John Wade Prentice. Parody functions here as a contestation of the elitist and thus acceptable black male body (no longer in crisis) appearing in a Hollywood movie for mass appeal and bourgeois consumption. The character that Poitier portrays is such a trophy of a black male that his success as a renowned physician is emphasized as if to overcompensate for the "disability" of his color.

Tar Baby's Christmas dinner scene parodies the politically correct Hollywood film, and the disastrous dinner is precipitated by the lovely placidity of appearances—Valerian's sleeping with his long-neglected wife and the long-awaited blooming of the "goddam hydrangea." Then the narrator shifts tone, mood, and focus, informing the reader that "NOBODY CAME" to Margaret's planned dinner, hence the invitation to the dreadlocked Son and servants (194) and the accompanying bedlam. When Son attributes Valerian's "regal comfort" in the French Caribbean to an act of land rape and imperialism outraging "Satan himself" (203), he is suddenly transformed into a historical figure who symbolizes the masses protesting their disinheritance. While Valerian vainly orders Son's expulsion, the proprietor becomes the emperor who has no clothes, and the two men's hostile verbal exchanges lead to the divestment of character identity. *Tar Baby's* narrative decentering of identity replaces the novel's earlier appearances of narrative synchronicity as manifested, for example, by the calmness and beauty of the island and the relations of the characters—for example, Valerian's wife Margaret and Ondine watch soap operas together like two friends. At the violent dinner, however, Morrison launches an assault against the staging of integration planks vis-à-vis popular films at a politically correct moment in our country's history. Ondine is reminded that she is a "cook," and Jade is revealed as a motherless orphan, rejecting maternally nursing women, Eloe's Aunt Rosa, and even Son (caring men can "mother" too). This is Morrison's critique of the distinct development of a self-absorbed African American ethos in a crass, postmodern society, relegating the well-being of a community to the pleasures of a lone individual.

Jazz

In *Jazz,* Morrison experiments with the syncopated and improvisational beat of jazz, appropriating the therapeutic music of anger and ecstasy to describe the lives of migrating characters who exist on the edge. Moreover, *Jazz* is devoid of an Ondine-like character, and the leitmotif of love and nurturance is turned upside down as if in a heartrending parody of love, subversively of the "new" Negro in *Jazz* but reverently in Morrison's distinguishing true love from sexual indulgence in the novel *Love.* Indeed in these two texts Morrison's parody of social conditions and hapless, motherless characters appears to stress the ruin that can occur when there is no cohesive maternal imago lovingly beckoning the misdirected or injured characters into a Baby Suggs–like cathartic Clearing. Like *Tar Baby,* the next two narratives depict Morrison's radical departure from her customary description of memorable maternal performances, and both books carry the textual weight of this maternal vacuum in narratives that appear fractured. Indeed, Morrison says that as music, jazz "always keeps you on the edge."[106] Music emerges in the novel as much a "character" as Joe Trace, his wife, Violet, and his young lover, Dorcas. The erratic mood of jazz provides the colorful but existentialist landscape of Langston Hughes's poor laboring masses rather than Alain Locke's new and educated Negro elites during the Harlem Renaissance. Morrison states, "I'm not sure that the other Renaissance, the Harlem one, was really ours,"[107] a reference perhaps to Jim Crow establishments in Harlem, such as the famed Cotton Club, which catered to "monied whites and gangsters."[108] Negro dancers, musicians, and singers were permitted into these cultured spaces only as entertainers.

In their writings on the period, Hughes and Locke present two different views of the Harlem Renaissance. In his titular essay "The New Negro" (1925), Locke writes jubilantly that something has occurred "in the life of the American Negro," who has a "new psychology" and "new spirit."[109] But in *The Big Sea* (1940), Hughes, writing retrospectively, criticizes Harlem Renaissance boasters such as Locke who believed that the coming-of-age of the new Negro would ameliorate racial strife. Hughes continues, "They thought the race problem had at last been solved through Art. They were sure the New Negro would lead a new life from then on in green pastures of tolerance created by Countee Cullen, Ethel Waters, Claude McKay, Duke Ellington, Bojangles, and Alain Locke." He adds, "I don't know what made any Negroes think that except that they were mostly intellectuals doing the thinking. The ordinary Negroes hadn't heard of the Negro Renaissance. And if they had, it hadn't raised their wages any."[110] In his study *When Harlem Was in Vogue,* David Levering Lewis puts Hughes's rejoinder more bluntly: "To suppose that a few superior people, who would not have filled a Liberty Hall quorum or Ernestine Rose's 135th Street library, were to lead ten million Afro-Americans into an era of opportunity and justice seemed irresponsibly delusional."[111]

These remarks prefigure Morrison's creation of *Jazz*'s central character, Joe Trace, who suffers from maternal abandonment as well as racial discrimination, as Morrison fuses familial and social discord to reveal her character's overwhelmingly stunted development. "I've been a new Negro all my life, but back then, back there, if you was or claimed to be colored, you had to be new and stay the same every day the sun rose and every night it dropped," cries Joe, the common Negro Everyman, verbally parodying Locke's new Negro awakening and exposing its vacuity for commoners like himself (129, 135). In her portrayal of Joe Trace, Morrison recasts the Harlem Renaissance through the lens of Hughes rather than that of Locke. Although *Jazz* covers the period of the Harlem Renaissance, she shifts the emphasis away from the era's vaunted pronouncement of the "new" Negro and onto a different and disturbing vision of Harlem as an illusionary haven because some artists thought the race quandary had been cleared. In this respect, Morrison adopts the art of parody as a countermimetic device to deride "those falsifying genres [such as Locke's essay] which offer wish-fulfillment in the place of sober realism" while providing "a model of sober and natural prose, which is better fitted to the realities of 'life as it is.'"[112]

That is, parody as Morrison uses it, whether verbal or dramatic and tragic, in *Jazz* allows her to create a referential backdrop of social and literary history against which she writes, offering what Bakhtin describes in another context as parody's serious but "intentionally exaggerated" critique, which highlights the author's caustic point of view.[113] As a result of her authorial attitude, Morrison's embracing of jazz, a composition she describes as leaving one "on edge," is intended to capture Joe's predicament as the Other, new Negro: poor, uneducated, and deprived. The scholar Farah Jasmine Griffin argues that the music in *Jazz* "defines and sustains their [the characters'] lives," and in another study she cites the "suffering" yet "spiritual" quality of the music.[114] This is true on one level, but while the edginess of jazz defines the characters' lives, as Griffin asserts, it does not sustain them, not even spiritually. Rather, jazz painfully underscores the intensity of their anxieties, driving Violet's "public craziness" (22), as she stops walking through Harlem and literally lies down in the street. She refuses to have children and denies her maternal instinct and yet kidnaps a young mother's baby to satisfy her suppressed maternal yearning, suggestive of complexities in her upbringing in terms of the family and motherhood. Joe is excessively driven by acts of "public craziness," such as rushing to a party in Harlem to murder the dancing Dorcas, all to the intoxicating mix of music and madness. Like the music, the city is deceptively seductive, for it has interesting people but "no high schools" and "no banks": bankrupt educationally and economically.

In the early twentieth century Joe, Violet, and Dorcas are a part of the Great Migration of Negroes leaving the Jim Crow South and the Midwest for New York City, exchanging one form of bodily entrapment for another that is deemed more liberal in the political and economic structure of race. They are drifting, motherless characters without a maternal proxy to fill the breach. Fifty-year-old Joe Trace acquires his name parodically after his unknown father abandons him "without a trace," and his "brain-blasted" mother, named "Wild," prefers the primitive but harmless nature of the woods to the "sophisticated" but hurtful realm of civilization. Like Joe, Violet and Dorcas are maternally rudderless. Violet's mother, Rose Dear, commits suicide, and Dorcas's mother and father are murdered in the East St. Louis race riots of 1917. Rootless, rudderless, and motherless, they travel to Harlem hoping to find a better existence. They seek freedom from Jim Crow barriers, looking, as Locke proclaimed, for a "new vision of opportunity, of social and economic freedom, of a spirit to seize, even in the face of an extortionate and heavy toll, a chance for the improvement of conditions."[115] However, in her parody of the new Negro, Morrison discloses that these migrating characters are as adrift in the North as they were in the South and the Midwest, and she explores their "tangle of pathology."

That is, *Jazz* links the meaningless hustle and bustle of three characters' lives to the social unrest and maternal crises of their past. An unskilled laborer turned salesman, Joe emerges as a complicated fusion of hero and villain, a lover of children on one hand and yet Dorcas's crazed executioner on the other, a polarity resulting not from his natural endowment but from his eccentric foundation. Morrison's unreliable but omniscient narrator details the trio's seminal act of violence, which emerges as a self-parody of their cultural dislocation and "Negro pathology." At the Harlem party where he finds Dorcas dancing with a younger man, a jealous Joe shoots and murders her. Afterward, Violet slashes the face of a dead Dorcas in her coffin, and the deceased girl's aunt "would have called the police after both of them if everything she knew about Negro life had made it even possible to consider" (74).

"Knowing" Negro life is a loaded term in Morrison's parody of Negro "pathology" because it is fraught with the tension of facts and stereotypes, both finding their way into studies by race experts who attempt to put the Negro struggle in historical perspective. In 1965 Daniel Patrick Moynihan wrote the study "The Negro Family: The Case for National Action," an eighty-page report submitted to President Lyndon Johnson for his War on Poverty program. Apparently well intended, Moynihan began chapter 5 of his report, "The Tangle of Pathology," with a placating and congratulatory introduction. He wrote, "That the Negro American has survived at all is extraordinary—a lesser people might simply have died out, as indeed others have. That the Negro community has not only survived, but has entered national affairs is the highest testament to the healing powers of the democratic ideal and the creative vitality of the Negro people."[116] Although armed with statistics on white and nonwhite families regarding their education, employment, head of household, children per household, narcotic use, and so forth, Moynihan concluded that Negro family life was unstable. This instability, he claimed, was largely a result of "Negro-life's" tangle of pathology and its primary matrifocal status, then 43. 9 percent to 15.4 percent in poor black and white families.[117] While he borrowed the term "tangle of pathology" from the black psychologist Kenneth Clark,[118] Moynihan's use of the phrase had the effect of racially highlighting Negro failure rather than America's long historical struggle with black oppression.

A major disappointment of Moynihan's study is that it left unacknowledged, as Elizabeth Grosz explains in a different framework in *Volatile Bodies*, the general cultural inseparability of the individual body and body politics. The body is geographically inscribed, Grosz submits, with societal markings that signify the politics of the environment and identity.[119] Significantly, the establishment of Jim Crow facilities throughout the country (marked "For Whites" and "For Coloreds") reinscribed the black body-in-crisis as alien and contaminated when compared to the white and national American body. Many blacks and whites were to "live the effects of their national identity directly on the body, which registers," Lauren Berlant submits, "the subject's legitimacy according to the degree to which she [or he] can suppress the [bodily] 'evidence,'"[120] as light-skinned Negroes did by passing for white, a cultural phenomenon in the 1920s. Morrison's characters Joe, Dorcas, and Violet are individual and collective parodies of black bodies-in-crises, which she deconstructs and then throws back at the system that stunted their families' identity formation. Morrison "fictions" the pathology of her characters' behavior but grounds the thorny issue of Negro pathology in their personal, political, and historical plight. Foucault remarks that writers can "fiction" history "on the basis of a political reality that makes it true, just as one fictions a politics not yet in existence [but] on the basis of a historical truth."[121] With Joe's schizophrenia in having seven separate lives, Morrison fuses the literary fiction of his and other characters' black familial hard luck with the history of black disenfranchisement with which many blacks simply could not cope, as Richard Wright hammered home.

Joe's reference to his seven lives as the Other *new*, "new Negro" includes his birth and harrowing maternal desertion in Virginia in 1873, his brief initiation into manhood by the hunter and surrogate father figure Henry Les Troy, and his walking to another section of Virginia and accidentally meeting Violet. His fourth change occurs in 1906, after he and Violet marry and en route to the North are moved "five times in four different cars to abide by Jim Crow laws" (127), reminiscent of Nel's experiences in *Sula*. During his fifth change, Joe moves from the overcrowded Mulberry Street tenements to Lenox Avenue in Harlem, although "light-skinned" Negroes, an inversion of white racists who screen spatial boundaries, attempted "to keep us out." His sixth mutation occurs during the summer race riots of 1917, as he becomes "brand new for sure because they almost killed me" (128). Finally, in 1919, he walked "every goddam step of the way" with the "three six nine," Morrison's historical allusion to the Harlem Hell Fighters, who were segregated from white American troops during World War I and led by the French. On February 17, 1919, the 369th Regiment of the Harlem Hell Fighters marched on Fifth Avenue, French-style in a dramatic phalanx formation, shoulder-to-shoulder, but "grim-faced" to the tune of jazz.

In the midst of his tribulation, it is noteworthy that Joe continues to seek maternal guidance. His mission of self-discovery is invariably related to his mother and the security of the maternal body, for he makes "three solitary journeys" to locate his mother, imploring, "You my mother? Yes. No. Both. Either. But not this nothing" (178). Through the symbolism of ropes, Morrison portrays Joe's and other motherless characters' tenuous hold on reality and identity. But the "rope broke" for him, as it did for Dorcas's aunt, who "carried that gathering rope with her always after the day on Fifth Avenue." The rope's breaking suggests their unraveling of reason and patience, due to a history of thwarted personal and cultural longings. Joe's seven lives, his unsuccessful quest to reach his mother, the Fifth Avenue march, and Dorcas's aunt's foreboding of her fate are all interconnected sketches of apocalyptic events, stressed by the thunderous beating of drums.

That Morrison withholds the maternal primacy from *Jazz* could suggest her perception of the 1920s as an incoherent period that was not "really ours" even though some Negro artists flourished. Psychoanalytically, *Jazz* emerges as speculation on a society in the absence of a formidable maternal persona, heroically combating social ills and familial wreckage as the overcoming matriarch Eva does in *Sula* and Pilate does in *Song of Solomon*. Instead, Morrison demonstrates the extensive moral damage of familial disruption with the loss of the mother as the embodiment of emotional cultivation. Psychologists cite "the fact that so many people regard bodily contact as the very essence of early mothering," with stroking and cuddling as a "basic precondition for psychological growth."[122] Joe, Violet, and Dorcas are deprived of maternal contact from the beginning, and each develops personality disorders, rendered famously in Joe's becoming many personalities and confessing to having "changed once too often. Made myself new one time too many" (129). Violet and Dorcas are similarly constructed. Violet has dual personalities: "*that* Violet, unsatisfied" and "*that* Violet should not have let the parrot go" (91, 92). Dorcas is described as "cold. All the way to the last she was dry-eyed. I [her friend Felice] never saw her shed a tear about anything" (212). Ensnared as the characters are in a web of bewilderment about themselves and the Jim Crow period, Joe's murder of Dorcas can be read as an existentialist act of moral relativity in a warped environment. After Dorcas's death, Violet and Joe seek redemption, attempting to learn more about the life they had killed and overkilled. As an Old Testament moralist, Morrison insists that defilers of human life retain something visible of their victims: Milkman keeps a lock of Hagar's hair; Beloved returns to haunt Sethe; and Violet and Joe keep Dorcas's picture on their fireplace mantel.

Love

The novel *Love* breaks with Morrison's traditional use of demonic parody, for it emerges as an inversion of love and the sexual manipulation of women's bodies. *Love* details the poisonous thrashing of love's innocence, and the novel is about not "how women love" but how the sanctity of love and the female body are desecrated in a postmodern society of moral relativity. The novel is more allegorical of moral qualities relating to good and evil, notwithstanding race and racism. However, like *Jazz*, *Love* falls short of a loving maternal prototype, leading to a missing element in a text of characters experiencing personal tragedies. The narrative moves through a span of time from 1912 to the 1990s, the ages of Jim Crow, the civil rights movement, and postmodern America, and includes a range of communities from the poor UP Beach to the upscale Sooker Bay and Silk. With an emphasis on a postmodern ethos, the narrative addresses a widening social malady of human fragmentation, particularly in its sexual parody of love in contradistinction to its moral allegory of childhood innocence and loss. Parody and allegory have two different functions in the novel, the former unmasking and disparaging the substitution of sex for love, and the latter disclosing each individual's story of lost love and grounding. Antithetical passions behind Morrison's sexual parody of love but an allegory of the child inside the male and female characters all suggest the distance between their exterior and interior selves, resulting in estrangement.

With Morrison's accentuation on character dissolution, maternal metaphors of transcendence have no place in *Love,* and women's maternal bodies do not occupy a sacred site of recovery or reverence. These bodies are, in fact, so ill treated that Sandler must remind his teenaged grandson that a "woman is an important somebody" (154), denouncing the reduction of the female body to sexual effigy. The omniscient narrator "L" is also obliged to cite her difference from the other sexed bodies, remarking, "I was born in rough weather. . . . in a downpour. You could say going from womb water straight into rain marked me" (64). While L's wisdom lies mainly in her ability as storyteller, summing up others' loveless lives, she is reduced to humming, a soulful endeavor in Morrison's work but an indication here of her marginalization in a society of "acid silence" (73). In his book review of *Love,* appropriately entitled "Hate," the critic Darryl Pinckney sums up Morrison's ironic treatment of the emotions her characters feel in the shadow of love, disclosed, I believe, allegorically.

The narrative repetition of the word "child" and the rhetoric of the image of childhood purity resonate with the novel's haunting sense of misplaced or vanished love, evidenced by Bill Cosey's legally willing "whatever nickels are left 'to my sweet Cosey child'" (88). His last drunken words become a mystery to the characters, and only the narrator L, who mercifully poisons him, claims to know the identity of his "sweet Cosey child," whom she declares is Heed, his child wife. But L hints at the possibility that Cosey's on-the-way and out-of-wedlock child with the prostitute Celestial could also be a candidate. However, the phrase "sweet Cosey child" and the word "nickels" have the symbolic ring of Orson Welles's sobriquet "Rosebud" in *Citizen Kane* and the protagonist's insatiable hunger for something of value irretrievably lost. Cosey shares this desire: he lost his own childhood innocence in the Jim Crow period as a youth made to spy on Negroes for his father, an Uncle Tom–type police informer.

Dialectically opposed to the strain of hate, the desire for love is expressed in the characters' wishful retention of a childhoodlike subjectivity in opposition to their learned social behavior in the looming adult world. Another example of this idea is presented early when two childhood friends, the wealthy Christine and the impoverished Heed, play together on Bill Cosey's Oceanside resort, blissfully unmindful of the society of wealth and materialism separating them. Heed is a resident of UP Beach, where poor women had numerous babies and the slogan "Death by Children" was created to describe them (104). Cosey's granddaughter Christine wears darling dresses and white ribbons in her hair and hails from the Sooker Bay community of Cosey's Oceanside resort of self-sufficient Negroes and the Silk residential area, where Cosey's mansion is located. May, Christine's mother and Bill Cosey's daughter-in-law, is described as an intruding "snake." She curses the girls' wholesomeness and motions to Heed, "Go away now. This [the resort] is private" (99, 78). The hissing sound, representing deception in *Jazz,* is associated here with the wily May and then Christine, who plots with her mother against Heed, who angrily burns Christine's mattress. "'She's going to kill us,' May hissed as mother and daughter stayed awake seething until 3 a.m." (134).

Love is replete with symbols of the Garden of Eden. These range from the ubiquitous descriptions of snakes and apples to other biblical allusions of an Edenic loss of incorruptibility, signifying a naked and unknowing Adam and Eve acquiring forbidden knowledge. Confronted by the mythic, crafty snake, which influences their decision to eat from the fruit tree, Adam and Eve become knowledgeable about good and evil. Similarly the female characters May, Christine, Heed, and Junior Viviane are allied with the symbolism of snakes and apples and, for the young girls, of forbidden sexual knowledge. While Darryl Pinckney remarks that the novel is mainly about "passion" and "how women love,"[123] there is no love in *Love,* recalling Pinckney's original pronouncement in the title of his review of *Love:* "Hate." Sex replaces love as a surrogate. "People with no imagination," the narrator theorizes, "feed it [love's absence] with sex—the clown of love" (63). As a clownish parody of love, sex and the manipulation of women's bodies suggest a vulgarity in *Love* that is missing even in *Jazz,* with its Negro pathologies, and that accentuates the novels' diverse social and literary agendas, as well as the enormous distinction Morrison makes between love and sex.

Parody in *Love* underscores Morrison's authorial need to demarcate the line separating love from sexual lust. Unseemly in its various guises, sexual coupling dominates the novel, although it is unrelated to and exists as a parody of the real thing: love with its accompanying portrait of romance and fidelity. Of characters from Bill Cosey to his child wife Heed, his granddaughter Christine, and the run-away Junior Viviane, the narrator L remarks that each has a story with a "monster in it . . . so they open their legs rather than their hearts where that folded child is tucked" (4, 5). The words "story," "monster," "legs," and "folded child" are telling in that they make known the strategies Morrison deploys (sexual parody and moral allegory) to deconstruct her characters' compromised ethical behavior. Mating occurs irresponsibly among those who have suffered a calamity and seek relief in sexual pleasure. Cosey's autoeroticism, observed by his granddaughter Christine; his long-standing affair with the beautiful but facially scarred prostitute Celestial; and his inappropriate pairing with his eleven-year-old child bride Heed occur only after the death of his first wife, Julia. She is presented as the only woman he "felt connected to" (111). This extraordinary display of authentic love and devotion is set apart from the raw profusion of sexual acts that lead to adulteries, abortions, and gang rapes. With Cosey's example, Morrison repeats the pattern of the loss of original love and its sexual barter with Heed, Christine, and Junior: the fighting trio of women. After losing Julia and Billy Boy, his son, the fiftyish Bill Cosey has affairs with "sporting women" but marries Heed, paying her family as she weds a man forty years her senior, a shocking union of two desperate bodies similar to the tragic combination of Dorcas and Joe Trace in *Jazz.*

Cosey's odd selection of Heed is connected not only to his loss of Julia but also to his forlorn childhood, illustrated by his boyish spying on a colored man "dragged through the street behind a four-horse wagon" (44). Of the poor children running after the wagon and crying for a father or a brother or an uncle, crying for a lost love, one "was a little girl," perhaps Heed. An adult Cosey regrets the girl's spoiled childhood, like his own, and seeks awkwardly to repair the damage by marrying Heed. Nicknamed Heed the Night, she is exposed to premature sexual awareness and then has an affair with a stranger and an abortion after the stranger returns to the Midwest. Heed's relationship with Christine, from whom she was separated in childhood, is marred for years after she marries Cosey. When Cosey dies, May, Christine, and Heed fight over his will, which was written arbitrarily on a regular luncheon menu. May hides that will, but Heed with Junior's aid recovers it from the attic. Heed forges the will, changing it to her and her siblings' financial benefit. As Heed matures and becomes possessive of her new proprietorship, Christine is sent away to a boarding school, where she acquires an education that she lords over Heed (26).

Of her many former lives, Christine had been the wife of a black American soldier, had stayed briefly in Germany, had returned alone to America, and had been mistress to Dr. Rio, who discarded her, after which she sought temporary refuge in the civil rights movement. As a lover-comrade to the revolutionary leader Fruit, Christine had one of multiple abortions because she, like *Jazz*'s Violet, rejected motherhood. She had "always been unsentimental about abortions, considering them as one less link in the holding chain and . . . not want[ing] to be a mother—ever" (164). The basis of her rejection of motherhood is related to May, who, like Pauline in *The Bluest Eye,* is an example of the archetypal bad mother: emotionally distant. However, unlike *The Bluest Eye,* where Mrs. MacTeer fills the gap and offers the lost daughter, Pecola, a temporary sanctuary, *Love* has no maternal alternate. Furthermore, Christine, like Jade in *Tar Baby* and Sula in *Sula,* has no special bond with the community and exists in the illusion of self-sufficiency, a death knell for Morrison's characters. Her return to One Monarch Drive, where she serves as cook and maid to Heed, forces her to recognize the importance of community even though she and Heed are at odds, a conflict influenced by the nonmaternal May.

As Christine's and May's troubled relations disclose, there are no loving maternal dyads in *Love,* with the exception of the briefly mentioned mother-daughter union of Vida and Dolly. Motherhood here, as in *Jazz,* becomes an outcast from responsible or sacrificing maternity. Acts of maternal sacrifice found in other Morrison novels are essentially nonexistent in *Love* and sparse in *Jazz;* there is instead bowdlerization of the maternal body, as Heed's singular and Christine's multiple abortions attest. Additionally, the sex-battered Celestial emerges as a parody of her name, Julia dies, and L, Heed, and Christine are deliberately childless. Female characters do not possess the desire of Morrison's maternal conquerors as seen, for example, in *Paradise*'s maternally driven Piedade and Consolata. The critic Paula Gallant Eckard posits that one of the fiercest of Morrison's sacrificing matriarchs, *Sula*'s Eva, who loses a leg to save her children, "provides the central metaphor of love and sacrifice."[124] But a host of Morrison's heroines can compete for this maternal distinction, including Pilate, who dies in Milkman's place. With the losses that Morrison's literary mothers experience, the author stresses the desperate choices they face in a denatured world of maternal hardships.

While the female characters in *Love* do not face these kinds of circumstances (and abort the possibility of having to do so), it is obvious that Morrison does not invest them with the implacable moral fiber of her legendary mothers. To this end, Morrison uses parody conservatively rather than rebelliously in *Love* to cordon off and guard love's inviolability from her characters' raw sexual impulses. Parody, as Morrison shows in *Jazz,* can be used to usurp the status quo in a celebration of its "subversive possibilities," which is "its essential characteristic,"[125] as seen in Morrison's hyperbole of the new Negro in a rabid Jim Crow epoch. Employed allusively rather than subversively in *Love,* parody now becomes in Morrison's hands a personal "imitation of another cultural production or practice,"[126] as Morrison mimics and protests Christine's cycle of abortions as a careless form of contraception, a symptom of individual and cultural breakdown. Her descriptions of Christine's "love" relationships render them as more playful than serious with men bearing such frolicsome names as Fruit and Rio.

Christine's s upheaval begins with her mother, May, and it is only after the death of the bad mother that Heed and Christine are reconciled. To effect their reconciliation, Morrison returns to their youth, adopting the imagery and language of childhood. Despite their acquired social behavior, Heed still retains "small, baby-smooth" hands (28), and Christine eats "every meal she could with it [a tiny spoon] to hold close the child it was given to and hold also the pictures it summoned" (22). In the attic the aging women rediscover the virtuousness of childhood. "Ush-hidagay. Ush-hidagay" is a gibberish language-sound that can be interpreted as signifying on Lyotard's postmodernist word games of self-knowledge in a fractured and restless society.[127] Christine and Heed's girlhood expression helps to facilitate their renewed sisterly bond before Heed dies in Christine's arms, both women summoning the innocence of youth that they had lost (194). Although the word games are mentioned sporadically, Morrison employs them to suggest the women's recapturing of their childhood innocence. Christine's and Heed's scarred lives are repeated in Junior Viviane's. She is the young, fatherless teen with hard "sci-fi" eyes who nonetheless has "the kind of eyes you see on those 'Save This Child' commercials" (66).

Junior comes to One Monarch Street in answer to an ad that the widowed Heed places, and she discovers in Bill Cosey's portrait a "stead[iness] while she robbed apples from the highest branch" (29, 30). The fruit refers to her sexual recklessness. In the house, inside the car, and around the town, Junior mates with the teen gardener Romen, whose grandparents, Vida and Sandler, worry about his becoming a young father with "some trashy teen mama" or, worse, "his contacting AIDS." Vida thinks of Romen's generation as "nervous" and frightening, "Nothing learned from her own childhood or from raising Dolly [his mother in the military] worked with them, and everywhere parents were flummoxed" (147, 148). In her home Vida requires Romen to wear "headphones" to listen to the earsplitting music of his generation as she recalls the relaxing air of "Moon Indigo" of her generation.

While she attempts to be motherly, it is Sandler who shields Romen, warning him about "bad cops, street slaughter, dope death, prison shivs, and friendly fire in white folks' wars" (150, 148). Like Heed, Christine, and Junior, Romen retains a measure of innocence, referred to as the "Real Romen." This particular feature is illustrated in his refusal to participate in the gang rape of a teen named "Faye or Faith." With his rebuff, Romen maintains faith with Sandler, who taught him the uniqueness of a "good good woman. She can be your mother, your wife, your girl-friend, your sister, or somebody you work next to" (154). Having been taught to respect the female body, Romen remembers and unties Faith's "mitten-tiny hands" from the gang's knotted binding while shedding "girl tears," showing his boyish-ness just as the girl's hands represent her innocent feminine essence (46, 47).

A parody of the sexualization of love, the novel *Love* is nostalgically evocative of old-fashioned values even as it questions the past as "pure" (147). In name symbolism alone, however, Heed's siblings represent an abstraction of moral alle-gorical qualities, drawn out and existing on the fringes of the narrative: Righteous Morning and Spirit, Solitude, Bride, Princess Starlight, Joy, and Welcome. While we neither see nor hear directly from these abstract, personified characters (Joy and Welcome die), they remain an evocation of a virtue-centered worldview held hostage by a postmodern period of confused values. "Once upon a time," the nar-rator reflects, "everybody knew everything. Once upon a time, a man could speak to another about his son or daughter, or a group of women would swoop down on a fast girl" to correct her (146, 147). This time in society has passed, as the novel laments.

Despite its attractive title implying romantic qualities of affection and loyalty, *Love*, like *Jazz*, is ironically one of Morrison's most trying novels. As moral allegory, *Love* rejects the idea of society having a morally neutral approach to standards of conduct, for Morrison draws an inviolate circle around love, human sexuality, and the female body. Society, she intimates, can be callous, but it can also be contested, as we see with the slave mother Sethe facing down an evil Schoolteacher. Rather than allowing slave society to define her, Sethe redefines herself and her children. In these and other instances, Morrison reveals that she is capable of creating ma-ternal metaphors of power that depict women as large as the oppressive history that she forces them to combat. That she is unwilling to continue this maternal patterning in *Jazz* and *Love* shows the range of her depth and her concern about postmodern America.

A Mercy

After the publication of *A Mercy*, which rewrites America's "origins' narrative," the journal *MELUS* devoted an entire issue to the work of Toni Morrison with interna-tional and national editors and scholars, attesting again to her global prominence. Significantly, in a novel that brings together Europeans, Native Americans, South

Americans, West Indians, Africans, and African American characters, Morrison inspires international scholars to analyze her authorial "exposing [of] societally sanctioned terror tactics" and her "ripping of all veils of racial and gender dichotomies and hierarchies," elsewhere and here, in her writing of a narrative of a "cautionary tale."[128] That is, *A Mercy* chronicles the early peopling of the colonies in the seventeenth century with European settlers and indentured servants (displacing Native Americans), African and Caribbean slaves, and free Negroes. Moreover the novel abounds with scenes of maternal loss and sacrifice, death and betrayal, and biblical symbolism. As demonic parody, though, the book mirrors the world the slaveholders made, especially in Virginia and Maryland, places of early English settlement. According to the historian Eugene D. Genovese, "The legal status of the slave during the seventeenth century, particularly in Virginia, still occasions dispute. We cannot be sure that the position of the earliest Africans differed markedly from the white indentured servant. The debate has considerable significance for the interpretation of race relations in American history."[129]

In my article "A Demonic Parody: Toni Morrison's *A Mercy*,"[130] I analyze the parodic elements of the novel more expansively, so here, after a summary of its history, the maternal issue is discussed. Morrison peoples this world with a motley assortment of characters. There are Willard and Scully, two ill-treated European indentured servants; a group of poor white indentured runaways; a respectable free Negro blacksmith who knows herbal medicine; and formerly poor but ambitious European landowners in Maryland and Virginia, the English/Dutchman Jacob Vaark and the Portuguese Senhor D'Ortega, respectively. There is also Vaark's wife, Rebekka, who is "shipped" from England "to anyone who would book her passage" (86). Working with Rebekka are three slave women: Lina, a Native American; Sorrow, a shipwrecked racial hybrid; and Florens, a black girl. Her *minha mae* (John Updike translates the term as "my mother" in Portuguese[131]) offers Rebekka for "a mercy" to Vaark, who was visiting Virginia, "where tobacco and slaves were married" (16), foreshadowing the tragic transformation of slavery. Morrison's parodic hypertext illuminates the uncultured background of the early Europeans and, ironically, their developing ethnocentrism and the "sustained violence" against blacks as lifelong slaves and against natives as outcasts, for those surviving genocide (16).

In her essay "Ruthless Epic Footsteps: Shoes, Migrants, and the Settlement of the Americas in Toni Morrison's *A Mercy*," European scholar Cathy C. Waegner follows Morrison's trope of shoes. Waegner links Morrison's metaphor of travel and shoes to the aggressive trekking of European characters to the New World, symbolized by the "deathfeet of the Europes [the native Lina's term for Europeans]." That is, the Europeans "trample on existing cultures, landscapes, and resources with thoughtlessly heavy tread and self-seeking avarice."[132] An indication of Morrison's encoding the changes of the New World, its violence and development of intractable race and class barriers, is found in her subtle reference to Bacon's Rebellion, as Waegner cites, but also in her reference to European diseases afflicting and killing the natives. "Morrison was fascinated," writes Waegner, "by [Nathaniel] Bacon's Rebellion, a poorly understood historical event. For Morrison, it was a moment of revolt involving all classes and ethnicities before the laws determining servitude and slavery were closely tied to race. In 1673, the 'people's war' was led by members of the local gentry against that very class, the rebels supported by a checkered army of blacks, some Natives, whites, mulattoes, freedmen, slaves, and the indentured."[133]

Parodying Bacon's Rebellion and its deadly aftermath, Morrison describes a band of misfits warring against hegemony—"an army of blacks, natives, whites." The result of these lower classes uniting, dangerously, against the powerful status quo was a "thicket of new laws authorizing chaos in defense of order. By eliminating manumission, gatherings, travel and bearing arms for black people only; by granting license to any white to kill any black" (11), the ruling class created a counterwar of divide and conquer. Morrison's A Mercy is a parodic inversion or, in Waegner's terms, a "counterpoise" of the patriotic "2007 Jamestown [Virginia] Jubilee, celebrating 400 years of the first permanent English settlement."[134] But the Native American novelist Leslie Marmon Silko explains in Ceremony that the settlement resulted in a devastating loss for the natives, which was repeated daily across the land. She laments, "Every day they had to look at the land, from horizon to horizon, and every day the loss was with them. It was the dead unburied, and the mourning of the lost going on forever."[135] Eventually the natives became internally colonized on reservations. The Native American Lina, who cites 1690 as a memorable year for the shoe-fetishistic, journeying Florens, now a slave in Maryland, is a survivor of the colonists' Indian wars. Morrison refers to groups of Native Americans later, as the violence had begun to peak in reality, being wiped out by a deadly, biological germ warfare against them. Morrison imitates this demonic incident in Native American history, connoting, like the aftermath of Bacon's Rebellion, its unimaginable wickedness.

Coupled with the loss of land, armed violence, broken treaties, and deliberate biological germ warfare against Native Americans, this last-mentioned act, perhaps the first in recorded history, combined with the others made the natives grist for the mill in mass genocide. Subtly or not, in regard to biological germ warfare, Morrison employs just one key word to connote its specific evil for coastal tribes such as the Powhatans: "had Lina been older, or tutored in healing, she might have eased the pain of her family and all the others dying around her: on mats of rush, lapping at the lake's shore, curled in paths within the village and in the forest beyond, but most tearing at blankets [emphasis added] they could neither abide nor abandon" (54). Howard Zinn explains that in 1763 the celebrated British general Jeffrey Amherst (Amherst, Massachusetts, took his surname around 1759, and Amherst College was named after the town) gave orders to a British commander negotiating land deals with the warring native chiefs. Amherst ordered the commander to give the natives "blankets from the small pox [sic] hospital."[136] In *American Holocaust*, the historian David E. Stannard explains that smallpox, influenza, and measles were the three "most rapid epidemic" diseases that Europeans brought to the New World and for which the natives had no immunity. The population of the Powhatan tribe in Jamestown, Virginia, for example, fell from 100,000 to 14,000 "because of English, French, and Spanish depredations and diseases." In contrast, the English population grew from 107 settlers in 1607 to 60,000 toward the end of the seventeenth century.[137]

Morrison's two striking descriptions of the colonies as peopled democratically by a diverse group of individuals and then divided violently along the boundaries of an intractable caste system convey the idea of the gradual social manufacturing of race and class, her parodic unmasking of permanent but socially constructed borders. Natives and blacks had begun to be separated even from a formerly downtrodden, backwater, throwaway group of European cultural upstarts. The English/Dutch tycoon Jacob Vaark had been a "ratty orphan become landowner" in Maryland, and he once worked in England as an agent for "the Company," another Morrison parody: in this case of Joseph Conrad's *Heart of Darkness* and its high-sounding, respectable, but deceptively named "The Company" and the "Eldorado Exploring Expedition"—imperial, capitalistic ventures exploiting Africa's natural resources. Having been tititlated by the luxury of riches, Vaark in Maryland begins to trade in slaves and rum produced by slave labor on the island of Barbados, easing his mind about his earlier sneering at D'Ortega for the latter's more immediate exploitation of human flesh: Vaark had identified D'Ortega and had "sneered at wealth dependent on a captured workforce" (32). Morrison's carefully selected slave settings (Virginia, Maryland, and Barbados) are embedded in history, as discussed in Stanley Elkins's *Slavery*, which states that "English colonial practice" for Negro slavery in Virginia and Maryland had "been drawn from Barbados any time after 1630" with an increase in the number of slaves.[138]

Like Vaark, D'Ortega has no cultured background. He is the "son of a cattleman" and "in line for nothing" (21), a reference to the old traditional order of a vaunted European aristocracy. Nevertheless he now wears "embroidered silk" and a periwig, a style imitated by his two young sons, suggesting their emerging social expectations. His wife, "Mistress D'Ortega," wears "loud perfume" and heavily powders her "face" (23). These are the colonies' unpolished nouveaux riches, the petite bourgeoisie. Kept wealthy by a plantation of bodily disfigured, scarred, and whipped slaves from Barbados and Portugal's Angola, D'Ortega still cannot repay a loan to Vaark, who recognizes D'Ortega's happenstance status. "Without a shipload of enslaved Angolans he would not be merely in debt; he would be eating from his palm instead of porcelain and sleeping in the bush of Africa rather than a four-post bed," Vaark muses. As compensation, the once-squeamish Vaark is offered Florens, whose mother sacrifices her to save her from the sexualization of female slaves, of which the mother is a victim. D'Ortega can depart with Florens, but not with her mother.

Structurally the novel opens with Florens narrating her personal trauma of maternal loss and displacement: she has a permanent "Mother hunger" (73), which she tries to manage with Lina's surrogate maternal care and her pursuit of an uninterested, independent Negro blacksmith. The narrative ends, symbolically, with Florens's *minha mae* attempting to satiate her daughter's hunger and explaining her reasons for sacrificing her daughter, just as Sethe in *Beloved* rationalizes to her ghostly daughter her far different form of sacrifice; both maternal actions signify their denatured worlds stripping motherhood of its pure naturalness. Florens's Angola mother, sold by Africans, experienced the shock and tragedy of the African Diaspora, the Middle Passage, and foreign enslavement on a colonial Virginia plantation. Thus Morrison connects a rapacious triumvirate of Africa, Europe, and the Americas—Brazilian slavery is referenced too. These three continents represent the indiscriminate display of the diabolism of avarice.

Florens's mother knows firsthand the trial of "terror" and is therefore unable to contemplate that kind of life for her daughter. In the concluding pages of *A Mercy*, the Virginia slave mother speaks lovingly to her Maryland daughter, speaking into the vast and welcoming infinite space within a "dynamic" situation "originating in an actual vacuum between two infinitely close bodies" of the mother-daughter dyad here, "speaking where infinity would really be actualized physically [and spiritually]" by a "power whose energy can never be closed up/closed off."[139] The wise mother anticipates the question that the daughter (whose soul/soles have grown "hard as cypress" [189]) is bound to ask: "Neither one [of the men on the plantation] will want your brother. I know their tastes. Breasts provide the pleasure more than simpler things. Yours are rising too soon and are becoming irritated by the cloth covering your little girl chest. And they see and I see them see" (190–91). The mother's final words recall Jacobs's keen observation about enslaved mothers. Slave mothers, Jacobs reflects, are careful about their children, especially their daughters: "The mother of slaves is very watchful. She knows there is no security for her children. After they have entered their teens she lives in daily expectation of trouble. . . . [Slavery] makes white fathers cruel and sensual."[140] That Florens is not exactly a teen but is quickly developing breasts—a "little girl chest" that is "rising too soon"—alerts the vigilant mother to take action.

With limited choices, the mother is willing to take a chance on Vaark, whose wife Rebekka has lost all her children, including the last, Patrician, a girl. But she is not willing to take a chance on D'Ortega, whose lasciviousness she knows from experience. "I know their tastes," she admits. Putting the welfare of her daughter before her own welfare, the Angolan mother manifests the same depth of maternal care that Morrison invests in all her loving maternal heroines. Conversely, Morrison shows the other side of mothering in *A Mercy*. Rebekka had learned from her mother that "religion . . . was a flame fueled by a wondrous hatred" (86). In her mother's world, an execution was witnessed as a "festivity as exciting as a king's parade" (88). The diabolism of Christian intolerance becomes a form of deadly theatrics rather than a display of the imperial venture of Conrad's explorers, but one theatrically managed by a forceful monarchy. Rebekka's mother is, therefore, a disabling, pseudo–power figure. She represents the paradoxical positioning of the maternal not as an enabling, creative fount of life but as a facilitator of patriarchal and monarchial religious restriction and repression. These are associated with death in the form of hangings, persecutions, and inquisitions. Morrison mimics the culture wars between the English and the natives as heathens, appropriating parody to illustrate and mock the colonists' religious hypocrisy. This does not bode well for Rebekka, but it explains Vaark's criterion for his future wife: that she be "unchurched" (23).

Beloved's Baby Suggs is "unchurched" but "holy"; thus Morrison's readers are given the task of trying to understand her distinction between an "unchurched" religious conversion and a "churched" or orthodox religious upbringing. Religious denominations in *A Mercy* reflect the same kind of narrowness that Rebekka's mother represents, sects including Protestants, Catholics, Separatists, Anglicans (a curate rapes the boyish Scully), Presbyterians, Baptists, and Anabaptists. Presbyterians are responsible for selling Lina to Vaark, naming and then abandoning the motherless native "without so much as a murmur of farewell" (60, 56), and for representing the church's lucrative involvement in slavery. Yet when the town's untouchable Vaark is dying from the "Pox" and the Baptists flee, the four loyal women stay with him: "All four—herself, Lina, Sorrow and Florens—sat down on the floor planks," after "haul[ing] him" into the house "through a cold spring rain" (104). But Scully notices Rebekka's change: "He did not dislike her, but looked on her behavior after the master's death and her own recovery not simply as the effects of ill health and mourning. She was a penitent, pure and simple, [w]hich to him meant that underneath her piety was something cold, if not cruel" (179). Rebekka whips Sorrow, advertises Florens for sale, and has Lina (who delivered her babies) accompany her to a church that the native savage cannot enter (182, 187).

Separated from her zealous mother by an ocean rather than a state, as Florens is, Rebekka subsumes the visage of her death mother, incapable of speaking lovingly into the infinity of space. She fills the chasm separating her from the "Mother hunger" felt by the other females. Hence, Rebekka is associated with death. Having become the archetypal death mother who loses her children and husband, she piously/deceptively recasts herself as a suffering female Job, the Old Testament patriarch who loses his children and is scorned by his false friends. Rather than cursing God and dying as his wife commands, Job remains faithful: "Though he slay me, yet will I trust in him."[141] Rebekka reflects on Job's crisis but lacks his faithfulness: "What shocked Job into humility and renewed fidelity was the message a [genuine] female Job would have known and heard every minute of her life"

(107). Feigning humility, Rebekka listens to the ghostly voices of her English female shipmates who offer her a "false comfort," consistent with her shallow but haughty life. After losing her children, Rebekka becomes envious of other mothers whose healthy babies remind her of her loss: "Each time one of hers died, she told herself it was anti-baptism that enraged her. But the truth was she could not bear to be around their undead, healthy children. More than envy, she felt that each laughing red-cheeked child of theirs was an accusation of failure, a mockery of her own" (108). After living in a house whose wide gates are covered by flowery and "gilded vines of serpent scales," and after scolding Jacob for building a third house, Rebekka now refuses to enter it in a display of penitence (176, 179).

Camouflaged by their flowery appearance, the wide gates to hell are the most prevalent of Morrison's biblical images, imitating the nine circles of hell in Dante's *Inferno*. Of the approximately nine times that Morrison refers to the ornate twin gates, most are associated with the alluring but deadly deception of sin: the wide iron gates of D'Ortega's plantation, inviting the envious Vaark (16, 31, 51); "the sinister gates that the smithy took two months to make" (59, 147, 175); and the "iron work aglitter" of gates, resembling deceptively the entrance to "heaven" (104). Since "thick vines" surround the "spectacular" gates and garden snakes (176, 188), it becomes clear that Morrison compares the feted European settlement of Jamestown, Virginia, to the fall of a Native American Eden. Rather than a celebration marking the jubilee event of Jamestown, Virginia, the act demands, as in Silko's novel, a ceremony for natives looking to heal themselves because of what for them was a major catastrophe, and Morrison agrees.

Critical reception of Morrison's novel varies between those critics who read successfully the "signs" the author refers to—"Other signs need more time to understand" (4)—and those who do not. Elizabeth McHenry, writing for the *Women's Review of Books,* reads them correctly. Although she never mentions the term "demonic parody," McHenry finds that Morrison's female characters and their narratives are reflective of the American Experiment and "speak volumes about the American past, its history of chattel slavery and racism, and the ambiguous nature of the freedom and opportunity it promised."[142] McHenry is less successful, however, in finding that "motherhood proves the undoing of so many of Morrison's women, [but] in this novel and others, it finally helps Sorrow to make sense of her own life and take ownership of it."[143] Once again, scholars who find motherhood so daunting an experience that it unhinges Morrison's maternal characters should take another look: not at motherhood but at the denatured forces in patriarchal society (slavery, racism, and genocide) that place women as mothers in fragile positions. McHenry understands this idea, writing that in *Beloved,* Morrison "meditates on the personal costs of slavery and the looming shadow it casts over parental and romantic love in African American contexts," but this critic still finds motherhood per se "problematic" for Morrison's literary mothers.

Problematizing Morrison's maternal characters for the social and political pathology in society that she has them confront is akin to blaming the victim. Instead the dysfunctional society is problematic because it makes motherhood and its natural rites of passage utterly impossible. *A Mercy*'s characters manifest the raw peopling of colonial America, its promising beginning and its devastating transformation: too hellish to be redeemed by a loving, creative maternal force. In *A Mercy* there is no cathartic Clearing, whose "sappiness" finds an earlier expression in the more fastidiously detailed trauma narrative *Beloved* when even Baby Suggs retreats to the Keeping Room, dying there. She gives up after Schoolteacher, trying to reclaim his slave-property, comes into her yard and asserts his authority. Such legalized tyranny in the finite world is perhaps the reason why *A Mercy*'s slave mother appeals to the infinite realm to communicate her message of love and sacrifice to her lost daughter: because the finite one of human bondage has closed off every opportunity to them. Into this world Morrison has the eternally damned Vaark return from the dead and revisit his wide-gated mansion. His revisitation is a demonic parody of the wandering soulless atrophy of those doomed to hell. In his treatise *Evil*, Terry Eagleton concludes that the damned lose even their "capacity to die, and, being unable to make an end, are doomed to eternal repetition."[144] On this didactic note, Morrison ends the starkest of her literary sermons on the gospel of social justice, rewriting the grand national myth of *E Pluribus Unum*.[145]

Home

Morrison returns to the boundaries of Jim Crow citizenship in *Home*, but also to the regenerating power of the maternal body/womb. Under 150 pages and shorter than *A Mercy*, her novella *Home* tells the story of a traumatized and discharged Korean war veteran, Frank Money, who leaves one combat zone overseas to return home to another combat zone in Jim Crow America in the 1950s. Frank's reconstitution is connected to his sister's rescue from a mad physician-scientist, Dr. Beauregard Scott, a "heavyweight Confederate" (62), who keeps a copy of Madison Grant's influential book on scientific racism, *The Passing of the Great Race; or, The Racial Basis of European History* (1916). A eugenicist, like Grant, who believes in the concept of Nordic supremacy amid a dangerous rising tide of lesser races and immigrants in America, "Dr. Beau" practices his scientific theory in private and on the poor, his work shrouded in secrecy. When Frank's young and uneducated sister, Ycidra, called Cee, goes to the doctor's house in Georgia looking for work, she inquires about her job and his profession and learns that "the doctor himself is the only one who really knows" (59). Less a sustaining narrative parody on history than a novella packed with parodic incidents on the trauma of war on battlefields abroad and at home, *Home* traces a broken vet's reinitiation into manhood and the women who assist him.

"Did you kill anybody?" asks the young son of Billy Watson, one of Frank Money's many regenerating agents on his way home to Georgia from the West Coast.

When Frank answers truthfully that killing had made him feel "bad," the lad with a sagging arm answers, "good" (32). In turn, Frank asks the innocent youth shot by a cop what he wants to be when he grows up, and he answers simply, yet profoundly, "a man" (32–33), implying, as the narrative does, a bounty on black manhood. Damaged and dead bodies, contaminated and emasculated Jim Crow bodies, pimped and prostituted bodies, boyish gangster bodies, and unprotected maternal bodies, abused or plundered and sterilized, all pervade the social landscape of *Home,* a title conveying the dictum that home is as much a centering of mind as it is a location of place, which the vet learns.

In his study *On Killing: The Psychological Cost of Learning to Kill in War and Society,* Dave Grossman relates the phenomenon of "combat stress" to the reality of "combat environment," so that relieving any soldier from the stress of a combat environment is believed to be "necessary to permit the soldier to return to a normal life."[146] But what Morrison does in *Home* is to surround Frank Money in Korea and in America with the prevalence of dead or shattered bodies, with no relief in sight from the violence of combat stress and combat environment, hence the pervasiveness of narrative trauma. During the war Frank sees the dead and dismembered bodies of his homeboys Mike and Stuff, the former "thrashing, jerking," and pleading "Don't tell Mama" (97), a grown but dying soldier retreating to the boyish innocence of childhood and the idealized maternal body. Stuff's white friend Red— "'Neck' was dropped" (98–99), from his name—lies pulverized, but his sobriquet (Redneck—neck suspended) is perhaps Morrison's allusion to President Truman's Executive Order 9981, which integrated the armed services in 1948 and ended the discrimination that blacks had faced in the military since George Washington's Revolutionary War in 1775. Frank kills a young Korean girl who is looking for food while tempting him sexually, a temptation he kills by murdering her. However, he disassociates himself from the murder of a child by referring to himself in the third person as "the guard" doing the killing (96). He suffers from bloodguilt and survivor's guilt, having killed and having stayed alive, unlike his friends.

Back home in Jim Crow America and traveling from Portland, Oregon, and Chicago, Illinois, to Lotus, Georgia, and home, Frank enters another combat zone where African Americans, even veterans, are reminded of their second-class citizenship. To separate the white and mainstream body from the black body, transportation systems were required legally to separate the races with the placement of partitions. Such laws read, "The conductor of each passenger train is authorized and required to assign each passenger to the car or the division of the car, when it is divided by a partition," for all "railroad companies are hereby required to provide separate cars or coaches for the travel and transportation of the white and colored passengers."[147] Parodying this hypotext of history, Morrison has Frank board a train and enter "a passenger car," where he "pushed through the green separation curtain and found a window seat" (26). The color green may have been the color of

Jim Crow partitions, but it also tropes on the name of Victor Green, a Harlem postal worker and civic leader who in the 1930s created *The Green Book,* which identified public places that served Negroes. Since Morrison inundates *Home* with regenerating agents, churches named "Redeemer" and "Zion" and characters such as Billy Watson too represent ways that blacks got around the humiliation of the system. Frank scans the "Green's travelers' book" (22–23) offered to him by Reverend Maynard, noting places "where he would not be turned away" (23).

Still, emasculated black male bodies appear throughout the text: from the "grown lawn boys" on buses going to work to mow lawns to the "publicly humiliated" husband on a train who could not protect himself or his wife from abusive whites throwing rocks (109, 24–25). These scenes and others remind Frank that "No car, no cab, no friends, no information, no plan—finding transportation from city to suburb in these parts were rougher than confronting a battlefield" (109). Haunting images of life as a battlefield for veterans and blacks are demoralizing to him. Along with scars from the military war and the reflection of dying friends and the blown-off hand of the young Korean girl he killed, Frank carries the scars of his tortured childhood, especially the memory of a black man's "body from a wheelbarrow" thrown "into a hole already waiting. One foot stuck up over the edge and quivered, as though it could get out, as though with a little effort it could break through the dirt being shoveled in. We [Frank, his sister, and Mike and Stuff] could not see the faces of the men doing the burying, only their trousers" (4), because of the children's size and the place of concealment. Here, Morrison references the men's unseen faces in a parody of anonymous, hooded Ku Klux Klan members who terrorized blacks. Philip Dray's book *At the Hands of Persons Unknown: The Lynching of Black America* cites Georgia, Mississippi, and Texas as the "dominant lynching states" in the Deep South.[148] Morrison's tracing of Frank's origin in Texas and his family's forced relocation to Georgia have the double impact of conveying their unrelieved suffering from one KKK state to another. When he is asked about his origins after Texas, he answers, "Korea, Kentucky, San Diego, Seattle, Georgia" (28), collapsing one foreign country and multiple American cities and states into a collective mass of ghastly memories, suggesting his homelessness.

In Georgia, Frank recovers his shattered manhood, which Morrison connects to her signature iconography of the regenerating feminine/maternal body. Frank's recoverability is related to three women: his sister, Ycidra; his lover, Lilly; and a community of maternal healers, led by Miss Ethel Fordham, a literary descendant of Morrison's respected matriarchs. An older and protective brother to Ycidra, Frank had assumed a maternal function to her due to their parents' inability to do so. When "Ida [the mother] asked Lenore [the stepgrandmother] if she would care for the baby because she could no longer see to her in the field, Lenore thought she would lose her mind . . . but agreed mainly because the four-year-old brother [Frank] was clearly the real mother to the infant" (87–88). Frank's mothering performance includes protecting his sister from uncaring relatives and a pervert who flashes her behind a tree. When he goes to Korea, Ycidra loses his protection and marries "a rat," who abandons her and becomes a guinea pig in Dr. Beau's eugenic experiment. With his secret sterilization of Ycidra, Dr. Beau becomes a parody of racist scientists and their experiments, which blacks endured. The most famous such experiment was the Tuskegee Syphilis Study Program in 1932. Unsuspecting rural blacks who had contracted syphilis were untreated by doctors in the U.S. Public Health Service to ascertain the effect of syphilis on the body: their blindness and death being the result. A copy of *The Passing of the Great Race* in Dr. Beau's possession signifies his acceptance of the practice of biological manipulation of controlled breeding so that the "better" races could outbreed the "lesser" races. Beau's two daughters being born with "great big heads" or "Cephalitis" (63) parodies with inversion the outlandish racial arrogance of scientists equating brain size with intelligence; and the doctor's description as a "small man" (64), like *Beloved's* Schoolteacher, suggests his myopia.

To save his bleeding and dying sister, Frank has to retrieve the "little-boy heart" inside himself because "deep inside her lived my secret picture of myself," a caring individual (104). This is accomplished with the help of another female. With the creation of the virginal Lily, whom Frank deflowers, Morrison submits to what Dave Grossman describes theoretically as the "linkage between sex and killing" in that both activities are "rites of manhood" because "battle like sex is a milestone in adolescent masculinity."[149] Indeed, when Frank gets the message from home that Ycidra is near death, his sexual relationship with Lily has peaked and his reinitiation into manhood is almost complete. Although Lily "displaced his disorder, his rage, and his shame," her response to Frank's leaving is noteworthy: "Their bed work, once so downright good to a young woman who had known no other, became a duty" (79). Frank thinks of their relationship as "medicinal, like swallowing aspirin" (107). Although the memories of his childhood with his sister and his sexual relationship with Lily are important to his recuperation, it lacks completion until he actually returns home, faces the town that he hates, overpowers the small doctor, and experiences a community of self-sacrificing maternal healers.

In a binary opposition to the remembered dead body in the wheelbarrow, Frank encounters a utopianlike society of laughing children and singing women. The Negro spiritual "Take me to the water, Take me to the water. To be baptized" (117) foreshadows the resurrection of both his sister and himself. Naturally, Morrison connects this final act of regeneration to the maternal bodies of women, led by "Miss Ethel" and "women [who] took turns nursing Cee" (119), in a ritual of homeopathic therapy that includes stopping her bleeding, curing her infection, douching her vagina, and positioning her open legs in the heat of a disinfecting sun. The women's attention to detail manifests what Ruddick identifies as the "discipline in attentive love" and the "radical self-renunciation" of mothering. Each woman has suffered a tragedy, but, as Ruddick avers about women performing maternal work, they have learned "to bracket their own desires,"[150] revealing their maternal altruism and sacrifice. Morrison details their personal traumas to underscore their selflessness, which is at the heart of maternal work for the greater good. Miss Ethel's two sons were murdered, and the other women endure bodily injuries affecting their sight and mobility. Still, they work, quilt, and sing while caring for Cee, who learns that she will "never have children to care about and give her the status of motherhood" (129). Yet she and Frank return to the town of remembered trauma, face the past, and locate and rebury the bones of the dead body in the wheelbarrow, having discovered his identity as "the man" who gave his life for the life of his son in a knife fight sponsored by racists. Manhood, like maternal care, requires sacrifice.

Predictably, critics comparing *Home* to Morrison's more celebrated novels, such as *Song of Solomon* and *Beloved*, find it lacking, not only due to its brevity but also because of the author's "circular enterprise" of discussing the brutality of the black experience and saying nothing new or "uplifting." Writing for London's *Guardian*, Sarah Churchwell singles out Morrison's finest novels but complains in general and about *Home* in particular, "Generational legacies, haunting[s], ghosts, and the persistent effects of racism and sexism are Morrison's enduring themes: they are big ones. But her novels about them are getting smaller, in every sense; she seems to be losing patience with her own stories."[151]

God Help the Child

Morrison's eleventh novel, published in 2015, deals with different kinds of bodies-in-crises, black and white children, while revisiting the familiar racist terrain of the African American experience, including the intraracism of blacks who have internalized their Herrenvolk status and seek refuge in having a near-white-skin privilege. This is one of the cursed legacies of slavery (besides black economic dispossession), and Harriet Beecher Stowe alludes to it in *Uncle Tom's Cabin* (1852). Stowe satirizes white-skin privilege among Louisiana's house slaves when the dark-skinned slave Dinah chastises the quadroon slave Rosa, who has described the former as "glum" because she "can't go to the [quadroon] ball." Acerbically, Dinah responds, "Don't want none o' your light-colored balls . . . makin' b'lieve you's white folks."[152] While Stowe ridicules the slaves' trumped-up, skin-privilege dialogue, the historian Joel Williamson writes of the seriousness of nineteenth-century, white-looking Negroes in New Orleans attending quadroon balls where "wealthy and cultured white men formally courted prospective mulatto mistresses," not as wives but as concubines.[153] Morrison opens *God Help the Child* with this historical allusion to one of slavery's sad reminders, as the white-looking mother, Sweetness, gives birth to a blue-black child, Lula Ann, and apologizes, absolving herself of guilt, as her light-skinned husband flees.

While *God Help the Child* has received mixed reviews,[154] based presumably on the absence of a long, sustaining narrative plot and interior character development, as we find in *Beloved,* for example (which the editor of the *New York Times Book Review* in 2006 declared the best American novel in twenty-five years, based on polling by prominent writers and critics), it generally follows the trajectory, though abbreviated, of *The Bluest Eye, Beloved, Home, Sula,* and *Song of Solomon. God Help the Child* describes bodies-in-crises too, often regenerated with the assistance of characters who assume a loving maternal function. This is especially true for Lula Ann, who is reborn as the black and beautiful Bride, unlike the unregenerate "black and ugly" Pecola Breedlove, who goes insane in *The Bluest Eye.* Also there is Raisin, a young white runaway, resembling an older Amy Denver in *Beloved,* who renames herself as she makes her way to Boston looking for carmine velvet to reclaim her life. Raisin, prostituted by her mother, just as Bride is unloved by hers, is renamed Rain. Together, Bride and Rain, resembling *Beloved*'s two throwaways, Amy and Sethe, are regenerated with the help of an aging but free-spirited white hippie couple, Evelyn and Steve.

These maternal surrogates first find Raisin stranded in the rain and take her to their home in nature's backwoods without electricity, as Morrison critiques contemporary society with its modern conveniences but ubiquitous Wal-Mart stores, patriotic but homeless veterans, and television sets on which "what passes for news is either gossip or a lecture of lies" (29). Afterward, Rain finds an injured Bride, who has become a cosmetics executive of her own firm, and after going for help returns to the site of the accident with Evelyn and Steve. It is Steve who "lifted" Bride out of her Jaguar, "asking no questions" and "position[ing] her in his arms" (84–85), similar to the male caregivers in *Beloved,* Paul D and Stamp Paid, rescuing and taking care of Sethe. Settled in the backwoods home of Evelyn and Steve, Bride, resting beneath a "Navajo blanket," notices the "light, unaided by electricity" (87), just as Miss Ethel and the community of women in *Home* bathe a recovering Cee in a bright landscape, the natural homeopathy of a loving home.

Bride and Rain are two of several formerly abused but fortunate children saved by the reinvention of themselves and the piloting of benign motherly forces. However, other children are not as fortunate, as Morrison provides a verisimilitude of the conditions of postmodern life and the psychosexual violence done to children by pedophiles, of whom a Google search reveals at least 60 percent are adult males. Pedophilia has a disturbing presence in the novel, which the inmate Sofia Huxley recognizes: "We were at the bottom of the heap of murderers, arsonists, drug dealers, bomb-throwing revolutionaries and the mentally ill. Hurting little children was their [other inmates'] idea of the lowest of the low" (66). But Sofia is innocent. Before Lula Ann was reborn as Bride and sought redress, she fingered Sofia, an innocent kindergarten teacher, who was found guilty of pedophilia along with her husband and then spends fifteen years in prison. Desperate for maternal love, Lula

Ann lied just to get close to her mother, who had refused even to touch her dark-skinned daughter. At the trial Sweetness responded approvingly as she and her daughter got media attention. A hypocrite and an example of the archetypal bad mother, Sweetness cautioned Lula Ann against exposing the *real* pedophile, their landlord, Mr. Leigh, whom she had seen "leaning over the short, fat legs of a child between his hairy white thighs" (54). As an adult, Bride seeks reconciliation with her former lover, Booker, who left her after she informed him of her attempt to apologize and pay Sofia, whom Booker had been led to believe is guilty of a crime that is tragically personal to him. As a kid, Booker lost his little but older brother, Adam, who was murdered along with several other boys by a male adult pedophile. It is on her way to Whiskey, California, seeking Booker that she meets Rain, Evelyn, Steve, and Queen, Booker's aunt, who lost contact with all of her children, especially Hannah, who disclosed her father's fondling of her to an unbelieving mother.

In her narrative proclivity in *God Help the Child* to offer examples of the bad mothering type—those who are capable of endangering the lives of their children —Morrison, stepping away from her superior mother characters, shifts her focus to the instability of some mothers. Sara Ruddick explains this poor model: "Real maternal power is not a stable quantity, but highly variable depending on techno-logical development, individual as well as collective economic resources, changing social and military policies, employment opportunities, housing practices, family arrangement, the mood, success, well-being, and age of her children." Moreover, Ruddick continues, real maternal power depends "of course, [on] her own health, energy, and non-maternal ambitions."[155] Of the abused children in *God Help the Child,* only Booker's brother, Adam, comes from a loving and nurturing family back-ground, perhaps one reason why "Adam's death had clouded him" (132). Booker recalls his "book-reading family" and "his mother's huge breakfast feats. Banquets really. Hot biscuits, short and flaky; grits, snow-white and tongue-burning hot; eggs beaten into pale saffron creaminess; sizzling sausage patties, sliced tomatoes, strawberry jam [and] freshly squeezed orange juice" (113). Booker's mother and father asked two questions of their children: "What have you learned that is true" (similar to *Song of Solomon*'s Pilate asking, "What is true?"); and "What problem do you have" (112). The questions, like the probable answers, are intended to im-press upon the children the power of critical thinking and their understanding of the meaningfulness of their lives in a society of predators and disingenuousness, recalling Morrison's narrative critique of the corporate media.

Conversely, both Rain and Bride had come from family backgrounds riddled by maternal trouble: economic deprivation for Rain. When asked, "If you saw your mother again what would you say to her," Rain answers bluntly, "Nothing. I'd chop her head off," for prostituting her daughter to cunnilingus-loving older men (102). Bride's maternal background is not so much related to economics as it is to the history of slavery and some African Americans' internalization of color pathology in a Herrenvolk country. Daughters placing their mothers in nursing homes or not visiting their mothers there are seen as reprobates in Morrison's fiction, guilty of betrayal. When Sula in the novel bearing her name places the matriarch Eva in a nursing home, the granddaughter is seen as Judas-like, betraying a strong and loving woman who has sacrificed her life not only for the lives of her children but also for the well-being of the Bottom community. Thus when Sweetness goes to a nursing home and Bride not only refuses to visit but only occasionally writes to her, Sweetness's birthing body is given no more respect than she had given to her daughter: little. As Sweetness had rejected her daughter, Lula Ann/Bride has now rejected her.

Reciprocity is a valued loving practice in *God Help the Child* for those considered worthy: indeed Rain saves Bride's life when she comes upon her in the woods in a crashed Jaguar and goes to inform Evelyn and Steve. In like manner, Bride saves Rain's life when she is shot with pellets by a group of racist white boys who refer to Bride as Rain's "Mammy" (105), in Evelyn and Steve's utopianlike society where the occupants have miraculously overcome "race." Bride steps in front of Rain and takes the pellets intended for the child. After Bride heals and leaves, Rain reflects, "My heart was beating fast because nobody had done that before. I mean Steve and Evelyn took me in, and all, but nobody put their own self in danger to save me" (105–6). Yet, Bride cannot extend this virtue of care to her mother, who hardly touched her. When Bride recalls Sofia's beating of her, she likens it tellingly to a maternal slap but "without the pleasure of being touched" (79).

In Ashley Montagu's important study *The Concept of Race,* he argues for a discontinuation of the word "race," stating that this term is "utterly erroneous and meaningless" and therefore should be "dropped from the vocabulary of the anthropologist, for it has done an infinite amount of harm and no good at all." Montagu is referring to the four or five divisions of humankind based not on "race" but on a distinction of what he refers to as the "physicogeographical history of man": environment, culture, and geography. In the scheme of things, he writes, "Complexions run into each other; forms follow the genetic character, and upon the whole, all are at last but shades of the same great picture, extending through all ages, and over all parts of the Earth."[156] Nevertheless in *God Help the Child* and other novels Morrison illustrates that perceptions rather than logical rationalizations about "race" have taken on a life of their own, resulting in her depictions of black bodies-in-crises. In *God Help the Child,* though, she consciously reverses a bad mother's color fetish as an outdated relic of slavery, which society in general and African Americans in particular must get over. Bride, who wears only white in striking contrast to her pure ebony skin, thinks of herself as being "stitched together" and having "personal glamour" in a "creative profession" that accepts her redefinition of herself (79).

Reunited with Booker, and pregnant, the white-clad Bride, a name metaphorically suggesting her ceremonial, rebirth readiness, regains her life-giving breast, notices the return of her pubic and underarm hairs, which she had lost previously. This new development is a display of the magical and transformative realism that Morrison associates with the navelless but life-affirming Pilate in *Song of Solomon*. Mothering is serious moral work in Morrison's narratives, as stated plainly in *Beloved:* "Unless carefree," or loose and irresponsible, "motherlove was a killer" (155). Responsible mothers have the life and death maternal instincts of preservation that Morrison gives even to her animals. In *God Help the Child*, upon hearing the voices of Bride and Rain, a doe, "watching the pair of humans, was as still as the tree, [which] she stood next to. The fawn nestled her flank"—after which "mother and child fled" (102), in safety, with the mother leading the way.

This chapter opens with Ira Katznelson's quotation about black history being "buried under a blanket of [American] history" and his idea that for all Americans to effect a true liberation in regard to knowing the totality of the black experience, writers must not "lift just one corner of that blanket" but "raise the entire cover."[157] Novel by novel this is what Morrison has done for her country. The "repetition" of her subject matter invites not "weariness," as England's Churchwell complains, but an acknowledgment of the depth and persistence of American racism, which has its long tentacles segmented into practically every facet of American life: from real estate to beauty culture; from cemeteries to police forces; from the media to the schools; from the stores to the parks; from the armed forces to the trains; from the hospitals to the medical professions, ad nauseum.

In the 1960s Martin Luther King Jr. cautioned African Americans against the "degenerating sense of nobodiness"[158] that the Jim Crow and de facto Jim Crow laws and practices were intended to induce in them, and which Morrison's narratives resist. Unlike Churchwell, another Morrison scholar understands her mission and asserts that Morrison refuses to "observe the carefully policed boundaries of . . . landscapes and the exclusionary definitions of national belonging."[159] Indeed, like the women writers discussed earlier, from Wheatley to Walker, Morrison does find something "uplifting" to write about: African Americans' enduring legacy of resistance to racism from one historical period to another. Inevitably this battle is powered by the energy of self-sacrificing maternal figures. "I thought that my mother was a powerful person, and the person more powerful than she, was her mother who was really powerful. And I had the grand experience of having my great-grandmother come to town. And who can be more powerful than your great-grandmother,"[160] asks Morrison rhetorically, giving readers the prototypes for her signature of formidable literary mothers and their sundry surrogates.

Afterword

Over a period of 245 years, the authors discussed here have given voice to a people who have always resisted their socially constructed identity in America. *Maternal Metaphors* analyzes the literary/political roles that these writers have played and continue to play in capturing crucial events in American history relating to the black body-in-crisis. Part 1 shows the tragedy and transformation of blacks from a state of slavery to a Herrenvolk democracy as written on Phillis Wheatley's, Harriet Jacobs's, and Charlotte Forten's enslaved and interstitial bodies as these writers morphed into a celebrated poet, a slave-mother/freedom fighter, and a democratic New England schoolmarm, respectively. Jessie Fauset's, Nella Larsen's, and Zora Neale Hurston's Jim Crow–segregated bodies were refashioned in afterimages of characters who redefined beauty in a mosaic of color. As seen in part 2, the other authors' impulses toward regeneration in their conflations of history, past and present, are no less vibrant: Paule Marshall's immigrants turned into mother-daughter warriors; Alice Walker's docile protagonists changed into evolving archetypes of clout; and Toni Morrison's pariahs became saviors.

Maternal iconography is a dominating feature in all their works. It is astonishing that this representation has a long, uninterrupted history in their literature: across time, genre, and geography. What do we make of their symbolic network of communication about the rhetoric of the image of the maternal body that each adopts in juxtaposition to the subordination of the gendered and racialized Other? Rebirth motifs are clear in their maternal imagery. But this alone does not explain their authorial preferences, for these writers do not reduce themselves or their characters to the strict biology of their bodies. By becoming and/or creating maternal figures as agents of social reform, these writers were envisioning a new paradigm for the political order: one in which women in general and black women in particular will have visibility, based on the real power of their factual and/or imagined recoverability from a history of trauma.

Notes

Introduction

1. Burke and Stets, *Identity Theory*, 112; Ellison, *Shadow and Act*, 28.
2. van den Berghe, *Race and Racism: A Comparative Perspective*, 29, 77, 18, 126.
3. Myrdal, *An American Dilemma*, 89.
4. Lerner, *The Creation of Patriarchy*, 39; Hirsch, *The Mother/Daughter Plot*, 36.
5. Hirsch, *The Mother/Daughter Plot*, 36.
6. Fox-Genovese, *Feminism without Illusion*, 125.
7. Morrison, *Beloved*, 162.
8. Alice Walker, *In Search of Our Mothers' Garden*, 233.
9. Michelle Boulous Walker, *Philosophy and the Maternal Body*, 116.
10. Cixous, "Sorties: Out and Out: Attacks/Ways Out/Forays," 95.
11. Michelle Boulous Walker, *Philosophy and the Maternal Body*, 109.
12. Cixous, "Sorties: Out and Out: Attacks/Ways Out/Forays," 97.
13. Spacks, "The Woman as Artist," 102.
14. Berlin, *Generations of Captivity*, 14.
15. van den Berghe, *Race and Racism: A Comparative Perspective*, 77.

Chapter 1. Phillis Wheatley's Seminaked Body as Symbol and Metaphor

1. Young, *Colonial Desire: Hybridity in Theory, Culture, and Race*, 29.
2. Michelle Boulous Walker, *Philosophy and the Maternal Body*, 135.
3. Reid-Pharr, *Conjugal Union*, 3–8; Adeeko, introduction, ix.
4. Gilligan, *In a Different Voice: Psychological Theory and Women's Development*, 17–21; Collins, *Black Feminist Thought*, 22–25, 124; "Feminist Ethics," in *Stanford Encyclopedia of Philosophy*, 13.
5. Adeeko, "Writing Africa under the Shadow of Slavery: Quaque, Wheatley, and Crowther," 14.
6. Carretta, *Phillis Wheatley: Biography of a Genius in Bondage*, 43.
7. Ibid., 44.
8. Mason, ed., *The Poems of Phillis Wheatley*, 52.
9. Ibid., 175.
10. Op. cit.
11. Jordan, *White over Black: American Attitudes toward the Negro, 1550–1812*, 20, 43.
12. Op. cit.
13. Carretta, *Phillis Wheatley: Biography of a Genius in Bondage*, 60.
14. Gould, *The Mismeasure of Man*, 404–8.
15. Ibid., 20, 404–8.
16. Ibid., 406.
17. Ibid., 410, 405.
18. Op. cit.
19. Foucault, *The Order of Things*, 161.
20. Lacan, "Towards a Genetic Theory of the Ego," 222–23.
21. Gates, *The Trials of Phillis Wheatley*, 5; Gilroy, *The Black Atlantic*, 152. In *Phillis Wheatley: Biography of a Genius in Bondage*, Carretta writes, "Such an examination would have been unnecessary. Most of the men named in the 'Attestation' had demonstrable direct as well as indirect ties to Phillis Wheatley herself. They already had ample evidence of her abilities" (103).

22. Carretta, *Phillis Wheatley Poems*, 8.

23. Jefferson, *Notes on the State of Virginia*, 139–40.

24. Yellin, *The Intricate Knot: Black Figures in American Literature, 1776–1863*, 11.

25. Finkelman, *Slavery and the Founders: Race and Liberty in the Age of Jefferson*, 192.

26. Irigaray, "Female Desire," 35.

27. Bennett, "Phillis Wheatley's Vocation and the Paradox of the 'Afric Muse,'" 69.

28. Mason, ed., *The Poems of Phillis Wheatley*, 203–4.

29. Ibid., 47.

30. Carretta, *Phillis Wheatley: Biography of a Genius in Bondage*, 38.

31. Hayden, "Classical Tidings from the Afric Muse: Phillis Wheatley's Use of Greek and Roman Mythology," 433.

32. Lerner, *The Creation of Patriarchy*, 141.

33. Bates, *From Classic to Romantic: Premise of Taste in Eighteenth-Century England*, 25.

34. Davidson, *A History of West Africa*, 5, 20, 27.

35. Carretta, *Phillis Wheatley: Biography of a Genius in Bondage*, 23.

36. Odell, ed., *Memoir and Poems of Phillis Wheatley*, 12.

37. Shields, "Phillis Wheatley's Struggle for Freedom in Her Poetry and Prose," 240–42.

38. Vassa, "Interesting Narrative of the Life of Olaudah Equiano or Gustavus Vassa, the African, Written by Himself," 12.

39. Shields, "Phillis Wheatley's Theoretics of the Imagination: An Untold Chapter in the History of Early American Literary Aesthetics," 347.

40. Mason, ed., *The Poems of Phillis Wheatley*, 53.

41. Scheick, *Authority and Female Authorship in Colonial America*, 118.

42. Ibid., 119.

43. Ibid., 120.

44. Op. cit.

45. Jones [Amiri Baraka], *Home: Social Essays*, 106.

46. Alice Walker, *In Search of Our Mothers' Garden*, 235–37.

47. Lerner, *The Creation of Patriarchy*, 222.

48. Erkkila, "Phillis Wheatley and the Black American Revolution," 236.

49. Bakhtin, *The Dialogic Imagination*, 304.

50. Krieger, *The Classic Vision*, 29.

51. Caputi, *Goddesses and Monsters*, 13.

52. Pollock, *George Whitefield and the Great Awakening*, 127, 224, 240, 247–49, 257, 268.

53. Benjamin Franklin, *Autobiography*, 117–18.

54. Op. cit.

55. Aubrey Williams, ed., *Poetry and Prose of Alexander Pope*, 331.

56. Mason, ed., *The Poems of Phillis Wheatley*, 55–57.

57. Jefferson, *Notes on the State of Virginia*, 139–40.

58. Mason, ed., *The Poems of Phillis Wheatley*, 55–57.

59. Bennett, "Phillis Wheatley's Vocation and the Paradox of the 'Afric Muse,'" 69.

60. Mason, ed., *The Poems of Phillis Wheatley*, 56.

61. Carretta, *Phillis Wheatley: Biography of a Genius in Bondage*, 78.

62. Mason, ed., *The Poems of Phillis Wheatley*, 185.

63. Ibid., 196.

64. Ibid., 83.

65. Waldstreicher, "The Wheatleyan Moment," 538.

66. Benjamin Franklin, *Autobiography*, 152–53.

67. Jordan, *White over Black: American Attitudes toward the Negro, 1550–1812*, 284. See also Gates, *The Trials of Phillis Wheatley*, 40–42.

68. Clarkson, *An Essay on the Slavery and Commerce of the Human Species, Particularly the African*, 125.

69. Gilroy, *The Black Atlantic*, xl.

70. Ibid., 17.

71. Mason, ed., *The Poems of Phillis Wheatley*, 198.

72. Ibid., 171.

73. Ibid., 197.

74. Isani, "The Contemporaneous Reception of Phillis Wheatley: Newspaper and Magazine Notices during the Years of Fame, 1765–1774," 261–63.

75. Foucault, *The Order of Things*, 160.

76. Somé, *The Healing Wisdom of Africa*, 124.

77. Ibid., 183.

78. Bassard, *Spiritual Interrogations*, 37.

79. Mason, ed., *The Poems of Phillis Wheatley*, 196n.

80. Ibid., 205–6.

81. Ibid., 209–10.

82. Twine, "Bearing Blackness in Britain," 105.

83. Mason, ed., *The Poems of Phillis Wheatley*, 107–8, 84n.

84. Odell, ed., *Memoir and Poems of Phillis Wheatley*, 18.

85. Ibid., 16.

86. Carretta, *Phillis Wheatley: Biography of a Genius in Bondage*, 172–73.

87. Mason, ed., *The Poems of Phillis Wheatley*, 167.

88. Mazyck, *George Washington and the Negro*, 45, 48, 51.

89. Ellis, *Founding Brothers*, 158.

90. Mazyck, *George Washington and the Negro*, 52–53.

91. Lossing, *The Pictorial Field-Book of the American Revolution*, 556.

92. Adeeko, introduction.

93. Carretta, *Phillis Wheatley: Biography of a Genius in Bondage*, ix, 195.

94. Goodman, *Of One Blood: Abolitionism and the Origins of Racial Equality*, 59. Goodman's analysis is worth repeating: "European travel accounts revealed that Africa was no Dark Continent, but a land of impressive rulers, industrious peoples, and productive economies. A black professor at Wittenberg University in Germany, several talented mulatto and black military men who commanded the respect of Europeans, a black druggist and mathematician in England, and the poet Phillis Wheatley in America, [all] were cited as a few examples among many of the triumph of gifted blacks over prejudice. Thomas Jefferson had denied that Phillis Wheatley's 'poems have any merit,' but Lydia Maria Child thought he would have 'judged differently, had he been perfectly unprejudiced.'"

Chapter 2. Harriet Jacobs's *Incidents in the Life of a Slave Girl*

1. Fitzhugh, "Cannibals All! or Slaves without Masters," 113.

2. Foucault, *Madness and Civilization*, 250.

3. Freud, "The Ego and the Id," 643.

4. Harriet Jacobs, *Incidents in the Life of a Slave Girl*, 208 (all subsequent references to this work are taken from the Signet edition in the bibliography).

5. Patterson, *Slavery and Social Death*, 175; Deborah Gray White, *Ar'n't I a Woman*, 35.

6. Husserl, "Material Things in Their Relation to the Aesthetic Body," 29.

7. Fox-Genovese, *Within the Plantation Household*, 47, 240. For Fox-Genovese's discussion of Dr. Flint's "rape" of Jacobs, see 392. Also see Hartman, *Scenes of Subjection: Terror, Slavery, and Self-Making in Nineteenth-Century America*, 107. Other scholars who advance charges of rape include Hopkins, "Seduction or Rape: Deconstructing the Black Female Body in Harriet Jacobs' *Incidents in the Life of a Slave Girl*"; Whitsitt, "Reading between the Lines"; and Vermillion, "Re-embodying the Self: Representations of Rape in *Incidents in the Life of a Slave Girl* and *I Know Why the Caged Bird Sings*." Whitsitt and Vermillion do not present hard evidence of rape but like others postulate that, in this instance, given Jacobs's "double voice of masking in the narrative" (Whitsitt, 77) and her ability to separate her "interior self" from "her body" (Vermillion, 247), she "masks" the truth of her experiences and maintains a degree of modesty, which is important to her.

8. Fox-Genovese, *Within the Plantation Household*, 47, 240; Hartman, *Scenes of Subjection: Terror, Slavery, and Self-Making in Nineteenth-Century America*, 97–98, 107–8.

9. Yellin, *Harriet Jacobs: A Life*, 144.

10. Stauffer, The *Black Hearts of Men: Radical Abolitionists and the Transformation of Race*, 241.

11. Kofman, *The Enigma of Woman: Woman in Freud's Writings*, 36, 39.

12. Torrey, *Freudian Fraud: The Malignant Effect of Freud's Theory on American Thought and Culture*, 250.

13. Freud, "Three Essays on the Theory of Sexuality," 248. For Freud's disclaimer of prejudices against women, see his essay "On Narcissism," 554–55.

14. Grosz, *Jacques Lacan: A Feminist Introduction*, 7–8, 130–31; Chodorow, *Femininities, Masculinities, Sexualities*, 1–4.

15. Chodorow, *Femininities, Masculinities, Sexualities*, 3.

16. Micale, "On the 'Disappearance' of Hysteria: A Study in the Clinical Deconstruction of a Diagnosis," 497, 499.

17. Gay, ed., *The Freud Reader*, 239.

18. Yellin, *Harriet Jacobs: A Life*, 40.

19. Du Bois quoted in Genovese, *The World the Slaveholders Made*, 140.

20. Yellin, *Harriet Jacobs: A Life*, 4, 7.

21. Bhabha, *The Location of Culture*, 193; Bhabha, "The Postcolonial Critic," 47–63.

22. I have taken these statistics from the following works: Myrdal, *An American Dilemma*, 133; Joel Williamson, *New People: Miscegenation and Mulattoes in the United States* (1980 edition), 63; and Zack, *Race and Mixed Race*, 75.

23. Yellin, *Harriet Jacobs: A Life*, 67.

24. Yellin, ed., *Harriet Jacobs: Incidents in the Life of a Slave Girl, Written by Herself*, 237.

25. Freud, "On Narcissism," 554–55.

26. Ibid., 555.

27. Tate, *Domestic Allegories of Political Desire*, 32.

28. Douglas, *The Feminization of American Culture*, 75.

29. Penzel, *Obsessive-Compulsive Disorders*, 349.

30. Freud, "Three Essays on the Theory of Sexuality," 266.

31. Yellin, *Harriet Jacobs: A Life*, 28.

32. Freud, "Three Essays on the Theory of Sexuality," 286.

33. Yellin, *Harriet Jacobs: A Life*, 57.

34. Hegel, *The Phenomenology of Mind*, 235.

35. Ibid., 237.

36. Freud, "The Ego and the Id," 646.

37. Op. cit.

38. Deborah Gray White, *Ar'n't I a Woman*, 7.

39. Hartman, *Scenes of Subjection: Terror, Slavery, and Self-Making in Nineteenth-Century America*, 98, 107–8.

40. Yellin, *Harriet Jacobs: A Life*, 26–27.

41. Ibid., 138–39.

42. Jordan, *White over Black: American Attitudes toward the Negro, 1550–1812*, 151.

43. Yellin, *Harriet Jacobs: A Life*, 50.

44. Freud, "On Narcissism," 551, 555.

45. Yellin, "Texts and Contexts of Harriet Jacobs' *Incidents in the Life of a Slave Girl: Written by Herself*," 262–63.

46. Op. cit. and Yellin, *Harriet Jacobs: A Life*, 157. Jacobs's self-sacrificing narrative and her sincerity and truthfulness receive further praise from Robert S. Levine. He contrasts "the happy ending" of Hannah Crafts's *The Bondwoman's Narrative* (circa 1855) and its "disgust at blackness" to the conclusion of narratives written by Jacobs, Douglass, and others who found their freedom ambiguous at best, given their sufferings (especially Jacobs's) and the racism they faced. "A happy ending, yet, but a disconcerting ending, too, completely inconsistent with the more troubled and ambivalent accounts we have of 'freedom' at the end of Douglass's *Narrative*, Harriet Jacobs's *Incidents*, Harriet Wilson's *Our Nig*, and perhaps most pertinently, Webb's *The Garies and Their Friends*. *Garies* concludes with a happy marriage and group gathering of free blacks and their white abolitionist friends, though with the disturbing suggestion of black vulnerability in racist Philadelphia." See Robert S. Levine, *Dislocating Race and Nation: Episodes in Nineteenth-Century American Literary Nationalism*, 175–76.

47. Op. cit.

48. These dates are based on the year of Jacobs's pregnancy and the year of Sawyer's marriage.

49. Freud, "Three Essays on the Theory of Sexuality," 255.

50. Yellin, *Harriet Jacobs: A Life*, 130. See also John Jacobs, "A True Tale of Slavery," 212.

51. Baur, *Hypochrondria, Woeful Imaginings*, 74.

52. Andrews, ed., *Classic African American Women's Narratives*, 200.

53. Yellin, introduction, xxx.

54. Yellin, *Harriet Jacobs: A Life*, 124.

55. Meyer's theory is cited in Grob, *The Mad Among Us: A History of the Care of America's Mentally Ill*, 143.

56. Yellin, *Harriet Jacobs: A Life*, 221.

57. Ibid., 136.

58. Carby, *Reconstructing Womanhood*, 61.

59. Stewart, "Revising 'Harriet Jacobs' for 1865," 718.

60. Yellin, *Harriet Jacobs: A Life*, 136.

61. Ibid., 236.

62. Ibid., 235, 259–60.

63. Grimké, *The Journals of Charlotte Forten Grimké*, 376.

64. Yellin, *The Harriet Jacobs Family Papers*, 426. See also Caleb Smith, "Harriet Jacobs among the Militants: Transformations in Abolition's Public Sphere, 1859–1861," 745.

Chapter 3. The Maternal Ideal

1. Grimké, *The Journals of Charlotte Forten Grimké*, ed. Stevenson, 319 (all subsequent references are taken from this edition of the *Journals*).

2. Ibid.

3. Winch, *A Gentleman of Color,* 62.

4. Ibid., 63.

5. Ibid., 65.

6. Ibid., 68, 75.

7. Ibid., 75.

8. Billington, introduction, 17; Douty, *Forten, the Sailmaker: Pioneer Champion of Negro Rights,* 80–81, and Winch, *A Gentleman of Color,* 77.

9. Douty, *Forten, the Sailmaker: Pioneer Champion of Negro Rights,* 183.

10. Grimké, *The Journals of Charlotte Forten Grimké,* ed. Stevenson, 175.

11. Winch, *A Gentleman of Color,* 260.

12. Ibid., 191.

13. Ibid., 330.

14. Ibid., 191.

15. Ibid., 334.

16. Ibid., 332.

17. Jeffrey, *The Great Silent Army of Abolitionism,* 104.

18. Douglas, *The Feminization of American Culture,* 47.

19. Ibid., 111.

20. Deborah Gray White, *Ar'n't I a Woman? Female Slaves in the Plantation South,* 56; Grimké, *The Journals of Charlotte Forten Grimké,* ed. Stevenson, 29.

21. Bush, "Lady Lives? Upper Class Women's Autobiographies and the Politics of Late Victorian and Edwardian Britain . . . ," 42.

22. Atkin, "'When Pincushions Are Periodicals': Women's Work, Race, and Material Objects in Female Abolitionism," 93.

23. Sanchez-Eppler, *Touching Liberty: Abolition, Feminism and the Politics of the Body,* 20.

24. Stowe, *Uncle Tom's Cabin,* 441.

25. Jeffrey, *The Great Silent Army of Abolitionism,* 103–4.

26. Gilman, "Black Bodies, White Bodies: Toward an Iconography of Female Sexuality in Late Nineteenth-Century Art, Medicine, and Literature," 235, 238.

27. Yellin, *Harriet Jacobs: A Life,* 149.

28. Jeffrey, *The Great Silent Army of Abolitionism,* 44.

29. Ibid., 64.

30. Gatewood, *Aristocrats of Color,* 7.

31. Butterfield, *Black Autobiography in America,* 2–3.

32. Ibid., 201.

33. Braxton, *Black Women Writing Autobiography,* 84, 90; Stevenson, introduction, in Stevenson, ed., *The Journals of Charlotte Forten Grimké,* 33.

34. Braxton, *Black Women Writing Autobiography,* 85. Also see Dunbar, *A Fragile Freedom: African American Women and Emancipation in the Antebellum City,* 148.

35. Gatewood, *Aristocrats of Color,* 8.

36. Du Bois, *The Souls of Black Folk,* 23.

37. Andrews, *To Tell a Free Story,* 196.

38. Pascal, *Design and Truth in Autobiography,* 5, 12.

39. Op. cit.

40. Op. cit.

41. Jeffrey, *The Great Silent Army of Abolitionism*, 174. For a discussion of Frederick Doug-lass's position on the possibility of blacks immigrating to Haiti upon the infamous Dred Scott decision and his own travels to England after John Brown's revolt, see also Robert S. Levine, *Dislocating Race and Nation: Episodes in Nineteenth-Century American Literary Nationalism*, 194–95.

42. Winch, *A Gentleman of Color*, 93.

43. Culley, *A Day at a Time: The Diary Literature of American Women from 1764 to the Present*, 10.

44. Winch, *A Gentleman of Color*, 347.

45. Ibid., 259.

46. Tompkins, *Sensational Designs . . .* , 123

47. This is a constant description in Journals 1, 2, and 3.

48. Dever, *Death and the Mother from Dickens to Freud*, 111. See also Freud, "Inhibitions," 130, 137.

49. Dever, *Death and the Mother from Dickens to Freud*, 7, 28.

50. Winch, *A Gentleman of Color*, 346.

51. Ibid., 345–46.

52. Chodorow, *The Reproduction of Mothering: Psychoanalysis and the Sociology of Gender*, 71, 86.

53. Peterson, *"Doers of the Word": African-American Women Speakers and Writers in the North (1830–1880)*, 219.

54. Ginzberg, *Women and the Work of Benevolence: Morality, Politics, and Class in the Nineteenth-Century United States*, 130, 139.

55. Von Frank, *The Trials of Anthony Burns*, 216.

56. Ibid., 181–82.

57. Ibid., 184.

58. Ibid., 199.

59. Ibid., 212.

60. Ibid., 205–6.

61. Op. cit.

62. Ibid., 194, 206.

63. Forten, *The Journal of Charlotte Forten*, ed. Billington, 24.

64. King, "I Have a Dream," 628.

65. Pascal, *Design and Truth in Autobiography*, 186.

66. Edmund Wilson, *Patriotic Gore: Studies in the Literature of the Civil War*, 240, 242.

67. Woods, *Black Majority*, 124.

68. Foner, *Reconstruction: America's Unfinished Revolution, 1863–1877*, 2.

69. Berg, *Mothering the Race: Women's Narratives of Reproduction, 1890–1930*, 18.

70. Ginzberg, *Women and the Work of Benevolence: Morality, Politics, and Class in the Nineteenth-Century United States*, 139.

71. Op. cit.

72. Sterling, ed., *We Are Your Sisters: Black Women in the Nineteenth Century*, 281.

73. Op. cit.

74. Ibid., 282.

75. Ibid.

76. Woods, *Black Majority*, 124.

77. Peterson, *"Doers of the Word": African-American Women Speakers and Writers in the North (1830–1880)*, 192.

78. Forten, "Life on the Sea Islands," 370–71.

---

79. Peterson, *"Doers of the Word": African-American Women Speakers and Writers in the North (1830–1880)*, 192, 219.

80. Sterling, ed., *We Are Your Sisters: Black Women in the Nineteenth Century*, 258.

81. Forten, "Life on the Sea Islands," 364. For further information on the topic of black women's labor of love in slavery and freedom, see Jacqueline Jones's award-winning study, *Labor of Love, Labor of Sorrow: Black Women, Work, and the Family, from Slavery to the Present*.

82. Peterson, *"Doers of the Word": African-American Women Speakers and Writers in the North (1830–1880)*, 192. See also Towne, *Letters and Diary of Laura M. Towne: Written from the Sea Islands of South Carolina, 1862–1884*, 310.

83. Stauffer, *The Black Hearts of Men: Radical Abolitionists and the Transformation of Race*, 21.

84. McFeely, *Frederick Douglass*, 383. In a previous publication—Moore, "When Meanings Meet: The Journals of Charlotte Forten Grimké"—I mistakenly cited Susan B. Anthony and not Elizabeth Cady Stanton as the author of this quotation.

85. Xavier, "Engaging George Campbell's Sympathy in the Rhetoric of Charlotte Forten and Ann Plato, African-American Women in the Antebellum North," 438.

86. Foner, *The Fiery Trial: Abraham Lincoln and American Slavery*, 290.

Chapter 4: Antiblack Aesthetics

1. McMahon, "Beauty," 232.

2. Du Bois, "Criteria of Negro Art," 753; Du Bois, *The Souls of Black Folk*, 10.

3. van den Berghe, *Race and Racism: A Comparative Perspective*, 18; Chinn, *Technology and the Logic of American Racism: A Cultural History of the Body as Evidence*, 80.

4. Robert E. Washington, *The Ideologies of African American Literature*, 45.

5. Huggins, *Harlem Renaissance*, 6–9, 53.

6. Lewis, *W. E. B. Du Bois: The Fight for Equality and the American Century, 1919–1963*, 180.

7. Op. cit.

8. Lowe, *Jump at the Sun: Zora Neale Hurston's Cosmic Comedy*, 142.

9. Kaplan, ed., *Zora Neale Hurston: A Life in Letters*, 518.

10. Foster, ed., "Postmodernism: A Preface," xv.

11. Du Bois, "The Black Codes," 409.

12. Michaels, "The Souls of White Folk," 188.

13. Blackmer, "The Veils of the Law: Race and Sexuality in Nella Larsen's Passing," 50.

14. Michaels, "The Souls of White Folk," 188–89.

15. Woodward, *The Strange Career of Jim Crow*, 70.

16. Ibid., 70–71.

17. Berlant, "National Brands/National Body: Imitation of Life," 131.

18. Cowan and McGuire, *Timelines of African American History*, 125–26.

19. Jordan, *The White Man's Burden*, 6.

20. Locke, "The New Negro," 966.

21. Kovel, *White Racism: A Psychohistory*, 18–19.

22. Ibid., 18.

23. Honour, ed., *The Image of the Black in Western Art*, vol. 4, *From the American Revolution to World War I*, 62.

24. Long, "The Outer Reaches: The White Writer and Blacks in the Twenties," 76.

25. Hutchinson, *The Harlem Renaissance in Black and White*, 21.

26. Klinkner and Smith, *The Unsteady March: The Rise and Decline of Racial Equality in America*, 9, 120–21.

27. Op. cit.

28. Hutchinson, *The Harlem Renaissance in Black and White*, 78.

29. Booker T. Washington, *Up from Slavery*, 85.

30. Du Bois, *The Souls of Black Folk*, 32.

31. Booker T. Washington, *Up from Slavery*, 86.

32. Harlan, ed., *The Booker T. Washington Papers*, vol. 1, *The Autobiographical Writings*, 96.

33. Kant, "Analytic of the Aesthetical Judgment," 130–31.

34. Du Bois, "Criteria of Negro Art," 757.

35. Turner, "W. E. B. Du Bois and the Theory of a Black Aesthetic," 46–54.

36. Du Bois, "Criteria of Negro Art," 757–58.

37. Adorno, *Aesthetic Theory*, 4.

38. Op. cit.

39. Although he uses the term "ungrammatical profundity" in another context, I borrow from Martin Luther King Jr's "Letter from a Birmingham Jail," 1865.

40. Larsen, *The Complete Fiction of Nella Larsen*, ed. Charles R. Larson, 56 (all subsequent references to Larsen's novels are taken from this source).

41. Baker, *Afro-American Poetics: Revisions of Harlem and the Black Aesthetic*, 166.

42. Sylvander, *Jessie Redmon Fauset, Black American Writer*, 31.

43. Robert E. Washington, *The Ideologies of African American Literature*, 45.

44. Sylvander, *Jessie Redmon Fauset, Black American Writer*, 47.

45. Ibid., 59.

46. Du Bois, "The Immediate Problem of the American Negro," 312.

47. Braithwaite, "The Novels of Jessie Fauset," 28.

48. Bone, *The Negro Novel in America*, 101–2.

49. Carby, *Reconstructing Womanhood*, 168; Christian, *Black Women Novelists: The Development of a Tradition, 1892–1976*, 41; duCille, *The Coupling Convention*, 87, 93.

50. Sylvander, *Jessie Redmon Fauset, Black American Writer*, 34.

51. Op. cit.

52. Goldman, *The Feminist Aesthetics of Virginia Woolf*, 118–19.

53. Jordan, *The White Man's Burden*, 70.

54. McDowell, *"The Changing Same": Black Women's Literature, Criticism, and Theory*, 61.

55. Gayle, *The Way of the New World*, 127. Gayle much preferred Hurston and her folk naturalism. See his article "Zora Neale Hurston: The Politics of Freedom."

56. Ahlin, *The 'New Negro' in the Old World: Culture and Performance in James Weldon Johnson, Jessie Fauset, and Nella Larsen*, 79–81.

57. Kuenz, "The Face of America: Performing Race and Nation in Jessie Fauset's *There Is Confusion*," 95–96, 97.

58. Kallen, "Democracy versus the Melting-Pot, Part One and Part Two," 217–20.

59. Kallen, "Excerpts," 3–4, 7.

60. Ibid., 3.

61. Kallen, "Democracy versus the Melting-Pot, Part One and Part Two," 217.

62. Kallen, "Excerpts," 3.

63. Gilbert and Gubar, "Ain't I a New Woman: Feminism and the Harlem Renaissance," 135.

64. Carby, *Reconstructing Womanhood*, 168.

65. Kuenz, "The Face of America: Performing Race and Nation in Jessie Fauset's *There Is Confusion*," 94–96.

66. Logan, *The Betrayal of the Negro*, 62; van den Berghe, *Race and Racism: A Comparative Perspective*, 15.

67. Ruddick, "Maternal Thinking," 214.

68. Ruddick, *Maternal Thinking: Toward a Politics of Peace*, 25.

69. Bone, *The Negro Novel in America*, 101.

70. McDowell, *"The Changing Same": Black Women's Literature, Criticism, and Theory*, 65.

71. Fabi, *Passing and the Rise of the African American Novel*, 105.

72. Brown, *Clotel, or The President's Daughter*, 6–8.

73. Christian, *Black Women Novelists: The Development of a Tradition, 1892–1976*, 44; Carby, *Reconstructing Womanhood*, 110.

74. Watson, "Twentieth-Century Mulatto Image: Novels of Passing, Protest, and the Black Bourgeoisie," 1–18.

75. Bernstein, *The Fate of Art: Aesthetic Alienation from Kant to Derrida and Adorno*, 17–18.

76. Ruddick, "Maternal Thinking," 214.

77. Joel Williamson, *New People: Miscegenation and Mulattoes in the United States* (1980 and 1995 editions), 119.

78. Op. cit.

79. "Editorial and Opinion," *Crisis*, April 15, 1915, 276–85.

80. Klinkner and Smith, *The Unsteady March: The Rise and Decline of Racial Equality in America*, 118.

81. Ibid., 119.

82. duCille, *The Coupling Convention*, 94–96; McDowell, *"The Changing Same": Black Women's Literature, Criticism, and Theory*, 75.

83. McDowell, *"The Changing Same": Black Women's Literature, Criticism, and Theory*, 75.

84. Grosz, *Volatile Bodies*, 117.

85. Cheryl Wall, *Women of the Harlem Renaissance*, 75, 216n.

86. Foster, ed., "Postmodernism: A Preface," xv.

87. McDowell, *"The Changing Same": Black Women's Literature, Criticism, and Theory*, 75.

88. Sylvander, *Jessie Redmon Fauset, Black American Writer*, 62, 84.

89. Kant, *Critique of Judgement*, 167.

90. Ibid., 166.

91. duCille, *The Coupling Convention*, 89.

92. Carby, *Reconstructing Womanhood*, 167.

93. Bone, *The Negro Novel in America*, 102.

94. duCille, *The Coupling Convention*, 88.

95. Kernal, *Kant's Aesthetic Theory*, 112.

96. Adorno, *Aesthetic Theory*, 57.

97. Hull, *Color, Sex and Poetry*, 17.

98. Thadious Davis, introduction, xvi, xvii.

99. Robert E. Washington, *Ideologies*, 78.

100. Lott, *Love and Theft: Blackface Minstrelsy and the American Working Class*, 119.

101. Ibid., 29

102. Ibid., 30.

103. Thadious Davis, introduction, xix.

104. Berg, *Mothering the Race: Women's Narratives of Reproduction, 1890–1930*, 128, 103.

105. Ahlin, *The 'New Negro' in the Old World: Culture and Performance in James Weldon Johnson, Jessie Fauset, and Nella Larsen*, 93.

106. Hostetler, "The Aesthetics of Race and Gender in Nella Larsen's *Quicksand*," 36.

107. Op. cit.

108. Thadious Davis, *Nella Larsen, Novelist of the Harlem Renaissance*, 27.

109. Charles R. Larson, introduction, in Larson, ed., *The Complete Fiction of Nella Larsen*, xii.

110. Op. cit.

111. Thadious Davis, *Nella Larsen, Novelist of the Harlem Renaissance*, 454.

112. See "Bans on Interracial Unions Offer Perspective on Gay Ones," *New York Times*, March 17, 2004. States with interracial bans struck down by the Supreme Court decision of 1967 included all southern states from West Virginia to Florida and Texas along with Oklahoma but also Missouri and Delaware.

113. Blackmer, "The Veils of the Law: Race and Sexuality in Nella Larsen's Passing," 50.

114. Senna, *Caucasia*, 303.

115. Thadious Davis, *Nella Larsen, Novelist of the Harlem Renaissance*, 27.

116. Sidonie Smith, *Subjectivity, Identity, and the Body: Women's Autobiographical Practices in the Twentieth Century*, 16.

117. Op. cit.

118. Stevens, "Sunday Morning," in Meyer, ed., *Poetry: An Introduction*, 427–29.

119. Thadious Davis, *Nella Larsen, Novelist of the Harlem Renaissance*, 280–81.

120. "Immanuel Kant (1724–1804): 'Theory of Aesthetics and Teleology' (*The Critique of Judgment*)."

121. Gayle, *The Way of the New World*, 126–27.

122. Horowitz, *New World Symphony: Dvorak in New York and Boston*.

123. Hayden White, "The Value of Narrativity in the Representation of Reality," 1.

124. Op. cit.

125. Thadious Davis, *Nella Larsen, Novelist of the Harlem Renaissance*, 4.

126. Hutchinson, *In Search of Nella Larsen: A Biography of the Color Line*, 224–39. See also Hutchinson's essay "*Quicksand* and the Racial Labyrinth," 543–44, 548.

127. Tanner, "Intimate Geography: The Body, Race, and Space in Larsen's *Quicksand*," 180.

128. Hutchinson, "*Quicksand* and the Racial Labyrinth," 547.

129. Thadious Davis, *Nella Larsen, Novelist of the Harlem Renaissance*, 7.

130. Ibid., 260–61.

131. In *An American Dilemma*, Myrdal writes, "True, there has developed recently a glorification of things African, especially in music and art, and there was a back-to-Africa movement after the First World War. But this is a reaction to discrimination from white people, on the one hand, and a result of encouragement from white people, on the other hand. Thus, even the positive movement away from American culture has its source in that culture. Negro race pride and race prejudice serve to fortify the Negro against white superiority" (928).

132. Tate, *Psychoanalysis and Black Novels*, 134; Tate, "Desire and Death in *Quicksand*, by Nella Larsen," 246.

133. Hutchinson, "*Quicksand* and the Racial Labyrinth," 570.

134. Tate, *Psychoanalysis and Black Novels*, 134–38.

135. Ibid., 132–33, 135, 138, 141.

136. Ibid., 131.

137. Op. cit.

138. Op. cit.

139. Ibid., 135.

140. Ibid., 140.

141. Kristeva, *Powers of Horror: An Essay on Abjection*, 13.

142. Kristeva, "Stabat Mater," 161.

143. Ibid.

144. Hayden White, "The Value of Narrativity in the Representation of Reality," 10.

145. Dever, *Death and the Mother from Dickens to Freud*, 45–46.

146. Ibid., 45.

147. Hutchinson, "*Quicksand* and the Racial Labyrinth," 566.

148. Cheryl Wall, *Women of the Harlem Renaissance*, 125–28.

149. Ibid., 131, 127.

150. James F. Wilson, *Bulldaggers, Pansies, and Chocolate Babies: Performance, Race, and Sexuality in the Harlem Renaissance*, 109–10.

151. McDowell, "*The Changing Same*": *Black Women's Literature, Criticism, and Theory*, 90.

152. Op. cit.

153. Butler, *Bodies That Matter*, 169; Thaggert, *Images of Black Modernism: Verbal and Visual Strategies of the Harlem Renaissance*, 67.

154. Thadious Davis, *Nella Larsen, Novelist of the Harlem Renaissance*, 325.

155. Op. cit.

156. Thadious Davis, *Nella Larsen, Novelist of the Harlem Renaissance*, 326.

157. I am basing my hypothesis on an account given of Negro spotters hired by white management in Washington, D.C., in 1922, discussed briefly in Adele Logan Alexander's family biography *Homelands and Waterways: The American Journey of the Bond Family, 1846–1926*, 455.

158. Twain, *The Tragedy of Pudd'nhead Wilson and the Comedy of Those Extraordinary Twins*, 140.

159. Berlant, "National Brands/National Body: Imitation of Life," 111.

160. Adorno, *Aesthetic Theory*, 88.

161. Berzon, *Neither White nor Black*, 143.

162. Litwack, *How Free Is Free? The Long Death of Jim Crow*, 39.

163. Bentley, *The Life of the Drama*, 241, 244.

164. Bermel, *Farce: A History from Aristophanes to Woody Allen*, 23.

165. McLendon, *The Politics of Color in the Fiction of Jessie Fauset and Nella Larsen*, 96.

166. Glasgow, *Madness, Masks, and Laughter: An Essay on Comedy*, 165.

167. Lewis and Ardizzone, *Love on Trial: An American Scandal in Black and White*, 161.

168. Ibid., 196.

169. Ibid., 133.

170. Jessica Milner Davis, *Farce*, 23.

171. Boyd, *Wrapped in Rainbows: The Life of Zora Neale Hurston*, 22.

172. Hemenway, *Zora Neale Hurston: A Literary Biography*, 56.

173. Ibid., 241, 273.

174. Ibid., 330.

175. Bone, *Down Home: A History of Afro-American Short Fiction from Its Beginning to the End of the Harlem Renaissance*, 123.

176. Simpson, ed., *The Local Colorists*, 1.

177. Op. cit.

178. Hurston, *Dust Tracks on the Road* (1984 edition), 18, 62.

179. Hurston, *Dust Tracks on the Road* (1995 edition), 600.

180. Hurston, "How It Feels to Be Colored Me," 153.

181. Hurston, "My Most Humiliating Jim Crow Experience," 163.

182. Montagu, *Man's Most Dangerous Myth: The Fallacy of Race*, 15.

183. Frydman, "Zora Neale Hurston, Biographical Criticism, and African Diasporic Vernacular Culture," 99.

184. Hurston, *Mules and Men* (1995), 83.

185. Hurston, *Mules and Men* (1978), 66–69.

186. Eagleton, *The Ideology of the Aesthetic,* 264.

187. Plant, *Every Tub Must Sit on Its Bottom,* 148–49.

188. Plant, *Zora Neale Hurston: A Biography of the Spirit,* 169.

189. Joel Williamson, *New People: Miscegenation and Mulattoes in the United States* (1980 and 1995 editions),111–13.

190. Hurston, *Moses, Man of the Mountain,* 577.

191. Hurston, *Dust Tracks on the Road* (1995), 733.

192. Ibid., 948.

193. Sylvander, *Jessie Redmon Fauset, Black American Writer,* 109.

194. Bone, *Down Home: A History of Afro-American Short Fiction from Its Beginning to the End of the Harlem Renaissance,* 140.

195. Kirschke, *Art in Crisis: W. E. B. Du Bois and the Struggle for African American Identity and Memory,* 143.

196. Carby, "The Politics of Fiction, Anthropology, and the Folk: Zora Neale Hurston," 80.

197. Davidson, *A History of West Africa,* 164.

198. Welch, *Africa: Before They Came,* 288.

199. Lawrence Levine, *Black Culture and Black Consciousness,* 112.

200. Op. cit.

201. Plant, *Every Tub Must Sit on Its Bottom,* 163.

202. Hurston, *Dust Tracks on the Road* (1995), 618.

203. Lowe, *Jump at the Sun: Zora Neale Hurston's Cosmic Comedy,* 147.

204. Ibid., 145.

205. Lacan, "The Signification of the Phallus," 282.

206. Hurston, *Jonah's Gourd Vine,* in *Hurston: Folklore, Memoirs, and Other Writings,* ed. Cheryl Wall, 31, 103 (subsequent references to this novel are taken from this edition).

207. Lowe, *Jump at the Sun: Zora Neale Hurston's Cosmic Comedy,* 136.

208. Hayden White, "The Value of Narrativity in the Representation of Reality," 19.

209. Hurston, "Sweat," 1003.

210. Ibid., 1001.

211. Plant, *Every Tub Must Sit on Its Bottom,* 163.

212. Booker T. Washington, *Up from Slavery,* 31, 41. See also Lowe, *Jump at the Sun: Zora Neale Hurston's Cosmic Comedy,* 98.

213. Plant, *Every Tub Must Sit on Its Bottom,* 121.

214. Lowe, *Jump at the Sun: Zora Neale Hurston's Cosmic Comedy,* 98.

215. Ibid.

216. Ibid., 123.

217. Hurston, *Dust Tracks on the Road* (1984 edition), 44–45.

218. Ibid., 48–49.

219. Lowe, *Jump at the Sun: Zora Neale Hurston's Cosmic Comedy,* 127.

220. Hemenway, *Zora Neale Hurston: A Literary Bibliography,* 231.

221. Boyd, *Wrapped in Rainbows: The Life of Zora Neale Hurston,* 271.

222. Hemenway, *Zora Neale Hurston: A Literary Biography,* 231.

223. Gates, *Signifying Monkey,* 184–85, 194, 198.

224. Ibid., 184–85.

225. Lowe, *Jump at the Sun: Zora Neale Hurston's Cosmic Comedy*, 156.

226. Hite, "Romance, Marginality, and Matrilineage: *The Color Purple* and *Their Eyes Were Watching God*," 48.

227. Kristeva, "About Chinese Women," 146.

228. Kawash, *Dislocating the Color Line: Identity, Hybridity, and Singularity in African-American Narrative*, 179.

229. Ibid.

230. Gen. 6:17.

231. Kawash, *Dislocating the Color Line: Identity, Hybridity, and Singularity in African-American Narrative*, 179.

232. Cheung, "Don't Tell: Imposed Silences in *The Color Purple* and *The Woman Warrior*," 162–74.

233. Lowe, *Jump at the Sun: Zora Neale Hurston's Cosmic Comedy*, 159.

234. Gen. 3:3.

235. Exod. 34:35.

236. Kristeva, "Stabat Mater," 161.

237. DuPlessis, "Power, Judgment, and Narrative in a Work of Zora Neale Hurston: Feminist Cultural Studies," 82.

238. Hurston, *Mules and Men* (1978 edition), 82.

239. Sollors, *Ethnic Modernism*, 60.

240. Macharia, "Queering Helga Crane: Black Nativism in Nella Larsen's *Quicksand*," 263, 258.

241. Op. cit.

242. Farebrother, *The Collage Aesthetic in the Harlem Renaissance*, 16, 17, 9, 115.

243. Carby, *Reconstructing Womanhood*, 174.

Chapter 5: Maternal Imprinting

1. Marshall, *Praisesong for the Widow*, 37 (all subsequent references to Marshall's texts are from works as cited in the bibliography).

2. Thorsson, "Dancing up a Nation: Paule Marshall's *Praisesong for the Widow*," 644–52. In regard to the dismantling of Jim Crow laws, in Kenneth B. Clark's essay "A Racial Progress and Retreat: A Personal Memoir," the social psychologist writes that while the Supreme Court voted unanimously to end Jim Crow segregation in 1954, with the famous *Brown v. Board of Education* case in Topeka, Kansas, the "euphoria was eclipsed." De facto segregation was the result in many northern as well as southern cities, a Herrenvolk democracy. Clark remarks, "The complexity and depth of American racism were reflected in the fact that, even while the Brown decision was opening doors to the civil rights movement, the seeds of racial backlash were being sown" (15).

3. Cruse, *The Crisis of the Negro Intellectual*, 207.

4. Ibid., 198.

5. Dance, "An Interview with Paule Marshall," 2.

6. Cudjoe, *Caribbean Women Writers*, 11.

7. Lowenthal, *West Indian Societies*, 42. See also Beckles, "Kalinago (Carib) Resistance to European Colonization of the Caribbean," 120.

8. Prince, *The History of Mary Prince, a West Indian Slave (Related by Herself)*, 191n.

9. Dance, "An Interview with Paule Marshall," 4.

10. Fanon, *The Wretched of the Earth*, 239–40, 232.

11. Simone A. James Alexander, *Mother Imagery in the Novels of Afro-Caribbean Women*, 8.

12. Church, *Language and the Discovery of Reality*, 39–40.

13. Barthes, *Image, Music, Text*, 32.

14. Campbell, *Myths to Live By,* 45–46.

15. Rich, *Of Woman Born,* 225–26, 237.

16. Kasinitz, *Caribbean New York,* 91. For a discussion of Anzia Yezierska and Paule Marshall, see Arthur Paris, "The Transatlantic Metropolis and the Voices of Caribbean Women," 84.

17. Tan, *The Joy Luck Club,* 142.

18. Hacker, *Two Nations,* 202.

19. Tan, *The Joy Luck Club,* 142.

20. Kasinitz, *Caribbean New York,* 42.

21. Wade-Gayles, "The Truths of Our Mothers' Lives: Mother-Daughter Relationships in Black Women's Fiction," 9.

22. Herman, *Too Long a Child: The Mother-Daughter Dyad,* 292.

23. Mary Helen Washington, "I Sign My Mother's Name." Washington argues that white feminists reveal a "bias toward Western white models [such as the Great Mother archetypal tale], which ignore African mythology" in illuminating the mother-daughter dyad. Yet, Washington confesses, "Without sufficient knowledge of African myths, I cannot trace Marshall's symbols back to their ultimate African sources," 159–60.

24. Rich, *Of Woman Born,* 225–26, 237.

25. Mary Helen Washington, "I Sign My Mother's Name," 160.

26. Barksdale, "Castration Symbolism in Recent Black American Fiction," 407.

27. Brecht, *Bertoldt Brecht Collected Plays,* 137.

28. Ellison, *Invisible Man,* 16.

29. Dance, "An Interview with Paule Marshall," 8.

30. Jung, "Phenomenology of the Self," 150; Kolar, "The (Post) Colonial Search for the Identity of Caribbean American (Grand) Daughters," 100.

31. Spillers, "*Chosen Place, Timeless People:* Some Figurations on the New World," 152.

32. Barthold, *Black Time,* 9, 10, 15.

33. Pettis, *Toward Wholeness in Paule Marshall's Fiction,* 1.

34. Kiple, *The Caribbean Slave,* 106.

35. Hamshere, *The British in the Caribbean,* 202.

36. Lowenthal, *West Indian Societies,* 5.

37. Ibid., 59.

38. Ibid., 46.

39. Op. cit.

40. Lamming, *In the Castle of My Skin,* xii.

41. Fanon, *Black Skin, White Masks,* 150.

42. Lowenthal, *West Indian Societies,* 39.

43. Ramchand, *The West Indian Novel and Its Background,* 4.

44. Dunn, *Sugar and Slaves,* 258.

45. Sandiford, "Paule Marshall's *Praisesong for the Widow:* The Reluctant Heiress, or Whose Life Is It Anyway," 373.

46. Barthold, *Black Time,* 9, 10, 15.

47. Davidson, *A History of West Africa,* 95–96.

48. Sandiford, "Paule Marshall's *Praisesong for the Widow:* The Reluctant Heiress, or Whose Life Is It Anyway," 380.

49. Campbell, *Myths to Live By,* 44.

50. Busia, "What Is Your Nation? Reconnecting Africa and Her Diaspora through Paule Marshall's *Praisesong for the Widow,*" 198. For Marshall's experience in Carriacou, see Marshall, *Triangular Road:*

A Memoir, 147. See also Pollard, "The World of Spirits in the Work of Some Caribbean Writers in the Diaspora," 27.

51. Brathwaite, "The African Presence in Caribbean Literature," 23.

52. Clement and Kristeva, *The Feminine and the Sacred,* 24.

53. McNeil, "The Gullah Seeker's Journey in Paule Marshall's *Praisesong for the Widow,*" 185.

54. Couser, "Oppression and Repression: Personal and Collective Memory in Paule Marshall's *Praisesong for the Widow* and Leslie Marmon Silko's *Ceremony,*" 108.

55. Sandiford, "Paule Marshall's *Praisesong for the Widow:* The Reluctant Heiress, or Whose Life Is It Anyway," 76, 384.

56. Cott, *The Grounding of Modern Feminism,* 9.

57. Harper, "The Colored People in America," 100.

58. Gutman, *The Black Family in Slavery and Freedom, 1750–1925,* 79.

59. Dance, "An Interview with Paule Marshall," 2, 4.

60. Hathaway, *Caribbean Waves: Relocating Claude McKay and Paule Marshall,* 123, 22.

61. Denniston, *The Fiction of Paule Marshall,* 165.

62. Lyotard, "The Postmodern Condition," 510.

63. Dance, "An Interview with Paule Marshall," 4, 19.

64. Rogoff, *The Cultural Nature of Human Development,* 17.

65. Nice, *Mothers and Daughters: The Distortion of a Relationship,* 79.

66. Pettis, *Toward Wholeness in Paule Marshall's Fiction,* 85.

67. Carissa Turner Smith, "Women's Spiritual Geographies of the African Diaspora: Paule Marshall's *Praisesong for the Widow,*" 720.

Chapter 6: The Phallic Maternal

1. Alice Walker, *The Color Purple,* 276 (all subsequent references to Walker's texts are from works included in the bibliography). The second quotation here is taken from Jung, "Aion: Phenomenology of the Self (The Ego, the Shadow, the Syzygy: *Anima/Animus*)," 151.

2. Litwack, *How Free Is Free? The Long Death of Jim Crow,* 130, 131.

3. Butler, *Bodies That Matter,* 1.

4. Jung, "Aion: Phenomenology of the Self," 152.

5. Kristeva, "Stabat Mater"; Irigaray, "This Sex Which Is Not One." Also see Mitchell and Rose, *Feminine Sexuality: Jacques Lacan and the école freudienne;* Mitchell, introduction, 17; and Grosz, *Jacques Lacan: A Feminist Introduction.* Grosz is among the first to argue that Juliet Mitchell's *Psychoanalysis and Feminism,* 1974, despite its problems, was responsible for the "radical rupture" in feminism regarding psychoanalysis (19).

6. Lacan, "The Signification of the Phallus," 285–87. See also Muller and Richardson, *Lacan and Language,* 3, 20–22.

7. Johnson, "The Frame of Reference: Poe, Lacan, Derrida," 243.

8. Alice Walker, afterword, 343. See also Wan Yahya et al., "Gender Representation in Alice Walker's Selected Novels," 238.

9. Irigaray, "This Sex Which Is Not One." Irigaray locates the "effects of the submission of humanity to the snares of language" in psychoanalytical discourse as that which must be resisted (103).

10. Jung, "Aion: Phenomenology of the Self," 142–43.

11. Ibid., 154.

12. Ibid., 142, 127.

13. Gaines, *Uplifting the Race: Black Leadership, Politics, and Culture in the Twentieth Century,* 255.

14. Jenkins, "Queering Black Patriarchy: The Salvific Wish and Masculine Possibility in Alice Walker's *The Color Purple*," 971.

15. Gaines, *Uplifting the Race: Black Leadership, Politics, and Culture in the Twentieth Century*, 235.

16. Muscio, *Cunt: A Declaration of Independence*, 1.

17. Jung, "Aion: Phenomenology of the Self," 145–47.

18. Op. cit.

19. Lauret, *Alice Walker*, 57.

20. Melissa Walker, *Down from the Mountaintop: Black Women's Novels in the Wake of the Civil Rights Movement, 1966–1989*, 110–11.

21. Alice Walker, *We Are the Ones We Have Been Waiting For*, 166.

22. Gatens, "Power, Bodies and Difference," 229.

23. King, *Why We Can't Wait*, 62, 64.

24. Nadel, "Reading the Body: *Meridian* and the Archeology of Self," 156, 158–59.

25. Also see Privett, "Dystopic Bodies and Enslaved Motherhood," 258.

26. Reference made to Alice Walker's *By the Light of My Father's Smile*.

27. Holt, *Alice Walker Banned*; Weir, "10 Most Hated Books."

28. Curtis D. Smith, *Jung's Quest for Wholeness*, 77.

29. Litwack, *How Free Is Free? The Long Death of Jim Crow*, 4–5.

30. Gates, "Color Me Zora," 243; Wendy Wall, "Lettered Bodies and Corporeal Texts," 262.

31. Cohn, *Transparent Minds: Narrative Modes for Presenting Consciousness in Fiction*, 26, 151. Cohn makes a distinction between the narrating and experiencing selves as set forth in the chapters "Psycho-Narration" and "Retrospective Techniques." He discusses the "range between two principal types: one dominated by a prominent narrator who, even as he focuses intently on an individual psyche, remains emphatically distanced from the consciousness he narrates" (26). However, Walker frequently ruptures this distance and attempts to merge the two Celies to reveal a single-minded consciousness and a whole rather than a split-conscious body. Walker is not totally successful as we see with the mature Celie still referring to men as "frogs." The second quote of the rebellion of Celie's letter writing is taken from McKever-Floyd, "'Tell Nobody but God': The Theme of Transformation in *The Color Purple*," 427.

32. Barker, *The Culture of Violence: Essays on Tragedy and History*, 113; Russell, "Homeward Bound: Transformative Spaces in *The Color Purple*," 196.

33. Chambers, "Narratorial Authority and 'The Purloined Letter,'" 285.

34. Irigaray, "This Sex Which Is Not One," 249.

35. Ibid., 252. See also Irigaray, *To Speak Is Never Neutral*, 94.

36. Butler, "The Lesbian Phallus and the Morphological Imaginary," 64–65. Also see de Lauretis, "Sexual Indifference and Lesbian Representation," 155–56.

37. hooks, "Reading and Resistance: *The Color Purple*," 285.

38. Barbara Smith, "The Truth That Never Hurts: Black Lesbians in Fiction in the 1980s," 50. While citing the "complex simplicity" of the novel, as does bell hooks, Smith, unlike hooks, hails the book as addressing an issue of sexual identity already prevalent in society, but she believes that Walker, a bisexual, did not go far enough. In Walker's refusal to address the polemics against lesbianism and, therefore, posit its legitimacy and disarm critics such as hooks, *The Color Purple* is "entirely lacking in self-scrutiny about the implications of lesbian identity" (62). Therefore, Smith essentially agrees with hooks, but for different reasons.

39. Lippa, *Gender, Nature, and Nurture*, 48.

40. Cohn, *Transparent Minds: Narrative Modes for Presenting Consciousness in Fiction*, 153.

41. Evelyn C. White, *Alice Walker: A Life*, 424. See also Dole, "The Return of the Father in Spielberg's *The Color Purple*." Dole accuses Spielberg of "white male supremacist fantasies" in the movie's depiction of black men (1).

42. Derrida, "The Purveyor of Truth," 188. I borrow the term "rephallization" from this essay on Edgar Allan Poe's work and Lacan's primary of the phallus, where Derrida quotes from Lacan: "Let us recall where Freud spells it out: on the mother's lack of a penis in which the nature of the phallus is revealed." He then responds, "After treating the Law and fetishism as a process of rephallicizing the mother (what has been stolen or detached from her)" must be returned.

43. Young-Bruehl, introduction. Here I am referring to Young-Bruehl's criticism of the "pleasure principle" as a sexual drive, governing "the sexual instinct in all its form."

44. Understandably, black male critics who read *The Color Purple* as thematically unrelenting in its attack on black men are not entirely without justification. Male critics often cited include David Bradley, who places *The Color Purple* at the "ground zero" level of a Hiroshima explosion; Philip M. Royster, who psychoanalyzes Walker as rewriting her alienation from her father; and Darryl Pinckney, who dismisses the novel as a "polemic" against black men in the timely rhetoric of white feminism in the 1970s, securing Walker's literary place in a new movement, which replaced the civil rights struggle. See Bradley, "Novelist Alice Walker: Telling the Black Woman's Story," 32; Royster, "In Search of Our Fathers' Arms: Alice Walker's Persona of the Alienated Darling," 347–70; and Pinckney, "Black Victims, Black Villains," 18. None of this criticism is without merit, although McDowell accuses Royster of practicing pop psychology and Jenkins argues that there is a "salvific wish" to restore the black patriarchal family romance. See McDowell, "Reading Family Matters," 79; and Jenkins, "Queering Black Patriarchy: The Salvific Wish and Masculine Possibility in Alice Walker's *The Color Purple*," 970. However, Walker "queers" this romance in a dismantling of patriarchy, having confessed her disappointment in males in the text *In Search of Our Mothers' Garden* when she adds, "I desperately needed my father and brothers to give me male models I could respect" (328). Both critics and feminists raise legitimate questions about the motivation behind Walker's gendered character portrayals—embedded as they are in the South of her personal experience and in the wider traumatic narrative on the lynching of black men in American history. Walker's male characterization appears to follow Barthes's three divisions of semiotic markers of identity, reflective of a personal symbolic consciousness, a paradigmatic consciousness, and a syntagmatic imagination. Each (personal, paradigmatic, and syntagmatic) contributes to a widening system of signs, mirroring black male behavior in Walker's novels. On all three levels, Walker's male characters are ensconced in a chain of images that recalls the kind of violence against women that she witnessed as a child, hence her development of a negative paradigm for the sketching of male characters. Barthes defines the syntagmatic consciousness as having a greater expansiveness than the first two, based on the symbolic and the homological. The syntagmatic consciousness, categorized as a "stereotyped syntagm," is "of the relations which unite signs on the level of discourse itself, i.e., essentially a consciousness of the constraints, tolerances, and liberties of the sign's associations." His description captures the sweeping program of Walker's stereotypical signifying on male behavior: it is the stereotype that black male critics reject, grounded, as they appear to be, in her early formative years. See Barthes, "The Imagination of the Sign," 212–15. Michael Awkward's acknowledging modern black women writers' "representation of black manhood . . . in desperate trouble" recalls Walker's mixed metaphors of the libidinal/castrated/rephallicized, black father figure in a Western phallic hegemony. See Awkward, "A Black Man's Place(s) in Black Feminist Criticism," 20. In his interview with Walker, Bradley opines that only elderly men such as Grange Copeland do well in her fiction while younger male figures remain chaff characters. See also Thielmann, "Alice Walker and the 'Man Question.'"

Thielmann agrees with McDowell and Jenkins in that in her refusal to glorify black men and to discuss black women's subjugation and sexual exploitation, Walker becomes a target of black male critics. Walker's major focus, however, according to Thielmann, is how both have been wounded by racism.

45. Winchell, *Alice Walker*, 115.

46. Richards, *On the Winds and Waves of Imagination: Transnational Feminism and Literature*, 125.

47. Ibid., 130–31.

48. Ibid., 130.

49. Lerner, *The Creation of Patriarchy*, 26–27.

50. Richards, *On the Winds and Waves of Imagination: Transnational Feminism and Literature*, 125.

51. Jung, *Man and His Symbols*, 5, 36.

52. Ibid., 36.

53. Op. cit.

54. Alice Walker, *Anything We Love Can Be Saved: A Writer's Activism*, 122–26.

55. Jung, "On the Relation of Analytical Psychology to Poetry," 321.

56. George, "Alice Walker's Africa: Globalization and the Province of Fiction," 354, 357, 359. For a discussion on the "uneasy themes" of what Africans do to other Africans as found in African postindependence novels (perhaps which explains George's sensitivity to Walker's *Possessing*), see Gauch, "Sampling Globalization in Calixthe Beyala's *Le petit prince de Belleville*," 204.

57. Jung, *Man and His Symbols*, 225.

58. Jung, "Aion: Phenomenology of the Self," 152.

59. Ibid., 155.

60. George, "Alice Walker's Africa: Globalization and the Province of Fiction," 364.

61. Jung, "Aion: Phenomenology of the Self," 152.

62. Alice Walker, *Anything We Love Can Be Saved: A Writer's Activism*, 34.

63. George, "Alice Walker's Africa: Globalization and the Province of Fiction," 357.

64. Ibid., 359.

65. Op. cit.

66. Warren and Wolff, "'Like the Pupil of an Eye': Sexual Blinding of Women in Alice Walker's Works," 1.

67. Thadious Davis, *Southscapes: Geographies of Race, Region & Literature*, 339, 347, 363.

68. Evelyn C. White, *Alice Walker: A Life*, 109.

69. Alice Walker, *Anything We Love Can Be Saved: A Writer's Activism*, 33, 34.

Chapter 7. Bodily Evidence

1. Katznelson, *When Affirmative Action Was White: An Untold History of Racial Inequality in Twentieth-Century America*, 178; Morrison, "The Site of Memory," 110 (all subsequent references to Morrison's novels are from works cited in the bibliography).

2. Swedish Academy, "Inscription." Toni Morrison, *The Nobel Lecture in Literature*, n.p.

3. Phiddian, "Are Parody and Deconstruction Secretly the Same Thing," 679.

4. Bakhtin, *The Dialogic Imagination*, 309.

5. Phiddian, "Are Parody and Deconstruction Secretly the Same Thing," 679.

6. Dentith, *Parody*, 55, 56.

7. Ibid., 189.

8. Jameson, *Postmodernism, or, the Cultural Logic of Late Capitalism*, 17.

9. Pérez-Torres, "Between Presence and Absence: *Beloved*, Postmodernism, and Blackness," 194.

10. Jameson, *Postmodernism, or, the Cultural Logic of Late Capitalism*, 17.

11. Dentith, *Parody*, 55–56.

12. Collins, "Conversation with Alice Childress and Toni Morrison," 4.

13. Wilkie and Hurt, "Jonathan Swift," 113.

14. Frye, *Anatomy of Criticism*, 148.

15. Massey and Denton, *American Apartheid: Segregation and the Making of the Underclass*, 67, 81. In his more recent study on black segregation in America, the sociologist Patrick Sharkey writes that over 70 percent of "African Americans who live in today's poorest, most racially segregated neighborhoods are from the same families that lived in the ghettos of the 1970s." See Sharkey, *Stuck in Place: Urban Neighborhoods and the End of Progress toward Racial Equality*, 9. See also Quayson, *Aesthetic Nervousness: Disability and the Crisis of Representation*, 86–87.

16. Grosz, *Volatile Bodies*, 23.

17. Ibid., 85.

18. Bell, "The Supreme Court & 1984 Term," 7.

19. Ellison, *Shadow and Act*, 28.

20. Michelle Boulous Walker, *Philosophy and the Maternal Body*, 135.

21. Miller, "Domination and Subordination," 75, 78; Bump, "Racism and Appearance in *The Bluest Eye*: A Template for an Ethical Emotive Criticism," 150.

22. Woodward, *The Strange Career of Jim Crow*, 18.

23. Van Buren, *The Modernist Madonna: Semiotics of the Maternal Metaphor*, 1.

24. Clark, *Prejudice and Your Child*, 42, 44–46; Goluboff, *The Lost Promise of Civil Rights*, 243. According to Kenneth Clark, white dolls in Jim Crow America were neither innocuous nor frivolous symbols of entertainment and play but a real political discourse on race and "beauty." Clark conducted "doll tests" in the 1940s and 1950s, testing black and white children in Arkansas, Massachusetts, and Pennsylvania. His results demonstrated the harmful effects white dolls had on the developing psyche of black girls. With his psychologist wife, Mamie, Clark developed projective tests of presenting four identical dolls to children ages three to seven. The dolls were similar except for color: two were brown and two were white. Testing the students' awareness of color, ethnicity, and desirability, the Clarks presented the following tasks to the children: "Give me the white doll; Give me the colored doll; and Give me the Negro doll." Then they said, "Give me the doll you like to play with" and "Give me the doll that is a nice color." The majority of the children demonstrated an unmistakable preference for white dolls. Clark remarked, "The fact that young Negro children would prefer to be white reflects their knowledge that society prefers white people. It is clear, therefore, that the self-acceptance or self-rejection found so early in a child's developing complex of racial ideas reflects the awareness and acceptance of the prevailing racial attitudes in his [or her] community." Clark describes one black girl who broke down and cried when he asked her to identify personally "with one of the dolls": she had characterized the colored dolls as "ugly and dirty." Perhaps the power of *The Bluest Eye* derives from Morrison's uncanny psychological portrayal of the damage that racism inflicts on a young girl such as Pecola, resulting in her feelings of race- and self-loathing, hence her request for a particular racial trope of beauty: blue eyes.

25. Hutcheon, *A Theory of Parody*, 32.

26. Dickerson, "Summoning SomeBody: The Flesh Made Word in Toni Morrison's Fiction," 197, 199, 202; Walters, *African American Literature and the Classicist Tradition: Black Women Writers from Wheatley to Morrison*, 114.

27. Bakhtin, *The Dialogic Imagination*, 309.

28. Page, *Dangerous Freedom: Fusion and Fragmentation in Toni Morrison's Novels*, 37, 35.

29. Tate, "Toni Morrison," 160.

30. Dentith, *Parody*, 39.

31. McDowell, *"The Changing Same": Black Women's Literature, Criticism, and Theory*, 104, 106, 108.

32. Grewal, *Circles of Sorrow, Lines of Struggle: The Novels of Toni Morrison*, 43.

33. Du Bois, "Black Reconstruction," 433.

34. Kluger, *Simple Justice*, 366.

35. Du Bois, "Black Reconstruction," 469.

36. Grewal, *Circles of Sorrow, Lines of Struggle: The Novels of Toni Morrison*, 43.

37. McDowell, *"The Changing Same": Black Women's Literature, Criticism, and Theory*, 105, 102.

38. Ibid.

39. Suranyi, *"The Bluest Eye* and *Sula:* Black Female Experience from Childhood to Womanhood," 20; Collins, "Shifting the Center: Race, Class, and Feminist Theorizing about Motherhood," 47.

40. Exod. 5:1.

41. Op. cit.

42. Rose, *Parody: Ancient, Modern, and Post-modern*, 128.

43. Gillespie and Kubitschek, "Who Cares? Women-Centered Psychology in *Sula*," 62.

44. Naylor, "A Conversation: Gloria Naylor and Toni Morrison," 125.

45. Phiddian, "Are Parody and Deconstruction Secretly the Same Thing," 686.

46. Story, "An Excursion into the Black World: The 'Seven Days' in Toni Morrison's *Song of Solomon*," 149–58.

47. Gilligan, *In a Different Voice: Psychological Theory and Women's Development*, 43; Sheng, "Toni Morrison's Gender Politics in *Song of Solomon*," 96.

48. Wilentz, "Civilizations Underneath: African Heritage as Cultural Discourse in Toni Morrison's *Song of Solomon*," 117.

49. Michelle Boulous Walker, *Philosophy and the Maternal Body*, 86.

50. Skerrett, "Recitations to the Griot: Storytelling and Learning in Toni Morrison's *Song of Solomon*," 195.

51. Mobley, "Call and Response: Voice, Community, and Dialogic Structures in Toni Morrison's *Song of Solomon*," 42, 48–51.

52. Phiddian, "Are Parody and Deconstruction Secretly the Same Thing," 686.

53. Grimshaw, ed., *Racial Violence in the United States*, 225, 316.

54. Ruas, "Toni Morrison," 97, 117.

55. Stepto, "Intimate Things in Place: A Conversation with Toni Morrison," 29. See also Dizard, "Toni Morrison, the Slave Narratives, and Modernism," 389, 390, 402.

56. Pérez-Torres, "Between Presence and Absence: *Beloved*, Postmodernism, and Blackness," 193.

57. Rose, *Parody: Ancient, Modern, and Post-modern*, 72.

58. Dentith, *Parody*, 74.

59. Krumholz, "The Ghosts of Slavery: Historical Recovery in Toni Morrison's *Beloved*," 114.

60. LaCapra, *History and Memory after Auschwitz*, 16.

61. Op. cit.

62. Eisenstein, *The Female Body and the Law*, 21, 22. Other informative analyses of motherhood and the body in *Beloved* are Ghasemi, "Negotiating Black Motherhood in Toni Morrison's Novels"; and Liscio, "*Beloved*'s Narrative: Writing Mother's Milk."

63. Mannix, *Black Cargoes*, 106.

64. Douglass, *Narrative of the Life of Frederick Douglass, an American Slave*, 39.

65. John Hope Franklin, *From Slavery to Freedom*, 178.

66. Hartman, *Scenes of Subjection: Terror, Slavery, and Self-Making in Nineteenth-Century America*, 98.

67. Foner, *Reconstruction: America's Unfinished Revolution, 1863–1877*, 2.

68. Barksdale, "Castration Symbolism in Recent Black American Fiction," 407.

69. Douglass, *Narrative of the Life of Frederick Douglass, an American Slave*, 48

70. McFeely, *Frederick Douglass*, 383.

71. Gould, *The Mismeasure of Man*, 409.

72. Barzun, *Race: A Study in Superstition*, 7.

73. Hayden White, *Tropics of Discourse: Essays in Cultural Criticism*, 185. In her perceptive essay, Dara Byrne discusses White's "logic of metaphor" as a trope of "differencing" in School-teacher's lessons on black inferiority/white superiority and finds Schoolteacher's lessons "integral to the fluidity of America's racist ideology in the public and private spheres." In my reading of Schoolteacher's measuring of the slaves' cranium, I place the emphasis on Morrison's parody of nineteenth-century scientific racism, which empirically establishes the "logic" behind "America's racist ideology," as Byrne argues in "'Yonder They Do Not Love Your Flesh': Community in Toni Morrison's *Beloved*: The Limitations of Citizenship and Property in the American Public Sphere."

74. Hayden White, *Tropics of Discourse: Essays in Cultural Criticism*, 185.

75. Demetrakopoulos, "Maternal Bonds as Devourers of Women's Individuation in Toni Morrison's *Beloved*," 1–2.

76. Henderson, "Toni Morrison's *Beloved*: Re-Membering the Body as Historical Text," 74.

77. Bakhtin, *The Dialogic Imagination*, 309.

78. Maquet, *Albert Camus: The Invincible Summer*, 46.

79. Ibid., 45–46.

80. Hill, "The All-Negro Communities of Oklahoma: The Natural History of a Social Movement," 254–68.

81. Page, "Furrowing All the Brows: Interpretation and the Transcendent in Toni Morrison's *Paradise*," 639.

82. Page Smith, *The Rise of Industrial America*, 648.

83. Dalsgard, "The One All-Black Town Worth the Pain: (African) American Exceptionalism, Historical Narration, and the Critique of Nationhood in Toni Morrison's *Paradise*," 233–48.

84. Page, "Furrowing All the Brows: Interpretation and the Transcendent in Toni Morrison's *Paradise*," 643.

85. Storace, "The Scripture of Utopia," 64–69.

86. Dalsgard, "The One All-Black Town Worth the Pain: (African) American Exceptionalism, Historical Narration, and the Critique of Nationhood in Toni Morrison's *Paradise*," 5.

87. Ibid., 4.

88. Ibid., 5.

89. Gatens, *Imaginary Bodies: Ethics, Power, and Corporeality*, 68. Also see Grosz, *Volatile Bodies*, 73.

90. Terry, "A New World Religion: Creolisation and Candomble in Toni Morrison's *Paradise*," 204–5.

91. Ibid., 23.

92. Bakhtin, *The Dialogic Imagination*, 302.

93. Page, "Furrowing All the Brows: Interpretation and the Transcendent in Toni Morrison's *Paradise*," 642.

94. Rody, *The Daughter's Return: African-American and Caribbean Women's Fictions of History*, 41.

95. Ibid., 10.

96. Watkins, "Talk with Toni Morrison," 46.

97. Rothstein, "Toni Morrison, in Her New Novel, Defends Women," C17

98. Ruas, "Toni Morrison," 105.

99. Docker, *Postmodernism and Popular Culture: A Cultural History,* 104.

100. Ruddick, *Maternal Thinking: Toward a Politics of Peace,* 39.

101. Koenen, "The One Out of Sequence," 73. See also Krumholz, "Blackness and Art in Toni Morrison's *Tar Baby,*" 269; and Scott, "*Song of Solomon* and *Tar Baby:* The Subversive Role of Language and the Carnivalesque," 32.

102. Foster, *Recodings: Art, Spectacle, and Cultural Politics,* 123.

103. Mulvey, "Visual Pleasure and Narrative Cinema," 586.

104. Op. cit.

105. Op. cit.

106. McKay, "An Interview with Toni Morrison," 155.

107. Christina Davis, "An Interview with Toni Morrison," 233.

108. Hughes, "From *The Big Sea,*" 1286.

109. Locke, "The New Negro," 961, 963.

110. Hughes, "From *The Big Sea,*" 1283, 1286.

111. Lewis, *When Harlem Was in Vogue,* 117.

112. Dentith, *Parody,* 74.

113. Bakhtin, *The Dialogic Imagination,* 81.

114. Griffin, *"Who Set You Flowin'?" The African-American Migration Narrative,* 194; Griffin, *Harlem Nocturne,* 164.

115. Locke, "The New Negro," 963.

116. Moynihan, "The Negro Family: The Case for National Action," 31.

117. Ibid., 29.

118. Clark, *Dark Ghetto.* See ch. 5, "The Pathology of the GHETTO," 81–110.

119. Grosz, *Volatile Bodies,* 117.

120. Berlant, "National Brands/National Body: Imitation of Life," 131.

121. Foucault, *Power/Knowledge: Selected Interviews & Other Writings, 1972–1977,* 193.

122. Schaffer, *Mothering,* 47.

123. Pinckney, "Hate," 21.

124. Eckard, *Maternal Body and Voice in Toni Morrison, Bobbie Ann Mason, and Lee Smith,* 53.

125. Dentith, *Parody,* 20.

126. Op. cit.

127. Lyotard, "The Postmodern Condition," 510.

128. Nicol and Terry, "Guest Editors' Introduction, Toni Morrison: New Directions." Other articles referenced include Fowler, "'Nobody Could Make It Alone': Fathers and Boundaries in Toni Morrison's *Beloved,*" 13; Atieh, "The Revelation of the Veiled in Toni Morrison's *Paradise:* The Whirling Dervishes in the Harem of the Convent," 104; and Babb, "*E Pluribus Unum?* The American Origins' Narrative in Toni Morrison's *A Mercy,*" 148.

129. Genovese, *The World the Slaveholders Made,* 227.

130. Moore, "A Demonic Parody: Toni Morrison's *A Mercy.*"

131. Updike, "Dreamy Wilderness," 112–13.

132. Waegner, "Ruthless Epic Footsteps: Shoes, Migrants, and the Settlement of the Americas in Toni Morrison's *A Mercy,*" 91.

133. Ibid., 102–3.

134. Ibid., 91. For Morrison's description of poor whites resembling slaves, Waegner cites Jordan and Walsh, *White Wars* [sic]: *The Forgotten History of Britain's White Slaves in America,* 2007.

135. Silko, *Ceremony,* 169.

136. Zinn, *A People's History of the United States, 1492–Present*, 86.

137. Stannard, *American Holocaust*, 68, 107, 98–99.

138. Elkins, *Slavery*, 41–42.

139. Irigaray, *To Speak Is Never Neutral*, 234. Irigaray is speaking on a theory of women's desire. I take some liberty in applying her theory to Morrison's mother-daughter dyad.

140. Harriet Jacobs, *Incidents in the Life of a Slave Girl*, 62, 56.

141. Book of Job, 13:15.

142. McHenry, "Into Other Claws," 16–17.

143. McHenry sees literary mothers as problematic in Morrison's fiction; I find the racist/sexist society as problematic, not the mothers. See also Wyatt, "Failed Messages, Maternal Loss, and Narrative Form in Toni Morrison's *A Mercy*," 131.

144. Eagleton, *Evil*, 59, 50.

145. Babb, "*E Pluribus Unum*? The American Origins Narrative in Toni Morrison's *A Mercy*," 147.

146. Grossman, *On Killing: The Psychological Cost of Learning to Kill in War and Society*, 48.

147. McKinstry, *While the World Watched*, 89.

148. Dray, *At the Hands of Persons Unknown: The Lynching of Black America*, lx.

149. Grossman, *On Killing: The Psychological Cost of Learning to Kill in War and Society*, 136.

150. Ruddick, *Maternal Thinking: Toward a Politics of Peace*, 122–23.

151. Churchwell, "*Home* by Toni Morrison—A Review," 1.

152. Stowe, *Uncle Tom's Cabin*, 214.

153. Joel Williamson, *New People: Miscegenation and Mulattoes in the United States*, (1995), 23.

154. Kara Wilson, "Kara Wilson Didn't Like Toni Morrison's New Book, 'God Help the Child'"; Evaristo, "*God Help the Child* Review—Toni Morrison Continues to Improve with Age."

155. Ruddick, *Maternal Thinking: Toward a Politics of Peace*, 36.

156. Montagu, ed., *The Concept of Race*, 3.

157. Katznelson, *When Affirmative Action Was White: An Untold History of Racial Inequality in Twentieth-Century America*, 178.

158. King, "Letter from a Birmingham Jail," 1857.

159. Terry, "'Breathing the Air of a World So New': Rewriting the Landscape of America in Toni Morrison's *A Mercy*," 145.

160. Koenen, "The One Out of Sequence," 79.

Bibliography

Adeeko, Adeleke. Introduction. *Research in African Literature* 40:4 (Winter 2009): ix.

———. "Writing Africa under the Shadow of Slavery: Quaque, Wheatley, and Crowther." Research in African Literature 40:4 (Winter 2009): 1–24.

Adorno, Theodor W. *Aesthetic Theory*. Ed. Gretel Adorno and Rolf Tiedemann. Translated by Robert Hullot-Kentor. Minneapolis: University of Minnesota Press, 1997.

Ahlin, Lena. *The 'New Negro' in the Old World: Culture and Performance in James Weldon Johnson, Jessie Fauset, and Nella Larsen*. Ed. Marianne Thormahlen and Beatrice Warren. Lund, Sweden: Lund University, 2006.

Alexander, Adele Logan. *Homelands and Waterways: The American Journey of the Bond Family, 1846–1926*. New York: Pantheon Books, 1999.

Alexander, Simone A. James. *Mother Imagery in the Novels of Afro-Caribbean Women*. Columbia and London: University of Missouri Press, 2001.

Andrews, William. *To Tell a Free Story*. Urbana: University of Illinois Press, 1986.

———, ed. *Classic African American Women's Narratives*. New York: Oxford University Press, 2003.

Atieh, Majda R. "The Revelation of the Veiled in Toni Morrison's Paradise: The Whirling Dervishes in the Harem of the Convent." *MELUS* 36:2 (Summer 2011): 89–107.

Atkin, Andrea M. "'When Pincushions Are Periodicals': Women's Work, Race, and Material Objects in Female Abolitionism." *American Transcendental Quarterly* 11:2 (June 1997): 93–114.

Awkward, Michael. "A Black Man's Place(s) in Black Feminist Criticism." In *Representing Black Men*, ed. Marcellus Blount and George P. Cunningham. 3–26. New York and London: Routledge, 1996.

Babb, Valerie. "*E Pluribus Unum*? The American Origins' Narrative in Toni Morrison's *A Mercy*." *MELUS* 36:2 (Summer 2011): 147–64.

Baker, Houston. *Afro-American Poetics: Revisions of Harlem and the Black Aesthetic*. Madison: University of Wisconsin Press, 1988.

Bakhtin, M. M. *The Dialogic Imagination*. Austin: University of Texas Press, 1981.

"Bans on Interracial Unions Offer Perspective on Gay Ones." *New York Times* (March 17, 2004), A16.

Barker, Francis. *The Culture of Violence: Essays on Tragedy and History*. Chicago: University of Chicago Press, 1993.

Barksdale, Richard K. "Castration Symbolism in Recent Black American Fiction." *College Language Association* 29:4 (June 1986): 400–413.

Barthes, Roland. *Image, Music, Text*. New York: Hill and Wang, 1977.

———. "The Imagination of the Sign." In *A Barthes Reader*, ed. Susan Sontag. New York: Hill and Wang, 1982.

Barthold, Bonnie J. *Black Time*. New Haven, Conn.: Yale University Press, 1981.

Barzun, Jacques. *Race: A Study in Superstition*. New York: Harper & Row, 1965.

Bassard, Katherine Clay. *Spiritual Interrogations*. Princeton, N.J.: Princeton University Press, 1999.

Bates, Walter Jackson. *From Classic to Romantic: Premise of Taste in Eighteenth-Century England*. New York: Harper & Row, 1946.

Baur, Susan. *Hypochondria, Woeful Imaginings*. Berkeley: University of California Press, 1988.

Beckles, Hilary McD. "Kalinago (Carib) Resistance to European Colonization of the Caribbean." In *Caribbean Slavery in the Atlantic World: A Student Reader,* ed. Verene Shepherd and Hilary McD. Beckles. Kingston, Oxford, and Princeton, N.J.: IRP, 2000.

Bell, Derrick. "The Supreme Court & 1984 Term." *Harvard Law Review* 99:4 (1985): 4–83.

Bennett, Paula. "Phillis Wheatley's Vocation and the Paradox of the 'Afric Muse.'" *PMLA* 113:1 (January 1998): 64–76.

Bentley, Eric. *The Life of the Drama.* New York: Atheneum, 1965.

Berg, Allison. *Mothering the Race: Women's Narratives of Reproduction, 1890–1930.* Urbana and Chicago: University of Illinois Press, 2001.

Berlant, Lauren. "National Brands/National Body: Imitation of Life." In *Comparative American Identities: Race, Sex, and Nationality in the Modern Text,* ed. Hortense J. Spillers. New York and London: Routledge, 1991.

Berlin, Ira. *Generations of Captivity.* Cambridge, Mass., and London: Belknap Press of Harvard University Press, 2003.

Bermel, Albert. *Farce: A History from Aristophanes to Woody Allen.* New York: Simon and Schuster, 1990.

Bernstein, J. M. *The Fate of Art: Aesthetic Alienation from Kant to Derrida and Adorno.* University Park: Pennsylvania State University Press, 1992.

Berzon, Judith R. *Neither White nor Black.* New York: New York University Press, 1978.

Bhabha, Homi K. *The Location of Culture.* New York and London: Routledge, 1994.

———. "The Postcolonial Critic." *Arena* 96 (Spring 1991): 47–63.

Billington, Ray Allen. Introduction. In *The Journal of Charlotte L. Forten,* ed. Ray Allen Billington. New York: Dryden Press, 1953.

Blackmer, Corrine E. "The Veils of the Law: Race and Sexuality in Nella Larsen's Passing." *College Literature* 22:3 (October 1995): 50–67.

Bone, Robert. *Down Home: A History of Afro-American Short Fiction from Its Beginning to the End of the Harlem Renaissance.* New York: Putnam's, 1975.

———. *The Negro Novel in America.* New Haven, Conn.: Yale University Press, 1965.

Boyd, Valerie. *Wrapped in Rainbows: The Life of Zora Neale Hurston.* New York: Scribner, 2003.

Bradley, David. "Novelist Alice Walker: Telling the Black Woman's Story." *New York Times* magazine, January 8, 1984, 25–37.

Braithwaite, William Stanley. "The Novels of Jessie Fauset." *Opportunity* 12:1 (1934): 24–28.

Brathwaite, Edward K. "The African Presence in Caribbean Literature." In *Slavery, Colonialism, and Racism,* ed. Sidney W. Mintz. New York: W. W. Norton, 1974.

Braxton, Joanne. *Black Women Writing Autobiography.* Philadelphia: Temple University Press, 1989.

Brecht, Bertoldt. *Bertoldt Brecht Collected Plays,* vol. 5, ed. Ralph Manheim and John Willett. New York: Pantheon Books, 1972.

Brown, William Wells. *Clotel, or The President's Daughter.* Ed. Joan E. Cashin. Armonk, N.Y. and London: M. E. Sharpe, 1996.

Bump, Jerome. "Racism and Appearance in *The Bluest Eye*: A Template for an Ethical Emotive Criticism." *College Literature* 37:2 (Spring 2010): 147–70.

Burke, Peter J., and Jan E. Stets. *Identity Theory.* New York: Oxford University Press, 2009.

Bush, Julia. "Lady Lives? Upper Class Women's Autobiographies and the Politics of Late Victorian and Edwardian Britain . . ." *Literature & History* 10:2 (October 2001): 42–61.

Busia, Akena P. "What Is Your Nation? Reconnecting Africa and Her Diaspora through Paule Marshall's *Praisesong for the Widow.*" In *Changing Our Own Words: Essays on Criticism, Theory, and*

Writing by Black Women, ed. Cheryl A. Wall. 196–211. New Brunswick and London: Rutgers University Press, 1989.

Butler, Judith. *Bodies That Matter.* New York: Routledge, 1993.

———. "The Lesbian Phallus and the Morphological Imaginary." In Judith Butler, *Bodies That Matter.* New York and London: Routledge, 1993.

Butterfield, Stephen. *Black Autobiography in America.* Amherst: University of Massachusetts Press, 1974.

Byrne, Dara. "'Yonder They Do Not Love Your Flesh': Community in Toni Morrison's *Beloved;* The Limitations of Citizenship and Property in the American Public Sphere." *Canadian Review of American Studies* 29:2 (January 1999): 25–59.

Campbell, Joseph. *Myths to Live By.* New York: Viking, 1972.

Caputi, Jane. *Goddesses and Monsters.* Madison and London: University of Wisconsin Press, 2004.

Carby, Hazel. "The Politics of Fiction, Anthropology, and the Folk: Zora Neale Hurston." In *New Essays on Their Eyes Were Watching God,* ed. Michael Awkward. New York: Cambridge University Press, 1990.

Carby, Hazel V. *Reconstructing Womanhood.* New York and Oxford: Oxford University Press, 1987.

Carretta, Vincent. *Phillis Wheatley: Biography of a Genius in Bondage.* Athens and London: University of Georgia Press, 2011.

———, ed. *Phillis Wheatley: Complete Writings.* New York: Penguin Books, 2001.

Chambers, Ross. "Narratorial Authority and 'The Purloined Letter.'" In *The Purloined Poe: Lacan, Derrida, and Psychoanalytic Reading,* ed. John P. Muller and William J. Richardson. Baltimore and London: Johns Hopkins University Press, 1988.

Cheung, King-Kok. "Don't Tell: Imposed Silences in *The Color Purple* and *The Woman Warrior.*" *PMLA* 103 (March 1988): 162–74.

Chinn, Sarah E. *Technology and the Logic of American Racism: A Cultural History of the Body as Evidence.* London and New York: Continuum, 2000.

Chodorow, Nancy. *Femininities, Masculinities, Sexualities.* Lexington: University Press of Kentucky, 1994.

———. *The Reproduction of Mothering: Psychoanalysis and the Sociology of Gender.* Berkeley, Los Angeles, and London: University of California Press, 1978.

Christian, Barbara. *Black Women Novelists: The Development of a Tradition, 1892–1976.* Westport, Conn.: Greenwood Press, 1980.

Church, Joseph. *Language and the Discovery of Reality.* New York: Vintage Books, 1966.

Churchwell, Sarah. "*Home* by Toni Morrison—A Review." *Guardian,* April 27, 2012.

Cixous, Héléne. "Sorties: Out and Out: Attacks/Ways Out/Forays." In *The Newly Born Woman.* Cixous with Catherine Clement. Translated by Betsy Wing. Minneapolis: University of Minnesota Press, 1986.

Clark, Kenneth B. *Dark Ghetto.* New York: Harper & Row, 1965.

———. *Prejudice and Your Child.* Boston: Beacon Press, 1955.

———. "A Racial Progress and Retreat." In *Race in America,* ed. Herbert Hill and James E. Jones Jr. Madison: University of Wisconsin Press, 1992.

Clarkson, Thomas. *An Essay on the Slavery and Commerce of the Human Species, Particularly the African.* Georgetown, K[sic]: J. N. Slyle, 1816.

Clement, Catherine, and Julie Kristeva. *The Feminine and the Sacred.* New York: Columbia University Press, 1998.

Cohn, Dorrit. *Transparent Minds: Narrative Modes for Presenting Consciousness in Fiction.* Princeton, N.J.: Princeton University Press, 1978.

Collins, Patricia Hill. *Black Feminist Thought*. London: HarperCollins Academic, 1991.

———. "Conversation with Alice Childress and Toni Morrison." In *Conversations with Toni Morrison*, ed. Danille Taylor-Cuthrie. Jackson: University Press of Mississippi, 1994.

———. "Shifting the Center: Race, Class, and Feminist Theorizing about Motherhood." In *Mothering: Ideology, Experience, and Agency*, ed. Evelyn Nakano Glenn, Grace Chang, and Linda Rennie Forcey. New York and London: Routledge, 1994.

Cott, Nancy. *The Grounding of Modern Feminism*. New Haven, Conn.: Yale University Press, 1987.

Couser, G. Thomas. "Oppression and Repression: Personal and Collective Memory in Paule Marshall's *Praisesong for the Widow* and Leslie Marmon Silko's *Ceremony*." In *Memory and Cultural Politics*, ed. Amritjit Singh, Joseph T. Skerrett Jr., and Robert E. Hogan. Boston: Northeastern University Press, 1996.

Cowan, Tom, and Jack McGuire. *Timelines of African American History*. New York: Roundtable Press, 1996.

Cruse, Harold. *The Crisis of the Negro Intellectual*. New York: William Morrow, 1967.

Cudjoe, Selwyn R. *Caribbean Women Writers*. Wellesley, Mass.: Calaloux Publications, 1990.

Culley, Margo. *A Day at a Time: The Diary Literature of American Women from 1764 to the Present*. Madison: University of Wisconsin Press, 1992.

Dalsgard, Katrine. "The One All-Black Town Worth the Pain: (African) American Exceptionalism, Historical Narration, and the Critique of Nationhood in Toni Morrison's Paradise." *African American Review* 35:2 (Summer 2001): 233–48.

Dance, Daryl Cumber. "An Interview with Paule Marshall." *Southern Review* 28:1 (Winter 1992): 1–20.

Davidson, Basil. *A History of West Africa*. New York: Anchor/Doubleday, 1966.

Davis, Christina. "An Interview with Toni Morrison." In *Conversations with Toni Morrison*, ed. Danielle Taylor-Guthrie. Jackson: University Press of Mississippi, 1994.

Davis, Jessica Milner. *Farce*. London: Methuen, 1978.

Davis, Thadious. Introduction. In Jessie Redmon Fauset, *Comedy: American Style*. New York: G. K. Hall & Co., 1995.

———. *Nella Larsen, Novelist of the Harlem Renaissance: A Woman's Life Unveiled*. Baton Rouge and London: Louisiana State University Press, 1994.

———. *Southscapes: Geographies of Race, Region & Literature*. Chapel Hill: University of North Carolina Press, 2011.

De Lauretis, Teresa. "Sexual Indifference and Lesbian Representation." *Theatre Journal* 40 (May 1988): 155–77.

Demetrakopoulos, Stephanie A. "Maternal Bonds as Devourers of Women's Individuation in Toni Morrison's *Beloved*." *African American Review* 26:1 (Spring 1992): 51–59.

Denniston, Dorothy H. *The Fiction of Paule Marshall*. Knoxville: University of Tennessee Press, 1995.

Dentith, Simon. *Parody*. New York and London: Routledge, 2000.

Derrida, Jacques. "The Purveyor of Truth." In *The Purloined Poe: Lacan, Derrida, and Psychoanalytic Reading*, ed. John P. Muller and William J. Richardson. Baltimore and London: Johns Hopkins University Press, 1988.

Dever, Carolyn. *Death and the Mother from Dickens to Freud*. Cambridge: Cambridge University Press, 1998.

Dickerson, Vanessa D. "Summoning SomeBody: The Flesh Made Word in Toni Morrison's Fiction." In *Recovering the Black Female Body: Self-Representations by African American Women*, ed. Michael Bennett and Vanessa D. Dickerson. New Brunswick and London: Rutgers University Press, 2001.

Dizard, Robin. "Toni Morrison, the Slave Narratives, and Modernism." *Massachusetts Review* 51:2 (Summer 2010): 389–405.

Docker, John. *Postmodernism and Popular Culture: A Cultural History.* Cambridge, Mass., and London: Cambridge University Press, 1994.

Dole, Carol M. "The Return of the Father in Spielberg's *The Color Purple.*" *Literature Film Quarterly* 24:1 (January 1996): 12–15.

Douglas, Ann. *The Feminization of American Culture.* New York: Noonday Press of Farrar, Straus and Giroux, 1977.

Douglass, Frederick. *Narrative of the Life of Frederick Douglass, an American Slave.* Boston and New York: Bedford Books, 1993.

Douty, Esther M. *Forten, the Sailmaker: Pioneer Champion of Negro Rights.* Chicago: Rand McNally, 1968.

Dray, Philip. *At the Hands of Persons Unknown: The Lynching of Black America.* New York: Random House, 2002.

Du Bois, W. E. B. "The Black Codes." In *Race, Class, and Gender in the United States,* ed. Paula S. Rothenberg. New York: St. Martin's Press, 1998.

———. "Black Reconstruction." In *Reconstruction: An Anthology of Revisionist Writings,* ed. Kenneth M. Stampp and Leon F. Litwack. Baton Rouge: Louisiana State University Press, 1969.

———. "Criteria of Negro Art." In *Norton Anthology of African American Literature,* ed. Henry Louis Gates and Nellie Y. McKay. New York: W. W. Norton, 1997.

———. "The Immediate Program of the American Negro." *Crisis* 9:6 (April 1915): 310–12.

———. *The Souls of Black Folk.* New York: Bantam Books, 1989.

duCille, Ann. *The Coupling Convention.* New York: Oxford University Press, 1993.

Dunbar, Erica Armstrong. *A Fragile Freedom: African American Women and Emancipation in the Antebellum City.* New Haven, Conn., and London: Yale University Press, 2008.

Dunn, Richard S. *Sugar and Slaves.* Chapel Hill: University of North Carolina Press, 1972.

DuPlessis, Rachel Blau. "Power, Judgment, and Narrative in a Work of Zora Neale Hurston: Feminist Cultural Studies." In *Critical Essays on Zora Neale Hurston,* ed. Gloria L. Cronin. New York: G. K. Hall, 1998.

Eagleton, Terry. *Evil.* New Haven, Conn., and London: Yale University Press, 2010.

———. *The Ideology of the Aesthetic.* Oxford: Basil Blackwell, 1990.

Eckard, Paula Gallant. *Maternal Body and Voice in Toni Morrison, Bobbie Ann Mason, and Lee Smith.* Columbia and London: University of Missouri Press, 2002.

"Editorial and Opinion." *Crisis,* April 15, 1915, 276–85.

Eisenstein, Zillah R. *The Female Body and the Law.* Berkeley: University of California Press, 1988.

Elkins, Stanley M. *Slavery.* New York: Grosset & Dunlap, 1963.

Ellis, Joseph. *Founding Brothers.* New York: Vintage Books, 2000.

Ellison, Ralph. *Invisible Man.* New York: Vintage Books, 1980.

———. *Shadow and Act.* New York: Random House, 1964.

Erkkila, Betsy. "Phillis Wheatley and the Black American Revolution." In *A Mixed Race: Ethnicity in Early America,* ed. Frank Shuffelton. New York: Oxford University Press, 1993.

Evaristo, Bernardine. "*God Help the Child* Review—Toni Morrison Continues to Improve with Age." *Guardian.* http://theguardian.com/books. April 19, 2015. Accessed May 16, 2015.

Fabi, M. Giulia. *Passing and the Rise of the African American Novel.* Urbana and Chicago: University of Illinois Press, 2001.

Fanon, Frantz. *Black Skin, White Masks.* New York: Grove Press, 1967.

———. *The Wretched of the Earth.* New York: Grove Press, 1963.

Farebrother, Rachel. *The Collage Aesthetic in the Harlem Renaissance*. Surrey, U.K., and Burlington, Vt.: Ashgate, 2009.

Fauset, Jessie Redmon. *The Chinaberry Tree: A Novel of American Life*. New York: AMS Press, 1969.

———. *Comedy, American Style*. New York: G. K. Hall, 1995.

———. *Plum Bum: A Novel without a Moral*. London and Boston, Melbourne and Henley: Pandora Press, 1985.

———. *There Is Confusion*. Boston: Northeastern University Press, 1989.

"Feminist Ethics." In *Stanford Encyclopedia of Philosophy*. http://plato.stanford.edu/entries/feminism ethics/. Accessed January 20, 2001, 13.

Finkelman, Paul F. *Slavery and the Founders: Race and Liberty in the Age of Jefferson*. New York: M. E. Sharpe, 2001.

Fitzhugh, George. "Cannibals All! or Slaves without Masters." In *Ante-Bellum: Writings of George Fitzhugh and Hinton Rowan Helper on Slavery*, ed. Harvey Wish. New York: Capricorn Books, 1960.

Foner, Eric. *The Fiery Trial: Abraham Lincoln and American Slavery*. New York and London: W. W. Norton, 2011.

———. *Reconstruction: America's Unfinished Revolution, 1863–1877*. New York: Harper & Row, 1989.

Forten, Charlotte L. *The Journal of Charlotte L. Forten*. Ed. Ray Allen Billington. New York: Dryden Press, 1953.

———. "Life on the Sea Islands." In *Classic African American Women's Narratives*, ed. William Andrews. New York: Oxford University Press, 2003.

Foster, Hal. *Recodings: Art, Spectacle, and Cultural Politics*. Port Townsend, Wash.: Bay Press, 1985.

———, ed. *The Anti-Aesthetic: Essays on Postmodern Culture*. Port Townsend, Wash.: Bay Press, 1983.

———, ed. "Postmodernism: A Preface." In *The Anti-Aesthetic: Essays on Postmodern Culture*. Port Townsend, Wash.: Bay Press, 1983.

Foucault, Michel. *Madness and Civilization*. New York: Vintage Books, 1965.

———. *The Order of Things*. New York: Vintage Books, 1991.

———. *Power/Knowledge: Selected Interviews & Other Writings, 1972–1977*. Ed. Colin Gordon. New York: Pantheon Books, 1980.

Fowler, Doreen. "'Nobody Could Make It Alone': Fathers and Boundaries in Toni Morrison's *Beloved*." *MELUS* 36:2 (Summer 2011): 13–33.

Fox-Genovese, Elizabeth. *Feminism without Illusion*. Chapel Hill: University of North Carolina Press, 1991.

———. *Within the Plantation Household*. Chapel Hill: University of North Carolina Press, 1988.

Franklin, Benjamin. *Autobiography*. New York: Doubleday, 1922.

Franklin, John Hope. *From Slavery to Freedom*. New York: Vintage Books, 1969.

Freud, Sigmund. "The Ego and the Id." In *The Freud Reader*, ed. Peter Gay. 628–58 New York: W. W. Norton, 1989.

———. "Inhibitions, Symptoms, and Anxiety." In *The Standard Edition of the Complete Psychological Works of Sigmund Freud*, vol. 20 (1925–1926). Translated by James Strachey. London: Hogarth Press, 1959.

———. "On Narcissism." In *The Freud Reader*, ed. Peter Gay. New York: W. W. Norton, 1989.

———. "Three Essays on the Theory of Sexuality." In *The Freud Reader*, ed. Peter Gay. New York: W. W. Norton, 1989.

Freydman, Jason. "Zora Neal Hurston, Biographical Criticism and African Diaspora Vernacular Culture." *MELUS: Multi-Ethnic Literature of the United States* 34 (Winter 2009): 99–88.

Frye, Northrop. *Anatomy of Criticism*. Princeton, N.J.: Princeton University Press, 1957.

Gaines, Kevin K. *Uplifting the Race: Black Leadership, Politics, and Culture in the Twentieth Century*. Chapel Hill and London: University of North Carolina Press, 1996.

Gatens, Moira. *Imaginary Bodies: Ethics, Power, and Corporeality*. New York and London: Routledge, 1996.

———. "Power, Bodies and Difference." In *Feminist Theory and the Body: A Reader*, ed. Janet Price and Margrit Shildrick. New York: Routledge, 1999.

Gates, Henry Louis. "Color Me Zora." In *Alice Walker: Critical Perspectives, Past and Present*, ed. Henry Louis Gates Jr. and K. A. Appiah. New York: Amistad, 1993.

———. *Signifying Monkey*. New York and Oxford: Oxford University Press, 1988.

———. *The Trials of Phillis Wheatley*. New York: Basic Books, 2003.

———, ed. *The Classic Slave Narratives*. New York: New American Library, 1987.

———, ed. *The Norton Anthology of African American Literature*. New York: W. W. Norton, 1997.

———, ed. *'Race,' Writing, and Difference*. Chicago: University of Chicago Press, 1986.

Gatewood, Willard B. *Aristocrats of Color*. Bloomington and Indianapolis: Indiana University Press, 1990.

Gauch, Suzanne. "Sampling Globalization in Calixthe Beyala's *Le petit prince de Belleville*." *Research in African Literatures* 41:2 (Summer 2010): 203–21.

Gay, Peter, ed. *The Freud Reader*. New York: W. W. Norton, 1989.

Gayle, Addison, Jr. *The Way of the New World*. New York: Anchor Press/Doubleday, 1975.

———. "Zora Neale Hurston: The Politics of Freedom." In *A Rainbow Round Her Shoulder*, ed. Ruthe T. Sheffrey. Baltimore: Morgan State University Press, 1982.

Genovese, Eugene D. *The World the Slaveholders Made*. New York: Vintage Books, 1971.

George, Olakunle. "Alice Walker's Africa: Globalization and the Province of Fiction." *Comparative Literature* 53:4 (Fall 2001): 354–70.

Ghasemi, Parvin. "Negotiating Black Motherhood in Toni Morrison's Novels." *CLA Journal* 53 (2010): 235–53.

Gilbert, Sandra M., and Susan Gubar. "Ain't I a New Woman: Feminism and the Harlem Renaissance." In *No Man's Land: The Place of the Woman Writer in the Twentieth Century*, ed. Sandra M. Gilbert and Susan Gubar. Vol. 3. New Haven, Conn.: Yale University Press, 1994.

Gillespie, Diane, and Missy Dehn Kubitschek. "Who Cares? Women-Centered Psychology in *Sula*." In *Toni Morrison's Fiction: Contemporary Criticism*, ed. David Middleton. New York and London: Garland, 2000.

Gilligan, Carol. *In a Different Voice: Psychological Theory and Women's Development*. Cambridge, Mass., and London: Harvard University Press, 1998.

Gilman, Sander L. "Black Bodies, White Bodies: Toward an Iconography of Female Sexuality in Late Nineteenth-Century Art, Medicine, and Literature." In *'Race,' Writing, and Difference*, ed. Henry Louis Gates. Chicago: University of Chicago Press, 1986.

Gilroy, Paul. *The Black Atlantic*. Cambridge, Mass.: Harvard University Press, 1993.

Ginzberg, Lori D. *Women and the Work of Benevolence: Morality, Politics, and Class in the Nineteenth-Century United States*. New Haven, Conn., and London: Yale University Press, 1990.

Glasgow, R. D. V. *Madness, Masks, and Laughter: An Essay on Comedy*. Madison-Teaneck: Fairleigh Dickinson University Press, 1995.

Goldman, Jane. *The Feminist Aesthetics of Virginia Woolf*. Cambridge: Cambridge University Press, 1998.

Goluboff, Risa L. *The Lost Promise of Civil Rights*. Cambridge, Mass., and London: Harvard University Press, 2007.

Goodman, Paul. *Of One Blood: Abolitionism and the Origins of Racial Equality.* Berkeley, Los Angeles, and London: University of California Press, 1998.

Gould, Stephen Jay. *The Mismeasure of Man.* New York and London: W. W. Norton, 1996.

Grewal, Gurleen. *Circles of Sorrow, Lines of Struggle: The Novels of Toni Morrison.* Baton Rouge: Louisiana State University Press, 1998.

Griffin, Farah Jasmine. *Harlem Nocturne.* New York: Basic, 2013.

———. *"Who Set You Flowin'?" The African-American Migration Narrative.* New York: Oxford University Press, 1995.

Grimké, Charlotte Forten. *The Journals of Charlotte Forten Grimké,* ed. Brenda Stevenson. New York: Oxford University Press, 1988.

Grimshaw, Allen D., ed. *Racial Violence in the United States.* Chicago: Aldine, 1969.

Grob, Gerald N. *The Mad among Us: A History of the Care of America's Mentally Ill.* New York: Free Press, 1994.

Grossman, Dave. *On Killing: The Psychological Cost of Learning to Kill in War and Society.* Boston, New York, and London: Little, Brown, 1996.

Grosz, Elizabeth. *Jacques Lacan: A Feminist Introduction.* London and New York: Routledge, 1990.

———. *Volatile Bodies.* Bloomington and Indianapolis: Indiana University Press, 1994.

Gutman, Herbert. *The Black Family in Slavery and Freedom, 1750–1925.* New York: Vintage Books, 1976.

Hacker, Andrew. *Two Nations.* New York: Scribners, 1992.

Hamshere, Cyril. *The British in the Caribbean.* Cambridge, Mass.: Harvard University Press, 1972.

Harlan, Louis R., ed. *The Booker T. Washington Papers.* Volume 1, *The Autobiographical Writings.* Urbana and Chicago: University of Illinois Press, 1972.

Harper, Frances Ellen Watkins. "The Colored People in America." In *A Brighter Coming Day. A Frances Ellen Watkins Harper Reader,* ed. Frances Smith Foster. New York: Feminist Press, 1990.

Hartman, Saidiya V. *Scenes of Subjection: Terror, Slavery, and Self-Making in Nineteenth-Century America.* New York: Oxford University Press, 1997.

Hathaway, Heather. *Caribbean Waves: Relocating Claude McKay and Paule Marshall.* Bloomington and Indianapolis: Indiana University Press, 1999.

Hayden, Lucy. "Classical Tidings from the Afric Muse: Phillis Wheatley's Use of Greek and Roman Mythology." *College Language Association* 35:4 (June 1992): 432–47.

Held, Virginia. *Feminist Morality.* Chicago: University of Chicago Press, 1993.

Hegel, G. W. F. *The Phenomenology of Mind.* Translated by J. B. Baillie. London and New York: George Allen & Unwin and Humanities Press, 1966.

Hemenway, Robert. *Zora Neale Hurston: A Literary Biography.* Urbana, Chicago, and London: University of Illinois Press, 1977.

Henderson, Mae. "Toni Morrison's *Beloved:* Re-Membering the Body as Historical Text." In *Beloved: A Casebook,* ed. William Andrews and Nellie Y. McKay. New York: Oxford University Press, 1999.

Herman, Nini. *Too Long a Child: The Mother-Daughter Dyad.* London: Free Association Books, 1989.

Hill, Mozell C. "The All-Negro Communities of Oklahoma: The Natural History of a Social Movement." *Journal of Negro History* 31 (Summer 1946): 254–68.

Hine, Darlene Clark, ed. *Black Women in the United States History.* Brooklyn: Carlson, 1990.

Hirsch, Marianne. *The Mother/Daughter Plot.* Bloomington: Indiana University Press, 1989.

Hite, Molly. "Romance, Marginality, and Matrilineage: *The Color Purple* and *Their Eyes Were Watching God.*" In *Reading Black, Reading Feminist,* ed. Henry Louis Gates. New York: Meridian, 1990.

Holt, Patricia. *Alice Walker Banned.* San Francisco: Aunt Lute Books, 1996.

Honour, Hugh, ed. *The Image of the Black in Western Art*, Volume 4, *From the American Revolution to World War I*. Cambridge, Mass., and London: Harvard University Press, 1989.

hooks, bell. "Reading and Resistance: *The Color Purple*." In *Alice Walker: Critical Perspectives, Past and Present*, ed. Henry Louis Gates Jr. and K. A. Appiah. New York: Amistad, 1993.

Hopkins, Patricia. "Seduction or Rape: Deconstructing the Black Female Body in Harriet Jacobs' *Incidents in the Life of a Slave Girl*." *Making Connections: Interdisciplinary Approaches to Cultural Diversity* 13:1 (September 2011): 4–20.

Horowitz, Joseph. *New World Symphony: Dvorak in New York and Boston*. October 6, 2001. http://216.239.100 www.gothamcenter.org. Accessed April 3, 2003.

Hostetler, Ann. "The Aesthetics of Race and Gender in Nella Larsen's *Quicksand*." *PMLA* 105:1 (January 1990): 35–46.

Huggins, Nathan. *Harlem Renaissance*. New York: Oxford University Press, 1971.

Hughes, Langston. "From *The Big Sea*." In *Norton Anthology of African American Literature*, ed. Henry Louis Gates Jr. and Nellie Y. McKay. New York: W. W. Norton, 1997.

Hull, Gloria T. *Color, Sex and Poetry: Three Women Writers of the Harlem Renaissance*. Bloomington and Indianapolis: Indiana University Press, 1987.

Hurston, Zora Neale. *Dust Tracks on the Road*. In Zora Neale Hurston, *Hurston: Folklore, Memoirs, and Other Writings*, ed. Cheryl Wall. New York: Library of America, 1995.

———. *Dust Tracks on the Road*. Urbana: University of Illinois Press, 1984.

———. "How It Feels to Be Colored Me." In Zora Neale Hurston, *I Love Myself When I Am Laughing . . .* New York: Feminist Press, 1979.

———. *Jonah's Gourd Vine*. In Zora Neale Hurston, *Hurston: Folklore, Memoirs, and Other Writings*, ed. Cheryl Wall. New York: Library of America, 1995.

———. *Moses, Man of the Mountain*. In Zora Neale Hurston, *Hurston: Novels and Stories*, ed. Cheryl Wall. New York: Library of America, 1995.

———. *Mules and Men*. Philadelphia: J. B. Lippincott, 1978.

———. "My Most Humiliating Jim Crow Experience." In Zora Neal Hurston, *I Love Myself When I Am Laughing . . .* New York: Feminist Press, 1979.

———. "Sweat." In *Norton Anthology of African American Literature*, ed. Henry Louis Gates and Nellie Y. McKay. New York: W. W. Norton, 1997.

———. *Their Eyes Were Watching God*. New York: Perennial Library, 1990.

Husserl, Edmund. "Material Things in Their Relation to the Aesthetic Body." In *The Body: Blackwell Readings in Continental Philosophy*, ed. Donn Welton. Malden, Mass.: Blackwell, 1999.

Hutcheon, Linda. *A Theory of Parody*. New York and London: Methuen, 1985.

Hutchinson, George. *The Harlem Renaissance in Black and White*. Cambridge, Mass., and London: Belknap Press of Harvard University Press, 1995.

———. *In Search of Nella Larsen: A Biography of the Color Line*. Cambridge, Mass., and London: Harvard University Press, 2006.

———. "*Quicksand* and the Racial Labyrinth." *Soundings: An Interdisciplinary Journal* 80:4 (Winter 1997): 543–71.

"Immanuel Kant (1724–1804): 'Theory of Aesthetics and Teleology' (*The Critique of Judgment*)." In *The Internet Encyclopedia of Philosophy*. http://www.utm.edu/research/iep/k/kantaest.htm. Accessed March 3, 2003.

Irigaray, Luce. "Female Desire." In *The Body*, ed. Donn Welton. Malden, Mass.: Blackwell, 1999.

———. "This Sex Which Is Not One." In *Writing On the Body: Female Embodiment and Feminist Theory*, ed. Katie Conboy, Nadia Medina, and Sarah Stanbury. New York: Columbia University Press, 1997.

———. *To Speak Is Never Neutral*. New York: Routledge, 2002.

Isani, Mukhtar Ali. "The Contemporaneous Reception of Phillis Wheatley: Newspaper and Magazine Notices during the Years of Fame, 1765–1774." *Journal of Negro History* 85·4 (Autumn 2000): 260–73.

Jacobs, Harriet. *Incidents in the Life of a Slave Girl*. New York: Signet Classic of New American Library, 2000.

Jacobs, John. "A True Tale of Slavery." In *Harriet Jacobs's Incidents in the Life of a Slave Girl*, ed. Jean Fagan Yellin. Cambridge, Mass., and London: Harvard University Press, 2000.

Jameson, Fredric. *Postmodernism, or, the Cultural Logic of Late Capitalism*. Durham, N.C.: Duke University Press, 1997.

JanMohamed, Abdul R. *Manichean Aesthetics*. Amherst: University of Massachusetts Press, 1983.

Jefferson, Thomas. *Notes on the State of Virginia*. Chapel Hill: University of North Carolina Press, 1954.

Jeffrey, Julie Roy. *The Great Silent Army of Abolitionism*. Chapel Hill: University of North Carolina Press, 1998.

Jenkins, Candace M. "Queering Black Patriarchy: The Salvific Wish and Masculine Possibility in Alice Walker's *The Color Purple*," *Modern Fiction Studies* 48:4 (Winter 2002): 969–1000.

Johnson, Barbara. "The Frame of Reference: Poe, Lacan, Derrida." In *The Purloined Poe: Lacan, Derrida, and Psychoanalytic Reading*, ed. John P. Muller and William J. Richardson. Baltimore and London: Johns Hopkins University Press, 1988.

Jones, Jacqueline. *A Dreadful Deceit. The Myth of Race from the Colonial Era to Obama's America*. New York: Basic Books, 2013.

———. *Labor of Love, Labor of Sorrow. Black Women, Work and The Family, from Slavery to the Present*. New York: Basic Books, 2010 Edition.

Jones, LeRoi [Amiri Baraka]. *Home: Social Essays*. New York: William Morrow, 1966.

Jordan, Don, and Michael Walsh. *White Cargo: The Forgotten History of Britain's White Slaves in America*. New York: New York University Press, 2008.

Jordan, Winthrop D. *The White Man's Burden*. New York: Oxford University Press, 1974.

———. *White over Black: American Attitudes toward the Negro, 1550–1812*. New York: W. W. Norton, 1977.

Jung, Carl. "Aion: Phenomenology of the Self (The Ego, the Shadow, the Syzygy: Anima/Animus)." In *The Portable Jung*, ed. Joseph Campbell. New York: Penguin Books, 1976.

———. *Man and His Symbols*. New York: Dell, 1968.

———. "On the Relation of Analytical Psychology to Poetry." In *The Portable Jung*, ed. Joseph Campbell. New York: Penguin Books, 1976.

———. "Phenomenology of the Self." In *The Portable Jung*, ed. Joseph Campbell. New York: Penguin Books, 1976.

Kallen, Horace. "Democracy versus the Melting-Pot." *Nation* (February 25, 1915): 217–20. See also "Excerpts from Horace Kallen's 'Democracy versus the Melting-Pot.'" http://www.american.edu/kdurr/kallen.html, 3–7. Accessed March 18, 2002, 1.

———. "Democracy versus the Melting-Pot, Part One and Part Two." *Nation* (February 25, 1915): 1–25.

Kant, Immanuel. "Analytic of the Aesthetical Judgment." In *Perspectives in Aesthetics: Plato to Camus*, ed. Peyton E. Richter. New York: Odyssey Press, 1967.

———. *The Critique of Judgement*. Oxford: Clarendon Press, 1964.

Kaplan, Carla, ed. *Zora Neale Hurston: A Life in Letters*. New York: Doubleday, 2001.

Kasinitz, Philip. *Caribbean New York*. Ithaca, N.Y.: Cornell University Press, 1992.

Katznelson, Ira. *When Affirmative Action Was White: An Untold History of Racial Inequality in Twentieth-Century America*. New York and London: W. W. Norton, 2005.

Kawash, Samira. *Dislocating the Color Line: Identity, Hybridity, and Singularity in African-American Narrative*. Stanford, Calif.: Stanford University Press, 1997.

Kernal, Salim. *Kant's Aesthetic Theory*. New York: St. Martin's Press, 1992.

King, Martin Luther, Jr. "I Have a Dream." In *The Bedford Reader*, ed. X. J. Kennedy, Dorothy M. Kennedy, and Jane E. Aaron. Boston and New York: Bedford/St. Martin's, 2006.

———. "Letter from a Birmingham Jail." In *Norton Anthology of African American Literature*, ed. Henry Louis Gates and Nellie Y. McKay. New York and London: W. W. Norton, 1997.

———. *Why We Can't Wait*. New York: New American Library, 1963.

Kiple, Kenneth F. *The Caribbean Slave*. New York: Cambridge University Press, 1984.

Kirschke, Amy Helene. *Art in Crisis: W. E. B. Du Bois and the Struggle for African American Identity and Memory*. Bloomington: Indiana University Press, 2007.

Klinkner, Philip A., with Rogers M. Smith. *The Unsteady March: The Rise and Decline of Racial Equality in America*. Chicago and London: University of Chicago Press, 1999.

Kluger, Richard. *Simple Justice*. New York: Alfred A. Knopf, 1976.

Koenen, Anne. "The One Out of Sequence." In *Conversations with Toni Morrison*, ed. Danielle Taylor-Guthrie. Jackson: University Press of Mississippi, 1994.

Kofman, Sarah. *The Enigma of Woman: Woman in Freud's Writings*. Ithaca, N.Y.: Cornell University Press, 1985.

Kolar, Stanislav. "The (Post) Colonial Search for the Identity of Caribbean American (Grand) Daughters." *Litteraria Pragensia: Studies in Literature and Culture* 20:39 (June 2010): 99–114.

Kovel, Joel. *White Racism: A Psychohistory*. New York: Columbia University Press, 1970.

Krieger, Murray. *The Classic Vision*. Baltimore and London: Johns Hopkins University Press, 1971.

Kristeva, Julie. "About Chinese Women." In *The Kristeva Reader*, ed. Toril Moi. New York: Columbia University Press, 1986.

———. *Powers of Horror: An Essay on Abjection*. Translated by Leon S. Roudiez. New York: Columbia University Press, 1982.

———. "Stabat Mater." In *The Kristeva Reader*, ed. Toril Moi. New York: Columbia University Press, 1986.

Krumholz, Linda. "Blackness and Art in Toni Morrison's Tar Baby." *Contemporary Literature* 49:2 (Summer 2008): 263–92.

———. "The Ghosts of Slavery: Historical Recovery in Toni Morrison's *Beloved*." In *Beloved: A Casebook*, ed. William L. Andrews and Nellie Y. McKay. New York: Oxford University Press, 1999.

Kuenz, Jane. "The Face of America: Performing Race and Nation in Jessie Fauset's *There Is Confusion*." *Yale Journal of Criticism* 12:1 (Spring 1999): 89–111.

Lacan, Jacques. "The Signification of the Phallus." In *Écrits: A Selection*, trans. Alan Sheridan. New York and London: W. W. Norton, 1977.

———. "Towards a Genetic Theory of the Ego." In *The Body*, ed. Donn Welton. Malden, Mass.: Blackwell, 1999.

LaCapra, Dominick. *History and Memory after Auschwitz*. Ithaca, N.Y., and London: Cornell University Press, 1998.

LaGrone, Kheven, ed. *Alice Walker's The Color Purple*. Amsterdam and New York: Rodopi, 2009.

Lamming, George. *In the Castle of My Skin*. New York: Schocken Books, 1983.

Larsen, Nella. *The Complete Fiction of Nella Larsen*. Ed. Charles R. Larson. New York: Anchor Books, 2001.

Larsen, Nella. *Passing*. In Nella Larsen, *The Complete Fiction of Nella Larsen*, ed. Charles R. Larson. New York: Anchor Books, 2001.

———. *Quicksand*. In Nella Larsen, *The Complete Fiction of Nella Larsen*, ed. Charles R. Larson. xi–xii. New York: Anchor Books, 2001.

Larson, Charles R., ed. Introduction. In *The Complete Fiction of Nella Larsen*. New York: Anchor Books, 2001.

Lauret, Maria. *Alice Walker*. New York: St. Martin's Press, 2000.

Lerner, Gerda. *The Creation of Patriarchy*. New York and Oxford: Oxford University Press, 1986.

Levine, Lawrence. *Black Culture and Black Consciousness*. New York: Oxford University Press, 1977.

Levine, Robert S. *Dislocating Race and Nation: Episodes in Nineteenth-Century American Literary Nationalism*. Chapel Hill: University of North Carolina Press, 2008.

Lewis, Earl, and Heidi Ardizzone. *Love on Trial: An American Scandal in Black and White*. New York: W. W. Norton, 2001.

Lewis, David Levering. *W. E. B. Du Bois: The Fight for Equality and the American Century, 1919–1963*. New York: Henry Holt, 2000.

———. *When Harlem Was in Vogue*. New York: Penguin Books, 1997.

Lippa, Richard A. *Gender, Nature, and Nurture*. Mahwah, N.J.: Lawrence Erlbaum Associates, 2002.

Liscio, Lorraine. "*Beloved's* Narrative: Writing Mother's Milk." *Tulsa Studies in Women's Literature* 11:1 (Spring 1992): 31–46.

Litwack, Leon F. *How Free Is Free? The Long Death of Jim Crow*. Cambridge, Mass., and London: Harvard University Press, 2009.

Locke, Alain. "The New Negro." In *Norton Anthology of African American Literature*, ed. Henry Louis Gates and Nellie Y. McKay. New York: W. W. Norton, 1997.

Logan, Rayford. *The Betrayal of the Negro*. New York: Collier Books, 1954.

Long, Richard. "The Outer Reaches: The White Writer and Blacks in the Twenties." In *Harlem Renaissance Re-Examined*, ed. Victor A. Kramer and Robert A. Russ. New York: Whitston, 1997.

Lossing, Benson J. *The Pictorial Field-Book of the American Revolution*. Volume 1. New York: Harper and Brothers, 1860.

Lott, Eric. *Love and Theft: Blackface Minstrelsy and the American Working Class*. New York and Oxford: Oxford University Press, 1993.

Lowe, John. *Jump at the Sun: Zora Neale Hurston's Cosmic Comedy*. Urbana and Chicago: University of Illinois Press, 1997.

Lowenthal, David. *West Indian Societies*. London: Oxford University Press, 1972.

Lyotard, Jean-Francois. "The Postmodern Condition." In *Literary Theory: An Anthology*, ed. Julie Rivkin and Michael Ryan. Malden, Mass., and Oxford: Blackwell, 1998.

Macharia, Keguro. "Queering Helga Crane: Black Nativism in Nella Larsen's *Quicksand*." *Modern Fiction Studies* 57:2 (Summer 2011): 254–75.

Mannix, Daniel. *Black Cargoes*. New York: Viking, 1962.

Maquet, Albert. *Albert Camus: The Invincible Summer*. New York: George Braziller, 1958.

Marshall, Paule. *Brown Girl, Brownstones*. New York: Feminist Press, 1981.

———. *The Chosen Place, the Timeless People*. New York: Vintage Books, 1984.

———. *Daughters*. New York: Penguin Group, 1991.

———. *The Fisher King*. New York: Simon & Schuster, 2000.

———. "From the Poets in the Kitchen." In Paule Marshall, *Reena and Other Stories*. New York: Feminist Press, 1983.

———. *Praisesong for the Widow*. New York: Penguin Group, 1983.

———. *Triangular Road: A Memoir.* New York: Basic Civitas Books, 2009.

Mason, Julian, ed. *The Poems of Phillis Wheatley.* Chapel Hill: University of North Carolina Press, 1989.

Massey, Douglass S., and Nancy A. Denton. *American Apartheid: Segregation and the Making of the Underclass.* Cambridge, Mass.: Harvard University Press, 1993.

Mazyck, Walter H. *George Washington and the Negro.* Washington, D.C.: Associated Publisher, 1932.

McDowell, Deborah. *"The Changing Same": Black Women's Literature, Criticism, and Theory.* Bloomington and Indianapolis: Indiana University Press, 1995.

———. "Reading Family Matters." In *Changing Our Own Words: Essays on Criticism, Theory, and Writing by Black Women,* ed. Cheryl A. Wall. New Brunswick, N.J., and London: Rutgers University Press, 1991.

McFeely, William S. *Frederick Douglass.* New York: Simon & Schuster, 1991.

McHenry, Elizabeth. "Into Other Claws." Review of *A Mercy* by Toni Morrison. *Women's Review of Books* 26:4 (July/August 2009): 16–17.

McKay, Nellie. "An Interview with Toni Morrison." In *Conversations with Toni Morrison,* ed. Danielle Taylor-Guthrie. Jackson: University Press of Mississippi, 1994.

McKever-Floyd, Preston L. "'Tell Nobody but God': The Theme of Transformation in *The Color Purple.*" *Crosscurrents* 57:3 (Fall 2007): 426–37.

McKinstry, Carolyn Maull. *While the World Watched.* Highlands Ranch, Colo.: Tyndale, 2011.

McLendon, Jacquelyn Y. *The Politics of Color in the Fiction of Jessie Fauset and Nella Larsen.* Charlottesville and London: University Press of Virginia, 1995.

McMahon, Jennifer Anne. "Beauty." In *The Routledge Companion to Aesthetics,* ed. Berys Gaut and Dominic McIver Lopes. New York and London: Routledge, 2001.

McNeil, Elizabeth. "The Gullah Seeker's Journey in Paule Marshall's *Praisesong for the Widow.*" *MELUS* 34:1 (Spring 2009): 185–209.

Micale, Mark S. "On the 'Disappearance' of Hysteria: A Study in the Clinical Deconstruction of a Diagnosis." *Isis, Journal of History of Science in Society* 84:3 (September 1993): 496–526.

Michaels, Walter Benn. "The Souls of White Folk." In *Literature and the Body,* ed. Elaine Scarry. Baltimore and London: Johns Hopkins University Press, 1988.

Miller, Jean Baker. "Domination and Subordination." In *Race, Class, and Gender in the United States,* ed. Paula S. Rothenberg. New York: St. Martin's Press, 1998.

Mitchell, Juliet, and Jacqueline Rose. *Feminine Sexuality: Jacques Lacan and the école freudienne.* New York and London: W. W. Norton, 1985.

Mobley, Marilyn Sanders. "Call and Response: Voice, Community, and Dialogic Structures in Toni Morrison's Song of Solomon." In *New Essays on Song of Solomon,* ed. Valerie Smith. Cambridge, Mass., and London: Cambridge University Press, 1995.

Montagu, Ashley. *Man's Most Dangerous Myth: The Fallacy of Race.* New York: Oxford University Press, 1974.

———, ed. *The Concept of Race.* New York: Free Press of Glencoe, 1964.

Moore, Geneva Cobb. "Archetypal Symbolism in Alice Walker's *Possessing the Secret of Joy.* *Southern Literary Journal* 33:1 (Fall 2000): 111–21.

———. "*Caucasia's* Migrating Bodies: Lessons in American History and Postmodernism." *Western Journal of Black Studies* 36:2 (Summer 2012): 108–18.

———. "A Demonic Parody: Toni Morrison's *A Mercy.*" *Southern Literary Journal* 44:1 (Fall 2011): 1–18.

———. "A Freudian Reading of Harriet Jacobs's *Incidents in the Life of a Slave Girl.*" *Southern Literary Journal* 38:1 (Fall 2005): 3–20.

————. "When Meanings Meet: *The Journals of Charlotte Forten Grimké*." In *Inscribing the Daily: Critical Essays on Women's Diaries,* ed. Suzanne L. Bunkers and Cynthia A. Huff. Amherst: University of Massachusetts Press, 1996.

————. "Zora Neale Hurston as Local Colorist." *Southern Literary Journal* 26:2 (Spring 1994): 25–34.

Morrison, Toni. *Beloved.* New York: Penguin Group/First Plume Printing, 1988.

————. *Beloved.* New York: First Vintage International Printing, 2004.

————. *The Bluest Eye.* New York: Penguin Books, 1970.

————. *God Help the Child.* New York: Alfred A. Knopf, 2015.

————. *Home: A Novel.* New York and Toronto: Alfred A. Knopf, 2012.

————. *Jazz.* New York: Plume, 1993

————. *Love.* New York: Alfred A. Knopf, 2003.

————. *A Mercy.* New York: Vintage International, 2008.

————. *Nobel Lecture in Literature* (1993). New York: Alfred A. Knopf, 1994.

————. *Paradise.* New York: Alfred A. Knopf, 1998.

————. "The Site of Memory." In *Inventing the Truth: The Art and Craft of MEMOIR,* ed. William Zinsser. Boston: Houghton Mifflin, 1987.

————. *Song of Solomon.* New York: Penguin, 1977.

————. *Sula.* New York: Plume, 1972.

————. *Tar Baby.* New York: Plume, 1982.

Moynihan, Daniel Patrick. "The Negro Family: The Case for National Action." In *The Moynihan Report and the Politics of Controversy,* ed. Lee Rainwater and William L. Yancey. Cambridge, Mass., and London: MIT Press, 1967.

Muller, John P., and William J. Richardson. *Lacan and Language.* New York: International Universities Press, 1982.

Mulvey, Laura. "Visual Pleasure and Narrative Cinema." In *Literary Theory: An Anthology,* ed. Julie Rivkin and Michael Ryan. Malden, Mass., and Oxford: Blackwell, 1998.

Muscio, Inga. *Cunt: A Declaration of Independence.* Seattle: Seal Press, 1998.

Myrdal, Gunnar. *An American Dilemma.* New York: Harper and Brothers, 1944.

Nadel, Alan. "Reading the Body: *Meridian* and the Archeology of Self." In *Alice Walker: Critical Perspectives, Past and Present,* ed. Henry Louis Gates Jr. and K. A. Appiah. New York: Amistad, 1993.

Naylor, Gloria. "A Conversation: Gloria Naylor and Toni Morrison." In *Conversations with Toni Morrison,* ed. Danielle Taylor-Guthrie. Jackson: University Press of Mississippi, 1994.

Nice, Vivien. *Mothers and Daughters: The Distortion of a Relationship.* New York: St. Martin's Press, 1992.

Nicol, Kathryn, and Jennifer Terry. "Guest Editors' Introduction, Toni Morrison: New Directions." *MELUS* 36:2 (Summer 2011): 7–12.

Odell, Margaretta, ed. *Memoir and Poems of Phillis Wheatley.* Boston: Isaac Knapp, 1838.

Page, Philip. *Dangerous Freedom: Fusion and Fragmentation in Toni Morrison's Novels.* Jackson: University Press of Mississippi, 1995.

————. "Furrowing All the Brows: Interpretation and the Transcendent in Toni Morrison's *Paradise*." *African American Review* 35:4 (December 2001): 637–49.

Paris, Arthur. "The Transatlantic Metropolis and the Voices of Caribbean Women." In *Caribbean Women Writers,* ed. Selwyn R. Cudjoe. Wellesley, Mass.: Calaloux Publications, 1990.

Pascal, Roy B. *Design and Truth in Autobiography.* Cambridge, Mass.: Harvard University Press, 1960.

Patterson, Orlando. *Slavery and Social Death*. Cambridge, Mass., and London: Harvard University Press, 1992.

Penzel, Fred. *Obsessive-Compulsive Disorders*. New York: Oxford University Press, 2000.

Pérez-Torres, Rafael. "Between Presence and Absence: *Beloved*, Postmodernism, and Blackness." In *Beloved: A Casebook*, ed. William L. Andrews and Nellie Y. McKay. New York: Oxford University Press, 1999.

Peterson, Carla L. *"Doers of the Word": African-American Women Speakers and Writers in the North (1830–1880)*. New York and Oxford: Oxford University Press, 1995.

Pettis, Joyce. *Toward Wholeness in Paule Marshall's Fiction*. Charlottesville and London: University of Virginia Press, 1995.

Phiddian, Robert. "Are Parody and Deconstruction Secretly the Same Thing?" *New Literary History* 28:4 (Autumn 1997): 673–96.

Pinckney, Darryl. "Black Victims, Black Villains." Review of *The Color Purple* by Alice Walker. *New York Review of Books* 34:1 (January 29, 1987): 17–20.

———. "Hate." Review of *Love* by Toni Morrison. *New York Review of Books* (December 4, 2003): 571.

Plant, Deborah. *Every Tub Must Sit on Its Bottom*. Urbana: University of Illinois Press, 1995.

———. *Zora Neale Hurston: A Biography of the Spirit*. Westport, Conn., and London: Praeger, 2009.

Pollard, Velma. "The World of Spirits in the Work of Some Caribbean Writers in the Diaspora." *Changing English, Studies in Culture and Education* 17:1 (March 2010): 27–34.

Pollock, John. *George Whitefield and the Great Awakening*. New York: Doubleday, 1972.

Prince, Mary. *The History of Mary Prince, a West Indian Slave (Related by Herself)*. In *The Classic Slave Narratives*, ed. Henry Louis Gates. New York: New American Library, 1987.

Privett, Katharyn. "Dystopic Bodies and Enslaved Motherhood." *Women: A Cultural Review* 18:3 (Winter 2007): 257–81.

Quayson, Ato. *Aesthetic Nervousness: Disability and the Crisis of Representation*. New York: Columbia University Press, 2007.

Ramchand, Kenneth. *The West Indian Novel and Its Background*. New York: Barnes & Noble, 1970.

Reid-Pharr, Robert. *Conjugal Union*. New York and Oxford: Oxford University Press, 1999.

Rich, Adrienne. *Of Woman Born*. New York: W. W. Norton, 1986.

Richards, Constance S. *On the Winds and Waves of Imagination: Transnational Feminism and Literature*. New York and London: Garland, 2000.

Richter, Peyton E., ed. *Perspectives in Aesthetics: Plato to Camus*. New York: Odyssey Press, 1967.

Rody, Caroline. *The Daughter's Return: African-American and Caribbean Women's Fictions of History*. New York: Oxford University Press, 2001.

Rogoff, Barbara. *The Cultural Nature of Human Development*. New York and Oxford: Oxford University Press, 2003.

Rose, Margaret. *Parody: Ancient, Modern, and Post-modern*. Cambridge and London: Cambridge University Press, 1993.

Rothenberg, Paula, ed. *Race, Class, and Gender in the United States*. New York: St. Martin's Press, 1998.

Rothstein, Mervyn. "Toni Morrison, in Her New Novel, Defends Women." *New York Times*, August 26, 1987, C17.

Royster, Philip M. "In Search of Our Fathers' Arms: Alice Walker's Persona of the Alienated Darling." *Black American Literature Forum* 20:4 (Winter 1986): 347–70.

Ruas, Charles. "Toni Morrison." In *Conversations with Toni Morrison*, ed. Danielle Taylor-Guthrie. Jackson: University Press of Mississippi, 1994.

Ruddick, Sara. "Maternal Thinking." In *Mothering: Essays in Feminist Theory*, ed. Joyce Trebilcot. Totowa, N.J.: Rowman & Allanheld, 1983.

———. *Maternal Thinking: Toward a Politics of Peace*. Boston: Beacon Press, 1995.

Russell, Danielle. "Homeward Bound: Transformative Spaces in *The Color Purple*." In *Alice Walker's The Color Purple*, ed. Kheven LaGrone. Amsterdam and New York: Rodopi, 2009.

Rydman, Jason F. "Zora Neale Hurston: Biographical Criticism, and African Diasporic Vernacular Culture." *MELUS* 34:4 (Winter 2009): 99–118.

Sanchez-Eppler, Karen. *Touching Liberty: Abolition, Feminism and the Politics of the Body*. Berkeley: University of California Press, 1993.

Sandiford, Keith A. "Paule Marshall's *Praisesong for the Widow*: The Reluctant Heiress, or Whose Life Is It Anyway?" *Black American Literature Forum* 20:4 (Winter 1986): 371–92.

Schaffer, Rudolph. *Mothering*. Cambridge, Mass.: Harvard University Press, 1977.

Scheick, William. *Authority and Female Authorship in Colonial America*. Lexington: University Press of Kentucky, 1998.

Scott, Joyce Hope. "*Song of Solomon* and *Tar Baby*: The Subversive Role of Language and the Carnivalesque." In *The Cambridge Companion to Toni Morrison*, ed. Justine Tally. Cambridge and New York: Cambridge University Press, 2007.

Senna, Danzy. *Caucasia*. New York: Riverhead Books, 1998.

Sharkey, Patrick. *Stuck in Place: Urban Neighborhoods and the End of Progress toward Racial Equality*. Chicago: University of Chicago Press, 2013.

Sheng, Qin. "Toni Morrison's Gender Politics in *Song of Solomon*." *Canadian Social Science* 7:2 (April 2011): 95–101.

Shields, John C. "Phillis Wheatley's Struggle for Freedom in Her Poetry and Prose." In *The Collected Works of Phillis Wheatley*, ed. John C. Shields. New York: Oxford University Press, 1989.

———. "Phillis Wheatley's Theoretics of the Imagination: An Untold Chapter in the History of Early American Literary Aesthetics." In *New Essays on Phillis Wheatley*, ed. John C. Shields and Eric Lamore. Knoxville: University of Tennessee Press, 2011.

Silko, Leslie Marmon. *Ceremony*. New York: Penguin, 1977.

Simpson, Claude M., ed. *The Local Colorists*. New York: Harper & Row, 1960.

Skerrett, Joseph. "Recitations to the Griot: Storytelling and Learning in Toni Morrison's *Song of Solomon*." In *Conjuring: Black Women, Fiction, and the Literary Tradition*, ed. Marjorie Pryse and Hortense Spillers. Bloomington and Indianapolis: Indiana University Press, 1985.

Smith, Barbara. "The Truth That Never Hurts: Black Lesbians in Fiction in the 1980s." In Barbara Smith, *The Truth That Never Hurts: Writings on Race, Gender, and Freedom*. New Brunswick, N.J.: Rutgers University Press, 1998.

Smith, Caleb. "Harriet Jacobs among the Militants: Transformations in Abolition's Public Sphere, 1859–1861." *American Literature* 84:4 (December 2012): 743–68.

Smith, Carissa Turner. "Women's Spiritual Geographies of the African Diaspora: Paule Marshall's *Praisesong for the Widow*." *African American Review* 42:3/4 (September 2008): 715–29.

Smith, Curtis D. *Jung's Quest for Wholeness*. Albany: State University of New York Press, 1990.

Smith, Page. *The Rise of Industrial America*. Volume 6. New York: McGraw Hill, 1984.

Smith, Sidonie. *Subjectivity, Identity, and the Body: Women's Autobiographical Practices in the Twentieth Century*. Bloomington and Indianapolis: Indiana University Press, 1993.

Smitherman, Geneva. *Talkin' and Testifyin': The Language of Black America*. Detroit: Wayne State University Press, 1986.

Sollors, Werner. *Ethnic Modernism*. Cambridge, Mass., and London: Harvard University Press, 2008.

Somé, Malidoma Patrice. *The Healing Wisdom of Africa*. New York: Penguin Putnam, 1998.

Spacks, Patricia Meyer. "The Woman as Artist." In *Women, Creativity, and the Arts*, ed. Diana Apostolos-Cappadona and Lucinda Ebersole. New York: Continnum, 1995.

Spillers, Hortense J. "*Chosen Place, Timeless People*: Some Figurations on the New World." In *Conjuring: Black Women, Fiction, and Literary Tradition*, ed. Marjorie Pryse and Hortense Spillers. Bloomington: Indiana University Press, 1985.

———, ed. *Comparative American Identities: Race, Sex, and Nationality in the Modern Text*. New York and London: Routledge, 1991.

Spillers, Hortense, and Marjorie Pryse, eds. *Conjuring: Black Women, Fiction, and Literary Tradition*. Bloomington: Indiana University Press, 1985.

Stampp, Kenneth M. *The Peculiar Institution: Slavery in the Ante-Bellum South*. New York: Vintage Books, 1989.

Stannard, David E. *American Holocaust*. New York: Oxford University Press, 1992.

Stauffer, John. *The Black Hearts of Men: Radical Abolitionists and the Transformation of Race*. Cambridge, Mass., and London: Harvard University Press, 2002.

Stepto, Robert. "Intimate Things in Place: A Conversation with Toni Morrison." In *Conversations with Toni Morrison*, ed. Danielle Taylor-Guthrie. Jackson: University Press of Mississippi, 1994.

Sterling, Dorothy, ed. *We Are Your Sisters: Black Women in the Nineteenth Century*. New York and London: W. W. Norton, 1997.

Steven, Wallace. "Sunday Morning." In *Poetry: An Introduction*, ed. Michael Meyer. Boston: Bedford Books, 1995.

Stevenson, Brenda, ed. Introduction. In *The Journals of Charlotte Forten Grimké*. 3–55. New York: Oxford University Press, 1988.

Stewart, Anna S. "Revising 'Harriet Jacobs' for 1865." *American Literature* 82:4 (December 2010): 701–24.

Storace, Patricia. "The Scripture of Utopia." Book Review of *Paradise* by Toni Morrison. *New York Times Review of Books* 45:10 (June 11, 1998): 64–69.

Story, Ralph. "An Excursion into the Black World: The 'Seven Days' in Toni Morrison's *Song of Solomon*." *Black American Literature Forum* 23:1 (Spring 1989): 149–58.

Stowe, Harriet Beecher. *Uncle Tom's Cabin*. New York: Bantam Books, 1981.

Sumler-Lewis, Janice. "The Forten-Purvis Women of Philadelphia and the American Anti-Slavery Crusade." In *Black Women in the United States History*, ed. Darlene Clark Hine. Brooklyn: Carlson, 1990.

Suranyi, Agnes. "*The Bluest Eye* and *Sula*: Black Female Experience from Childhood to Womanhood." In *The Cambridge Companion to Toni Morrison*, ed. Justine Tally. Cambridge: Cambridge University Press, 2007.

Sylvander, Carolyn Wedin. *Jessie Redmon Fauset: Black American Writer*. New York: Whitston, 1981.

Tan, Amy. *The Joy Luck Club*. New York: Ivy Books, 1989.

Tanner, Laura E. "Intimate Geography: The Body, Race, and Space in Larsen's *Quicksand*." *Texas Studies in Literature and Language* 51:2 (Summer 2009): 179–202.

Tate, Claudia. "Desire and Death in *Quicksand*, by Nella Larsen." *American Literary History* 7:2 (Summer 1995): 234–60.

———. *Domestic Allegories of Political Desire*. New York: Oxford University Press, 1992.

———. *Psychoanalysis and Black Novels*. New York and Oxford: Oxford University Press, 1998.

———. "Toni Morrison." In *Conversations with Toni Morrison*, ed. Danielle Taylor-Guthrie. Jackson: University Press of Mississippi, 1994.

Terry, Jennifer T. "'Breathing the Air of a World So New': Rewriting the Landscape of America in Toni Morrison's *A Mercy*." *Journal of American Studies* 48:1 (February 2014): 127–45.

———. "A New World Religion: Creolisation and Candomble in Toni Morrison's *Paradise*." In *Toni Morrison and the Bible,* ed. Shirley A. Stave. New York and Oxford: Peter Lang, 2006.

Thaggert, Miriam. *Images of Black Modernism: Verbal and Visual Strategies of the Harlem Renaissance.* Amherst and Boston: University of Massachusetts Press, 2010.

Thielmann, Pia. "Alice Walker and the 'Man Question.'" In *Critical Essays on Alice Walker,* ed. Ikenna Dieke. Westport, Conn., and London: Greenwood Press, 1999.

Thorsson, Courtney. "Dancing up a Nation: Paule Marshall's *Praisesong for the Widow.*" *Callaloo* 30:2 (Spring 2007): 644–52.

Tompkins, Jane. *Sensational Design: The Cultural Work of American Fiction, 1790–1860.* New York: Oxford University Press, 1985.

Torrey, E. Fuller, M.D. *Freudian Fraud: The Malignant Effect of Freud's Theory on American Thought and Culture.* New York: HarperCollins, 1992.

Towne, Laura M. *Letters and Diary of Laura M. Towne: Written from the Sea Islands of South Carolina, 1862–1884.* Ed. Rupert Sargent Holland. Cambridge: Riverside Press, 1912.

Turner, Darwin T. "W. E. B. Du Bois and the Theory of a Black Aesthetic." In *Harlem Renaissance Re-Examined,* ed. Victor A. Kramer and Robert A. Russ. New York: Whitson, 1997.

Twain, Mark. *The Tragedy of Pudd'nhead Wilson and the Comedy of Those Extraordinary Twins.* New York: Oxford University Press, 1996.

Twine, France Winddance. "Bearing Blackness in Britain." In *Ideologies and Technologies of Motherhood,* ed. Helena Ragone and France Winddance Twine. New York and London: Routledge, 2000.

Updike, John. "Dreamy Wilderness." Review of *A Mercy* by Toni Morrison. *New Yorker* 84:35 (November 3, 2008): 112–13.

Van Buren, Jane Silverman. *The Modernist Madonna: Semiotics of the Maternal Metaphor.* Bloomington and Indianapolis: Indiana University Press, 1989.

Van den Berghe, Pierre. *Race and Racism: A Comparative Perspective.* New York, London, and Sydney: John Wiley, 1967.

Vassa, Gustavus. "Interesting Narrative of the Life of Olaudah Equiano, or Gustavus Vassa, the African, Written by Himself." In *Great Slave Narratives,* ed. Arna Bontemps. 1–192.. Boston: Beacon Press, 1969.

Vermillion, Mary. "Reembodying the Self: Representations of Rape in *Incidents in the Life of a Slave Girl* and *I Know Why the Caged Bird Sings.*" *Biography* 15:3 (Summer 1992): 243–60.

Von Frank, Albert J. *The Trials of Anthony Burns.* Cambridge, Mass., and London: Harvard University Press, 1998.

Wade-Gayles, Gloria. "The Truths of Our Mothers' Lives: Mother-Daughter Relationships in Black Women's Fiction." *SAGE, a Scholarly Journal on Black Women* 1:2 (Fall 1984): 8–12.

Waegner, Cathy C. "Ruthless Epic Footsteps: Shoes, Migrants, and the Settlement of the Americas in Toni Morrison's *A Mercy*." In *Post-national Enquiries: Essays on Ethnic and Racial Border Crossings,* ed. Jopi Nyman. 91–112. Newcastle upon Tyne: Cambridge Scholars, 2009.

Waldstreicher, David. "The Wheatleyan Moment." *Early American Studies* 9:3 (Fall 2011): 522–51.

Walker, Alice. Afterword. In Alice Walker, *The Third Life of Grange Copeland.* New York: Pocket Books, 1988.

———. *Anything We Love Can Be Saved: A Writer's Activism.* New York: Random House, 1997.

———. *By the Light of My Father's Smile.* New York: Random House, 1998.

———. *The Color Purple.* New York: Pocket Books, 1982.

———. *In Search of Our Mothers' Garden.* New York: Harcourt Brace Jovanovich, 1983.

———. *Meridian.* New York: Pocket Books, 1986.

———. *Possessing the Secret of Joy.* New York: Pocket Books, 1992.

———. *The Temple of My Familiar.* New York: Pocket Books, 1990.

———. *The Third Life of Grange Copeland.* New York: Pocket Books, 1988.

———. *We Are the Ones We Have Been Waiting For.* New York: New Press, 2006.

Walker, Melissa. *Down from the Mountaintop: Black Women's Novels in the Wake of the Civil Rights Movement, 1966–1989.* New Haven, Conn., and London: Yale University Press, 1991.

Walker, Michelle Boulous. *Philosophy and the Maternal Body.* New York and London: Routledge, 1998.

Wall, Cheryl. *Women of the Harlem Renaissance.* Bloomington and Indianapolis: Indiana University Press, 1995.

———, ed. *Changing Our Own Words: Essays on Criticism, Theory, and Writing by Black Women.* New Brunswick, N.J.: Rutgers University Press, 1989.

Wall, Wendy. "Lettered Bodies and Corporeal Texts." In *Alice Walker: Critical Perspectives,* ed. Henry Louis Gates Jr. and K. A. Appiah. New York: Amistad, 1993.

Walters, Tracey L. *African American Literature and the Classicist Tradition: Black Women Writers from Wheatley to Morrison.* New York and London: Palgrave Macmillan, 2007.

Wan Roselezam Wan Yahya, Maryam Aminian, and Emily Abd Rahman. "Gender Representation in Alice Walker's Selected Novels." *International Journal of the Humanities* 8:1 (2010): 231–44.

Warner, Anne Bradford. "Harriet Jacobs at Home in *Incidents in the Life of a Slave Girl. Southern Quarterly* 45:3 (April 2008): 30–47.

Warren, Nagucyalti, and Sally Wolff. "'Like the Pupil of an Eye': Sexual Blinding of Women in Alice Walker's Works." *Southern Literary Journal* 31:1 (Fall 1998): 1–16.

Washington, Booker T. *Up from Slavery.* New York: Doubleday Pocket Book, 1940.

Washington, Mary Helen. "I Sign My Mother's Name." In *Mothering the Mind,* ed. Ruth Perry and Martine Watson. New York: Holmes and Meier, 1984.

Washington, Robert E. *The Ideologies of African American Literature.* Lanham, Md.: Rowman & Littlefield, 2001.

Watkins, Mel. "Talk with Toni Morrison." In *Conversations with Toni Morrison,* ed. Danielle Taylor-Guthrie. Jackson: University Press of Mississippi, 1994.

Watson, Reginald Wade. "Twentieth-Century Mulatto Image: Novels of Passing, Protest, and the Black Bourgeoisie." *CLA Journal* 54:1 (September 2010): 1–18.

Weir, John. "10 Most Hated Books." *Advocate,* June 24, 1997, 91–96.

Welch, Galbraith. *Africa: Before They Came.* New York: William Morrow, 1965.

White, Deborah Gray. *Ar'n't I a Woman? Female Slaves in the Plantation South.* New York and London: W. W. Norton, 1999.

White, Evelyn C. *Alice Walker: A Life.* New York and London: W. W. Norton, 2004.

White, Hayden. *Tropics of Discourse: Essays in Cultural Criticism.* Baltimore and London: Johns Hopkins University Press, 1978.

———. "The Value of Narrativity in the Representation of Reality." In *On Narrative,* ed. W. J. T. Mitchell. Chicago and London: University of Chicago Press, 1981.

Whitsitt, Novian. "Reading between the Lines." *Frontiers: A Journal of Women Studies* 31:1 (March 2010): 73–88.

Wilentz, Gay. "Civilizations Underneath: African Heritage as Cultural Discourse in Toni Morrison's *Song of Solomon.*" In *Toni Morrison's Fiction: Contemporary Criticism,* ed. David Middleton. New York and London: Garland, 2000.

Wilkie, Brian, and James Hurt. "Jonathan Swift." In *Literature of the Western World,* ed. Brian Wilkie and James Hurt. 113–16. New York: Macmillan, 1984.

Williams, Aubrey, ed. *Poetry and Prose of Alexander Pope.* Boston: Houghton Mifflin, 1969.

Williamson, Joel. *New People: Miscegenation and Mulattoes in the United States.* New York: Free Press, 1980.

———. *New People: Miscegenation and Mulattoes in the United States.* Baton Rouge: Louisiana State University Press, 1995.

Wilson, Edmund. *Patriotic Gore: Studies in the Literature of the American Civil War.* New York: Oxford University Press, 1962.

Wilson, James F. *Bulldaggers, Pansies, and Chocolate Babies: Performance, Race, and Sexuality in the Harlem Renaissance.* Ann Arbor: University of Michigan Press, 2011.

Wilson, Kara. "Kara Wilson Didn't Like Toni Morrison's New Book, 'God Help the Child.'" *Artnews* .com. April 20, 2015. Accessed May 16, 2015.

Winch, Julie. *A Gentleman of Color.* New York: Oxford University Press, 2002.

Winchell, Donna Haisty. *Alice Walker.* New York: Twayne, 1992.

Woods, Peter. *Black Majority.* New York: Alfred A. Knopf, 1974.

Woodward, C. Vann. *The Strange Career of Jim Crow.* New York: Oxford University Press, 1966.

Wyatt, Jean. "Failed Messages, Maternal Loss, and Narrative Form in Toni Morrison's *A Mercy.*" *Modern Fiction Studies* 58:1 (Spring 2012): 128–51.

Xavier, Silvia. "Engaging George Campbell's Sympathy in the Rhetoric of Charlotte Forten and Ann Plato, African-American Women in the Antebellum North." *Rhetoric Review* 24:4 (2005): 438–56.

Yellin, Jean Fagan. *Harriet Jacobs: A Life.* New York: Basic Books, 2004.

———. *The Intricate Knot: Black Figures in American Literature, 1776–1863.* New York: New York University Press, 1972.

———. Introduction. In *Harriet Jacobs: Incidents in the Life of a Slave Girl, Written by Herself,* ed. Jean Fagan Yellin. Cambridge, Mass., and London: Harvard University Press, 2000

———. "Texts and Contexts of Harriet Jacobs' *Incidents in the Life of a Slave Girl: Written by Herself.*" In *The Slave's Narrative,* ed. Charles T. Davis and Henry Louis Gates Jr. New York: Oxford University Press, 1985.

———, ed. *The Harriet Jacobs Family Papers.* Volume 2. Chapel Hill: University of North Carolina Press, 2008.

———, ed. *Harriet Jacobs, Incidents in the Life of a Slave Girl, Written by Herself.* Cambridge, Mass., and London: Harvard University Press, 2000.

Young, Robert J. C. *Colonial Desire: Hybridity in Theory, Culture and Race.* London and New York: Routledge, 1995.

Young-Bruehl, Elisabeth. Introduction. In *Freud on Women: A Reader,* ed. Elizabeth Young-Bruehl. 3–47. New York: W. W. Norton, 1990.

Zack, Naomi. *Race and Mixed Race.* Philadelphia: Temple University Press, 1993.

Zinn, Howard. *A People's History of the United States, 1492–Present.* New York: HarperPerennial, 1995.

Index